Lecture Notes in Computer Science   7662

Commenced Publication in 1973
Founding and Former Series Editors:
Gerhard Goos, Juris Hartmanis, and Jan van Leeuwen

Priya Narasimhan
Peter Triantafillou (Eds.)

Middleware 2012

ACM/IFIP/USENIX
13th International Middleware Conference
Montreal, QC, Canada, December 3-7, 2012
Proceedings

 Springer

Volume Editors

Priya Narasimhan
Carnegie Mellon University
Electrical and Computer Engineering Department
4720 Forbes Avenue
Pittsburgh, PA 15213, USA
E-mail: priya@cs.cmu.edu

Peter Triantafillou
University of Patras
Department of Computer Engineering and Informatics
University Campus
26504 Rio, Greece
E-mail: peter@ceid.upatras.gr

ISSN 0302-9743   e-ISSN 1611-3349
ISBN 978-3-642-35169-3   e-ISBN 978-3-642-35170-9
DOI 10.1007/978-3-642-35170-9
Springer Heidelberg Dordrecht London New York

Library of Congress Control Number: 2012952143

CR Subject Classification (1998): C.2, H.4, D.2, H.3, K.6.5, D.4.6

LNCS Sublibrary: SL 2 – Programming and Software Engineering

Typesetting: Camera-ready by author, data conversion by Scientific Publishing Services, Chennai, India

Printed on acid-free paper

Springer is part of Springer Science+Business Media (www.springer.com)

Preface

This edition marks the 13th ACM/IFIP/USENIX Middleware Conference. The first conference was held in the Lake District of England in 1998, and its origins reflected the growing importance of middleware and the realization that middleware represented an active, rigorous, growing and evolving research discipline in its own right. The definition of the term "middleware" has also evolved in the past decade, but retains, at its core, the notion of different levels/layers of abstractions in distributed-computing systems. Since its inception, the *Middleware Conference* has remained a premier forum for the discussion of innovations and recent advances in the design, implementation, experimentation, deployment, and usage of middleware systems.

The 2012 Middleware Conference included a variety of papers spanning the design, implementation, deployment, and evaluation of middleware for next-generation platforms such as cloud computing, mobile services, peer-to-peer systems, pub/sub middleware, Internet of Things, etc., along with middleware support to enable attributes such as availability, scalability, diagnosis, security, privacy, etc.

The Research Track of the conference this year reflected a very strong technical program, with 24 papers accepted out of 125 submissions. The Industrial Track of the conference accepted 6 papers out of 22 additional submissions. The papers were judged based on originality, contribution, presentation quality, relevance to the conference, and potential impact on the field. This year, two innovations were introduced. First, the reviewing process included an author-feedback phase; this proved to be successful in bringing the authors and the Program Committee members closer and helped to increase fairness, reducing chance variability and improving the quality of the program. Second, a new paper submission category, namely that of Systems and Experiences, was introduced with great success; there were more than 20 submissions to this category and 4 of them were selected for inclusion into the program.

The program also included workshops on topics such as adaptive/reflective middleware, embedded middleware, multi-device middleware, and middleware for cloud management and Internet computing. Other important pillars of the conference were a poster and a demo session, as well as tutorials. To highlight and mentor the next-generation of middleware researchers, the conference program also included a doctoral symposium.

It is our privilege to have had the opportunity to serve as the Program Chairs of the 2012 Middleware Conference and we would like to thank everyone who made the conference so successful. The Organizing Committee, particularly General Chair Bettina Kemme, provided continuous support, guidance, and leadership. The Program Committee did a thorough and timely job of evaluating submissions. The Steering Committee provided advice, insights from previous conferences, as well as a sense of continuity. Last but not least, we would like to thank the authors – the outstanding quality of the papers is a testament to the dedication and the efforts of our authors to this field and their lasting, impactful research contributions to the 2012 ACM/IFIP/USENIX Middleware Conference.

December 2012   Priya Narasimhan
                                                             Peter Triantafillou

Organization

Middleware 2012 was organized under the joint sponsorship of the Association for Computing Machinery (ACM), the International Federation for Information Processing (IFIP), and USENIX.

Organizing Committee

General Chair

Bettina Kemme   McGill University, Canada

Program Committee Chairs

Priya Narasimhan   Carnegie Mellon University, USA
Peter Triantafillou   University of Patras, Greece

Industrial Track Chairs

Michael Spreitzer   IBM, USA
Jan de Meer   SmartSpaceLab, Germany

Workshop Chair

Marta Patiño-Martinez   Technical University Madrid, Spain

Posters and Demo Chair

Eric Wohlstadter   University of British Columbia, Canada

Sponsorship Chair

Fred Douglis   EMC Backup Recovery Systems, USA

Local Arrangements Chair

Wenbo He   McGill University, Canada

Web Chair

Muthucumaru Maheswaran   McGill University, Canada

Proceedings Chair

Kévin Huguenin   EPFL, Switzerland

Registration Chair

Kamal Zellag	McGill University, Canada

Publicity Chairs

Soila Kavulya	Carnegie Mellon University, USA
Jiaqi Tan	DSO National Labs, Singapore;
	Carnegie Mellon University, USA
Rolando Martins	University of Porto, Portugal

Steering Committee

Gordon Blair	Lancaster University, UK (Chair)
Jan De Meer	SmartSpaceLab, Germany
Fred Douglis	EMC Backup Recovery Systems, USA
Hans-Arno Jacobsen	University of Toronto, Canada
Roy Campbell	University of Illinois at Urbana-Champaign, USA
Brian F. Cooper	Google, USA
Jean Bacon	University of Cambridge, UK
Cecilia Mascolo	University of Cambridge, UK
Indranil Gupta	University of Illinois at Urbana-Champaign, USA
Guruduth Banavar	IBM, USA
Anne-Marie Kermarrec	INRIA, France
Fabio Kon	University of São Paulo, Brazil
Paulo Ferreira	INESC, Portugal
Luís Veiga	INESC, Portugal
Rui Oliveira	Universidade do Minho, Portugal

Program Committee

Jean Bacon	University of Cambridge, UK
Ken Birman	Cornell University, USA
Gordon Blair	Lancaster University, UK
Rajkumar Buyya	University of Melbourne, Australia
Roy Campbell	University of Illinois Urbana-Champaign, USA
Antonio Casimiro	University of Lisbon, Portugal
Antonio Carzaniga	University of Lugano, Switzerland
Lucy Cherkasova	HP Labs, USA
Brian Cooper	Google, USA
Dilma da Silva	IBM Research, USA
Xavier Defago	JAIST School of Information Science, Japan
Tudor A. Dumitras	Symantec Research, USA
Amr El-Abbadi	University of California, Santa Barbara, USA

Referees

Manoj Agarwal
Srikanta Bedathur
Kyle Benson
Norman Bobroff
Ioannis Boutsis
Jeff Cleveland
Kashif Sana Dar
Mamadou Diallo
Ngoc Do
Aaron Elmore
Gerhard Fohler
Sylvain Frey
Alfredo Goldman
Danny Hughes
Manos Kapritsos
Nicolas Le Scouarnec
Vincent Leroy
Huan Li
Miguel Liroz
Dionysis Logothetis
P. Michael Melliar-Smith
Shicong Meng
Jonathan Michaux
Iris Miliaraki
Hatem Mohamed

Faisal Nawab
Yanik Ngoko
Emanuel Onica
Partha Pal
Navneet Kumar Pandey
Yannis Patlakas
Aaron Paulos
Padmanabhan Pillai
Lucas Provensi
Zhijing Qin
Reza Rahimi
Jerry Rolia
Georgios Siganos
Abhishek Singh
Julian Stephen
Vinaitheerthan Sundaram
Yuzhe Tang
Patrick Valduriez
Jose Valerio
Narasimha Raghavan Veeraragavan
Luís Veiga
Ming Xiong
Apostolos Zarras
Ye Zhao

Sponsoring Institutions

International Federation for Information Processing
http://www.ifip.org

Association for Computing Machinery
http://www.acm.org

Advanced Computing Systems Association
http://www.usenix.org

McGill University
http://www.mcgill.ca

Corporate Sponsors

      EMC Corporation
http://www.emc.com

   IBM
http://www.ibm.com

      Hewlett-Packard Company
www.hp.com

B B N   BBN Technologies
TECHNOLOGIES   http://www.bbn.com

Table of Contents

Publish/Subscribe Middleware

Big-Data and Cloud Computing

Availability, Security and Privacy

CrowdMAC: A Crowdsourcing System
for Mobile Access

Ngoc Do[1,*], Cheng-Hsin Hsu[2,**], and Nalini Venkatasubramanian[1]

[1] Dept. of Information and Computer Science, University of California, Irvine, USA
[2] Dept. of Computer Science, National Tsing Hua University, Hsin-Chu, Taiwan

Abstract. Staggering growth levels in the number of mobile devices and amount of mobile Internet usage has caused network providers to move away from unlimited data plans to less flexible charging models. As a result, users are being required to pay more for short accesses or under-utilize a longer-term data plan. In this paper, we propose CrowdMAC, a crowdsourcing approach in which mobile users create a marketplace for mobile Internet access. Mobile users with residue capacity in their data plans share their access with other nearby mobile users for a small fee. CrowdMAC is implemented as a middleware framework with incentive-based mechanisms for admission control, service selection, and mobility management. CrowdMAC is implemented and evaluated on a testbed of Android phones and in the well known Qualnet simulator. Our evaluation results show that CrowdMAC: (i) effectively exercises the trade-off between revenue and transfer delay, (ii) adequately satisfies user-specified (delay) quality levels, and (iii) properly adapts to device mobility and achieves performance very close to the ideal case (upper bound).

Keywords: Crowdsourcing, wireless networks, resource allocation optimization.

1 Introduction

Recent years have witnessed a dramatic increase in the number of mobile Internet users due to the tremendous popularity of smartphones and tablets; market forecasts point out that although only 13.3% worldwide cellular users have smartphones in 2011, the ratio is expected to reach 31.0% by 2016 [4]. In some regions, the number of smartphone users actually has exceeded that of feature phone users at the time of writing. For example, more than 46% of U.S. adults own smartphones in early 2012 [6], in Japan the smartphone penetration rate exceeds 95%. A key use of smartphones is to gain access to the Internet. Market reports place the number of mobile Internet users at 1.2 billion worldwide; the National Communications Commission of Taiwan reports that 68% of cellphone

---

* N. Do and N. Venkatasubramanian are partially supported by National Science Foundation, grants #1059436 and #1057928.
** C. Hsu is partially supported by the National Science Council (NSC) of Taiwan, grant #100-2218-E-007-015-MY2.

P. Narasimhan and P. Triantafillou (Eds.): Middleware 2012, LNCS 7662, pp. 1–20, 2012.

users opt for data plans [3]. The staggering number of data plan users forces cellular service providers to deploy costly infrastructure and purchase expensive spectrum, so as to maintain quality-of-service. The resultant traffic surge has also backfired at the mobile users, as the cellular service providers have moved away from unlimited data plans to tiered services [5], and may consider time-dependent pricing [18], which in turn may increase user's monthly bill.

Existing data plans often require 1- to 3-year contracts, and may not have too many options in terms of monthly traffic quotas. This results in low quota utilization, e.g., the worldwide average unused data quota is as high as 61% [4]. Studies indicate that 48.6% of AT&T data plan users incur very low monthly traffic (lower than the least expensive 300-MB data plan), and 81% of these users have a residue quota of more than 100 MBs every month [8]. The aforementioned statistics reveal that: (i) light mobile Internet users may find the contracts and relatively high data plan quotas less appealing, and (ii) other mobile Internet users may have residue data plan quotas. We argue that these two types of users could form a virtual community or marketplace, similar to My Virtual Neighbor [7], and share the resources with each other.

In this paper, we present *CrowdMAC*, a *crowdsourcing* solution for providing on-demand mobile Internet access. Crowdsourcing refers to open platforms, that enable "loose sharing of resources between undefined publics" that may be human or online. Crowdsourcing platforms often incorporate human participation [15] allowing entities to outsource tasks to individuals and gain information from the collective processing. In CrowdMAC, mobile users in need of Internet access (or network connectivity in general) leverage the ability of other nearby users to provide access to the resource – i.e., mobile Internet. In particular, light mobile Internet users may completely avoid data plans, and *hire* other mobile Internet users with residue resources (e.g., data plan quotas, battery) to transfer data to/from the Internet for them. The hired mobile Internet users are referred to as *mobile Access Points (mobile APs)*, and the hiring mobile Internet users are referred to as *mobile devices* throughout this paper. The mobile devices and mobile APs communicate with each other via short-range wireless networks, such as WiFi ad hoc, WiFi Direct [2] and Bluetooth, and hence do not incur significant traffic overhead over the cellular networks. This kind of sharing is called *tethering*, and is widely used among mobile devices belonging to the same user. Some cellular service providers, including Verizon Wireless, Clearwire, and Sprint sell dedicated mobile gateways [23], which essentially are mobile APs. Cooperative use of multiple access networks (Cellular, WiFi, Bluetooth, and etc.) is becoming increasingly feasible; enabling rich mobile applications using such hybrid access networks is a current topic of research [11, 13, 14, 16, 19, 21].

Matching mobile devices with nearby mobile APs is not an easy task – the following challenges arise in creating a meaningful incentive-based design that ensures robust data transfer despite dynamics of mobile users and connectivities.

1. How does a mobile AP make an admit/reject decision upon receiving a request from a mobile device? Admitting a larger number of requests brings

higher revenues, but causes buffer overflow and a longer end-to-end delay for file transfer. Higher delays may turn users away from the system.

2. How does a mobile device select a mobile AP and a corresponding service (Cellular or WiFi network)? Services charge different fees and provide different qualities of service.

3. How do mobile devices and mobile APs deal with uncertain channel conditions caused by mobility? The system has to solve the situation where a mobile device is moving out of its range before its file is completely transferred to the mobile AP. Similarly, a mobile AP's direct Internet access link may be disconnected due to mobility.

4. How does the system handle the associated security issues and legal implications of sharing mobile access? How does this scheme fit into the ISP/network provider ecosystem?

In this paper, we focus on the mechanisms to enable crowdsourced mobile access to the Internet where mobile APs with direct access are able to offer connectivity to mobile devices without easy direct access (i.e., challenges 1, 2 and 3). In particular, CrowdMAC implements incentive-based mechanisms for admission control, service selection and mobility handling in a distributed middleware framework described in Section 2. The proposed mechanisms are implemented directly on off-the-shelf Android devices and require no changes to the underlying network boxes such as cellular base stations and WiFi Hotspots. Challenge 4 (i.e., security and integration with ISPs/providers) is a topic of future work; we discuss our views on this in Section 7.

2   CrowdMAC: Architecture and Approach

In this section, we describe the design principles and architecture of the Crowd-MAC crowdsourcing system that enables mobile devices to hire mobile APs to upload and download data.

2.1   Hardware and Network Architecture

Fig. 1 illustrates the hardware components in the proposed system architecture that include the following parties.

- **Mobile Device:** A device wishes to upload/download a file, but currently does not have a *last connection* to the Internet.
- **Mobile AP:** A mobile AP is also a mobile device which possesses a last connection(s) to the Internet via cellular base stations or WiFi Hotspots. We assume that mobile APs possess data plans with network service providers, and are thus able to send/receive control messages to/from the Internet. In our proposed system, a mobile AP is willing to transfer data for a mobile device for fees. In Fig. 1, A, C, and D are mobile APs willing to transfer data for mobile device B.

  A mobile AP may have one or more last connections over either cellular base stations or WiFi Hotspots. The last connections correspond to different

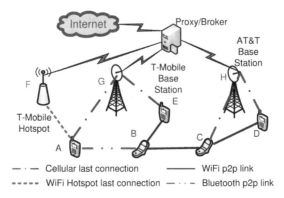

Fig. 1. Network architecture of the proposed system

service providers, which charge the mobile AP at various prices. Moreover, transferring data over different wireless networks consumes diverse local resources, including battery levels and CPU cycles. Hence, each mobile AP may set a different price for transferring data over each last connection. Because a mobile AP may simultaneously transfer data over multiple last connections, it can concurrently offer multiple transfer **services**. Hence, by service, we refer to a specific last connection of a mobile AP.

– **Proxy/Broker:**[1] The system consists of a proxy/broker located behind last connections that keeps records of data amount transferred by mobile APs for mobile devices and the corresponding payments. It ensures that data is transferred from/to the Internet through mobile APs in totality and correctly.

Note that although C in Fig. 1 has a last connection, it may access the Internet through mobile AP D at times of poor connectivity. Nonetheless, we assume that a smartphone can be either a mobile device or a mobile AP, but not both simultaneously in this paper.

2.2 Software Architecture

CrowdMAC is envisioned as a distributed middleware system that resides on mobile devices, mobile APs, and the network proxy/broker. A mobile AP may provide concurrently multiple services, each for a last connection. Fig. 2 depicts the key software components/modules in CrowdMAC: (i) AAA Module, (ii) Control Plane Module, (iii) Data Plane Module, and (iv) Connection Manager. Fig. 2 also illustrates the operational workflow of a CrowdMAC session. Without loss of generality, we illustrate the system workflow using a data upload scenario, and minor modifications required for a download session.

---

[1] Multiple proxies/brokers can be used to scale the system. Proxies/brokers can be offered by: (i) a service provider, (ii) an alliance of multiple providers, or (iii) a third-party company.

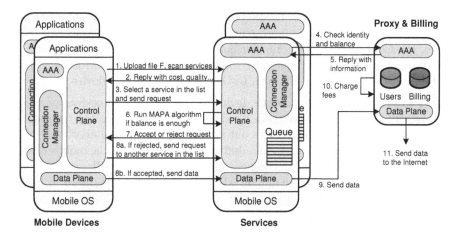

Fig. 2. Components and workflow (upload case) in the middleware system

AAA Module. This module maintains information about users in the system and their mobile access sessions via databases at the proxy/broker. Mobile devices and mobile APs register themselves with the proxy/broker and provide identity information stored in database *User*. During operation, logs are maintained about the amount of data transferred by mobile APs for mobile devices and the corresponding monetary fees in database *Billing*. Our initial implementation uses a prepaid option. Mobile devices (i.e., users) make a monetary deposit to their account before they can use services provided by mobile APs. Prior to transferring data for a mobile device, the mobile AP accesses the proxy/broker to verify if the mobile device is able to cover the fees for the transfer.

Control Plane Module. The control plane modules at different nodes cooperate to establish and maintain connectivity between a mobile device that requests access and the mobile APs that enable this access for a fee. When a mobile device wishes to use a service provided by a mobile AP, it first establishes a connection to the mobile AP through a discovery process in the Control Plane. Mobile devices and mobile APs discover one another as follows. When a user has a file to upload, the Control Plane at the mobile device executes a *service scan* by broadcasting a one-hop message with the size of the file. The Control Plane at the surrounding mobile APs respond to the scan message with the corresponding fees to transfer the file to the Internet. The price of each service is a function of the last connection cost and the local resource consumption dependent on the data amount transferred. It can be manually set by the mobile AP owner. Once the mobile device finds a list of services, it will select a service in the list and send a request containing its identity stored in its AAA to the corresponding mobile AP to use the service. If there is no service found, the mobile device will wait for some time before repeating the scan process. Upon receiving a request from the mobile device, the Control Plane communicates with the proxy/broker through the AAA component to authenticate the user. The identity information provided in the user request is used to verify the mobile device's balance at the billing server. If the balance cannot cover the fees, the request is rejected. Otherwise, the Control Plane goes further one more step. It makes a decision if it should admit or reject the request by running an admission control algorithm, *MAPA*, and then replies the decision to the requesting mobile device.

Data Plane Module. If the mobile device requesting service receives an *admit* response, its Control Plane triggers its Data Plane to start transferring data. Otherwise, it will remove the service out of the list, and choose another service to send the request. In the case of an admitted upload request, the mobile device reads the file and begins transmitting data packets to the Data Plane at the mobile AP. The Data Plane at the mobile AP maintains a **FIFO Queue** to buffer the receiving packets and transmits the buffered packets to the proxy/broker over its last connection. The proxy/broker then transmits the packets to the Internet. Once the whole file is successfully uploaded, the Data Plane at the mobile AP sends a confirmation back to the mobile device.

Connection Manager. This component manages network interfaces available on the device. It notifies the Control Plane and the Data Plane the availability of surround mobile devices and APs and the breakage of connections.

3   CrowdMAC Admission Control

We next present an admission control algorithm, called **MAPA** (Mobile AP Admission control) that allows a service to admit or reject requests from mobile devices based on the characteristics of the incoming requests, their potential to generate increased revenue for the service and the current set of ongoing commitments made by the service. Key design criteria of the admission control algorithm include: (a) maximizing long term revenue (measured as average revenue over time); (b) ensuring overall stability of the system (implying no buffer overflows at the service); and (c) providing a distributed and practical implementation.

We characterize the problem and develop an algorithm to enable admission control decision using a Lyapunov optimization framework. The Lyapunov approach is well suited to creating an operational framework for the mobile access crowdsourcing problem in this paper since it provides: (a) a meaningful theoretical underpinning for stability analysis of the dynamic execution environment and (b) the inherent queuing theoretic based modeling that is well suited to the network transmission problem. Using Lyapunov framework for designing admission control algorithms has been studied in [17,20] for cellular base stations and WiFi Hotspots where resources are not an issue. Our problem considered here is much more challenging because mobile APs are resource constrained, and thus ensuring stability of CrowdMAC must consider this fact.

3.1   Basic Models and Problem Formulation

Consider a network consisting of a set of mobile APs M, a set of mobile devices D, and a set of wireless links L. Let us also assume that time is divided into slots of t units and requests are made by mobile devices to mobile APs for wireless services in a specific time slot. The following terminologies are used in developing the problem.

Services. Each mobile AP m provides a set of services S_m – which in our case represents disparate last hop connections. Let S be a set of all services in the network. When mobile device d wishes to upload a file to the Internet, it selects a service s_m provided by mobile AP m and waits for an accept or reject decision from s_m.

Monetary Costs. Mobile device d, who wishes to upload/download a file with size f_d through a service, must pay a price or cost, which is a function of f_d. In this paper, this is the revenue earned by the service and we consider this as monetary cost. If d selects service s_m provided by mobile AP m, d will be charged a cost denoted by $C(s_m, f_d)$. Typically, $C(s_m, f_d)$ incorporates two subcosts: (a) a local resource consumption cost, $C_r(s_m, f_d)$, that captures the cost incurred due to use of resources at m , and (b) a provider cost, $C_p(s_m, f_d)$, paid by the mobile AP to the network provider (e.g., telco) for covering the data plan cost of s_m's last connection[2]. Hence, $C(s_m, f_d) = C_r(s_m, f_d) + C_p(s_m, f_d)$.

The exact choice of the cost function is immaterial to our admission control technique. Our system works well with any non-decreasing concave function $C(s_m, f_d)$. For example, energy consumption, a dominating portion of the local resource cost for mobile devices, $C_r(s_m, f_d)$, can be modeled as a non-decreasing concave function of the amount of transmitted data [12]. Similarly, a mobile AP m with a 200 MB, \$10 data plan may employ a linear function such as $C_p(s_m, f_d) = \frac{10 f_d}{200(1024)^2}$ to represent the provider cost.

Workload Arrival and Departure. A mobile AP m may have many mobile devices requesting to use its services for file upload/download. We assume that each mobile device has only one file to upload/download at a time, and the maximum file size is F_{max}. A mobile device approaches m when it wants to use m's services, and departs when it completes the transmission or moves out of m's range. Let $R_{s_m}(t)$ denote the set of mobile devices requesting to use service s_m provided by m in time slot t, and $A_{s_m}(t)$ denote the total workload requested from service s_m in time slot t. That is, $A_{s_m}(t) = \sum_{d \in R_{s_m}(t)} f_d$. Assume that $A_{s_m}(t) \leq A_{max} \quad \forall s_m, t$, where A_{max} is the maximum possible workload at any mobile AP. We assume that mobile device arrival rate to m is i.i.d over time slot. Every time slot, s_m admits a set of mobile devices $r_{s_m}(t) \in R_{s_m}(t)$ with an admitted workload of $a_{s_m}(t) \leq A_{s_m}(t)$. The time average data amount admitted to s_m is defined: $\bar{a}_{s_m} \triangleq \lim_{t \to \infty} \frac{1}{t} \sum_{\tau=0}^{t-1} \mathbb{E}\{a_{s_m}(\tau)\}$.

If a mobile device moves out of m's range and has not completed transmission of the file, it finds another mobile AP to upload the remaining file. We let $g_{s_m}(t)$ be the residual data that was not sent via s_m due to disconnections between the mobile AP and mobile devices. Assume that $g_{s_m}(t) \leq g_{max} \quad \forall s_m, t$. The time average residual data not sent via s_m is: $\bar{g}_{s_m} \triangleq \lim_{t \to \infty} \frac{1}{t} \sum_{\tau=0}^{t-1} \mathbb{E}\{g_{s_m}(\tau)\}$.

---

[2] For simplicity, we consider the provider cost also includes cost paid for the proxy/broker provider.

Network Capacity. For each link l in L, let $\mu_l(t)$ and $\theta_l(t)$ denote the amount of data transferred through link l and the maximum capacity of link l at time slot t. Thus, $\mu_l(t) \leq \theta_l(t)$. Value $\theta_l(t)$ depends on channel quality while $\mu_l(t)$ depends on the available data for transfer and $\theta_l(t)$. We assume that channel quality is i.i.d over time slots. We denote θ_{max} as the maximum channel capacity under any quality channel, i.e., $\theta_l(t) \leq \theta_{max} \quad \forall l, t$.

We denote $\mu_{s_m}^{out}(t)$ as the amount of data transmitted out of service s_m in time slot t. $\mu_{s_m}^{out}(t) = \mu_l(t)$ if l is s_m's last connection for the upload case, or $\mu_{s_m}^{out}(t) = \sum_{d \in \Gamma_{s_m}(t)} \mu_{m-d}(t)$ for the download case where $\Gamma_{s_m}(t)$ denote a set of mobile devices that s_m is serving. The time average outgoing data amount from s_m is defined as: $\bar{\mu}_{s_m}^{out} \triangleq \lim_{t \to \infty} \frac{1}{t} \sum_{\tau=0}^{t-1} \mathbb{E}\{\mu_{s_m}^{out}(\tau)\}$.

We define the total incoming data amount to s_m at time slot t as $\mu_{s_m}^{in}(t) = \sum_{d \in \Gamma_{s_m}(t)} \mu_{d-m}(t)$ for the upload case, or $\mu_{s_m}^{in}(t) = \mu_l(t)$ where l is the last connection for the download case. We denote ϑ_{max} as the maximum incoming data amount to any service at any time slot, i.e., $\mu_{s_m}^{in}(t) \leq \vartheta_{max} \quad \forall s_m, t$. The time average incoming data amount at s_m is defined as: $\bar{\mu}_{s_m}^{in}(t) \triangleq \lim_{t \to \infty} \frac{1}{t} \sum_{\tau=0}^{t-1} \mathbb{E}\{\mu_{s_m}^{in}(\tau)\}$.

Problem Formulation. Given a set of mobile devices $R_{s_m}(t)$ arriving at service s_m and requesting to use service s_m with workload $A_{s_m}(t)$, s_m determines a set of mobile devices $r_{s_m}(t)$ to be admitted for using the service such that:

$$\max: \quad \bar{C}_{s_m} = \lim_{t \to \infty} \frac{1}{t} \sum_{\tau=0}^{t-1} \sum_{d \in r_{s_m}(\tau)} \mathbb{E}\{C(s_m, f_d)\}; \tag{1a}$$

$$\text{st:} \quad \bar{\mu}_{s_m}^{in} \leq \bar{\mu}_{s_m}^{out}; \tag{1b}$$

$$\bar{a}_{s_m} \leq \bar{g}_{s_m} + \bar{\mu}_{s_m}^{in}. \tag{1c}$$

Objective function (1a) indicates that s_m attempts to maximize the time average revenue while maintaining its system's stability over time as shown in constraint (1b). Constraint (1c) is to ensure that admitted data will be transmitted to s_m unless the mobile device leaves the range of the mobile AP.

3.2 Our Proposed Admission Control Algorithm - MAPA

To solve the problem (1a)-(1c), we design an admission control algorithm using the Lyapunov framework. To ensure the two constraints (1b) and (1c), we maintain a real queue and a virtual queue for each service s_m in S presented below.

Real Queue and the System Stability - Constraint (1b). Data transmitted to/from mobile devices from/to s_m is stored at a queue before it can be transmitted further. Each service has one real queue to store request data; let $Q_{s_m}(t)$ denote the queue backlog, which is the number of bytes in that queue, at the beginning of time slot t for service s_m. The queue backlog's evolution is expressed as:

$$Q_{s_m}(t+1) \triangleq \max(Q_{s_m}(t) - \mu_{s_m}^{out}(t) + \mu_{s_m}^{in}(t), 0). \tag{2}$$

We define **stability** of our system as finite average queue backlog:

$$\bar{Q}_{s_m} \triangleq \lim_{t \to \infty} \sup \frac{1}{t} \sum_{\tau=0}^{t-1} \mathbb{E}\{Q_{s_m}(\tau)\} < \infty. \tag{3}$$

Notice that if (3) is maintained then constraint (1b) is satisfied. In real implementations, the real queue at mobile devices can be ignored, as a mobile device
may read files on-demand rather than prefetching them into memory.

Virtual Queue and the Admitted Data - Constraint (1c): To satisfy constraint (1c) without breaking the Lyapunov framework, we employ the concept
of a virtual queue that captures the projected load over time based on requests
admitted by the service. Each service s_m maintains a virtual queue $U_{s_m}(t)$ that
is just a software counter, i.e. does not hold actual data packets. $U_{s_m}(0)$ is set
to 0 and $U_{s_m}(t)$ evolves over time as follows:

$$U_{s_m}(t+1) \triangleq \max(U_{s_m}(t) - g_{s_m}(t) - \mu_{s_m}^{in}(t) + a_{s_m}(t), 0). \tag{4}$$

Lemma 1. *If the virtual queue is stable, i.e.,*

$$\bar{U}_{s_m} \triangleq \lim_{t \to \infty} \sup \frac{1}{t} \sum_{\tau=0}^{t-1} \mathbb{E}\{U_{s_m}(\tau)\} < \infty. \tag{5}$$

then constraint (1c) is satisfied.[3]

We define **a revenue weight** V that works as a control parameter providing a
trade-off between revenue and stability. By employing the Lyapunov framework
with the real queue, the virtual queue, and parameter V, we translate the original
problem (1a)-(1c) to another optimization problem that can be solved by 3 tasks
presented in the following algorithm.

The MAPA algorithm, summarized in Algorithm 1, solves the problem in a
distributed manner, and can be directly deployed on off-the-shelf devices without
requiring modifications of the existing softwares at cellular base stations and
WiFi Hotspots. It works as follows. Every time slot, every service s_m performs
three tasks: (1) determining which mobile devices requesting to use s_m will be
admitted; (2) determining if mobile devices that s_m is serving should transmit
data to s_m's real queue or not; and (3) transmitting data out of the real queue
$Q_{s_m}(t)$ whenever the queue is not empty.

To do task (1), service s_m needs to solve the problem (6a)–(6b). It does
that by going through every mobile device d in $R_{s_m}(t)$, and calculates $e_d = VC(s_m, f_d) - U_{s_m}(t)f_d$. If $e_d \geq 0$, then d is admitted. Otherwise, d is rejected.
Therefore, the procedure's complexity is $O(n)$.

Service s_m performs task (2) to control congestion. In the case of admitted
upload requests, every time slot, if s_m observes that the real queue backlog

---

[3] The proofs of our lemmas and theorems throughout this paper are omitted without
breaking the flow, due to the space limitations.

is larger than the virtual queue backlog, s_m broadcasts a *STOP* message to request mobile devices not to transmit data in the current time slot. In the case of admitted download requests, the service generates threads to download data packets from the Internet and put the packets into the real queue. At the beginning of a time slot, if there is congestion at the real queue, the service stops the threads from downloading during the time slot.

Algorithm 1. Admission Control and Transmission Schedule

---

1. **Admission Control Procedure** : Every time slot t, service s_m selects a set of mobile devices $r_{s_m}(t)$ from $R_{s_m}(t)$ such that the following maximization condition is satisfied:

$$\text{max:} \quad \sum_{d \in r_{s_m}(t)} (VC(s_m, f_d) - U_{s_m}(t)f_d); \tag{6a}$$

$$\text{st:} \quad r_{s_m}(t) \in R_{s_m}(t). \tag{6b}$$

2. **Transmission Schedule for Incoming Data**: Every time slot t, s_m schedules transmission for incoming data such that if $Q_{s_m}(t) - U_{s_m}(t) > 0$, it does not allow mobile devices to transmit data to the service as well as download data from the Internet.

3. **Transmission Schedule for Outgoing Data**: Every time slot t, s_m always transmits data out of the service if its real queue has data to send.

3.3 Performance Analysis for the MAPA Algorithm

Let's denote $C^*_{s_m}$ as the maximum time average revenue of the problem (1a)–(1c) achieved by some stationary randomized algorithm. We first show that MAPA achieves a time average revenue $\bar{C}$ arbitrarily close to $C^*_{s_m}$.

Theorem 1 (Revenue Lower Bound). *Our MAPA algorithm achieves a lower bound of the time average revenue:*

$$\bar{C}_{s_m} = \lim_{T \to \infty} \frac{1}{T} \sum_{\tau=0}^{T-1} \sum_{d \in r_{s_m}(\tau)} \mathbb{E}\{C(s_m, f_d)\} \geq C^*_{s_m} - \frac{\beta}{V}, \text{ where} \tag{7}$$

$$\beta = \frac{1}{2}[\max(\theta_{max}, \vartheta_{max})^2 + \max(g_{max} + \vartheta_{max}, A_{max})^2]. \tag{8}$$

Next, we show there is a trade-off O(1/V, V) between the achieved revenue and the quality-of-services in the MAPA algorithm.

Theorem 2 (Worst Case Bounds on Real and Virtual Queues). *MAPA provides worst case bounds of the service's real and virtual queue size:*

$$U_{s_m}(t) \leq Vy^*_{s_m} + A_{max} = U^*_{s_m}; \quad Q_{s_m}(t) \leq Vy^*_{s_m} + A_{max} + \vartheta_{max} = Q^*_{s_m}, \tag{9}$$

where y_{s_m} is a service based function with respect to f_d ($f_d \leq F_{max}$) defined as $y_{s_m} = \frac{C(s_m, f_d)}{f_d}$ and $y^*_{s_m}$ is the maximum value of y_{s_m}, $Q^*_{s_m}$ and $U^*_{s_m}$ indicate the maximum queue backlog of s_m's real queue and virtual queue.

The above two theorems illustrate the trade-off between the time average revenue and the worst case queue bounds. If service s_m increases its time average revenue $O(1/V)$, then the size of both real and virtual queues increases $O(V)$. For example, when queue sizes reach infinity, s_m achieves the time average revenue arbitrarily close to the optimal value.

However, note that a large queue size may lead to high end-to-end delay. The following lemma shows that MAPA leads to a linear relationship between the end-to-end delay and the backlogs of the real and virtual queues.

Lemma 2 (Relating Queue Size and Delay). *Let's denote the current backlogs of the real and virtual queues as $Q^o_{s_m}$ and $U^o_{s_m}$, respectively. Assume that the incoming and outgoing data rates $\mu^{in}_{s_m}$ and $\mu^{out}_{s_m}$ of service s_m are unchanged over time slots. The MAPA algorithm achieves the worst case delay T to send all data in the real and virtual queues to the Internet:*

$$T = \hat{t} + \hat{T} \qquad slots, \ where \qquad (10)$$

$$\hat{t} = \max(0, \lceil \frac{Q^o_{s_m} - U^o_{s_m}}{\mu^{out}_{s_m}} \rceil); \quad \hat{Q}^o_{s_m} = \max(0, Q^o_{s_m} - \hat{t}\mu^{out}_{s_m}); \qquad (11)$$

$$\hat{T} = \begin{cases} \lceil \frac{\hat{Q}^o_{s_m} + U^o_{s_m}}{\mu^{out}_{s_m}} \rceil & if \ \mu^{in}_{s_m} \geq \mu^{out}_{s_m}; \\ \lceil \frac{\hat{Q}^o_{s_m}}{\mu^{out}_{s_m}} + \frac{U^o_{s_m}}{\mu^{in}_{s_m}} \rceil + 2 & if \ 2\mu^{in}_{s_m} > \mu^{out}_{s_m} > \mu^{in}_{s_m}; \\ \lceil \frac{U^o_{s_m}}{\mu^{in}_{s_m}} \rceil & if \ \mu^{out}_{s_m} \geq C\mu^{in}_{s_m} \ (C \geq 2). \end{cases} \qquad (12)$$

Selection of Parameter V. We have shown that V controls the trade-off between time average revenue and the delay. Two heuristics to select V are:

- *Bounding memory consumption*: Let M^* be memory bound at a service. Per Theorem 2, we have $Q^*_{s_m} = Vy^*_{s_m} + A_{max} + \vartheta_{max} \leq M^*$, which enables us to pick a V value satisfying the memory bound.
- *Delay quality*: The delay quality is a quality-of-service metric for a service to deliver all data currently admitted in the virtual queue and buffered in the real queue to the Internet. Let T_{s_m} be the bounded delay quality, service s_m wishes to offer. If T_{s_m} is small, the amount of data admitted and buffered is small. That leads to a short transfer delay to deliver data to the Internet and a low revenue for the service. According to Lemma 2, T_{s_m} is the upper bound of T. In the worst case, we have $Q^o_{s_m} = Q^*_{s_m}$ and $U^o_{s_m} = U^*_{s_m}$. We set the minimum data rate incoming to s_m to be $\mu^{in}_{s_m}$ and the minimum outgoing data rate from the service to be $\mu^{out}_{s_m}$. Plugging $Q^*_{s_m}$, $U^*_{s_m}$, $\mu^{out}_{s_m}$ and $\mu^{in}_{s_m}$ into Lemma 2, we estimate V by (9) such that T is bounded by T_{s_m}.

4 Handling Mobile Device and Mobile AP Mobility

Due to mobility, connections between mobile devices and services as well as last connection may be lost. Fundamental to our approach is the ability to monitor the liveness of a link. For a service provided by the mobile AP, once it detects the disconnection, it removes the mobile device from the list of the devices it is serving, updates the virtual queue, and drops the mobile device's packets out of the real queue. For the mobile device, it stops using that service, and scans for another service. Advanced technologies such as WiFi Direct [2] on Android OS 4.0.4 support APIs to detect the disconnection quickly. For other network technologies, we broadcast HELLO messages to detect the breakage. In addition to liveness monitoring, CrowdMAC incorporates the following techniques to support continuity of upload/download under mobility conditions.

Technique 1 - File Segmentation for easy management and recovery: We divide each large file into smaller sized chunks and transmit each chunk independently. This is to reduce the transfer time and consequently enable successful delivery of chunks, despite connectivity changes. Once chunks have been sent, missing packets and chunks are retransmitted.

Technique 2 - Service Selection and Mobility Awareness: When multiple mobile APs are available, a mobile device can choose one from them using one of the following strategies:

1. *Cost Based Service Selection*: The mobile device simply chooses the service with the lowest cost.
2. *Delay Quality Based Service Selection*: The mobile device picks the service with the best delay quality (as defined in Section 3.3).
3. *Mobility Based Service Selection*: The mobile device chooses a service based on reliability of the link from itself to the service. We assume that mobile devices and APs travel using a well known Random Waypoint model. Link reliability is determined by estimating link duration that indicates how long a link is likely to last. The mobile device picks the service with the longest link duration. The duration of link l denoted as $\delta_l(t)$ can be estimated using existing efforts, such as Qin and Zimmermann [22] using an analytical model to estimate the link duration based on GPS readings.

Technique 3 - Incentives to Constrain Mobility during file transfer: We employ charging schemes to motivate mobile devices and mobile APs to constrain mobility during file transfer. In file download scenarios, consider a situation in which a mobile device d requests to download a file f_d. The file has been downloaded in the real queue, but just part of that has been sent to the mobile device because the mobile device moves out of the service's range. This is unfairness to the mobile AP because it had to pay for the Internet access cost $C_p(s_m, f_d)$ to download the file. To address this issue, the mobile AP divides the file into multiple smaller chunks. Each time when the service starts downloading a chunk c_d, the mobile device will be charged a fee $C_p(s_m, c_d)$. Once the mobile device fully receives the whole chunk from the service, it pays the remaining fee $C_r(s_m, c_d)$. If the service fails to download the chunk, it returns $C_p(s_m, c_d)$ to the mobile device. Note that if the service does not receive a confirmation of receiving a chunk from the mobile device, it will not download the next chunk. With this mechanism, both sides, the mobile device and the service, have motivation to

 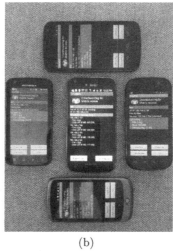

         (a)   (b)

Fig. 3. Our Android based testbed: (a) a screenshot of our system on a mobile device and (b) an experiment with 5 different types of mobile phones

maintain the link stability until the whole chunk is successfully downloaded. In file upload scenarios, incentive provision is simpler. Fees are charged on what the service uploads through the broker/proxy. While the mobile device is motivated to keep the link stable to complete the transfer, the mobile AP is incentivized to keep the last connection stable to earn the revenue.

5   Testbed Implementation: A Proof-of-Concept

Our Testbed and Settings. We implement our middleware on an Android based testbed which consists of a Linux server and multiple Android smartphones located in the University of California, Irvine. An interesting thing is our implementation does not depend on synchronized timers among mobile devices and mobile APs. The admission control procedure in Algorithm 1 runs once for each request, rather than in every single time slot. That is, whenever a mobile device has a file to transfer, it sends a request to a mobile AP. That mobile AP then invokes the MAPA algorithm right away, and immediately sends back the accept/reject decision. Also, the transmission scheduling procedure in Algorithm 1 keeps track of the backlogs of virtual and real queues on mobile APs. Once a mobile AP sends a STOP message, the corresponding mobile device stops transmitting data to that mobile AP. Since MAPA does not require synchronized timers, it can be readily implemented in the CrowdMAC system.

We deploy our system on multiple types of Android phones: a Samsung Galaxy SII as a mobile AP connecting to the T-Mobile network, and four mobile devices including Google Nexus, Nexus S, HTC Nexus One and Motorola Atrix. The phones run Android OS versions from 2.3.6 to 4.0.4. They are placed in a labroom with no mobility and connect to each other over a WiFi peer-to-peer network using WiFi Tether [1]. The mobile AP is equipped with a data plan of $30 for 5 GB, and it charges $5 per GB for local resource consumption. The T-Mobile network is measured to have bandwidth between 311 and 748 Kbps throughout our experiments. In each experiment, each mobile device uploads 50 equal-sized files. For each file, a mobile device sends a request to the mobile AP and waits for its decision. If the request is rejected, the mobile device waits for 2 secs before it resends the request. The mobile device skips the current file if the its request is rejected for 5 times. Fig. 3 presents our system's GUI and the phones in an experiment.

Experimental Results. We consider two metrics (i) *Revenue*, which is the total revenue generated by the service in each experiment, and (ii) *Transfer delay*, which is the average per-file transfer time, from the instant a request is admitted to the instant when the last packet is transferred.

Reliable transfer. We repeat the experiments with various parameter $V \in [0, 1500]$, and we consider two file sizes: 512 KB and 1 MB. Across all experiments, we find that all the admitted requests lead to successful file uploads. This confirms that the proposed CrowdMAC system and MAPA algorithm do work.

Trade-off between revenue and transfer delay. Fig. 4 presents the revenue and transfer delay under different V. This figure shows that smaller V leads to fewer admitted requests, and thus lower revenue. Furthermore, fewer admitted requests means lighter-loaded networks, and thus shorter transfer delay. For example, with $V = 10$, the mobile AP only admits half of the 512 KB files at the end; while with $V = 1000$, the mobile AP admits all the requests. Fig. 4 shows the effectiveness of V: the MAPA algorithm supports wide ranges of revenues and transfer delays.

User-specified delay quality level. We next evaluate the V selection heuristic proposed in Sec. 3.3. We consider the heuristic that maps a delay quality level, between 45 and 135, to a suitable V value. Fig. 5 presents the revenue and transfer delay achieved by various delay quality levels. We make two observations. First, higher delay quality level leads to more admitted requests, which in turn results in high revenue and transfer delay. Second, Fig. 5(b) reveals that the average transfer delay is always smaller than the delay quality level specified by the user throughout our experiments.

6   Simulation Based Evaluation

6.1   Settings

We implement our middleware system in Qualnet 5.02 [9]. In simulations, we use WiMAX to simulate last connections from mobile APs to the Internet and use IEEE 802.11 in ad hoc mode to simulate links among mobile devices and mobile APs. We configure the WiMAX range to cover all mobile APs, and we set the 802.11 range to be 120 m. Two-Ray model is used as the propagation model and UDP is used as the transport protocol in our simulations. Simulation time is set long enough such that all files can be completely transferred.

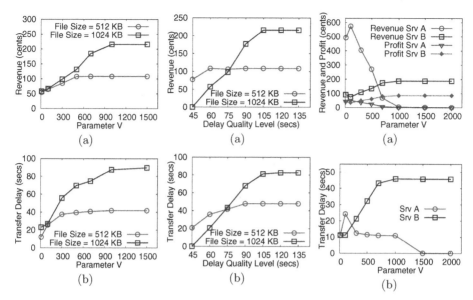

Fig. 4. Diverse Parameter V: (a) revenue and (b) transfer delay

Fig. 5. Diverse user-specified delay quality level: (a) revenue and (b) transfer delay

Fig. 6. Trade-off between: (a) revenue and profit, and (b) transfer delay

We follow the current data plan prices of T-Mobile [10] to design the cost functions. We define three cost functions: (1) $S_1 = \frac{10 \times 100x}{2 \times (1024)}$ cent/KB ($10 for 200 MB), (2) $S_2 = \frac{30 \times 100x}{5 \times (1024)^2}$ cent/KB ($30 for 5 GB), and (3) $S_3 = \frac{5 \times 100x}{(1024)^2}$ cent/KB ($5 for 1 GB) where x is the amount of transferred data in KB. S_1 and S_2 cover the Internet access cost, and S_3 covers the local resource consumption cost. Each mobile AP may decide to employ one of the cost functions, or adapt a linear combination of two of them.

In Section 5, we examine our system with networks with a single service. In this section, we investigate our system's performance with more than one service, so as to exercise two different service selection strategies. In addition to the two metrics described earlier, we consider metrics: (i) *Profit*: the total monetary cost (C_r) charged by a service for its local resource consumption after each simulation, (ii) *Cost*: the total cost paid by a mobile device on average for each file, (iii) *End-to-end delay*: the average delay per file from the instant a mobile device scans services to the instant when the last packet reaches destination; (iv) *Number of interruptions*: the average number of disconnections during each file transfer, and (v) *Overhead*: the ratio between the total traffic amount and the total file size. We ran each simulation five times with different random seeds, and plotted the averages of the results obtained in all runs. If not otherwise specified, we consider all mobile devices to select the service based on the cost. By default, we use the same V value for all mobile APs. In the following two sections, we consider the static and mobile scenarios, respectively.

6.2   Evaluation Under Static Scenarios

We configure a network with a WiMAX base station, two mobile APs, and seven mobile devices. Each mobile AP offers a service, and we call them service A and B, respectively. Service A employs a more expensive cost function of $S_1 + S_3$, and B employs a cheaper cost function of $S_2 + S_3$. All mobile devices are in the range of both mobile APs. In each simulation, every mobile device sequentially transfers 50 equal-sized files. We conduct each simulation with two file sizes: 512 KB and 1 MB. Due to the space limitations, we present the results with 512 KB files if not otherwise specified.

Generality of the MAPA Algorithm. We compare MAPA against two baseline algorithms: *ALL* and *ONE*. In ALL, a service always accepts request from mobile devices no matter how much workload it is carrying on. Hence, it aims to maximize its revenue. In ONE, a service always rejects request unless it is serving no request. Thus, ONE is designed for service to provide best service quality to one request. Different from ALL and ONE, MAPA employs a parameter V. We vary $V \in [0, 2000]$, and repeat the simulations with MAPA. We find that ALL and ONE achieve similar revenue, profit, and end-to-end delay as MAPA with $V = 10$ and $V = 2000$, respectively. Hence, MAPA is a general algorithm for diverse quality-of-service needs.

Trade-off between Revenue and Transfer Delay. We plot the resulting profit and transfer delay in Fig. 6. Fig. 6(a) shows that, with a small V, service A achieves higher revenue due to its higher Internet access cost. This in turn leads to higher workload and longer transfer delay as illustrated in Fig. 6(b). With a larger V, service B achieves higher revenue because its maximum workload is raised. With $V > 1000$, service B accepts all requests and achieves the highest possible revenue, at the expense of long transfer delay. Fig. 6 reveals the trade-off between revenue and transfer delay.

V's Implication on Profit. Fig. 6(a) reveals that service B makes higher profit than A when $V \in [100, 2000]$. This can be attributed to B's lower Internet access cost. In fact, with $V \in [100, 600]$, service B makes higher profit even when A achieves high revenue. With $V \in [0, 100]$, service A makes higher profit, because B has saturated its maximum workload. Service A has a larger maximum workload due to its higher cost.

User-Specified Delay Quality Level. We consider the heuristic, presented in Sec. 3.3, which maps a delay quality level to a suitable V value. We vary the delay quality level of B from 45 to 172 secs. Service A sets its delay quality level to be half of B's. Fig. 7 presents the simulation results, in which x-axis is the delay quality level of service B. This figure shows that when the delay quality level of B $\leq$ 60 secs, mobile devices completely avoid service A. This is because the delay quality level for A is too short for 512 KB files. Once the delay quality is large enough, service A starts to receive requests, and its revenue and profit increase. At the delay quality of 75 secs (i.e., 150 secs on the x-axis), service A accepts all requests. That leads to the saturated revenue and transfer delay at service A as shown in Figs. 7. We make another observation: the transfer

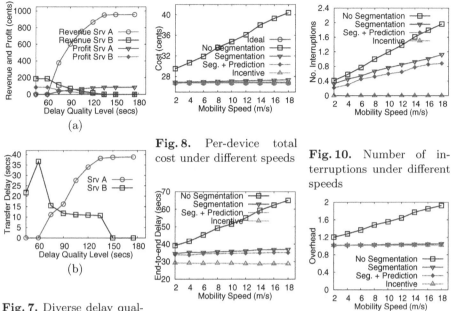

Fig. 7. Diverse delay quality level: (a) revenue and profit, and (b) transfer delay

Fig. 8. Per-device total cost under different speeds

Fig. 9. End-to-end delay per file under different speeds.

Fig. 10. Number of interruptions under different speeds

Fig. 11. Traffic overhead of our system

delay is always lower than the delay quality level specified by the users in our simulations. This reveals the effectiveness of our heuristic.

6.3 Evaluation under Mobility Scenarios

Mobile users may move around when they are participating in CrowdMAC. To evaluate the performance of our system under user mobility, we set up a 700×700 m^2 network with 40 devices. Among these devices, there are 8 stationary mobile APs connecting to a WiMAX base station and offering Internet access services. The other mobile devices travel with Random Waypoint model unless otherwise specified and download 50 files with a size of 512 KB. A mobile device downloads only one file each time, and starts the next download 30 secs after it finishes the previous one. Mobile APs are randomly placed in the network such that they cover about 65% of the network area. Some mobile APs are placed overlapped such that a mobile device can have a chance to discover more than one mobile AP. We configure all mobile APs to use the same cost functions S_2 and S_3. Unless otherwise specified, mobile devices select service using cost based strategy.

Impact of Techniques Handling Mobility. We repeat the simulations with different mobility handling techniques, and plot the results in Figs. 8–11. The considered techniques are:

1. *Ideal*: The expected cost under no exceptions, such as link breakages. This is the minimum cost a mobile device could possibly pay.
2. *No Segmentation*: No specific technique is applied. Each file is transferred in its entirety.
3. *Segmentation*: The performance achieved by using technique File Segmentation for handling mobility.
4. *Segmentation + Prediction*: The performance of the combination of two techniques: File Segmentation and Mobility based Service Selection.

Fig. 8 shows that No Segmentation pays the highest cost up to 42 cents to download the files, i.e., 16 cents higher than Ideal, at the speed of 18 m/s. It is because the increase of the speed leads to a higher link breakage frequency and a higher amount of data which is downloaded to the real queue yet transferred to the mobile device. The Segmentation technique significantly improves the performance. Segmentation leads to the cost close to Ideal, only 1 cent higher to download 25 MB at the high speed of 18 m/s. Segmentation + Prediction even reduces the cost more, approximately equal to Ideal at that speed.

Fig. 9 shows that the end-to-end delay of No Segmentation is approximately twice higher than that of Segmentation. Segmentation + Prediction further reduces the end-to-end delay to 2 secs shorter than that of Segmentation. The higher end-to-end delay can be attributed to more link breakages due to the mobility. We plot the number of interruptions in Fig. 10, which confirms our conjecture. Last, Fig. 11 reports the relative overhead achieved by different techniques. This figure clearly shows that CrowdMAC produces negligible traffic overhead. It also reveals the effectiveness of File Segmentation.

Impact of the Incentive Mobility. We have shown that CrowdMAC works well even when mobile devices follow a random mobility model. Next we consider a more realistic mobility model, denoted as *Incentive Mobility Model*. In this model, the mobile devices, after selecting services, try to keep the links between themselves and the services stable, rather than moving fast and causing link breakage. This is done in order to ensure continuity for ongoing services that have already been charged. Mobile devices that are not transferring files follow the Random Waypoint model.

We plot the system performance under the Incentive Mobility Model in Figs. 8–11, labelled by *Incentive*. CrowdMAC achieves much better performance under this realistic mobility model. In particular, Incentive: (i) achieves the same minimum cost as Ideal, (ii) more than 10 secs shorter end-to-end delay than Segmentation + Prediction, and (iii) never suffers from interruptions.

7   Related Work and Concluding Remarks

Modern mobile phones have been extended to incorporate multiple networking interfaces beyond traditional cellular and WLAN capabilities; this enables them to form opportunistic networks using technologies such as WiFi Direct [2], WiFi Tether [1] and Bluetooth. Opportunistic networks complement infrastructure networks with new capabilities to support throughput enhancement [13, 21] and peer-to-peer cellular traffic offloading [14,16,19]. Efforts have explored techniques to enhance throughput for mobile devices that suffer from low cellular data rates by selecting proxies that are in fact mobile devices with high cellular link rates [13,21]. Recent research has also proposed solutions [14,16,19] for mobile devices to cooperatively disseminate data. For example, in [14,19], nearby mobile devices cooperate to stream live videos; in these schemes, selected mobile devices are scheduled to receive part of videos over cellular networks and relay the received data to other mobile phones over WiFi peer-to-peer networks.

To our best knowledge, CrowdMAC is the first effort to developing a crowd-sourcing system to motivate mobile users for sharing Internet access. We showed how to design and implement a middleware framework that incorporates a Lyapunov based admission control algorithm for mobile APs to serve multiple requesting mobile devices optimally and stably, strategies for mobile devices to select mobile APs appropriately, and techniques for handling device and AP mobility. CrowdMAC has been implemented and evaluated on a testbed of diverse Android phones with varying capabilities indicating feasibility of the approach. Our experimental and simulation results show that CrowdMAC: (i) effectively exercises the trade-off between revenue and transfer delay, (ii) adequately satisfies user-specified (delay) quality level, and (iii) properly adapts to device mobility and achieves performance very close to the ideal case (upper bound).

Future Work. The Lyapunov based approach in this paper lends itself well to a practical implementation. One can also consider an alternate game theoretic formulation that models the interaction between mobile devices and mobile APs as a multiparty game. The ability to embed the game theoretic approach into a real system in a dynamic setting is challenging – this is our future work.

To realize a broader and wide-scale deployment of our crowdsourcing scheme, our future work will also address two key concerns. The first concern is that of security. Mechanisms are required to protect a users' file as it passes through arbitrary (and potentially untrusted) nodes, networks and middle-boxes; this includes protection from DOS attacks and from malicious services. How to leverage cryptographic techniques to provide such end-to-end security is our current aim. The second concern is the need for a tighter integration of the proposed scheme into the ISP/provider ecosystem so as to mesh with the business objectives of telcos and service providers. Creating localized networks to support data exchange is becoming a commodity technology. We believe that the ability to crowd-source/share local wireless access can offer a new perspective that may change the scale and scope of mobile data delivery just as VoIP has changed the landscape of telephony today.

References

1. Android WiFi tether (2009), http://code.google.com/p/android-wifi-tether/
2. Wi-Fi certified Wi-Fi Direct: Personal, portable Wi-Fi that goes with you anywhere, any time (2010), http://www.wi-fi.org/Wi-Fi_Direct.php
3. National communications commission (2011), http://www.ncc.gov.tw/

4. Traffic and market data report (2011),
   http://hugin.info/1061/R/1561267/483187.pdf
5. Why Verizon dropped its unlimited data plan (and what you can do about it)
   (2011), http://moneyland.time.com/2011/06/23/why-verizon-
   dropped-its-unlimited-data-plan/
6. 46% of American adults are smartphone owners (2012),
   http://pewinternet.org/ /media//Files/Reports/2012/Smartphone
   %20ownership%202012.pdf
7. My virtual neighbor (2012), http://www.myvirtualneighbor.com/
8. Nearly half of AT&T subscribers would pay less by switching to a metered plan
   (2012), http://tinyurl.com/86kcgyj
9. Qualnet network simulator (2012),
   http://code.google.com/p/android-wifi-tether/
10. T-Mobile data plan (2012),
    http://www.t-mobile.com/shop/plans/mobile-broadband-plans.aspx
11. Balasubramanian, A., Mahajan, R., Venkataramani, A.: Augmenting mobile 3G
    using WiFi. In: Proc. of MobiSys, San Francisco, USA, pp. 209–222 (2010)
12. Balasubramanian, N., Balasubramanian, A., Venkataramani, A.: Energy consump-
    tion in mobile phones: A measurement study and implications for network appli-
    cations. In: Proc. of IMC, Chicago, IL, pp. 280–293 (2009)
13. Bhatia, R., Li, L., Luo, H., Ramjee, R.: ICAM: Integrated cellular and ad hoc
    multicast. IEEE Transactions on Mobile Computing 5(8), 1004–1015 (2006)
14. Do, N., Hsu, C., Jatinder, S., Venkatasubramanian, N.: Massive live video distri-
    bution over hybrid cellular and ad hoc networks. In: Proc. of IEEE WoWMoM,
    Lucia, Italy, pp. 1–9 (2011)
15. Franklin, M., Kossmann, D., Kraska, T., Ramesh, S., Xin, R.: CrowdDB: Answering
    queries with crowdsourcing. In: Proc. of ACM SIGMOD, Athens, Greece, pp. 61–72
    (2011)
16. Han, B., Hui, P., Kumar, V., Marathe, M., Shao, J., Srinivasan, A.: Mobile
    data offloading through opportunistic communications and social participation.
    IEEE/ACM Transactions on Mobile Computing 11(5), 821–834 (2012)
17. Huang, L., Neely, M.: The optimality of two prices: Maximizing revenue in a
    stochastic communication system. IEEE/ACM Transactions on Networking 18(2),
    406–419 (2010)
18. Joe-Wong, C., Ha, S., Chiang, M.: Time-dependent broadband pricing: Feasibility
    and benefits. In: Proc. of IEEE ICDCS, Minneapolis, MN, pp. 288–298 (2011)
19. Keller, L., Le, A., Cici, B., Seferoglu, H., Fragouli, C., Markopoulou, A.: MicroCast:
    cooperative video streaming on smartphones. In: Proc. of ACM MobiSys, Lake
    District, United Kingdom (2012)
20. Lotfinezhad, M., Liang, B., Sousa, E.: Optimal control of constrained cognitive
    radio networks with dynamic population size. In: Proc. of IEEE INFOCOM, San
    Diego, CA, pp. 1–9 (2010)
21. Luo, H., Meng, X., Ramjee, R., Sinha, P., Li, L.: The design and evaluation of uni-
    fied cellular and ad-hoc networks. IEEE Transactions on Mobile Computing 6(9),
    1060–1074 (2007)
22. Qin, M., Zimmermann, R.: Improving mobile ad-hoc streaming performance
    through adaptive layer selection with scalable video coding. In: Proc. of ACM
    Multimedia, Augsburg, Germany, pp. 717–726 (2007)
23. Yeh, S., Talwar, S., Wu, G., Himayat, N., Johnsson, K.: Capacity and coverage
    enhancement in heterogeneous networks. IEEE Wireless Communications 18(3),
    32–38 (2011)

Pogo, a Middleware for Mobile Phone Sensing

Niels Brouwers and Koen Langendoen

Delft University of Technology
{n.brouwers,k.g.langendoen}@tudelft.nl

Abstract. The smartphone revolution has brought ubiquitous, power-ful, and connected sensing hardware to the masses. This holds great promise for a wide range of research fields. However, deployment of experiments onto a large set of mobile devices places technological, or-ganizational, and sometimes financial burdens on researchers, making real-world experimental research cumbersome and difficult. We argue that a research infrastructure in the form of a large-scale mobile phone testbed is required to unlock the potential of this new technology.

We aim to facilitate experimentation with mobile phone sensing by providing a pragmatic middleware framework that is easy to use and fea-tures fine-grained user-level control to guard the privacy of the volunteer smart-phone users. In this paper we describe the challenges and require-ments for such a middleware, outline an architecture featuring a flexible, scriptable publish/subscribe framework, and report on our experience with an implementation running on top of the Android platform.

Keywords: Mobile Middleware, Mobile Phone Sensing, Mobile Test Beds.

1   Introduction

Modern smartphones are rapidly becoming ubiquitous and are even supplanting the desktop PC as the dominant mode for accessing the Internet [7]. They are equipped with a powerful processor and a wide range of sensors that can be used to infer information about the environment and context of a user. These capabil-ities and the rapidly growing number of smartphones offer unique opportunities for a great number of research fields including context-aware computing [25], reality mining [11], and community sensing [5,20]. Basically, the smartphone revolution will enable experimentation at scale in real-world settings; an excit-ing prospect.

To date most efforts have focused on building monolithic mobile applica-tions that are tested in small-scale lab environments. Real-world deployment is a labor-intensive process, which involves recruiting participants, acquiring de-vices, deploying software updates, and so on. Because the barrier for deployment onto a large number of devices is high, many applications and experiments are never able to leave the desk of the researcher. This is a serious drawback that needs to be addressed as history has shown that small-scale systems often show quite different behavior when put to the test in the real world [21].

P. Narasimhan and P. Triantafillou (Eds.): Middleware 2012, LNCS 7662, pp. 21–40, 2012.

The challenge for running large-scale experiments is no longer the hardware, as affordable smart phones equipped with various sensors are ubiquitously available, but the software engineering involved in creating and installing the application code to read, process, and collect the desired information. Indiscriminately gathering all possible sensor data on the device and sending it back to a central server is infeasible due to bandwidth, power consumption, and privacy concerns. Hence, on-line analysis and filtering is required [6]. Since researchers rarely get their algorithms right on the first try, quick (re-)deployment of mobile sensing applications is essential for the experimental process, but typical application stores are not suitable for this. Finally, there is a large administrative overhead involved with managing large groups of test subjects, especially when multiple experiments need to be carried out, which is something which ideally should be hidden from scientists and end-users.

We strongly believe that providing an easy to use, large-scale testbed of mobile phones carried by ordinary people will be a game changer for many types of experimental research. Overall our aim is to unlock the true potential of mobile phone sensing by developing a research infrastructure that can be used by a broad range of researchers to easily and quickly deploy experiments. In this paper we introduce *Pogo*, a middleware infrastructure for mobile phones that provides easy access to sensor data for the research community. By installing the *Pogo* middleware, which is as simple as downloading an application from the application store, a phone is added to a shared pool of devices. Researchers can request a subset of those devices, and remotely deploy their own executable code onto them. We make the following contributions in this work:

1. We present the design rationale behind *Pogo*, motivate our choices, and compare them against related work.
2. We describe the implementation of our middleware and demonstrate its feasibility it using a real-world Wi-Fi localization experiment.
3. We propose and evaluate a novel scheme for automatically synchronizing data transmissions with that of other applications, dramatically reducing energy consumption.

The rest of this paper is structured as follows. We introduce related work in Section 2, and present our design choices in Section 3. Section 4 describes the implementation of *Pogo*. We evaluate our middleware in Section 5, and finally conclusions and future work are presented in Section 6.

2   Related Work

In this section we introduce several sensor processing and collection frameworks that have been proposed in the fields of context-aware computing and mobile phone sensing, as well as some systems that have been developed for tracking smartphone usage. We will make a detailed comparison between these works and *Pogo* when we present its design in Section 3.

Context-aware computing is a field that uses sensor data to infer information about the *context* of a user. Examples of contexts are user location, emotional state, and transportation mode. Middleware built for this purpose aids developers by providing sensor abstractions and off-the shelf classifiers, and help reduce energy consumption by scheduling sensors intelligently.

Jigsaw [23] is a framework for continuous mobile sensing applications. It uses a pipeline architecture, with different pipes for each sensor, and has the ability to turn individual stages on or off depending on need and resource availability. It has classifiers for accelerometer and audio data built-in, and reduces power consumption by scheduling GPS sampling in a smart way. The *Interdroid* platform [19] aims to provide a toolkit for the development of 'really smart' applications, and focuses on integrating mobile phones and cloud computing. Applications contain a client and server part, the latter of which can be uploaded to a remote server in the cloud where it can run to support the client. *Mobicon* [22] proposes a *Context Monitoring Query* language (CMQ), which can be used by applications to specify the type of context information they require. The middleware then intelligently plans sensor usage in order to reduce power consumption. However, the data processing in context-aware systems is geared towards assisting the user, and therefore do not include functionality for collecting data at a central server or for remotely deploying sensing tasks.

Mobile phone sensing middleware aims to turn smartphones into mobile sensors. The aim is to collect data about user behavior or the environment in which a user moves around, and send it to a central point for further analysis. One such project is *AnonySense* [8]. Tasks are written in a domain-specific language called *AnonyTL*, which has a Lisp-like syntax. These tasks are matched to devices using predicates based on the context of the device, such as its location. Another relevant project is *Cartel* [4], which is a software and hardware infrastructure comprising mobile sensing nodes on cars. Remote task deployment, although limited in nature, is supported through runtime configuration of parameters like the type and rate of sensor information reported by the mobile devices; continuous queries written in SQL submitted to a central server further process and filter this data, providing additional adaptability. A much more flexible approach is offered by *PRISM* [10], which allows deployment of executable binaries at the mobile devices themselves. Method call interposition is used to sandbox running applications for security and privacy reasons. *Crowdlab* [9] proposes an architecture for mobile volunteer testbeds that allows low-level access to system resources, and employs virtualization technologies to run sandboxed applications concurrently with the host operating system.

Phone Usage Traces *SystemSens* [14] and *LiveLab* [26] are end-to-end logging tools for measuring smart phone useage, and can be useful for diagnosing other running applications. They collect data about wireless connectivity, battery status, cpu usage, screen status, and so on. Both offload the collected traces to a central server only when the phone is charging in order to save energy. *MyExperience* [15] is a more flexible system that can also capture sensor data and user context, and is even able to ask the user for feedback through an on-screen survey. MyExperience can be configured using XML files with support for scripting, and behavior can be updated in the field by sending scripts through SMS or e-mail. Output is stored in a local database that is synchronized periodically with a central one.

3   Design

In this section we look at several design aspects of *Pogo*, compare alternative options and discuss how they fit in with the related work, and finally motivate our choices. Note that many of these considerations have architectural consequences, as is reflected in Section 4.

3.1   Testbed Organization

The most straightforward way to structure a testbed is to have a central server and a set of mobile devices in a master-slave setup. The phones collect and process data locally, and send it to the server where it is stored, possibly after further processing. This model is followed by most middleware, including PRISM [10] and AnonySense [8]. However, such a strongly centralized server component must also have a front-end where scientists can upload scripts, download data, and manage their device pool, which introduces a considerable implementation overhead. Moreover, since researchers share devices between them and multiple sensing applications run concurrently on each device there is an inherent many-to-many relationship between researchers and end-users.

We have therefore opted for a design where both parties, the researchers and the test subjects, run the *Pogo* middleware, with a central server acting only as a communications switchboard between them. This way researchers can interact directly with end-user devices without having to go through a web interface or logging into a server. There are three types of stake holders in a *Pogo* testbed. First, the *device owners* contribute computational and sensing resources to the system by running *Pogo* on their phones. The *researchers* run *Pogo* on their computers and consume these resources by deploying experiments. The *administrator* of the testbed decides which devices are assigned to which researchers. In a way the administrator acts as a broker who brings together people who offer and consume resources. The connections between researchers and device owners are double blind, with the administrator having only personal information about the researchers who use the system.

3.2   Deployment

An important consideration is how experiments are delivered to the mobile devices. Remote deployment is a basic functionality of any testbed and supports the development of new algorithms and techniques by enabling researchers to test hypotheses and benchmark solutions. It is, however, also a vital requirement for running long-term sensing studies, which may need to deal with changing requirements, new hardware developments, and new insights, or simply require maintenance to correct programming errors.

Broadly speaking there are two methods of deployment found in literature. *Pull-based* systems present the user with a list of applications that can be downloaded. Common examples are the iPhone *App Store*[1] and Android's *Play Store*[2]. The choice for which application runs on which device lies solely with the user. In contrast, *push-based* systems allow researchers to send their applications to remote devices without interaction from the user. This can be manual, like in Prism [10] or Boinc [1], or automatic based on device capabilities or context, as is the case with AnonySense [8].

Note that pull-based systems often have a push component, in the form of application updates that are installed automatically. The Play Store has an updating mechanism where new versions can be pushed to Google's servers by developers. End-users that have the application installed will be notified of such updates and can choose to either update manually, or let Android manage this automatically. Depending on the updating method, it may take anywhere from a few hours to several days for a device to get the latest version. In our experience, these long update times are not suitable for quick redeployment and experimentation. What is more, the update process on the phone stops the application if it is running and it has to be restarted by the user. This means that automated updates result in regular downtime even with the most committed users due to the time it takes for them to notice that the application has been killed.

For *Pogo* we have chosen a push-based system because we believe it is most suitable for rapid deployment and experimentation. Of course, this means that users are not able to choose what kind of applications are running on their phones. We therefore allow users to select the types of information their wish to share, so that they retain full control over their own privacy.

3.3   Participation

Participation by the general public is an important aspect of our approach and we employ several strategies and incentives to attract users to our testbed. First of all the barrier for participation is kept as low as possible. The goal is to have volunteers just click once on the *Pogo* icon in their application store, which will automatically start the download, installation, and execution of the middleware on their phone. There is no registration process after the application has been installed. This implies an opportunistic approach in which the middleware runs silently in the background; only if a user wants to change the default settings (e.g., about privacy) or remove the middleware completely does he need to take action. We guarantee complete anonymity and give the user full control over what information he wishes to share, and these settings can be changed at any time from the application interface.

We expect that research institutions will recruit nodes among employees and students, possibly rewarding the latter group with study credit. We are also investigating monetary incentives such as Amazon's Mechanical Turk[3]. We have

---

[1] http://www.apple.com/itunes
[2] http://play.google.com/
[3] https://www.mturk.com/mturk/welcome

a central server that can keep track of when devices are online and what data they are sharing, which would be the basis for assigning rewards. A third option is to distribute smart phones for free with the understanding that the recipients run the middleware and share their data [17].

3.4   Experiment Description

There are several approaches to writing mobile sensing experiments. Runtime-configurable systems such as Cartel [4], and domain-specific languages like CMQ [22] and AnonyTL [8], are easy to execute and sandbox. Moreover, notation is generally short and concise, and accessible to researchers and programmers with little domain experience. On the other hand, deployment systems like PRISM [10] and CrowdLab [9] allow native applications to be deployed on remote nodes, giving total flexibility, but at the cost of requiring complex sandboxing techniques, like method call interposition or hardware virtualization, to keep malicious or malfunctioning code from degrading user experience or breaking privacy.

We feel that the expressiveness of general programming languages is neccesary if *Pogo* is to support the wide range of applications that we envision. The example application that we describe in Section 4.1 implements a clustering algorithm that could not be expressed in a simple DSL or query language. While it is true that middleware can be extended with new functionality if desired, doing so would require updating the application for the entire installed base, which is exactly the kind of deployment overhead we wish to avoid.

We argue that simplicity and flexibility do not have to be competing constraints. *Pogo* applications are written in JavaScript, a popular and accessible programming language. We expose a small, yet powerful programming API of only 11 methods that abstracts away the flow of information between sensors and scripts, and between phones and data collecting PCs. In this way, developers do not need to know anything about smartphones or Android in order to be able to write *Pogo* experiments. Sandboxing is straightforward as the scripting runtime can be used to control what functionality the application is allowed to use.

3.5   Programming Abstractions

The choice of a generic programming language over a DSL means that we must provide an application programming interface (API) to developers that exposes the kind of functionality required for mobile sensing applications. We identified the following requirements. First, applications need to be able to *access sensor data*, either by reading them directly or by listening for updates. Second, there should be a facility for *periodically executing code*. Third, a means of *communicating with a central point* (the researcher) is required so that findings can be reported. Finally, some means of *breaking up large experiments into smaller components* is not a functional requirement per se, but makes complex applications such as the one described in Section 4.1 more manageable.

Starting from the simplest option, we have considered exposing a rich API to the scripting runtime. This approach is taken by PhoneGap[4], a popular toolkit for developing portable mobile applications with HTML5 and JavaScript. For example, the accelerometer can be read by calling the `navigator.accelerometer.getCurrentAcceleration` method. However, such an API grows quickly as more sensors are added, and a lot of 'glue' code is required to interface between the native platform API and JavaScript. Moreover, consider the case where two scripts are running on the same device, and both are requesting a Wi-Fi access point scan at regular intervals. It would be sufficient to scan at the highest of the two frequencies to serve both scripts, but this energy-saving optimization cannot be made without some form of coordination.

The API requirements essentialy boil down to an exchange of *data* and *events* between loosely coupled entities; sensors, scripts, and devices. Two popular abstractions for this type of communication are *tuple spaces* [16] and *publish-subscribe* [13]. A tuple space is a shared data space where components interact by inserting and retrieving data. In a publish-subscribe system, components *publish* information to a central authority, the so-called *message broker*. Other components can then *subscribe* to this information and are notified when new data become available. In terms of capabilities, the two techniques are roughly equivalent [3]. We have chosen publish-subscribe for *Pogo* mostly because of implementation advantages. First, in a publish-subscribe system a sensor component can easily query whether there are other components interested in its output. If not, the sensor can be turned off to save energy. Second, subscriptions in *Pogo* optionally carry parameters that can be used to add details such as a requested sampling rate. Finally, the model is event-based, which fits our choice for JavaScript.

4   Implementation

In this section we describe our implementation of *Pogo*, which is written in Java and runs on Android smartphones as well as on desktop PCs and servers. The Android platform was chosen because of its ubiquity (at the time of writing Android had 50.9% market share[5]), and because it supports the type of background processing required for mobile phone sensing tasks. *Pogo* runs on Android 2.1 and up, and currently stands at 10,666 source lines of Java code, of which 5,170 lines are common, 2,948 are Android-specific, and 2,548 belong to the PC version.

4.1   Example Application

Before we describe our implementation in detail, we believe it is helpful to present an application to both give a concrete example of the type of experiments we envision, as well as to provide a running example with which to illustrate the

---

[4] http://www.phonegap.com
[5] http://www.gartner.com/it/page.jsp?id=1924314

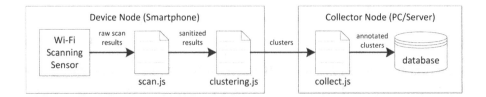

Fig. 1. Data-flow of the localization application. The `scan.js` script requests Wi-Fi access points scans from the Wi-Fi sensor, sanitizes them, and sends them to `clustering.js`. This script clusters the scans and sends cluster characterizations to the `collect.js` script running on the collector node, which in turn pushes them into a database.

various implementation details. We chose a meaningful, real-world localization application for this purpose. The goal of the application is to find locations where the user spends a considerable amount of time, such as the home, the office, and so on. We do this by periodically sampling Wi-Fi access points, and clustering these scan results based on similarity. The clusters found in this way characterize a 'place' where the user dwelled.

Figure 1 shows the data flow of the application. The `scan.js` script obtains scan results from the Wi-Fi scanning sensor. It sanitizes the raw results by removing locally administered access points, and normalizes received signal strength (RSSI) values so that 0 and 1 correspond to -100 dBM and -55 dBM respectively. These values are then picked up by the `clustering.js` script that extracts clusters (locations) using a modified version of the DBSCAN clustering algorithm [12]. The modification in this case is that we use a sliding window of 60 samples from which we extract core objects. Clusters are 'closed' whenever a user moves away from the place it represents (when a sample is found that is not reachable from the cluster). The distance metric used is the cosine coefficient. When a cluster is closed, a sample is selected that best characterizes the cluster[6] and sent to the server along with entry and exit timestamps. The `collect.js` script running on the collector node collects these cluster characterizations and uses Google's geolocation service [18] to convert them into a longitude, latitude pair. The annotated places are then pushed into a database.

This example illustrates a number of key features of *Pogo*. The location clustering is performed on the device so as to avoid sending raw access point scans to the collector and hence minimize communication cost, which shows the advantages of on-line processing. The flexibility of our scripting environment allows us to write complex sensing applications and even run custom clustering algorithms when desired. Applications can easily be broken down into a set of cooperating scripts, and communication between them flows seamlessly across the wireless networking boundary.

---

[6] The nearest neighbour to the mean of all scan results is selected.

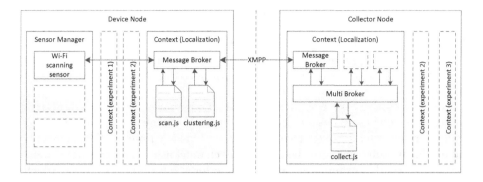

Fig. 2. A device- and collector node running the localization application

4.2   Node Architecture

In *Pogo* both the researchers and device owners are running the same middleware; the only functional difference between them is that researcher nodes are operating in *collector* mode, which gives them the ability to deploy scripts. We therefore do not have to write an extensive server application. Instead, we use an off-the-shelf open source instant messaging server to manage communication between device- and collector nodes.

Figure 2 shows the anatomy of two *Pogo* node instances, a device and collector node running the example application presented in Section 4.1. Scripts belonging to a certain experiment run inside a so-called *context*, which acts as a sandbox; scripts can only communicate within the same experiment. Each context has a counterpart on a remote node, and communication between them flows over the XMPP protocol, as we will describe Section 4.6.

Each context has a *message broker* associated with it where scripts can subscribe to- and publish data. Since contexts have counterparts on remote devices, so do message brokers. The brokers on either end synchronize with each other so that the publish-subscribe mechanism works seamlessly across the network boundary. Since contexts on collector nodes can have more than one remote context associated with them, a *multi broker* is used to make the communication fan out over the different devices. Note that message exchange can only happen between a device- and collector node, device nodes can never communicate with each other directly.

Finally, sensors live inside a *sensor manager*. They are able to publish data to, or query subscriptions from, all contexts. All a script needs to do in order to obtain sensor data is to subscribe to it. This also works across the network; a script running on a collector node that subscribes to battery information will automatically receive voltage measurements from all devices in the experiment.

4.3   Publish-Subscribe Framework

Communication between sensors, scripts, and devices uses a topic-based publish-subscribe paradigm [13], where *messages* (events) are published on *channels*.

For example, the Wi-Fi scanning sensor publishes its output on the `wifi-scan` channel, and scripts that wish to consume this data simply subscribe to this channel. Messages are represented as a tree of key/value pairs, which map directly onto JavaScript objects so that they can be passed between Java and JavaScript code seamlessly. Messages are serialized to JSON[7] notation when they are to be delivered to a remote node.

A subscription in *Pogo* can have a parameter object associated with it. Scripts can use this to be more specific about the information they are interested in. For example, a script may request location updates, but only from the GPS sensor. It can do this by subscribing to the `locations` channel using the `provider:'GPS'` parameter. Another example is the `scan.js` script in our running example, which requests access point scans every minute. The scanning interval in this case is also passed using the parameters (`interval:60000`).

Given the battery constraints of mobile devices it would be wasteful to have sensors draw power when their output is not being consumed. The framework therefore allows sensors to listen for changes in subscriptions to the channels they publish on. Sensors can enable or disable scanning based on this information, and change their behavior depending on the subscription parameters.

4.4 Scripting

Scripts are executed using Rhino[8], a JavaScript runtime for Java, which allows for seamless integration of the two languages. In the interest of security however, we hide the Java standard library and of course all of the Android API from the application programmer. Instead, we expose only a small programming interface, shown in Table 1.

The `setDescription()` and `setAutostart()` functions can be placed in the script body to set script parameters. If automatic starting of a script is turned off, it will not run until the user explicitly starts it through the UI. The description of the script will be shown in the UI as well. The `print()` function prints a debug message that can be viewed on the phone, while the `log` and `logTo` functions can be used to write lines of text to permanent storage. The `publish` and `subscribe` function expose the message passing framework to a script. The `parameters` argument to `subscribe` is optional and is used to add parameters to a subscription. For example, the following line:

```
1 subscribe('wifi-scan', handleScan, { interval : 60 * 1000 });
```

requests a wifi scan result once per minute. The returned `Subscription` object can be used to control whether a subscription is active or not. The `release` method deactives a subscription, while `renew` can be used to reactivate it at a later time. Note that these methods have no effect when the subscription is inactive or active respectively.

An object can be 'frozen' with the `freeze` function, which means it will be serialized to permanent storage. Each script can have only one such object at any

---

[7] http://www.json.org/
[8] http://www.mozilla.org/rhino/

Table 1. *Pogo* JavaScript framework API

```
setDescription(description)
setAutoStart(start)
print(message1[, ...[, messageN]])
log(message1[, ...[, messageN]])
logTo(logName, message1[, ...[, messageN]])
publish(channel, message)
Subscription subscribe(channel, function[, parameters])
freeze(object)
object thaw()
String json(object)
setTimeout(function, delay)
```

given time, and `freeze` will always overwrite any preexisting data. This stored object can be retrieved using `thaw`. These two methods make it possible to have data persist through script stop/start cycles and updates. The `json` function serializes an object to a string using JSON notation. The `setTimeout` method works in much the same way as it does in a browser, allowing a function to be scheduled for execution at some point in the future.

4.5   Event Scheduling

Handling (timed) events requires some special attention on mobile devices because power management has to be taken into account. When the screen is turned off and there are no ongoing activities such as a phone call being made, Android will put the CPU to sleep to conserve energy. Applications can prevent the CPU from going to sleep by acquiring a *wake lock*, and this is essential for many asynchronous sensing tasks. Consider the example where an application requests a Wi-Fi access point scan. If the CPU is not kept awake during the 1-2 seconds the process generally requires, the application will not be notified upon scan completion. When the CPU is in deep sleep, it can be awoken only by events such as incoming calls, or the user pressing a hardware button. Alternatively, an application may want to schedule a wake-up call periodically, which it can do by setting a so-called *alarm*.

The *Pogo* framework abstracts away the complexities of setting alarms and managing wake locks through a *scheduler* component that executes submitted tasks in a thread pool, and supports delayed execution. Using a thread pool has the advantage that components that execute code periodically do not have to maintain their own threads and are therefore more light-weight. A typical example is a sensor component that samples at a given interval. When there are no tasks to execute, the CPU can safely go to sleep.

The scheduler is also used when calling JavaScript subscription handlers and functions that have been scheduled for execution using the `setTimeout` method. A script can have multiple subscriptions, so in theory multiple Java threads could execute code belonging to the same script. However, since JavaScript does not have facilities to handle concurrency, the threads are synchronized so that only a single thread will run code from a given script at any time.

To keep incorrect or malicious code from locking up the system and draining the battery, all calls to JavaScript functions by the framework must complete within a certain timeframe. If the JavaScript function does not return in time, it is interrupted and an exception is thrown. The default timeout is set to 100ms.

4.6   Communication

Pogo relies on the XMPP protocol[9], which was originally designed for instant messaging. Using an instant messaging protocol is helpful because associations between devices and researchers can be captured as buddy lists, or *rosters* in XMPP parlance. These are stored at the central server and can therefore be easily managed by the testbed administrator. The XMPP server we use, Openfire[10], has an easy-to-use web interface for this purpose.

Mobile phones frequently switch between wireless interfaces as the user moves in- or out of range of access points and cell towers. Unfortunately there is no transparent TCP handover between these interfaces, causing stale TCP sessions and even dropped messages. This message loss problem is recognized in the XMPP community and although several extensions have been proposed[11], these have yet to be implemented in popular server and client libraries. *Pogo* detects, using the Android API, when the active network interface changes and automatically reconnects on the new interface. We have implemented our own end-to-end acknowledgements on top of XMPP to recover from message loss.

Messages that are to be transferred over the XMPP connection are not sent out immediately for two reasons. First, when there is no wireless connectivity, messages should be stored and sent out at a later time when connectivity has been restored. Second, sending small amounts of data over a 2G/3G connection has been shown to be extremely energy inefficient due to the overhead associated with switching between the different energy states of a modem, as we will elaborate upon in the next section. We exploit the fact that data gathering applications generally allow for long latencies in message delivery. Messages are therefore buffered at the device and sent out in batches. Buffered messages are stored in an embedded SQL database to ensure that no messages are lost should a device reboot or run out of battery.

4.7   Tail Detection

Data transmission over a 2G/3G internet connection is costly due to the tail energy overhead involved [2,24]. In a nutshell, data transmission triggers the modem to go into a high-power state, where it stays for a considerable amount of time after the transmission itself has ended. Figure 3 shows an energy trace

---

[9] http://xmpp.org/

[10] http://www.igniterealtime.org/projects/openfire/

[11] i.e. XEP184, XEP198.

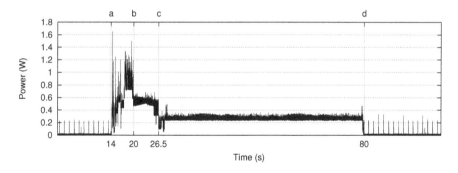

Fig. 3. Tail energy due to 3G transmissions. The 3G ramp-up starts at a. After data transmission has ended (point b), the modem stays in high-energy mode (DCH) for approximately six seconds until c. Finally, there is a long tail where the modem stays in medium-energy mode (FACH) for another 53.5 seconds between c and d. The small spikes before a and after d are due to the duty cycling of the modem. The trace was obtained under the same conditions as described in Section 5.2 on the KPN network.

taken from a Samsung Galaxy Nexus smartphone. The event marked a shows the modem being triggered by a transmission (in this case the phone checking for new e-mail). It takes several seconds for the actual transmission to begin as the modem negotiates a private channel with the cell tower, leading to the so-called *ramp-up* time. After the transmission has ended at event b, the modem waits in high energy mode to see if there is further data until point c, after which it goes into a medium-energy mode, where it stays for a further 56 seconds. The time from b to d, 60 seconds in this example, is commonly referred to as the *tail-energy* of a transmission, and periodically transfering small packets of information could easily cause this overhead to dominate the overall energy consumption of the application.

To avoid generating many tails it is possible to either flush the transmit buffer at long intervals (i.e. once per hour), or simply delay transfer until the phone is plugged into the charger. However, there are typically many applications already present on a mobile phone that periodically trigger a 3G tail. Examples are background processes that check for e-mail, instant messaging applications, and turn-based multi-player games. *Pogo* detects when other applications activate the modem, and if it has data to send, takes advantage of this opportunity to push it out before the modem has moved to a lower power state. In this way *Pogo* is able to avoid generating tail energy of its own by synchronizing its transmissions with that of other applications. Since most users typically set their phones to check for new e-mail every so many minutes, *Pogo* almost never generates its own tail.

The implementation of this scheme requires some special consideration. The general idea is to periodically read the number of bytes received and transmitted on the 2G/3G network interface using the Android API, and fire a transmission event when these numbers change. The exact length of the tail we are trying

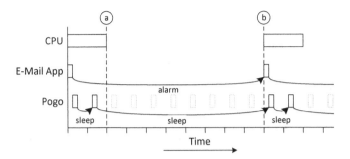

Fig. 4. *Pogo* running alongside an e-mail application that periodically checks for new mail. The horizontal blocks show when the CPU, e-mail app, and *Pogo* are active.

to detect depends on the mobile carrier, but we typically wish to catch the high-power tail which is measured in seconds.

Periodic sampling at such intervals becomes problematic due to energy overhead incurred when waking up the CPU. As explained in the previous section, Android will put the CPU to sleep when there are no wake locks held by any applications, and can only be woken up explicitly by setting an alarm. When the alarm fires, the CPU will be woken up and start executing pending tasks. The processor will stay awake for typically more than a second before going back to sleep, even if there is nothing for it to do. With a sampling interval measured in seconds the overhead from keeping the CPU awake would be considerable.

We therefore use a side-effect of how Java's `Thread.sleep` method is implemented on Android. When the processor is in sleep mode, the timers that govern the sleeping behavior are also frozen, which means that the thread will only continue to execute after the CPU has been woken up by some other process. We use this to detect when the CPU is woken up by another application, possibly a background service that wants to engage in data transmission.

Figure 4 shows a situation where an e-mail application periodically checks for new mail. The e-mail app uses the alarm functionality of Android to ensure that the CPU is woken up. *Pogo* checks for network activity every second, but uses `Thread.sleep` instead of alarms. At event *(a)*, the CPU goes to sleep because there are no wake locks preventing it from doing so. With the CPU sleeping, the *Pogo* thread is no longer running. At event *(b)*, the alarm set by the e-mail app fires and the CPU is brought out of sleep mode. The *Pogo* thread continues and is eventually unblocked when its timer runs out. It can then detect the network traffic and push out its own data.

5   Evaluation

In this section we evaluate *Pogo* in three ways. We first validate the suitability of our programming model for mobile sensing applications in Section 5.1. In Section 5.2 we show, using power traces obtained from a modern Android smartphone, that our mechanism for avoiding tail-energy significantly reduces

Table 2. Code complexity for *Pogo* applications. Size is given in bytes.

Application	File	SLOC	Size
`Localization example`	`scan.js`	41	1,414
	`clustering.js`	155	4,096
	`collect.js`	18	469
	total	**214**	**5,979**
`RogueFinder`	`roguefinder.js`	28	799
	`collect.js`	5	100
	total	**32**	**899**

the energy overhead of *Pogo*. Finally, we present our experience with a real-world experiment in Section 5.3.

5.1   Program Complexity

We implemented the example application described in Section 4.1. Table 2 shows the source lines of code count[12] for the application. The `clustering.js` script is by far the largest, mainly due to the modified DBSCAN clustering algorithm, as well as functionality for calculating the cosine coefficient. Still, the entire application takes up only 214 lines of code.

We also wanted to compare our programming model against related work. Listing 1 shows the RogueFinder application written in AnonyTL, as it appears in [8]. This program sends Wi-Fi access point scans to the server once per minute, but only if the device is within a given geographical location (represented by a polygon). We implemented an equivalent program for *Pogo*, a fragment of which is shown in Listing 2. First, a subscription is created to scan for access points on line 5. This subscription is then immediately released because scanning should only be activated within the designated area (line 9). On line 11, the application subscribes to location updates, and toggles the Wi-Fi subscription based on the device location. Note that the `locationInPolygon` method was omitted for brevity. The total size for this application can be found in Table 2.

The RogueFinder application illustrates the trade-off between DSLs and our JavaScript-based approach. First, we had to implement the `locationInPolygon` function to simulate AnonyTL's `In` construct, as this was not a part of our API. Second, toggling the Wi-Fi scanning sensor depending on the user location required extra work (lines 11-16). Third, a second script running on the collector node (`collect.js`) is required to get the data off the device. Still, we would argue that this increase in complexity is an acceptable price to pay for the flexibility that *Pogo* offers over application-specific solutions such as AnonyTL.

5.2   Power Consumption

We validate the tail detection mechanism described in Section 4.7 by taking detailed power measurements from a Samsung Galaxy Nexus phone. We set up

---

[12] Empty lines and comments are not counted.

Listing 1. The RogueFinder application in AnonyTL.

```
1 (Task 25043) (Expires 1196728453)
2   (Accept (= @carrier 'professor'))
3   (Report (location SSIDs) (Every 1 Minute)
4     (In location
5       (Polygon (Point 1 1) (Point 2 2)
6       (Point 3 0))))
```

Listing 2. The RogueFinder application for *Pogo* (fragment).

```
1 function start()
2 {
3   var polygon = [{ x:1, y:1}, { x:2, y:2 }, { x:3, y:0 }];
4
5   var subscription = subscribe('wifi-scan', function(msg) {
6     publish(msg, 'filtered-scans');
7   }, { interval : 60 * 1000 });
8
9   subscription.release();
10
11  subscribe('location', function(msg) {
12    if (locationInPolygon(msg, polygon))
13      subscription.renew();
14    else
15      subscription.release();
16  });
17 }
```

a single e-mail account and configured it to be checked at 5 minute intervals. We and ran experiments both with- and without *Pogo* running alongside it. In the experiments where *Pogo* was running it was sampling the battery sensor every minute. Because of the synchronization mechanism these values were reported in batches of five whenever the e-mail application checked for updates. We inserted a 0.33Ω shunt between the battery voltage line and sampled the voltage drop over the shunt using a National Instruments NI USB-6009 14-bit ADC. The phone was running stock firmware, Android 4.0 (Ice Cream Sandwitch), with all background processes such as location services disabled.

We obtained one-hour traces with- and without *Pogo* running and compared the energy consumption. Because the length of the 3G tail depends on carrier settings we repeated this experiment with each of the three major mobile carriers in The Netherlands. With each comparison we took the trace without *Pogo* running as the base line and calculated the increase in power consumption as a percentage of that value. The results are shown in Table 3.

Table 3. Power consumption with- and without *Pogo* running on a Samsung Galaxy Nexus with e-mail being checked every five minutes. When *Pogo* is running, it reports battery voltage sampled once per minute.

Carrier	Without *Pogo*	With *Pogo*	Increase
KPN	277.59 J	288.76 J	4.09%
T-Mobile	182.05 J	194.3 J	6.73%
Vodafone	205.47 J	218.98 J	6.57%

Table 4. Results of the localization experiment. The size columns show the size in bytes of the raw data set.

User	Scans	Size	Locations	Size	Match	Partial
User 1	25,562	6,278,929	230	89,514	95%	96%
User 2a	11,474	3,082,356	121	48,048	86%	90%
User 2b	6,745	2,139,525	93	44,154	97%	100%
User 3	33,224	9,064,727	1282	437,527	80%	83%
User 4	32,092	12,664,291	274	139,572	92%	97%
User 5	33,549	11,836,962	333	197,433	95%	98%
User 6	34,230	14,426,142	158	77,251	89%	96%
User 7	35,637	9,305,313	703	181,389	96%	98%
User 8	34,395	11,618,974	329	141,634	95%	97%

The differences between the different carriers are substantial. We observed very long tails on the KPN network (Figure 3 shows such a tail), resulting in a higher total energy consumption than on the other two networks. On the other hand we found the differences in energy consumption on the same network due to *Pogo* to be marginal, with a maximum of 6.57% increase in total consumption on the Vodafone network. This shows that *Pogo* can report data regularly with minimal energy overhead by automatically synchronizing its tranmission with other background processes.

5.3   Experimental Results

We tested *Pogo* by deploying the localization application described in Section 4.1 and let it run for 24 days. Of the 8 participants, 6 were given a Samsung Galaxy Nexus to use as their primary phone. The other two preferred to use their own phone, a Sony Ericsson Xperia X10 mini and a Samsung Nexus S. The latter participant experienced some issues with his phone however and later switched to a Galaxy Nexus, and we denote this user's two sessions as 2a and 2b respectively. One of the participants did not have mobile Internet and had to rely on Wi-Fi to offload his data periodically (user 7). The application additionally logged all Wi-Fi scan results to SD card, and these raw traces were collected after the experiment as ground truth.

Table 4 shows an overview of the results. In total we collected 246,908 access point scans for a total of 76,7MB of raw data, and found 3,525 user locations[13] for a total of 1.3MB of raw data. In other words, we reduced the total amount of data transferred by 98.3% by making use of on-line clustering as opposed to sending all data back to the collector node. To see what the quality of the data was like, we ran our clustering algorithm over the raw traces and compared the output with what was received at the collector node. We found that there were inconsistencies between the two data sets. First, some clusters were missing at the collector node, or had a later start time. This was due to the clustering algorithm being interrupted half-way through building a cluster, losing its program state. When *Pogo* resumed it would only report the latter half of the dwelling session, hence the difference in cluster start times. This would happen if a phone was rebooted, ran of out battery, or when we uploaded a new version of the script.

Furthermore, we found that for two users we were missing large numbers of clusters, specifically in certain time periods. This was because we had configured *Pogo* to drop messages older than 24 hours if there was no Internet connectivity. We had not anticipated that this would become an issue since all participants had regular Internet access. However, user 2a made a trip abroad and turned off data roaming for cost reasons, resulting in messages being purged after a day. User 3 experienced problems with his 3G Internet access resulting in two days of missing data.

The 'match' column in Table 4 shows the percentage of clusters found in the post-processed data set that exactly matched the ones gathered by the collector node. The 'partial' column shows the percentage of nodes that were matched only partially due to the problems described. We have since added the `freeze` and `thaw` methods to preserve application state across clean application restarts which will help reduce the problem of *Pogo* scripts being interrupted, and improve data quality.

6   Conclusions

The smart phone revolution is rapidly changing the field of mobile data gathering. Modern phones have very capable processing hardware, ubiquitous Internet connectivity, and a range of interesting sensor modalities, which makes them – in principle – an ideal platform for all kinds of information collection tasks. In reality though, experiments with large collections of mobile devices are rare, and only carried out by a handful of experts, due to a string of complicating factors.

In this paper we presented *Pogo*, our proposed middleware for building large-scale mobile phone sensing test beds. *Pogo* takes a pragmatic approach and gives researchers a subset of the available mobile devices for them to deploy experiments on. These experiments are written in JavaScript, and use a publish-subscribe framework that abstracts away the details of communication between

---

[13] Note that these are not unique locations, but rather sessions of a user staying at some place.

mobile devices and researchers' computers. Users are given fine-grained control over what sensor information they wish to share to protect their privacy

We have demonstrated the feasibility of our implementation with a real-world use case involving eight users and running for 24 days. We argue that the programming model we developed for *Pogo* is easy to use, yet flexible enough to build complex applications. Finally, we have shown, through detailed power measurements, that *Pogo* is capable of offloading its sensor data at a very low energy overhead – as little as 4% – by synchronizing its transmissions with other background processes present on the device.

Pogo is a work in progress. In the future we would like to implement power modelling to estimate the resource consumption of individual scripts. We would also like to automate the assignment process between devices and researchers based on information such as device capabilities and geographical location. Finally, we are planning on contributing *Pogo* to the mobile phone sensing community as an open-source project in the near future.

References

1. Anderson, D.P.: Boinc: A system for public-resource computing and storage. In: Proceedings of the 5th IEEE/ACM International Workshop on Grid Computing, GRID 2004, pp. 4–10. IEEE Computer Society, Washington, DC (2004)
2. Balasubramanian, N., Balasubramanian, A., Venkataramani, A.: Energy consumption in mobile phones: a measurement study and implications for network applications. In: IMC 2009, pp. 280–293 (November 2009)
3. Busi, N., Zavattaro, G.: Publish/subscribe vs. shared dataspace coordination infrastructures. is it just a matter of taste? In: WETICE 2001 Proceedings of the 10th IEEE International Workshops on Enabling Technologies: Infrastructure for Collaborative Enterprises, pp. 328–333 (2001)
4. Bychkovsky, V., Chen, K., Goraczko, M., Hu, H., Hull, B., Miu, A., Shih, E., Zhang, Y., Balakrishnan, H., Madden, S.: The CarTel mobile sensor computing system. In: 4th int. conf. on Embedded Networked Sensor Systems, SenSys 2006, Boulder, Colorado, USA, pp. 383–384 (November 2006)
5. Campbell, A.T., Eisenman, S.B., Lane, N.D., Miluzzo, E., Peterson, R.A.: People-centric urban sensing. In: 2nd Int. Conference on Wireless Internet, WiCon 2006, Boston, MA (August 2006)
6. Chu, D., Kansal, A., Liu, J., Zhai, F.: Mobile apps: It's time to move up to CondOS. In: 13th Workshop on Hot Topics in Operating Systems, HotOS XIII, Napa, CA, pp. 1–5 (May 2011)
7. Cisco: Cisco visual networking index: Global mobile data traffic forecast update (2010-2015), http://www.cisco.com/en/US/solutions/collateral/ns341/ns525/ns537/ns705/ns827/white_paper_c11-520862.html (Febraury 2011)
8. Cornelius, C., Kapadia, A., Kotz, D., Peebles, D., Shin, M., Triandopoulos, N.: Anonysense: privacy-aware people-centric sensing. In: 6th Int. Conf. on Mobile Systems, Applications, and Services, MobiSys 2008, pp. 211–224 (June 2008)
9. Cuervo, E., Gilbert, P., Wu, B., Cox, L.: Crowdlab: An architecture for volunteer mobile testbeds. In: Communication Systems and Networks, COMSNETS, Bangalore, India, pp. 1–10 (Janaury 2011)

10. Das, T., Mohan, P., Padmanabhan, V.N., Ramjee, R., Sharma, A.: PRISM: platform for remote sensing using smartphones. In: 8th int. conf. on Mobile Systems, Applications, and Services, MobiSys 2010, San Francisco, CA, pp. 63–76 (June 2010)

11. Eagle, N., Pentland, A.: Reality mining: sensing complex social systems. Personal Ubiquitous Computing 10, 255–268 (2006)

12. Ester, M., Peter Kriegel, H.S.J., Xu, X.: A density-based algorithm for discovering clusters in large spatial databases with noise, pp. 226–231. AAAI Press (1996)

13. Eugster, P.T., Felber, P.A., Guerraoui, R., Kermarrec, A.M.: The many faces of publish/subscribe. ACM Computing Surveys 35, 114–131 (2003)

14. Falaki, H., Mahajan, R., Estrin, D.: Systemsens: a tool for monitoring usage in smartphone research deployments. In: Proceedings of the Sixth International Workshop on MobiArch, MobiArch 2011, pp. 25–30. ACM, New York (2011)

15. Froehlich, J., Chen, M.Y., Consolvo, S., Harrison, B., Landay, J.A.: Myexperience: a system for in situ tracing and capturing of user feedback on mobile phones. In: MobiSys 2007, pp. 57–70. ACM, New York (2007)

16. Gelernter, D.: Generative communication in linda. ACM Transactions on Programming Languages and Systems 7, 80–112 (1985)

17. Glater, J.D.: Welcome, freshmen. have an ipod (2008), http://www.nytimes.com/2008/08/21/technology/21iphone.html?ref=education

18. Google geolocation API. (November 2009), http://code.google.com/p/gears/wiki/GeolocationAPI

19. Kemp, R., Palmer, N., Kielmann, T., Bal, H.: The smartphone and the cloud: Power to the user. In: MobiCloud 2010, Santa Clara, CA, pp. 1–6 (October 2010)

20. Krause, A., Horvitz, E., Kansal, A., Zhao, F.: Toward community sensing. In: 7th Int. Conf. on Information Processing in Sensor Networks, IPSN 2008, St. Louis, Missouri, USA, pp. 481–492 (April 2008)

21. Langendoen, K., Baggio, A., Visser, O.: Murphy loves potatoes: Experiences from a pilot sensor network deployment in precision agriculture. In: 14th Int. Workshop on Parallel and Distributed Real-Time Systems (WPDRTS), Rhodes, Greece (April 2006)

22. Lee, Y., Iyengar, S.S., Min, C., Ju, Y., Kang, S., Park, T., Lee, J., Rhee, Y., Song, J.: Mobicon: a mobile context-monitoring platform. Commun. ACM 55(3), 54–65 (2012)

23. Lu, H., Yang, J., Liu, Z., Lane, N.D., Choudhury, T., Campbell, A.T.: The jigsaw continuous sensing engine for mobile phone applications. In: 8th ACM Conference on Embedded Networked Sensor Systems, SenSys 2010, Zürich, Switzerland, pp. 71–84 (November 2010)

24. Qian, F., Wang, Z., Gerber, A., Mao, Z.M., Sen, S., Spatscheck, O.: Characterizing radio resource allocation for 3g networks. In: Proceedings of the 10th Annual Conference on Internet Measurement, IMC 2010, pp. 137–150. ACM, New York (2010)

25. Schilit, B., Adams, N., Want, R.: Context-aware computing applications. In: First Workshop on Mobile Computing Systems and Applications, Santa Cruz, CA, pp. 85–90 (December1994)

26. Shepard, C., Rahmati, A., Tossell, C., Zhong, L., Kortum, P.: Livelab: measuring wireless networks and smartphone users in the field. SIGMETRICS Perform. Eval. Rev. 38(3), 15–20 (2011)

m.Site: Efficient Content Adaptation for Mobile Devices

Aaron Koehl and Haining Wang

Department of Computer Science
College of William and Mary
Williamsburg, VA, USA

Abstract. Building a mobile user interface can be a time consuming process for web site administrators. We present a novel approach for adapting existing websites to the mobile paradigm. In contrast to existing technologies, our approach aims to provide a trio of functionality, ease of use, and scalability for large web communities. A site administrator visually selects objects within a web page, and assigns one or more attributes to page objects from a rich collection of pre-defined page modifications. Our proposed system then generates code for a multi-session, php-based proxy server to provide dynamic mobile content adaptations based on the attributes selected. The modifications encapsulate complex page interactions and provide a simplified interface to mobile users. The proxy server is augmented with a highly efficient and standards-compliant browser residing on the server to interpose on behalf of a resource-constrained mobile client. Adaptations such as pre-rendering of content can be cached and shared across users to amortize load. We build a prototype and evaluate its efficacy on a complex web application driving a busy online community with nearly 66,000 members.

Keywords: mobile content adaptation, web application proxy.

1 Introduction

Web site administrators and content providers continually aim to accommodate an ever-increasing user base, yet doing so requires supporting a diverse set of browsing platforms. As a consequence, site administrators are forced to balance site accessibility and dependability against the costs of supporting multiple platforms. For instance, due to varying DOM (document object model) implementations within popular web browsers, object accesses in JavaScript are often written in such a way that if one function fails because of browser incompatibility, another function must be written to take over, with the idea that eventually a compatible function will be invoked. Such support issues are not limited to scripting. Differences in supported image formats, support for transparency, variation in supported fonts, subtle discrepancies in CSS rendering, incompatibilities caused by user-installed plugins, availability of media extensions such as Flash and SilverLight, and browser quirks modes [6] between versions must all

P. Narasimhan and P. Triantafillou (Eds.): Middleware 2012, LNCS 7662, pp. 41–60, 2012.
© IFIP International Federation for Information Processing 2012

be taken into consideration to guarantee support for a large audience. Although there are productivity tools that help in this regard, correctly supporting a diverse set of clients is still a time consuming process. Ultimately, it is the content administrators and site owners who suffer revenue loss when a user's browsing experience is compromised.

Support for mobile browsing introduces considerable complexity to the equation, as mobile browsers are limited in their capabilities, and even the extents of those limitations vary greatly between devices. In addition to diverse client software environments, the device's screen size, network bandwidth, and computational ability can compromise the user's browsing experience if disregarded by the site's administrator. Whereas great strides have been made in providing capable mobile architectures, there is a considerable gap between mobile browsing and the richness provided on even low-end desktop platforms. Supporting higher computational power is at odds with the small form factor, heat output, and battery life expected of today's smart phones, such as the BlackBerry, iPhone, and Android.

Currently, site administrators of large and dynamic template-based websites such as online communities often do not have the time, skill, or capability to deploy specialized templates for mobile users, although these websites must consider the demands and needs of the growing mobile market. To tackle the problem faced by site administrators, we propose a cross-cutting approach to content adaptation for mobile browsing. Content adaptation (screen scraping) is an effective way to alter the presentation for resource constrained clients, without involving changes to logic at the database or scripting layer. It is important to emphasize that (1) content adaptation employs a multitude of techniques, and (2) content adaptation techniques do not portend a single correct method, instead we recognize a design space in which content adaptation systems make various tradeoffs.

We therefore develop **m.Site**, a productivity framework that enables site administrators to dynamically adapt content for the mobile web with minimal effort, yet still allows for advanced, programmed customizations. m.Site does not rely on special browsers or remote third party services, is uninvasive with respect to code modification, preserves the platform-independence of the web by not requiring device-specific API's, and provides the site administrator with an efficient and cost-effective way to customize very complicated dynamic web sites.

Our design goal is to make the use of m.Site as simple as possible. We accomplish this by introducing an *attribute* paradigm, where page objects are identified in a visual tool, and attributes are selected and applied from a menu. These attributes embody well-known techniques such as image fidelity transformation, to complex subpage interactions. The visual tool generates php shell code for a server-side proxy, which is responsible for downloading page content, applying page transformations and attributes, managing cookie jars and multiple users, and marshaling interactions between the mobile client and the originating web page. Figure 1 shows the architecture of m.Site at-a-glance. Available to the

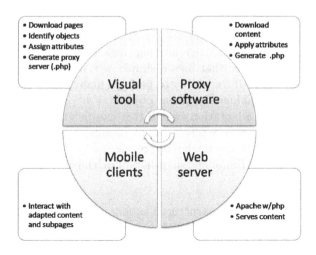

Fig. 1. High-level overview of the m.Site architecture

server side proxy is an arsenal of web scraping and DOM-manipulation tools, as well as an embedded WebKit [5] browser, which can be used as one of several pre-rendering engines or to execute code. By simplifying the interface and reducing or eliminating the need to write transformation code, we expect administrators will more readily adapt existing web sites for the mobile web.

Our work is motivated by scalability issues found with previous research in this area. The Highlight [21] system employs a remote control metaphor, in which server-side web browser instances are used to maintain state for each client. The resource consumption makes this approach infeasible for large web communities with thousands of concurrent users.

While providing similar high-level features, we instead generate code for a lightweight proxy that can handle the majority of the content adaptation: page slicing, state management, and DOM manipulation, calling on the web browser only when needed as a graphical rendering engine, or for browser-specific functionality. In this way, we also expose the opportunity for the proxy to cache and amortize rendering costs and general content adaptations across multiple users. Cookie security, session management, manipulation via jQuery, and AJAX requests can all be satisifed independently of a heavyweight browser, providing much of the browser's functionality without the associated scalability issues.

We build a prototype of our system and evaluate its efficacy on a complex web application driving a busy online community with nearly 66,000 members. Summarily, this paper makes the following contributions:

- A code generator that produces a low-overhead, multi-session proxy server to support adapted pages. This proxy server manages sessions, keeping browsing sessions open in a stateful manner, without the overhead of a browser running on the server for each user [21];

- A php-based proxy capable of using a highly efficient and standards-compliant browser running on the server in a disconnected state;
- Server-side caching to amortize rendering costs across many client sessions;
- A visual admin interface that uses a simple *attribute* paradigm to provide site administrators with the ability to perform many complex modifications for both visible and hidden document objects;
- A pluggable content adaptation system that can be extended with multiple rendering engines to produce HTML, static images, PDF, plain text, or Flash content at any point in the rendering process;
- Support for producing thumbnail snapshots of rich media content for resource-constrained devices.

The remainder of this paper is structured as follows. Section 2 surveys related work and existing techniques for adapting mobile content. Section 3 describes the m.Site framework as well as the benefits provided by the attribute system. Section 4 evaluates the efficacy of the framework on a live site, and finally Section 5 concludes.

2   Related Work

m.Site is a productivity framework aimed at allowing site content adaptation post-hoc, for mobile devices. Architecturally, systems that allow content adaptation exist either on the client or as a middleware proxy on the server.

Both client and proxy solutions for content adaptation have been proposed over the years, influenced by varying needs of the user and site administrator, as well as evolving technology in resource-constrained devices. Fudzee and Abawajy [17] provide a high level classification for content adaptation systems, and further argue for their viability as an attractive solution. m.Site is a dynamic, proxy-based content adaptation system colocated on the web server, as our motivation is on the site administrator's need to support as diverse and broad of a user base as possible.

Remote display protocols (e.g. thin clients) are not new [23]. However, several systems have been proposed specifically for mobile devices [16,14], which offload computation from a mobile device to a more capable server, while sending graphical updates and metadata to the device. While thin clients are a relevant technology, they require the installation of client-side software to manage the interaction. Also similar are specialized accelerated mobile browsers such as Opera [9] and Skyfire [10]. m.Site ascribes to the offloading approach, but proposes lightweight graphical updates to be disseminated using an ordinary, default mobile browser.

Client-side browser plugins [1,3] can provide the user with many tools to customize a site's layout. A plugin injects Javascript into the downloaded page and manipulates the layout using DOM functions. These systems have trouble with dynamic page changes, as they often use static XPaths and basic heuristics to locate objects on the page. However, there has been research into making client content adaptation systems more robust [12], allowing customizations to be reused in spite of content changes. Still, Javascript is limited to modifying objects in the DOM tree. m.Site allows for more sophisticated content adaptation techniques in addition to Javascript manipulation.

Systems such as [18,19] allow content adaptations to persist based on the inputs of a corpus of users. Sharing of scripts within GreaseMonkey communities [2] provides a static analog to this. Unfortunately, client side software solutions all suffer from the same problem when aiming to serve a large user base. Users are reluctant to install or use new browsers and plugins other than the default, and thus site administrators cannot rely upon these techniques for layout and content adaptation, especially of mobile visitors.

Proxy based systems allow more sophisticated content adaptation techniques, extending even to rich multimedia types [26]. FlashProxy [20] allows Flash content to execute remotely on the server yet be displayed on a mobile device. Employing a binary rewriting technique to interpose on behalf of the browser, events trapped on the proxy are sent to the client's browser via a Javascript RPC system, maintaining interactivity. m.Site addresses rich media concerns by allowing snapshots of rich media content to be generated, but leaves the interactivity of Flash, movies, and Silverlight to their respective plugin developers.

A number of proxy-based content adaptation systems have been proposed, which aid in navigating pages on mobile devices [21,25]. Bickmore and Schilit devise a system [11] to analyze and modify a web page based on heuristics and rules, for instance to adapt all images to a lower fidelity.

Automated techniques for page adaptation are promising but not always widely applicable [24]. Chen et al. propose a system to automatically analyze and split a page into subpages to reduce horizontal scrolling [13]. Xiao et al. extend this approach to allow a page to be split into a hierarchical structure [25]. Tools such as Apple's DashCode [4] can be used to simultaneously author a mobile and web application, avoiding a dual-maintenance scenario, but sites must be rewritten to use such a tool. Automated techniques provide a good starting point for adapting page content, and could be used in conjunction with a framework such as m.Site.

A hybrid approach for enhancing mobile navigation is to use a proxy to generate thumbnail overviews of site content. Annotated thumbnails and page splitting enhance navigation by reducing the input effort of browsing a site [25]. m.Site allows the creation of annotated thumbnails as well as multiple levels of page splitting. Note that a page of low-fidelity thumbnail links can load an order of magnitude faster than rendering complicated site content on a mobile device, by reducing both bandwidth and computational effort.

The Highlight system [21] employs a modified Firefox browser located on a proxy server. A user interacts with modified content sent to the mobile browser, which in turn remotely controls the browser session maintained on the server. While this keeps sessions separate and allows for dynamic content, it does not scale well. In contrast, the m.Site framework uses Apple's WebKit [5] library for server side rendering, but only when absolutely necessary. Most of the DOM

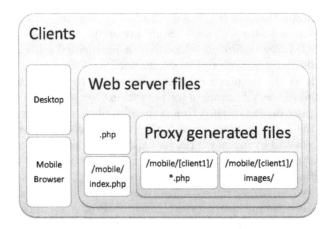

Fig. 2. m.Site organization

manipulation and content adaptation can occur outside of the context of the web browser, while keeping the ability for the proxy to maintain state and sessions for multiple users, and exposing additional cross-session optimizations such as caching of pre-rendered objects.

3   System Architecture

m.Site consists of two major components: a visual tool that the site administrator uses to reshape the site content, and a proxy server that dynamically applies attributes and generates the reauthored pages. Figure 1 provides a high-level overview of the m.Site architecture, while Figure 2 presents how m.Site is organized on the server.

3.1   Site Administrator Tools

In order to be as productive as possible, we develop a visual tool for providing site administrators a live view of the site. Once a page is loaded, the administrator is able to highlight page objects using a point and click approach, to select DOM objects on the page. A separate dock exists for non-visual objects, such as CSS, Javascript functions, head-section content, `doctype` tags, and cookies. The selected objects can be subsequently assigned any number of special attributes that ultimately affect their display on the client. Once a page is downloaded, the proxy system dynamically identifies these objects, applies any defined adaptations, applies any default rules for unidentified objects, generates the appropriate subpages and content, and redirects the user to a newly generated entry page.

It is possible that graphical objects split from the main page cannot be rendered without JavaScript and associated CSS, that is, objects may have intra-page dependencies. These dependencies can be identified in the visual tool.

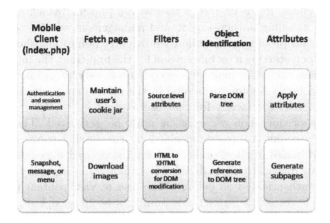

Fig. 3. Role of the Rendering Proxy

If a dependent object is to be rendered on the client, the appropriate CSS and JavaScript dependencies can be satisfied by assigning an attribute, which provides the object to the browser.

The typical work flow to mobilize a site is to load a site's page into the tool, visually select relevant objects, and choose attributes to apply (if any). A more advanced work flow delivers more control, and may include matching objects and content with regular expressions, image fidelity manipulation, defining of cacheable objects, and more sophisticated adaptation techniques, such as pre-rendering CSS on the server but rendering text on the client. As with most authoring tools, such techniques will be heavily dependent on the site being adapted.

3.2 Proxy Server

Upon completion, the visual tool generates a php file from shell template code. This shell code becomes a proxy for the originating page, and handles user session authentication, cookie jars, and high-level session administration, such as deletion of cookies. The proxy also handles downloading of the originating page on demand, http authentication on behalf of the client, and any error handling should the page be unavailable. Figure 3 highlights the main tasks performed by the proxy.

After a page is downloaded by the proxy, the attribute system and filters are invoked to apply any attributes defined by the site administrator. This includes locating any objects that need to be modified within the page, and performing any DOM manipulation. The proxy then creates a subdirectory for the user, generates one or more static subpages, and creates any supporting images and files as needed—the contents of which are controlled by the attribute system as shown in Figure 2.

The mobile client begins its interaction with a php file, which contains code responsible for handling authentication and management specific to m.Site sessions, as well as for providing a mobile-friendly entry point (snapshot and menu) into the site. Upon starting a mobile session for the first time, the mobile browser is issued a session cookie for maintaining state on the server. All of the files generated during a user's session are stored in the file system under a (protected) subdirectory created specifically for that user.

If the snapshot does not yet exist, it must be generated. The proxy first loads the user's cookie jar (as determined by the session cookie), and issues a page fetch on behalf of the mobile client for the desired page, which includes downloading any images to be rendered. The cookie jar is necessary as the proxy itself must be authenticated on behalf of the user to view content privy to that user. For publicly accessible forums, this would not be an issue, but typical online communities provide access to private forums and user setting pages that require authentication.

Once the page is fully downloaded, the HTML rendering engine can be employed to generate a snapshot of the page, save a low-fidelity version of that snapshot to an image file, and generate an appropriate HTML/Javascript overlay to use the snapshot as a menu to other subpages. At the end of this phase, the snapshot image and HTML can be sent to the client browser while the rest of the subpages are generated. The user should be satisfied with seeing a familiar screen shot and branding from the desired site.

For subpages, any attributes that need to be applied at the raw source level can be applied at this point, which we refer to as the filter phase. This can include extremely simple filters such as changing the `doctype` and `title`, or blanketly removing `css` and `script` tags. Slightly more complex filters would include rewriting all images to reference a low-fidelity image cache or different server. The page could be completely adapted after just a few simple filters, avoiding a DOM parse altogether, and assuming the snapshot is served from the cache, the work of the proxy could be done at this point.

For more complex modifications, a DOM parse is necessary. The m.Site framework has the capabilities of the popular source formatting tool HTML Tidy [22] compiled in. This library is applied at the filter phase, and is used to convert HTML to XHTML, which enables parsing by the wide array of XML/DOM manipulation tools available, as most of the XML-based tools won't handle malformed XML. The m.Site framework is modular enough to allow different libraries to be employed for DOM parsing (and subsequent filters based on the DOM tree), though for the next phase it is tightly integrated with the DOM parse provided by WebKit.

At the end of the attribute phase, all newly-allocated subpages are written to the file system in the client's session directory (see Figure 1). Any pre-rendered images are written to the client's image subdirectory, and any newly-generated shared images are written to the public cache. Some of the more powerful attributes call for m.Site to generate the server side php code to manage any interactions required as a result of the custom attributes, for instance, to satisfy AJAX requests.

Mobile Client Detection. Detection of a mobile device can be accomplished in a number of ways, but common practice is to use a set of heuristics that are kept up-to-date with new browsers and devices[1]. For our purposes, it is assumed that the client is already identified, and has either been automatically redirected to the proxy, or has explicitly chosen to use the proxy service for a particular page. Note that not all pages require a proxy to be mobile-friendly.

Object Identification. As a page is loaded for the first time, the proxy server must have a way to identify objects on the page, so that attributes and content adaptations can be applied.

The m.Site framework supports multiple object identification techniques, including source-level rules and heuristics. As in other systems [12,1], a DOM-based approach is supported using XPath. Similarly, objects can be identified using new CSS 3 selector support, since the framework integrates a server-side port of the popular jQuery [8] DOM manipulation library. Page modifications can be made directly to a parsed DOM. Likewise, modifications can also be made at the source level, rather than by manipulating the DOM tree, which can expose some optimizations.

3.3   Attribute System

The power of the m.Site framework originates from the very rich attribute system, which makes it possible to customize a site's layout and adapt its content for mobile browsers. The attributes provide a site administrator with fine-grained control over the rendering of pages, and also provides new adaptation techniques not available in other systems, such as partial pre-rendering, a subset of which is described below.

Pre-rendering. For complex pages, considerable time is spent in a mobile browser downloading content, parsing, rendering CSS and HTML, and fetching additional images. A page, subpage, object, or object group can be marked to be completely rendered on the server side into a single graphic, saving much computational effort on the mobile device. Additional attributes allow the rendered image's fidelity to be lowered, reducing network bandwidth. In the index page of our test site, this technique can reduce wall-clock load time by a factor of 5. Pre-rendered objects can be dynamically linked to subpages, creating a mobile-friendly menu.

Page Splitting. Any object, object group, or page can be split and set to render in its own separate HTML file, thus creating a subpage. If the subpage is combined with the pre-rendering attribute, it will be made up of simple pre-rendered images. Otherwise, the HTML making up that object will still be intact, and will be delivered to and rendered on the client's browser. For instance, a long column of links may be identified and moved to its own page.

---

[1] See [7] for more information about the detection of a mobile device.

Sub-subpages. Subpages can also be further split into more subpages. When a subpage is split, it allows for a hierarchical navigation reminiscent of that provided by [25].

Object Dependencies. When a subpage is set to be rendered in its entirety on the client side (HTML and CSS rather than a pre-rendered graphic), certain objects such as scripts that are needed to render the subpage may only exist in the master document or other subpages. By identifying these dependencies in the visual tool, we allow Javascript, CSS, and other objects to be pulled into the subpage as needed. This allows both non-visual and visual contents to be repeated in multiple subpages. The approach taken in other systems is to repeat head content on all subpages [25]. Unfortunately, this approach misses cases, where Javascript and other functionality are located in the body of pages. m.Site allows scripts and other content to be pulled from any portion of the page, and duplicated on as many subpages as is desired. Similarly, content such as ads, and navigational aids such as jump-menus can be made to appear on every subpage. Since any object can be duplicated on any subpage, this provides superior control over regular page-splitting approaches.

Javascript Insertion / Removal. Javascript functions can be dynamically inserted into the HTML source before rendering on the server, as well as after rendering. For instance, to modify how the server renders, one script can be used to manipulate the DOM tree to control certain layout elements, akin to [1]. For the client, a second script can be inserted to create a mobile-friendly navigational menu from the rendered elements. This is sort of modification cannot be realized by using Javascript-based content adaptation systems alone, such as [1,12].

Object Insertion, Removal, Relocation, and Replacement. When adapting a mobile layout, we allow HTML, CSS, and Javascript to be manipulated by the proxy. Objects can be inserted, for instance, to support adding an ad to the bottom or a breadcrumb navigational element at the top of each subpage. Objects can be hidden (via CSS style properties) when it arrives on the client, or stripped out of the source completely. Objects can also be relocated or duplicated into disparate subpages. Lastly, objects can be replaced entirely. For instance, if a mobile-friendly version of a client Javascript API exists, the desktop-based library can be replaced outright. Another example is the replacement of a logout button with a get parameter, which allows cookies to be cleared on the proxy.

Partial CSS Rendering. A complicated CSS design can take much time to render on a mobile device. Sometimes, it is desirable to take a portion of CSS code, replace the text with stretched one-pixel placeholders (to allow the layout engine to properly size the object), and take a snapshot of the rendered object. We call this partial pre-rendering. The proxy takes responsibility for rendering the graphical component, but uses Javascript to render the text on the device. Thus, the rendered object can then be used as a background in a static subpage, while the device only needs to draw text in the proper location.

Image Fidelity. As one would expect of content adaptation systems, objects can be passed to a post-processor before being made available to the client, allowing for manipulations in image fidelity and cropping. The attribute system is used to supply parameters to the post processor. For instance, when a full page is rendered into a high-fidelity png, it can consume upwards of 600K. This would take considerable time and bandwidth to send to the device. A post-processor can produce a reduced-fidelity jpg at 25-50k. When displaying a zoomed-out overview page on a small device screen, the lowered image fidelity is not noticeable, and only results in a faster load and rendering time.

Search. Search functionality is inherently lost when a web page is rendered on the server side. Although restructuring the mobile layout into subpages reduces the need to search, sometimes searchability is desired even on subpages, despite the associated costs. Thus, we allow an attribute to be defined as "searchable". At rendering time, a sorted word index is built on the server from the textual content read from the web page. The rendered location of each word is stored in a Javascript array along with the word list, and the ordered search index is then inserted into the subpage along with a Javascript binary search function. In order for the client to make use of the search functionality, the site administrator must define an HTML element (button or link) to make the initial Javascript call. Thus, the search attribute effectively allows pre-rendered images to be searched.

Object Caching. Certain areas of a site may be defined as cachable across sessions, amortizing the initial pre-rendering cost across many users. Once a cacheable object is rendered, it is placed into a pre-render cache on the server and can be used by the attribute system as needed. Using the properties of the cache attribute, for instance, a cached snapshot of the main page of a site can be set to expire after an hour.

Sometimes it is necessary to be able to maintain interactivity for portions of a site. For instance, some areas of the site may be protected with HTTP authentication. If the proxy comes across a page that requires user input, the client is redirected to a lightweight HTTP authentication page. Once authenticated, the proxy stores this information and uses it on behalf of the client. Authentication information is stored and maintained separately across users. HTTP authentication can be set with the application of a single attribute.

Overall, the m.Site framework leverages these rich attributes to provide site administrators with as much control over the mobilization of the site as possible.

4   Evaluation

In this section, we describe how the m.Site framework can be applied in a real-world setting—a complex, template-driven dynamic web site. We present the modification of the various content elements on the site's main page as well as those attributes that we ultimately select for deployment on the site. Finally, we show our experimental results.

4.1 Anticipated Load

The site used for testing runs the popular vBulletin [15] forum software for online communities. As of 2012, the site receives an average 2.2 million hits per day with as many as 1200 users online at a time, and with a historical doubling of traffic every 18 months. Like many catering to a growing and diverse community of users understand, the site's membership has grown large enough to expect streamlined mobile access. Hence, this load drives the need for a scalable and cost-effective mobilization solution. As vBulletin encompasses an active and broad community of site administrators with varying skills and capabilities, it is essential to provide a framework that is both accessible and useful, yet to be so it must be scalable, cost-effective, and have minimal deployment requirements.

4.2 Target Usage

Figure 4 shows the main page of the test site rendered from a desktop machine at its native resolution. The site starts with a logo and leader board banner advertisement, followed by a box of navigational links and a login form. Below this is a transient box used for announcements, followed by a long list of about 30 forum descriptions (clipped for space) and links to each forum's most recent post. Underneath the forum listing is a display showing which members are logged in, with links to each online member's public profile. Toward the bottom is a box of site statistics, a list of birthdays, public calendar entries, and finally some additional navigational links. This layout is a nearly unmodified default template reminiscent of thousands of online forums, and as such serves as a suitable test candidate.

The entry page of the test site requires a total of 224,477 bytes to be received from the network, inclusive of all images, external Javascripts (of which there are about 12), and CSS files. On the BlackBerry Tour smart phone (528 MHz processor), wall clock rendering time for this forum listing page is 20 seconds. For a grounded comparison, a modern desktop browser renders the page in about 1.5 seconds. Over WiFi, a 3rd-generation iPod Touch (600 MHz) using the WebKit-based Safari renders the page in 4.5 seconds, and 9 seconds over 3G.

Over time, the page has grown more complex to suit the desktop user. For what is tantamount to a magazine's table of contents, 20 seconds can be a burdensome wait. Table 1 draws a comparison. By using m.Site to render a snapshot of the page on the server side, the user perceives a significant reduction in latency, and unlike text-based content adaptation, the site administrator still delivers a branded look. The snapshot is overlayed using an image map with links to content areas defined with the subpage attribute.

Though page load performance will be less of an issue as more modern, standards-compliant mobile browsers become the norm, the site administrator can still take advantage of content adaptation to mitigate the small form factor, and facilitate quick access to information on-the-go. Even with the incredibly responsive zoom capability of the iPod Touch, for many core site requests, only a small amount of information is needed from the web page. For instance, looking

Fig. 4. SawmillCreek.org Test site rendered at full resolution

up flight cancellations in an airport usually only requires a small subset of the functionality provided by most airlines on their web pages.

Fully zoomed in its native resolution, the BlackBerry Tour (480x325 browser area) displays only a small window into the normal site, as shown by the upper left box drawn in Figure 4. Such a small viewing window requires considerable scrolling to read, both vertically and horizontally. Indeed, this is not even wide enough to display a common leader board banner ad of 728 pixels wide, and obviates the need to adapt this banner by replacing it with a mobile-specific version. Ideally, this is done by selecting the ad and applying an attribute that directs its replacement at the source level.

Just as an HTML page can take many forms, m.Site attributes can be applied in many different ways, depending on the needs of the site administrator. A mobile visit to an online weather site or movie theater should probably focus

Table 1. Comparison of wall-clock time from initial request to browsable page

Device	Wall-clock Time
BlackBerry Tour browser page load	20 sec.
Snapshot page generation	2 sec.
Cached snapshot page to Blackberry	5 sec.
iPhone 4 via 3G	20 sec.
iPhone 4 via WiFi	4.5 sec.
Desktop browser page load	1.5 sec.

on providing local weather or show times as quickly as possible, then perhaps national forecasts or box office descriptions. Recognizing that a mobile visit to an online woodworking community is akin to reading a magazine, the focus of our content adaptation on the entry page is to connect the reader with interesting threads as efficiently as possible, while maintaining the site's branding. Such a decision is an important factor in determining which content to display more prominently, while it should not cause functionality to be hidden on that basis alone. Thus, even though we will employ attributes to emphasize the forum listing, other functionality on the page will still be accessible to the user via subpages (rather than removed altogether).

4.3   Applying Attributes to the Test Site

A user will typically perform one of two actions when visiting the main page: either logging in to access the site's private areas, or browsing the forum listing for interesting topics. Whereas the structure remains the same, the links on the forum listing page continually change content as new discussion threads are added. We detail how both of these areas are adapted for a mobile user as follows.

Upon visiting the site, the mobile user is presented with a quick-loading, cached snapshot of the entire site. Application of this attribute gives the user the satisfaction of an immediate response upon visiting the site. The snapshot is pre-rendered, saved at low fidelity, and stored in a public cache for 60 minutes. The image itself is also scaled down to prevent the user from having to zoom in before clicking. The main idea is to present the user with the site's overall branding and an efficient means of diving into the desired site content.

The subpage attribute allows document fragments to be moved into subpages, along with dependent CSS and Javascript snippets. As shown in Fig. 5, we have applied the subpage attribute to the login form. Clicking the snapshot, where the login form would have been, links the user to the login form subpage. The login form elements have multiple dependencies in the original HTML source, including CSS and Javascript, which are satisfied by inserting the dependent scripts underneath the head tag in the subpage using a copy attribute.

The logo box (table and image) is also copied (rather than moved) to the top of the login subpage, but the `src` attribute of the image is set to a mobile-specific

Fig. 5. SawmillCreek.org login form subpage rendered as a result of applying page-splitting, image replacement, and css injection attributes

version of the logo. Figure 5 shows a screen shot of the adapted login subpage rendered on a BlackBerry Storm.

All of the defined subpage attributes contribute to an image map overlay, which is automatically generated for the main page snapshot. For each subpage generated, the coordinates and extents of the original document elements must be queried from the DOM, (in this case, the top left corner, height, and width), and are used to draw clickable rectangular image map regions on the snapshot. Each region links to its corresponding subpage. The queried coordinates map to the original-size document, but since the snapshot is scaled down, the m.Site framework implicitly translates the coordinates as well.

The site navigation links below the login box in the original site do not scale down at all. When viewed on a small display, the result is a single horizontal line of links (constructed as a table) that necessitates a horizontal scrollbar. To mitigate, we apply an attribute to transform the DOM, stripping the links from the segment and rewriting the HTML to list the links vertically, into two columns.

Whereas the default action for a subpage attribute is to render into a separate HTML file, setting one more attribute can allow the subpage to be loaded asynchronously and on demand into a `div` element in the current page. That is, any subpage can set to render into the current document using an asynchronous http request (AJAX). The m.Site framework injects the needed Javascript functions and creates appropriate `div` containers to enable this functionality on those pages that require it. The container is hidden and empty by default. When displayed, it can be centered in the viewport. Thus, it gives the appearance of being able to "activate" otherwise static portions of the pre-rendered snapshot, all without reloading the page. This has the added advantage of saving bandwidth and latency by not having to reload and parse large amounts of CSS and Javascript. The site's navigation links are loaded asynchronously through this method.

4.4   AJAX Support

Consider for a moment, the most typical use of asynchronous Javascript calls on a given website: a user clicks on a link, causing data to be retrieved into a DIV element, circumventing the cost of a full page load. At the low level, a user clicks on a link, triggering a Javascript onClick event, which in turn instantiates an asynchronous call to the server (usually a GET request), whose response is then marshaled to another Javascript function serving as a handler to populate a DIV element.

On mobile devices that support AJAX, such as Apple's iPad, iPhone, and Google Droid phones, no content adaptation is needed to maintain the original interactivity of the website. That is, the original asynchronous calls can be employed on these mobile devices, saving full-page rendering costs as is the case on desktop platforms. However, the next subsection shows how content adaptation can be used for these devices.

For non-AJAX capable devices, like the Blackberry's browser, content adaptation can be employed to restore AJAX-like interactivity. Previous work highlights a "remote browser in a proxy" metaphor [21] as a solution, but unfortunately, this solution does not scale well. How then, can AJAX interactivity be maintained without a remote browser?

As it turns out, the solution is simple—rewrite the link that gets sent to the device, and embed an additional function for the proxy to satisfy the request. For example, the following onClick handler for a "Show Picture" thumbnail loads a larger picture version when clicked:

```
$("#picframe").load('site.php?do=showpic&id=1')
```

The original site has a server-side AJAX request handler invoked when the action showpic and an id are supplied to the script. Upon validation (proper session, security, and accessible id), the desired image is displayed. This link would be adapted, using server-side jQuery, with a static call to the proxy, as follows:

```
proxy.php?action=1&p=1
```

This illustration is invariably simple, but is easily extended. When a site is integrated with the Google API and Yahoo (YUI) DOM API's, the link translation is more complex, but just as easily performed by the framework. Why not replace the link with a direct call to site.php? In more complex instances the returned result is rarely a simple picture, and often contains XML or JSON and must be massaged via Javascript. This can be handled easily and efficiently in the php-based proxy augmented with server-side jQuery. Using a CSS3-style pattern allows the content adaptation to be more robust to changes. The proxy's action is no more than a function, and the parameter p is its parameter representing the id in the original call.

4.5   AJAX Evaluation

Many popular "apps" for Apple's iPad and iPhone platforms are site-specific content-adaptation applications, which make navigation of data and page intensive sites more convenient for mobile users, in spite of the fact that these devices do already support AJAX, Javascript, and many HTML5 features.

To evaluate our approach, we choose to adapt a portion of the popular classified listing engine (CraigsList.com) using our proxy. Craigslist users browse pages of classified listings organized by category and sorted by date; clicking on a link brings the user to a new page with the contents of the selected ad. The evaluation device is a 1st-generation iPad and we want to take advantage of its extra screen real estate, to help the user locate desired information faster.

Craigslist does not ordinarily require any AJAX requests, which for a mobile device means an overuse of the browser's tiny back button, and continual reloading of pages. Rather than designing a platform specific application through the Apple developer network, we develop a browser-based content adaptation application for Craigslist, which simplifies navigation by *adding* asynchronous data loads.

Figure 6 shows the before-and-after results using our prototype. On the top left is the original site rendered in Google Chrome containing a page of links to classified ads. The second and third snapshots show the links and text identified in the administrator tool, and the proxy code. The last illustration is the result of content adaptation applied to the original page.

The adapted site is split into two DIV panes, with the left pane containing the list of classified listings, and the right pane containing the detailed classified listing. When an ad in the left pane is clicked, an AJAX call is dispatched to the proxy in the manner previously described. The proxy checks the cache for the downloaded page, and if it does not exist, fetches the page from CraigsList, performs the content adaptation, and outputs it to the iPad as an AJAX response. The result is a much more enjoyable browsing experience on the mobile device.

4.6   Limits to Scalability

As mentioned previously, our work is motivated by acknowledged scalability issues with the approach used in [21]. In that system, a costly browser instance is required for every client request. The core of our approach is to mitigate this cost, by (1) amortizing rendering costs across multiple clients where possible, and (2) only using a full-scale browser instance when absolutely necessary for server-side graphical rendering. In most cases, the server-side browser metaphor is maintained by our proxy as a lightweight and scalable substitute.

To illustrate the improvement offered by our approach, we conduct a series of tests to measure the throughput (i.e., the number of satisfied requests) under various load conditions. We simulate repeated client requests for a remote site, while we vary the percentage of requests that require instantiation of a full browser instance. Our tests are performed on commodity dual-core hardware running Windows Vista, Qt, and WebKit, and do not make use of a thread

Fig. 6. Adding AJAX calls to enhance Craig's List for the iPad

pool of browser instances. Using a browser pool can potentially violate security assumptions if shared by multiple clients.

Figure 7 shows our results. The tests are performed three times per data point, each over a one minute measurement window. The interarrival times between full-scale rendering requests are randomly distributed. A U[0,1] random number is assigned to each request; if the number exceeds the percentage being tested, the request is marked as not requiring a browser instance. As the figure depicts, by limiting the number of requests requiring a graphical render, we are able to increase the number of satisifed requests from 224 to 29038, two orders of magnitude. We expect similar results on non-commodity server hardware as well. For many sites like our test site, rendering the main snapshot is only required once per hour and can be shared by multiple users. Caching and amortizing rendering costs over thousands of clients makes the cost negligible.

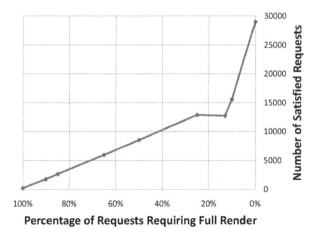

Fig. 7. Increased scalability with addition of lightweight proxy for majority of requests

5   Conclusion

As more and more users access the Web via mobile devices, it becomes essential for site administrators to adapt content for mobile users. However, mobilizing existing content through templates and custom redesign is a costly, tedious, and time-consuming process. Thus, tools to streamline the process are in great demand. In this paper, we have presented the m.Site framework, a powerful set of tools that bolster productivity and provide site administrators with the ability to adapt web content for their mobile users. With a visual tool, a familiar *attribute* paradigm, and an extensible server-side framework, a site administrator can quickly generate code for content adaptation proxies that streamline site functionality. By building a pluggable framework and only calling on a browser instance when absolutely necessary, we have improved the scalability issues from previous work. We have built a prototype of m.Site and validated its effectiveness as a content adaptation tool on real online community websites.

Acknowledgements. We are grateful to the anonymous referees for their insightful feedback. This work was partially supported by NSF grant 0901537 and ARO grant W911NF-11-1-0149.

References

1. Greasemonkey (2009), `http://www.greasespot.net`
2. Greasemonkey user scripts (2009), `http://www.userscripts.org`
3. Platypus firefox extension (2010), `http://platypus.mozdev.org`
4. Apple dashcode (2012), `http://developer.apple.com/tools/dashcode/`
5. Apple webkit html engine (2012), `http://webkit.org`

6. Browser compatibility information (2012), http://www.quirksmode.org
7. Detect mobile browsers (2012), http://detectmobilebrowsers.mobi
8. jquery, the write less, do more, javascript library (2012), http://www.jquery.com
9. Opera-mini browser (2012), http://www.opera.com
10. Skyfire mobile browser (2012), http://www.skyfire.com
11. Bickmore, T., Schilit, B.: Digestor: Device-independent access to the world wide web. In: Proc. WWW-6, Santa Clara, CA, pp. 655–663 (1997)
12. Bila, N., Ronda, T., Mohomed, I., Truong, K., de Lara, E.: Pagetailor: Reusable end-user customization for the mobile web. In: ACM MobiSys 2007, San Juan, Puerto Rico (June 2007)
13. Chen, Y., Ma, W.-Y., Zhang, H.-J.: Detecting web page structure for adaptive viewing on small form factor devices. In: Proceedings of the 12th International Conference on World Wide Web, New York, NY, USA (2003)
14. Deboosere, L., Vankeirsbilck, B., Simoens, P., De Turck, F., Dhoedt, B., Demeester, P., Kind, M., Westphal, F., Taguengayte, A., Plantier, T.: Mobithin management framework: design and evaluation. In: 3rd International Workshop on Adaptive and Dependable Mobile Ubiquitous Systems, London, United Kingdom, (July 13-17, 2009)
15. I. B. Inc. vbulletin forum software (2012), http://www.vbulletin.com
16. Kim, J., Baratto, R., Nieh, J.: Pthinc: a thin-client architecture for mobile wireless web. In: 15th International Conference on World Wide Web (WWW), Edinburgh, Scotland (2006)
17. Md. Fudzee, M., Abawajy, J.: A classification for content adaptation systems. In: 10th International Conference on Information Integration and Web-Based Applications & Services, Linz, Austria (2008)
18. Mohomed, I., Cai, J., de Lara, E.: Urica: Usage-aware interactive content adaptation for mobile devices. In: 1st ACM European Conference on Computer Systems (EuroSys 2006), Leuven, Belgium (2006)
19. Mohomed, I., Scannell, A., Bila, N., Zhang, J., de Lara, E.: Correlation-based content adaptation for mobile web browsing. In: ACM/IFIP/USENIX International Conference on Middleware, Newport Beach, CA (2007)
20. Moshchuk, A., Gribble, S., Levy, H.: Flashproxy: transparently enabling rich web content via remote execution. In: 6th International Conference on Mobile Systems, Applications, and Services (Mobisys), Breckenridge, CO (2008)
21. Nichols, J., Hua, Z., Barton, J.: Highlight: a system for creating and deploying mobile web applications. In: 21st Annual ACM Symposium on User Interface Software and Technology (UIST 2008), Monterey, CA (2008)
22. Raggett, D.: Html tidy, http://tidy.sourceforge.net
23. Richardson, T., Stafford-Fraser, Q., Wood, K., Hopper, A.: Virtual network computing. IEEE Internet Computing 2(1), 33–38 (1998)
24. Schilit, B., Trevor, J., Hilbert, D., Koh, T.: m-links: An infrastructure for very small internet devices. In: 7th Annual International Conference on Mobile Computing and Networking (Mobicom 2001), Rome, Italy (2001)
25. Xiao, X., Luo, Q., Hong, D., Fu, H., Xie, X., Ma, W.: Browsing on small displays by transforming web pages into hierarchically structured subpages. ACM Trans. Web 3(1), 1–36 (2009)
26. Zhang, Y., Guan, X., Huang, T., Cheng, X.: A heterogeneous auto-offloading framework based on web browser for resource-constrained devices. In: International Conference on Internet and Web Applications and Services, pp. 193–199 (2009)

MORENA: A Middleware for Programming NFC-Enabled Android Applications as Distributed Object-Oriented Programs

Andoni Lombide Carreton, Kevin Pinte, and Wolfgang De Meuter

Software Languages Lab, Vrije Universiteit Brussel,
Pleinlaan 2, 1050 Brussels, Belgium
{alombide,kpinte,wdmeuter}@vub.ac.be

Abstract. NFC is a wireless technology that allows software to interact with RFID tags and that is increasingly integrated into smartphones and other mobile devices. In this paper, we present MORENA: a middleware that treats NFC-enabled programs as distributed object-oriented programs in which RFID tags are represented as intermittently connected remote objects. We draw inspiration from the ambient-oriented programming paradigm to represent these objects as first-class remote references which only offer asynchronous communication with the tag to which they refer. This allows the programmer to implement mobile applications that read from or write to RFID tags without having to handle every single fault manually and without blocking the entire application during read or write operations. We built MORENA on top of the Android platform and evaluated our abstractions by implementing a representative application running on NFC-enabled Android phones using MORENA.

Keywords: RFID, mobile applications, Android, pervasive computing.

1 Introduction

The Internet of Things [1][2] research vision can now be implemented using mainstream hardware. Smartphones and other mobile devices are increasingly equipped with NFC (Near Field Communication) chips that allow to read and write a wide range of RFID tags. The most prominent ones are high-end phones running Google's Android platform [3], such as Google's Nexus S. One of the reasons is that companies such as Google are interested in mobile payment applications, such as Google Wallet [4]. However, such applications are only a fraction of what is possibly with an NFC-enabled smartphone. Unfortunately, current APIs that allow the programmer to implement NFC-enabled applications are designed for very specific scenarios (such as mobile payment) and hence exhibit a number of drawbacks that make developing more complicated applications hard and error-prone.

P. Narasimhan and P. Triantafillou (Eds.): Middleware 2012, LNCS 7662, pp. 61–80, 2012.
© IFIP International Federation for Information Processing 2012

1.1   Drawbacks of the Android NFC API

MORENA (MObile RFID-ENabled Android middleware) is designed around the Google Android NFC API, currently to our knowledge the most advanced NFC API for mobile devices that is available in the mainstream. This API is designed to cover the bare essentials to allow the programmer to implement NFC-enabled applications while not having to deal with every single hardware detail. Still, it suffers from a number of drawbacks, which we describe below.

Synchronous Communication. Read and write operations on RFID tags are blocking operations in the Android NFC API. This means that a program performing such operations is suspended until these operations succeed or fail. Since these operations are slow in comparison with the rest of the program, the application becomes unresponsive when not carefully used. Therefore, the documentation of the API strongly recommends to run RFID operations in a separate thread. This burdens the programmer with manual concurrency management, which is hard and error-prone.

Coupling in Time. Reading or writing RFID tags frequently fails because the tag in question is out of range. Especially with tiny NFC chips as the ones found in mobile devices, failure is the rule instead of the exception. Manually dealing with faults requires every single RFID operation to be protected with exception handling code, further complicating the application code. In many cases, operations will succeed shortly after their first failed attempt because of a small change in the physical environment, such as an RFID tag that is positioned differently with respect to the smartphone. This causes the programmer to write looping code merely for retrying failed operations. We say that communication is coupled in time.

Manual Data Conversion. The Android NFC API abstracts away the low-level memory layout of RFID tags. Still, the programmer must manually convert application-specific data that has been read from or that will be written to an RFID tag. This means that when RFID operations are separately developed from the application logic, the application programmer must have internal knowledge of these operations to understand how he or she should convert application-specific data to a suitable representation for storage on the RFID tags' memory. This is error-prone because the API does not enforce specific data conversions to be associated with specific applications and RFID tags.

Tight Coupling with Activity-Based Architecture. Android applications are always *activities*: special Java objects representing an Android GUI with a thread of execution. It is via these activities that the application is notified of I/O and user interface events (by means of *intents*) such as RFID events. Although this event-driven API makes it straightforward to override a number of callbacks that capture these events and directly undertake the necessary actions in the activity code, it also introduces a tight coupling of the RFID operations with activities (i.e. the user interface). This makes it harder to perform RFID operations outside of the context of such an activity.

1.2 Ambient-Oriented Programming

In this paper, we consider interaction with an RFID tag a distributed computing problem as opposed to traditional I/O. More specifically, we draw inspiration from the *ambient-oriented programming* paradigm [5], which is a programming paradigm targeting distributed systems consisting of mobile devices interconnected via unreliable, ad hoc wireless networks. Indeed, NFC can be regarded as an unreliable, ad hoc wireless communication technology while RFID tags can be considered as simple remote devices.

We have previously integrated RFID into ambient-oriented programming [6] by relying on non-mainstream RFID hardware and by building dedicated abstractions into an ambient-oriented research language called AmbientTalk [7]. In this work, we crystallize the ideas behind this research into an implementation on top of mainstream hardware (namely Android smartphones) and using mainstream programming technology (namely the Android platform in the Java language). The concepts from ambient-oriented programming discussed below are carried over as follows.

Tracking of Connectivity. Ambient-oriented programs must keep track of which services become available and unavailable as devices roam. Similarly, an RFID-enabled application must be able to keep track of which RFID tags are currently in and out of range and be notified of changes in the connectivity with the tags it is interacting with.

Asynchronous Communication. All distributed programming systems have primitives for sending and receiving data across the network. Ambient-oriented programming requires these primitives to be non-blocking: a process or thread of control should not be suspended if the operation cannot be completed immediately. This requirement is based on the fact that in an unreliable network, communicating parties can often be unavailable, and making a communication operation block until the communicating party is available may lead to unacceptable delays. Non-blocking communication is also known under the term *asynchronous communication*, the style of communication now also popular in rich web applications using AJAX that should not block the web interface. Similarly, for RFID-enabled applications, communication with an intermittently connected RIFD tag should not block the application when the tag is temporarily out of communication range.

Decoupling in Time. Unreliable wireless connections require communication models that can abstract from the network connectivity between communicating processes. It should be possible for two processes to express communication independently of their connectivity. This significantly reduces the case-analysis for the programmer, which can reason in terms of a fully connected network by default, and can deal with border cases in an orthogonal way. Similarly, exchanging data with an intermittently connected RFID tag is prone to many failures. In many cases, multiple attempts at reading from or writing to an RFID tag's memory are needed before an operation succeeds. This should happen without immediately signaling an error for every single fault to the programmer. Instead, the implementation should retry these operations without blocking the application or signaling an error.

First-Class References to Remote Objects. Decoupling in time is achieved by storing sent messages in an intermediary data-structure. This makes it possible for communicating parties to interact across unreliable connections, because the logical act of information sending is decoupled from the physical act of information transmission, allowing for the information to be saved and transmitted at a later point in time when the connection between both parties is restored.

In AmbientTalk, remote services and RFID tags are represented as remote objects which are always referred to by a remote reference called a *far reference*. These far references (first proposed in the E language [8]) are first class, encapsulate the identity of a remote object and store messages directed towards the remote objects that could not be sent due to physical phenomena. Additionally, far references encapsulate a thread of control that, in response to connectivity changes with the object which it refers to, attempts to forward its stored messages (in the correct order). Far referencers offer an asynchronous interface such that the programmer can register observers on it to be notified of connectivity changes and messages being successfully sent or timed out.

1.3   Approach

It was our goal to integrate the concepts described above into mainstream technology such as the Android platform. This is achieved by providing a middleware that readily integrates with the Android platform (version 4.0 and up). In short, the Android NFC API models RFID operations as **file I/O**, while MORENA treats RFID operations as **network communication**. Additionally, MORENA tackles the remaining drawbacks in the Android NFC API, namely manual data conversion and the tight coupling of the API with the activity-based architecture.

In the next section, we describe the abstractions offered by MORENA for interacting with RFID-tagged objects as if they where remotely connected software objects which are automatically converted to the correct data format for reading from and writing to RFID tags. Thereafter in Section 3, we descend one level deeper into the MORENA middleware which allows the programmer to deal with references to RFID tags directly and allows to encode custom encoding strategies for Java objects. Subsequently, in Section 4 we discuss the application of MORENA in a representative application. Section 5 discusses related work and finally, Section 6, details future work on MORENA and concludes this paper.

2   RFID-Enabled Android Applications as Distributed Object-Oriented Programs

As mentioned in the introduction, the main idea is to no longer treat RFID communication as a form of I/O, but to come up with a suitable representation for RFID tags such that they can be treated as first-class remote objects. A second objective is to loosen the coupling with activity-based architecture of the Android API.

MORENA offers two layers of abstraction. On the highest level, the programmer uses special Java objects called *things* which are causally connected to a specific RFID tag and which can be automatically converted to the correct data format to be read from or written to RFID tags. The lower level requires the programmer to interact through a reference with the bare RFID tag, but allows to come up with custom data conversion strategies (a good example is storing specific fields of an object directly on the RFID tag while other fields are stored in some external database). This section is about the highest level where the programmer uses things.

2.1   Things

Consider an application where facilities offer guests access via their smartphones or tablets to their WiFi access points by swiping over an RFID tag that contains the credentials for connecting to the WiFi network. Using the things abstraction, an object that is read from and written to RFID tags must be a thing. Consider the WifiConfig class that allows us to create such things defined below.

```java
public class WifiConfig extends Thing {
  public String ssid_;
  public String key_;

  public WifiConfig(
      ThingActivity<WifiConfig> activity,
      String ssid,
      String key) {
    super(activity);
    ssid_ = ssid;
    key_ = key;
  }

  public boolean connect(WifiManager wm) {
    // Connect to ssid_ with password key_
  };
}
```

WifiConfig things are simple objects containing two fields, the SSID and password of a WiFi network. All fields that are not declared **transient** are serialized when the thing is stored on an RFID tag. In this case, both fields are stored.

Serialization of things happens by converting Java objects to the JSON format using Google's own serialization library (GSON) built into the Android platform. GSON performs deep serialization of all JSON-serializable fields, but does not support cycles in the object graph to serialize.

Creating a thing requires passing the Android activity in its constructor, as shown in the example. MORENA offers a dedicated activity called `ThingActivity` which is parametrized with the type of things the activity is interacting with. In this case, this is the `WifiConfig` thing type. Internally, such a `ThingActivity` captures all low level Android events (such as the ones typically signaled by means of intents) and triggers the correct actions on the associated thing objects. This frees the programmer from dealing with Android activities directly for every single operation or event.

2.2   Initializing Things

In this section we discuss the initialization of empty RFID tags using things. On the level of abstraction discussed in this section, the programmer can make use of several callbacks that can be overridden on the `ThingActivity`. The one to use for initializing things is the one overridden below.

```
@Override
public void whenDiscovered(EmptyRecord empty) {
  empty.initialize(
    myWifiThing,
    new ThingSavedListener<WifiConfig>() {
      @Override
      public void signal(WifiConfig thing) {
        toast("WiFi joiner created!");
      }
    },
    new ThingSaveFailedListener() {
      @Override
      public void signal() {
        toast("Creating WiFi joiner failed, try again.");
      }
    });
}
```

It is triggered each time an empty RFID tag is detected. It is triggered with an `EmptyRecord`, which is a special thing object denoting an empty tag. Its `initialize` method is used to initialize it with a thing object that at that moment in time is not bound yet to a particular RFID tag. Note that initializing a thing involves writing data to the RFID tag to store the serialized thing in its memory. Since this is an operation that may be long lasting (compared to other computations) and since it may frequently fail, MORENA enforces that it happens asynchronously. For this, `initialize` takes in this case three arguments: the thing to store on the empty tag, a listener object that will be invoked when the thing is successfully initialized, and an object listener that will be invoked when the operation fails given a default timeout. Various overloaded versions of initialize exist, such that for example the failure listener can be omitted or the timeout value can be manually specified. We chose to expect two different listener objects as opposed to a single listener object implementing two different callbacks: one for success and one for failure. The reason is flexibility: these tiny listener objects are usually created by directly implementing an interface, while at the same time, in many cases different success listeners are needed while only a single or handful failure listeners are required (or the other way around). Separating them into separate first-class objects introduces more syntax, but prevents code duplication in such situations.

2.3   Discovering and Reading Things

Just like the whenDiscovered callback for detecting empty RFID tags shown above, there is an overloaded variant that can be used to detect things that are already initialized. In our example application, it is overridden as follows:

```
@Override
public void whenDiscovered(WifiConfig wc) {
    toast("Joining Wifi network " + wc.ssid_);
    wc.connect();
}
```

This callback will be triggered every time an RFID is scanned which contains a thing of type WifiConfig. Upon scanning, the data is deserialized and passed as a WifiConfig argument to this callback.

For ease of programming, such a thing object like wc encapsulates a cached version of this deserialized object which allows synchronous access to its fields and methods. This is used in the example above to call the connect method which connects the Android device to the WiFi network specified in the wc.

However, synchronous access is not without danger since other devices might have concurrently updated the thing stored in the RFID tag's memory. In this case, no problem can occur because immediately after detecting the thing, the connect method is called. For critical cases, the programmer must rely on the asynchronous operations discussed in Section 3.

2.4   Saving Modified Things

The programmer is free to modify thing objects. However, this will render them inconsistent with their serialized counterpart stored on the corresponding RFID tag. To write through any changes performed on a thing to the tag memory, the programmer must explicitly *save* the object. Since such a save operation involves writing the serialized thing onto the tag, which is a long-lasting operation that may frequently fail, MORENA enforces save operations to happen asynchronously. The code snippet below shows how saving a modified thing happens.

Analogous to thing initialization discussed earlier in Section 2.2, a success listener and a failure listener can be supplied to be notified of a successful or

```
myWifiConfig.ssid_ = "MyNewWifiName";
myWifiConfig.key_  = "MyNewWifiPassword";

myWifiConfig.saveAsync(
  new ThingSavedListener<WifiConfig>() {
    @Override
    public void signal(WifiConfig wc) {
      toast("WiFi joiner saved!");
    }},
  new ThingSaveFailedListener() {
    @Override
    public void signal() {
      toast("Saving WiFi joiner failed, try again.");
    }});
```

failed save. Again, various overloaded versions of the saveAsync method exist, depending on which callbacks must be specified and whether the timeout value should be different from the default one. Since we are dealing with NFC technology, which only has a range of a few centimeters, we assume that race conditions are nigh impossible if no exuberantly large timeout values are chosen by the programmer. One of the future features of MORENA that we are investigating is providing alternative protection mechanisms against such race conditions.

2.5   Broadcasting Things

Other than using a phone's built-in NFC chip for reading and writing RFID tags, the Android NFC API allows to use this same wireless communication technology to exchange data in an ad hoc fashion between two phones in NFC communication range. This technology is called *Beam*. The Beam API is largely similar to the API for communication with RFID tags, which it means it suffers from the same drawbacks, namely synchronous communication, coupling in time, manual data conversion and a strong coupling with the activity-based architecture. MORENA allows to easily exchange thing objects between phones over an NFC connection using beam. In our example application, users can connect other users to the WiFi network by bringing their phones close together and broadcasting a WifiConfig thing. This happens as follows.

```
myWifiConfig.broadcast(
  new ThingBroadcastSuccessListener<WifiConfig>() {
    @Override
    public void signal(WifiConfig wc) {
      toast("WiFi joiner shared!");
    }},
  new ThingBroadcastFailedListener<WifiConfig>() {
    @Override
    public void signal(WifiConfig wc) {
      toast("Failed to share WiFi joiner, try again.");
    }});
```

As one can see from the broadcast method used above, this is again an asynchronous operation (as it may frequently fail), adhering to the interface used before in this paper.

The reception of such a thing object using broadcast, causes the standard whenDiscovered callback of the receiving ThingActivity to be invoked. Remember from our example application that upon reception it will connect the Android device to the WiFi network stored on the tag. Things received via broadcast will not be bound to a particular RFID tag (although they can later be by initializing empty tags with them).

3 RFID-Tagged Objects by Reference

In this section, we descend a level of abstraction lower in the MORENA middleware. It offers a reference abstraction to RFID-tagged objects instead of thing objects to the programmer, which allows for asynchronous read and write operations with custom data conversion strategies. The thing abstractions are built directly on top of this layer of abstraction. For the sake of brevity, we use a simple example application that allows to read and write strings onto RFID tags supplied by the user.

3.1 Detecting RFID Tags

Detecting RFID tags already happens in an event-driven manner by activities in the Android API. MORENA offers a TagDiscoverer class that captures these events generated by a specific activity and uses them to generate *tag reference* objects: the objects that represent remote references to RFID tags in MORENA.

Consider a simple Android application that simply shows plain text stored on the last scanned RFID tag and allows the user to overwrite it with new content. One could create a TagDiscoverer subclass as shown below.

```
private class MyTagDiscoverer extends TagDiscoverer {
  @Override
  public void onTagDetected(TagReference ref) {
    readTagAndUpdateUI(reference);
  }
  @Override
  public void onTagRedetected(TagReference ref) {
    readTagAndUpdateUI(reference);
  }
}
```

This subclass overrides two methods that can be used to track the connectivity of an RFID tag: onTagDetected for a tag that has never been detected before, and onTagRedetected for a tag that has already previously been detected. These methods are called with a tag reference as sole argument, which can subsequently be used to interact with the RFID tag (as explained below in Section 3.2). In this simple application, the user interface showing the contents of the last scanned tag is updated with the contents of the tag (the implementation of readTagAndUpdateUI is shown in Section 3.2).

TagDiscoverers are instantiated by passing them the activity (of type NFCActivity) that generates the RFID events and a MIME type that identifies the type of data that the tag contains such that the correct intent is triggered by the activity. Tags containing other types of data are disregarded. Typically, this data type is defined per application, as shown below for our example application.

```
new MyTagDiscoverer(
  this,
  TEXT_TYPE,
  new NdefMessageToStringConverter(),
  new StringToNdefMessageConverter());
```

Additionally, TagDiscoverers are associated with two converter objects that are responsible for converting objects for storage on RFID tags and data read from an RFID tag back into the correct object. These converter objects are explained later in Section 3.2. The idea is to encapsulate data conversion within TagDiscoverers and the TagReferences they generate. This way, an NFCActivity can easily use multiple tag references without worrying about data conversion. Once a TagDiscoverer is instantiated, the programmer must no longer worry about activities.

3.2 The Tag Reference Abstraction

Once a tag reference is obtained (either through a TagDiscoverer or by parameter passing), it offers a non-blocking event-driven API in its own right for asynchronously reading from and writing data from the tag. Additionally, it keeps a queue of buffered read and write operations that are still waiting to be processed (for example because the RFID tag to which it points is temporarily unavailable). Tag references encapsulate a private event loop that uses its own thread of control to sequentially check if the first message in the queue can be processed. If it fails, it just remains in the queue. If it succeeds, the registered event listener on this asynchronous operation is triggered and the operation is removed from the queue, after which the tag reference attempts to execute the next scheduled operation. It is guaranteed that a message is never processed before previously scheduled messages are processed first. If an operation times out, it is removed from the queue as well and the next operation is attempted, but this time the failure listener associated with the operation is triggered (if there is one).

Listeners associated with these non-blocking tag reference operations are always asynchronously scheduled for execution in the activity's main thread, which frees the programmer of manual concurrency management. It also means that usually all statements after a tag reference operation in the code are executed first before the listeners are executed. Synchronization of operations must happen by nesting these listeners.

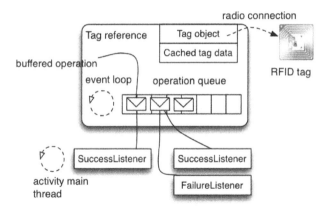

Fig. 1. The tag reference abstraction

The tag reference abstraction is depicted schematically in figure 1. In addition to the bare Android tag object, it also encapsulates a cached version of the contents of the RFID tag, which is updated after each read and write operation. Although it provides synchronous access to these cached data, the programmer must be aware that if a tag is not seen for some time, its contents might have changed and an asynchronous read is a better option.

Within one Android activity, only a single unique tag reference can exist to the same RFID tag. Behind the scenes, TagDiscoverer instances use a private TagReferenceFactory that generates tag references for tags that are detected for the very first time, and subsequently reuses these references when tags are redetected and a reference to them is requested. It is however the programmer's responsibility to garbage collect unused tag references, as this is application specific and usually driven by external events (as opposed to internal references). For future versions of MORENA, we are investigating leasing strategies [9] that allow the application to obtain a lease on an RFID tag for a limited amount of time, after which it expires and the reference to the tag can be safely garbage collected.

In the two subsequent sections, we describe the asynchronous interface offered by the tag reference abstraction.

Reading RFID Tags. Below is the implementation of the private method that is called by the TagDiscoverer class of our simple example application.

As we showed in Section 3.1, when a new tag is detected or a previously detected tag is redetected, this method is called with the obtained tag reference. The tag reference is used for asynchronously reading the tag. If this does not succeed within a predefined timeout, an error is shown to the user. If it succeeds within the predefined timeout, the user interface is updated with the cached data of the tag reference.

```
private void readTagAndUpdateUI(TagReference ref) {
  tagReference_ = ref;
  ref.read(
    new TagReadListener() {
      @Override
      public void signal(TagReference ref) {
        handleTagRead(ref);
      }},
    new TagReadFailedListener() {
      @Override
      public void signal(TagReference ref) {
        handleTagReadFailed();
      }});
}
```

Writing RFID Tags. Writing tags using a tag reference happens in a similar fashion. The listener shown below is triggered by our simple example application when the user clicks the button that causes new text being inputted by the user to be written to the last seen RFID tag.

```
private OnClickListener saveButtonListener =
  new OnClickListener() {
    public void onClick(View button) {
      String toWrite = // Get text from EditText field
      tagReference_.write(
        toWrite,
        new TagWrittenListener() {
          @Override
          public void signal(TagReference ref) {
            handleTagRead(ref);
          }},
        new TagWriteFailedListener() {
          @Override
          public void signal(TagReference ref) {
            handleTagWriteFailed();
          }});
    }
  };
```

It just gets the data from a text field, which is afterwards automatically converted to the appropriate format by the tag reference. This way, data conversion is defined per tag reference and given such a tag reference, the programmer must no longer worry about it.

Just like for reading tags, we allow to register separate listener objects for successful writes and failed writes. In the success listener, the user interface is updated with the new cached data of the tag (which is the data that has been physically written on it, otherwise this listener would not have been triggered). In the failure listener, an error message is shown to the user.

Converting Objects for Storage on RFID Tags. Converting objects for storage on RFID tags and converting data read from RFID tags back to objects happens on a per-tag reference and per-TagDiscoverer basis. This decouples detection of tags and data conversion from the NFCActivity. Implementing these converters requires some knowledge about the Android NFC API, namely its implementation of the NDEF[1] (NFC Data Exchange Format) standard [10].

The class shown below implements a converter for converting data read from an RFID tag into a string for our example application.

```
private class NdefMessageToStringConverter
  implements NdefMessageToObjectConverter {
    @Override
    public Object convert(NdefMessage ndefMessage) {
      return new String(
        (ndefMessage.getRecords()[0]).getPayload());
    }
};
```

In our simple example application, tags contain just a single record containing a string.

The class shown below implements the corresponding converter for converting a string back to the NDEF format for storage on an RFID tag's memory.

```
private class StringToNdefMessageConverter
  implements ObjectToNdefMessageConverter {
    @Override
    public NdefMessage convert(Object o) {
      String toConvert;
      if (o == null) { toConvert = ""; }
      else { toConvert = (String)o; }
      NdefRecord r = new NdefRecord(
        NdefRecord.TNF_MIME_MEDIA,
        TEXT_TYPE,
        new byte[0], // No id.
        toConvert.getBytes(Charset.forName("UTF-8")));
      return new NdefMessage(new NdefRecord[]{ r });
    }
};
```

The details are not of great importance to this paper. It simply creates a byte representation of the string in the correct charset and stores it in a single NdefMessage object contained into a new NdefRecord. This record specifies the type of tags on which TagDiscoverers filter.

---

[1] NDEF messages are in essence lists of byte arrays (NDEF records) in which the data must be stored.

3.3   Interaction with Other Phones Using Beam

Similar to interaction with RFID tags, we built an asynchronous, event-driven
API for exchanging beamed messages. Being notified of an asynchronously received beam message happens by registering a `BeamReceivedListener`, such as
shown below.

```
new MyBeamListener(
  this,
  TEXT_TYPE,
  new NdefMessageToStringConverter());
```

Just like a `TagDiscoverer`, its constructor takes an `NFCActivity` as first
argument, the tag MIME type and a read converter. This allows that the
`BeamReceivedListener` autonomously converts received NDEF messages to objects without the programmer needing to worry about the activity which signals
the low-level events.

Below is the implementation of the subclass instantiated above.

```
private class MyBeamListener extends BeamReceivedListener {
    @Override
    public void onBeamReceived(Object o) {
      // Set text of EditText field.
    }
}
```

The programmer must override the `onBeamReceived` callback to react on
a received beam message. The data transported in the beam message is
automatically converted into an object using the read converter of the
`BeamReceivedListener`.

In contrast to the interaction with RFID tags, beaming does not happen by
means of a reference abstraction. The reason is that beaming is an undirected
operation that broadcasts a message to any device willing to accept the beamed
data. Instead, beaming messages to other phones happens using `Beamer` objects
that again encapsulate data conversion to decouple this from the activity. The
instantiation of the `Beamer` object used by our example application is shown
below. The first argument is the `NFCActivity`.

```
private Beamer beamer_ = new Beamer(
  this,
  new StringToNdefMessageConverter());
```

Just like for RFID operations, beaming messages must happen asynchronously,
using the beam method that is used below in the listener that is triggered when
the user clicks the beam button.

```
private OnClickListener beamButtonListener =
  new OnClickListener() {
    public void onClick(View button) {
      String toBeam = // Get text from EditText field
      // Beaming is undirected.
      beamer_.beam(
        toBeam,
        new BeamSuccessListener() {
          @Override
          public void signal() {
            handleBeamSucceeded();
          }},
        new BeamFailedListener() {
          @Override
          public void signal() {
            handleBeamFailed();
          }});
    }
  };
```

When this button is clicked, the data to be beamed is retrieved from a text field
in the user interface and passed to the asynchronous beam operation. To detect
a successful beam operation, it takes a listener as second argument. To detect
if the beamed message times out, as a third argument it takes another listener.
These listeners are optional and are the only way to be notified of the state
of the asynchronous operation. It exhibits the same behavior as performing an
asynchronous write operation on an RFID tag.

Of particular importance is the fact that data conversions are now encapsulated in TagDataConverter objects, which are associated with TagReference,
TagDiscoverer, Beamer and BeamReceivedListener objects. This means
that a single activity can use multiple TagDiscoverers generating different
TagReferences and different Beamers and BeamReceivedListeners all with
their separate data conversion strategies that are automatically applied when
exchanging data with RFID tags or using Beam.

3.4   Filtering Events

As discussed earlier in this section, the only way to distinguish between interesting scanned tags or interesting received beam messages and non-interesting
ones, is to filter on the tag type (as is done by the TagDiscoverers and
BeamReceivedListeners). Since this is a rather coarse-grained way of filtering, the programmer finds himself implementing filtering behavior manually
and scattered over the application code. This is why TagDiscoverers and
BeamReceivedListeners offer an additional method that can be optionally
overridden by the programmer.

For `TagDiscoverers`, this `checkCondition` method is a predicate that will be applied on the tag reference generated or retrieved by the `TagDiscoverer`, as shown below.

```java
private class MyTagDiscoverer extends TagDiscoverer {
  // ... Same as before ...
  @Override
  public boolean checkCondition(TagReference ref) {
    // ... condition ...
  }
}
```

A typical pattern is that the cached data of the tag reference is used to filter on.

For `BeamReceivedListeners`, a similar predicate can be applied on the object received in the beam message, as shown below.

```java
private class MyBeamListener extends BeamReceivedListener {
  // ... Same as before ...
  @Override
  public boolean checkCondition(Object o) {
    // ... condition ...
  }
}
```

Only when these predicates are satisfied, the listeners are triggered.

4   Evaluation

In this section, we compare two versions of the WiFi sharing application used as an example throughout this paper. The first version is based on the standard NFC API of the Android platform. The second is almost exactly the same application[2], but built on top of the MORENA middleware[3]. The focus of our work is reducing the effort that is needed to develop an RFID-enabled Android application. As a metric we chose to count the lines of code needed for implementing particular RFID subproblems in the application. These subproblems are **(1) event handling** (e.g. to be notified of detected tags), **(2) data conversion, (3) failure handling, (4) read/write functionality**, and finally **(5) concurrency management** (to prevent blocking the application on tag I/O).

Figure 2 shows two graphs comparing both implementations. The graph on the left-hand side shows a comparison of the number of lines of code dedicated to each subproblem. The total number of RFID-related lines of code for the hand-crafted implementation is 197 and for the implementation based on MORENA 36 (a reduction by a factor 5).

---

[2] We will discuss the differences at the end of this section.

[3] The source of these experiments and the MORENA middleware can be downloaded at: http://soft.vub.ac.be/amop/research/rfid/morena/files

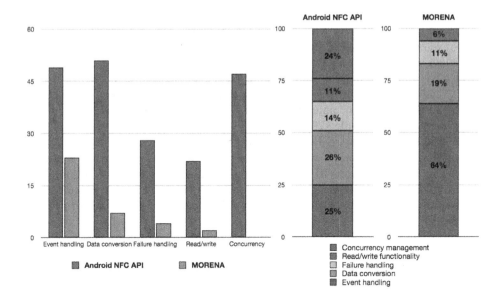

Fig. 2. Comparison of handcrafted RFID code and MORENA code

The right-hand side shows the percentages that the RFID subproblems constitute to the total count. We observe that MORENA shifts the focus to event handling and frees the programmer of any concurrency management. This is to be expected because MORENA's asynchronous communication abstractions take care of concurrency automatically at the expense of more event-driven code.

This leads us to a final note on this comparison. MORENA not only simplifies dealing with RFID technology, it also holds another bonus over the handcrafted implementation. Thanks to its asynchronous communication abstractions, operations that fail due to tag disconnections are automatically retried, which is not incorporated in the handcrafted version, in which the user must manually reattempt the operation. Furthermore, in the MORENA version, multiple write operations can be batched until a tag comes in range, while in the handcrafted solution the user can only attempt to write as soon as a tag is in range. Implementing the same behavior in the handcrafted version will further complicate the implementation. In short, MORENA not only significantly reduces the complexity of implementing RFID-enabled Android applications, but in comparison to naively using the Android NFC API offers a better user experience as well.

5   Related Work

Typical application domains for RFID technology are asset management, product tracking and supply chain management. In these domains RFID technology is usually deployed using traditional RFID middleware, such as Aspire RFID [11] and Oracle's Java System RFID Software [12]. RFID middleware applies filtering, formatting or logic to tag data captured by a reader such that the data can be processed by a software application. Such traditional middleware uses a setup where several RFID readers are embedded in the environment, controlled by a single application agent. These systems rely on a backend database which stores the information that can be indexed using the identifier stored on the tags. They use this infrastructure to associate application-specific information with the tags, although some of them allow to store information directly on the tags, such as for example WinRFID.

WinRFID [13] is an RFID middleware that is entirely based on the .NET Framework and Windows services, which are specified in XML. Services can read from and write data onto RFID tags using an object-oriented abstraction. The tag data is also specified in XML and is converted back and forth to a simplified and compressed format when written onto tag memory. The main drawback of WinRFID however is that the devices and/or services have to be explicitly registered into a registry component, such that the services can contact this registry to interact with for example RFID readers that were a-priori registered.

Fosstrak [14] (formerly named Accada) is an open source RFID middleware platform that is based on the Electronic Product Code standards [15]. Fosstrak offers a virtual tag memory service (VTMS) that similarly to our approach facilitates writing application-specific data to RFID tags asynchronously. However, Fosstrak only supports writing key-value pairs.

In contrast to MORENA, the systems discussed above do not target mobile applications running on for example smartphones. Still, in the literature one can find interesting mobile applications making use of RFID, such as home care [16] or the tracking of personal belongings [17]. This reinforces our idea that there is a need for better programming abstractions in this domain. Conversely, MORENA does not target industrial applications which have to deal with a massive amount of RFID tags, and thus require greater scalability. We are currently investigating how to carry over some of MORENA's concepts into such a middleware.

An alternative distributed computing paradigm to the ambient-oriented programming, on which MORENA is based, is distributed tuple spaces. In [18], RFID tags are used to store application-specific data and form a distributed tuple space that is dynamically constructed by all tuples stored on the tags that are in reading range. Mobile applications interact by means of traditional tuple space operations. However, there is no way to control on which specific tag tuples will be stored.

6   Conclusion and Future Work

In this paper, we have presented MORENA, a middleware that aims at raising the level of abstraction on which developers can build RFID-enabled Android applications. We have evaluated the abstractions offered by MORENA by implementing a mobile RFID-enabled application using the bare essentials provided by the Android platform and comparing the implementation to an implementation based on MORENA. We observe that using MORENA significantly eases the development of mobile RFID-enabled Android applications.

The main feature that remains to be added in a future version of MORENA is a leasing mechanism which has two goals. The first goal is to protect cached thing objects from data races when other RFID-enabled devices are able to write new data on their corresponding RFID tags. The second goal is to allow cached objects to be garbage collected automatically. The mechanism that we envision is to write a locking timestamp and a device ID on the RFID tag's memory by the device willing to interact with the tag. Only if this succeeds, the device is granted exclusive access. The timestamp dictates for how long the device has exclusive access to the memory of the tag. Beyond this timestamp, the lease expires and the device looses its exclusive access, unlocking the tag for interaction with other devices. The assumption made here is that the clock drift among Android devices is small enough to exclude practically all race conditions.

To summarize, the abstractions offered by the MORENA middleware make developing mobile RFID-enabled Android applications easier as follows:

Automatic Conversion of Thing Objects. MORENA's thing objects can be used as regular Java objects, but can in addition be seamlessly read from or written to RFID tags.

Tracking of Connectivity. MORENA offers an event-driven interface such that an application can be notified if a *particular* RFID tag is in or out of communication range.

First-Class References to RFID Tags. In MORENA, RFID tags are uniquely linked to tag references or thing objects.

Asynchronous Communication and Decoupling in Time. MORENA offers asynchronous and fault-tolerant operations for reading or writing the RFID tags' memories, reducing the case analysis for the programmer and freeing the programmer from manual concurrency management to keep the application responsive.

Looser Coupling from the Activity-Based Architecture. MORENA encapsulates the low-level NFC API which is tightly coupled to Android activities into thing objects, tag references or other higher level abstractions such that applications become less coupled to the user interface.

Support for Beam. Just like reading and writing things to and from RFID tags, using the same abstractions, things can be broadcasted to other phones using NFC.

References

1. Atzori, L., Iera, A., Morabito, G.: The internet of things: A survey. Computer Networks 54(15), 2787–2805 (2010)
2. Kortuem, G., Kawsar, F., Sundramoorthy, V., Fitton, D.: Smart objects as building blocks for the internet of things. IEEE Internet Computing 14, 44–51 (2010)
3. Komatineni, S., MacLean, D., Hashimi, S.Y.: Introducing the android computing platform. In: Pro Android 3, pp. 1–20. Apress (2011)

4. Handa, R., Maheshwari, K., Saraf, M.: Google Wallet - A Glimpse Into the Future of Mobile Payments. GRIN Verlag GmbH (2011)
5. Dedecker, J., Van Cutsem, T., Mostinckx, S., D'Hondt, T., De Meuter, W.: Ambient-Oriented Programming in AmbientTalk. In: Thomas, D. (ed.) ECOOP 2006. LNCS, vol. 4067, pp. 230–254. Springer, Heidelberg (2006)
6. Lombide Carreton, A., Pinte, K., De Meuter, W.: Software abstractions for mobile rfid-enabled applications. In: Software: Practice and Experience (2011)
7. Van Cutsem, T., Mostinckx, S., Gonzalez Boix, E., Dedecker, J., De Meuter, W.: Ambienttalk: object-oriented event-driven programming in mobile ad hoc networks. In: XXVI International Conference of the Chilean Computer Science Society, pp. 3–12. IEEE Computer Society (2007)
8. Miller, M.S., Tribble, E.D., Shapiro, J.S.: Concurrency Among Strangers: Programming in E as Plan Coordination. In: De Nicola, R., Sangiorgi, D. (eds.) TGC 2005. LNCS, vol. 3705, pp. 195–229. Springer, Heidelberg (2005)
9. Gray, C., Cheriton, D.: Leases: an efficient fault-tolerant mechanism for distributed file cache consistency. In: SOSP 1989: Proceedings of the Twelfth ACM Symposium on Operating Systems Principles, pp. 202–210. ACM Press, New York (1989)
10. Madlmayr, G., Ecker, J., Langer, J., Scharinger, J.: Near field communication: State of standardization. In: Michahelles, F. (ed.) Proceedings of the International Conference on the Internet of Things 2008, vol. 1, p. 6. ETH Zürich (March 2008)
11. Kefalakis, N., Leontiadis, N., Soldatos, J., Gama, K., Donsez, D.: Supply chain management and NFC picking demonstrations using the AspireRfid middleware platform. In: ACM/IFIP/USENIX Middleware 2008, pp. 66–69. ACM, New York (2008)
12. Oracle (Sun Developer Network), Developing auto-id solutions using sun java system rfid software
13. Prabhu, B.S., Su, X., Ramamurthy, H., Chu, C.-C., Gadh, R.: Winrfid – a middleware for the enablement of radio frequency identification (rfid) based applications. White paper, UCLA – Wireless Internet for the Mobile Internet Consortium (January 2008)
14. Floerkemeier, C., Roduner, C., Lampe, M.: Rfid application development with the accada middleware platform. IEEE Systems Journal, Special Issue on RFID Technology 1, 82–94 (2007)
15. EPCGlobal Standards Overview (September 2010), http://www.epcglobalinc.org/standards
16. Sidén, J., Skerved, V., Gao, J., Forsström, S., Nilsson, H.-E., Kanter, T., Gulliksson, M.: Home care with nfc sensors and a smart phone. In: Proceedings of the 4th International Symposium on Applied Sciences in Biomedical and Communication Technologies, ISABEL 2011, p. 150:1–150:5. ACM, New York (2011)
17. Watfa, M.K., Kaur, M., Daruwala, R.F.: IPurse: An Innovative RFID Application. In: Zhou, M. (ed.) ISAEBD 2011, Part IV. CCIS, vol. 211, pp. 531–538. Springer, Heidelberg (2011)
18. Mamei, M., Quaglieri, R., Zambonelli, F.: Making tuple spaces physical with rfid tags. In: Symposium on Applied computing, pp. 434–439. ACM, New York (2006)

Fmeter: Extracting Indexable Low-Level System Signatures by Counting Kernel Function Calls

Tudor Marian[1], Hakim Weatherspoon[2], Ki-Suh Lee[2], and Abhishek Sagar[3]

[1] Google
[2] Cornell University
[3] Microsoft Corp.

Abstract. System monitoring tools serve to provide operators and developers with an insight into system execution and an understanding of system behavior under a variety of scenarios. Many system abnormalities leave a significant impact on the system execution which may arise out of performance issues, bugs, or errors. Having the ability to quantify and search such behavior in the system execution history can facilitate new ways of looking at problems. For example, operators may use clustering to group and visualize similar system behaviors. We propose a monitoring system that extracts formal, indexable, low-level system signatures using the classical vector space model from the field of information retrieval and text mining. We drive an analogy between the representation of kernel function invocations with terms within text documents. This parallel allows us to automatically index, store, and later retrieve and compare the system signatures. As with information retrieval, the key insight is that we need *not* rely on the semantic information in a document. Instead, we consider only the statistical properties of the terms belonging to the document (and to the corpus), which enables us to provide both an efficient way to extract signatures at runtime and to analyze the signatures using statistical formal methods. We have built a prototype in Linux, Fmeter, which extracts such low-level system signatures by recording all kernel function invocations. We show that the signatures are naturally amenable to formal processing with statistical methods like clustering and supervised machine learning.

Keywords: Information retrieval, term-frequency inverse document frequency, indexable system signatures.

1 Introduction

System monitoring is key to understanding system behavior. Developers and operators rely on system monitoring to provide information necessary to identify, isolate, and potentially fix performance bottlenecks and hidden bugs. Unfortunately, as computer systems become increasingly complex, understanding their execution behavior to identify such performance bottlenecks and hidden bugs has become more difficult. Furthermore, large scale system deployments, like the present-day datacenters that power cloud services, require increasingly complex automatic system monitoring infrastructures [1–3].

One issue is that existing monitoring solutions have not been designed to enable the extraction of low-overhead, low-level, system signatures that are sufficiently expressive

P. Narasimhan and P. Triantafillou (Eds.): Middleware 2012, LNCS 7662, pp. 81–100, 2012.
© IFIP International Federation for Information Processing 2012

to be used in automatic analysis by formal methods. For example, instruction level monitoring in software and breakpoint debugging incur prohibitive overheads; system call tracing is both expensive and not expressive enough; hardware counters by themselves provide little amounts of specialized information while hardware counter assisted profiling is not expressive enough since it relies on sampling. By contrast, high-level metrics, like the number of completed transactions per second are overly general and application specific, and are unable to capture with sufficient fidelity low-level system behavior.

Another issue is that few monitoring solutions provide a systematic and formal way to leverage past diagnostics in future problem detection and resolution [4]. Instead, system monitoring has traditionally been performed in an ad-hoc fashion, using anything from printf/printk statements, debuggers, operating system process tracers, runtime instrumentation [5], to logging libraries, kernel execution tracing [6], low-level hardware counters [7,8], generalized runtime statistics [9,10], and system call monitoring [11] to name a few.

In this paper we introduce Fmeter—a novel monitoring technique that efficiently extracts *indexable* low-level system descriptions, or signatures, which accurately capture the state of a system at a point in time. Every low-level signature is essentially a feature vector where each feature roughly corresponds to the number of times a particular operating system's kernel function was invoked. Fmeter draws inspiration from the field of information retrieval, which showed that counting words in a document is sufficiently powerful to enable formal manipulations of document corpora. Likewise, Fmeter does not rely on any additional contextual information, like call stack traces, function parameters, memory location accesses, and so on.

By construction, embedding kernel function calls into the vector space model [12] yields formally indexable signatures of low-level system behavior. Developers and operators can automatically analyze system behavior using conventional statistical techniques such as clustering, machine learning, and similarity based search against a database of previously labeled signatures. For example, Fmeter enables operators to instrument entire datacenters of production-ready machines with the flip of a switch, and provides a way to automatically diagnose problems. At the very least, Fmeter enables operators to prune out the space of potential problems. By contrast, expending human expertise to perform forensic analysis in such an environment on a large number of individual systems is intractable.

Fmeter occupies a new point in the design space of monitoring systems that yield low-level system signatures. Unlike low level statistical profilers (e.g., Oprofile [7]) which only capture the most frequent events in their event space, Fmeter records every single kernel function invocation, therefore there are no events that fly under the radar—as long as they belong to Fmeter's event space to begin with. This is an important feature of Fmeter since bugs typically reside in cold code. (Section 2.1 formally defines what is the precise contribution of each kernel function invocation count to a signature.) Moreover, Fmeter signatures are insensitive to nondeterminism and are machine independent.

Since Fmeter does not need to collect any detailed contextual information (like entire stack traces), generating and retrieving signatures can be more efficient than general-purpose function tracers. As we demonstrate in Section 4, we leverage this knowledge

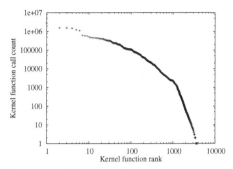

Fig. 1. Kernel function call count during boot-up

of the problem domain to render the Fmeter prototype more efficient than the default Ftrace [6] kernel function tracer. Like Ftrace, Fmeter has virtually zero runtime overhead if it is not enabled. However, unlike the Ftrace function tracer, Fmeter does not collect any additional semantic information with each function call. The Fmeter runtime overhead introduced by signature generation is sufficiently low that signature generation can be turned on at production time for long continuous periods of time. Generating and logging signatures over such long continuous time intervals increases the likelihood of success of post-mortem analysis of crashed systems.

Our contributions are as follows:

– We provide a novel method for extracting indexable low-level system signatures by embedding kernel function calls into the vector space model. The signatures are naturally amenable for formal statistical manipulations, like clustering, machine learning / classification, and similarity based search.
– We introduce Fmeter—an efficient prototype implementation of a monitoring system capable of generating and retrieving the low-level system signatures continuously over long periods of time, in real-time, and with little overhead.
– We show that the signatures are sufficiently powerful to capture meaningful low-level system behaviors which can be accurately classified by conventional unsupervised and supervised machine learning techniques. Furthermore, the signatures are also sufficiently precise for automatic classifiers to unambiguously distinguish even between system behaviors that differ in subtle ways.

The rest of the paper is structured as follows. Section 2 discusses our motivation, insight, approach, and challenges for creating an indexable signature via embedding kernel function calls into a classical vector space model. We describe our Fmeter design and implementation in 3. In Section 4, we evaluate Fmeter and our proposed approach. We discuss limitations to our approach and design in Section 5. Finally, we discuss related work and conclude in Sections 7 and 8.

2 Methodology

To extract meaningful, low-level system signatures that are also formally indexable, we turned to the discipline of information retrieval (IR) and text mining for inspiration.

The information retrieval community has had a long and proven track record of developing successful statistical techniques for automatic document indexing and retrieval. In particular, the IR discipline has shown that simple statistics computed over the document's terms are sufficiently powerful to yield information which can be formally analyzed. For example, search engines typically throw away semantic information (e.g., they do not parse sentences and paragraphs) and use term frequencies mechanically for scoring and ranking a document's relevance given an input query.

Like the frequency of words in documents, function invocations appear to follow a power-law like distribution. Figure 1 shows invocation counts of 3815 functions of the Linux kernel version 2.6.28 invoked on a Dell Power Edge R710 four way quad core x86 Nehalem platform from the late boot-up stage until the login prompt was spawned. It shows that some functions are called more frequently than others. This behavior is also consistent with the role of instruction-caches in exploiting temporal locality of code. Such heavy-tailed distributions have been observed often in the real-world. A classic example of such a power-law is the distribution of wealth in the world, the distribution in rankings of U.S. cities by population, and the distribution of document terms in a large corpus of natural language [13]. For example, the word frequency in the whole of Wikipedia [14], reported on November 27, 2006, follows a shape similar to that of Figure 1. Such distributions have been thoroughly analyzed by statisticians, economists, computer scientists and mathematicians alike, and various analytical modes have been proposed—e.g., power-laws can be mathematically modeled by preferential attachment, also referred to as the "rich get richer" effect.

2.1 Low-Level System Signatures

Our key insight is that we extract low-level system signatures by mapping the concepts of information retrieval and text mining to system behavior. In our model, the information retrieval concept of a "term" corresponds to a kernel function call, while the concept of a "document" corresponds to a period of low-level system activity, or function calls, over a predetermined period of time. (The kernel function calls should *not* be confused with the system calls exported by the kernel through it's application binary interface.) The "corpus" then corresponds to a collection of low-level system activities. Like in the classical vector space model [12], we disregard the semantic information in a document and consider only the statistical properties of the terms belonging to the document (and to the corpus). In our case, we disregard the sequence of kernel function calls (the "call stack" trace), the function parameters, memory location accesses, or hardware device state manipulation. Instead, we rely solely on counting the kernel function invocations, which is significantly cheaper and introduces less overhead.

We use the term frequency-inverse document frequency (tf-idf) model to represent documents, and thus system signatures, as weight vectors. The weight vector for a document j is $\mathbf{v_j} = [w_{1,j}, w_{2,j}, \ldots, w_{N,j}]^T$ where N is the number of "terms," i.e., the total number of kernel functions. Each weight $w_{i,j} = tf_{i,j} \times idf_i$, or the product of the term frequency, and the inverse document frequency. The term frequency is given by: $tf_{i,j} = \frac{n_{i,j}}{\sum_k n_{k,j}}$ where $n_{i,j}$ is the number of times the term (function) i appears (was called) in document (during the monitoring run) j. Essentially the term frequency counts the number of times a term appears in a document, and normalizes it by the size of the document. Normalization is required to prevent bias towards longer documents (or in our case towards longer runs) which would implicitly have a higher term count by sheer virtue of their length (duration of execution).

The inverse document frequency is used to diminish the weight of terms that occur very frequently in the entire corpus, which is the case for example with prepositions in text documents, or multiplexed functions like the `ioctl`, `ipc` and `execve` system calls, or virtual memory management internal routines during the boot-up phase (the top ranked kernel functions as seen in Figure 1). The inverse document frequency is computed as: $idf_i = \log \frac{|D|}{1+|\{d:i\in d\}|}$ where $|D|$ is the size of the corpus, or in our case the number of monitored low-level system activities, and the term $|\{d : i \in d\}|$ represents the number of documents containing the term i.

Fmeter collects low-level system *signatures* as weight vectors $\mathbf{v_j}$ (for each signature j), by counting the number of times each kernel function was called during a given time-interval. More precisely, the set of distinct kernel functions induce the orthonormal basis for the weight vectors $\mathbf{v_j}$. Each distinct kernel function corresponds to one of the unit-vectors, i.e., versors, that together span the space in which every system signature is defined to be a point.

Since each signature is represented as a vector belonging to the same vector space, we can express signature similarities as the similarity between the vectors. One such measure is the cosine similarity between two vectors—the cosine of the angle between the two vectors: $\cos\theta = \frac{\mathbf{x}\cdot\mathbf{y}}{||\mathbf{x}||\,||\mathbf{y}||}$; $||\cdot||$ is a vector norm and $\mathbf{x}\cdot\mathbf{y}$ the dot product between the two vectors. Alternatively, one may specify a *distance metric*, like the Minkowski distance induced by the L_p norm: $d_p(\mathbf{x},\mathbf{y}) = \left(\sum_i |x_i - y_i|^p\right)^{\frac{1}{p}}$. Unless specified otherwise, throughout this paper we compare vectors using the Euclidean distance, i.e., the distance metric induced by the L_2 norm. Furthermore, certain formal methods require we normalize the vectors, in which case we rely on the L_2 norm as well.

Fmeter retrieves such formal, indexable, low-level system signatures by embedding kernel function invocations into the classical vector space model [12]. Our approach was inspired by the information retrieval and text mining literature. By broadly ignoring the semantics of "documents," we balance the delicate act of constructing effective low-level signatures while incurring low signature retrieval overhead, and in the process we gain the opportunity to manipulate the signatures using conventional statistical tools.

2.2   Statistical Data Analysis

The low-level system signatures collected by Fmeter are indexable, hence they can be manipulated by formal data analysis methods like unsupervised and supervised machine learning, similarity based search, and so on.

Clustering is a typical unsupervised learning technique that groups together vectors (and therefore low-level system signatures) that are naturally close to each other, or similar, based on a given distance metric. When used in conjunction with system signatures, clustering can identify similar low-level behaviors. A typical clustering algorithm also returns the *centroid* of each grouping assignment. The centroid of a cluster of signatures can then be used as a *syndrome* which characterizes a manifestation of a common behavior, e.g., an undesired behavior. Clustering can therefore be used to detect system behaviors which are similar to past pathological behaviors or previously encountered problems. A key property of clustering is that it allows for unknown behaviors to be classified as similar to some syndrome S, even though the unknown behaviors may belong to a distinct class of their own (i.e., clustered together, the unknown signatures yield a centroid which is closest to S). Section 4.2 contains our evaluation of Fmeter signature clustering.

Unlike unsupervised learning methods like clustering, supervised learning requires labeled training data to construct a predictive model. The model is subsequently used to make predictions about unlabeled data. For example, if an operator has access to a labeled training data set containing both signatures of buggy / compromised device driver behavior and signatures of normal behavior exercised by a correct device driver, future unlabeled instances of buggy device driver behavior may be identified by a classifier. Section 4.2 contains a detailed evaluation of such machine learning using Fmeter signatures as training, validation, and test data.

We envision an environment in which an operator has access to a database of labeled low-level system signatures describing many instances of normal and abnormal behavior, and perhaps the necessary steps to remedy problems. The signatures are retrieved and stored from systems whose behavior has been forensically identified and labeled. For example, signatures can be retrieved from systems that operate within normal parameters, as well as from systems that have been identified to exert certain bugs, performance issues, and any unwanted behavior (like the system reacting to a denial of service attack or a system being compromised and acting as a spam-bot and so on). Once the root cause of the problem is found for some abnormal behavior, Fmeter can then be used to generate a large number of `tf-idf` signatures with low overhead. These signatures are subsequently labeled appropriately, and stored in the database for future training references by classifiers. Likewise, signatures can be clustered to obtain syndrome centroids. By labeling similar vectors and syndrome centroids with semantic meaning, an operator may later determine automatically whether a system has some property or is behaving in an undesired fashion.

Interestingly, clustering may also be applied recursively. Applying meta-clustering on the retrieved cluster centroids, we can determine which entire classes, not just individual signatures of behaviors, are similar to one another. If two classes of system behaviors are similar with respect to their `tf-idf` signatures, it means they are similar in the way they invoke the kernel's functions. We can therefore schedule concurrently executing tasks that rely on the same kernel code-paths (and implicitly the same in-kernel data-structures) on cores that share a cache domain (e.g., the L3 cache for an Intel Nehalem microarchitecture). For a monolithic kernel (the only kind we instrument with Fmeter) such an assignment boosts performance due to improved cache locality while executing in kernel-mode [15]. For example, Fmeter logging over large time intervals would enable such a cache-aware task assignment feedback loop; as shown in Section 4.1, Fmeter signature retrieval and logging is sufficiently cheap to render such logging feasible (and can be switched on and off at runtime).

3   Extracting Signatures

Instrumenting every existing application to count all possible function calls is unrealistic. Instead, we only instrument the operating system kernel, since all applications depend on it to varying degrees. User-mode applications typically request services from the kernel through a well defined application binary interface (ABI). Fmeter reduces the size of the possible feature-space by limiting its dimensionality to a subset that is both manageable and contains significant low-level information. However, unlike statistical (kernel and otherwise) profilers, Fmeter triggers upon every kernel function call. Fmeter keeps track of how many times each kernel function is called, and exports this information to user-space through the debugfs [16] file system interface.

Since function names are not sufficient as unambiguous identifiers (e.g., a kernel may have duplicate static functions), we identify kernel functions by their start address. Absolute addresses work since unlike relocatable code, the kernel symbols are loaded at the same address across reboots, however, using addresses means that the signatures are not valid across different kernel versions. We consider this limitation to be minor given the target Fmeter environment, namely that of compute clouds which run a small number of managed virtual machine / bare-metal kernels. Function symbols that reside in runtime loadable modules introduce further complications since modules are relocated at load time. Initially Fmeter identified functions in modules using a tuple comprising of the module name, version, and function offset within the module. However, we observed that different version drivers may contain mostly the same code (confirmed after we compared disassembled modules one function at a time) but adding even the slightest modifications at some point in the module changes all subsequent offsets. Therefore we decided that Fmeter does not instrument functions that live within runtime loadable kernel modules, and signatures will only capture the behavior of modules by virtue of the calls the modules make into the core-kernel. This means that Fmeter effectively reduces the dimensionality of the feature space, a technique that is commonly used throughout machine learning (e.g., to select only the most meaningful features based on principal component analysis, and prune out the otherwise low-impact features).

The Linux kernel already provides several facilities to intercept and execute ad-hoc handlers when kernel functions start or finish executing. For example, the Kernel Dynamic Probes (Kprobes) [5] subsystem may be used to graft breakpoint instructions at runtime, and call into implanted handler routines (these routines may live in runtime loadable modules as well, hence new ones can be coded as needed). Unlike Kprobes, which incur the runtime overhead of inserting a breakpoint, executing the handler, and single-stepping through the breakpointed instruction, the Ftrace [6] infrastructure shifts most of the overhead at kernel compile time and during the kernel boot-up phase. In particular, when compiled with gcc's -pg flag, all kernel functions are injected with a call to a special mcount routine, a technique similar to the way in which the ATOM [17] platform converted a program into its own profiler. The mcount routine must be implemented in assembly because the call does not follow the conventional C–ABI. During kernel boot-time, the mcount call sites are iterated over and recorded in a list, and are subsequently converted into noops. The saved list can later be used at runtime to dynamically and selectively convert any of the call-sites back into trace calls.

Currently, Ftrace implements several tracers in this manner, e.g., a function call tracer to trace all kernel functions, a function graph tracer that probes functions both upon entry and exit hence providing the ability to infer call-graphs, a tracer of context switches and wake-ups between tasks, and so on. Since the Ftrace subsystem supports a large variety of tracers, it encompasses a general purpose machinery that generically logs retrieved data to user-space through the debugfs interface. More precisely, Ftrace relies on large fixed size circular buffers to store traced information, and individually recorded information has variable size (e.g., function traces and call-graphs). Moreover, the circular buffer management is fairly complex since it has to be accessed in an SMP-safe fashion to protect against concurrent updates since the kernel executes concurrently on all available processors. Although the Ftrace circular buffer available in the kernel version we started with (version 2.6.28) was deemed to be somewhat lock-heavy [18] with impact on performance, there have since been various attempts to replace it with a wait-free alternative [18, 19]. Wait-free FIFO buffers [20, 21] are difficult to prove correct and are prone to subtle race-conditions and errors, which is why their adoption into the mainline Linux kernel has been slow.

Since Ftrace is not extensible, i.e., new tracers cannot be added in a non-invasive way, we implemented the Fmeter tracing to rely only on the mcount kernel functionality and did not make use of the conventional ring-buffers. Instead, we constructed an efficient data structure which takes advantage of the structure of the monitored data to further reduce overheads. Conceptually, Fmeter requires only a small, fixed size array that maps kernel function address to an integer value denoting invocation count. Fmeter creates this mapping at boot-time, right after the kernel introspects itself and records the mcount sites for all traced kernel functions. To access and update the mapping during normal operation, we provide a specialized mcount routine.

The function-to-invocation map is slightly more involved. Fmeter actually maintains a set of per-CPU indices, each index mapping a kernel function to a cache aligned 8 byte integer value. The integer value is incremented each time the corresponding function is invoked while running on the current CPU. Each per-CPU index is allocated as a series of free pages, and each page contains an array of "slots." Before a kernel function executes for the first time, the mcount routine is invoked. Our specialized mcount routine replaces the call site that triggered its call with a call to a custom-built stub for the original kernel function whose preamble invoked mcount in the first place. There will be one such stub dynamically created by the specialized mcount routine for every instrumented function. All subsequent calls to the instrumented kernel function will execute the custom, personalized stub from then on.

The custom stub for each kernel function is generated by embedding two indices into the stub code itself. The first index identifies the page in the page list which constitutes the per-CPU data buffer. The second index identifies the corresponding slot on the selected page corresponding to the invoked function. The indices are generated at boot-time, when the mappings between function addresses and invocation counts are allocated. When invoked, each individual stub disables preemption to prevent the current task from being scheduled out and potentially moved on a different CPU, follows the mapping by way of the two embedded indices, increments the corresponding invocation count, and re-enables preemption before returning.

Enabling and disabling preemption is a cheap operation that amounts to integer arithmetic on a value in the current task's process control block. It is cheaper than atomic operations like the `lock;inc` instructions used by the Linux kernel spinlocks and cheaper than compare-and-swap instructions used, for example, by wait-free circular buffers. Note that lock-free constructs do not absolve such atomic operations from generating expensive cache-coherency traffic over the cross-core interconnect.

A user-space daemon periodically reads the function invocation counts from debugfs and logs them to disk. The normalizing step during the `tf-idf` score computation ensures that the collection period does not have a major influence on the signatures; though it can be configured. The logging daemon reads all kernel function invocation counts twice (before and after the time interval) and computes the difference which is later transformed into `tf-idf` scores, once an entire corpus is generated.

4   Evaluation

We begin our evaluation by measuring the overhead introduced by Fmeter. To quantify the overhead, we perform a set of micro- and macro-benchmarks. We then proceed to show the efficacy of statistical data analysis methods. We employ unsupervised (clustering) and supervised (classification) machine learning techniques to retrieve information and to monitor system behavior.

Throughout our experiments we use a Dell PowerEdge R710 server equipped with a dual socket 2.93GHz Xeon X5570 (Nehalem) CPU. Each CPU has four cores and 8MB of shared L3 cache, and is connected through its private on-chip memory controller to 6GB of RAM, for a total of 12 GB of cache-coherent NUMA system memory. The Nehalem CPUs support hardware threads, or hyperthreads, hence the operating system manages a total of 16 processors. The R710 machine is equipped with a Serial Attached SCSI disk and two Myri-10G NICs, one CX4 10G-PCIE-8B-C+E NIC and one 10G-PCIE-8B-S+E NIC with a 10G-SFP-LR transceiver; the server is connected back to back to an identical twin R710 server (the twin server is only used during experiments involving network traffic). The R710 server runs a vanilla Linux kernel version 2.6.28 in three configurations: with the Ftrace subsystem disabled, with the Ftrace function tracer turned on, and patched with Fmeter instead of Ftrace respectively.

4.1   Micro- and Macro-Benchmarks

This section demonstrates the overhead of using Fmeter while deployed to monitor systems in-production. We compare against a vanilla kernel with Linux Ftrace function tracer turned both on and off. When Ftrace is turned off the overhead is zero, whereas if it is turned on, recording every kernel function call incurs additional overhead. Kernel functions are behind all system calls which applications use, they are responsible for handling events, like interrupts, and they are also directly called by kernel threads. Fmeter implements its own technique of utilizing the `mcount` call to record data in dedicated per-CPU data slots while incurring low overhead. By contrast, the Ftrace collection mechanism is more involved, since more information is recorded, e.g. function call-traces, and passed to user-space.

Table 1. LMbench: Linux kernel in vanilla configuration, with Ftrace function tracer on, and with Fmeter on

Test	Baseline μs	Ftrace μs	Fmeter μs	Slowdown Ftrace	Fmeter	Ratio
AF_UNIX sock stream latency	4.828 ± 0.585	27.749 ± 2.649	7.393 ± 0.867	5.748	1.531	3.753
Fcntl lock latency	1.219 ± 0.209	6.639 ± 0.039	3.024 ± 0.649	5.446	2.481	2.195
Memory map linux.tar.bz2	206.750 ± 0.590	1800.520 ± 4.486	317.125 ± 1.368	8.709	1.534	5.678
Pagefaults on linux.tar.bz2	0.677 ± 0.008	3.678 ± 0.008	0.866 ± 0.009	5.433	1.279	4.249
Pipe latency	2.492 ± 0.010	12.421 ± 0.042	3.201 ± 0.081	4.985	1.285	3.881
Process fork+/bin/sh -c	1446.800 ± 18.678	6421.000 ± 11.124	1831.590 ± 7.546	4.438	1.266	3.506
Process fork+execve	672.266 ± 6.663	3094.380 ± 14.093	847.289 ± 3.227	4.603	1.260	3.652
Process fork+exit	208.914 ± 6.951	1116.800 ± 10.880	268.275 ± 1.910	5.346	1.284	4.163
Protection fault	0.185 ± 0.009	0.607 ± 0.011	0.286 ± 0.006	3.280	1.544	2.125
Select on 10 fd's	0.231 ± 0.001	1.410 ± 0.001	0.277 ± 0.001	6.110	1.199	5.096
Select on 10 tcp fd's	0.261 ± 0.001	1.798 ± 0.004	0.326 ± 0.001	6.897	1.251	5.512
Select on 100 fd's	0.897 ± 0.002	9.809 ± 0.001	1.321 ± 0.008	10.941	1.474	7.424
Select on 100 tcp fd's	2.189 ± 0.002	26.616 ± 0.242	3.308 ± 0.023	12.160	1.511	8.046
Semaphore latency	2.890 ± 0.072	6.117 ± 0.236	2.084 ± 0.062	2.117	0.721	2.936
Signal handler installation	0.113 ± 0.000	0.280 ± 0.000	0.127 ± 0.001	2.473	1.119	2.209
Signal handler overhead	0.909 ± 0.010	3.124 ± 0.009	1.072 ± 0.005	3.435	1.179	2.914
Simple fstat	0.100 ± 0.001	0.852 ± 0.006	0.145 ± 0.002	8.550	1.458	5.864
Simple open/close	1.193 ± 0.004	11.222 ± 0.019	1.873 ± 0.014	9.410	1.571	5.991
Simple read	0.101 ± 0.000	1.196 ± 0.007	0.171 ± 0.000	11.893	1.701	6.990
Simple stat	0.721 ± 0.002	7.008 ± 0.021	1.067 ± 0.012	9.720	1.480	6.567
Simple syscall	0.041 ± 0.000	0.210 ± 0.000	0.053 ± 0.000	5.156	1.303	3.958
Simple write	0.086 ± 0.000	1.012 ± 0.004	0.130 ± 0.001	11.723	1.511	7.759
UNIX connection cost	15.328 ± 0.057	81.380 ± 0.260	21.919 ± 1.339	5.309	1.430	3.713

Table 1 shows the overhead incurred by Ftrace and Fmeter with respect to a vanilla un-instrumented kernel during the lmbench [22] micro-benchmark (the results represent average latencies in μs along with standard error of the mean). Overall, Fmeter incurs significantly less overhead than Ftrace. At best, Ftrace is as little as 2.125 times slower than Fmeter, whereas in the worst case Ftrace it is as high as 8.046 times slower than Fmeter. On average, Fmeter is 1.4 times slower than a vanilla kernel, whereas Ftrace is about 6.69 times slower than the un-instrumented kernel. It is important to note that lmbench tests exert unusual stress on very specific kernel operations by executing them in a busy-loop which is uncommon and typically considered an anomaly in real-world production-ready environments.

Table 2. (a) apachebench scores, vanilla (un-instrumented) kernel, Ftrace kernel function tracer on, and with Fmeter on; (b) Linux kernel compile time

Configuration	Requests per second	Slowdown
vanilla	14215.2 ± 69.6931	0.00 %
fmeter	10793.3 ± 77.7275	24.07 %
ftrace	5524.93 ± 33.4601	61.13 %

(a)

	Unmodified	Ftrace	Fmeter
real	57m58.961s	89m56.821s	56m43.264s
user	47m50.175s	49m5.492s	46m24.890s
sys	7m59.642s	41m31.300s	9m45.817s

(b)

Table 2(a) displays the results of a HTTP server macro-benchmark. We used the standard `apachebench` tool, which was configured to send 512 concurrent connections (1000 times in closed-loop for a total of 512000 requests) and we used a single 1400 byte HTML file as the target served by the apache httpd web server. The apache HTTP server and the `apachebench` client ran both on the same machine to eliminate any network-induced artifacts. All tests were conducted 16 times for each configuration, and we report the average along with the standard error of the mean. The Table shows a 24% slowdown in the number of requests completed per second for Fmeter and a 61% slowdown for Ftrace. As with lmbench, the test stresses the system to magnify overheads by issuing a large number of concurrent connections.

Finally, Table 2(b) depicts the time elapsed while compiling the Linux kernel, as reported by the `time` utility (not the bash `time` command), atop various configurations. As expected, the time spent in user-mode (under the row labeled `user`) is roughly the same irrespective if a vanilla kernel is used, or whether one of the Ftrace function tracer or the Fmeter subsystems are enabled instead. However, unlike user-mode code which is not instrumented, the kernel code is, and the numbers shown in the Table (under the row labeled `sys`) reveal that while Fmeter slows down the kernel compilation by about 22%, Ftrace slows it down by no less than 420%, i.e. it is 5.2 times slower. The numbers are consistent with the Fmeter and Ftrace design which only rely on the instrumentation of the kernel code-paths. In general, applications that rely little on the operating system's kernel functionality, e.g., those applications that issue few system calls (like the scientific programs that crunch numbers), would show a lower overhead. However it also implies that there are less opportunities for meaningful system signatures to be collected by Fmeter when such applications are running, thereby reducing the efficacy of our system profiling methodology altogether.

4.2   Clustering and Supervised Machine Learning

Next we show the amenability of signatures retrieved with Fmeter towards statistical data analysis techniques. We extract the signatures while performing workloads in a controlled environment. First, we show that supervised machine learning can be applied to distinguish with high accuracy amongst the signatures extracted while performing three different workloads. Second, we evaluate the efficacy of the same machine learning classifiers in distinguishing between highly similar behaviors, as induced by subtle modifications in the code of a network interface device driver. The device driver resides in an un-instrumented kernel module, hence the signatures retrieved only account for the core-kernel functions the driver calls *into* (i.e., none of the functions of either driver are instrumented). Our assumption is that such subtle device driver modifications are characteristic of compromised or buggy systems which are otherwise exceedingly hard to forensically analyze.

And third, we show that signatures retrieved during the same workloads can be automatically clustered together and accurately distinguished from signatures belonging to different workloads. We employ the same set of signatures used to previously evaluate the supervised machine learning. Since clustering is an unsupervised learning method, system operators may rely on it to identify specific behaviors without having access to labeled signatures. Operators may categorize whether a particular behavior of interest is similar to a previously observed syndrome by comparing the behavior's signatures with syndrome signatures.

Throughout the evaluation we employ conventional, though state-of-the-art, machine learning algorithms and information retrieval measurement techniques.

Supervised Machine Learning. First we show how supervised machine learning can distinguish with high accuracy between Fmeter signatures corresponding to different system behaviors. We then proceed to evaluate the efficacy of machine learning classifiers in distinguishing between highly similar system behaviors—as induced by subtle modifications in the code of a network interface controller's device driver which resides in an un-instrumented kernel module. For the former experiment, we collected a set of signatures from three different tasks in a controlled fashion. The tasks in question were:

- kernel compile (`kcompile`)
- secure copy of files over the network (`scp`)
- dbench disk throughput benchmark (`dbench`)

All three tasks ran on the same system—our Dell PowerEdge R710 server—without interference from each-other. The Fmeter logging daemon collected the signatures every 10 seconds. For every workload type we retrieved roughly 250 distinct signatures, which we subjected to our machine learning methods.

There are many available types of supervised classifiers one can use, e.g. decision trees, Neural Networks, Support Vector Machines (SVMs), Gaussian mixture models, and naïve Bayes, not to mention ensemble techniques that combine one or more classifiers of the same (e.g., bagging and boosting of decision trees) or different type to perform classification. Based on our previous experience, we chose to use the SVM^{light} [23, 24] classifier, which is an implementation of Vapnik's Support Vector Machine [25]. We are considering experimenting with a hand-crafted C4.5 decision tree package that supports high dimension vectors and is capable of performing boosting and bagging.

In a nutshell, SVMs construct a hyperplane that separates the vectors in the training set such that the separation margin is maximized (i.e., the hyperplane is chosen such that it has the largest distance to the nearest training data points of any class). Since the vectors in the training example may not be linearly separable by a hyperplane in the vector-space defined by the features, SVMs rely on kernel-functions (not to be confused with the operating system's in-kernel functions traced by Fmeter) to construct the hyperplane in a higher dimensional space. Classifying is performed in a straightforward manner, simply by determining on which "side" of the hyperplane an example point/vector resides.

A common practice for evaluating the performance of a machine learning algorithm when one does not have a large data set is to use a technique called K-fold cross validation. As we only collected signatures for 30 or 60 minutes every 10 seconds, we did not create a very large data set, therefore we performed K-fold cross validation. We split the positive and negative signatures into K sets of equal sizes (modulo K). We merge the positive signatures of set i with the negative signatures of set i, $\forall i \in \{0, K-1\}$, thus creating K folds. For each fold i, we set it aside and mark it as the *test data*. Fold $((i+1) \bmod K)$ is marked as the *validation data*, and the remaining folds are concatenated together and marked as the *training data*. Then we proceed to repeatedly train the SVM^{light} classifier on the training data while using the validation data to incrementally tune the parameters of the classifier, if any. Once the classifier parameters are chosen based on the performance on the validation data (e.g., choosing the parameters that maximize accuracy), the classifier is evaluated a single time on the test data. (Note that to ensure correctness, the test set should be used only once, to assess the performance of a fully trained classifier.) We report the average metrics obtained by evaluating the classifier on the test data for each of the K folds—without further training the model.

Table 3. Clustering: SVM^{light} averaged accuracy, precision, and recall over all 10-folds

Signature grouping	Baseline Accuracy (%)	Test set (average± std. dev., over all folds)		
		Accuracy (%)	Precision (%)	Recall (%)
dbench(+1), kcompile(−1)	51.797	100.00±0.00	100.00±0.00	100.00±0.00
scp(+1), kcompile(−1)	51.177	99.39±0.99	99.28±1.54	99.56±1.38
scp(+1), dbench(−1)	50.619	100.00±0.00	100.00±0.00	100.00±0.00
dbench(+1), kcompile ∪ scp (−1)	65.589	100.00±0.00	100.00±0.00	100.00±0.00
scp (+1), kcompile ∪ dbench (−1)	66.432	99.57±0.69	99.17±1.76	99.56±1.38
kcompile (+1), scp ∪ dbench (−1)	67.977	99.57±0.69	99.56±1.38	99.09±1.92

Table 4. Myri10ge: SVM^{light} averaged accuracy, precision, and recall over all 8-folds

Signature comparison	Baseline Accuracy (%)	Test set (average± std. dev., over all folds)		
		Accuracy (%)	Precision (%)	Recall (%)
myri10ge 1.4.3 (+1), 1.5.1(−1)	50.765	100.00±0.00	100.00±0.00	100.00±0.00
myri10ge 1.5.1 (+1), 1.5.1 LRO off(−1)	50.25	100.00±0.00	100.00±0.00	100.00±0.00
myri10ge 1.4.3 (+1), 1.5.1 LRO off(−1)	51.015	100.00±0.00	100.00±0.00	100.00±0.00

We did not spend significant time searching the parameter space for either of the experiments. Instead, we simply set the SVM's kernel parameter to the default polynomial function, and we searched the parameter space of the trade-off between training error and margin, also known as the C parameter. Note that the signature vectors were scaled into the unit-ball using the L_2 norm—a common SVM classification practice.

We begin by evaluating the performance of the SVM classifier while distinguishing between the same three distinct workloads. Our classifier expects only two distinct classes labeled +1 and −1 respectively, therefore, since we have a total of three workloads we perform the following experiments. First, we apply the SVM classifier to datasets containing signatures from all possible combinations of two distinct classes, which yields the following groupings: scp (+1) vs. kcompile (−1), scp (+1) vs. dbench (−1), and kcompile (+1) vs. dbench (−1). Next, we apply the SVM classifier to groupings in which we label the signatures from one of the workloads to be of class +1 and the remaining signatures from the other two workloads to be of class −1. We repeat the groupings for every workload, yielding three possible combinations (e.g., the first one being scp of class +1 and kcompile ∪ dbench of class −1).

Table 3 depicts the SVM performance in terms of accuracy, precision, and recall on the test set, averaged over all 10-folds. The SVM has been previously calibrated on the validation set. We also report the accuracy baseline, which is computed by reporting on the accuracy of a pseudo-classifier that always chooses the class with the label of the majority signatures. For example, if a dataset contains 100 data points of class +1 and 150 data points of class −1, then the baseline accuracy would be $\frac{150}{250} = 0.6$ (or 60%). Table 3 shows the SVM classifier to perform remarkably well. In particular, it is able to perfectly distinguish the workloads in three of the signature groupings, and performs almost as good for the remaining groupings. (To get a better intuition of the classifier's performance it is important to compare the reported accuracy with the baseline accuracy.)

Next, we evaluate how well can machine learning tell apart signatures generated by systems that only differ in subtle ways. For this experiment, the core kernel remains the same, and we only alter the myri10ge device driver for the Myri10G NIC. Further, the device driver resides in a runtime loadable module, which Fmeter does not instrument, therefore the possible set of kernel functions that are being counted by Fmeter does not change. Instead, Fmeter records the signatures that contain the driver's behavior by virtue of the core-kernel symbols (i.e., functions) the driver calls *into*.

We chose the following three scenarios for the monitored system: (**i**) running with the myri10ge driver version 1.5.1 and default load-time parameters, (**ii**) running with the myri10ge driver version 1.4.3 and default load-time parameters, and (**iii**) running with the myri10ge driver version 1.5.1 but with the load-time parameter set to disable the large receive offload (LRO) capability. The first scenario provides a baseline for "normal" mode of operation, while the second and third scenarios provide various degrees of diverging modes of operation. For example, the scenario in which the LRO is disabled may correspond to a compromised system that maliciously loaded a runtime module/extension which increases the propensity of the machine to DDOS attacks. Likewise, the scenario in which we use an older version of the driver may be indicative of a buggy or a compromised vital subsystem. As a matter of fact, we disassembled the two driver versions (with `objdump`) and compared the un-relocated binary representation of the functions code. With respect to the older version of the driver, 24 functions were altered in the newer version, one function (`myri10ge_get_frag_header`) was removed, and 11 new functions were added. Of the newly added functions, only one was ever called during our workloads, namely `myri10ge_select_queue`. (Recall that none of these functions, or any other functions defined within the loadable drivers for that matter, belong to the Fmeter vector space.)

We ran Netperf [26] TCP stream tests between the two twin servers with the receiver machine running the Fmeter instrumented kernel and the three myri10ge driver variants. During the Netperf runs, we were able to achieve 10Gbps line rate. By contrast, if the conventional Ftrace kernel function tracer is on, we were able to only achieve a throughput of little more than half the line rate, which indicates that the overall overhead introduced by Fmeter was acceptable. Table 4 shows the results of the SVM classifier on all folds of the test set (we used eight-fold cross validation), after the C parameter was calibrated on the validation set. Our classifier achieves perfect accuracy, prediction, and recall in all cases. (The case in which we compared the version 1.4.3 of the driver against version 1.5.1 with LRO disabled was supposed to be a baseline indicator that is easier to classify than the other two.)

Signature Clustering. Next we subject the Fmeter signatures to an unsupervised learning method such as clustering. We use the same three workloads we already evaluated our supervised machine learning against in Section 4.2, namely `scp`, `kcompile` and `dbench`. This choice of workload also allows us to directly compare how the unsupervised clustering stacks against the supervised machine learning.

We implemented two standard well-known clustering algorithms, namely agglomerative hierarchical clustering, and K-means respectively. Both clustering algorithms use the Euclidean distance (as induced by the L_2 norm), while the agglomerative hierarchical clustering is of the complete-, single-, and average-linkage flavors. We only report on the single-linkage variant throughout the paper since the results for complete- and average-linkage are similar.

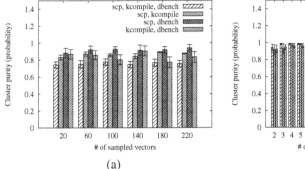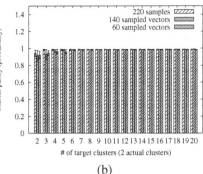

(a)   (b)

Fig. 2. (a) K-means cluster purity (probability) given the number of (equally) sampled vectors from each class; (b) K-means cluster purity for scp and dbench signatures with respect to different number of target clusters (the K parameter).

Although the hierarchical clustering algorithm is more precise than the K-means algorithm, it is computationally more expensive, and it requires a notoriously hard to choose "height-cut" for automatic evaluation given more than two distinct classes. By contrast, the K-means algorithm converges significantly faster, and since the target number of resulting/expected clusters (i.e., the K parameter) is already given as an input parameter, it is straightforward to automatically evaluate the quality of the clustering result. We chose to use the K-means algorithm as our primary clustering unsupervised learning mechanism.

There are various metrics for evaluating the quality of clustering, like *purity*, *normalized mutual information*, *Rand index*, or the *F-measure*. We chose to use *purity*, since it is both simple and transparent. In particular, to compute the purity of a clustering, each resulting cluster is assigned to its most frequent class, and the accuracy of the assignment is measured by counting the number of correctly assigned signatures divided by the total number of signatures.

Figure 2(a) shows the cluster purity between all four permutations of the three workloads on the y-axis. We used the K-means algorithm, with the K parameter set for the actual number of clusters, i.e., $K = 3$ for the clustering of scp, kcompile, and dbench, and $K = 2$ otherwise. On the x-axis, the Figure depicts the number of signatures randomly selected, without replacement, from each workload class (the same number of signatures were selected from the kcompile workload as were selected from the scp, and dbench workloads). The results are averaged over 12 runs, with the error bars denoting standard error of the mean. There are three observations. First, the purity scores are high, denoting good clustering. Second, the clustering performance increases only slightly as the number of signatures increases, hence a small number of signatures are sufficient to properly determine each cluster's *centroid*. And third, the quality of the clusters for $K = 3$ and vectors sampled from each of the workloads available is lower than the quality of clusters yielded by K-means with $K = 2$ and vectors sampled only from two separate workloads, irrespective of which two workloads were sampled. This means that clustering effectiveness appears to decrease as more classes (corresponding to different workloads) are considered.

At this point it is important to note that high purity is easy to achieve by simply increasing the number of expected clusters; in the case of K-means by increasing the value of the parameter K. In particular, if there are as many clusters as there are vectors (signatures), then the purity evaluates to 1.0. We proceed to leverage this property to show the quality of the clustering results. Figure 2(b) shows the purity of clustering signatures from the scp and dbench workloads, by increasing the number of target / expected clusters (we simply varied the parameter K of the K-means algorithm). As the Figure shows, the purity scores converge rapidly to the maximum value of 1.0 while the standard error of the mean decreases at the same time. The intuition is that there are very few (1, 2, or 3) additional clusters that capture the clustering "mistakes" made by the ideal clustering (where K is set to the actual number of classes, $K = 2$ in this case). The additional separate clusters group together these incorrectly classified signatures.

Compared to supervised machine learning, clustering on the same sets of signatures performs worse. Nevertheless, clustering is still a useful statistical analysis method, since it can naturally group signatures belonging to many classes. Furthermore, we can apply meta-clustering on the retrieved cluster centroids to determine which classes of behaviors, and hence not just individual signatures which are instances of behaviors, are closer to one another. Determining which system behaviors are similar in the way they use the operating system kernel functions can then be leveraged for low-level optimizations (e.g., improve cache locality).

5   Limitations

Fmeter uses the Ftrace infrastructure, as such, it only traces kernel function calls. We recognize that the kernel makes extensive use of function inlining and pre-processor macros (e.g., common list, hash-table, and even page table traversals) which we are unable to capture with our current methodology. Likewise, processes that require very little kernel intervention, like scientific applications, are likely to be all assigned similar signatures that are very close to the null/zero vector, which makes them harder to distinguish from one another, irrespective of the learning machinery.

Moreover, we recognize that the process of performing a measurement introduces uncertainty itself by interfering with the collected data. For example, the user-space daemon that logs signatures to disk interferes with the monitored system by virtue of using the kernel's pseudo file system and the kernel's proper file and storage subsystem (buffer cache, VFS, ext3, block layer, and so on). However, all retrieved signatures are perturbed uniformly by the logging.

6   Future Work

Currently, the overhead introduced by Fmeter is much higher than the overhead of statistical profiling tools like oprofile. Nevertheless, the Fmeter overhead is also significantly lower than that of the precise profiling tools like the ones relying on the conventional Ftrace kernel function tracer. Since the kernel function invocations follow a power-law distribution (see Figure 1), a straightforward optimization to the Fmeter counting infrastructure would be to maintain a fast cache that holds the call counts for the top N hottest functions. Using a sufficiently small cache to account for the most popular kernel functions could lower the overheads, e.g., by decreasing the cache pollution incurred while following the Fmeter stubs. The value of N can be experimentally chosen based on the size of the processor caches.

We also plan to explore using Fmeter signatures to perform meta-clustering on already retrieved cluster centroids. Being able to apply clustering methods in such a recursive fashion would allow us to determine which entire classes, not just instances of behavior, are similar in the way they invoke the kernel functionality. We can thus leverage this information to better schedule concurrently executing tasks that rely on the same kernel code-paths (and implicitly the same in-kernel data-structures) on processor cores that share a cache domain (e.g., the L3 cache for an Intel Nehalem microarchitecture). Such assignments have the potential to boost the overall performance of monolithic kernels due to improved cache locality while executing in kernel-mode.

7 Related Work

System Monitoring Based on Indexable Signatures. There have been several prior approaches that monitored system calls [11, 27, 28] to build some model which can be used to detect deviations from normal behavior. Furthermore, recent work [4, 29] has shown how indexable signatures can be used to capture essential system characteristics in a form that facilitates automated clustering and similarity based retrieval. Formal methods, like K-means clustering and the L_2 norm are then used to compare similarities among system states. Our work uses the statistical vector space model [12] to represent the system execution in a given time frame. Fmeter demonstrates how indexable signatures in low-level system monitoring (based on *all* kernel function calls, as opposed to just the system calls) can be generated with low overhead and used in a running high performance system. Like prior work, we too use existing information retrieval techniques to facilitate formal manipulation of Fmeter's signatures.

System Monitoring Using Performance Counters. The most commonly used monitoring tools record system variables for performance tuning and failure diagnostics. Oprofile [7] and DCPI [30] use hardware performance counters, and ProfileMe [31] uses instruction-level counters to periodically collect long-term system usage information. Such powerful post-processing utilities aid in visualizing and identifying potential performance bottlenecks. With such statistics, it is possible, for example, to understand and analyze the behavior of Java applications [32]. Since these tools focus on a small and limited set of predefined performance counters, it becomes impossible to look up arbitrary system behavior of interest in the logs. Fmeter differs from these tools by allowing execution sequences (low-level system signatures) to be indexed and later retrieved.

Chopstix [8] expands the use of individual counters by monitoring a diverse set of system information. These "vital signs" provide a wider picture of system execution at a given point in time. Along the same lines are tools such as CyDAT, Ganglia, CoMoN and Artemis [9, 10, 33, 34] which focus on monitoring distributed systems and cater to the fast growing cloud computing environments. The visualization methods for such tools are important for understanding interactions amongst the nodes in a cluster due to the large volumes of logs and heterogeneity in platforms.

System Monitoring Based on Logging. System logging is used in another area of system monitoring. System operators, developers and automatic trainers can extract error conditions in the logs and use machine learning techniques to predict indicated errors [35–38]. Alternatively, system state signatures can be recorded and searched for automatic diagnosis [39]. There is also a dedicated set of tracers which allows isolating non-deterministic system behavior and heisenbugs [40, 41] and replaying execution from the logs [42] to reproduce error conditions or perform fault correction on the fly [43, 44]. In addition, statistical induction techniques exist for automated performance diagnosis and management at the server application level [45]. Fmeter differs from these tools since it is able to generate indexable low-level signatures in a running system with low overhead (see Section 4.2).

System Monitoring Based on Indexing Logs. Signature based system monitoring has also inspired methodologies which focus on post-processing of logs to generate useful inferences. This class of methods attempts to generate inferences based either on identifying some signatures in the log data or finding anomaly-based aberrations [46, 47]. Our method is a generalization of such analysis which can be used for both signature-based retrieval and anomaly detection. Alternatively, use of fine-grained control flow graphs as signatures has also been proposed as a useful malware detection strategy [48]. Moreover, similarity based measures working at the application level on a diverse set of system attributes have shown to be successful [49]. Latest work shows a novel path of combining source code analysis and runtime feature creation into console log mining for anomaly detection [50, 51]. Our approach explores a similar way of applying machine learning and information retrieval techniques, yet using a different class of low-level signatures (and an efficient, specific signature extraction method).

8 Conclusion

We present Fmeter, a monitoring infrastructure that extracts formal, indexable, low-level system signatures by embedding kernel function calls into the classical vector space model. Fmeter represents system signatures as `tf-idf` weight vectors by disregarding the semantic information in a document and consider only the statistical properties of the terms belonging to the document (and to the corpus). In our case, we disregard the sequence of kernel function calls (the "call stack" trace), the function parameters, memory location accesses, hardware device state manipulation and so on. Instead, we rely on as little information as possible, namely counting the kernel function calls. This approach is sufficient to provide meaningful and effective system signatures, while incurring low system overhead. Further, the signatures are naturally amenable for statistical information retrieval manipulations, like clustering, machine learning, and information retrieval. We demonstrate the efficacy of Fmeter by yielding near-perfect results during clustering and supervised classification of various system behaviors.

Availability

The Fmeter source code is published under BSD license and is freely available at `http://fireless.cs.cornell.edu/fmeter`.

References

1. Hellerstein, J.L.: Engineering autonomic systems. In: ICAC 2009 (2009)
2. Schroeder, B., Pinheiro, E., Weber, W.D.: DRAM errors in the wild: a large-scale field study. In: SIGMETRICS 2009 (2009)
3. Dean, J.: Designs, Lessons and Advice from Building Large Distributed Systems. Keynote Talk: LADIS 2009 (2009)
4. Cohen, I., Zhang, S., Goldszmidt, M., Symons, J., Kelly, T., Fox, A.: Capturing, indexing, clustering, and retrieving system history. In: SOSP 2005 (2005)
5. Mavinakayanahalli, A., Panchamukhi, P., Keniston, J., Keshavamurthy, A., Hiramatsu, M.: Probing the guts of kprobes. In: Linux Symposium 2006 (2006)
6. Ftrace - Function Tracer, http://lwn.net/Articles/322666/
7. Oprofile, http://oprofile.sourceforge.net
8. Bhatia, S., Kumar, A., Fiuczynski, M.E., Peterson, L.: Lightweight, high-resolution monitoring for troubleshooting production systems. In: OSDI 2008 (2008)
9. Cretu-Ciocarlie, G.F., Budiu, M., Goldszmidt, M.: Hunting for problems with artemis. In: Proceedings of WASL (2008)
10. Massie, M.L., Chun, B.N., Culler, D.E.: The Ganglia Distributed Monitoring System: Design, Implementation, and Experience. In: Proceedings of Parallel Computing (2004)
11. Sekar, R., Bendre, M., Dhurjati, D., Bollineni, P.: A fast automaton-based method for detecting anomalous program behaviors. In: Proceedings of the 2001 IEEE Symposium on Security and Privacy (SP), pp. 144–155 (2001)
12. Salton, G., Wong, A., Yang, C.S.: A vector space model for automatic indexing. Communications of the ACM 18(11), 613–620 (1975)
13. Booth, A.D.: A "law" of occurrences for words of low frequency. Information and Control 10(4), 386–393 (1967)
14. Grishchenko: http://wikipedia.org/wiki/File:Wikipedia-n-zipf.png
15. Boyd-Wickizer, S., Morris, R., Kaashoek, M.F.: Reinventing scheduling for multicore systems. In: HotOS 2009 (2009)
16. Debugfs, http://lwn.net/Articles/115405/
17. Srivastava, A., Eustace, A.: ATOM - A System for Building Customized Program Analysis Tools. In: PLDI 1994 (1994)
18. Edge, J.: A lockless ring-buffer, http://lwn.net/Articles/340400/
19. Edge, J.: One ring buffer to rule them all? http://lwn.net/Articles/388978/
20. Brandenburg, B.B., Anderson, J.H.: Feather-trace: A light-weight event tracing toolkit. In: OSPERT 2007 (2007)
21. Krieger, O., Auslander, M., Rosenburg, B., Wisniewski, R.W., Xenidis, J., Da Silva, D., Ostrowski, M., Appavoo, J., Butrico, M., Mergen, M., Waterland, A., Uhlig, V.: K42: building a complete operating system. In: EuroSys (2006)
22. Staelin, C.: lmbench: Portable Tools for Performance Analysis. In: USENIX ATC 1996 (1996)
23. Joachims, T.: Svm^{light}, http://svmlight.joachims.org/
24. Joachims, T.: Learning to Classify Text Using Support Vector Machines. Dissertation. Springer (2002)
25. Vapnik, V.N.: The Nature of Statistical Learning Theory. Springer (1995)
26. Netperf, http://netperf.org/
27. Forrest, S., Hofmeyr, S.A., Somayaji, A., Longstaff, T.A.: A sense of self for unix processes. In: IEEE Symposium on Security and Privacy (1996)
28. Li, P., Gao, D., Reiter, M.K.: Automatically Adapting a Trained Anomaly Detector to Software Patches. In: Balzarotti, D. (ed.) RAID 2009. LNCS, vol. 5758, pp. 142–160. Springer, Heidelberg (2009)

29. Bodik, P., Goldszmidt, M., Fox, A., Woodard, D.B., Andersen, H.: Fingerprinting the data-center: automated classification of performance crises. In: EuroSys 2010 (2010)
30. Anderson, J.M., Berc, L.M., Dean, J., Ghemawat, S., Henzinger, M.R., Leung, S.T.A., Sites, R.L., Vandevoorde, M.T., Waldspurger, C.A., Weihl, W.E.: Continuous profiling: where have all the cycles gone? In: SOSP 1997 (1997)
31. Dean, J., Hicks, J.E., Waldspurger, C.A., Weihl, W.E., Chrysos, G.: Profileme: hardware support for instruction-level profiling on out-of-order processors. In: MICRO 1997 (1997)
32. Sweeney, P.F., Hauswirth, M., Cahoon, B., Cheng, P., Diwan, A., Grove, D., Hind, M.: Using hardware performance monitors to understand the behavior of java applications. In: Proceedings of the 3rd Virtual Machine Research and Technology Symposium, VM (2004)
33. DiFatta, C., Klein, D.V., Poepping, M.: Carnegie mellon's cydat: Harnessing a wide array of telemetry data to enhance distributed system diagnostics. In: Proceedings of WASL (2008)
34. Park, K., Pai, V.S.: Comon: a mostly-scalable monitoring system for planetlab. SIGOPS Oper. Syst. Rev. 40(1), 65–74 (2006)
35. Salfner, F., Tschirpke, S.: Error log processing for accurate failure prediction. In: WASL 2008 (2008)
36. Sandeep, S.R., Swapna, M., Niranjan, T., Susarla, S., Nandi, S.: Cluebox: A performance log analyzer for automated troubleshooting. In: WASL 2008 (2008)
37. Fulp, E.W., Fink, G.A., Haack, J.N.: Predicting computer system failures using support vector machines. In: Proceedings of WASL (2008)
38. Hauswirth, M., Sweeney, P.F., Diwan, A., Hind, M.: Vertical profiling: understanding the behavior of object-priented applications. In: OOPSLA 2004 (2004)
39. Redstone, J., Swift, M.M., Bershad, B.N.: Using computers to diagnose computer problems. In: Proceedings of HotOS, pp. 91–86 (2003)
40. Musuvathi, M., Qadeer, S., Ball, T., Basler, G., Nainar, P.A., Neamtiu, I.: Finding and reproducing heisenbugs in concurrent programs. In: OSDI 2008 (2008)
41. Ronsse, M., Christiaens, M., Bosschere, K.D.: Cyclic debugging using execution replay. In: Proceedings of the International Conference on Computational Science-Part II 2001 (2001)
42. Guo, Z., Wang, X., Tang, J., Liu, X., Xu, Z., Wu, M., Kaashoek, M.F., Zhang, Z.: R2: An application-level kernel for record and replay. In: OSDI 2008 (2008)
43. Tucek, J., Lu, S., Huang, C., Xanthos, S., Zhou, Y.: Triage: diagnosing production run failures at the user's site. In: SOSP 2007 (2007)
44. Qin, F., Tucek, J., Zhou, Y., Sundaresan, J.: Rx: Treating bugs as allergies - a safe method to survive software failures. ACM Trans. Comput. Syst. 25, 7 (2007)
45. Cohen, I., Goldszmidt, M., Kelly, T., Symons, J., Chase, J.S.: Correlating instrumentation data to system states: a building block for automated diagnosis and control. In: OSDI 2004 (2004)
46. Sequeira, K., Zaki, M.: Admit: anomaly-based data mining for intrusions. In: KDD 2002 (2002)
47. Ghosh, A.K., Schwartzbard, A.: A study in using neural networks for anomaly and misuse detection. In: Proceedings of the 8th conference on USENIX Security Symposium 1999 (1999)
48. Bonfante, G., Kaczmarek, M., Marion, J.Y.: Control flow graphs as malware signatures. In: Proceedings of the International Workshop on the Theory of Computer Viruses (2007)
49. Lane, T., Brodley, C.E.: Temporal sequence learning and data reduction for anomaly detection. ACM Trans. Inf. Syst. Secur. 2(3), 295–331 (1999)
50. Xu, W., Huang, L., Fox, A., Patterson, D., Jordan, M.I.: Detecting large-scale system problems by mining console logs. In: SOSP 2009 (2009)
51. Lou, J.G., Fu, Q., Yang, S., Xu, Y., Li, J.: Mining invariants from console logs for system problem detection. In: USENIX ATC 2010 (2010)

SPADE: Support for Provenance Auditing in Distributed Environments

Ashish Gehani and Dawood Tariq

SRI International

Abstract. SPADE is an open source software infrastructure for data provenance collection and management. The underlying data model used throughout the system is graph-based, consisting of vertices and directed edges that are modeled after the node and relationship types described in the Open Provenance Model. The system has been designed to decouple the collection, storage, and querying of provenance metadata. At its core is a novel provenance kernel that mediates between the producers and consumers of provenance information, and handles the persistent storage of records. It operates as a service, peering with remote instances to enable distributed provenance queries. The provenance kernel on each host handles the buffering, filtering, and multiplexing of incoming metadata from multiple sources, including the operating system, applications, and manual curation. Provenance elements can be located locally with queries that use wildcard, fuzzy, proximity, range, and Boolean operators. Ancestor and descendant queries are transparently propagated across hosts until a terminating expression is satisfied, while distributed path queries are accelerated with provenance sketches.

1 Introduction

The origin of SPADE [59] can be traced to a discussion in 2006 with a member of the BaBar [5] project at SLAC [58]. BaBar consists of more than 500 physicists and engineers, maintains petabytes of information in databases, and processes large volumes of data using computational Grids that consist of computer clusters in multiple administrative domains. One conclusion from the discussion was that despite the long history of research in distributed computing, the issue of how to ascertain the security of data in Grid environments (with hundreds of users from scores of independent organizations) was still open to debate.

Extant filesystems reported minimal information about the history of stored data, leaving the task of maintaining such records to individual applications. While knowledge of lineage would allow the trustworthiness of data to be ascertained, support to answer such queries was limited (typically to determining the time and user involved in the original creation and last modification of a file). The gap provided the impetus to create SPADE in 2008 as a distributed service for collecting, certifying, and querying the provenance of Grid data [56].

The first version (SPADEv1) tackled a combination of fundamental challenges, including provenance growth and verification latency, as well as practical concerns, such as the need to support legacy environments. SPADEv1 used selective provenance replication to increase distributed availability while limiting the storage overhead [15].

P. Narasimhan and P. Triantafillou (Eds.): Middleware 2012, LNCS 7662, pp. 101–120, 2012.

It aggregated, reordered, and query-specifically pruned provenance elements to improve latency and reliability when verifying responses [18], and embedded provenance *witnesses* (precursors of *sketches* [17,39]) as hints to reduce extraneous remote connections in distributed provenance queries [18].

To collect provenance without modifying applications or the operating system, events from a user space filesystem [50] were fused with process-related information from /proc (on Linux). Unmodified applications could ensure that a file's provenance was transparently transferred across network connections. This was accomplished by appending the provenance to the content if the filename was suitably augmented when the file was opened for reading, and analogously extracting and recording the appended provenance at the other end if the file was saved with an augmented filename [16].

In late 2009, the NIGHTINGALE project [45] began experimental use of SPADEv1. NIGHTINGALE involved experts from 15 universities and corporations concurrently developing parts of a speech technology toolchain that processed terabytes of data on hundreds of computers. We expected that the provenance of intermediate outputs would be used to optimize the subsequent steps in workflows. In practice, application-generated metadata was maintained for this. Instead, SPADEv1 was used to locate bottlenecks in distributed workflows by adding support to capture input and output attributes and recording them in the provenance. It was also actively used to identify code and data dependencies when releasing new versions of the toolchain.

Given the number of institutions involved, we anticipated that provenance certification would be widely employed, but it was not. We learned that SPADEv1's design meant certification was finer-grained than warranted in many situations. Similarly, the architecture imposed a high overhead for incorporating additional provenance attributes, experimenting with novel storage and indexing models, and handling provenance from diverse sources. This motivated a redesign in 2010.

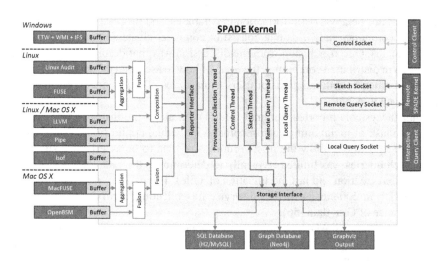

Fig. 1. SPADEv2 has a cross-platform kernel that decouples the collection, storage, and querying of provenance metadata derived from applications, operating systems, and network activity

SPADEv2 is the second generation of our data provenance collection, management, and analysis software infrastructure. The underlying data model used throughout the system is graph-based, consisting of vertices and directed edges, each of which can be labeled with an arbitrary number of annotations (in the form of key-value pairs). These annotations can be used to embed the domain-specific semantics of the provenance.

The system has been completely re-architected to decouple the production, storage, and utilization of provenance metadata, as illustrated in Figure 1. At its core is a novel *provenance kernel* that mediates between the producers and consumers of provenance information, and handles the persistent storage of records. The kernel handles buffering, filtering, and multiplexing incoming metadata from multiple provenance sources. It can be configured to commit the elements to multiple databases, and responds to concurrent queries from local and remote clients. The kernel also supports modules that operate on the stream of provenance graph elements, allowing the aggregation, fusion, and composition of provenance elements to be customized by a series of filters.

SPADEv2 supports the Open Provenance Model [42,47] and includes controlling *Agent*, executing *Process*, and data *Artifact* node types, as well as dependency types that relate which process *wasControlledBy* which agent, which artifact *wasGeneratedBy* which process, which process *used* which artifact, which process *wasTriggeredBy* which other process, and which artifact *wasDerivedFrom* which other artifact. Table 1 illustrates how each of these nodes and dependencies represented.

Table 1. SPADE can emit provenance graphs in Graphviz [21] syntax with Open Provenance Model (OPM) semantics. The encoding of the provenance elements is summarized here. Provenance domain semantics are added to the vertices and edges as annotations.

OPM Node	Node Encoding	Graph Representation
Agent vertex	Red octagon	Agent
Process vertex	Blue rectangle	Process
Artifact vertex	Yellow ellipse	File

OPM Dependency	Dependency Encoding	Graph Representation
WasControlledBy edge	Purple arrow (from *Process* to *Agent*)	Process → Agent
WasGeneratedBy edge	Red arrow (from *Artifact* to *Process*)	Artifact → Process
Used edge	Green arrow (from *Process* to *Artifact*)	Process → Artifact
WasTriggeredBy edge	Blue arrow (from *Process* to *Process*)	Process → Process
WasDerivedFrom edge	Yellow arrow (from *Artifact* to *Artifact*)	Artifact → Artifact

2   Provenance Kernel

The kernel is designed to be extensible in four ways. A *reporter* can be added to collect provenance activity about a new domain of interest. A *filter* can be inserted to perform a new transformation on provenance events in the kernel. A *storage* system can be introduced to record provenance in a new format. A *sketch* can be used to optimize the distributed querying. The kernel is written in Java and uses a combination of the runtime's dynamic classloading and abstract classes to facilitate the concurrent addition and removal of reporters, filters, sketches, and storage through the *control client*. A different abstract class defines the framework for each type of extension and how it interfaces with the kernel.

The control client maintains a history of commands, and allows a combination of extensions to be saved to or loaded from a configuration file. When the control client shuts the kernel down, callbacks are invoked in all extensions to shut them down gracefully (flushing buffered data as necessary) and the kernel's configuration is saved so it can be automatically loaded the next time it runs.

When SPADEv2 is activated on a computer, the provenance kernel is launched as a daemon that runs in the background. Its functionality can be invoked on demand with low latency and imposes low overhead when not in active use. Initially, the kernel is blind to provenance reporting, deaf to control and query clients, and mute about events it has learned of. It uses saved configuration information, if available, to spawn threads for each of the tasks described in Table 2.

Table 2. The SPADE kernel is multi-threaded to allow provenance reporting, local and remote querying, and reconfiguration of the kernel to operate concurrently

Thread	Service Provided
Provenance Collection	Reporters queue events programmatically in buffers that must then be emptied by a thread in the kernel. The thread extracts the events, filters them, and commits them to local storage.
Remote Queries	Each kernel is implicitly part of a peer-to-peer provenance overlay, with a thread handling provenance queries from remote kernels.
Sketches	A kernel on another computer may need a provenance sketch to optimize its distributed queries. Such requests are processed through a separate port and thread.
Local Queries	Interactive use with query clients requires extra information, including user prompts and error reporting, to be multiplexed with the responses to queries, and is therefore handled by a thread that is distinct from the one for remote queries.
Kernel Control	Since the kernel operates as a background system service, it uses a thread to listen for connections on a control port that then processes commands received from the control client.

When a provenance event occurs, SPADEv1 blocked until the activity had been completely recorded. This had the advantage that the provenance records were always synchronized with the state of the system (from which provenance events were derived). However, it had the disadvantage that application performance was adversely impacted by the latency introduced during input and output operations. The design choice had been made to support workflows that used the provenance of intermediate data to decide subsequent steps. In practice, the tight coupling was seldom necessary.

The SPADEv2 kernel provides a non-blocking interface for reporting provenance events. While this ensures that the monitoring overhead for provenance collection is minimal, it introduces a new concern. In scenarios where the rate at which provenance is being reported varies significantly, there are periods when the kernel cannot process events at the rate that they are arriving. In this situation, some events are lost. To mitigate this, SPADEv2 creates separate *buffers* for each provenance reporter to enqueue events into. A thread in the kernel then dequeues events when the load permits, processes the events through any configured filters, and sends the results to persistent storage.

3   Generating Metadata

Although users do maintain provenance records manually (in the form of scientific laboratory notebooks, for example), automating the generation and collection of provenance metadata substantially reduces their burden, improves reproducibility, aids in debugging, and increases the utility of their data to other researchers. To facilitate this, SPADEv2 includes a number of reporters that transparently transform computational activity into provenance events that are sent to the kernel.

```
putVertex(Agent a);
putVertex(Process p);
putVertex(Artifact a);

putEdge(Used u);
putEdge(WasControlledBy wcb);
putEdge(WasDerivedFrom wdf);
putEdge(WasGeneratedBy wgb);
putEdge(WasTriggeredBy wtb);
```

Fig. 2. A *reporter* emits a provenance element by calling the appropriate function, which queues it in a buffer. The kernel multiplexes elements from the buffers of all reporters.

Each reporter utilizes the same interface to the kernel, abstracted in Figure 2. This holds regardless of whether the provenance elements are manually curated, application emitted, logged by a workflow engine, or from the operating system's audit trail. The domain semantics are captured as annotations on the vertices and edges.

3.1   Operating System Provenance

The advantages of collecting data provenance at the operating system level are that it provides a broad view of activity across the computer and that it does not require applications to be modified. The approach has a number of limitations, including the fact that this may provide too much extraneous information and not enough detail about particular applications that are of interest. A significant consideration for software maintainability is how the system activity is obtained. Implementing a kernel module or modifying system libraries requires a substantial investment in adapting the collection mechanism to each currently available and future version of the operating system.

An alternative approach relies on utilizing the auditing mechanisms of each operating system, which typically have stable programming interfaces across operating system versions. The disadvantage of the technique is that it is limited to the information exposed in the audit trail, which does not include records of interprocess communication through shared memory, graphical user interface events, or keyboard input. Nevertheless, the provenance collected suffices for characterizing the batch computing workloads that are the staple of scientific computing workflows. In particular, this includes the process's name, owner, group, parent, host, creation time, command line, environment variables, and a file's name, path, host, size, and modification time. The types of provenance collected at the operating system level are summarized in Table 3.

Linux (System-wide): An audit trail is needed for the Common Criteria certification of systems used by U.S. Government agencies. Linux vendors interested in sales to this market contributed kernel changes to monitor activity across the entire host and generate corresponding audit events. These are accessible through a Unix socket (*/var/run/audispd_events*) after activating a system service (*audispd*) with an appropriate plug-in. SPADEv2's Linux reporter configures the audit system to generate records for *exec()*, *fork()*, *clone()*, *exit()*, *open()*, *close()*, *read()*, *write()*, *clone()*, *truncate()*, and *rename()* system calls.

Since Java does not support reading from Unix sockets, a utility written in C serves as a bridge. The audit records are then parsed in the Java component of the reporter. Reporting *read()* and *write()* events poses two challenges. First, the Linux audit records contain only a file descriptor, so a mapping between descriptors and filenames has to be built using information from *open()* calls. Second, reporting *read()* and *write()* events would provide enough provenance metadata that system responsiveness would noticeably degrade. Consequently, these two calls are not reported. Instead, the flags of *open()* calls are used to infer whether a process is reading or writing a file. If detailed input and output records are needed, the alternative Linux reporter that focuses on selected filesystem activity can be utilized.

Process-related information is obtained from two sources. When a system call occurs, the kernel generates an audit record. The reporter extracts the process identifier from this record. This identifier is then used to obtain further details about the process from the Linux /proc filesystem, if available. Since the audit record is created in the kernel but used in user space, it may be reporting the action of a process that has already terminated, with no corresponding information available under /proc. In this case, other elements of the audit record (such as the name, owner, and group of the process) are used. On the surface, the approach employed appears to introduce a *time-of-check-to-time-of-use* race condition. However, this is not the case since process identifiers are allocated serially. A problem would manifest only if the process identifier value wrapped through the entire possible range within the time window between the check and use.

We found that network-related system calls (such as *connect()* and *accept()*) report only the remote IP address and port information. The source IP address and port are not recorded, preventing connections from being completely disambiguated. This weakness is partially addressed by the Network reporter.

Linux (Selected activity): The hooks and module needed to support FUSE [14] user space filesystems are present in all Linux kernels, starting with version 2.6.14. In particular, interposition can be limited to file activity in a specific directory, eliminating the monitoring of calls to files outside the subtree. This allows detailed provenance to be recorded with low overhead for workloads that are localized to a single subtree (as is the case with many scientific and engineering applications), including annotations on *used* and *wasGeneratedBy* edges for the time spent in *read()* and *write()* calls.

The reporter includes C code that is linked against the FUSE shared library that handles communication with the kernel. This code is invoked when *read()*, *write()*, *rename()*, *truncate()*, *link()*, *symlink()*, *readlink()*, and *unlink()* filesystem calls occur, and the arguments to each call are passed via the Java Native Interface (JNI) [31] to Java code that transforms the filesystem event into appropriate provenance elements. The identifier of the process that made the filesystem call is used to extract more information about the process from the Linux /proc filesystem. Since the system call is blocked during this step, the process record will always be present and the information extracted will be current and accurate.

If a process does not interact with the filesystem, it will not trigger a FUSE event. In this situation, no information would be collected about the process. To mitigate this limitation, information about all ancestor processes is also extracted and added to the provenance record. In this context, it is worth noting that when a process exits, the Linux kernel changes the parent of all child processes to the parent of the exiting process. This can result in multiple (consistent) accounts of the lineage of a single process.

Android (System-wide): Google's mobile device platform, Android, uses a Linux kernel. We therefore assumed that the audit-based Linux reporter would be usable for collecting data provenance. However, a number of challenges arose, including the absence of audit code in the Linux kernel for ARM processors, and the audit daemon *auditd*'s dependence on *glibc* functions not present in Android's replacement *bionic* library. Using our patch (that is now part of Linux kernel 3.3) and modified audit utilities, SPADEv2 can collect Android provenance. It is worth noting that this is lower-level activity than would be generated by a reporter that instrumented Android's Dalvik virtual machine. Interactions between applications are captured using the transaction log (in /proc) of the Binder inter-process communication mechanism.

Mac OS X (System-wide): The Basic Security Module (BSM) system was designed by Sun Microsystems. It includes a framework for generating, accessing, and parsing audit records in a documented format. Apple had it ported to Mac OS X to obtain Common Criteria certification. The open source version is maintained as OpenBSM [46]. The Mac OS X kernel reports system events in real time. A process with sufficient privilege can access the resulting records by reading the named pipe /dev/auditpipe. Using an *ioctl()* system call, the pipe can be configured to specify which system events are of interest. The system-wide Mac OS X reporter consists of C code that runs with *setuid*, configures the pipe, and then forwards the output to unprivileged Java code where it is parsed and used to generate appropriate provenance events. The set of system calls monitored includes *fork()*, *exit()*, *kill()*, *read()*, *write()*, *create()*, and *rename()*.

Each audit record includes the identifier of the process responsible for the action. Since OpenBSM can be configured to record the command line arguments and environment variables when a process is invoked, in principle the audit records should have sufficient process-related information. However, the OpenBSM subsystem on OS X Snow Leopard does not audit the *spawn( )* system call, which is used by the *Finder* to launch applications. Therefore, even though *fork( )* and *exec( )* calls are audited, a significant amount of process-related provenance is lost (since processes started with *spawn( )* are not observed). To address this limitation, the reporter extracts the process identifier and obtains further information about the process with the *ps* utility. This approach cannot collect information about a short-lived process that may have terminated before *ps* was invoked. It is worth noting that the serial allocation of process identifiers ensures that information about the wrong process is never collected.

Since system-wide activity is monitored, only the first read from and write to a file by a process are recorded to minimize the performance overhead. The alternative Mac OS X reporter (that focuses on selected filesystem activity) can record details about reads and writes, should that level of detail be needed. Further, when network connections occur, the BSM records generated have invalid IP addresses on OS X Snow Leopard and OS X Lion, preventing the construction of provenance artifacts to represent connections. The Network reporter attempts to address this weakness.

Mac OS X (Selected activity): An alternative reporter for Mac OS X that leverages the MacFUSE [37] user space filesystem was developed to limit provenance collection to a subtree in the filesystem. This facilitates managing the overhead associated with recording *read()* and *write()* calls. The reporter contains C code that is called when *read(), write(), rename(), link(), symlink(), readlink()*, and *unlink()* calls occur. Each invocation results in a call through JNI to Java code that converts the filesystem event into a corresponding provenance event.

Information about the process that made a filesystem call is obtained with the *ps* utility. In contrast to the system-wide reporter, where the invocation of *ps* is not synchronized with the system call being audited, here the filesystem call blocks during the invocation of *ps*, ensuring that metadata is collected even for short-lived processes.

As with the Linux FUSE-based reporter, a process that does not interact with the filesystem does not trigger the collection of its provenance. This prevents descendant processes from being linked to ancestor processes, and creates a problem in practice with gaps in provenance chains. To mitigate this issue, when information is collected about a process, records are constructed for all known ancestor processes as well.

Though MacFUSE requires administrator privileges to be installed (since it uses a Mac OS X kernel extension), it is used by numerous other software packages and may already be installed and available on the user's system. This is of particular utility in situations where the user does not have permission to install a *setuid* program (as is needed for the system-wide Mac OS X reporter).

Windows (System-wide): Microsoft's Event Tracing for Windows (ETW) [10] framework allows application developers to use system-level information for debugging and performance analysis. Since ETW provides a documented interface for collecting information about operating system activity, we used it to generate provenance records. However, ETW provides process identifiers only in event descriptions, necessitating the use of Microsoft's Windows Management Instrumentation (WMI) [66] framework to obtain details such as a process's name, binary location, creation time, and command line.

When ETW generates file events, it records the associated filenames internally but does not make them available until the end of the tracing session. This prevents the online generation of provenance artifacts. Microsoft's Windows Driver Kit (WDK) [63] includes the Installable File System (IFS) Kit [28], which can be used to write filters that intercede on filesystem calls. We developed an IFS filter to monitor file creation, reads, and writes.

Consequently, our initial Windows reporter consisted of C++ code that interfaced with the ETW, WMI, and IFS subsystems. The C++ code has been replaced by an invocation of the *Process Monitor* tool [49], which interfaces with the Windows subsystems and emits a log. The Windows reporter now parses the events in the log and transforms them into provenance elements that are sent to the SPADEv2 kernel.

The approach of relying on an external tool to collect system activity resolved three issues. First, it allows the reporter to run on all versions of Windows released after 2000. In contrast, the initial reporter supported only a single version of the operating system since the programming interfaces of ETW and WMI differ across releases of Windows. Second, it eliminates the need for IFS driver signing since Process Monitor has a signed kernel driver. Third, it eliminates a dependency on Microsoft source code that could not be redistributed with SPADEv2 due to an incompatible license.

Table 3. In this summary of operating system provenance reporting, a check mark in a cell indicates that the operation listed in the column is recorded by the reporter listed in the row. The last row depicts the Open Provenance Model semantics of the operation.

	Open File for Reading	Open File for Writing	Read File	Write File	Rename File	Create Link	Transmit Data	Receive Data	Create Process
Linux	✓	✓							✓
Mac	✓	✓			✓				✓
Windows			✓	✓			✓	✓	✓
Selected			✓	✓	✓	✓			
Network							✓	✓	
Provenance Semantics	File ← Process	Process ← File	File ← Process	Process ← File	Process → New File (Old File)	File ← Link	Process ← Connection	Connection ← Process	Parent Process ← Child Process

Network: SPADE aims to support provenance queries about distributed computations. Whereas SPADEv1 was limited to noting the relationship between a source and destination file when a remote copy occurred, SPADEv2 explicitly models a network connection as a pair of *network artifacts* connected by *used* and *wasGeneratedBy* edges.

Network artifacts (depicted by green diamonds in Table 3) are distinguished by the property that each endpoint can independently construct the same artifact without explicit coordination. This allows the complete decentralization of provenance collection in distributed systems while still ensuring that subgraphs from different hosts can be reassembled into a coherent reconstruction of distributed data provenance. SPADEv2 implements network artifacts with this property combining the time the connection was initiated with the IP addresses and TCP or UDP ports of the two endpoints.

None of the Linux or Mac OS X reporters have access to correct source and destination IP address and TCP or UDP port information. Consequently, a separate reporter uses the *lsof* [35] utility in repeat mode to poll the operating system and periodically retrieve a list of recent connections. These are transformed into provenance semantics and then sent to the SPADEv2 kernel. While the reporter is not asynchronously notified of new connections, it is able to report network provenance metadata within a second of the connection's occurrence. The synchronous inspection of network activity means that short-lived connections are unlikely to be reported.

3.2 Application Provenance

An advantage of collecting data provenance from the operating system, as described in Section 3.1, is that applications can be monitored without any provenance-specific modifications. However, instrumentation at this level of abstraction results in an operating system process being modeled as a monolithic entity. Since intra-process data flow (such as memory reads and writes) is not recorded, internal application-level dependencies cannot be differentiated. Further, the provenance semantics of interest in an application may manifest at a higher level of abstraction than operating system interfaces. SPADEv2 includes two types of support for collecting application-level data provenance on both Linux and Mac OS X.

Domain-Specific Language: In late 2010, scientists at SRI were managing large volumes of mass spectroscope data. They were interested in using SPADEv2 to track the computational manipulation of the records. Since the steps were performed in MAT-LAB [40], we needed a mechanism to communicate provenance information from an external application to the SPADEv2 kernel.

One possible approach would have been to create a dynamically linked library with functions for reporting provenance metadata, similar to Harvard's Core Provenance Library [38]. We adopted an alternative approach for a number of reasons. First, the target application's source would have to be available, which is not the case for commercial applications such as MATLAB. Second, determining where to insert the calls to the provenance reporting functions would require extensive study of the target application's codebase. Third, the library would reside in the address space of the target application, leaving the issue of communicating the metadata to the SPADEv2 kernel unresolved.

Instead, we developed a reporter that creates a named pipe, continuously reads from it, parses any information it retrieves, and constructs appropriate provenance elements that are then sent to the SPADEv2 kernel. Provenance metadata can be sent to the reporter by any source that can write to a named pipe, including external applications

and users interested in manually adding provenance records. The provenance metadata
must be stated in a simple OPM-inspired domain-specific language. The corresponding
context-free grammar is shown in Backus-Naur Form in Figure 3.

```
        <provenance> ::= <provenance> <element> | <element>
           <element> ::= <node> | <dependency>
              <node> ::= <node-type> <node-id> <annotation-list>
         <node-type> ::= type: <vertex-type>
       <vertex-type> ::= Agent | Process | Artifact
           <node-id> ::= id: <vertex-id>
         <vertex-id> ::= <unique-identifier>
   <annotation-list> ::= <annotation-list> <annotation> | <annotation>
        <annotation> ::= <key> : <value>
        <dependency> ::= <dependency-type> <start-node> <end-node>
                         <annotation-list>
   <dependency-type> ::= type: <edge-type>
         <edge-type> ::= WasControlledBy | WasGeneratedBy | Used |
                         WasTriggeredBy | WasDerivedFrom
        <start-node> ::= from: <vertex-id>
          <end-node> ::= to: <vertex-id>
```

Fig. 3. The grammar for the domain-specific language that can be used by external applications
to report Open Provenance Model metadata to the SPADEv2 kernel

Compiler-Based Instrumentation: Manually instrumenting an application to emit
provenance metadata requires a substantial effort. This becomes decreasingly tenable as
the scale of the software system increases. To address this, we developed LLVM-based
[34] compiler support to automate the process of instrumenting an application to emit
intra-process provenance information at function call granularity [61].

In many instances, the function call level of abstraction corresponds to what the user
is interested in. However, this may still result in reporting far more information than the
user is interested in since every function call will be reported. To avoid overwhelming
the user with extraneous information, we allow only the functions that are of interest to
be specified. The program sources are statically analyzed to obtain the application's call
graph, which is then traversed in a reverse reachability analysis to identify which functions should be reported. Provenance metadata about all other functions is discarded.

An advantage of recording provenance at the finer application function call level
is that it reduces the process-level *dependency aliasing* that results when collecting
provenance using system calls. For example, the provenance of data transmitted over a
network connection includes all the files read until that point by the server, if provenance
is collected at the operating system level. If individual threads read different files and
sent them to distinct network connections, well-structured code would allow function
call level provenance to distinguish the dependencies.

In practice, users are interested in the values of arguments to function calls. However, providing meaningful information about the arguments requires knowledge of
their types, which is often lost in the process of compiling from the source language

to LLVM's intermediate representation, *bitcode*. Since provenance instrumentation is inserted in the bitcode, only pointers to such values can be reported.

4 Persistent Storage

SPADEv1 used a relational database to store the provenance metadata as it was being collected. This meant that provenance collection could proceed only at the rate that transactions could be committed to the database. Graph queries were constructed as SQL queries, with repeated self-joins to compute the transitive closures necessary to answer path queries. The addition of new attributes resulted in changes to the relational schema. Each of these contributed to performance degrading as the provenance graphs grew in size. For users collecting large volumes of provenance metadata and primarily initiating graph queries, a graph database seemed to be a better option.

Despite the limitations of storing provenance in SQL databases, it remained an attractive option for some users. This is the case if the quantity of provenance is smaller (as is the case when provenance is collected from a source reporting it at a higher level of abstraction or over a shorter span of time), the query workload is well supported by relational operators, or the user has SQL infrastructure and experience that can be leveraged.

SPADEv2 allows arbitrary types of persistent storage to be used as a back end. It does this by defining an abstract storage interface. An adapter for a back end implements the subset of the storage interface that the repository can support. The query interface forwards requests without interpreting them. This allows the SPADEv2 kernel to utilize the native query capabilities of each type of storage.

Neo4j: Neo4j [44] is a high-performance cross-platform graph database with support for transactions. It allows vertices and edges to be typed and annotated, provides a rich set of graph querying functionality, and incorporates Apache Lucene [36] indexing of the graph data. Lucene provides Boolean, wildcard, fuzzy, proximity, range, boosting, and grouping operators for flexible querying. Neo4j is the default database used by SPADEv2.

SQL: To facilitate storing provenance in SQL databases, SPADEv2 includes a JDBC-based [30] storage adapter. By default, the SQL adapter uses the cross-platform embedded relational database, H2 [27]. However, it can also use an alternative JDBC-compliant database, such as MySQL [43], by specifying the driver at activation. The adapter supports recording provenance elements in vertex and edge tables, and SQL queries over these tables, but does not implement graph functionality in the storage interface, such as path queries.

After the SQL storage has been loaded, every provenance node is added as a new row in the table of vertices. When an annotation has a key that has not previously been observed, the table's schema is extended with a new column for the key. The value in an annotation is stored in the cell corresponding to the row of the vertex and the column of the key. Incoming dependencies are similarly added to the table of edges, with the schema continuously evolved to handle new keys in annotations on edges.

Graphviz: Graphviz [21] was created in 1988 by AT&T Research to facilitate graph visualization. Over the years, visualization and analysis tools have adopted the Graphviz DOT language for storing and manipulating graph data. Once the SPADEv2 Graphviz storage is loaded, every provenance element and dependency is output in DOT syntax to a file. This file can then be used with Graphviz tools that employ a variety of graph layout algorithms, as well as a wide range of other graph visualization applications. Querying is not supported by the Graphviz storage.

5 Filtering

Automated provenance collection can result in large volumes of metadata. As more information is generated and stored, both the precision and performance of queries start to degrade. One strategy to address this is to abstract the information and filter out elements if possible. In addition, when provenance is collected from multiple sources, normalizing and reconciling the streams before they are committed to persistent storage can improve subsequent query precision and performance. Therefore, the SPADEv2 kernel supports aggregation, fusion, and composition *filters* that can be used to normalize and reconcile provenance elements [19].

Temporal Aggregation: In environments where numerous low-level events are generated, *aggregation* can mitigate information overload. For example, the provenance elements of a group of readings that are close in value and from a network of sensors can be combined into one provenance element that describes the set of sensors and the value range. An analogous incentive is present for the provenance of data from cyber-physical systems such as SCADA process controllers, but with aggregation occurring over the time variable instead of the spatial one of sensor networks. When the readings do not change, the provenance elements can be aggregated into one that includes the interval of invariance. SPADEv2 includes a filter with the same motif for operating system provenance, where the provenance of a non-interleaved sequence of reads or writes can be replaced with a single provenance element that has an annotation added to describe the start and end points of the sequence.

Multi-source Fusion: When two or more reporters report provenance about the same phenomena, the semantics of the reported events may overlap. If the reporters operate at similar levels of abstraction, *fusion* allows distinct provenance elements (generated by different reporters) to be combined to provide a more complete representation of the same underlying phenomenon. As an example, reporters that capture events across the whole operating system typically report with coarse temporal granularity. A reporter that focuses on selected filesystem activity can track and add annotations about the exact quantity of time spent for each `read()` or `write()` operation for application profiling. SPADEv2 includes a filter to reconcile the two perspectives through fusion keyed on a common key (such as the process identifier), allowing a single view of operating system activity with the input and output times added to the appropriate *used* and *wasGeneratedBy* edges.

Cross-Layer Composition: When reporters operate at different levels of abstraction, *composition* can relate the activity with an *isAbstractedBy* edge. For example, the *Process* vertex for a function call can have an *isAbstractedBy* edge to the operating system

Process vertex of the application in which the call occurred. Such edges can be used to connect provenance from the LLVM-based intra-process level provenance reporter described in Section 3.2 and an operating system-level provenance reporter described in Section 3.1.

6   Evaluation

To evaluate the performance of SPADEv2, we measured the overhead of collecting provenance while building and running the Apache Web server [4] and running the BLAST genome sequence alignment tool. SPADEv2 was run in the background on Mac OS X 10.6.8, Linux Fedora 17, and Windows 7 with system-wide reporters. All experiments were performed on a 2.4 GHz Intel Core i5 machine with 4 GB of memory.

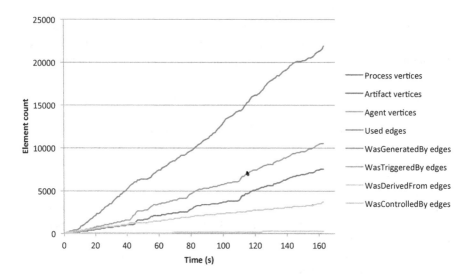

Fig. 4. Number of provenance elements generated over time during the build process of the Apache Web server on Linux is reported

To provide insight into the rate at which provenance elements are generated, Figure 4 shows the count of different types of provenance elements as they are emitted while the Apache Web server is being built. The Linux reporter for selected activity was used to collect the provenance metadata.

Figure 5 reports the time to build the Apache Web server on Windows, Mac OS X, and Linux. This time is reported for an unmodified system as well as one that has been augmented with SPADEv2 to collect provenance with a system-wide reporter. The comparison is intended to provide an understanding of the overhead incurred by collecting provenance during a compute-intensive task. The Windows reporter imposes a 53% overhead during the Apache build, presumably because a wide range of system calls are invoked and audited. On Mac OS X and Linux, the overhead was less than 10% and 5%, respectively.

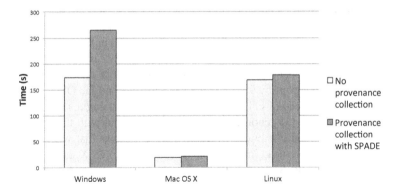

Fig. 5. Time to build the Apache Web server on multiple operating systems is measured here

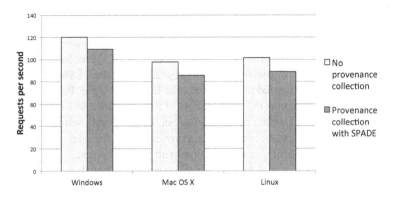

Fig. 6. Number of requests that can be handled by the Apache Web server on Windows, Mac OS X, and Linux is measured to understand the overhead of collecting provenance during normal opertation

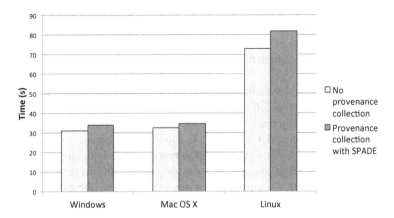

Fig. 7. The time to run the BLAST genome sequence alignment tool on multiple operating systems is measured to understand the overhead of collecting provenance during a heavy workload

To understand the overhead of collecting provenance when a service is running, the Apache Web server was run on Windows, Mac OS X, and Linux. In each case, the rate at which the Web server is able to handle requests is reported in Figure 6. This is done for both an unmodified system as well as one where SPADEv2 is running and collecting provenance with a system-wide reporter. When provenance is being collected, the performance of Apache drops by 9% on Windows and 12% on Mac OS X and Linux.

To estimate the overhead of collecting provenance when using a scientific application, we ran the BLAST [3] genome sequence alignment tool with the *influenza* data set [29] from the National Institutes of Health. Figure 7 shows that when provenance is being collected, the overhead imposed on Windows, Mac OS X, and Linux is 9%, 6%, and 12%, respectively. Since the tool invokes a limited number of system calls, the difference in overheads is likely an artifact of the set of calls being utilized.

7 Related Work

Data provenance has a range of applications. HP SRC's Vesta [24] uses it to make software builds incremental and repeatable. Lineage File System [55] records the input files, command line options, and output files when a program is executed. Its records are stored in a database that can be queried to reconstruct the lineage of a file. Provenance-Aware Storage System [51] augments this with details of the software and hardware environment. The provenance of Datalog programs has been tracked with semi-rings [22].

Several Grid environments account for data provenance in their design. $^{my}Grid$ [67] with Taverna [2] allows biologists to add application-level annotations of the data's provenance. This is then stored in the user's repository, although it does not enable other users of the data to determine its provenance. The Provenance Aware Service Oriented Architecture (PASOA) project [41] arranges for data transformations to be reported to a central provenance service [60], which can be queried by other users as well. The more recent ES3 model [13] extracts provenance information automatically from arbitrary applications by monitoring their interactions with their execution environment and logs them to a customized database. While ES3 logs events at a more abstract level than PASS, it follows the same centralized model of metadata logging. The approach ensures that the provenance does not have to be replicated. However, in the event that the metadata is heavily accessed, the latency of performing remote lookups can degrade application performance.

A number of distributed systems have been built to help scientists track their data. Chimera [11] allows a user to define a workflow, consisting of data sets and transformation scripts. The system then tracks invocations, annotating the output with information about the runtime environment. CMCS [48] is a toolkit for chemists to manage experimental data derived from fields like combustion research. It is built atop WebDAV [64], a Web server extension that allows clients to modify data on the server. ESSW [12] is a data storage system for earth scientists. If a script writer uses its libraries and templates, the system will track lineage so that errors can be tracked back to maintain the quality of data sets. A number of systems track the provenance of database elements, including Trio [65], DBNotes [6], and Perm [20]. Trio also allows the source of uncertainty to be traced. VisTrails [57] tracks the provenance of visualization workflows. Bose and

Frew's survey [7] identifies a number of other projects that aid in retrieving the lineage of scientific data.

PASS describes global naming, indexing, and querying in the context of sensor data [53]. PA-NFS [52] enhances NFS to record provenance in local area networks. Harvard's PQL [26] describes a new language for querying provenance and leverages the query optimization principles of semi-structured databases. However, it does not consider distributed naming explicitly. SPADEv2 addresses the issue by using storage identifiers for provenance vertices that are unique to a host and requiring distributed provenance queries to disambiguate vertices by referring to them by the host on which the vertex was generated as well as the identifier local to that host.

ExSPAN [68] allows the exploration of provenance in networked systems and extends traditional relational models for storing and querying provenance metadata, while SPADEv2 supports both graph and relational database storage and querying. PASS has explored the use of clouds [53,54]. Provbase [1] uses Hbase, an open-source implementation of Google's BigTable [9], to store and query scientific workflow provenance. IBM researchers have proposed a provenance index that improves the execution of forward and backward provenance queries [32]. A number of efforts, including SPADEv2, have recently considered how to compress provenance [68,39]. Query optimization techniques on compressed provenance data has also been examined [25].

The Open Provenance Model (OPM) [42,47] facilitates interoperability between systems by providing a common model for describing provenance. Several projects provide OPM-compliant provenance, including SPADEv2 [59], PASS [52], VisTrails [8], and Tupelo [62]. An OPM profile [23] provides conventions for modeling distributed aspects of provenance, such as transactions. However, query interoperability and global naming are not addressed.

8 Conclusion

SPADEv2 provides a cross-platform distributed data provenance collection, filtration, storage, and querying service. It defines reporters that can be inserted between an application and the operating system, between functions of an application, or at arbitrary user-defined interfaces. Once inserted, the infrastructure operates as middleware, monitoring the targeted applications and enabling provenance analysis for a variety of purposes, including facilitating experiment reproducibility, distributed debugging, and determining dependencies when sharing data and code. We empirically compared and reported the cost of running applications with and without the middleware.

Acknowledgments. We thank Maisem Ali, Basim Baig, Nathaniel Husted, Minyoung Kim, Florent Kirchner, Hasnain Lakhani, Tanu Malik, Ian Mason, Ligia Nistor, Sharjeel Qureshi, Aditya Rajgarhia, Hassen Saïdi, Fareed Zaffar, and Jian Zhang for their contributions.

This material is based upon work supported by the National Science Foundation under Grants OCI-0722068 and IIS-1116414. Any opinions, findings, and conclusions or recommendations expressed in this material are those of the authors and do not necessarily reflect the views of the National Science Foundation.

References

1. Abraham, J., Brazier, P., Chebotko, A., Navarro, J., Piazza, A.: Distributed storage and querying techniques for a semantic Web of scientific workflow provenance. In: IEEE International Conference on Services Computing (2010)
2. Nedim Alpdemir, M., Mukherjee, A., Paton, N.W., Fernandes, A.A.A., Watson, P., Glover, K., Greenhalgh, C., Oinn, T., Tipney, H.: Contextualised Workflow Execution in MyGrid. In: Sloot, P.M.A., Hoekstra, A.G., Priol, T., Reinefeld, A., Bubak, M. (eds.) EGC 2005. LNCS, vol. 3470, pp. 444–453. Springer, Heidelberg (2005)
3. Altschul, S.F., Madden, T.L., Schaffer, A.A., Zhang, J., Zhang, Z., Miller, W., Lipman, D.J.: Gapped BLAST and PSI-BLAST: A new generation of protein database search programs. Nucleic Acids Research 25 (1997)
4. Apache Web Server (Version 2.2.22), `http://httpd.apache.org/`
5. BaBar, `http://www-public.slac.stanford.edu/babar/`
6. Bhagwat, D., Chiticariu, L., Tan, W.-C., Vijayvargiya, G.: An annotation management system for relational databases. In: 30th ACM International Conference on Very Large Data Bases (2004)
7. Bose, R., Frew, J.: Lineage retrieval for scientific data processing: A survey. ACM Computing Surveys 37(1) (2005)
8. Callahan, S., Freire, J., Santos, E., Scheidegger, C., Silva, C., Vo, H.: VisTrails: Visualization meets data management. In: ACM SIGMOD International Conference on Management of Data (2006)
9. Chang, F., Dean, J., Ghemawat, S., Hsieh, W., Wallach, D., Burrows, M., Chandra, T., Fikes, A., Gruber, R.: BigTable: A distributed storage system for structured data. 7th USENIX Symposium on Operating Systems Design and Implementation (2006)
10. Event Tracing for Windows, `http://msdn.microsoft.com/en-us/library/bb968803.aspx`
11. Foster, I.T., Vckler, J.-S., Wilde, M., Zhao, Y.: A virtual data system for representing, querying, and automating data derivation. In: Scientific and Statistical Database Management Conference (2002)
12. Frew, J., Bose, R.: Earth System Science Workbench: A data management infrastructure for earth science products. In: Scientific and Statistical Database Management Conference (2001)
13. Frew, J., Metzger, D., Slaughter, P.: Automatic capture and reconstruction of computational provenance. Concurrency and Computation 20(5) (2008)
14. Filesystem in Userspace, `http://fuse.sourceforge.net`
15. Gehani, A., Lindqvist, U.: Bonsai: Balanced lineage authentication. In: 23rd Annual Computer Security Applications Conference. IEEE Computer Society (2007)
16. Gehani, A., Kim, M., Zhang, J.: Steps toward managing lineage metadata in Grid clusters. In: 1st Workshop on the Theory and Practice of Provenance (2009)
17. Gehani, A., Kim, M., Malik, T.: Efficient querying of distributed provenance stores. In: 8th ACM Workshop on the Challenges of Large Applications in Distributed Environments (2010)
18. Gehani, A., Kim, M.: Mendel: Efficiently verifying the lineage of data modified in multiple trust domains. In: 19th ACM International Symposium on High Performance Distributed Computing (2010)
19. Gehani, A., Tariq, D., Baig, B., Malik, T.: Policy-based integration of provenance metadata. In: 12th IEEE International Symposium on Policies for Distributed Systems and Networks (2011)

20. Glavic, B., Alonso, G.: Perm: Processing provenance and data on the same data model through query rewriting. In: 25th International Conference on Data Engineering (2009)
21. Graphviz, http://www.graphviz.org/
22. Green, T., Karvounarakis, G., Tannen, V.: Provenance semirings. In: 26th ACM Symposium on Principles of Database Systems (2007)
23. Groth, P., Moreau, L.: Representing distributed systems using the Open Provenance Model. Future Generation Computer Systems 27(6) (2011)
24. Heydon, A., Levin, R., Mann, T., Yu, Y.: The Vesta Approach to Software Configuration Management. Technical Report 168, Compaq Systems Research Center (2001)
25. Heinis, T., Alonso, G.: Efficient lineage tracking for scientific workflows. In: ACM SIGMOD International Conference on Management of Data (2008)
26. Holland, D.A., Braun, U., Maclean, D., Muniswamy-Reddy, K., Seltzer, M.: Choosing a data model and query language for provenance. In: 2nd International Provenance and Annotation Workshop (2008)
27. H2, http://www.h2database.com
28. Installable File System, http://msdn.microsoft.com/en-us/windows/hardware/gg463062.aspx
29. Influenza Data, National Institutes of Health, ftp://ftp.ncbi.nlm.nih.gov/genomes/INFLUENZA/influenza.faa
30. Java Data Base Connectivity, http://www.oracle.com/technetwork/java/overview-141217.html
31. Java Native Interface, http://java.sun.com/docs/books/jni/
32. Kementsietsidis, A., Wang, M.: On the efficiency of provenance queries. In: 25th International Conference on Data Engineering (2009)
33. Linux Audit, http://people.redhat.com/sgrubb/audit/
34. LLVM, http://llvm.org
35. lsof, ftp://lsof.itap.purdue.edu/pub/tools/unix/lsof
36. Apache Lucene, http://lucene.apache.org/core/old_versioned_docs/versions/3_0_1/queryparsersyntax.html
37. MacFUSE, http://code.google.com/p/macfuse/
38. Macko, P., Seltzer, M.: A general-purpose provenance library. In: 4th USENIX Workshop on the Theory and Practice of Provenance (2012)
39. Malik, T., Gehani, A., Tariq, D., Zaffar, F.: Sketching Distributed Data Provenance. In : Liu, Q., Bai, Q., Giugni, S., Williamson, D., Taylor, J. (eds.) Data Provenance and Data Management in eScience. SCI, vol. 426, pp. 85–108. Springer, Heidelberg (2013)
40. MATLAB, http://www.mathworks.com/products/matlab/
41. Miles, S., Deelman, E., Groth, P., Vahi, K., Mehta, G., Moreau, L.: Connecting scientific data to scientific experiments with provenance. In: 3rd IEEE International Conference on e-Science and Grid Computing (2007)
42. Moreau, L., Clifford, B., Freire, J., Futrelle, J., Gil, Y., Groth, P., Kwasnikowska, N., Miles, S., Missier, P., Myers, J., Plale, B., Simmhan, Y., Stephan, E., Van den Bussche, J.: The Open Provenance Model core specification (v1.1). Future Generation Computer Systems (2010)
43. MySQL, http://www.mysql.com/
44. Neo4j, http://neo4j.org/
45. Novel Information Gathering and Harvesting Techniques for Intelligence in Global Autonomous Language Exploitation, http://www.speech.sri.com/projects/GALE/
46. OpenBSM, http://www.trustedbsd.org/openbsm.html
47. Open Provenance Model, http://openprovenance.org/

48. Pancerella, C., Hewson, J., Koegler, W., Leahy, D., Lee, M., Rahn, L., Yang, C., Myers, J.D., Didier, B., McCoy, R., Schuchardt, K., Stephan, E., Windus, T., Amin, K., Bittner, S., Lansing, C., Minkoff, M., Nijsure, S., van. Laszewski, G., Pinzon, R., Ruscic, B., Wagner, A., Wang, B., Pitz, W., Ho, Y.L., Montoya, D., Xu, L., Allison, T.C., Green Jr., W.H., Frenklach, M.: Metadata in the collaboratory for multi-scale chemical science. In: Dublin Core Conference (2003)

49. Process Monitor, Windows Sysinternals, http://technet.microsoft.com/en-us/sysinternals/bb896645.aspx

50. Rajgarhia, A., Gehani, A.: Performance and extension of user space file systems. In: 25th ACM Symposium on Applied Computing (2010)

51. Muniswamy-Reddy, K.-K., Holland, D.A., Braun, U., Seltzer, M.: Provenance-aware storage systems. In: USENIX Annual Technical Conference (2006)

52. Muniswamy-Reddy, K.-K, Braun, U., Holland, D.A., Macko, P., Maclean, D., Margo, D., Seltzer, M., Smogor, R.: Layering in provenance systems. In: USENIX Annual Technical Conference (2009)

53. Muniswamy-Reddy, K.-K., Macko, P., Seltzer, M.: Making a Cloud provenance-aware. In: 1st USENIX Workshop on the Theory and Practice of Provenance (2009)

54. Muniswamy-Reddy, K.-K., Macko, P., Seltzer, M.: Provenance for the Cloud. In: 8th USENIX Conference on File and Storage Technologies (2010)

55. Lineage File System, http://crypto.stanford.edu/~cao/lineage.html

56. Scalable Authentication of Grid Data Provenance, http://www.nsf.gov/awardsearch/showAward.do?AwardNumber=0722068

57. Silva, C.T., Freire, J., Callahan, S.: Provenance for visualizations: Reproducibility and beyond. Computing in Science and Engineering 9(5) (2007)

58. SLAC National Accelerator Laboratory, http://www.slac.stanford.edu/

59. Support for Provenance Auditing in Distributed Environments, http://spade.csl.sri.com/

60. Szomszor, M., Moreau, L.: Recording and Reasoning over Data Provenance in Web and Grid Services. In: Meersman, R., Schmidt, D.C. (eds.) CoopIS/DOA/ODBASE 2003. LNCS, vol. 2888, pp. 603–620. Springer, Heidelberg (2003)

61. Tariq, D., Ali, M., Gehani, A.: Towards Automated Collection of Application-Level Data Provenance. In: 4th USENIX Workshop on the Theory and Practice of Provenance (2012)

62. Tupelo project, NCSA, http://tupeloproject.ncsa.uiuc.edu/node/2

63. Windows Driver Kit, http://msdn.microsoft.com/en-us/windows/hardware/gg487428.aspx

64. WebDAV, http://www.webdav.org/

65. Widom, J.: Trio: A system for integrated management of data, accuracy and lineage. In: 2nd Conference on Innovative Data Systems Research (2005)

66. Windows Management Instrumentation, http://msdn.microsoft.com/en-us/library/aa394582(v=VS.85).aspx

67. Zhao, J., Goble, C.A., Stevens, R., Bechhofer, S.: Semantically Linking and Browsing Provenance Logs for E-science. In: Bouzeghoub, M., Goble, C.A., Kashyap, V., Spaccapietra, S. (eds.) ICSNW 2004. LNCS, vol. 3226, pp. 158–176. Springer, Heidelberg (2004)

68. Zhou, W., Sherr, M., Tao, T., Li, X., Loo, B., Mao, Y.: Efficient querying and maintenance of network provenance at Internet-scale. In: ACM SIGMOD International Conference on Management of Data (2010)

VScope: Middleware for Troubleshooting Time-Sensitive Data Center Applications

Chengwei Wang[1], Infantdani Abel Rayan[3], Greg Eisenhauer[1],
Karsten Schwan[1], Vanish Talwar[2], Matthew Wolf[1], and Chad Huneycutt[1]

[1] Georgia Institute of Technology
[2] HP Labs.
[3] Riot Games

Abstract. Data-Intensive infrastructures are increasingly used for on-line processing of live data to guide operations and decision making. VScope is a flexible monitoring and analysis middleware for troubleshooting such large-scale, time-sensitive, multi-tier applications. With VScope, lightweight anomaly detection and interaction tracking methods can be run continuously throughout an application's execution. The runtime events generated by these methods can then initiate more detailed and heavier weight analyses which are dynamically deployed in the places where they may be most likely fruitful for root cause diagnosis and mitigation. We comprehensively evaluate VScope prototype in a virtualized data center environment with over 1000 virtual machines (VMs), and apply VScope to a representative on-line log processing application. Experimental results show that VScope can deploy and operate a variety of on-line analytics functions and metrics with a few seconds at large scale. Compared to traditional logging approaches, VScope based troubleshooting has substantially lower perturbation and generates much smaller log data volumes. It can also resolve complex cross-tier or cross-software-level issues unsolvable solely by application-level or per-tier mechanisms.

Keywords: Cloud, Data Center, Management, Troubleshooting.

1   Introduction

In the 'big data' era, live data analysis applications are becoming easy to scale, as well as being lucrative for or even critical to a company's operation. For instance, by continuously analyzing the live number of page views on its products, an e-commerce website can run a dynamic micro-promotion strategy in which when over 3000 customers are looking at a product for over 10 seconds, an extra 20% discount appears on the web page to increase sales. Other mission-critical examples for e-commerce sites are click fraud and spam detection.

The importance of live data analysis is underscored by the recent creation of real-time or 'streaming' big data infrastructures[1], which include Flume, S4, Storm, Chukwa, and others [5,28,25,29,11,23,15]. Conceptually, these are based

---

[1] In this paper we use the term 'real-time' to refer a latency restriction within seconds or hundreds of milliseconds.

P. Narasimhan and P. Triantafillou (Eds.): Middleware 2012, LNCS 7662, pp. 121–141, 2012.
© IFIP International Federation for Information Processing 2012

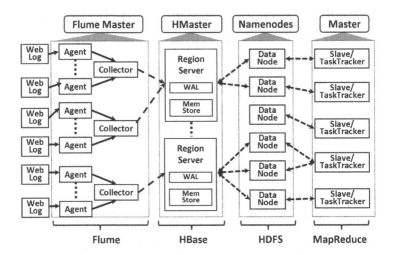

Fig. 1. A typical real-time web log analysis application composed from Flume, HBase, HDFS, and Hadoop. In Flume, *agents* reside in web or application servers, collecting logs and converting them into key-value pairs. *Collectors* receive and aggregate the local results and insert them into HBase, a distributed, scalable key-value store by which users can query the analysis results on-the-fly. HBase consists of *region servers* that are equipped with a memory cache, termed *MemStore*, and a Write Ahead Log (WAL). The data are first written to the WAL and MemStore before being asynchronously persisted to the back-end distributed file system, HDFS, which is typically shared by other data-intensive batch systems, such as Hadoop-based MapReduce codes used for off-line, long-term analyses. Each tier can scale to 1000s of servers or virtual machines.

on the well-established paradigm of stream- or event-based processing [16,2,1], but their attractiveness stems from the fact that they can be easily integrated with other elements of 'big data' infrastructures, such as scalable key-value stores and MapReduce systems, to construct multi-tier platforms spanning thousands of servers or consolidated virtual servers in data centers. A sample platform integrating Flume and other data-intensive systems is depicted in Figure 1.

Crucial to maintaining high availability and performance for these multi-tier applications, particularly in light of their stringent end-to-end timing requirements, is *responsive troubleshooting* – a process involving the timely detection and diagnosis of performance issues. Such troubleshooting is notoriously difficult, however, for the following reasons:

– *Holistic vs. tier-specific troubleshooting.* As illustrated in Figure 1, each tier is typically a complex distributed system with its own management component, e.g. HBase or Flume masters. Developed by different vendors and/or managed by different operation teams, tier-specific management can improve the availability of individual tiers, but is not sufficient for maintaining an entire application's end-to-end performance, a simple reason being that issues visible in one tier may actually be caused by problems located in another. Needed are holistic systems to efficiently track problems across tiers.

- *Dynamic, per-problem functionality.* Problems in complex, large-scale systems arise dynamically, and for each class of problems, there may be different detection, analysis, and resolution methods. Troubleshooting, therefore, is an inherently dynamic activity, involving on-line capabilities to capture differing metrics and to diagnose/analyze them with potentially problem- and situation-specific methods[36].
- *Scalable, responsive problem resolution.* In latency-sensitive applications like the one in Figure 1, to maintain desired timing, troubleshooting must be conducted both with low perturbation and with high responsiveness: issues must be detected, diagnosed, and repaired without missing too many events and while maintaining availability for other ongoing actions.
- *System-level effects.* Holistic troubleshooting must extend beyond a single application, to also identify the system-level bottlenecks that can arise in today's consolidated data center or cloud computing systems.

Previous troubleshooting systems have not addressed all of these challenges. Solutions that monitor 'everything all the time' [26,39,27], including both application and system-level events, do not scale for detailed diagnostics via say, debug-level logging or tracing with consequent high levels of perturbation. This is shown in Figure 2, where continuously logging application-level debugging events on all of its nodes slows down an application's performance by more than 10 times over the baseline. Sampling [30,31,14,7] for some of the components and/or for some period of time may not only miss important events, affecting troubleshooting effectiveness, but will also bring

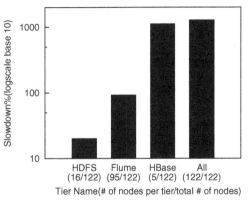

Fig. 2. E2E performance slowdown (i.e. latency increase) % caused by debug-level logging at different tiers of the architecture shown in Figure 1

about serious performance issues when using a homogeneous and/or random sampling strategy across all nodes, e.g., with Dapper [31]'s use of a uniform, low (1/1000) sampling rate. In Figure 2, debug-level logging in the Flume application's HBase tier, the smallest portion of the system (5/122 VMs), results in over 10 times slowdown, which is more than an order of magnitude of the perturbation imposed by debug-level logging in the Flume tier, which has the majority of nodes (95/122). Thus, it is inadvisable to use a high sampling rate for the HBase tier, whereas such a strategy for the Flume tier will likely lead to only modest additional perturbation. An alternative troubleshooting approach chosen by GWP [30] is to randomly pick some set of machines. This may work well if that set is in the HDFS tier, but will be prohibitively costly if the HBase tier is picked. Other approaches, like those taken by Fay [14] and Chopstix [7] to set sampling rates based on the event population, still remain unaware of application level perturbation, resulting in the same issue as the one faced by GWP. We, therefore, conclude that *a more flexible system is needed for efficient troubleshooting, where methods can differ for each behavior, tier, and type of analysis being performed.*

The VScope middleware presented in this paper makes it possible (1) to adjust and tune troubleshooting dynamically – at runtime – for individual tiers and across tiers, (2) to dynamically deploy any analysis action(s) needed to understand the metric data being captured in the ways required by such troubleshooting, and (3) to do so in ways that meet the perturbation/overhead requirements of target applications. To achieve those ends, VScope, as a flexible monitoring and analysis system, offers the following novel abstractions and mechanisms for troubleshooting latency-sensitive, multi-tier data center applications:

1. *Dynamic Watch, Scope, and Query.* VScope abstracts troubleshooting as a process involving repeated *Watch*, *Scope*, and *Query* operations. Respectively, these (i) detect performance anomalies, (ii) 'zoom-in' to candidate problematic groups of components or nodes, and (iii) answer detailed questions about those components or nodes using dynamically deployed monitoring or analysis functions. VScope can operate on any set of nodes or software components and thus, can be applied within a tier, across multiple tiers, and across different software levels.

2. *Guidance.* Replacing the current manual 'problem ticket' mechanisms used in industry, VScope based troubleshooting is directed by on-line 'guidance', realized by the *Watch* and *Scope* operations that first detect abnormal behavior, followed by exploring candidate sources for such behavior, and only then initiate more detailed queries on select entities. The current implementations of *Watch* and *Scope* support both 'horizontal guidance', to track potential problems across different tiers of a multi-tier application, and 'vertical guidance', to understand whether problems are caused by how applications are mapped to underlying machines.

3. *Distributed Processing Graphs (DPGs).* All VScope operations are realized by DPGs, which are overlay networks capable of being dynamically deployed and reconfigured on any set of machines or processes, supporting various types of topologies and analysis functionalities. First introduced in our previous work [36], where we proposed the basic architecture of DPGs and investigated an impact model of metric number/size and various DPG topologies, along with other factors, this paper presents DPG implementation, APIs, and commands, based on which we build VScope's troubleshooting functionality.

VScope's capabilities and performance are evaluated on a testbed with over 1000 virtual machines (VMs). Experimental results show the VScope runtime negligibly perturbs system and application performance, and requires mere seconds to deploy 1000 node DPGs of varying topologies. This results in fast operation for on-line queries able to use a comprehensive set of application to system/platform level metrics and a variety of representative analytics functions. When supporting algorithms with high computation complexity, VScope serves as a 'thin layer' that occupies no more than 5% of their total latency. Further, by using guidance that correlates system- and application-level metrics, VScope can locate problematic VMs that cannot be found via solely application-level monitoring, and in one of the use cases explored in the paper, it operates with levels of perturbation of over 400% less than what is seen for brute-force and most sampling-based approaches.

2   System Design and Implementation

2.1   Goals and Non-goals

The design of VScope is driven by the following goals: (1) *flexibility*: to initiate, change, and stop monitoring and analysis on any set of nodes at any time, supported by operators for dynamically building and controlling user-defined actions for runtime troubleshooting; (2) *guided operation*: programmable methods for detecting potential problems and then tracking interactions that may contribute to them, between tiers and across software levels, thereby focusing troubleshooting in ways that can reduce overheads and improve effectiveness; and (3) *responsiveness and scalability*: to deploy troubleshooting methods with low delay at scales of 1000+ nodes.

VScope is designed to be a general platform rather than a set of ad hoc analysis algorithms/solutions. VScope does not replace operator involvement, but aims to facilitate their troubleshooting efforts. Further, while VScope may be used to seek the root causes of failures, its current implementation lacks functionality like an off-line diagnostic database and a rich infrastructure for determining and using decision trees or similar diagnostic techniques. Also, the methods presently implemented in VScope focus on persistent performance problems that will likely render an application inoperable after some time, i.e., when there are frequent or repeated violations of certain performance indicators that persist if they are not addressed. Having determined potential sources of such problems, VScope can then trigger certain actions for mitigation or recovery, but it assumes such functionality to be supported by other subsystems (e.g., inherent to specific applications/tiers or software levels) or housed in some external system for problem resolution [9].

2.2   VScope Overview

The system architecture of VScope is depicted in Figure 3(a). The machines (VMs or physical machines) in the target application are managed by a server called *VMaster*. Operators use VScope operations, DPG commands, or scripts with the DPG API, in a console called *VShell* provided by *VMaster*. *VMaster* executes those commands by deploying DPGs on requested machines to process their monitoring metrics, and it returns results to operators. In detail, it starts a *DPGManager* to create a new DPG, which essentially, is an overlay network consisting of processing entities named *VNodes* residing on application machines. The *DPGManager* dynamically deploys *VNodes* equipped with assigned functions on specified machines, and connects them with a specified topology. *VNodes*

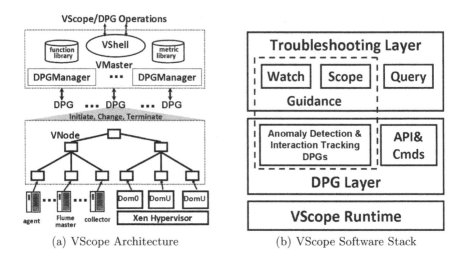

(a) VScope Architecture   (b) VScope Software Stack

Fig. 3. VScope System Design

collect and process monitoring metrics, transmit metrics or analysis results to other *VNodes* or the *DPGManager*, which in turn relays results to *VMaster*. *DPGManager* can initiate, change, or terminate its DPG on-the-fly.

In *VMaster*, the *metric library* defines monitoring metric types and associated collection functions. The *function library* defines the user-defined and default metric analysis functions, including those used in guidance (see Section 2.5). The above metrics and functions can be dynamically deployed into DPGs for various troubleshooting purposes.

The VScope software stack, described in Figure 3(b), has three layers. The troubleshooting layer exposes basic operations in *VShell*: *Watch*, *Scope*, and *Query*, which will be described in Section 2.3. The *Watch* and *Scope* operations constitute the *guidance mechanism*, where *Watch* notifies the operator when and where end-to-end anomalies happen, and *Scope* provides the potential candidate nodes contributing to the anomalies. Operators (or automated decision engines) can then use *Query* for in-depth analysis on those candidates yielded by guidance. These operations are built upon the DPG layer. In particular, the guidance mechanism (*Watch* and *Scope*) relies on an anomaly detection DPG and on interaction tracking DPGs. The DPG layer also exposes API and management commands to offer finer grain controls and customization. The lowest layer, the VScope runtime, is comprised of a set of daemon processes running on all nodes participating in the VScope system (i.e., the machines hosting the application and additional management machines running VScope). This runtime maintains the connections between machines and implements dynamic DPG creation and management. In virtualized data centers, the VScope runtime can be installed in hypervisors (e.g., Dom0 in Xen), in the virtual machines hosting the application(s) being monitored, in both, and/or in specialized management engines [21,24]. Our testbed uses a VScope installation in the Xen hypervisor as well as in the VMs hosting the Flume application.

2.3   Troubleshooting Operations

Watch. The *Watch* operation monitors a list of metrics on a set of nodes[2], and its current implementation applies to them an anomaly detection function in order to detect and report anomalous behaviors for any specified metrics. The parameters of the *Watch* operation described in Table 1 show its ability to monitor metrics on any VScope node, using detection function specified with *detectFunc*. Sample functions used in our work include thresholding

Table 1. Arguments of Watch(*Optional)

Argument	Description
nodeList*	a list of nodes to monitor
metricList	a list of metric types
detectFunc*	detection function or code
duration*	duration
frequency*	frequency

key performance indicators (KPI), such as request latency and statistics like those based on entropy described in [37]. The frequency and duration of the *Watch* operation are also configurable. In our Flume application, the *Watch* operation continuously executes on all the Flume *agent* nodes, monitoring their end-to-end message latencies and detecting the nodes with latency outliers. Internally, *Watch* is implemented using an anomaly detection DPG explained in Section 2.5.

Scope. The *Scope* operation (described in Table 2) discovers a set of nodes interacting with a particular node specified by argument *source*, at a time specified by argument *timestamp*. This operation guides troubleshooting by informing operators which nodes are related to the problematic node when the anomaly happens. Based on this guidance, operators can deploy a DPG on those nodes (or some subset of them) for further diagnosis, using the *Query* operation. For instance, for the Flume application, 'horizontal guidance' identi-

Table 2. Arguments of Scope(*Optional)

Argument	Description
nodeList*	a list of nodes to explore
graph	name of interaction graph
source	node in interest
timestamp*	interaction at a specific time
distance	number of edges
direction*	backward, forward or both

fies the HBase *region servers* with which some specified Flume *agent* is interacting via a Flume *collector*, and 'vertical guidance' tracks the mappings between a physical machine and the VMs it hosts. By default, the output of *Scope* is a list of nodes directly interacting with the *source*. *distance* and *direction* are optional arguments, where the former specifies indirect interactions by setting the value > 1, and the latter specifies the 'direction' of interaction, for instance, 'receiving requests from' or 'sending requests to'.

In a nutshell, *Scope* works by searching an in-memory, global graph abstraction that describes interactions between every pair of nodes. Multiple types of interaction graphs are supported, covering a range of interactions from event level to network and system levels. These are shown in Table 7 and are specified

---

[2] A node is a physical or a VM running the VScope runtime in example application.

with the argument *graph*. The creation and continuous update of the global graph is implemented using an interaction tracking DPG explained in Section 2.5.

Query. The *Query* function collects and analyzes metrics from a specified list of nodes, and provides results to query initiators. *Query* has two modes – *continuous* mode and *one-shot* – the latter being helpful when running monitoring or analysis actions that have high overheads. *Query* (including *query* with 'continuous' mode) is designed with the 'pull' model, i.e., the *VMaster* requests (pulls) metrics/results from *VNodes*. Conversely, *watch* is designed with the 'push' model, i.e., *VNodes* periodically report basic metrics or anomaly detection results to the *VMaster*.

Table 3. Arguments of Query(*Optional)

Argument	Description
nodeList*	a list of nodes to query
metricList*	a list of metric types
queryFunc	analytics function or code
mode*	continuous or one-shot

2.4   Flexible DPGs

DPG as the Building Block. All VScope operations described in Section 2.3 are implemented via DPGs. A DPG consists of a set of processing points (*VNodes*) to collect and analyze monitoring data. It can be configured in multiple topologies to meet varying scale and analysis requirements. For example, it can be configured as a hierarchical tree or as a peer-to-peer overlay or, when operating at smaller scales, as a centralized structure. Managed by a *DPGManager*, a DPG can be dynamically started on a specified set of nodes, where each *VNode* runs locally on a designated node and executes functions specified in VScope operations. These functions are stored as binaries in the *function library*, and they can be dynamically linked. As a result, DPGs are flexible in terms of topology, functions executed, and metric types. Further, DPG outputs can be (i) presented immediately to the VScope user in *VShell*, (ii) written into rotating logs, or (iii) stored as off-line records in a database or key-value store. The last two configurations are particularly important when historical data is needed for troubleshooting. The use case in Section 4.2 uses rotating logs to store past metric measurements.

DPG API and Management Commands. Figure 4 describes the DPG core API and sample topologies, with details shown in Table 4. The *create()* method automatically creates any size topology of type point-to-point (P), centralized (C), or hierarchy (H) for some specified list of nodes. Topology specifics are configurable, e.g., besides the number of nodes, one can specify the branching factor of a hierarchical

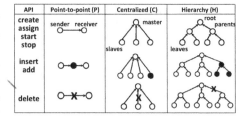

Fig. 4. DPG API and Topologies

Table 4. Pseudo Functions for DPG API

DPG create (list, topology, spec)	Create a DPG with a specified topology
int add (src, dst, DPG)	Add a link from *VNode* src to *VNode* dst
int assign (func, spec, list, DPG)	Assign function to a list of *VNodes*
int start (DPG)	Start a DPG
int stop (DPG)	Stop an operating DPG
int insert (new, src, dst, DPG)	Insert a new *VNode* between existing *VNodes*
int delete (src, dst, DPG)	Delete a link from *VNode* src to *VNode* dst

topology. *Create()* returns a unique DPG ID for reference in subsequent operations, and in the *assign()* method, the parameter *func* is a registered function ID. When a DPG is running, one can call the *assign()* to change the functionality on any *VNode* or use the *insert()* and *delete()* methods to change the DPG. The DPG API is exposed as commands in *VShell*, as well, and there are additional auxiliary management commands like *list* (listing metric types, functions, or DPGs) and *collect* (returns the metric collection function).

Though operators can just use VScope operations without knowing the underlying DPG logic, new topologies, new operations and customization of existing functionality can be added easily through direct use of DPG APIs, which is not described in detail here because of space constraints.

2.5   Implementation

VScope Runtime. The VScope runtime is implemented with EVPath [1], a C library for building active overlay networks. Metric collection uses standard C libraries, system calls, and JMX (at application level). Metrics are encoded in an efficient binary data format [1], and a standard format template is used to define new metric types. Built-in metrics and functions are listed in Table 5 and Table 6. As shown in the tables, VScope has a comprehensive set of metrics across application, system and platform levels, and a variety of representative analytics functions that are implemented with standard C libraries and other open source codes [13]. The DPGs associated with these functions have different topologies. For instance, *Pathmap*, PCA (Principle Component Analysis) and K-Clustering are implemented as centralized DPGs, as they require global data.

Table 5. Basic Metrics

Level	Basic Metrics
Appli-cation	E2E Latency, JMX/JVM Metrics Flume/HBase/HDFS INFO Logs
Virtual Machine	VCPU, Memory, I/O Metrics Network Traffic, Connections
Dom0 & System	CPU, I/O and Memory Metrics Paging, Context Switch Metrics

Table 6. Built-in Functions

	DPG	Algorithms
Watch	Hierarchy	MAX/MIN/AVE, Entropy, Top-K
Scope	Centralized	Pathmap[3]
Query	Centralized	K-Clustering, PCA

Algorithm 1. Parallel Graph Aggregation

---

1. On each leaf node, generate an adjacency list (where each record is
   [vertex ID, connected vertices]) sorted by vertex IDs, and send it to parent
2. On each parent or root node, merge n sorted
   adjacency lists as follows:

   i. Create an array P with size of n storing current vertex ID in each adjacency list.
   ii. If multiple IDs in P are the same and they are the smallest, merge their records
   into a new record, else take the record with the smallest vertex ID in P as the
   new record. (essentially an n-way sorting of n vertex ID arrays)
   iii. Place the new record into the merged adjacency list.
   iv. Update P to reflect the next record in each adjacency list.
   v. Repeat ii to iv until all the records in n adjacency lists are visited.

End-to-End Anomaly Detection. The *Watch* operation is implemented using a DPG with a hierarchical topology in which the leaves are all of the nodes of the web log analysis application. This DPG collects the end-to-end latency on each Flume *agent*, which is defined as the duration between the time when a new log entry is added and the time it (or its associated result) appears in HBase. This is measured by creating a test log entry on each *agent*, querying the entry in HBase, and computing the difference. The latencies are then aggregated through the tree using Entropy-based Anomaly Testing (EbAT) [37,35], a lightweight anomaly detection algorithm, to output the agents that are outliers. Other algorithms for anomaly detection and ranking are investigated in [38,34].

Interaction Tracking. Table 7 shows the built-in global graphs supported by *Scope*, covering a range of interactions from event level to network and system levels. For each graph type, in our implementation, a DPG is deployed and continuously run on all the nodes to construct and update the corresponding graph structure in *VMaster*. There are two ways to track the global interactions, *centralized* or *distributed*. For interactions like the causality graph implemented using *Pathmap* [3], a DPG collects metrics from leaves,

Table 7. VScope Interaction Graphs

	Interaction	DPG
Causality Graph	Event Flow between Nodes	Centralized Using Pathmap
Connection Graph	Network Connection	Distributed Using Netstat
Virtual Graph	Dom0-DomU Mapping	Distributed Using Libvirt
Tier Graph	Dependency between Tiers	Distributed Static Config.

compresses them at intermediate nodes, and then constructs the graph at the DPG root. An alternate distributed implementation of graph construction uses parallel analysis in which the leaves analyze metrics to generate a local graph (e.g., in the connection graph, it is the ingress and egress connections on a node), the local graphs are aggregated at parent nodes to create partial graphs which are finally aggregated at the root to produce the global graph. The current prototype uses adjacency lists to represent graphs and employs the parallel algorithm shown in Algorithm 1 to merge adjacency lists.

3 Experimental Evaluation

Experiments are conducted on a testbed running 1200 Xen VMs hosted by 60 physical server blades using Ubuntu Linux (20 VMs per server). Every server has a 1TB SATA disk, 48GB Memory, and 16 CPUs (2.40GHz). Each VM has 2GB memory and at least 10G disk space.

3.1 VScope Base Overheads

We install VScope on every VM in a host and vary the number of *VNodes* on each VM. Each *VNode* collects the metrics shown in Table 5, and sends them to a separate DPG. As shown in Table 8, CPU and Memory overheads to the VM are negligible even when there are 50 *VNodes* (1000 concurrent DPGs in the host). With continuous anomaly de-

Table 8. VScope Runtime Overheads

DPG# in Host	VNode# in VM	CPU Usage Increase	Memory Usage Increase
20	1	< 0.01%	0.02%
100	5	< 0.01%	0.02%
1000	50	< 0.01%	0.03%

tection and via interaction tracking, VScope imposes only 0.4% overhead on the end-to-end latency of application described in Section 4. In contrast and as shown in Section 4, heavyweight VScope operations, like those performing tracing or logging may incur considerable overheads, due to the innately high costs of those data collection methods. These facts demonstrate the utility of continuously using the 'thin' VScope layer, which does not add notable costs, and then, only using heavier weight data collection and analysis methods when needed. Further, by having the 'thin' layer point out 'where' and 'when' such heavier weight methods are to be used, the inevitably high overheads of using those methods can be reduced.

3.2 DPG Deployment

Fast deployment of DPGs is critical for timely troubleshooting. We evaluate this by measuring the latency for deploying a hierarchical DPG on more than 1000 VMs, each of which has one *VNode*. The topology has a height of 2, and the total number of leaf VMs varies from 125 to 1000.

As expected, Figure 5(a) shows increased deployment times (presented as latency on the Y-Axis) with increased DPG sizes. However, latency remains within 5 seconds even at the scale of 1000 VMs. This would be considered sufficient for current troubleshooting delay requirements stated in [8] (typically 1 hour), but it also suggests the utility of future work on DPG reuse – to use and reconfigure an existing DPG, when possible, rather than creating a new one, or to pre-deploy DPGs where they might be needed. Deploying moderate scale DPGs with hundreds of nodes, however, usually happens within 1 second, suggesting that such optimizations are not needed at smaller scale. Also note that deployment latency varies with different branching factors (bf). At scales less than 750, deploying

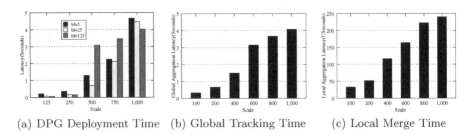

(a) DPG Deployment Time   (b) Global Tracking Time   (c) Local Merge Time

Fig. 5. Efficient DPG Deployment and Guidance Mechanism

the DPG with bf 125 has larger latency than those with smaller bf values; this is because parent nodes construct their subtrees in parallel and the parents in the DPG with bf 125 have the biggest subtrees.

3.3   Interaction Tracking

The *Scope* operation relies on efficient methods for interaction tracking. We evaluate a distributed DPG (used for connection graph) by creating a two-level, hierarchical DPG with bf 25. We vary its number of leaves from 125 to 1000, and for this test, each VM has a randomly generated local interaction graph represented by an adjacency list with 1000 vertex entries with each vertex connected to 1000 randomly generated vertices. We measure the total latency from the time the first local graph is generated by leaf VMs to the time when the respective merged graph is created at the root. We also measure the average time of local processing incurred during the per-node aggregation of connection graph information in order to study the dominant factor in total latency.

As shown in Figure 5(b), the total latency for generating a global graph increases as the system scales, but it remains within 4 seconds for 1000 VMs, where each VM has a 1000×1000 local connection graph. This means that the system can generate such a global graph at a resolution of every 4 seconds. Total latency is mainly due to the queuing and dequeuing time on *VNodes* plus network communication time. This is shown by the small measured local aggregation latency in Figure 5(c). At the same time, since these latencies increase linearly with the total number of inputs, parallel aggregation is a useful attribute to maintain for large scale systems. We also note that the local graphs occupy a fair amount of memory, which suggests opportunities for additional optimizations through use of more efficient internal data structures. Finally, the analytics actions taken by *Scope* utilize the *Pathmap* for centralized interaction tracking. In Section 3.4, Figure 6 shows that it can generate a 1000 VM graph within 8 seconds.

In summary, the *Scope* operation's current implementation is efficient for the long running enterprise codes targeted in our work, but it may not meet the requirements of real-time codes such as those performing on-line sensing and actuation in highly interactive settings like immersive games.

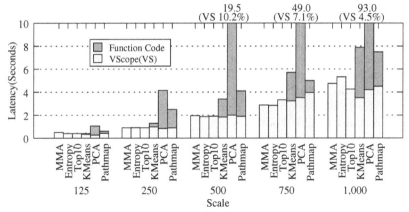

Fig. 6. Analytics Microbenchmark Performance

3.4 Supporting Diverse Analytics

We use the algorithms in Table 6 as micro-benchmarks to measure the base performance of VScope operations. Tests randomly generate a 1000×1000 matrix of float numbers on each VM, and vary the size of the hierarchical DPG (bf=25) from 125 to 1000 leaf VMs. We measure the latency for analyzing the data on all leaf VMs at each scale. For centralized algorithms, the parent *VNodes* only relay the data. For the Top-K algorithm, we calculate the top 10 numbers. We conduct K-Means clustering with 5 passes.

Figure 6 shows latency breakdowns as well as the total latency of each function. In general, most of the algorithms operate within seconds, with increasing latencies for rising scales. Algorithms with high computational complexity are more costly, of course, but for such 'heavyweight' algorithms, especially for PCA, although the total latencies are over 1.5 minutes at the scale of 1000 VMs, the base VScope implementation contributes only about 4.5% to these delays, and this contribution decreases as the system scales.

4 Experiences with Using VScope

This section illustrates the utility of VScope for troubleshooting, using the application described in Figure 1 (VScope's DPG architecture was also investigated in other use cases in [36,19].) The application's Flume tier has 10 *collectors*, each of which is linked with 20 *agents*. The HBase tier has 20 *region servers*, and the HDFS tier has 40 *datanodes*[3]. Experiments use web request traces from the World Cup website [18] to build a log generator that replays the Apache access logs on each of 200 *agent* VMs. Each *agent* reads the new entries of the log and sends them to its *collector*. The *collector* combines the *ClientID* and *ObjectID* as the keyword and the log content as the value, then places the record into HBase.

---

[3] Each tier has one master node, and in HBase, 5 *region servers* serve as the ZooKeeper quorum. For simplicity, we do not 'count' masters when discussing scale.

The log generator generates 200 entries per second. The worst case end-to-end latency in the problem-free scenario is within 300 milliseconds.

The VScope runtime is installed on all of the VMs and in addition, on all physical machines (i.e., Xen's Dom0s). In accordance with standard practice for management infrastructures [21,36], one additional dedicated VM serves as *VMaster*, and 5 dedicated VMs serve as parent *VNodes* in the two-level hierarchy DPGs used for troubleshooting. Two use cases presented below validate VScope's utility for efficient troubleshooting.

4.1   Finding Culprit Region Servers

The first VScope use case crosses multiple tiers of the Flume application. The objective is to find some 'culprit' *region server* exhibiting prolonged execution times. Those are difficult to detect with standard HBase instrumentation because debug-level logging in *region servers* to trace their request processing times [6] generates voluminous logs and high levels of perturbation to the running server(s). Hence troubleshooting using brute force methods might quickly find a culprit by turning on all of the *region servers'* debug-level logging and then analyzing these logs (in some central place), but this would severely perturb the running application. Alternative methods that successively sample some random set of servers until a culprit is found would reduce perturbation but would likely experience large delays in finding the culprit server. More generally, for multi-tier web applications, while bottleneck problems like the 'culprit' *region server* described above commonly occur, they are also hard to detect, for several reasons. (1) Dynamic connectivity – the connections between the Flume and HBase tiers can change, since the *region server* to which a collector connects is determined by the keyword region of the collector's current log entry. (2) Data-Driven concurrency – HBase splits the regions on overloaded *region servers*, causing additional dynamic behavior. (3) Redundancy – a *region server* is typically connected by multiple *collectors*. As a result, one 'culprit' *region server* exhibiting prolonged processing times may affect the end-to-end latencies observed on many *agents*.

We synthetically induce server slowdown, by starting garbage collection (GC) in the Java Virtual Machine (JVM) on one of the *region servers*. This prolonged disturbance eventually slows down the Flume *agents* connected to the *region server* via their *collectors*. Experimental evaluations compare VScope, the brute-force, and the sampling-based approaches for finding the culprit *region server*. The VScope approach follows the 3 steps illus-

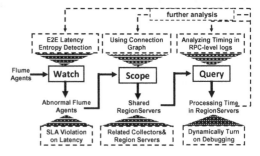

Fig. 7. Steps using VScope operations

trated in Figure 7. (1) A user at a *VShell* console issues a *Watch* operation to find which *agents* have prolonged end-to-end latencies.

(2) Use the *connection graph* (chosen from Table 7) and the *Scope* operation to find the connected *collectors* and the *region servers* to which they connect. In these guidance actions, the *connection graph* is the *graph* parameter, the problematic *agent* node is the *source*, and '2' is used as the *distance* parameter. The output will be the *collector* and associated *region servers*. By iteratively 'Scoping' all anomalous *agents*, we find that they share 5 *collectors*. Furthermore, the *Scope* operation returns the set of *region servers* in use by these collectors, and we can determine that they have 4 *region servers* in common. Therefore, we select those four as candidate culprits. Under the assumption of only one culprit *region server*, this operation will succeed because the culprit affects all of these *collectors*. While it will be rare to have multiple culprit *region servers* in a short period of time, in that case, more candidates may be chosen, but they still constitute only a small set of all *region servers*.

(3) Here, VScope has narrowed down the search for the problematic *region server*, and we can now use the *Query* operation to turn on debug-level logging for the candidates. We note that the *region servers* yielded by the *Scope* operation will always include the culprit, because VScope tracks all connections. The user will still have to carefully examine the region server logs to find the problem, but instead of having 20 candidates (the brute-force approach), there are just 4. If the examination is done sequentially (by gathering and examining logs one server at a time) to minimize perturbation, the user can expect to examine 2 logs on the average (requiring 20 minutes of logging and .45GB of data) with VScope, as op-posed to 10 logs (requiring 100 minutes of logging and 2GB of data) with the brute-force approach. If log gathering is per-formed in parallel to save time, the in-formation provided by VScope allows the retrieval of just 4 logs (0.9GB) vs. 20 logs

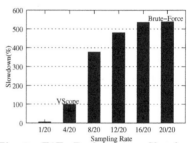

Fig. 8. E2E Performance Slowdown (i.e. E2E latency increase) % w.r.t Sampling Rate (# of sampled region servers / total # of region servers)

(4.1GB) by the brute-force approach. Note that, as shown in Figure 8, simulta-neously logging on multiple region servers has a non-linear effect upon system performance. Simultaneous logging on only 4 servers (with VScope) slows the overall system down by 99.3%, but logging on all servers (brute-force) slows it by 538.9%. Compromise approaches like random sampling might log on more than one, but fewer than the total number of candidate region servers, hoping to trade off perturbation with 'time-to-problem-discovery'. However, the inher-ent randomness makes their performance nondeterministic. In contrast, VScope rationally narrows the set of possible bad region servers, thus improving the ex-pected perturbation, log data sizes, and time to resolution in both average and worst cases.

These results validate the importance of VScope's 'guided' operation that explicitly identifies the nodes on which troubleshooting should focus, in contrast to methods that use sampling without application knowledge or that employ non-scalable exhaustive solutions. They also demonstrate VScope's ability to assist with cross-tier troubleshooting. We note that, for sake of simplicity, this use case assumes the root cause to be within the *region servers*. This assumption can be removed, of course, and in that case, operators can apply further analysis as shown in Figure 7 by iteratively using VScope operations.

4.2   Finding a 'Naughty' VM

Previous research has shown the potential for running real-time application in virtualized settings [22]. However, VMs' resource contention on I/O devices can degrade the end-to-end performance of the application. A typical scenario is that some 'naughty' VM excessively uses a physical NIC shared by other VMs on the same physical host, thereby affecting the performance of the real-time VMs. Potential 'naughty' VMs could be those that run MapReduce *reducers* and exchange voluminous data with a number of other nodes (e.g. *mappers*), or those running HDFS *datanodes* and replicating large files. Contention could also stem from management operations like VM migration and patch maintenance [32].

There are remedies for contention issues like those above. They include migrating the 'naughty' VMs and/or changing network scheduling. VM migration can involve long delays, and changes to VMs' network scheduling may involve kernel reboots that are unsuitable for responsive management. The solution with which we experiment performs traffic shaping for the 'naughty' VM on-the-fly, in the hypervisor, without involving guest VMs. To do so, however, support is needed to first locate the troublesome VM. VScope running in the Dom0s of our virtualized infrastructure provides such support. Specifically, VScope deploys *VNodes* in each host's Dom0, using the virtualization graph in Table 7 to track mappings between VMs and hypervisors.

We emulate the 'naughty' VM issue by deploying a VM with a Hadoop *datanode* and *tasktracker*, on the host where a 'good' VM is running one of the 200 Flume *agents*. This scenario is chosen to emulate co-running a real-time web log analysis application with a batch system using Hadoop for long term analysis on the data generated

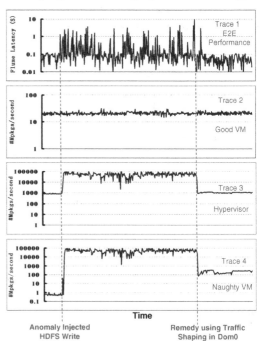

Fig. 9. Using VScope to Find a 'Naughty' VM

by the real-time application. In this case, a problem is created by starting a HDFS benchmarking job called 'TestDFSIO write', which generates 120 2GB files with 4 replicas for each file in HDFS. This 'naughty VM' generates 3 files (we have 40 *slaves* in the Hadoop configuration. Every *slave* carries out 3 map tasks, each of which writes a 2G file to HDFS, and replicates them via the network. VScope is used to find that naughty VM, so that its communications can be regularized via Dom0 traffic shaping.

The monitoring traces in Figure 9 demonstrate VScope's troubleshooting process. Trace 1 presents the latency data generated by the *Watch* operation. Latency rises after the anomaly is injected. Using 1 second as the threshold for an end-to-end performance violation, after 20 violations are observed within 5 minutes, the *Watch* operation reports an anomaly and its location, i.e., the 'good' VM. After the anomaly is reported, troubleshooting starts for the VM by querying basic VM level metrics, including the *number of packages per second* represented by Trace 2^4, where we find that metrics in the VM do not show abnormal behavior. In response, we use the *Scope* operation to find which physical machine is hosting the VM and then *Query* its aggregate packet rate. With these guided actions, Trace 3 shows that the shared NIC is exchanging a large number of packets, in contradiction to the low packet rate in the 'good' VM. The next step is to further *Scope* the virtualization graph to find the other VMs running on the same physical host and then *Query* the network metrics of their VIFs[5]. The 'naughty' VM is easily found, because its respective VIF consumes the majority of the packets for the physical NIC, as shown in Figure 9:Trace 4. The correctness of the diagnosis obtained via VScope is demonstrated by applying traffic shaping in Dom0, which involves using TC to throttle the bandwidth of the 'naughty' VM. It is apparent that this action causes the end-to-end latency of the good VM to return to normal (see Trace 1). In Trace 3, the hypervisor packet rate goes down, and in Trace 4 the network consumption of the 'naughty' VM also sinks, as expected, but it still has its share of network bandwidth.

5   Related Work

Aggregation systems like SDIMS[39] and Moara[20] are most related to VScope in terms of flexibility. SDIMS provides a flexible API to control the propagation of reads and writes to accommodate different applications and their data attributes. Moara queries sub-groups of machines rather than the entire system. In both systems, flexibility is based on dynamic aggregation trees using DHTs (Distributed Hash Tables). VScope's approach differs in several ways. First, VScope can control which nodes and what metrics to analyze; neither SDIMs nor Moara provides this level of granularity. SDIMS only controls the level of propagation along the tree, and Moara chooses groups based on attributes in the query (e.g., CPU utilization). Second, the analysis functions in SDIMS

---

[4] We only show NIC-related metrics for succinctness.

[5] A VIF is the logical network interface in Dom0 accepting the packets for one VM and in our configuration, each VM has a unique VIF.

and Moara are limited to aggregation functions, while arbitrary functions can be used with VScope, including those performing 'in transit' analysis. Third, like other monitoring or aggregation systems, including Ganglia[26], Astrolabe[33], and Nagios[27], SDIMS and Moara focus on monitoring the summary of system state, while VScope's can also be used for in-depth troubleshooting, including debugging and tracing, supported by basic metric aggregation like that performed in the *Watch* operation.

GWP[30], Dapper[31], Fay[14], Chopstix[7] are distributed tracing systems for large scale data centers. VScope is similar in that it can monitor and analyze in-depth system or application behaviors, but it differs as follows. First, instead of using statistical (Fay and Chopstix leverage *sketch*, a probabilistic data structure for metric collection) or random/aggressive sampling (as used in GWP and Dapper), VScope can look at any set of nodes, making it possible to implement a wide range of tracing strategies (including sampling) through its guidance mechanism. Second, those tracing systems use off-line analysis, while VScope can analyze data on-line and in memory, to meet the latency restriction for troubleshooting real-time applications.

HiTune[12] and G^2[17] share similarity with VScope in that they are general systems for troubleshooting 'big-data' applications. HiTune extracts the dataflows of applications, using Chukwa for data collection and Hadoop for dataflow analysis. G^2 is a graph processing system that uses code instrumentation to extract runtime information as a graph and a distributed batch processing engine for processing the queries on the graph. VScope differs in its focus on on-line troubleshooting, whereas HiTune and G^2 are mainly for off-line problem diagnosis and profiling. Further, HiTune and G^2 are concerned with analyzing within a single application tier, while VScope troubleshoots across multiple application tiers. Other troubleshooting algorithms and systems, such as Pinpoint[10], Project5[4], and E2EProf[3], target traditional web applications while VScope focuses on real-time data-intensive applications.

6   Conclusions

VScope is a flexible, agile monitoring and analysis system for troubleshooting real-time multi-tier applications. Its dynamically created DPG processing overlays combine the capture of monitoring metrics with their on-line processing, (i) for responsive, low overhead problem detection and tracking, and (ii) to guide heavier weight diagnosis entailing detailed querying of potential problem sources. With 'guidance' reducing the costs of diagnosis, VScope can operate efficiently at the scales of typical data center applications and at the speeds commensurate with those applications' timescales of problem development. The paper provides evidence of this fact with a real-time, multi-tier web log analysis application.

Our ongoing work is further developing VScope's notion of guided operation, one idea being to automatically generate certain sequences of guidance actions from the previous manual actions taken by operators. We will also investigate other guidance options. To extend scalability to the 10,000+ machines of today's large scale data center applications run by web companies like Google or

Amazon, it may also be useful to pre-position DPGs into potentially critical subsystems and/or reconfigure existing DPGs, instead of deploying new ones when investigating problems via detailed queries.

References

1. The evpath library, http://www.cc.gatech.edu/systems/projects/EVPath
2. Abadi, D., Carney, D., Çetintemel, U., Cherniack, M., Convey, C., Lee, S., Stonebraker, M., Tatbul, N., Zdonik, S.: Aurora: a new model and architecture for data stream management. The VLDB Journal 12(2), 120–139 (2003)
3. Agarwala, S., Alegre, F., Schwan, K., Mehalingham, J.: E2eprof: Automated end-to-end performance management for enterprise systems. In: Proceedings of the 37th Annual IEEE/IFIP International Conference on Dependable Systems and Networks, DSN 2007, pp. 749–758. IEEE, Washington, DC (2007)
4. Aguilera, M.K., Mogul, J.C., Wiener, J.L., Reynolds, P., Muthitacharoen, A.: Performance debugging for distributed systems of black boxes. In: Proceedings of the 19th ACM symposium on Operating systems principles, SOSP 2003 (2003)
5. Apache. Cloudera flume, http://archive.cloudera.com/cdh/3/flume/
6. Apache. Hbase log, http://hbase.apache.org/book/trouble.log.html
7. Bhatia, S., Kumar, A., Fiuczynski, M.E., Peterson, L.: Lightweight, high-resolution monitoring for troubleshooting production systems. In: Proceedings of the 8th USENIX Conference on Operating Systems Design and Implementation, OSDI 2008, pp. 103–116. USENIX Association, Berkeley (2008)
8. Bodik, P., Goldszmidt, M., Fox, A., Woodard, D.B., Andersen, H.: Fingerprinting the datacenter: automated classification of performance crises. In: Proceedings of the 5th European Conference on Computer Systems, EuroSys 2010, pp. 111–124. ACM, New York (2010)
9. Candea, G., Kawamoto, S., Fujiki, Y., Friedman, G., Fox, A.: Microreboot - a technique for cheap recovery. In: Proceedings of the 6th Conference on Symposium on Opearting Systems Design & Implementation, OSDI 2004 (2004)
10. Chen, M.Y., Kiciman, E., Fratkin, E., Fox, A., Brewer, E.: Pinpoint: Problem determination in large, dynamic internet services. In: Proceedings of the 2002 International Conference on Dependable Systems and Networks, DSN 2002, pp. 595–604. IEEE Computer Society Press, Washington, DC (2002)
11. Condie, T., Conway, N., Alvaro, P., Hellerstein, J.M., Elmeleegy, K., Sears, R.: Mapreduce online. In: Proceedings of the 7th USENIX Conference on Networked Systems Design and Implementation, NSDI 2010 (2010)
12. Dai, J., Huang, J., Huang, S., Huang, B., Liu, Y.: Hitune: dataflow-based performance analysis for big data cloud. In: Proceedings of the 2011 USENIX Conference on USENIX Annual Technical Conference, USENIXATC 2011 (2011)
13. De Hoon, M., Imoto, S., Nolan, J., Miyano, S.: Open source clustering software. Bioinformatics 20(9), 1453–1454 (2004)
14. Erlingsson, U., Peinado, M., Peter, S., Budiu, M.: Fay: extensible distributed tracing from kernels to clusters. In: Proceedings of the Twenty-Third ACM Symposium on Operating Systems Principles, SOSP 2011, pp. 311–326 (2011)
15. Facebook. Scribe, https://github.com/facebook/scribe/wiki
16. Gedik, B., Andrade, H., Wu, K.-L., Yu, P.S., Doo, M.: Spade: the system s declarative stream processing engine. In: Proceedings of the 2008 ACM SIGMOD International Conference on Management of Data, SIGMOD 2008, pp. 1123–1134 (2008)

17. Guo, Z., Zhou, D., Lin, H., Yang, M., Long, F., Deng, C., Liu, C., Zhou, L.: g^2: a graph processing system for diagnosing distributed systems. In: Proceedings of the 2011 USENIX Annual Technical Conference, USENIXATC 2011 (2011)
18. Hewlett-Packard. Worldcup98 logs, http://ita.ee.lbl.gov/
19. Hu, L., Schwan, K., Gulati, A., Zhang, J., Wang, C.: Net-cohort: Detecting and managing vm ensembles in virtualized data centers. In: Proceedings of the 9th ACM International Conference on Autonomic Computing, ICAC 2012 (2012)
20. Ko, S.Y., Yalagandula, P., Gupta, I., Talwar, V., Milojicic, D., Iyer, S.: Moara: Flexible and scalable group-based querying system. In: Issarny, V., Schantz, R. (eds.) Middleware 2008. LNCS, vol. 5346, pp. 408–428. Springer, Heidelberg (2008)
21. Kumar, S., Talwar, V., Kumar, V., Ranganathan, P., Schwan, K.: vmanage: loosely coupled platform and virtualization management in data centers. In: Proceedings of the 6th International Conference on Autonomic Computing, ICAC 2009, pp. 127–136. ACM, New York (2009)
22. Lee, M., Krishnakumar, A.S., Krishnan, P., Singh, N., Yajnik, S.: Supporting soft real-time tasks in the xen hypervisor. In: Proceedings of the 6th ACM SIG-PLAN/SIGOPS International Conference on Virtual Execution Environments, VEE 2010, pp. 97–108. ACM, New York (2010)
23. LinkedIn. Kafka, http://sna-projects.com/kafka/design.php
24. Mansour, M.S., Schwan, K.: I-RMI: Performance Isolation in Information Flow Applications. In: Alonso, G. (ed.) Middleware 2005. LNCS, vol. 3790, pp. 375–389. Springer, Heidelberg (2005)
25. Marz, N.: Twitter's storm, https://github.com/nathanmarz/storm
26. Massie, M.L., Chun, B.N., Culler, D.E.: The ganglia distributed monitoring system: Design, implementation and experience. Parallel Computing (2003)
27. L. Nagios Enterprises. Nagios, http://www.nagios.org/documentation.
28. Neumeyer, L., Robbins, B., Nair, A., Kesari, A.: S4: Distributed stream computing platform. In: IEEE International Conference on Data Mining Workshops, ICDMW 2010, pp. 170–177 (December 2010)
29. Rabkin, A., Katz, R.: Chukwa: a system for reliable large-scale log collection. In: Proceedings of the 24th International Conference on Large Installation System Administration, LISA 2010, Berkeley, CA, USA, pp. 1–15 (2010)
30. Ren, G., Tune, E., Moseley, T., Shi, Y., Rus, S., Hundt, R.: Google-wide profiling: A continuous profiling infrastructure for data centers. In: Micro. IEEE (2010)
31. Sigelman, B.H., Barroso, L.A., Burrows, M., Stephenson, P., Plakal, M., Beaver, D., Jaspan, S., Shanbhag, C.: Dapper, a large-scale distributed systems tracing infrastructure. Technical Report dapper-2010-1, Google (April 2010)
32. Soundararajan, V., Anderson, J.M.: The impact of management operations on the virtualized datacenter. In: Proceedings of the 37th Annual International Symposium on Computer Architecture, ISCA 2010, pp. 326–337 (2010)
33. Van Renesse, R., Birman, K.P., Vogels, W.: Astrolabe: A robust and scalable technology for distributed system monitoring, management, and data mining. ACM Trans. Comput. Syst. 21, 164–206 (2003)
34. Viswanathan, K., Choudur, L., Talwar, V., Wang, C., MacDonald, G., Satterfield, W.: Ranking anomalies in data centers. In: The 13th IEEE/IFIP Network Operations and Management Symposium, NOMS 2012, pp. 79–87 (2012)
35. Wang, C.: Ebat: online methods for detecting utility cloud anomalies. In: Proceedings of the 6th Middleware Doctoral Symposium, MDS 2009 (2009)

36. Wang, C., Schwan, K., Talwar, V., Eisenhauer, G., Hu, L., Wolf, M.: A flexible architecture integrating monitoring and analytics for managing large-scale data centers. In: Proceedings of the 8th ACM International Conference on Autonomic Computing, ICAC 2011, pp. 141–150. ACM, New York (2011)
37. Wang, C., Talwar, V., Schwan, K., Ranganathan, P.: Online detection of utility cloud anomalies using metric distributions. In: The 12th IEEE/IFIP Network Operations and Management Symposium, NOMS 2010, pp. 96–103 (2010)
38. Wang, C., Viswanathan, K., Choudur, L., Talwar, V., Satterfield, W., Schwan, K.: Statistical techniques for online anomaly detection in data centers. In: The 12th IFIP/IEEE International Symposium on Integrated Network Management, IM 2011, pp. 385–392 (2011)
39. Yalagandula, P., Dahlin, M.: A scalable distributed information management system. In: Proceedings of the 2004 Conference on Applications, Technologies, Architectures, and Protocols for Computer Communications, SIGCOMM 2004, pp. 379–390. ACM, New York (2004)

SOFTScale: Stealing Opportunistically for Transient Scaling

Anshul Gandhi[1], Timothy Zhu[1], Mor Harchol-Balter[1], and Michael A. Kozuch[2]

[1] Carnegie Mellon University
[2] Intel Labs

Abstract. Dynamic capacity provisioning is a well studied approach to handling *gradual* changes in data center load. However, *abrupt* spikes in load are still problematic in that the work in the system rises very quickly during the setup time needed to turn on additional capacity. Performance can be severely affected even if it takes only 5 seconds to bring additional capacity online.

In this paper, we propose SOFTScale, an approach to handling load spikes in multi-tier data centers without having to over-provision resources. SOFTScale works by opportunistically stealing resources from other tiers to alleviate the bottleneck tier, even when the tiers are carefully provisioned at capacity. SOFTScale is especially useful during the transient overload periods when additional capacity is being brought online.

Via implementation on a 28-server multi-tier testbed, we investigate a range of possible load spikes, including an artificial doubling or tripling of load, as well as large spikes in real traces. We find that SOFTScale can meet our stringent 95th percentile response time Service Level Agreement goal of 500ms without using any additional resources even under some extreme load spikes that would normally cause the system (without SOFTScale) to exhibit response times as high as 96 seconds.

1 Introduction

Data centers play an important role in today's IT infrastructure. Government organizations, hospitals, financial trading firms, and major IT companies, such as Google, Facebook and Amazon, all rely on data centers for their daily business activities. A primary goal for data center operators is to provide good response times to users; these response time targets typically translate to some response time Service Level Agreements (SLAs). A secondary goal is to reduce operational costs by exploiting the variability in user demand. By scaling capacity to match current demand, operators can either: (i) reduce power consumption by turning off unneeded servers, or (ii) save on rental costs by releasing unneeded virtual machines, or (iii) get additional work done by repurposing unneeded servers for other tasks.

Data center services today are often organized as multiple tiers. Typically, one of these tiers is an *application tier* that processes requests, and another tier is the *data tier* that is responsible for efficiently delivering data back to the application tier. While it is possible to physically collocate the application tier and the data tier on the same servers, dividing the architecture into physically different

P. Narasimhan and P. Triantafillou (Eds.): Middleware 2012, LNCS 7662, pp. 142–163, 2012.

tiers is preferable because it makes it easier to scale and manage the individual tiers [1–3]. The data tier is stateful, and is almost never turned off [4, 5], even if there is a significant drop in load [6]. The application tier, on the other hand, is usually stateless and can be dynamically scaled using existing reactive [7–9], predictive [10, 11] or mixed [3, 12, 13] approaches, *provided that the load does not change too abruptly.*

Unfortunately, abrupt changes in load, or load spikes, are all too common in today's data centers. Important events, such as the September 11 attacks [14, 15], earthquakes or other natural disasters [16], slashdot effects [17], Black Friday shopping [18], or sporting events, such as the Super Bowl [19] or the Soccer World Cup [20], are common causes of load spikes for website traffic. Service outages [21] or server failures [22] can also result in abrupt changes in load caused by a sharp drop in capacity. While some of the above events are predictable, most of them *cannot* be predicted in advance.

Abrupt changes in load are especially problematic since adding capacity requires some time, which we call *setup time*, denoted by t_{setup}. Even if we instantaneously detect a spike in load, it will still take the system at least the setup time to add the required capacity. In our lab, the setup time for turning on an additional server is approximately 5 minutes. Likewise, the setup time needed to create virtual machines (VMs) can range anywhere from 30 seconds – 1 minute if the VMs are locally created (based on our measurements using kvm [23]) or 5 – 10 minutes if the VMs are obtained from a cloud computing platform (see, for example, [24]). All these numbers are extremely high, and can result in long periods where the SLA is violated.

Throughout the paper, we focus on the performance of the system during the setup time following a load spike. Since no additional capacity can be added during the setup time, the system has a fixed number of servers online, and we refer to such a system as the **baseline**. A typical SLA requires that the 95th percentile of response time, denoted by T_{95}, stay below 500ms[1]. In this paper, we consider the more difficult goal of meeting the T_{95} requirements during the setup time (i.e., after the onset of the spike, and before additional servers can be brought online). This is equivalent to saying that *no more than 5% of all requests that arrive during the setup time are allowed to exceed the 500ms response time.* In addition to the T_{95} (which measures over the entire setup time), in some plots, we also show the "instantaneous T_{95}", which is the 95th percentile of response times collected every second.

Consider a system which has the appropriate number of application servers turned on to ensure that the 95th percentile of response times stays below 500ms at the current load of 15% of peak load. Here, peak load refers to the maximum load that our system can handle (see Section 2 for details of our experimental testbed). Now, imagine that the load suddenly increases to 30%. The time needed to turn on the necessary additional servers is the setup time, say 5 minutes. We say that our system can "handle" a load jump if $T_{95} \leq 500ms$ during the setup

---

[1] Our choice of SLA is motivated by recent studies [3, 10, 25] which indicate that 95th percentile guarantees of several hundred milliseconds are typical.

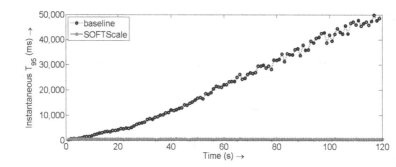

Fig. 1. Using SOFTScale, we can meet response time SLAs even under a 15% to 30% load jump. Note that the y-axis ranges from 0s to 50s.

time. As shown in Figure 1, our baseline system is not able to handle the 15% to 30% load jump. The black dots in Figure 1 show the increase in instantaneous T_{95} during the first two minutes of the setup time under the baseline, where the system is clearly under-provisioned during this time. The data for Figure 1 is generated from experiments running on our implementation testbed using a key-value based workload (see Section 2 for full details of our experimental testbed). As shown in the figure, instantaneous T_{95} increases rapidly over time, reaching 50 seconds after only two minutes. Even if future hardware reduces this setup time to 10 seconds, we see that instantaneous T_{95} can be well over 3 seconds.

In order to avoid setup times, data center operators typically over-provision capacity at all times (since load spikes are often unpredictable). For example, to handle a 15% to 30% load jump, one needs to over-provision resources by a factor of 2. Clearly, such an approach is quite expensive.

We propose SOFTScale, an approach that allows data centers to handle load spikes without having to over-provision resources and incur costs. SOFTScale leverages the fact that the data tier in a multi-tier data center is always left on [4–6]. Thus, during the setup time following a load spike, we can use these "always on" data tier servers to do some of our application work. SOFTScale involves running the application tier software on the data tier servers, where this software is only used during the setup time. We refer to this notion as "stealing" of the data tier capacity. SOFTScale requires no additional resources and can even handle a doubling of load, so long as the final load is not too high. Returning to our example where the load instantaneously doubles from 15% to 30%, we see that SOFTScale, denoted by the flat gray line in Figure 1, allows the instantaneous T_{95} to stay within the 500ms SLA at all times. While stealing from the data tier can increase the latency of data operations, the overall benefit of being able to meet SLAs during setup times makes a compelling case for using SOFTScale. Note that one could theoretically use SOFTScale even after the setup time, however, the (non-zero) increase in latency of data operations as a result of using SOFTScale suggests otherwise. The SOFTScale middleware is depicted in Figure 2, and is described in detail in Section 3.4.

Almost all papers on dynamic capacity management (see, for example, [7–11, 3, 12, 13]) deal with new approaches to scale capacity in response to changes in load. However, such approaches can be ineffective during the setup time, as shown in Figure 1. SOFTScale is a complementary solution that aims to improve performance *specifically during the setup time*, and is meant to be used in conjunction with any existing dynamic capacity management approach.

While the concept behind SOFTScale seems obvious, there are some practical difficulties that may have led researchers to dismiss this idea as "unworkable", hence the lack of publications on this idea. First, there's the question of *when* is SOFTScale useful. Since the data tier is provisioned to handle peak load, invoking SOFTScale when the data tier is already bottlenecked will lead to SLA violations. Second, there's the question of *how much* can we steal from the data tier. If we end up stealing too much from the data tier, the overall system performance might degrade. Third, there's the fear that running application work on the data tier servers will interfere with data delivery work, and can possibly lead to SLA violations. Finally, there's the fear that implementing SOFTScale is too complicated.

In this paper, we demonstrate via implementation that the SOFTScale middleware is a practical solution that allows us to meet response time SLAs even when load increases suddenly by a factor of 2, provided that the load is not too high. In particular, this paper makes the following contributions:

- We determine *load regimes* for which SOFTScale can be successfully applied to handle load spikes (see Section 3.1). This addresses the question of *when* to invoke SOFTScale. Further, identifying load regimes where SOFTScale is *not* beneficial avoids accidental overload of the data tier.
- We determine *how much* data tier capacity can be leveraged by SOFTScale for a given load (see Section 3.2). This enables us to steal the *right amount* of capacity from the data tier without hurting overall response time.
- We show that it is possible to avoid interference between the application work and the data delivery work on the data servers by simply *isolating* these processes to different CPU cores (see Section 3.3).
- We outline the steps needed to implement the SOFTScale middleware (see Section 3.4). In our testbed, we implemented SOFTScale by adding less than a thousand lines of code in the Apache load balancer.
- We present an analytical model that estimates the system performance under SOFTScale (see Section 3.5), which allows us to predict the performance of SOFTScale for a range of multi-tier systems.

We evaluate SOFTScale via implementation on a 28-server multi-tier testbed hosting a key-value based application built along the lines of Facebook or Amazon. Our implementation results show that SOFTScale can be used to handle instantaneous load spikes (see Section 4.1), load spikes seen in real-world traces (see Section 4.2) as well as load spikes caused by server failures (see Section 4.3). To fully investigate the applicability of SOFTScale, we experiment with multiple setup times ranging from 5 minutes (see Section 4) all the way down to 5 seconds (see Section 5). Our results indicate that SOFTScale can provide huge benefits across the entire spectrum of setup times. We also investigate the applicability of SOFTScale in future server architectures which may have a larger number of

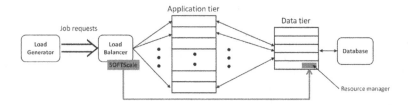

Fig. 2. Our experimental testbed

CPU cores per server. Our results (see Section 6) indicate that SOFTScale will be even more beneficial in such cases.

2   Our Experimental Testbed

Figure 2 illustrates our experimental testbed. The gray components make up SOFTScale, and will be described in detail in Section 3.4. We employ one server as the front-end load generator running httperf [26]. Another server is used as a load balancer running the Apache HTTP Server, which distributes incoming PHP requests to the application servers. Each application server communicates with the data tier, which in our setup comprises memcached servers, to retrieve data required to service the requests. Another server is used to store the entire data set, a billion key-value pairs, on a database.

Throughout this paper we measure power consumption and use that as a proxy for all operational (resource) costs. We monitor the power consumption of individual servers by reading the power values from the power distribution unit. The idle power consumption for our servers is about 140W (with C-states enabled) and the average power consumption for our servers when they are busy or in setup is about 200W. The setup time for our servers is about $t_{setup} = 5$ minutes. However, we also examine the effects of lower t_{setup}[2]. We replicate this effect by not routing requests to a server if it is marked for sleep. When the server is marked for setup, we wait t_{setup} seconds before sending requests to it.

2.1   Workload

We design a key-value workload to model realistic multi-tier applications such as the social networking site, Facebook, or e-commerce sites like Amazon [25]. Each generated request (or job) is a PHP script that runs on the application server. A request begins with the application server requesting a value for a random key from the memcached servers. The memcached servers provide the value, which itself is a collection of new keys. The application server then again requests values for these new keys from the memcached servers. This process can continue

---

[2] Lower setup times could either be a result of using sleep states (which are prevalent in laptops and desktop machines, but are not well supported for server architectures yet), or using virtualization to quickly bring up virtual machines.

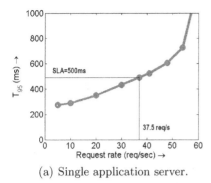
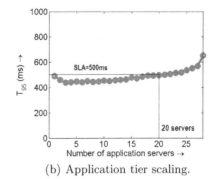

(a) Single application server.   (b) Application tier scaling.

Fig. 3. Figure (a) shows that a single application server can handle 37.5 req/s per server. Figure (b) shows that once we have more than 20 application servers, they can no longer handle 37.5 req/s per server because the memcached tier becomes the bottleneck.

iteratively. In our experiments, we set the number of iterations to correspond to an average of roughly 2,200 key-value requests per job, which translates to a mean service time of approximately 200 ms, assuming no resource contention. The job size distribution is highly variable, with the largest job requiring roughly 20 times as many key-value requests as the smallest job.

In this paper, we use the Zipf [27] distribution to model the popularity of the initial random key request. To minimize the effects of misses in the memcached layer (which could result in an unpredictable fraction of the requests violating the response time SLA), we tune the parameters of the Zipf distribution so that only a negligible fraction of requests miss in the memcached layer.

2.2   Provisioning

In order to demonstrate the effectiveness of SOFTScale, we tune our implementation testbed to have no spare capacity at the memcached tier at peak load. Our memcached tier comprises 5 servers, each with a 6-core Intel Xeon X5650 processor and 48GB of memory. However, we offline two cores[3] per server to be consistent with the specifications that were published by Facebook [28], leaving us with 4-core memcached servers. We now determine how many application servers we need to fully saturate the memcached tier.

Each of our application servers is a powerful 8-core (dual-socket) Intel Xeon E5520 processor-based server. We run an experiment where we have one application server and all five memcached servers, and we flood the system. We find that the application server can handle at most 37.5 req/s without violating the SLA, as shown in Figure 3(a).

---

[3] Observe that weakening the memcached servers greatly hurts SOFTScale in that there is less capacity to steal, but we do this purposely to create a fully saturated memcached tier.

We now examine how well the system scales as we add more application servers. Ideally, if we have x application servers, the system should be able to handle a maximum request rate of at least $37.5 \times x$ req/s without violating the 500ms SLA. Figure 3(b) shows our scaling results, where we vary the number application servers from 1 to 28, and use a request rate of 37.5 req/s times the number of application servers. We see that the system scales perfectly up to 20 application servers. Once we have more than 20 application servers, we see that they can no longer handle 37.5 req/s per server. This is because at this *peak load*, which corresponds to $37.5 \times 20 = 750$ req/s, the memcached tier starts becoming a bottleneck. We validate our claim by ensuring that the other components in the system, namely the load generator, the load balancer, and the application servers, are not a bottleneck. Further, by monitoring the network bandwidth, we ensure that it is not a bottleneck. With this ratio of 20 application servers to 5 memcached servers, we ensure that the memcached tier is saturated. Thus, at least 5 memcached servers are needed to handle peak load (using more than 5 memcached servers only improves the performance of SOFTScale). This 4:1 ratio of application servers to memcached servers is consistent with Facebook [29].

Based on the above experiments, we conclude that the 5 memcached servers can handle at most 750 job req/s before they become a bottleneck. Thus, in our experiments, we limit our total request rate to 750 req/s, which we also refer to as peak load or 100% load. At peak load, we do not have any spare capacity on the memcached servers. Thus, we cannot "steal" any resources from memcached servers at high load without violating the 500ms SLA.

When running the system, the 5 memcached servers are always kept on. By contrast, the number of application servers needed at any time is $\lceil \frac{r}{37.5} \rceil$, where r is the current request rate into the system. For example, if the current request rate is 15% of the peak (or 112 req/s), we provision $\lceil \frac{112}{37.5} \rceil = 3$ application servers. Now, if the load suddenly doubles from 15% (112 req/s) to 30% (225 req/s), we need 6 application servers in total. Thus, the 3 application servers that are currently on, become the bottleneck.

3   SOFTScale

The key idea behind SOFTScale is to leverage the computational power at the always on data tier servers to do some of our application work during the setup time while additional application tier capacity is being brought online. The motivation behind this idea is that, while our memcached servers are provisioned to have exactly the right amount of resources at high load (for our system, peak load is 750 req/s), there are extra resources available at low load. Thus, when the system load is low, we should be able to "steal" resources from the memcached servers to offset some of the workload at the bottlenecked application servers.

SOFTScale works by enhancing the Apache load balancer to route some of the application requests to the memcached servers during load spikes. Note that the software needed to process the application work will first have to be installed on the data tier servers. For our experimental testbed, this only involved installing

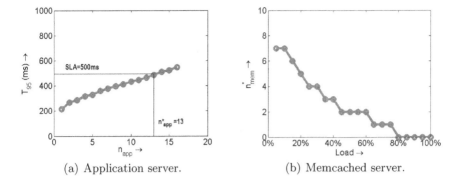

(a) Application server.   (b) Memcached server.

Fig. 4. Figure (a) shows that we should invoke SOFTScale whenever the number of requests at the application server exceeds 13. Figure (b) shows n^*_{mem}, the optimal number of application requests that can be simultaneously handled by a memcached server without violating the 500ms SLA, as a function of the total system load.

the Apache web server with PHP support on the memcached servers. Further, our application software does not consume a lot of memory.

While SOFTScale sounds like a promising idea, exploiting the full potential of SOFTScale is challenging. We now describe SOFTScale by discussing the design decisions behind the algorithm.

3.1   When to Invoke SOFTScale?

SOFTScale must be invoked *as soon as there is a spike in load*. A spike in load could be caused *either* by an increase in request rate *or* by a loss in application tier capacity (server failures or service outages).

If the spike in load is caused by a sudden increase in request rate, then the obvious approach to detect this spike would be to monitor request rate periodically. Unfortunately, request rate is a time-average value, and is thus not instantaneous enough to detect load spikes. We propose monitoring the *number of active requests* at each application server, n_{app}, to detect load spikes. If the system is under-provisioned because the request rate is too high, then n_{app} will immediately increase. Monitoring n_{app} is fairly straightforward, and many modern systems, including the Apache load balancer, already track this value.

Spikes in load can also be caused by a sudden loss in application tier capacity (server failures or service outages). In this case, request rate cannot be used to detect the spike. Fortunately, n_{app} is immediately responsive to server failures, since it increases instantaneously when the application tier capacity drops.

We must invoke SOFTScale when n_{app} becomes so high that the T_{95} SLA is in danger of being violated. In particular, if n^*_{app} is the maximum number of simultaneous requests that a single application server can handle without violating the SLA, then we invoke SOFTScale as soon as n_{app} exceeds n^*_{app} for all application servers. Of course, one can also be conservative and invoke SOFTScale even when n_{app} is below n^*_{app}.

An easy way to determine n^*_{app} is by profiling the application servers. We run a closed-loop experiment with a single application server where we fix the number of simultaneous requests in the system (n_{app}), and monitor T_{95}. Figure 4(a) shows our results. We see that, for our system, $n^*_{app} = 13$. This same technique (profiling the application servers) can be used for determining n^*_{app} for different systems as well. Note that n^*_{app} corresponds to the 37.5 req/s that each application server can handle. Since we provision the application tier so as not to exceed 37.5 req/s at each server, *a reading of $n_{app} > 13$ indicates overload*. Thus, we invoke SOFTScale as soon as the load balancer detects that n_{app} has exceeded 13 for all the application servers.

3.2   How Much Application Work Can Memcached Handle?

Now that we know *when* to invoke SOFTScale (and thus, *when* to attempt to steal resources from the data tier), the next design question is: *how much* can we steal? The memcached servers are primarily responsible for providing data to the application work. Thus, we cannot overload memcached servers with too much application work. Figure 4(b) shows n^*_{mem}, the maximum number of application requests that a memcached server can handle simultaneously without violating the SLA. We see that n^*_{mem} depends on the overall system load, as should be expected. When the system load is low ($< 20\%$), each memcached server can handle almost half the work capacity of an application server, whereas when the load is high ($\geq 80\%$), memcached servers cannot handle any application work. Details on how we determine n^*_{mem} in Figure 4(b) can be found in [30].

3.3   Need for Isolation

While we have successfully overloaded the functionality of the memcached servers, we have not eliminated interference between the memcached work and the application work at the memcached servers. One way of reducing interference is to "isolate" these two processes at the memcached servers, by partitioning the four cores at the memcached server between the memcached work and the application work. We achieve this core isolation by using the `taskset` command in Linux. A logical way of partitioning the cores is in a 2:2 ratio, with 2 cores dedicated to memcached work and 2 cores dedicated to application work. However, we find that the performance of SOFTScale improves greatly if we *dynamically* adjust the partitioning based on total system load. For example, when the system load is extremely low, we can get away with restricting memcached to only one core at each memcached server and reserving the remaining three cores for application work in case of a load spike (1:3 partitioning). On the other hand, when the system load is very high, we need all four cores for memcached work (4:0 partitioning). Figure 5 shows n^*_{mem} for the memcached servers with dynamic isolation and without any isolation (same as Figure 4(b)). Note the four discrete horizontal levels for dynamic isolation. These refer to a 4-core partitioning between the memcached work and application work in the ratio of 1:3, 2:2, 3:1

and 4:0 respectively. We see that dynamic isolation greatly enhances the capacity of memcached servers to handle application work. Henceforth, when we use SOFTScale, it will be implied that we are referring to SOFTScale with dynamic isolation. Details on how we obtain Figure 5 can be found in [30].

3.4   The SOFTScale Algorithm

We are now ready to describe our SOFTScale algorithm, which is implemented in the load balancer, and is depicted in gray in Figure 2. We send application requests to the application servers, via Join-the-Shortest-Queue routing, as long as any server has less than n^*_{app} simultaneous requests. If all of the application servers have at least n^*_{app} requests, SOFTScale is invoked. SOFTScale sends any additional requests above the n^*_{app} requests to the memcached servers. The resource manager (see Figure 2) at each memcached server is responsible for invoking the software that will serve the incoming application requests. In our case, this software is the Apache web server with PHP support, which is invoked upon boot. The resource manager also isolates the application work from the memcached work. We limit the number of requests that we send to each memcached server to n^*_{mem}. Recall that n^*_{mem}, which is the optimal number of simultaneous application requests that a memcached server can handle, is not a constant, and in fact varies with load as specified in Section 3.3 and Figure 5. Note that $n^*_{mem} = 0$ if load is greater than or equal to 80% of peak load. Thus, SOFTScale will not send application requests to the memcached servers if load is high. Once we have n^*_{mem} requests at all memcached servers, then we load balance additional requests among the application servers.

3.5   An Analytical Model for Estimating SOFTScale's Performance

We now present a simple analytical model that allows us to estimate the range of load jumps that SOFTScale can handle for a given multi-tier system. Let k_{app} and k_{mem} denote the total number of application servers and memcached servers in the system, respectively. If the current system load is x% of the peak load, where $0 \leq x \leq 100$, then the number of application servers on is roughly $k_{app} \cdot \frac{x}{100}$, assuming the application tier is dynamically scaled. Suppose that each memcached server can handle n^*_{mem} simultaneous application requests at load x%. Then, the total number of application requests that the memcached tier can handle is $k_{mem} \cdot n^*_{mem}$. Note that the number of simultaneous requests that the system can handle without SOFTScale at load x% is $k_{app} \cdot \frac{x}{100} \cdot n^*_{app}$, where n^*_{app} is the number of simultaneous requests than an application server can handle. Thus, at x% load, the fraction of additional load that the system can handle with SOFTScale is:

$$\text{Fraction of additional load that SOFTScale can handle} \approx \frac{k_{mem} \cdot n^*_{mem}}{k_{app} \cdot \frac{x}{100} \cdot n^*_{app}} \quad (1)$$

Equation (1) suggests that the additional load that SOFTScale can handle goes down as the system load (x%) increases, as expected (note that n^*_{mem} also drops with system load, as shown in Figure 5). As we will show in Sections 4.1 and 6, Equation (1) matches our experimental results for SOFTScale's performance. Thus, we can use Equation (1) to predict SOFTScale's performance for systems whose k_{app}, k_{mem}, n_{app}^* or n_{mem}^* values are different from ours.

4   Results

We now evaluate the performance of SOFTScale for a variety of load spikes. We start in Section 4.1, where we consider a range of *instantaneous* load jumps and characterize the space of jumps that SOFTScale can handle. Then, in Section 4.2, we examine the performance of SOFTScale under real-world load spikes. Finally, in Section 4.3, we examine the performance of SOFTScale for load spikes that are caused by service outages or server failures. For all the experiments in this section, we consider $t_{setup} = 5$ minutes, which is the setup time for our servers. Later, in Section 5, we examine SOFTScale under lower setup times.

4.1   Characterizing the Range of Load Jumps that SOFTScale Can Handle

In this section, we consider *instantaneous* jumps in load, as shown in Figure 6, and examine the system *only during the setup time*. We assume the system is properly provisioned for the initial load, and thus, is *under-provisioned* after the load jump, during the setup time. Under SOFTScale, although the application tier is under-provisioned during the setup time, we can use the memcached tier to compensate. By contrast, under the "baseline" architecture, we are limited to the capacity of the under-provisioned application tier. We compare SOFTScale with the "baseline" architecture by examining the following metrics: T_{95}, the 95th percentile of response times during the 5 minute setup time, and P_{avg}, the average power consumed by the application servers and the memcached servers during the setup time. Note that P_{avg} is proportional to the amount of resources being used, and can thus be thought of as a proxy for operational costs. For a given load jump, if the system has $T_{95} \leq 500ms$, we say that it can "handle" the load jump.

   Figure 7(a) shows the effect of SOFTScale on T_{95} for specific load jumps. We choose these specific load jumps since they correspond to the maximum jump that SOFTScale can handle at each of the initial loads. For example, if the initial load is 10% of the peak, then SOFTScale can handle a maximum jump of 10% → 29%, where the load changes instantaneously from an initial load of 10% to a final load of 29%. We see that SOFTScale provides huge benefits in T_{95}, as long as the final load is less than 50%. In particular, the T_{95} under SOFTScale is less than 500ms for the 10% → 29% jump, as compared with 96s under the baseline. Likewise, SOFTScale lowers T_{95} from 64s to less than 500ms for the 20% → 35%, and from 38s to less than 500ms for the 30% → 45% load jump. SOFTScale provides these performance improvements by opportunistically stealing resources from the memcached servers to handle the critical application work.

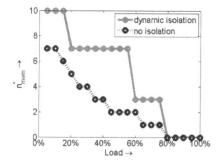

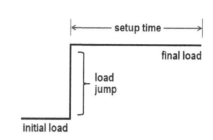

Fig. 5. The figure illustrates enhancement in SOFTScale using dynamic isolation

Fig. 6. The figure illustrates the load jumps we use in our experiments. Note that we only evaluate the system during the setup time.

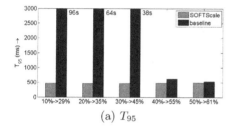

(a) T_{95}

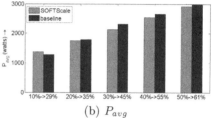

(b) P_{avg}

Fig. 7. SOFTScale meets $T_{95} = 500ms$ SLA without consuming any extra resources for a range of load jumps

When the load jumps from $40\% \rightarrow 55\%$ and $50\% \rightarrow 61\%$, SOFTScale still provides improvement in T_{95}, but these improvements are not as dramatic. This is because the memcached tier is optimally provisioned (see Section 2.2), and thus has very little spare capacity at high loads.

By contrast, the baseline architecture (no SOFTScale) would have to resort to significant over-provisioning to handle the load jumps. For example, for the $10\% \rightarrow 29\%$ jump, the baseline would have to over-provision the application tier by about 190% to meet SLA goals during the setup time. Clearly, this is a huge waste of resources.

Figure 7(b) plots P_{avg}, the average power consumed by the application servers and the memcached servers, for SOFTScale and the baseline. We see that SOFTScale does not consume any additional power as compared to baseline. This is because the total amount of work done by all servers under SOFTScale and under baseline is about the same, for a given load level. Thus, P_{avg}, which is a proxy for operational costs, does not change significantly when using SOFTScale.

Figure 8 shows the full set of results for SOFTScale. In Figure 8(a), the gray region shows the solution space, or regimes, of load jumps that SOFTScale can handle without violating the 500ms SLA, while the black region shows the load jumps that the baseline can handle without violating the SLA. Note that

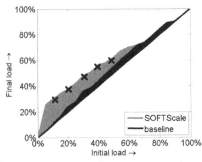 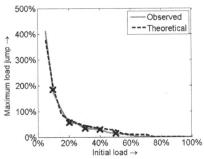

(a) Solution space for $t_{setup} = 5$ minutes.   (b) Improvement for $t_{setup} = 5$ minutes.

Fig. 8. Full range of results for SOFTScale. The crosses in the figures refer to the specific load jump cases shown in Figure 7. Note that SOFTScale's solution space in Figure (a) is a superset of the baseline's solution space.

SOFTScale's solution space is a superset of the baseline's solution space. The crosses in the figure refer to the specific load jump cases we showed in Figure 7, namely the maximum load jumps that SOFTScale can handle for each of the initial loads.

Since the system is optimally provisioned (see Section 2), the baseline cannot handle any significant load jumps. In particular, when the initial load is either too low or too high, the baseline cannot handle any load jumps. However, because of the inherent elasticity in the system, the baseline can handle some small load jumps when the initial load is moderate. For example, when the initial load is 20%, the black region indicates that baseline can handle a maximum jump of $20\% \rightarrow 24\%$.

By contrast, SOFTScale can handle a much larger range of load jumps as compared to the baseline. For example, when the initial load is 20%, the gray region indicates that SOFTScale can handle a maximum jump of $20\% \rightarrow 35\%$.

In Figure 8(b), we plot the maximum load jump (in %) that SOFTScale can handle for each initial load using the solid gray line. Again, the crosses in the figure refer to the specific load jump cases we showed in Figure 7. For example, the first cross from the left corresponds to the $10\% \rightarrow 29\%$ load jump, which amounts to a 190% jump in load. The dashed line shows our estimates for the maximum load jump that SOFTScale can handle, given by Equation (1) (with a few extra % due to the elasticity in the system). We see that our estimates match our implementation results. As expected, Figure 8(b) shows that SOFTScale can handle huge jumps when the initial load is low, but can only handle moderate load jumps when the initial load is high.

4.2   Spikes in Real-World Traces

In addition to evaluating SOFTScale under instantaneous load jumps (as in Section 4.1), we also evaluate SOFTScale under the real-world traces, Pi Day [31],

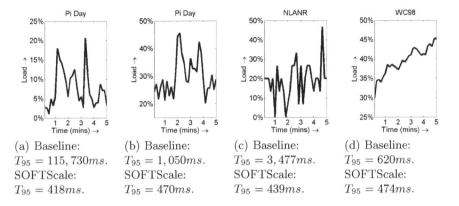

(a) Baseline:
$T_{95} = 115, 730ms$.
SOFTScale:
$T_{95} = 418ms$.

(b) Baseline:
$T_{95} = 1, 050ms$.
SOFTScale:
$T_{95} = 470ms$.

(c) Baseline:
$T_{95} = 3, 477ms$.
SOFTScale:
$T_{95} = 439ms$.

(d) Baseline:
$T_{95} = 620ms$.
SOFTScale:
$T_{95} = 474ms$.

Fig. 9. Real-world trace snippets used for our experiments

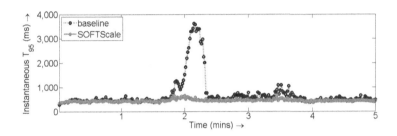

Fig. 10. The plot illustrates the superiority of SOFTScale over the baseline for the Pi Day [31] trace in Figure 9(b)

NLANR [32] and WC98 [20], shown in Figure 9. We re-scale each trace so that the peak load corresponds to 750 req/s, and then consider five minute (t_{setup}) snippets that highlight load spikes. The load numbers in Figure 9 correspond to the post-scaled traces. We assume the system is well provisioned at time $t = 0$, and then examine the system performance for the next five minutes, during which additional capacity is being brought online.

Although the initial load ranges from 5% to 30% across the different traces, SOFTScale achieves a T_{95} of less than 500ms for all cases (see Figures 9(a) to 9(d)). By contrast, the baseline results in a T_{95} of over 115s in Figure 9(a), where the load quadruples from 5% to 20%. In Figure 9(b), where the load roughly doubles from 25% to 46%, the T_{95} under the baseline is just over a second, in contrast to SOFTScale's 470ms. The superiority of SOFTScale over the baseline for the trace in Figure 9(b) is further illustrated in Figure 10, which depicts the instantaneous T_{95} (collected every second) over the trace.

4.3 Spikes Created by Server Faults

Thus far, we considered the case where load spikes are caused by a sudden increase in request rate. However, load spikes can also result because of a sudden

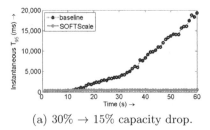
(a) 30% → 15% capacity drop.

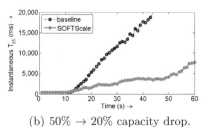
(b) 50% → 20% capacity drop.

Fig. 11. SOFTScale provides significant benefits even when load spikes are caused by a sudden drop in capacity. In the figures above, we drop capacity at the 10s mark.

drop in capacity. Service outages [21] and server failures [22] are common causes for a sudden (and unpredictable) drop in capacity. SOFTScale is useful regardless of the cause of load spikes since SOFTScale is invoked when the number of jobs at a server increases (see Section 3.1). We now illustrate the fault-tolerance benefits of SOFTScale.

Consider a system that is well provisioned to handle 30% initial load. Suppose a failure takes down half of the provisioned capacity, resulting in a system that can now only handle 15% load. We refer to this as a 30% → 15% capacity drop. Figure 11(a) shows our experimental results for instantaneous T_{95} (collected every second) under a 30% → 15% capacity drop, which is triggered at the 10s mark. Apache's load balancer is very quick to recognize that some of the application servers are offline, and thus stops sending additional requests to them. In Figure 11(a), while SOFTScale successfully handles the capacity drop, the baseline completely falls apart. The power consumption for SOFTScale and the baseline are about the same, and are thus omitted due to lack of space.

Figure 11(b) shows our experimental results for instantaneous T_{95} under a very severe 50% → 20% capacity drop, which is produced by taking down 6 of the 10 application servers at the 10s mark. This time, we see that instantaneous T_{95} rises sharply for both SOFTScale and the baseline. However, the rate at which instantaneous T_{95} increases under SOFTScale is significantly lower than that under the baseline. Thus, we conclude that SOFTScale is useful even when load spikes are caused by a sudden drop in capacity.

5   Lower Setup Times

While production servers today are only equipped with "off" states that necessitate a huge setup time (t_{setup} = 5 minutes for our servers), future servers may support sleep states, which can lower setup times considerably. Further, with virtualization, the setup time required to bring up additional capacity (in the form of virtual machines) might also go down. In this section, we analyze SOFTScale for the case of lower setup times by tweaking our experimental testbed as discussed in Section 2. Intuitively, for low setup times, one might ex-

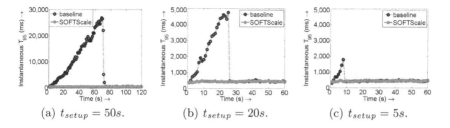

Fig. 12. Effect of t_{setup} on instantaneous T_{95} for a 15% → 30% jump in load

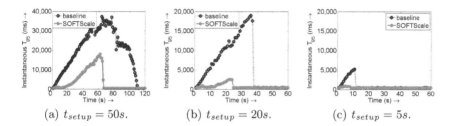

Fig. 13. Effect of t_{setup} on instantaneous T_{95} for a 20% → 50% jump in load

pect that SOFTScale is not needed since instantaneous T_{95} should not rise too much during the setup time. This turns out to be false.

Figure 12 shows our experimental results for instantaneous T_{95} under the 15% → 30% load jump, for a range of t_{setup} values. We change the scale for Figure 12(a) to fully capture the effect of the 50s setup time. Recall from Figure 8(a) that SOFTScale can handle the 15% → 30% load jump, even if $t_{setup} = 5$ minutes. Thus, it is not surprising that SOFTScale can handle the 15% → 30% load jump for $t_{setup} = 50$s, 20s and 5s in Figure 12.

By contrast, the instantaneous T_{95} for the baseline quickly grows and exceeds the 500ms SLA during the entire setup time duration, even for the $t_{setup} = 5$s case. However, the instantaneous T_{95} values for the baseline are not too high under lower setup times. This is because *when the setup time is low, the overload period is very short.* Observe that instantaneous T_{95} does not drop immediately after the setup time because of the backlog created during the setup time.

Figure 13 shows our experimental results for instantaneous T_{95} under the 20% → 50% load jump. Recall from Figure 8(a) that SOFTScale *cannot* handle the 20% → 50% load jump when $t_{setup} = 5$ minutes. In Figure 13, we see that instantaneous T_{95} rises sharply during the setup time for both SOFTScale and the baseline. However, the rate at which instantaneous T_{95} increases under SOFTScale is at most half that under the baseline.

Figure 14 shows the full set of results for SOFTScale for the case of $t_{setup} = 20$s. In Figure 14(a), we show the solution space of load jumps that SOFTScale and the baseline can handle without violating the 500ms T_{95} SLA (over the 20s setup time). The crosses in the figure refer to the specific load jump cases we showed in Figures 12 and 13. We see that SOFTScale can handle a much larger

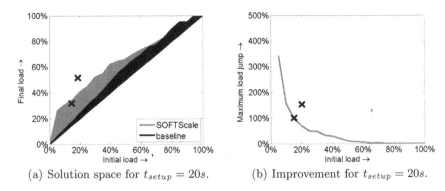

(a) Solution space for $t_{setup} = 20s$.   (b) Improvement for $t_{setup} = 20s$.

Fig. 14. Full range of results for SOFTScale under $t_{setup} = 20s$. The crosses in the figures refer to the specific load jump cases shown in Figures 12 (15% → 30% load jump) and 13 (20% → 50% load jump).

range of load jumps (gray region) as compared to the baseline (black region), just as we observed in Figure 8(a) for $t_{setup} = 5$ minutes. In Figure 14(b), we plot the maximum load jump (in %) that SOFTScale can handle for each initial load. Again, as expected, SOFTScale can handle huge jumps when the initial load is low, but can only handle moderate jumps when the initial load is high.

It is very interesting to note that the performance degradation caused by load spikes for the baseline case does not go away even when the setup time is really low. Thus, *there is a need for SOFTScale even under low setup times*. Comparing Figures 8 and 14, we see that the range of load jumps that the baseline (and SOFTScale) can handle increases only slightly under the much lower setup time of 20s. The reason that this increase is so small is that most of the "damage" to T_{95} has already occurred after only a few seconds.

6   Future Architectures

In our implementation testbed (see Section 2), we use 4-core servers for the memcached tier. In the near future, it is likely that 4-core processors will be replaced by 8 (or more) core processors, even though their memory capacity is unlikely to increase significantly [33]. Thus, we would still need just as many memcached servers. On the other hand, data replication needs may require additional memcached servers. In either case, the memcached tier will now have more spare compute capacity that can be exploited by the application tier via SOFTScale. In this section, we investigate the performance of SOFTScale for the case where we have 8-core memcached servers.

Figure 15 shows n^*_{mem}, the optimal number of application requests that a memcached server can handle simultaneously without violating the 500ms SLA, for 8-core and 4-core memcached servers. We see that using 8-cores allows us to put a lot more application work on the memcached servers. Thus, SOFTScale should be able to handle much higher load jumps with 8-core memcached servers.

Figure 16(a) shows the full set of results for SOFTScale and the baseline, both with 8-core memcached servers, for the case of $t_{setup} = 5$ minutes. We see that SOFTScale with 8-core memcached servers can handle a significantly larger range of load jumps. For example, SOFTScale can handle a $10\% \rightarrow 50\%$ load jump as compared to the maximum jump of $10\% \rightarrow 29\%$ using 4-core memcached servers, as was shown in Figure 8(a). Further, SOFTScale can now handle load jumps even when the load is as high as 80%, since the memcached work requires at most 4 cores at peak load (see Section 2), still leaving 4 cores at each memcached server for application work. We also estimated the maximum load jump that SOFTScale can handle via Equation (1), and found that our estimates match our implementation results. Figure 16(b) shows the full set of results for SOFTScale for the case of $t_{setup} = 20s$. These results are very similar to those in Figure 16(a). Thus, even though there is a cost (monetary cost and increased power consumption) involved in switching to 8-core memcached servers, it might make sense to deploy these servers for the memcached tier to handle severe load spikes using SOFTScale.

7   Prior Work

There is a lot of prior work that deals with dynamic capacity management. These works can be classified into reactive [7–9], predictive [10, 11] and mixed [3, 12, 13] approaches. While these approaches can handle gradual changes in load, they cannot handle abrupt changes, especially load spikes that occur almost instantaneously. This claim was also verified by other authors [34].

There has been some prior work specifically dealing with load spikes [34, 35]. Chandra et al. [34] show that existing dynamic capacity management algorithms are not good at handling flash crowds in an internet data center. In order to handle flash crowds, the authors advocate either having spare servers that are always available (over-provisioning), or finding a way to lower setup times. However, as our work shows (see Figures 12(c) and 13(c)), even a 5s setup time can result in severe SLA violations. Further, by using SOFTScale, we do not have to pay for any additional resources, which is not the case when over-provisioning via spare servers. Lassettre et al. [35] propose a short-term forecasting approach to handle load spikes for a multi-tier system with a setup time of 30s. While [35] is very effective at handling load spikes that gradually build over time, it is not well suited for the instantaneous load spikes we consider in this paper since the forecasting in [35] itself requires at least 10s, and we have shown that even a 5s setup time is detrimental. Observe that SOFTScale is actually complementary to the above approaches, and can be used in conjunction with them.

There has also been recent work looking at data spikes, where a particular web object becomes extremely popular. Data spikes can be handled by caching or replication (see, for example [4]), and are not the focus of our paper.

To handle load spikes for small websites with only static content, a possible solution is to host their content on a cloud computing platform. These platforms are able to handle load spikes by over-provisioning more economically since they

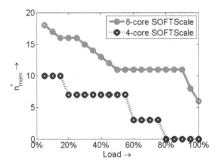

Fig. 15. Using 8-core memcached servers significantly enhances SOFTScale's ability to handle load jumps

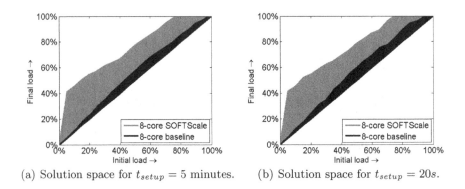

(a) Solution space for $t_{setup} = 5$ minutes. (b) Solution space for $t_{setup} = 20s$.

Fig. 16. Full range of results for SOFTScale with 8-core memcached servers under (a) $t_{setup} = 5$ minutes and (b) $t_{setup} = 20s$. We see that 8-core memcached servers provide huge benefits for SOFTScale regardless of the setup time.

host multiple websites, and load spikes on individual websites are often not correlated (statistical multiplexing) [36]. For multi-tiered cloud computing environments, SOFTScale can be used in conjunction with statistical multiplexing.

Finally, there is also a lot of prior work [37–40] that deals with managing overload conditions by allowing for performance degradation. Some of the popular techniques that have been used to regulate performance degradation include admission control and request prioritization. By contrast, SOFTScale handles load spikes without any performance degradation, provided the load is not high. If the load is high, SOFTScale can be coupled with techniques like those in [37–40] to minimize the damage caused by load spikes.

8   Conclusion

In this paper, we consider load spikes, which are all too common in today's data centers [18, 19, 14, 15, 20–22]. Our results in Figures 12 and 13 show that ignoring load spikes can result in severe SLA violations, even if it takes only 5 seconds of setup time to bring capacity online. The obvious solution of over-provisioning resources is quite expensive since load spikes are often unpredictable.

We propose SOFTScale, an approach to handling load spikes in multi-tier data centers without consuming any extra resources. In multi-tier data centers, the application tier is typically stateless, and can be dynamically provisioned, whereas the data tier is stateful, and is always left on. SOFTScale works by opportunistically stealing resources from the data tier to alleviate the overload at the application tier during the setup time needed to bring additional application tier capacity online. Since tiers in a data center are typically carefully provisioned for peak load, SOFTScale must steal from the data tier without hurting overall performance. SOFTScale does this by first determining how much spare capacity can be stolen from the data tier without violating SLAs at different load levels, and then dynamically isolating the application work and the data delivery work at the data tier to avoid interference.

Our implementation results on a 28-server testbed demonstrate that SOFTScale can handle various load spikes for a range of setup times (see Figures 8 and 14). Specifically, SOFTScale can handle instantaneous load jumps ranging from $5\% \rightarrow 25\%$ to $50\% \rightarrow 61\%$, even when the setup time is 5 minutes. SOFTScale works extremely well for real-world load spikes (see Figure 9), and significantly improves performance (typically a 2X – 100X factor improvement) when compared to the baseline. Even more benefits are possible for future many-core servers (see Figure 16).

While our implementation testbed mimics a web site of the type seen in Facebook or Amazon with an application tier and a memcached tier, we believe SOFTScale will also be applicable when the memcached tier is replaced by any other data tier. Since the data tier is stateful, there will always be a subset of servers that will not be turned off. Thus, SOFTScale can leverage these servers to alleviate the bottleneck at the application tier during load spikes.

References

1. Eckerson, W.W.: Three tier client/server architecture: Achieving scalability, performance, and efficiency in client server applications. Open Information Systems 10 (January 1995)
2. Schussel, G.: Client/server: Past, present and future (September 2006), http://www.dciexpo.com/geos/dbsejava.htm
3. Urgaonkar, B., Chandra, A.: Dynamic provisioning of multi-tier internet applications. In: ICAC 2005, Washington, DC (2005)
4. Trushkowsky, B., Bodík, P., Fox, A., Franklin, M.J., Jordan, M.I., Patterson, D.A.: The SCADS director: scaling a distributed storage system under stringent performance requirements. In: FAST 2011, San Jose, CA, USA (2011)
5. Bryant, R., Tumanov, A., Irzak, O., Scannell, A., Joshi, K., Hiltunen, M., Lagar-Cavilla, A., de Lara, E.: Kaleidoscope: cloud micro-elasticity via VM state coloring. In: EuroSys 2011, Salzburg, Austria (2011)
6. Atikoglu, B., Xu, Y., Frachtenberg, E., Jiang, S., Paleczny, M.: Workload analysis of a large-scale key-value store. In: Sigmetrics 2012, London, UK (2012)

7. Leite, J.C., Kusic, D.M., Mossé, D.: Stochastic approximation control of power and tardiness in a three-tier web-hosting cluster. In: ICAC 2010, Washington, DC, USA (2010)
8. Nathuji, R., Kansal, A., Ghaffarkhah, A.: Q-clouds: Managing performance interference effects for QoS-aware clouds. In: EuroSys 2010, Paris, France (2010)
9. Padala, P., Hou, K.Y., Shin, K.G., Zhu, X., Uysal, M., Wang, Z., Singhal, S., Merchant, A.: Automated control of multiple virtualized resources. In: EuroSys 2009, Nuremberg, Germany (2009)
10. Krioukov, A., Mohan, P., Alspaugh, S., Keys, L., Culler, D., Katz, R.: NapSAC: Design and implementation of a power-proportional web cluster. In: Green Networking 2010, New Delhi, India (2010)
11. Horvath, T., Skadron, K.: Multi-mode energy management for multi-tier server clusters. In: PACT 2008, Toronto, ON, Canada (2008)
12. Gmach, D., Krompass, S., Scholz, A., Wimmer, M., Kemper, A.: Adaptive quality of service management for enterprise services. ACM Trans. Web 2(1), 1–46 (2008)
13. Gandhi, A., Chen, Y., Gmach, D., Arlitt, M., Marwah, M.: Minimizing data center SLA violations and power consumption via hybrid resource provisioning. In: IGCC 2011, Orlando, FL, USA (2011)
14. LeFebvre, W.: CNN.com: Facing A World Crisis. Invited Talk, USENIX ATC (2002)
15. Hu, J., Sandoval, G.: Web acts as hub for info on attacks. CNET news (Septemper 2001)
16. Wald, L.A., Schwarz, S.: The 1999 southern california seismic network bulletin. Seismological Research Letters 71, 401–422 (2000)
17. Adler, S.: The Slashdot Effect: An Analysis of Three Internet Publications, http://ssadler.phy.bnl.gov/adler/SDE/SlashDotEffect.html
18. Constine, J.: Walmart's black friday disaster: Website crippled, violence in stores (November 2011), http://techcrunch.com/2011/11/25/walmart-black-friday
19. Ohlson, K.: Victoria's secret knows ads, not the web. Computer World (February 1999)
20. Arlitt, M., Jin, T.: Workload characterization of the 1998 world cup web site. IEEE Network (1999)
21. Pachal, P.: Amazon apologizes for cloud outage, issues credit to customers. PCMag. (April 2011)
22. Schroeder, B., Pinheiro, E., Weber, W.D.: DRAM errors in the wild: a large-scale field study. In: SIGMETRICS 2009, Seattle, WA, USA (2009)
23. Kivity, A., Kamay, Y., Laor, D., Lublin, U., Liguori, A.: kvm: the Linux virtual machine monitor. In: Linux Symposium 2007, Ottawa, ON, Canada (2007)
24. Amazon Inc.: Amazon Elastic Compute Cloud, http://aws.amazon.com/ec2/
25. DeCandia, G., Hastorun, D., Jampani, M., Kakulapati, G., Lakshman, A., Pilchin, A., Sivasubramanian, S., Vosshall, P., Vogels, W.: Dynamo: Amazon's highly available key-value store. In: SOSP 2007, Stevenson, WA, USA (2007)
26. Mosberger, D., Jin, T.: httperf—A Tool for Measuring Web Server Performance. ACM Sigmetrics: Performance Evaluation Review 26, 31–37 (1998)
27. Newman, M.E.J.: Power laws, Pareto distributions and Zipf's law. Contemporary Physics 46, 323–351 (2005)
28. LaPedus, M.: Facebook Wants New and Cheaper Memories (November 2011), http://semimd.com/blog/2011/11/08/facebook-wants-new-and-cheaper-memories
29. Personal communication with Facebook

30. Gandhi, A., Zhu, T., Harchol-Balter, M., Kozuch, M.: SOFTScale: Stealing Opportunistically For Transient Scaling. Technical Report CMU-CS-12-111. Carnegie Mellon University (2012)
31. Andersen, D.G.: Trace of web site activity on Pi day (3/14/2011) from domains hosted by angio.net. Personal Communication (December 2011)
32. National Laboratory for Applied Network Research. Anonymized access logs, `ftp://ftp.ircache.net/Traces/`
33. Kim, Y., Seshadri, V., Lee, D., Liu, J., Mutlu, O.: A case for exploiting subarray-level parallelism (SALP) in DRAM. In: ISCA 2012, Portland, OR, USA (2012)
34. Chandra, A., Shenoy, P.: Effectiveness of dynamic resource allocation for handling internet flash crowds. Technical Report TR03-37, Department of Computer Science, University of Massachusetts at Amherst (November 2003)
35. Lassettre, E., Coleman, D.W., Diao, Y., Froehlich, S., Hellerstein, J.L., Hsiung, L.S., Mummert, T.W., Raghavachari, M., Parker, G., Russell, L., Surendra, M., Tseng, V., Wadia, N., Ye, P.: Dynamic Surge Protection: An Approach to Handling Unexpected Workload Surges with Resource Actions that Have Lead Times. In: Brunner, M., Keller, A. (eds.) DSOM 2003. LNCS, vol. 2867, pp. 82–92. Springer, Heidelberg (2003)
36. Elson, J., Howell, J.: Handling flash crowds from your garage. In: USENIX ATC 2008, Boston, MA, USA (2008)
37. Urgaonkar, B., Shenoy, P.: Cataclysm: Scalable overload policing for internet applications. Journal of Network and Computer Applications 31(4), 891–920 (2008)
38. Adya, A., Bolosky, W.J., Chaiken, R., Douceur, J.R., Howell, J., Lorch, J.: Load management in a large-scale decentralized file system. MSR-TR 2004-60 (2004)
39. Voigt, T., Tewari, R., Freimuth, D., Mehra, A.: Kernel mechanisms for service differentiation in overloaded web servers. In: USENIX ATC 2001, Boston, MA, USA (2001)
40. Cherkasova, L., Phaal, P.: Session-based admission control: A mechanism for peak load management of commercial web sites. IEEE Trans. Comput. 51 (June 2002)

Taking Garbage Collection Overheads Off the Critical Path in SSDs

Myoungsoo Jung, Ramya Prabhakar, and Mahmut Taylan Kandemir

The Pennsylvania State University

Abstract. Solid state disks (SSDs) have the potential to revolutionize the storage system landscape, mostly due to their good random access performance, compared to hard disks. However, garbage collection (GC) in SSD introduces significant latencies and large performance variations, which renders widespread adoption of SSDs difficult. To address this issue, we present a novel garbage collection strategy, consisting of two components, called *Advanced Garbage Collection* (AGC) and *Delayed Garbage Collection* (DGC), that operate collectively to migrate GC operations from busy periods to idle periods. More specifically, AGC is employed to defer GC operations to idle periods in advance, based on the type of the idle periods and on-demand GC needs, whereas DGC complements AGC by handling the collections that could not be handled by AGC. Our comprehensive experimental analysis reveals that the proposed strategies provide stable SSD performance by significantly reducing GC overheads. Compared to the state-of-the-art GC strategies, P-FTL, L-FTL and H-FTL, our AGC+DGC scheme reduces GC overheads, on average, by about 66.7%, 96.7% and 98.2%, respectively.

1 Introduction

Over the past decade, different computing domains, ranging from high performance computing and enterprise server platforms to embedded systems, are adopting SSDs [1] [2], due to their technical merits such as good random access performance, low power consumption, higher robustness to vibrations and temperature, and higher read/write bandwidth than hard disks [3]. NAND flash capacity is increasing by two to four times every two years [4] and SSD prices are expected to continue to fall to the extent of becoming cheaper than high-speed hard disk [5], which can in turn enable widespread deployment in diverse computing domains.

Modern SSDs internally employ a flash translation layer (FTL), managing two intrinsic properties of NAND flash memory to emulate it as a block device: first, no write is allowed before erasing a block, called the *erase-before-write* property. Second, NAND flash makers adopt a write sequence in a block due to the page-level program disturbance behavior [6] [7], which has a deep relationship with modern NAND flash memory reliability and data integrity. In addition to the erase-before-write property, this *in-order-update* property in a block necessitates *out-of-place updates* for write operations. To enable such out-of-place updates

P. Narasimhan and P. Triantafillou (Eds.): Middleware 2012, LNCS 7662, pp. 164–186, 2012.

in the SSD, FTL remaps the logical addresses that conventional block devices provide to the physical addresses presented by the NAND flash memory. In addition, the FTL employs a garbage collector, which reclaims the invalid pages, incurred during the out-of-place update process. At a high-level, the garbage collector relocates valid pages in certain blocks to new blocks, which are prepared in advance, and erases them in order to make rooms for new writes. This operation is referred to as *garbage collection* (GC).

The biggest problem with existing garbage collectors is that their worst-case latency can be as high as 64~128 times than that of normal write operations [8] [9]. Our own experiments show that GCs introduce numerous blocking I/Os, and once a GC operation begins, the response time of write operations on SSD increases substantially. Further, GC overheads significantly reduce available bandwidth in most recent commercial SSDs. Unfortunately, this interaction between the GC and writes introduces significant performance variations/degradations during I/O, which may not be acceptable in many I/O-intensive computing environments.

Motivated by this, most current FTLs optimize mapping policies to minimize the number of GC invocations and hide their undesired latency. For example, existing buffer management schemes are specialized to reduce the number of writes to NAND flash. Also, some SSDs employ partial block cleaning techniques [10] [11] that attempt to provide stable GC performance by balancing the number pages/blocks between production and consumption of them using an extra non-volatile buffer. However, there is yet another dimension to avoiding GC overheads. Specifically, *the presence of idle I/O times in workloads can be exploited by shifting garbage collections from busy periods to other periods where they can be accommodated with minimum performance penalty.*

In this paper, we propose a novel GC strategy, an approach that removes GC overheads and provides stable I/O performance in SSDs during the I/O congestion periods. Our proposed GC strategy consists of two components, called *Advanced Garbage Collection* (AGC) and *Delayed Garbage Collection* (DGC). More specifically, AGC tries to secure free blocks and remove on-demand GCs from the critical path *in advance*, so that users do not experience GC-induced latencies during the I/O-intensive periods, whereas DGC handles the collections that AGC could not handle, by delaying them to future idle periods. Since our approach mainly reschedules garbage collections, it can work with any existing FTL.

Shifting GC operations however can increase program/erase (PE) cycles, which makes the life time of SSDs shorter. For example, if a garbage collector heedlessly reclaim blocks, which have the potential to be further utilized or used for new writes, it can introduce unnecessary PE cycles in relocating valid pages within them. To prevent this problem, we propose two different implementations for AGC, called *look-ahead garbage collection* and *proactive block compaction*, based on the duration of the idle period under consideration and the style of GC detection. Specifically, the look-ahead GC utilizes short idle periods and reclaims block based on the online information extracted from a device-level queue,

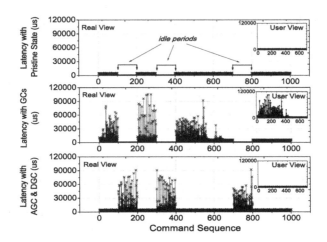

Fig. 1. Overview and comparison of SSD latencies with/without our proposed GC strategies (AGC and DGC), tested by random write pattern with 2048KB request size. Note that AGC and DGC shift GC overheads to idle periods (as shown in the real view), thereby providing stable I/O performance like a pristine state (as shown in the user view).

whereas the proactive block compaction targets long idle periods and perform GCs only related to fully utilized blocks.

As shown in Figure 1, the main **goal** behind our strategies is to perform as many GCs as possible in the *idle periods*. Our **contributions** in this paper can be summarized as follows:

- *Eliminating GC Overheads:* When using our garbage collection strategies, applications do not experience GC overheads. This is because our strategies successfully migrate on-demand GCs from busy periods to idle periods. Experimental results show that our proposed GC strategies result in stable I/O performance under various types of workloads.

- *Avoiding Additional GC Operations:* The proposed schemes (AGC and DGC), when applied together, do not increase the original number of GC operations. They only reschedule the GC operations that would be invoked soon by speculating their GC activities and identifying appropriate idle periods based on their durations (short or long). If the frequency with which idleness occurs is not high enough, then the GC invocations are postponed to future idle periods without affecting latency of I/O operations. As a result, we do not incur any additional GC operations.

- *Compatibility with Underlying FTL Schemes:* Most optimized garbage collectors proposed in the literature need additional non-volatile (NV) blocks on the SSD and/or require customized FTLs for successful execution. In contrast, our proposed schemes do *not* require any extra NV blocks or major modifications to the existing data structures, and can therefore work with diverse FTLs.

To test the effectiveness of our GC schemes, we implemented them in a simulator that models bus-level transactions and collected statistics using a variety of workloads. Our experimental results show that the proposed schemes reduce GC overheads (without causing additional write/erase operations) between 66.7% and 98.2%, in terms of the worst-case response time. Further, our schemes prepare free blocks in advance to help prevent the block thrashing problem. Consequently, they reduce the number of block erase operations by 16.6%, compared to a conventional FTL.

2   Background and Related Work

2.1   Flash Translation Layer

The NAND-based flash consists of physical *blocks*; a physical block is the erase unit and is composed of several *pages*, which are the read/write units in the NAND flash. One of the drawbacks of the NAND flash is that a page needs to be updated in-place within the block. In addition, writes to a formerly written page are not allowed before erasing the entire block corresponding to it. Since a block is much larger than a page and an erase operation is more expensive than a write operation, the NAND flash alone is not sufficient to build an SSD. Therefore, a *Flash Translation Layer* (FTL) is required within the SSD to prepare physical blocks ahead of time. Whenever an SSD receives write requests, it forwards them to a temporal block called an *update block*. The FTL then serves requests by physically (in-place) writing them into a block. This allows logical out-of-order update by mapping addresses between the in-place and out-of-place update sequences.

The FTL also hides the latency of block erase and unnecessary read/write operations in copying valid pages that are live in a block [8] [12]. Similarly, to provide data consistency and coherence between the original block (also called the *data block*) and the update block, the FTL internally maintains mapping information and address translations. In this way, by internally managing the flash specific characteristics, the FTL provides compatibility with commodity storage systems. Typically, based on the number of the data block(s) and update block(s) in a logical block, FTLs are classified into three types. Block-mapping FTL manages a logical block by combining one data and one update block (1:1 mapping). Hybrid mapping FTLs manage a logical block by composing n data block(s) and m update block(s) ($n : m$ mapping). Finally, pure-page mapping FTLs leverage only update blocks for serving I/Os, and can allocate them in any physical page location.

2.2   Garbage Collection

If the FTL does not have enough free pages in its update block, it has to perform GC in an attempt to reclaim available blocks to which write request, can be forwarded. This type of GC is referred to as *update block reclaiming GC*.

Similarly, in cases where the FTL has insufficient free blocks, it should secure free blocks by evicting some other logical blocks, called *free block reclaiming GC*. These processes require migrating all valid pages from the update and original blocks to a new free block (called *page migration*) and erasing these two blocks. Thus, *the GC latencies are typically much larger than that of normal I/O operations*. In addition, the FTL carries out these GC operations during runtime on a need-basis, meaning that the collections are postponed as long as the SSD can accept new data and are only performed when required. The reason why GCs are executed on demand is that a block erase operation, which is part of the garbage collection activity, can significantly affect the SSD's lifetime and reliability [8]. For example, if a garbage collector heedlessly reclaim blocks, which have the potential to be further utilized or used for new writes, it can introduce unnecessary program/erase (P/E) cycles for relocating valid pages within them. Due to this property, GC latencies typically piggyback on ordinary I/O requests, leading potentially to very high I/O latencies. Several FTL based studies [9] [8] attempted to reduce GC overheads and hide their latencies. Other approaches like the real-time GC [10] and the partial block cleaning [11] [13] aimed to provide stable GC performance by balancing the number pages/blocks between the production and consumption of them using an extra non-volatile buffer.

3   Impact of Garbage Collection in Commercial SSDs

To measure the impact of GCs in state-of-the-art SSDs, we evaluated their latencies and bandwidth with/without GCs.[1]

Latency Impact: Figures 2a and 2b plot normal latencies and extra latencies due to GCs, respectively. In this empirical test, we used a 256GB MLC-based SSD which employs two 128MB internal DRAM buffers and measure latencies of individual I/O operations using ULINK's DriveMaster [14]. The DriverMaster is a commercial tool that captures detailed storage-level latencies and tests SSDs in a physical level. We wrote data with 1MB transfer size into the SSD using a random pattern. While a pristine SSD was used for the normal latency test, we later filled the SSD completely and introduced a one hour period before evaluating the GC latencies. As illustrated in Figure 2, GCs introduce numerous blocking I/Os, and once a GC operation begins, the response time for write operations increases substantially. Further, irrespective of the large amount of idleness that we artificially introduced, high latencies of GC are observed from the beginning of the GC latency test.

Bandwidth Impact: From a system designer viewpoint, throughput might be a more important performance metric. In this test, we measured performance with/without GCs of four commercial SSDs (three 64GB, 256GB and 160GB MLC-based SSDs and one 120GB SLC-based SSD) using Intel Iometer [15]. Figures 3a and 3b plot bandwidth with the pristine state and bandwidth with

---

[1] All SSDs we tested (e.g., 64GB, 256GB, 160GB MLC-based SSDs and 120GB SLC-based SSD) were deployed in 2010 ~ 12.

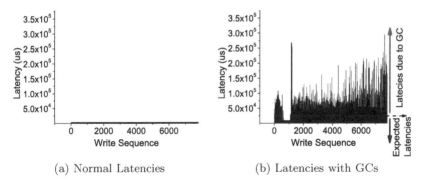

(a) Normal Latencies   (b) Latencies with GCs

Fig. 2. Latency comparison for a random write access pattern with 1MB request size using a real MLC-based SSD

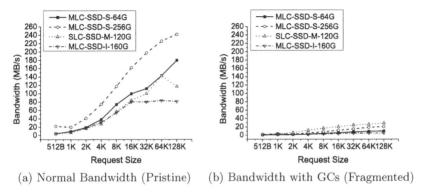

(a) Normal Bandwidth (Pristine)   (b) Bandwidth with GCs (Fragmented)

Fig. 3. System throughput for four state-of-the-art SSDs (different vendors and NAND types). Note that all SSDs tested suffer from significant performance degradation once garbage collections begin.

fragmented state, respectively. To make an SSD fragmented, we first wrote 4KB data in random order and fully utilized its storage space. Similar to the latency impact test, we artificially introduced a one hour idle time before evaluating this bandwidth impact test. As shown in Figure 3, GC overheads significantly reduce available bandwidth in all four commercial SSDs tested, regardless of the idle time introduced.

4   High Level View of GC Scheduling

To avoid performance degradation and variations caused by GCs, we propose novel garbage collection strategies. Unlike previous GC strategies that reduce the number of GC invocations or GC overheads at runtime, our proposed GC strategies fully utilize device-level idle times, which are invisible to the user, to perform GC activities. To efficiently exploit such idle times, we classify them into two groups based on their lengths. Using our idle period classification, we then invoke different types of GCs to ensure that the user does not experience long GC-induced latencies. Our approach allows the other components of FTL to work without any modification, making our approach highly portable.

4.1   Idle Period Classification

Short Idle Periods: Several applications exhibit short idle intervals interleaved with parallel I/O requests in a device-level command queue [16], which allows a storage system to determine actual data transfer times and implement out-of-order execution of I/O commands. To enable this, most host interface protocols bring I/O commands, along with preinformation including request type, addresses and request size, to the storage system before the actual data transfer begins.

To measure how many commands with their preinformation are available at a given time and the duration of idle periods, we executed Intel Iometer workloads [15] and employed a 265GB MLC-based SSD that used in Figure 2. The LeCroy protocol analyzer [17] is used for analyzing the SATA protocol at the physical layer. We observed that 3-17 commands are delivered to the device-level command queue in parallel before the actual data communication starts, and the storage-level idle times experienced by the I/O requests vary between 1.8 μs and 15.2 ms, based on the operation type and transfer size.

This storage-level short idle periods that we measured can be detected by looking through the I/O commands with their preinformation. Specifically, one can preview I/O commands in the queue before they get executed, and identify the short idle intervals between successive I/O commands. Even though this interval is short, one benefit gained from utilizing these short idle intervals is that it allows one to investigate a request through preinformation and accurately predict what will happen to the request during the idle time. Each short idle period can be expressed as follows:

$$T_{short-idle} = t_{start_{i+1}} - (t_{start_i} + t_{exe_i} * l_i) \qquad (1)$$
$$: \forall i, 1 < i \leq n,$$

where $i+1$ denotes the index of the I/O command following the ith I/O command in the queue, t_{start_i} denotes actual transfer start time, t_{exe_i} is the execution time based on a page, and l_i is the page length of I/O command i. Clearly, short idle periods exist only if $T_{short-idle}$ is larger than zero and there are I/O commands sitting in the queue (i.e., at least two commands). Here, n depends on the queue size accommodated by the host interface nuance. For example, NCQ [16] provides 32 entries, whereas TCQ [18] typically provides 256 entries. AGC exploits just two entries for previewing the I/O commands.

Long Idle Periods: We also observed that many applications exhibit relatively long idle periods with no enqueued I/O commands. We classify an idle period as a long idle period if its length is larger than a certain threshold [19] [20] [21]. The fraction of I/O instructions that experience these long idle periods ranges between 38% and 83% under various workloads tested [22] [23] when the threshold is set to 1 sec. Note that, to detect these idle periods, we cannot take advantage of the device-level command queue and preinformation since it is empty most of the time. Consequently, long idle periods should be handled differently.

Depending on whether idle periods are short, long or none, our proposed strategies schedule GC operations and secure free blocks differently.

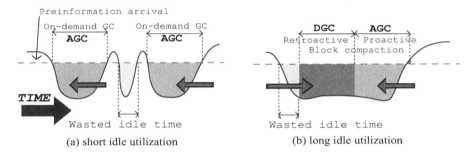

(a) short idle utilization   (b) long idle utilization

Fig. 4. A high-level view of our proposed GC strategy and idle time utilization

4.2   Shifting Garbage Collection Overheads to Idle Periods

We start by observing that scheduling a GC on an arbitrary idle period can introduce extra block reclaimings (P/E cycles) and reduce opportunities for block reuse. This can in turn potentially shorten SSD lifetime and affect its reliability. Therefore, in our proposed schemes, we migrate the GC operations to *carefully-chosen* idle periods without increasing the original number of GC operations. We also minimize the overheads incurred by on-demand GC invocations by securing the available free blocks as much as possible in advance during the idle periods.

We explore two different strategies for shifting GC overheads, depending on the amount of idleness and on-demand GC needs, as shown in Figure 4. First, short idle periods are mainly exploited by shifting on-demand GCs that will be invoked during busy periods (Figure 4a). In this case, the garbage collector monitors upcoming device-level I/O tasks to determine when a collection will be needed and performs the necessary tasks *proactively*. If there is no on-demand GC need, the garbage collector performs block compactions to reclaim fully-occupied blocks thereby retrieving free blocks in advance (Figure 4b). We refer to this strategy as the *Advanced GC (AGC)*. Second, if the amount of short idleness is not sufficient to avoid on-demand GC invocations at a certain point, our proposed GC strategies prevent them from being invoked on the critical path by delaying the GC execution (Figure 4b); we refer to this strategy as the *Delayed GC (DGC)*. In other words, AGC shifts GC activities to idle periods in advance, whereas DGC handles the on-demand collections that AGC could not handle, by delaying the GC invocations to future idle periods.

These different GC strategies based on the type of idle periods and GC needs allow our strategies to shift GCs from busy periods to idle periods, as illustrated in Figure 1. At the same time, they help us minimize the potential side effects on SSD reliability and eliminate the extra storage space requirement in the SSD for the operation of the proposed schemes.

5   Implementation of Our GC Strategies

Recall that we quantified the impact of garbage collection on commercial SSDs in Section 3. To alleviate the overheads caused by garbage collections, we classified the types of idle periods in Section 4 and presented a high-level view of our proposed approach. We next describe the technical details of AGC and DGC in Sections 5.1 and 5.2, respectively. Section 5.3 discusses how AGC and DGC works together.

5.1   Details of Advanced GC Strategy (AGC)

AGC tries to remove the on-demand GCs from the critical path and secure free blocks in advance so that users do not experience long GC-induced latencies during the I/O congestion periods. Depending on the type of the idle period we are dealing with, one can implement AGC in two different ways. The look-ahead garbage collection (Section 5.1) is a type of AGC that targets on-demand collections by utilizing short idle periods, whereas the proactive block compaction (Section 5.1) secures free blocks by utilizing long idle periods.

Look-Ahead Garbage Collection. To shift GC invocations to earlier idle periods, this scheme exploits the device-level command queue and short idle periods. It starts by calculating the number of GC operations that can be executed in short idle periods. In this step, the look-ahead GC checks the queue entries and extracts I/O request information such as the length of I/O request and the Logical Sector Number (LSN) and associated Logical Block Number (LBN). It then finds the Physical Block Numbers (PBNs) corresponding to the LBN by looking up the mapping table of the underlying FTL. The look-ahead garbage collector then checks whether the available space, especially the number of free pages, is sufficient to service the I/O request of the specified size (length). If not, an update block reclaiming GC is required.

Once the need for GC is identified, our scheme next calculates a GC latency in order to accurately perform on-demand GC in advance. Let κ denote the number of physical blocks per logical block (e.g., in a block mapping scheme, the value of κ is one. On the other hand, if the system employs a 2:8 hybrid mapping scheme, κ can be up to ten). Further, let t_{load}, t_{write}, and t_{erase} denote execution latencies for page load (read), page write and block erase operation, respectively, and let t'_{write} represent the time for writing metadata to confirm the fact that a certain physical block was erased after GC (this helps to ensure mapping consistency in the FTL). Since the look-ahead GC knows PBN(s) for the logical block and has all the relevant mapping information, it can determine the number of valid pages for the PBN(s); say, n_{page}^{valid}. In this way, for each I/O command i that is involved in the GC, its GC latency (T_{gc_i}) can be calculated using the following expression:

$$T_{gc_i} = \underbrace{(t_{load} + t_{write}) * n_{page}^{valid}}_{page\ migration} + \overbrace{(t_{erase} + t'_{write}) * \kappa}^{block\ cleaning}. \qquad (2)$$

This expression captures the page migration latency for each valid page from the update/data block to a free block, as well as the block cleaning latency for these blocks. Typically, t'_{write} is approximately the same as the latency it takes to write one page (t_{write}). This is because the metadata is designed to fit in a single page to reduce the overhead of storing the metadata itself. The total amount of time taken by the look-ahead GC to perform collections over n blocks is given by ($\sum_{i=1}^{n} T_{gc_i}$). Using the GC latencies of individual blocks, we determine the number of blocks (n) that can be reclaimed at runtime, under the constraint that the total GC time for the determined number of blocks is less than or equal to the short idle time given by Equation (1). Once AGC determines the number of blocks, n, to be claimed, it performs look-ahead GCs for these n blocks in advance.

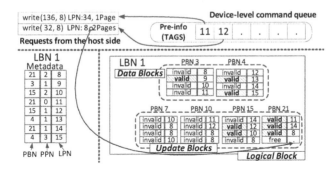

Fig. 5. An example of the look-ahead GC with a hybrid mapping scheme. By inquiring the mapping information, our AGC scheme figures out that the GC for LBN 1 will be invoked soon.

For instance, in Figure 5, the look-ahead GC identifies the request with an LSN of 32 and I/O size of eight sectors. Since the logical block corresponding to that request has only one free page, our scheme executes the GC operation in the short idle time. In addition to providing stable and better SSD performance, this implementation performs GCs *only when* an on-demand GC is about to occur and the short idle periods are suitable to perform GC. Therefore, it ensures a similar level of reliability compared to a standard FTL.

Proactive Block Compaction. In order to exploit long idle times that could not be exploited by the look-ahead GC, we propose a proactive block compaction mechanism strategy. In this strategy, we detect the blocks (in a logical block) that are fully occupied with valid/invalid pages, and compact them in advance during the long idle periods. Compacting blocks involves enforcing all valid pages from the fully-occupied physical block to a new, clean block, and removing the invalid pages in the former by erasing them. Consider as an example Figure 6 where we have two fully-occupied blocks, namely, LBN 5 and LBN 32768. AGC can compact these two blocks in advance during long idle periods. In order to avoid the scanning penalty required to identify the fully-occupied blocks, we add the LBN of the fully-occupied block to the AGC job list, while the FTL is serving the I/O requests so that the blocks can be compacted *proactively* without scanning the entire storage address space.

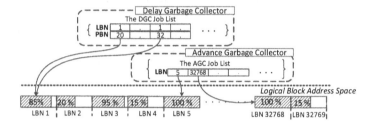

Fig. 6. Job lists for AGC and DGC

Even though proactive block compaction is relatively simple, it can be very effective in practice as far as enhancing idle time utilization and securing free blocks are concerned. It should be noted that the proactive block compaction mechanism is executed *only if* the number of free blocks is less than the free block threshold (i.e., an on-demand GC would be invoked very soon). Therefore, similar to the look-ahead GC mechanism discussed earlier, this proactive block compaction mechanism also minimizes the number of unnecessary erase operations, which in turn helps to improve SSD endurance and reliability.

Incremental Garbage Collection. One concern regarding AGC is that it could lead to undesired performance degradations and prevent the GC latencies from being hidden, if idle periods are too short or do not occur frequently enough. To avoid this, our implementation of AGC splits GC activities into smaller ones delimited by *checkpoints*, and performs the GCs step-by-step based on the checkpoints. As illustrated in Figure 7, the checkpoints are inserted at the end of every NAND I/O completion point and constitute the boundaries across the neighboring GC steps. Inspired by the checkpointing strategy described by [24], AGC incrementally performs a given GC operation one step at a time; this is referred to as the *Incremental Garbage Collection (Incremental GC)* in the remainder of this paper.

Whenever AGC reaches a checkpoint, the incremental GC determines whether further collections can be performed or not by checking the device-level queue. If there are no I/O requests until the next checkpoint, it goes ahead and executes

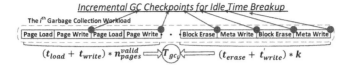

Fig. 7. Checkpointing for incremental GC. At each checkpoint, by checking the device-level queue, the garbage collector can decide whether it can perform further collections or not.

the next step of the GC operation. The same procedure is repeated as long as there are no I/O requests. If on the other hand AGC detects an I/O request at a particular checkpoint, it postpones the remaining GC steps to the next idle period. To do this, it marks the current GC job status and inserts this marked status information into another job list that is managed by DGC (this will be revisited in Section 5.2). This incremental GC operation allows AGC to avoid the potential drawbacks of very short idle periods, and smoothly pass the control of GC operations to DGC. As a result, the SSD is able to serve the bursty I/O requests that can potentially create very short idle periods.

5.2   Details of Delayed GC Strategy (DGC)

Even though idle periods are typically long enough [20] [22] [25] for AGC to prepare available free blocks ahead of time and execute GC in advance, in cases where idleness does not occur frequently, AGC may not be very successful. The main goal behind our *Delayed Garbage Collection Strategy* (DGC) is to address this situation by delaying GC invocations. Its operation can be divided into two steps as explained below.

Update Block Replacement. As stated earlier, the main reason why GCs degrade system performance is *page migrations*. To avoid this degradation, DGC defers the page migration activity to *future* idle periods. Whenever an on-demand GC occurs in a busy period, DGC allocates free block(s) as update block(s). Normally, commodity FTLs migrate valid pages from the update and data blocks to an allocated free block. In contrast, DGC skips this process and serves the urgent I/O requests. Rather than migrating pages, DGC adds the LBN and PBN(s) corresponding to the migration into a job list it maintains (called the *DGC job list*). This delayed page migration activity is later resumed in a future idle period by the DGC's retroactive block compaction (see Section 5.2).

   The free block allocation carried out by DGC is similar to what a standard FTL would do during GC. The only difference is that DGC allocates the block as an update block (not a free block). Since the FTL already has an update block (but it is garbage), DGC intercepts the update block information and replaces the PBN of the update block with the allocated free block's PBN in the FTL mapping table. In this way, the FTL treats the allocated free block (called the delay block) as an update block, and is not required to manage the block mapping information. It explicitly manages replacing/updating a block for preserving consistency during

information mapping. Further, DGC maintains this information using the DGC
job list and hides this information from the FTL until the page migration process
completes. In the meantime, if there is an I/O request, the FTL serves that request
based on the available mapping information. This replacement and interception
procedure is called the *Update Block Replacement*.

The main advantage of the update block replacement is that, as soon as
the SSD receives an I/O request, it can serve the request without migrating
the valid pages, even when AGC could not handle on-demand GCs in advance.
Another benefit is that DGC does not require any additional NV memory space
for delaying on-demand GCs, which is essential resources of prior works [11] [13].
This is because it replaces the update block with free blocks that belong to the
FTL address space. Note that the mappings employed by the FTL and DGC do
not interfere with each other, and this allows DGC to work with various other
mapping schemes used in current FTLs.

Retroactive Block Compaction. When
there is no I/O congestion, DGC performs page migrations and returns the
relevant delay block and update/replace
block to the free block space. The blocks
returned DGC can be recycled as normal free blocks. To return a block, DGC
first extracts the LBN and PBN for a
replace/update block from the DGC job
list. It then queries the PBN for the data
and delay blocks by using FTL's block-
level mapping table. That is, it looks up
the mapping table entry for the LBN extracted from the DGC job list and gets
the corresponding PBN from the table.

Once DGC collects all PBN(s) for the
blocks related to the delayed logical block,
it retroactively compacts the blocks and
returns them to the original state (i.e., as
free blocks). While compacting, DGC migrates valid pages deferred from all PBNs
for each delay, replace/update, and data
block. This page migration is simply executed by reading and writing pages in
an ascending order. We want to point
out that the number of pages requiring
migration is less than or equal to the number of pages in a logical block, independent of the number of delay and data
blocks involved. Thus, the migration cost
of DGC is the same as that of original GC.

```
if irp.command != empty then
    if ftl.checkOnDemandGc(irp)
    then
        /* delay the on-demand GC   */
        UpdateBlockReplacement(irp)
        insertEntry(DgcJobList,
        irp.getLbn())
    /* call the FTL service        */
    ftl.ServeIo(irp.command, irp.lsn,
    irp.sectors)
else
    targetLbn := getDgcLbn(DgcJobList)
    /* DGC                         */
    if targetLbn != nullblock then
        consumed = RetroactiveBlock-
        Compaction(targetLbn)
    /* AGC                         */
    idleType :=
    checkIdleType(CommandQueue,
    consumed)
    if idleType = short then
        /* Calculate GC latency using
           Equation 1 & 2            */
        idletimes :=
        getIdleTime(CommandQueue,
        consumed) requiredTimes :=
        speculateExecutionTime()
        while idletimes ≥
        requiredTimes do
            LookaheadGc(irp)

    else if idleType = long then
        ProactiveBlockCompaction(irp)
```

Algorithm 1:
IssueCommands(IoRequestPacket
irp) of our proposed AGC+DGC
algorithm. Note that the SSD just
forwards I/O requests to the underlying FTL without performing
any GC during the busy periods.

During busy periods, DGC preferentially reads and writes pages to the delay block rather than the replace/update block to guarantee data consistency. The reason behind this order is that the delay block contains the latest data when compared to the data in the replace/update block(s). This also helps DGC to improve block utilization and reduce the amount of I/O activity while performing the collections since the replace/update block(s) can be erased without any read or write operation in the ideal case.

5.3   Putting the Two Schemes Together

When our two schemes, AGC and DGC, are applied together we expect that most GCs are invoked by AGC; DGC will be invoked only if the idleness at hand is insufficient or the number of free blocks secured by AGC is not enough. In fact, we observed during our experiments that the fraction of idle periods DGC handles accounts for at most 20%, and AGC manages the rest. Algorithm 1 describes the steps involved in integrating DGC and AGC (called the *AGC+DGC scheme*). In summary, if an I/O request triggers an on-demand GC, DGC delays page migration to future idle periods using the *update block replacement* mechanism. During idle periods, DGC first performs *retroactive block compaction* **only if** a delayed GC block exists. And, AGC is invoked based on the type of idle period at hand. Specifically, if the idle period is short (just enough to perform the required GC), *look-ahead garbage collection* is invoked. Finally, *proactive block compaction* is invoked when the idle period is long. In each implementation, GC is performed incrementally, as explained in Section 5.1.

6   Experimental Evaluation

To evaluate the effectiveness of our AGC and DGC, we introduced them in a event simulation platform whose a typical SSD storage stack is fully implemented, including flash drivers, translation layers, and host interface controllers. Our simulator also models multiple channels and ways with a bus transaction-level clock accuracy such that different types of idleness can be accurately simulated with diverse workloads we tested.

SSD Configuration. We implemented two different SSD-based disk arrays;

• **6SSDs-RAID:** The first disk array was setup based on the original MSN file server storage configuration [22], which consists of 6 disks (Disk0 $\sim$ Disk5). In this default array, we introduced six of 64GB SSDs and each SSD, which replaces each disk of MSN storage server, has 4 channels and 4 ways architecture. Further, we categorize this SSD array based on each disk of write-intensity.

- *6SSDs-RAID-LO* is the group of SSD0, 1, 2, and 3 with low I/O intensive workloads of which the fraction of write amount is under 20% of total I/Os.
- *6SSDs-RAID-HI* is another SSD group, consisting SSD4 and 5 with high I/O intensive workloads of which the write fraction of total I/Os is 80%.

• **3SSDs-RAID:** Another disk array leverages three SSDs, in which each individual SSD composes of 8 channels and 8 ways (128GB). This disk array was configured to measure performance impacts on a different SSD configuration. In this 3SSDs-RAID, disk0 and disk1 (of the MSN server) are replaced by SSD0, disk2 and disk5 are replaced by SSD1, and disk3 and disk4 are replaced by SSD2.

Both SSD arrays in RAID-0 configuration are viewed by the OS as a single device. Even though we model a Samsung K9KGA0B0M MLC NAND flash[2] [26] in our simulations, our proposed GC strategies can be applied to other NAND flash device models as well. Due to limitations of space, we are not able to show our evaluation on other devices, but the performance behaviors with the most current version of NAND flash packages (two planes and dual dies architecture) are very similar to the results shown in this section.

FTL Implementation. We implemented a log-structured FTL (*L-FTL*) and a 2:8 hybrid mapped FTL (*H-FTL*) on the SSD-based disk array models [12] [8]. We also implemented a partial GC scheme based FTL (*P-FTL*) [11] [13] [10]. After some initial experiments, the percentage of free blocks and GC threshold are set to 3% and 1%, respectively, of the total SSD address space[3]. We also introduced a 14 GB extra space to P-FTL for each SSD in the 6SSDs-RAID and 28GB extra spaces to it for each SSD in the 3SSDs-RAID based on the results from the write buffer analysis [11]; these extra spaces are used as the non-volatile write buffer in an attempt to serve urgent I/Os and provide real-time support, and managed through the page-level mapping scheme in P-FTL, instead of employing a block-level mapping scheme.

Workloads. Enterprise traces tested are collected from the MSN file storage server over 5 days [22] [23]. The total I/O traffic studied was up to 1.8TB. Important characteristics of our traces are given in Table 1. In the traces used, 34.6% of idle intervals were long (larger than 1 sec) and less than 29.5% were short, and 35.9% of the requests were back-to-back with no idle time in between.

It should be mentioned that each I/O request of any trace we simulate has a time stamp associated with it, and all the different approaches we tested (for reducing GC overheads) take advantage of scheduling the I/O requests based on the corresponding time stamps (using NCQ). Our bus-transaction level simulator extracts access time information from the I/O commands, using which we synchronize the global timer of the simulator and check the I/O latencies at the end of every I/O completion. This enables us to accurately record idle/busy periods on the SSDs.

---

[2] This has 128 pages per a block. Based on a 4 KB page size, read, write and block erase latencies are 183.2 us, 860.36 us, and 2 ms, respectively.

[3] Some industries employ even higher GC thresholds with more free blocks, which renders SSDs expensive. Since there is a variety of configurations for GC threshold, we choose a lower bound value for our evaluation. We believe that alleviating GC overheads in our configuration (more complex) can be reduced the GC problem in such expensive SSDs configuration based on write amplification analysis with over-provisioning and spare factors [27].

Table 1. Important characteristics of our traces. The last column gives % of I/O requests containing sufficiently long idle (> 1 sec) periods.

	The number of I/O requests	Total amount of requests (KB)	Total amount of writes (KB)	Idle Periods (%)
Disk0	1,509,397	32,490,240	3,051,918	38.6
Disk1	2,221,728	35,383,340	17,722,159	81.3
Disk2	500	1,958	1,958	56.6
Disk3	4,352	2,392,445	2,387,767	83.0
Disk4	12,627,396	117,607,983	24,835,283	42.4
Disk5	12,981,710	130,033,924	31,777,436	41.3
Total	29,345,083	317,909,889	79,776,520	64.1

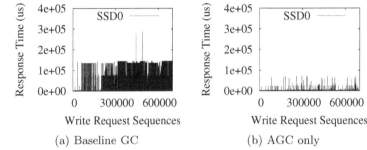

(a) Baseline GC   (b) AGC only

Fig. 8. Performance of AGC with relatively low I/O intensive workloads (SSD 0 of 6SSDs-RAID)

6.1 Performance Comparison

We first evaluate the performance of our two GC strategies (AGC and DGC) using 6SSDs-RAID in isolation. Figures 8 and 9 plot the response times of SSD0 of 6SSDs-RAID-LO and SSD5 of 6SSDs-RAID-HI, respectively. As illustrated in Figure 8, AGC alone successfully hides almost all on-demand GCs in SSD0, leaving nothing for DGC. We see from Figure 9b, however, that AGC alone is not very successful with the high I/O intensive workloads. During the high write-intensive periods, a few on-demand GCs are invoked due to the very small amount of short idle periods in SSD5. Even though the number of these on-demand GC invocations is small, the FTL uses up available free blocks for new requests, which introduces more on-demand GC invocation. In a worst-case scenario, AGC suffers from both increased amount of GC invocations and short idle periods as the execution progresses. This is the reason why AGC requires DGC to handle such on-demand GCs. One can see from Figure 9c that DGC alone successfully hides the GC latencies until four million write requests are served. However, as soon as the available free blocks run out, DGC starts performing on-demand GCs. One can also see from this result that DGC needs AGC, which supplies free blocks, enabling the former to defer on-demand GCs. Both AGC and DGC, when applied individually, increase the number of GCs compared to the baseline GC, which is used to perform on-demand GC of L-FTL (see Figure 9a). However, when they are applied together, they successfully hide GC latencies, as illustrated in Figure 9d, and the total number of GCs does *not* exceed the baseline case (Section 6.5). In the rest of our experiments, we focus on this integrated AGC+DGC scheme.

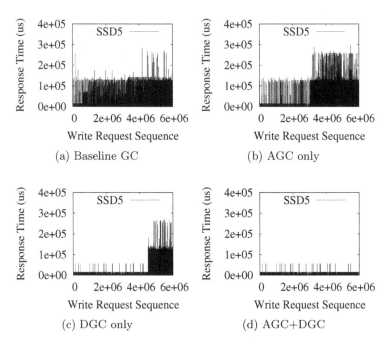

Fig. 9. Performance comparison of different garbage collection strategies (SSD5 of 6SSDs-RAID with high I/O intensive workloads)

6.2   Worst Case Response Time

Figure 10 plot the worst-case response times (WCRTs) 6SSDs-RAID. We see from these graphs that, WCRT ranges from 131 ms to 311 ms in 6SSDs-RAID-LO, under both the L-FTL and H-FTL schemes. However, in both P-FTL and AGC+DGC we observe negligible WCRTs, which results in completely hiding the GC latencies from the I/O operations. We further observe that AGC+DGC reduces the WCRT by 65.2%, 98.6% and 96.4%, on average, over P-FTL, L-FTL and H-FTL, respectively. This is because AGC+DGC performs on-demand GCs only during the idle periods, and consequently, users experience no GC overheads during their I/O services.

However, in 6SSDs-RAID-HI, P-FTL's WCRT behavior fluctuates due to the *write buffer block thrashing* problem.[4] This causes P-FTL to perform out of order writes for a while and, as a result, WCRTs become ten times worse as

---

[4] This problem arises when the free pages in the write buffer (NV buffer) to which P-FTL writes urgent data are no longer available.

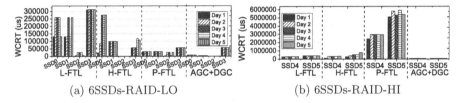

(a) 6SSDs-RAID-LO

(b) 6SSDs-RAID-HI

Fig. 10. Worst-case response time (WCRT) analysis for 6SSDs-RAID. (a) With low I/O intensive workloads, P-FTL and AGC+DGC show deterministic behaviors while the performances of L-FTL and H-FTL fluctuate over time. (b) With high I/O intensive workloads, P-FTL experiences very high WCRT, whereas AGC+DGC continues to provide stable I/O performance.

compared to the L-FTL case. In contrast, AGC+DGC still serves I/O requests within the predefined latencies, and achieves about 53 ms latency, including the theoretic minimum for I/O processing, while the other approaches suffer from the performance fluctuations and experience long WCRT under heavy I/O requests. Further, SSDs supported by our AGC+DGC do *not* incur any GC latencies during busy periods, even in execution phases with very low idle times ($\leq 10\%$). This is because AGC eliminates on-demand GCs using idle times, and DGC postpones the GC latencies by shifting them to future idle periods, as plotted in Figure 11c. Figure 11 also explains how our proposed GC strategies collectively take GC overheads off the critical path. While L-FTL and H-FTL (see Figures 11a and 11b) incur GC latencies during the busy periods, AGC+DGC incurs (see

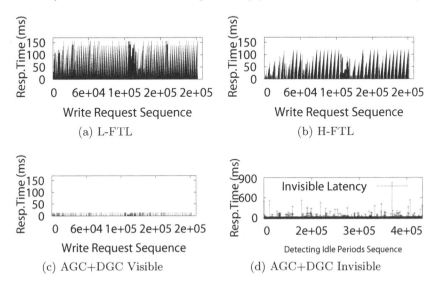

(a) L-FTL

(b) H-FTL

(c) AGC+DGC Visible

(d) AGC+DGC Invisible

Fig. 11. Response times for a write intensive section (where the fraction of I/O executions with no idle time is account for about 90%). While H-FTL removes about 40% of the GC related overheads, AGC+DGC hides all on-demand GC latencies.

Figure 11d) GC latencies *only* during the idle periods, which are not perceived by applications. This clearly shows that AGC+DGC provides stable and better SSD performance with no on-demand GCs taking place during the busy periods.

6.3   Excess Waiting Time

Figure 12 plots the amount of excess waiting time (EWT)[5] in 6SSDs-RAID. One can observe from Figure 12a that H-FTL significantly cuts down the GCs by maximizing the block-level locality. It also dramatically reduces the number of page migrations introduced by GCs. However, it can also be seen that, as the execution progresses (from day 1 to day 5), occurrences of EWTs increase, due to the shortage of available free blocks. To secure free blocks, H-FTL had to merge up to ten blocks into two logical blocks, and merge approximately fifteen thousand times a day, generating significant overheads. In contrast, P-FTL and AGC+DGC successfully hide GC overheads at runtime (and thereby All EWT of them is zero). However, the frequency of EWTs in H-FTL is less than that in P-FTL with high write intensive workloads (see Figure 12b). In this case, P-FTL could not fully hide GC latencies when the NV buffer was completely used by the large amount of I/O requests. This is because P-FTL incurs much longer latencies than H-FTL, due to the write buffer thrashing problem, which is the same as the one causing high WCRT.

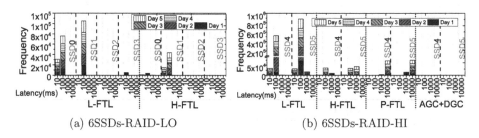

(a) 6SSDs-RAID-LO   (b) 6SSDs-RAID-HI

Fig. 12. Excess waiting time (EWT). The x-axis represents the upper bound on EWT. (a) L-FTL and H-FTL experience I/O blocking problem stemming from GCs while P-FTL and AGC+DGC have no such problem. (b) With heavy writes, even though P-FTL results in fewer GC invocations, its GC latencies are much longer than others

On the other hand, our scheme successfully hides GC latencies because AGC can ahead secure available blocks (delay blocks) to DGC even under high write intensive workloads. Further, because of update block replacement scheme, the delay blocks are the same as the free blocks, thereby not requiring any extra blocks to manage different mapping schemes. Our proposed strategy essentially eliminates on-demand GCs by exploiting different types of idle periods and thus leads to stable GC latencies.

---

[5] EWT is defined as the difference between the actual wait time and the marginal response time (in this paper, it is assumed to be 30 *ms*).

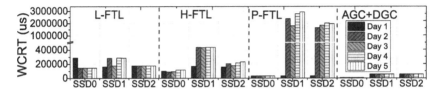

Fig. 13. Worst-case response time (WCRT) analysis for the 3SSDs-RAID

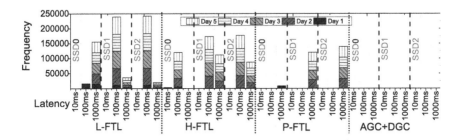

Fig. 14. Excess waiting time (EWT) analysis for the 3SSDs-RAID

6.4   Performance Compariosn of 3SSDs-RAID

Figure 13 and Figure 14 illustrate, respectively, WCRTs and EWTs for 3SSDs-RAID. In both WCRT and EWT analyses, performance of the 3SSDs-RAID is similar to 6SSDs-RAID except for P-FTL. Specifically, in day 1, P-FTL guarantees deterministic performance with the zero EWT value on even high write-intensive workloads (SSD1 and SSD2 of 3SSDs-RAID) because each SSD of 3SSDs-RAID has a larger storage capacity than an SSD in the 6SSDs-RAID configuration. In other words, P-FTL is more tolerant to update block reclaiming GC overheads as its NV buffer has more physical pages. However, as the amount of writes increases, the available physical pages also run out. As a result, P-FTL could not satisfy the deadline requirements again. 3SSDs-RAID with P-FTL has about 50% less impact on the write block thrashing problem compared to 6SSDs-RAID, mainly because, in addition to the larger physical pages on the NV buffer, P-FTL itself can secure abundant free block resource as well, thereby reducing potential GC overheads during free block reclaiming. However, due to reasons similar to the case of 6SSDs-RAID, over the time, P-FTL makes 3SSDs-RAID performance worse than L-FTL and H-FTL. While the performance of P-FTL depends mainly on the size of NV buffer and are not able to essentially take GC overheads off the critical path of SSDs, AGC+DGC satisfies the performance requirements irrespective of different SSD configuration chosen and the I/O traffics tested.

6.5   Side-Effects of AGC and DGC

Figure 15a plots the breakdown of GCs across different collection schemes. Since AGC is responsible for preparing the free blocks, it is desired that the contribution of the AGC be larger than that of the DGC. We see that, as expected, AGC executes for at least 80% of the total number of GCs. As a result, DGC is able to secure enough free blocks when it performs update block replacement to delay GCs. We want to point out that the proactive block compaction is applied in a majority of the AGC operations. The proactive block compaction does not execute until the number of free blocks is less than the free block threshold (even though it is under the underlying FTL's GC threshold (3%)). Therefore, our scheme does not introduce any unnecessary erases, and thus reduces the potential side-effects of GC.

Figure 15b presents the average block erase counts under different free block thresholds when executing AGC. In this figure, the dotted vertical line indicates L-FTL's average erase count per block, which is twenty one. Since AGC is performed only if the target GC block is fully occupied or if an on-demand GC is to be invoked very soon, it only migrates

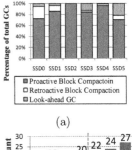

(a)

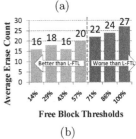

(b)

Fig. 15. (a) Garbage collection type breakdown of total collection. (b) Block erase impact by free block threshold.

necessary GC activities from busy period, thereby minimizing side effect in terms of SSD reliability.

We observed that the free block threshold should be less than 71% for the average erase count of the proactive block compaction in AGC to be comparable to L-FTL. If the proactive block compaction shifts on-demand GCs beyond this threshold, it makes wear-leveling characteristics worse than L-FTL. Interestingly, the erase counts with low free block thresholds are better than L-FTL. This is because preparing free blocks using fully-occupied blocks in advance helps to prevent the log block thrashing problem (in L-FTL), which can introduce improper erase operations. In our experiments, the best free block threshold for satisfying the wear-leveling requirement was found to be less than 43% of the original GC threshold.

7   Conclusions

We proposed novel a garbage collection strategy consisting of two main components, called *Advanced Garbage Collection* (AGC) and *Delayed Garbage Collection* (DGC), that cooperate in hiding GC overheads in SSDs. AGC tries to secure free blocks in advance and remove on-demand GCs from the critical path so that users do *not* experience GC latencies during I/O congestion. In comparison, DGC handles GC invocations that could not be handled by AGC by differing them to future idle periods. Our experimental analysis using both enterprise workloads and high performance I/O workloads indicate that the proposed strategies (AGC and DGC) provide stable I/O performance. Compared to three state-of-the-art GC strategies, P-FTL, L-FTL and H-FTL, our integrated scheme (AGC+DGC) reduces GC overheads dramatically.

Acknowledgment. We would like to thank anonymous reviewers for their constructive feedback. This work is supported in part by NSF grants 1017882, 0937949, and 0833126 and DOE grant DESC0002156.

References

1. Caulfield, A.M., et al.: Understanding the impact of emerging non-volatile memories on high-performance, IO-intensive computing. In: SC (2010)
2. Kgil, T., Roberts, D., Mudge, T.: Improving NAND flash based disk caches. In: ISCA (2008)
3. Caulfield, A.M., Grupp, L.M., Swanson, S.: Gordon: Using flash memory to build fast, power-efficient clusters for data-intensive applications. In: ASPLOS (2009)
4. Lee, S.W., et al.: A case for flash memory SSD in enterprise database applications. In: FAST (2011)
5. EMC: Raw drive capacity cost trends,
   `http://wikibon.org/w/images/a/a4/emcrawdrivecapacitycosttrends.jpg`
6. Micheloni, R., et al.: Inside NAND Flash Memories. Springer (2010)
7. Caulfield, A.M., et al.: Characterizing flash memory: Anomalies, observations,and applications. In: SC (2009)
8. Kang, J.U., et al.: A superblock-based flash translation layer for NAND flash memory. In: EMSOFT (2006)
9. Lee, S.W., et al.: FAST: An efficient flash translation layer for flash memory. In: EUC Workshops (2006)
10. Chang, L.P., Kuo, T.W.: Real-time garbage collection for flash-memory storage systems of real-time embedded systems. TECS (2004)
11. Choudhuri, S., Givargis, T.: Deterministic service guarantees for NAND flash using partial block cleaning. In: CODESS+ISSS (2008)
12. Kim, J., et al.: A space-efficient flash translation layer for Compact Flash systems. In: TCE (2002)
13. Jung, M., Yoo, J.: Scheduling garbage collection opportunistically to reduce worst-case I/O performance in SSDs. In: IWSSPS (2009)
14. ULINK technology, `http://www.ulinktech.com/`
15. Intel, `http://www.iometer.org/`
16. Intel, Seagate: Serial ATA Native Command Queuing: An Exciting New Performance Feature for Serial ATA. Intel and Seagate (July 2003)
17. LeCroy, `http://www.lecroy.com/`
18. T10: Technical Committee T10 (2009), `http://www.t10.org/`
19. Colarelli, D., Grunwald, D.: Massive arrays of idle disks for storage archives. In: SC (2002)
20. Mi, N., et al.: Efficient management of idleness in storage systems. The ACM Transactions on Storage Journal (2009)
21. Golding, R., et al.: Idleness is not sloth. In: USENIX ATC (1995)

22. Narayanan, D., et al.: Migrating server storage to SSDs: Analysis of tradeoffs. In: EuroSys (2009)
23. SNIA: IOTTA Repository (2006), http://iotta.snia.org/
24. Kim, J.H., et al.: Incremental Merge Methods and Memory Systems Using the Same. U.S. Patent #2006004971A1 (January 5, 2006)
25. Narayanan, D., et al.: Everest: Scaling down peak loads through I/O off-loading. In: EuroSys (2008)
26. Samsung Electorincs: K9GAG0B0M. In: Data Sheet (2008)
27. Hu, X.Y.: et al.: Write amplification analysis in flash-based solid state drives. In: SYSTOR (2009)

Unifying Thread-Level Speculation and Transactional Memory*

João Barreto[1], Aleksandar Dragojevic[2], Paulo Ferreira[1],
Ricardo Filipe[1,**], and Rachid Guerraoui[2]

[1] INESC-ID/Technical University Lisbon, Portugal
{joao.barreto,paulo.ferreira}@inesc-id.pt, rfilipe@gsd.inesc-id.pt
[2] EPFL, Switzerland
{aleksandar.dragojevic,rachid.guerraoui}@epfl.ch

Abstract. The motivation of this work is to ask whether Transactional Memory (TM) and Thread-Level Speculation (TLS), two prominent concurrency paradigms usually considered separately, can be combined into a hybrid approach that extracts untapped parallelism and speed-up from common programs.

We show that the answer is positive by describing an algorithm, called TLSTM, that leverages an existing TM with TLS capabilities. We also show that our approach is able to achieve up to a 48% increase in throughput over the base TM, on read dominated workloads of long transactions in a multi-threaded application, among other results.

1 Introduction

Multicore architectures are already the norm for most commodity computing devices. This trend calls for concurrent programs that expose enough parallelism to maximize the utilization of such increasing computational resources. Yet, concurrent programs are significantly more difficult to code than sequential ones.

In recent years we have witnessed increasing efforts from the research community to develop new emerging paradigms that ease the challenge of extracting parallelism from non-trivial programs. Thread-Level Speculation (TLS) [1, 2] and Transactional Memory (TM) [3] are perhaps the most prominent examples of such efforts. State-of-the-art solutions from both paradigms have already proved to extract considerable parallelism from a wide range of programs, while hiding complex concurrency issues away from the programmer [4, 5].

However, more than easily coding concurrent programs that yield *some* parallelism, we want concurrent programs that expose *as much parallelism as the ever increasing hardware thread count*. This goal becomes dramatically more challenging as affordable multicore machines include more and more cores each

---

* This work was partially supported by FCT (INESC-ID multi-annual funding) through the PIDDAC Program funds and by FCT project specSTM (PTDC/EIA-EIA/122785/2010).
** Contact author.

year. While 4-core processors supporting up to eight simultaneous hardware threads are already regarded as commodity hardware, 8-core, 16-core and even chips with tens or hundreds of cores promise to be an affordable reality soon [6].

Unfortunately, when examined individually, both TLS and TM have crucial limitations that hinder one's ability to extract high parallelism from most sequential programs.

On the one hand, TLS departs from a sequential program, breaks it into fine-grained tasks, and tries to automatically parallelize such tasks in a speculative fashion. For the sake of correctness, TLS ensures that any data dependencies stemming from the original sequential program order are respected in the speculatively parallelized execution. However, experience from the TLS systems proposed so far suggests that, for most programs, such data dependencies severely restrict the number of tasks that any TLS can parallelize effectively (i.e., without incurring in expensive rollbacks) [7]. Recent results show that even the most successful TLS systems rarely go beyond a relatively modest horizon of parallelization depth without rollback (e.g. less than 6 parallel tasks with SpLIP TLS [4]).

On the other hand, TM involves the programmer in the parallelization effort, by requiring him to explicitly fork the program into multiple threads. By carefully reasoning about the semantics of the application being parallelized, the programmer can thereby eliminate many data dependencies that were originally implicit across the original sequential program. Hence, in theory, higher levels parallelism are now attainable.

However, hand-parallelizing a program into many fine-grained threads is far from trivial. It requires a careful reasoning about the semantics of the application being parallelized, since the programmer must assert if the work performed by the parallelized tasks is actually commutative. Furthermore, it demands a thrifty understanding of the actual overheads of thread creation and management, so that the programmer can determine whether fine-grained tasks will actually introduce speed-up if parallelized. Hence, the programmer will typically choose a monolithic organization of coarse-grained threads. This is evident in the most representative TM benchmarks [8–10] and applications [11, 12]. In other words, the programmer is dissuaded from exposing the full fine-grained parallelism that the underlying application effectively contains.

Therefore, when facing the challenge of parallelizing a sequential program to run on a next-generation multicore machine, the programmer will most likely get disappointing results with either approach separately, TLS or TM.

While the research community places its efforts in exclusively improving one approach alone, we advocate that the time has come to question a hybrid direction: *Can TLS and TM be combined into a unified solution that would extract untapped parallelism (and speed-up) from our common applications?* If this hybrid approach proves to be feasible, programmers would first be asked to hand-parallelize their programs into coarse-grained threads using the TM paradigm. Each thread in the multi-threaded program would then be further parallelized into finer-grained parallel tasks, in a TLS fashion.

To the best of our knowledge, this paper is the first to give a positive answer to the above question, proving that TM and TLS do add up. We take a middleware approach, focusing on Software Transactional Memory (STM) and Software Thread-Level Speculation (STLS). Our main contribution is a unified STM+STLS middleware called *TLSTM*. *TLSTM* relies on standard techniques, such as compile time code inspection, to speculatively break each transaction in a multi-threaded STM program into multiple tasks that will run in parallel. If no conflicts arise among the multiple tasks, then the transaction can commit earlier. *TLSTM* can even be more optimistic and speculatively execute future transactions of a thread, even when the current transaction in that thread is still active. If the speculation proves to be successful and every transaction commits, then further parallelism is accomplished.

TLSTM extends an existing STM, SwissTM [13]. The key insight is that a SwissTM transaction is used as speculative execution unit that supports two concepts: STM transactions (defined by the user) and TLS speculative tasks (automatically created at compile or run-time). An STM transaction is seen as a sequence of one or more TLS speculative tasks, which can run out-of-order in a speculative fashion, until they commit sequentially.

Our implementation of TLSTM[1] achieves up to a 48% speedup over SwissTM, when running on a multi-threaded benchmark of long transactions, with three speculative tasks inside each transactional memory thread. Furthermore, we also study several scenarios and applications where STLS does not provide any help to the STM runtime.

The remainder of the paper is organized as follows. Section 2 defines the STM+TLS model we wish to support. Section 3 then describes the TLSTM algorithm. We evaluate TLSTM on Section 4. Section 5 surveys related work on STM and STLS. Finally, Section 6 draws conclusions and discusses future work.

2   A Unified TM+TLS Model

We start by defining the novel model we want to support. Programmers can manually fork and join *user-threads* in their programs. Since critical sections might exist due to shared memory locations, programmers are also responsible for hand delimiting such critical sections as *user-transactions*. Together, the user-threads and their user-transactions comprise the hand-parallelized program. For presentation simplicity, we assume that user-transactions are flat (i.e., non-nested); however, the model can easily be extended to consider user-transaction nesting.

When executed, each user-thread's program will be further decomposed into speculative tasks, which will run in parallel in a speculative fashion. A task's boundaries lie either outside of a user-transaction's code, or inside a user-transaction's code. In case the task's boundaries lie inside of a user-transaction's code, they can either be the same as the user-transaction's boundaries or they can represent just a fraction of that user-transaction.

---

[1] Open source available at http://www.gsd.inesc-id.pt/project-pages/specSTM

The life cycle of a successful task goes through a number of states: initially, the task is *running;* once the task has executed its last instruction, it is said to be *completed;* finally, it becomes *committed* when the task's effects become visible to all other tasks and cannot be undone. We say that a task is *active* if it is either running or completed. If the speculative execution of some task tsk is found to be inconsistent with the expected outcome of the sequential execution of tsk's user-thread (causing an intra-thread conflict), or tsk's execution is inconsistent with the execution of other user-threads (inter-thread conflict), then tsk must rollback, and is said to have *aborted*.

Hereafter, when a task tsk_1 runs code that precedes (in program order) the code executed by task tsk_2, we say that tsk_1 *is from the past of* tsk_2 (whereas tsk_2 *is from the future of* tsk_1). Within the collection of active tasks of a user-thread, we distinguish one *current task,* which corresponds to the earliest running task of the user-thread. This corresponds to the task that is running the code that the user-thread would be running if executing with no thread level parallelism. All the active tasks in the future of the current task are called *out-of-order tasks.* As soon as the current task completes, the next task in program order becomes the new current task.

The accesses performed by tasks belonging to the same user-thread must behave as if they ran sequentially. More precisely, our model ensures that any read from a task tsk_1 observes all the writes that tasks from tsk_1's past should perform and does not observe values written by future tasks.

Our model ensures that user-transactional correctness (more concretely, the opacity criteria [14]) is preserved across user-transactions, even when user-transactions are actually executed by multiple tasks running out of order. Only after every task belonging to the same user-transaction has completed its execution can the user-transaction commit.

3   TLSTM, A First Unified STM+TLS Middleware

A first naive solution to the STM+TLS problem that one might consider would be to simply run TLS on top of each thread of an existing multi-threaded STM application (either software-based or hardware-based), with no modifications on any of the two components. However, the correctness of conventional TLS algorithms relies on the assumption that the underlying (single-threaded) program exclusively accesses thread-local variables. Clearly, this no longer holds in the STM+TLS model.

Hence, we must look towards an integrated approach, i.e. a single runtime that fully supports the unified TM+TLS model that Section 2 introduced. TLSTM is a hybrid runtime that extends an existing STM, SwissTM [13], with TLS capabilities in order to support the unified STM+TLS model we described. SwissTM is a state-of-the-art STM system that supports optimistic read-write conflict detection and pessimistic write/write conflict detection, which has been shown to outperform other relevant STMs.

Therefore, before presenting TLSTM, Section 3.1 starts by describing the baseline SwissTM algorithm. Section 3.2 then discusses the hard challenges that we needed to tackle when leveraging SwissTM with support for TLS. Section 3.3 finally introduces the TLSTM algorithm.

3.1   The Baseline STM: SwissTM

In SwissTM, a global commit counter, called *commit-ts*, is used as a wall clock that is incremented by every non-read-only user-transaction on commit. SwissTM maintains a global lock table. Each location is mapped to a pair of locks, *r-lock* (read) and *w-lock* (write) from the global table. *r-lock* can either hold a version number or the *locked* value. *w-lock* can either hold a write-log entry or the *unlocked* value. Any user-transaction wishing to write must first obtain the location's *w-lock*. This eagerly prevents write/write conflicts between user-transactions.

Writes are performed in temporary copies, and only applied on the actual location once the associated user-transaction commits. During commit, the user-transaction acquires the *r-lock* of each location that the user-transaction wrote to. This prevents other user-transactions from reading the written locations and, as a result, observing inconsistent states. Upon successful commit, the *r-lock* is unlocked and contains the new *commit-ts* value, hence denoting the instant where the new value of the location was made visible to every other user-transaction.

SwissTM uses lazy counter-based validation [15, 16] to detect read/write conflicts. Each user-transaction maintains a version timestamp, *valid-ts*, denoting a point in the logical commit time for which all the values that the user-transaction has observed so far are guaranteed to be valid. Whenever the user-transaction reads some location that has a higher version than its *valid-ts*, the user-transaction needs to extend its *valid-ts* to the version being read. This requires traversing the user-transaction's read-log to validate that each version read so far remains valid at the new *valid-ts*, i.e. it has not been overwritten in the meantime.

3.2   Leveraging SwissTM with Thread-Level Speculation: Main Challenges

The key insight is that what used to be a SwissTM transaction is now used as a task in TLSTM. A user-transaction will now consist of a sequence of one or more tasks, which are automatically/manually created at compile or runtime, and can run out-of-order in a speculative fashion.

However, extending an STM (such as SwissTM) with TLS support is far from trivial. In the following, we discuss all the main challenges and give an intuitive overview of how TLSTM tackles each of them.

Ensure Low Overhead. A major part of the unified runtime's overhead comes from conflict detection. Besides the inter-thread conflicts of SwissTM, TLSTM must also detect and resolve the intra-thread conflicts resulting from TLS. There are several TLS techniques we can employ, but bluntly doing so would incur unacceptable overheads in conflict detection. Thus we must ensure that the overhead of the unified runtime is much smaller than the overhead of the sum of its parts. This requires that TLSTM reuses most of SwissTM's data structures and procedures, and adds minimal complexity to conflict detection.

Conceptually, two types of intra-user-thread conflicts may arise: *write-after-read* (WAR), where a task writes to a location that a future task already read from; and *write-after-write* (WAW), where a task wants to write to a location already written by a future task.

WAR conflicts are discovered through a new task validation procedure that starts by validating the read-log inherited from SwissTM, which records the reads performed from committed state. Then this procedure validates a new task-read-log, similar to SwissTM's read-log, which records the reads performed from writer tasks of the task's past. First, this validation checks if any of the values read from committed state were speculatively written by running tasks from the task's past. Second, this validation must ensure that each value the task has read from a past writer task has not been updated by a task from the writer task's future. If any of these situations has occurred, we abort the task performing validation. We check the need for this validation at read, write and commit time.

In the case of WAW conflicts we cannot rely on SwissTM's write-write conflict handling alone. If we did so, we could easily have intra-thread deadlocks when a future task wrote to a location and waited for its past tasks to complete in order to commit. This task might be stuck waiting forever if a past task wishes to write to that same location, which in turn would be indefinitely waiting for the location's write-lock to be released.

This problem requires a very small addition to SwissTM's write-write conflict handling. If a task wishes to acquire a write-lock that is held by a past task from the same user-thread, the task wishing to acquire the lock aborts. If, otherwise, it was a future task that write-locked the location, that future task will be signaled to abort. By following this task contention management approach we have only one running task writing on a certain location at a time.

Before committing a task, TLSTM must also ensure that all past tasks have completed and cannot be aborted because of intra-thread conflicts. TLSTM achieves this by *serializing commits* of tasks belonging to the same user-thread, along with the previously explained intra-thread conflict detection.

We ensure this by associating each task with a monotonically increasing *serial number* in the scope of the task's user-thread, and once the commit step of some task starts, the task waits for tasks from the same user-thread with lower serial numbers to complete before committing.

Transaction Commit. The transaction commit procedure in TLSTM needs to take into account the reads and writes performed by every single task of the user-transaction, in order to preserve atomicity. Thus, transaction commit differs substantially from SwissTM's, since it is performed by the last task of the user-transaction in program order, which we call the commit-task.

When committing a user-transaction, the commit-task validates the reads of all tasks of the user-transaction. When committing to memory the values of a write user-transaction, the commit-task needs to update all values written by all tasks of the user-transaction. Intermediate tasks take no part in validating reads or updating writes of the user-transaction, while waiting for the commit-task to commit the user-transaction.

Transaction Abort. As in commits, transaction abort in TLSTM involves a coordinated effort from the multiple parallel tasks that comprise the user-transaction. This challenge is especially difficult as some of such tasks might still be running when the abort decision is taken.

When a task receives the abort transaction signal it waits until all tasks from its user-transaction have received that signal. Then, the last task of the aborting user-transaction clears every write-lock of all tasks in its user-transaction and resets the tasks' state to their last known correct values. Finally, the last task signals every past task of its user-transaction to restart, before restarting itself.

Preventing Inter-thread Deadlocks. Since TLSTM supports multiple threads, TLSTM must ensure that there are no deadlocks between tasks of different user-threads writing to several locations.

Imagine the scenario of an application with two user-threads running two tasks each ($T_{A,1}$ represents task 1 from thread A and so on): $T_{A,1}$, $T_{A,2}$, $T_{B,1}$, $T_{B,2}$. $T_{A,2}$ holds the write-lock to location X and $T_{B,2}$ holds the write-lock to location Y. Assume that $T_{A,1}$ wants to write to Y and $T_{B,1}$ wants to write to X and that TLSTM inherits the inter-thread contention manager from SwissTM. Hence, when a task holds the write-lock of a location and tasks from other user-threads want to write to that location, they have to wait for the current writer to commit.

Both tasks $T_{A,1}$ and $T_{B,1}$ will be blocked waiting for the lock owners to abort or commit, but the contention manager will not signal the lock owners to abort and the lock owner tasks will not commit because they are waiting for their past tasks to complete (as a consequence of *serializing commits*).

In order to solve this problem, the inter-thread contention manager must be task-aware, so that it makes decisions according to the user-thread's set of tasks and not for each task individually.

Whenever an inter-thread conflict is detected between two tasks, the contention manager aborts the more speculative one, i.e. the one that has fewer tasks from its past that are still running. Not only does this strategy favor tasks with higher probability of completing successfully, but it also prevents starvation. If contending user-transactions have the same number of completed tasks, then TLSTM employs traditional STM contention management algorithms. Currently, TLSTM implements the two phase greedy contention manager for this case.

Inconsistent Reads. TLS and STM can induce out of order reads that may trigger undesirable effects. For example, picture $T_{A,1}$ writing NULL to location X and then allocating a new object to X. If $T_{A,2}$ reads the intermediate value of X it will crash because of a NULL pointer exception.

While in STM these are prevented through atomicity, as read operations only read values from the user-transaction itself or from committed state. In TLS values can be read from running tasks, which may result in reading intermediate and inaccurate values [4].

Therefore, in a unified runtime it is not possible to prevent all inconsistent reads, so TLSTM needs to detect and take care of those coming from TLS. In TLSTM, when a task reads a location the task needs to check if the location it is reading from is valid. Unfortunately, this validation also takes a toll on correct read operations.

3.3   Algorithm

We now describe in detail how TLSTM overcomes the challenges discussed in the previous section, thereby leveraging SwissTM with TLS support. Algorithms 1 to 3 present the pseudo-code of TLSTM. The following sections explain each aspect of the algorithm in detail.

For each user-thread, the runtime supports up to a fixed number of simultaneously active tasks, called *speculative depth* (SPECDEPTH). Each task is assigned a unique user-thread identifier and a unique serial number which represents the task's position in program order.

Any technique for decomposing each user-thread into tasks can be employed, which is orthogonal to our model and out of the scope of this paper, as long as it ensures that a task does not span across the boundaries we presented earlier. Several standard techniques can be used for user-thread decomposition, from loop iteration speculation (e.g. spec-DOALL and spec-DOACROSS [17]), to procedure fall-through speculation [18], at either compile-time and/or execution-time.

Task, User-Transaction and User-Thread State. Each task maintains the following state inherited from SwissTM:

- *valid-ts*, a timestamp denoting the instant where the read accesses performed by this task are guaranteed to be valid;
- *read-log* and *write-log* tables, each one used to store location entries that were read (resp. written) by the task;

Furthermore, each task also maintains the following new state:

- *tid*, the task's user-thread identifier;
- *serial*, the program order of this task within its user-thread;
- *tx-start-serial* and *tx-commit-serial*, which denote the first and last task, respectively, from the task's user-transaction in program order;
- *try-commit*, a flag that indicates whether this is the last task in the user-transaction;
- *last-writer*, which holds the serial of the last known writer task of the user-thread. Used to check if task validation is required;

Each user-thread maintains the following state, shared by every task running on behalf of this user-thread:

- *completed-task* and *completed-writer*, denoting the serial identifiers of the last completed task and last completed writer task of the user-thread;

- *owners*[*SPECDEPTH*], an array of pointers to the state of each task in the user-thread.

For a given task *tsk* of user-thread *thr*, its state can be obtained at index [*tsk.serial* mod *SPECDEPTH*] of the *thr.owners* array.

Starting a Task. By definition, a task can only start when the number of active tasks in the given user-thread is lower than the *SPECDEPTH* limit. Once that condition is satisfied, the task is assigned the next serial number in its user-thread and its initial state is saved in the corresponding position of the *owners* array (line 2 alg. 1). If the task belongs to an user-transaction, its start and commit-serial are assigned. The *last-writer* of the new task is assigned the value of the last completed writer of that task's user-thread (line 3 alg. 1). The *valid-ts* of the new task is initialized with the current value of the global counter *commit-ts* (line 4 alg. 1).

Reading. Before reading, the task consults the location's write-lock. In TLSTM, a location's write-lock is either unlocked or points to the location's redo-log. In sum, the location's redo-log has the last speculative write-log entry for that location. TLSTM's write-log entry complements that of SwissTM with the serial number and user-thread identifier of the task that owns the write-log entry, as well as links to entries from past tasks which also wrote to that entry's location.

There are two possible branches for a read operation on a location, depending on whether the location is write-locked by the task's own user-thread or not. If the location is not write-locked by the task's user-thread, i.e. the location is either write-locked by another user-thread or unlocked, TLSTM follows the same procedure as SwissTM: the task reads the location's committed value from memory (line 16 alg. 1).

If, otherwise, the location has been write-locked by the task's user-thread, the task needs to read from the most recent speculative value. This value was either written by the task itself or a past task. The task traverses the redo-log until it finds the entry the task itself wrote to, or a past task wrote to (line 8 alg. 1). If it was the task itself to write to that location, the task can simply return the written value (line 10 alg. 1), since the task's reads from its own writes do not need to be validated.

If, instead, the last speculative value was written by a past task, the task first checks if that past task has already completed. If the past writer task has not completed yet, the task waits until the past task has completed in order to proceed (line 11 alg. 1). TLSTM implements this restriction to simplify the WAR conflict validation procedure. This procedure would have to additionally check the number of writes a past task had performed on the location, in order to validate intra-thread reads done from running tasks.

Afterwards, the task performs validation looking for WAR conflicts, which may have occurred between the current task and the past task that just completed (line 13 alg. 1). If all went well, the task creates a new entry in the task-read-log and adds the location and the validation information (task's serial number) to that log (line 14 alg. 1).

In order to detect dangerous inconsistent reads that could crash the application TLSTM uses several known techniques from previous STLSs [4].

Writing. The task starts by checking if the location has been write-locked by the task itself (line 36 alg. 2). If it has, it just needs to update the logged value, like SwissTM does.

If this is not the case, three situations may occur, depending on whether the lock is:

Write-locked by Another Task from the Same User-Thread. If the location is write-locked by a future task, the future task is signaled to abort, since the task is from the past of the location's current writer in program order (line 47 alg. 2).

If the location is write-locked by a past task, TLSTM needs to check if that past task has already completed (line 45 alg. 2). If the past task is still running, the task will rollback since it is from the future of the location's current writer in program order. If the past task has completed, TLSTM locks the location for writing and adds a new entry to the redo-log which previously owned the write-lock (line 51 alg. 2).

Write-locked by a Task from Another User-Thread. In this case (line 41 alg. 2), the task calls the contention manager in order to decide whether the writer task or the current owner of the write-lock must abort. If the contention manager decides the owner of the write-lock must abort, the writer task waits until the write-lock is eventually unlocked.

Unlocked. This means the present task is the only active task writing to that location. Here the task atomically locks the location's write-lock by $compare - and - swap$, creates a new redo-log that owns the location, assigns the redo-log to the write-lock and continues. Finally, the task performs inter-thread validation, just like SwissTM. Additionally, the task performs intra-thread validation looking for WAR conflicts that may have occurred in the meantime.

Commit. The commit of a user-transaction is carried out by its last task (in program order), called the *commit-task* , once the commit-task and all preceding tasks have completed (line 66 alg. 3). The commit step is very similar to SwissTM, with a few modifications. The commit-task must now consider the read-logs and write-logs of every task of the user-transaction (and not just its own logs) when validating read-logs or committing writes.

Every user-transaction now needs to check for possible validation at commit time, whereas on SwissTM only write user-transactions needed to (line 78 alg. 3). The reason why read user-transactions can no longer proceed without checking for validation is because each task of the user-transaction may have completed at different points in time. This means some tasks of the same user-transaction may have different valid-ts values, thus TLSTM cannot rely on the commit-task's valid-ts alone. If all tasks of a user-transaction have the same valid-ts, then the commit-task can skip this validation.

Algorithm 1. Pseudo-code representation of TLSTM

```
 1 function start(serial, program-thread-id, try-commit, start-serial, commit-serial)
 2     task-init(serial, ptid, try-commit, start-serial, commit-serial);
 3     last-writer ← uthread[tsk.ptid].completed-writer;
 4     tsk.valid-ts ← commit-ts;

 5 function read-word(tsk, addr)
 6     (r-lock, w-lock) ← map-addr-to-locks(addr);
 7     if is-locked-by-my-thread(w-lock, tsk) then
 8         while w-lock and w-lock.serial > tsk.serial do
 9             w-lock = w-lock.previous-entry;
10         if w-lock.serial = tsk.serial then return read(addr);
11         while uthread[tsk.ptid].completed-task < w-lock.serial − 1 do
12             if abort-transaction then  rollback(tsk);
13         if uthread[tsk.ptid].completed-writer > last-writer and not
           validate-task(tsk) then rollback(tsk);
14         add-to-task-read-log(tsk, w-lock, w-lock.serial);
15         return read(addr);
16     return SwissTM-read-commited-value(addr);

17 function validate-task(tsk)
18     for log-entry in tsk.task-read-log do
19         if is-locked-by-my-thread(log-entry.w-lock) then
20             w-lock = log-entry.w-lock;
21             if w-lock.serial = tsk.serial then
22                 w-lock = w-lock.previous-entry;
23             if w-lock = NULL or log-entry.serial ≠ w-lock.serial then
24                 return false;
25         else  return false;
26     for log-entry in tsk.read-log do
27         if is-locked-by-my-thread(log-entry.w-lock) then
           w-lock = log-entry.w-lock;
28         while w-lock do
29             if w-lock.serial >= serial then
30                 w-lock = w-lock.previous-entry;
31             else  return false;
32     return true;
```

Algorithm 2. Pseudo-code representation of TLSTM

---

33 function *write-word*(*tsk, addr, value*)
34   if *aborted-internally* then *rollback*(*tsk*);
35   (*r-lock, w-lock*) ← *map-addr-to-locks*(*addr*);
36   if *is-locked-by-my-task*(*w-lock, tsk*) then
37   *update-log-entry*(*w-lock, addr, value*);
38   return;

39   while *true* do
40   if *abort-transaction* then *rollback*(*tsk*);
41   if *is-locked-by-other-thread*(*w-lock*) then
42   if *cm-should-abort*(*tsk, w-lock*) then *rollback*(*tsk*);
43   else continue;

44   if *w-lock.serial* < *tsk.serial* then
45   if *uthread[tsk.ptid].completed-task* < *w-lock.serial* then *rollback*(*tsk*);

46   else
47   *owners[w-lock.serial].aborted-internally* = *true*;
48   continue;

49   *previous-entry* = *w-lock*;
50   *log-entry* ← *add-to-write-log*(*tsk, w-lock, addr, value , ptid, serial, previous-entry*);
51   if *compare&swap*(*w-lock, w-lock, log-entry*) then break;

52   if *read*(*r-lock*) > *tsk.valid-ts* and not *extend*(*tsk*) then *rollback*(*tsk*);
53   if *uthread[tsk.ptid].completed-writer* > *last-writer* and not *validate-task*(*tsk*) then *rollback*(*tsk*);

54 function *cm-should-abort*(*tsk, w-lock*)
55   *task-progress* = *uthread[tsk.ptid].completed-task* - *tsk.start-serial*;
56   *owner-progress* = *uthread[w-lock.ptid].completed-task* − *w-lock.owner.start-serial*;
57   if *task-progress* > *owner-progress* then
58   *w-lock.owner.abort-transaction* = *true*;
59   return *false*;

60   if *task-progress* < *owner-progress* then return *true*;
61   if *cm-task-stronger-than-owner*(*tsk, w-lock.owner*) then
62   *w-lock.owner.abort-transaction* = *true*;
63   return *false*;

64   return *true*;

Algorithm 3. Pseudo-code representation of TLSTM

```
65  function commit(tsk)
66      while uthread[tsk.ptid].completed-task < tsk.serial - 1 do
67      |   if aborted-internally then  rollback(tsk);
68      if abort-transaction then rollback-transaction(start-serial);
69      if uthread[tsk.ptid].completed-writer ≠ last-writer then
70      |   if validate-task(tsk) = false then  rollback(tsk);
71      if not tsk.try-commit then
72          if not is-read-only(tsk) then
73          |   uthread[tsk.ptid].completed-writer = serial;
74          uthread[tsk.ptid].completed-task = serial;
75          while uthread[tsk.ptid].completed-task < tsk.commit-serial do
76          |   if abort-transaction then rollback(tsk);
77          return;
78      if (abort-serial = validate(tx)) > 0 then
79      |   rollback-transaction(abort-serial);
80      if not is-read-only(tx) then
81          for write-log in tx do
82              for log-entry in write-log do
83              |   write(log-entry.r-lock, locked);
84          ts ← increment&get(commit-ts);
85          if (abort-serial = validate(tx)) > 0 then
86          |   rollback-transaction(abort-serial);
87          for write-log in tx do
88              for log-entry in write-log do
89                  write(log-entry.addr, log-entry.value);
90                  if log-entry.w-lock = log-entry then
91                  |   write(log-entry.r-lock, ts);
92                  write(log-entry.w-lock, unlocked);
93          uthread[tsk.ptid].completed-writer = serial;
94      uthread[tsk.ptid].completed-task = serial;

95  function rollback-transaction(start-serial)
96      for write-log in tx do
97          for log-entry in write-log do
98          |   write(log-entry.w-lock, log-entry.previous-entry);
99          write-log.clear();
100     uthread[tsk.ptid].completed-writer = start-serial-1;
101     uthread[tsk.ptid].completed-task = start-serial-1;
102     abort-transaction =false;
103     for i=start-serial TO serial-1 do
104     |   owners[i].abort-transaction = true;
105     rollback(tsk);
```

The commit of the user-transaction then proceeds as in SwissTM, locking the write-logs' read-locks (line 83 alg. 3), incrementing the commit timestamp and validating the user-transaction (line 85 alg. 3). Then, the commit-task updates the values in main memory with the new values from the write-logs of all the user-transaction's tasks (line 89 alg. 3). At the end, the commit-task releases the read and write locks associated with the updated values (line 92 alg. 3).

Finally, the commit-task updates the completed-writer counter if it belongs to a write user-transactions, and updates the completed-task counter to signal the completion of the task and user-transaction (line 93 alg. 3).

Intermediate tasks of a user-transaction just have to update the completed-writer counter, if they have written anything, and the completed-task counter (line 74 alg. 3). Then, they start waiting until all future tasks of the user-transaction have completed, and thus the user-transaction has committed, so that the task can exit safely.

Aborts. Aborting a single task follows the same procedure of SwissTM's user-transaction abort. TLSTM needs to abort a single task when an intra-thread WAR or WAW conflict is detected. Intra-thread WAW conflicts are checked for in two distinct places. First, WAW conflict verification is performed when a task wishes to write to a location (line 34 alg. 2). TLSTM could perform this verification on read operations too, but that would incur in more overhead for the most common read operation. Second, TLSTM checks for intra-thread WAW conflicts at commit time, while waiting for all past tasks to complete. When all past tasks have completed and the task has not aborted due to a WAW conflict, the task needs to be validated for previously undetected WAR conflicts (as explained in Section 3.2). If WAR conflict validation fails, the task must be individually aborted.

There are also situations where a task may need to abort its entire user-transaction (every single task of the user-transaction to which the aborting task belongs to) because of an inter-thread write-write conflict. The first situation occurs at commit time, if the task passed WAR conflict validation (line 68 alg. 3). The second situation occurs also at commit time, while an intermediate task waits for the future tasks of its user-transaction to commit (line 76 alg. 3).

We chose to abort every single task of the aborting user-transaction because of the simplicity of this approach. The alternative would be to abort only the user-transaction's tasks that wrote to the location that triggered the write-write conflict, and the user-transaction's tasks that read those speculative values. Discovering all these tasks would be very complex, since TLSTM would need to traverse the write-log of each task in the user-transaction in search of the location that triggered the abort and mark those tasks for abort. Then TLSTM would need to traverse the task-read-log of each task of the user-transaction in search for the locations written by the tasks marked to abort and also mark the tasks where TLSTM finds those locations.

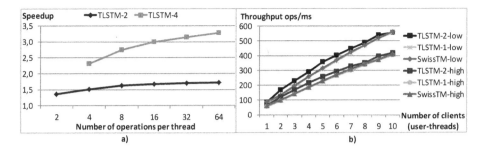

Fig. 1. a) Speedup in the red-black tree's throughput for TLSTM with 2 and 4 tasks and 1 thread vs SwissTM with 1 thread; b) Throughput of TLSTM with 1 and 2 tasks per thread vs SwissTM, with an increasing number of threads on STAMP's Vacation

4   Evaluation

This section evaluates a TLSTM prototype, which was implemented in C++, based on the C++ implementation of the SwissTM STM, using POSIX threads. The measurements discussed next were obtained using a quad AMD Opteron 6272 with 64 cores total for the STAMP Vacation application and a SPARC Enterprise T5120 server with up to 64 hardware threads for the remainder of the benchmarks. Each result measures the throughput of the respective runtime in operations per second and is the average of three repeated experiments.

We want to determine answers to two main questions: *1) can our unified TLS+STM approach effectively achieve speed-up from simple STM programs?*; and *2) in which kind of applications is TLSTM more advantageous, and in which applications is it not a good approach?*

We started by looking at a modified version of the traditional Red-black Tree micro-benchmark in order to figure out if task size had any impact on the unified runtime's performance. In this modified version each thread runs a transaction that performs a number of lookup operations, which are read-only, to the Red-Black Tree. We can easily split those transactions into several tasks that execute fewer operations each, e.g. if a transaction runs four operations in total, we can split it into two tasks that run two operations each.

From this experiment we can see that task size does indeed have an impact on the runtime's performance (Figure 1.a). For larger task sizes we obtain a better throughput ratio, for both two and four tasks per user-thread, from which we can deduce that our approach has better performance in applications with large transactions which can be split into large tasks.

Therefore, we started looking at the STAMP application suite [9] in search of applications with large transactions that could be easily split into several parallel tasks. However, most of STAMP's applications had either very small transactions or no further parallelization potential. One application stood out though, the Vacation application which implements an online transaction processing system for travel reservations. A client can issue several operations to the system,

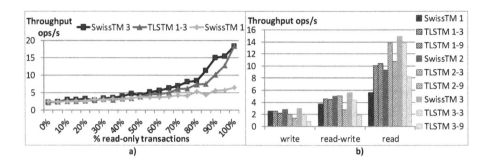

Fig. 2. a) Throughput of TLSTM with 1 thread and 3 tasks vs SwissTM with 1 thread and 3 threads; b) Throughput of SwissTM vs TLSTM with 3 and 9 tasks per thread, with up to 3 threads; Both on STMBench7 long traversals only

e.g. reserve a plane ticket, reserve an hotel or rent a car, and each operation is encapsulated in a transaction.

Since these operations are quite small, similar in size to the red-black tree micro-benchmark operations, we modified the Vacation benchmark taking into account the red-black tree results. We picture each client issuing eight operations at a time, which now incorporate an application server transaction and can be easily split into two tasks, executing four operations each. We still mimic the low and high contention scenarios of the original Vacation application.

The results of this experiment (Figure 1.b) show us that a unified TLS+STM runtime using two task per user-thread improves the throughput of applications with a self-imposed limit to the number of spawned user-threads, in this case the number of concurrent clients being served. Interestingly, both low and high contention scenarios of this application show the same behavior, which we assume to occur because of the very low contention between operations, even in the higher contention scenario. We can also see that TLSTM with one task per user-thread has a very similar throughput to SwissTM, with both lines overlapping most of the time, on both scenarios. This suggests that there are applications where TLSTM can be used as a replacement to SwissTM.

Another interesting reference benchmark for STMs that includes large transactions is STMBench7 [8], which has a wide range of operations on a very large shared data structure. From these operations we targeted those which could be automatically split into tasks by a compiler or runtime, in which the set of "Long Traversals" operations stood out. It was also the most computationally intensive set of operations, which made it a perfect candidate to parallelize even further. Most of the remainder operations were either non-divisible or very short, so they would not benefit from parallelization too much. The shared data structure of STMBench7 is built as a tree of objects, with three branches departing from the root, each with arbitrary depth. Therefore, it made sense to split the "Long Traversals" which traverse the whole tree in multiples of three tasks.

The experiment on figure 2.a compares the performance of running one and three user-threads in SwissTM to one user-thread in TLSTM with three tasks.

By comparing TLSTM with three tasks and one user-thread to SwissTM with three user-threads we can see how much does the programmer gain if he is capable of hand-parallelizing more code into transactions, instead of relying on automated code division and a unified TLS+STM runtime. But if he does rely on such a runtime, we can see that TLSTM is most beneficial for read-dominated workloads. In fact, for 100% read-only transactions TLSTM achieves practically full speedup. In contrast, TLSTM already performs worse than the base STM for write-dominated workloads.

The problem lies within STMBench7's write "Long Traversals". These write-transactions have a high intra-thread conflict rate (several tasks writing to the same location). Such conflicts translate into the observed decrease in perfor-mance, since these transactions will execute almost serially. This is the worst case scenario for TLSTM. In write-transactions with a low conflict rate, such as those of the STAMP's Vacation application, we see that TLSTM performs close to the observed behavior on read-only transactions.

For the last of our experiments, we consider the default settings that STM-Bench7 originally defines [8]: *write-dominated workload* (10% read operations); *read-write workload* (60% read operations); and *read-dominated workload* (90% read operations).

This last experiment aims at studying how TLSTM behaves as the number of user-threads grows, and how such performance compares to SwissTM running the same number of user-threads. We can see in figure 2.b that TLSTM with three tasks decreases its performance when going from two to three user-threads, whereas SwissTM scales quite acceptably on read-write and read-dominated workloads. This is an effect of the increased contention in the workload. The inter-thread abort procedure is substantially more complex in TLSTM than in SwissTM, thus hindering its performance in scenarios where contention is higher (more conflicts and rollbacks).

However, we can see that for read-dominated workloads TLSTM with three tasks outperforms SwissTM by 80% on one user-thread and 48% on two user-threads. By increasing the number of user-threads we increase the level of con-tention even further, thus providing diminishing returns. When executing an inter-thread abort, all of the user-thread's tasks must be aborted. Thus, the inter-thread abort procedure's performance is directly influenced by the number of tasks in the user-thread. In order to measure this influence, we experimented on TLSTM with nine tasks and up to three user-threads (Figure 2.b).

In the case of one user-thread in the read-dominated workload, we can achieve even more speedup with nine TLSTM tasks than with three. But as soon as we get to use two user-threads, the inter-thread contention becomes high enough to harm TLSTM's performance. We can see this is a trend for increasing numbers of user-threads, on any type of workload. This fact suggests that the inter-thread abort procedure is one of the major bottlenecks in the unified approach of TLSTM.

We conclude that each application using TLSTM will have to find a sweet spot between the number of user-threads and tasks in use. Too many user-threads may prevent scalability of the application, while too many tasks may dramatically hinder the performance of the hybrid runtime. For STMBench7's "Long Traversals" this spot seems to be two user-threads with three tasks each, in order to achieve maximum performance.

5   Related Work

Originally introduced in the seminal paper from Herlihy and Moss [3], the interest and advancement in the STM area has grown dramatically in recent years, incited by the advent of affordable multicore processors. Still, most STM programs are still organized as a monolithic collection of a relatively small number of coarse-grained threads. Evidence of this is found in most benchmarks (e.g. [8, 9, 19, 20]) and representative applications of STM.

A distinct research direction that has similar goals as STM is automatic parallelization of sequential programs. Classically, this approach focused on automatically identifying tasks that have no data dependencies (e.g. independent loop iterations) and executing them in parallel. On the other hand, the approach of Thread-Level Speculation (TLS) developed over the last decade has a more aggressive technique for extracting parallelism from sequential programs [1, 2, 21–23]. Rather than parallelizing only provable independent tasks, TLS executes tasks in parallel speculatively and relies on the runtime detection of violations to the sequential semantics of the original program to discard the changes to the program state and restart the affected tasks.

While the first proposed TLS solutions relied on hardware support, recently there has been a growing focus on software approaches. Solutions such as [17, 24–27, 4] are examples of successful efforts towards Software TLS that can yield substantial speed-ups from sequential programs. Still, the conservative nature of TLS constitutes a key limitation to the level of parallelism that it can extract. While proposed TLS systems have been shown to achieve considerable speed-ups (e.g. 77% on average according to Oancea et. al. [4]), most non-trivial programs that do not fit in the category of embarrassingly parallel problems have relatively low bounds on the level of conflict-free speculation.

Most of the run-time support of Software TLS has close resemblance with an STM run-time. For instance, writes are speculative, as they may need to be undone; accesses must be validated for conflicts; tasks have a commit stage; and tasks can be aborted, and restarted. Departing naturally from such an observation, a number of recent Software TLS solutions rely on an underlying simplified STM run-time to offer TLS to single-threaded programs [28]. These solutions are radically different than our proposal: while TLSTM combines STM and TLS, allowing each thread in a transactional multi-threaded programs to be automatically parallelized, TLS solutions relying on STM only address the case of single-threaded programs.

To the best of our knowledge, the only work that addresses TLS support on multi-threaded programs is due to Martinez and Torrelas [29]. However, their approach is fundamentally different from ours, as it only tries to speculatively execute and synchronize threads that would otherwise be blocked waiting on a barrier, lock or flag. Unifying STM and TLS in a common run-time implies solving a number of fundamentally different problems.

In the context of replicated STMs there are some recent examples of systems that employ automatic speculative parallelization to hide the expensive latency of distributed transaction commit [30, 31]. In contract to our contribution, these solutions are proposed in a distinct context (distributed STMs) and limit speculation to one transaction that runs in parallel while the preceding transaction is awaiting commitment.

6   Concluding Remarks

The rapidly increasing core count of commodity machines is demanding highly parallel programs. We claim that the time has come to question a hybrid direction that unifies two prominent research directions of parallel programming that, up to now, have been working (almost) separately with very similar goals.

This paper shows that, although unifying TLS and TM in a hybrid middleware introduces hard challenges, they can be overcome and untapped parallelism potential can be discovered. We describe our experience with a first proof of concept, the TLSTM algorithm. Our results obtained with trivial and non-trivial benchmarks confirm that STM and STLS do add up successfully for some workloads. Our results also show that there is still a considerable amount of improvement to be made towards devising a unified STM+STLS solution that scales gracefully with both the number of hand-parallelized threads and the number of automatically spawned speculative tasks.

Our preliminary work shows that issues such as transaction rollback and commit are now much more complex (due to the multiple tasks that may comprise each user-transaction), and future work should focus on their negative impact on the overall throughput. The location redo-logs have also showed to add substantial overhead. Hence, different approaches for handling speculative writes (e.g. in-place writes [4]) should be studied.

References

1. Sohi, G.S., Breach, S.E., Vijaykumar, T.N.: Multiscalar processors. In: 25 Years of the International Symposia on Computer Architecture (selected papers), ISCA 1998, pp. 521–532. ACM, New York (1998)
2. Hammond, L., Willey, M., Olukotun, K.: Data speculation support for a chip multiprocessor. In: SIGPLAN Not., vol. 33, pp. 58–69 (1998)
3. Herlihy, M., Moss, J.E.B.: Transactional memory: Architectural support for lock-free data structures. In: Proceedings of the 20th Annual International Symposium on Computer Architecture (1993)
4. Oancea, C.E., Mycroft, A., Harris, T.: A lightweight in-place implementation for software thread-level speculation. In: Proceedings of the Twenty-First Annual Symposium on Parallelism in Algorithms and Architectures, pp. 223–232 (2009)

5. Dragojević, A., Felber, P., Gramoli, V., Guerraoui, R.: Why stm can be more than a research toy. Commun. ACM 54(4), 70–77 (2011)
6. Howard, J., Dighe, S., Hoskote, Y., Vangal, S., Finan, D., Ruhl, G., Jenkins, D., Wilson, H., Borkar, N., Schrom, G., Pailet, F., Jain, S., Jacob, T., Yada, S., Marella, S., Salihundam, P., Erraguntla, V., Konow, M., Riepen, M., Droege, G., Lindemann, J., Gries, M., Apel, T., Henriss, K., Lund-Larsen, T., Steibl, S., Borkar, S., De, V., Van Der Wijngaart, R., Mattson, T.: A 48-core ia-32 message-passing processor with dvfs in 45nm cmos. In: Solid-State Circuits Conference Digest of Technical Papers (ISSCC), 2010 IEEE International, pp. 108–109 (February 2010)
7. Oplinger, J.T., Heine, D.L., Lam, M.S.: In search of speculative thread-level parallelism. In: Proceedings of the 1999 International Conference on Parallel Architectures and Compilation Techniques. PACT 1999 (1999)
8. Guerraoui, R., Kapalka, M., Vitek, J.: Stmbench7: a benchmark for software transactional memory. SIGOPS Oper. Syst. Rev. 41, 315–324 (2007)
9. Cao Minh, C., Chung, J., Kozyrakis, C., Olukotun, K.: STAMP: Stanford transactional applications for multi-processing. In: IISWC 2008: Proceedings of The IEEE International Symposium on Workload Characterization (September 2008)
10. Ansari, M., Kotselidis, C., Watson, I., Kirkham, C.C., Luján, M., Jarvis, K.: Leetm: A non-trivial benchmark suite for transactional memory. In: ICA3PP (2008)
11. Zyulkyarov, F., Gajinov, V., Unsal, O.S., Cristal, A., Ayguadé, E., Harris, T., Valero, M.: Atomic quake: using transactional memory in an interactive multiplayer game server. In: PPoPP 2009: Proceedings of the 14th ACM SIGPLAN Symposium on Principles and Practice of Parallel Programming, pp. 25–34 (2009)
12. Carvalho, N., Cachopo, J.: a., Rodrigues, L., Silva, A.R.: Versioned transactional shared memory for the fénixedu web application. In: Proceedings of the 2nd Workshop on Dependable Distributed Data Management, pp. 15–18 (2008)
13. Dragojević, A., Guerraoui, R., Kapalka, M.: Stretching transactional memory. In: Proceedings of the 2009 ACM SIGPLAN Conference on Programming Language Design and Implementation, pp. 155–165. ACM (2009)
14. Guerraoui, R., Kapalka, M.: On the correctness of transactional memory. In: PPoPP 2008: Proceedings of the 13th ACM SIGPLAN Symposium on Principles and Practice of Parallel Programming (2008)
15. Dice, D., Shalev, O., Shavit, N.: Transactional Locking II. In: Dolev, S. (ed.) DISC 2006. LNCS, vol. 4167, pp. 194–208. Springer, Heidelberg (2006)
16. Felber, P., Fetzer, C., Riegel, T.: Dynamic performance tuning of word-based software transactional memory. In: Proceedings of the 13th ACM SIGPLAN Symposium on Principles and Practice of Parallel Programming, pp. 237–246 (2008)
17. Kim, H., Raman, A., Liu, F., Lee, J.W., August, D.I.: Scalable speculative parallelization on commodity clusters. In: Proceedings of the 2010 43rd Annual IEEE/ACM International Symposium on Microarchitecture, MICRO 43 (2010)
18. Chen, M.K., Olukotun, K.: Exploiting method-level parallelism in single-threaded java programs. Proceedings of the 1998 International Conference on Parallel Architectures and Compilation Techniques, PACT 1998 (1998)
19. Gajinov, V., Zyulkyarov, F., Unsal, O.S., Cristal, A., Ayguade, E., Harris, T., Valero, M.: Quaketm: parallelizing a complex sequential application using transactional memory. In: Proceedings of the 23rd International Conference on Supercomputing, ICS 2009, pp. 126–135. ACM (2009)
20. Watson, I., Kirkham, C., Luján, M.: A study of a transactional parallel routing algorithm. In: Malyshkin, V.E. (ed.) PaCT 2007. LNCS, vol. 4671, pp. 388–398. Springer, Heidelberg (2007)

21. Steffan, J.G., Colohan, C.B., Zhai, A., Mowry, T.C.: A scalable approach to thread-level speculation. In: Proceedings of the 27th Annual International Symposium on Computer Architecture, ISCA 2000, pp. 1–12 (2000)
22. Steffan, J.G., Colohan, C., Zhai, A., Mowry, T.C.: The stampede approach to thread-level speculation. ACM Trans. Comput. Syst. 23, 253–300 (2005)
23. Liu, W., Tuck, J., Ceze, L., Ahn, W., Strauss, K., Renau, J., Torrellas, J.: Posh: a tls compiler that exploits program structure. In: Proceedings of the Eleventh ACM SIGPLAN Symposium on Principles and Practice of Parallel Programming, pp. 158–167. ACM, New York (2006)
24. Oancea, C.E., Mycroft, A.: Software thread-level speculation: an optimistic library implementation. Proceedings of the 1st International Workshop on Multicore Software Engineering, IWMSE 2008, 23–32 (2008)
25. Devabhaktuni, S.: Softspec: Software-based speculative parallelism via stride prediction. In: Master's thesis, M.I.T (1999)
26. Cintra, M., Llanos, D.R.: Toward efficient and robust software speculative parallelization on multiprocessors. In: Proceedings of the ninth ACM SIGPLAN Symposium on Principles and Practice of Parallel Programming, pp. 13–24 (2003)
27. Rundberg, P., Stenström, P.: An all-software thread-level data dependence speculation system for multiprocessors. Journal of Instruction-Level Parallelism (2001)
28. Mehrara, M., Hao, J., Hsu, P.C., Mahlke, S.: Parallelizing sequential applications on commodity hardware using a low-cost software transactional memory. In: Proceedings of the 2009 ACM SIGPLAN Conference on Programming Language Design and Implementation, PLDI 2009, pp. 166–176 (2009)
29. Martínez, J.F., Torrellas, J.: Speculative synchronization: applying thread-level speculation to explicitly parallel applications. In: Proceedings of the 10th International Conference on Architectural Support for Programming Languages and Operating Systems, ASPLOS-X, pp. 18–29. ACM, New York (2002)
30. Kemme, B., Pedone, F., Alonso, G., Schiper, A., Wiesmann, M.: Using optimistic atomic broadcast in transaction processing systems. IEEE Trans. on Knowl. and Data Eng. 15(4), 1018–1032 (2003)
31. Palmieri, R., Quaglia, F., Romano, P.: Osare: Opportunistic speculation in actively replicated transactional systems. In: Proceedings of the 2011 IEEE 30th International Symposium on Reliable Distributed Systems, SRDS 2011, pp. 59–64. IEEE Computer Society Press, Washington, DC (2011)

Message-Passing Concurrency
for Scalable, Stateful, Reconfigurable Middleware

Cosmin Arad[1,2], Jim Dowling[1,2], and Seif Haridi[1,2]

[1] KTH Royal Institute of Technology, Stockholm, Sweden
[2] Swedish Institute of Computer Science, Kista, Sweden
{cosmin,jdowling,seif}@sics.se

Abstract. Message-passing concurrency (MPC) is increasingly being used to build systems software that scales well on multi-core hardware. Functional programming implementations of MPC, such as Erlang, have also leveraged their stateless nature to build middleware that is not just scalable, but also dynamically reconfigurable. However, many middleware platforms lend themselves more naturally to a stateful programming model, supporting session and application state. A limitation of existing programming models and frameworks that support dynamic reconfiguration for stateful middleware, such as component frameworks, is that they are not designed for MPC.

In this paper, we present Kompics, a component model and programming framework, that supports the construction and composition of dynamically reconfigurable middleware using stateful, concurrent, message-passing components. An added benefit of our approach is that by decoupling our component execution model, we can run the same code in both simulation and production environments. We present the architectural patterns and abstractions that Kompics facilitates and we evaluate them using a case study of a non-trivial key-value store that we built using Kompics. We show how our model enables the systematic development and testing of scalable, dynamically reconfigurable middleware.

Keywords: component model, message-passing, compositional concurrency, dynamic reconfiguration, multi-core execution, reproducible simulation, distributed systems architecture.

1 Introduction

In recent times, there has been a marked increase in the use of programming languages and frameworks that support message-passing concurrency (MPC) to build high performance servers [1, 2]. The main reasons for the renewed interest in MPC are that it scales well on multi-core hardware architectures and that it provides a simple and *compositional* concurrent programming model, free from the quirks and idiosyncrasies of locks and threads. Another reason is that high performance non-blocking sockets map easily to MPC applications. In addition to this, functional programming implementations of MPC, such as Erlang [3] and Scala actors [4], have the benefit of being suitable for building middleware that is dynamically reconfigurable. Due to its stateless nature and support for

P. Narasimhan and P. Triantafillou (Eds.): Middleware 2012, LNCS 7662, pp. 208–228, 2012.

message passing, Erlang supports the construction of software that can be safely upgraded online. Message processing can be temporarily suspended in modules marked for upgrade, and the problem of transferring state from the old module to the new module is largely avoided.

The challenge we address in this paper is how to provide support for both MPC and dynamic reconfiguration in a framework for building high-performance middleware that lends itself more naturally to a stateful programming model, supporting session and application state. Existing stateful programming models and frameworks that support dynamic reconfiguration, such as component frameworks [5], are not designed for MPC support and they do not decouple their execution model from component code. As a result, they cannot run the same code in both simulation and production environments.

In previous work on dynamically reconfigurable middleware, component models, such as OpenCom [5] and Fractal [6], developed mechanisms such as explicit dependency management, component quiescence, and reconfigurable connectors for safely adapting systems online. However, the style of component interaction, based on blocking interface invocation, precludes compositional concurrency in these models making them unsuited to present day multi-core architectures.

Our work is also relevant within the context of popular non-blocking socket frameworks that are used to build high performance event-driven server applications [7], such as Lift [1] and Twitter's Finagle [8] for Scala, and Facebook's Tornado [9] for Python. Kompics' asynchronous event programming framework allows it to seamlessly integrate different non-blocking networking frameworks (such as Netty, Apache Mina, and Grizzly)[1] as pluggable components.

Kompics is a message-passing, concurrent, and hierarchical component model with support for dynamic reconfiguration. The broad goal of Kompics is to raise the level of abstraction in programming distributed systems. We provide constructs, mechanisms, architectural patterns, as well as programming, concurrency, and execution models that enable programmers to construct and compose reusable and modular distributed abstractions. We believe this is an important contribution because it lowers the cost and accelerates the development and evaluation of more reliable distributed systems. The other main motivation for our asynchronous event programming framework is performance, particularly for high-concurrency networked applications.

Through a case-study of a scalable key-value store, we show that the performance of traditional event-driven programming does not have to come at the cost of more complex programs. Using encapsulation, components can hide event-driven control flow and support component reuse. We leverage encapsulation when testing Kompics systems, by enabling the same component code to be run in both simulation and production systems. To support the easy specification of simulation experiments, we introduce a domain-specific language that provides constructs for generating simulation experiment scenarios containing thousands of nodes.

---

[1] http://www.jboss.org/netty;
   http://mina.apache.org; http://grizzly.java.net

A summary of our key principles in the design of Kompics are as follows. First, we tackle the increasing complexity of modern distributed systems through hierarchical abstraction. Second, we decouple components from each other to enable dynamic system evolution and runtime dependency injection. Third, we decouple component code from its executor to enable different execution environments.

2   Component Model

Kompics is a component model targeted at building distributed systems by composing protocols programmed as event-driven components. Kompics components are reactive state machines that execute concurrently and communicate by passing data-carrying typed events, through typed bidirectional ports, connected by channels. This section introduces the conceptual entities of our component model and its programming constructs, its execution model, as well as constructs enabling dynamic reconfiguration, component life-cycle and fault management.

2.1   Concepts in Kompics

The fundamental Kompics entities are events, ports, components, event handlers, subscriptions, and channels. We introduce them here and show examples of their definitions with snippets of Java code. The Kompics component model is programming language independent, however, we use Java to illustrate a formal definition of its concepts.

Events. Events are passive and immutable *typed* objects having any number of typed attributes. The type of an attribute can be any valid type in the host programming language. New event types can be defined by sub-classing old ones. Here are two example event type definitions in Java[2]:

```
1  class Message extends Event {
2      Address source;
3      Address destination;
4  }
```

```
1  class DataMessage extends Message {
2      Data data;
3      int sequenceNumber;
4  }
```

In our Java implementation of Kompics, all event types are descendants of a root type, Event. We write DataMessage⊆Message to denote that DataMessage is a subtype of Message. In diagrams, we represent an event using the ◆Event graphical notation, where Event is the event's type, e.g., Message.

Ports. Ports are *bidirectional* event-based component interfaces. A port is a gate through which a component communicates with other components in its environment by sending and receiving events. A port allows a specific set of event types to pass in each direction. We label the two directions of a port as *positive* $(+)$ and *negative* $(-)$. The *type* of a port specifies the set of event types that can traverse the port in the positive direction and the set of event types that can traverse the port in the negative direction. Concretely, a port type definition

---

[2] We omit the constructors, getters, setters, access modifiers, and import statements.

consists of two sets of event types: a "positive" set and a "negative" set. There is no sub-typing relationship for port types.

Here are two example port type definitions in Java[3]:

```
1 class Network extends PortType {{
2     positive(Message.class);
3     negative(Message.class);
4 }}
```

```
1 class Timer extends PortType {{
2     indication(Timeout.class);        //positive
3     request(ScheduleTimeout.class);//negative
4     request(CancelTimeout.class);   //negative
5 }}
```

In this example we define a Network port type which allows events of type Message (or a subtype thereof) to pass in both ('+' and '−') directions. The Timer port type allows ScheduleTimeout and CancelTimeout events to pass in the '−' direction and Timeout events to pass in the '+' direction.

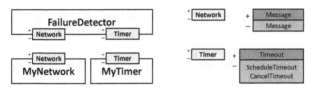

Fig. 1. The MyNetwork component has a **provided** Network port. MyTimer has a **provided** Timer port. The FailureDetector has a **required** Network port and a **required** Timer port. In diagrams, a provided port is figured on the top border, and a required port on the bottom border of a component.

Conceptually, a port type can be seen as a service or protocol abstraction with an event-based interface. It accepts *request* events and delivers *indication* or *response* events. By convention, we associate requests with the '−' direction and responses or indications with the '+' direction. In our example, a Timer abstraction accepts ScheduleTimeout requests and delivers Timeout indications. A Network abstraction accepts Message events at a sending node (*source*) and delivers Message events at a receiving node (*destination*) in a distributed system.

A component that *implements* a protocol or service will *provide* a port of the type that represents the implemented abstraction. Through this provided port, the component will receive the request events and trigger the indication events specified by the port's type. In other words, for a provided port, the '−' direction is incoming to the component and the '+' direction is outgoing from the component.

In Figure 1, the MyNetwork component provides a Network port and the MyTimer component provides a Timer port. In diagrams, we represent a port using the ⁝Port graphical notation, where Port is the type of the port, e.g., Network. We represent components using the Component notation.

When a component *uses* a lower level abstraction in its implementation, it will *require* a port of the type that represents the abstraction. Through a re-

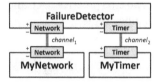

Fig. 2. *channel*₁ connects the provided Network port of MyNetwork with the required Network port of the FailureDetector. *channel*₂ connects the provided Timer port of My-Timer with the required Timer port of the FailureDetector.

quired port, a component sends out the request events and receives the indication/response events specified by the port's type, i.e., for required ports, the '−' direction is outgoing from the component and the '+' direction is incoming to the component.

Channels. Channels are first-class bindings between component ports. A channel connects two *complementary* ports of the *same* type. For example, in Figure 2, *channel*₁ connects the provided Network port of MyNetwork with the required Network port of the FailureDetector. This allows, e.g., Message events sent by the FailureDetector to be received by MyNetwork.

Channels forward events in both directions in FIFO order. In diagrams, we represent channels using the ▬*channel*▬ graphical notation. We omit the channel name when it is not relevant.

Handlers. An event handler is a first-class procedure of a component. A handler accepts events of a particular type (and subtypes thereof) and it is executed *reactively* when the component receives such events. During its execution, a handler may trigger new events and mutate the component's local state. The handlers of one component instance are *mutually exclusive*, i.e., they are executed sequentially. This alleviates the need for synchronization between different event handlers of the same component accessing the component's mutable state, which greatly simplifies their programming.

Here is an example event handler definition in Java:

```
1 Handler<Message> handleMsg = new Handler<Message>() {
2   public void handle(Message message) {
3     messages++;  // ← component-local state update
4     System.out.println("Received from " + message.source);
5 }};
```

In diagrams, we use the ⟨h⟨Event⟩⟩ graphical notation to represent an event handler, where *h* is the handler's name and Event is the type of events accepted by the handler, e.g., Message.

Subscriptions. A subscription binds an event handler to one component port, enabling the handler to handle events that arrive at the component on that port. A subscription is allowed only if the handler's accepted event type, E, is allowed to pass by the port's type definition. In other words, E must be one of (or a subtype of one of) the event types allowed by the port's type definition to pass in the direction of the handler.

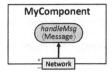

Fig. 3. The *handleMsg* event handler is **subscribed** to the required Network port of MyComponent. As a result, *handleMsg* will be executed whenever MyComponent receives a Message event on this port, taking the event as an argument.

Figure 3 illustrates the *handleMsg* handler from our previous example being subscribed to a port. In diagrams, we represent a subscription using the $\longrightarrow$ graphical notation.

In this example, the subscription of *handleMsg* to the Network port is allowed because Message is in the positive set of Network; *handleMsg* will handle all events of type Message or a subtype of Message, received on this Network port.

Components. Components are event-driven state machines that execute *concurrently* and communicate *asynchronously* by message-passing. In the host programming language, components are objects consisting of any number of local state variables and event handlers. Components are modules that export and import event-based interfaces, i.e., provided and required ports. Each component is instantiated from a component definition.

Here is an example component definition in Java:

```
 1 class MyComponent extends ComponentDefinition {
 2   Positive<Network> network = requires(Network.class); // ← required port
 3   int messages;                                        // ← local state
 4   public MyComponent() {                               // ← component constructor
 5     System.out.println("MyComponent created.");
 6     messages = 0;
 7     subscribe(handleMsg, network);
 8   }
 9   Handler<Message> handleMsg = new Handler<Message>() { ... };
10 }
```

In this example we see the component definition of MyComponent, illustrated in Figure 3. Line 2 specifies that the component has a required Network port. The *requires* method returns a reference to a required port, *network*, which is used in the constructor to subscribe the *handleMsg* handler to this port (line 7). The type of the required port is Positive⟨Network⟩ because, for required ports the positive direction is incoming into the component. Both a component's ports and event-handlers are first-class entities which allows for their dynamic manipulation.

Components can encapsulate subcomponents to hide details, reuse functionality, and manage system complexity. Composite components enable the control and dynamic reconfiguration of entire component ensembles as if they were single components. Composite components form a containment hierarchy rooted at a Main component (see Figure 4). Main is the first component created when the runtime system starts and it recursively creates all other sub-components. Since there exist no components outside of Main, Main has no ports.

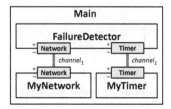

Fig. 4. The Main component encapsulates FailureDetector, MyNetwork, and MyTimer

Here is the Main component specification in Java:

```
1  class Main extends ComponentDefinition {
2    Component net, timer, fd;          // ← subcomponents
3    Channel channel1, channel2;        // ← channels
4    public Main() {                    // ✓ constructor
5      net = create(MyNetwork.class);
6      timer = create(MyTimer.class);
7      fd = create(FailureDetector.class);
8      channel1 = connect(net.provided(Network.class), fd.required(Network.class));
9      channel2 = connect(timer.provided(Timer.class), fd.required(Timer.class));
10   }
11   public static void main(String[] args) {
12     Kompics.bootstrap(Main.class);
13 }}
```

In our Java implementation, the Main component is also a Java main class (lines 11-13 show the *main* method). When executed, this will invoke the Kompics runtime system, instructing it to bootstrap, i.e., to instantiate the root component using Main as a component specification (line 12).

In lines 5-7, Main creates its subcomponents and saves references to them. In line 8, it connects MyNetwork's provided Network port to the required Network port of the FailureDetector. As a result, $channel_1$ is created and saved. Unless needed for dynamic reconfiguration (see Section 2.6), channel references need not be saved.

Components are *loosely coupled*: a component does not know the type, availability, or identity of any components with which it communicates. Instead, a component only "communicates" with its ports and it is up to the component's environment to wire up the communication.

Explicit component dependencies (required ports) enable dynamic reconfiguration of the component architecture, a fundamental feature for evolving, long-lived systems.

2.2   Kompics Operations

While presenting the Kompics concepts we have already introduced some of the basic operations on these concepts: *subscribe*, *create*, and *connect*. These have counterparts that undo their actions: *unsubscribe*, *destroy*, and *disconnect*, and these have the expected semantics. Here is the code for *destroy* and *disconnect* using our previous example:

Fig. 5. MyComponent handles one MyMessage event and triggers a MyMessage reply on its required Network port

```
1  class Main extends ComponentDefinition {
2    Component net, timer, fd;         // ← subcomponents
3    Channel channel1, channel2;       // ← channels
4    public undo() {                   // ✓ some method
5      disconnect(net.provided(Network.class), fd.required(Network.class));
6      disconnect(timer.provided(Timer.class), fd.required(Timer.class));
7      destroy(net);    destroy(timer);        destroy(fd);
8  }}
```

A fundamental command in Kompics is *trigger*, which is used to (asynchronously) send an event through a port. In the next example, MyComponent handles a MyMessage event due to its subscription to its required Network port. Upon handling the first message, MyComponent triggers a MyMessage reply on its Network port and then it unsubscribes its *handleMyMsg* handler, thus handling no further messages.

Figure 5 illustrates MyComponent. In diagrams, we denote that an event handler may trigger an event on some port, using the ⬥Event→ graphical notation.

```
1  class MyComponent extends ComponentDefinition {
2    Positive<Network> network = requires(Network.class);
3    public MyComponent() { // ← component constructor
4      subscribe(handleMyMsg, network);
5    }
6    Handler<MyMessage> handleMyMsg = new Handler<MyMessage>() {
7      public void handle(MyMessage m) {
8        trigger(new MyMessage(m.destination, m.source), network);
9        unsubscribe(handleMyMsg, network); // ← reply only once
10 }};}
```

2.3   Publish-Subscribe Event Dissemination

Components are unaware of other components in their environment. A component can communicate, i.e., handle received events and trigger events, only through the ports visible within its scope. The ports visible in a component's scope are its own ports and the ports of its immediate sub-components. Ports and channels forward triggered events toward other connected components, as long as the types of events triggered are allowed to pass by the respective port type specifications. Hence, component interaction is dictated by the connections between components as configured by their enclosing parent component.

Component communication follows a message-passing publish-subscribe model. An event triggered (published) on a port is forwarded to other components by all channels connected to the other side of the port (Figure 6). As an optimization, our runtime system avoids forwarding events on channels that

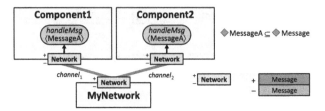

Fig. 6. When MyNetwork triggers a MessageA on its provided Network port, this event is forwarded by both *channel₁* and *channel₂* to the required Network ports of Component1 and Component2, respectively

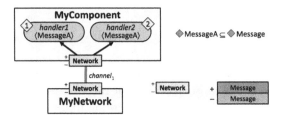

Fig. 7. When MyNetwork triggers a MessageA event on its Network port, this event is delivered to the Network port of MyComponent and handled by both *handler1* and *handler2*, sequentially (figured with yellow diamonds), in the order in which the two handlers were subscribed to the Network port

would not lead to any compatible subscribed handlers. An event received on a port is handled by all compatible handlers subscribed to that port (Figure 7).

2.4 Component Initialization and Life-Cycle

Every component provides a special Control port used for initialization, life-cyle, and fault management. Figure 8 illustrates the Control port type and a component that declares an Init, a Start, and a Stop handler. Typically, for each component definition that requires state initialization one defines a specific initialization event (subtype of Init) which contains component-specific configuration parameters.

An Init event is guaranteed to be the first event handled. When a component subscribes an Init event handler to its Control port in its constructor, the component will not handle any other event before a corresponding Init event.

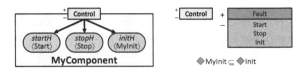

Fig. 8. Every Kompics component provides a Control port by default. To this Control port, the component can subscribe Start, Stop, and Init handlers. In general, we do not illustrate the control port in component diagrams.

```
1 class MyComponent extends ComponentDefinition {
2   int myParameter;
3   public MyComponent() { // ← component constructor
4     subscribe(handleStart, control); // ← similar for Stop
5     subscribe(handleInit, control);
6   }
7   Handler<MyInit> handleInit = new Handler<MyInit>() {
8     public void handle(MyInit init) {
9       myParameter = init.myParameter;
10   }};
11  Handler<Start> handleStart = new Handler<Start>() {
12    public void handle(Start event) {
13      System.out.println("started");
14 }};}
```

Start and Stop events allow a component (which handles them) to take some actions when the component is activated or passivated. A component is created *passive*. In the passive state, a component can receive events but it will not execute them. (Received events are stored in a port queue.) When activated, a component will enter the *active* state (executing any enqueued events). Handling life-cycle events is optional for a component.

To activate a component, a Start event is triggered on its control port, and to passivate it, a Stop event is triggered on its control port. Here is an example snippet of code possibly executed by a parent of *myComponent*:

```
1   trigger(new MyInit(42), myComponent.control());
2   trigger(new Start(), myComponent.control());
3   trigger(new Stop(), myComponent.control());
```

When a composite component is activated (or passivated), its subcomponents are recursively activated (or passivated). The *bootstrap* construct, introduced in the Main component example, both creates and starts the Main component.

2.5 Fault Management

Kompics enforces a fault isolation and management mechanism inspired by Erlang [3]. A software fault or exception thrown and not caught within an event handler is caught by the runtime system, wrapped into a Fault event and triggered on the Control port, as shown in Figure 9.

A composite component may subscribe a Fault handler to the control port of its subcomponents. The component can then replace the faulty subcomponent with a new instance (through dynamic reconfiguration) or take other appropriate actions. If a Fault is not handled in a parent component it is further propagated to the parent's parent and so on until it reaches the Main component. If not

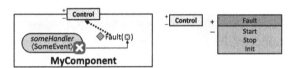

Fig. 9. Uncaught exceptions thrown in event handlers are caught by the runtime, wrapped in a Fault event and triggered on the control port

handled anywhere, ultimately, a system fault handler is executed which dumps the exception to standard error and halts the execution.

2.6 Dynamic Reconfiguration

Kompics enables the dynamic reconfiguration of the component architecture without dropping any of the triggered events. In addition to the ability to dynamically create and destroy components, connect and disconnect ports, subscribe and unsubscribe handlers, Kompics supports four channel commands to enable safe dynamic reconfiguration: *hold, resume, plug,* and *unplug.* The *hold* command puts the channel on hold. The channel stops forwarding events and starts queuing them in both directions. The *resume* command has the opposite effect, resuming the channel. When a channel resumes, it first forwards all enqueued events, in both directions, and then keeps forwarding events as ususal. The *unplug* command, unplugs one end of a channel from the port where it is connected, and the *plug* command plugs back the unconnected end to a (possibly different) port.

To replace a component *c1* with a new component *c2* (with similar ports), *c1*'s parent, *p*, puts on hold and unplugs all channels connected to *c1*'s ports; then, *p* passivates *c1*, creates *c2* and plugs the unplugged channels into the respective ports of *c2* and resumes them; *c2* is initialized with the state dumped by *c1* and activated. Finally, *p* destroys *c1*.

3   Implementation

We have implemented Kompics in Java. In this section we discuss some of the implementation details related to the runtime system, component scheduling, different modes of execution, and component dependency management. Kompics is publicly released as an open-source project. The source code for the Java implementation of the Kompics runtime, component library, and case studies presented here, are all available online at http://kompics.sics.se.

Java Runtime and Network I/O. Our Java runtime system implements the Kompics concepts and operations as well as the Kompics execution model. The Kompics runtime system supports pluggable component schedulers, decoupling component behaviour from component execution. In particular, this enables the ability to use different component schedulers to execute the same (unchanged) component-based system in different modes: parallel multi-core execution and deterministic simulation. Next subsection highlights the default scheduler.

We implemented a rich library of components and ports that provide basic distributed systems abstractions. For example, we have three different implementations for the Network abstraction using Apache MINA, Netty, and the Grizzly network library, respectively. Each of these components implements automatic connection management, message serialization, and Zlib compression. The choice of implementations is configurable - for example, CATS in section 4 uses Grizzly with Kyro for message serialization.

Multi-core Component Scheduling. The Kompics execution model admits an implementation with one lightweight thread per component. However, as Java has only heavyweight threads, we use a pool of worker threads for concurrently executing components. Every component is marked as *idle* (if it has no events awaiting execution), *ready* (if it has one or more events waiting in ports to be executed in handlers), or *busy* (if an event is currently being executed in a handler). Each worker has a dedicated queue of *ready* components. Workers process one event in one component at a time and one component cannot be processed by multiple workers at the same time. Thus, the Kompics execution model guarantees that handlers of a single component instance execute mutually exclusively.

Workers may run out of ready components to execute, in which case they engage in *work stealing* [10]. Work stealing involves a *thief*, a worker with no ready components contacting a *victim*, the worker with the highest number of ready components, and stealing a batch of half of its ready components. Stolen components are moved from the victim's work queue to the thief's work queue. From our experiments, batching shows a considerable performance improvement over stealing small numbers of ready components. To improve concurrency, the work queues are implemented as lock-free queues, meaning that the victims and thieves can concurrently consume ready components from their queues.

By designing components as reactive state machines and scheduling them using a pool of worker threads, we provide a simple programming model that leverages multi-core machines without any extra programming effort.

Deterministic Simulation Mode. We provide a special scheduler for reproducible system simulation. The system code is executed in deterministic simulation provided it does not attempt to create threads. In simulation mode, the system's bytecode (including any binary libraries) is instrumented to intercept all calls for the current time and return the simulated time. Therefore, without editing any of its source code, the system can be executed deterministically in simulated time. Library code for secure random number generators is also instrumented to use the same seed and achieve determinism. Attempts to create threads are also intercepted and the simulation halts since it would not be able to guarantee deterministic execution.

Testing and Programming in the Large. Kompics supports test-driven development through both unit-testing and integration-testing. Firstly, since components are implemented in Java classes, a component can be mocked, so that the individual handlers can be unit-tested. Secondly, integration tests (tests covering more than one component) can be implemented as Java unit tests running the tested subsystem in simulation mode, enabling systems to be built and validated using standard continuous integration platforms. To this end, we used Apache Maven to organize the structure and manage the artifacts of the Kompics component library. The complete framework counts more than 100 modules. We organize the various Kompics concepts into *abstraction* and *component* packages. An abstraction package contains a port together with the request and indication events of that port. A component package contains the implementation of one component with some component-specific events (typically subtypes of events defined in required ports). The source code for an abstraction or component package is organized as a Maven module and the binary code is packaged into a Maven artifact, a JAR archive annotated with meta-data about the package's version, dependencies, and pointers to web repositories from where (binary) package dependencies are automatically fetched by Maven.

In general, abstraction packages have no dependencies and component packages have dependencies on abstraction packages for both the required and provided ports. This is because a component implementation will use event types defined in abstraction packages, irrespective of the fact that an abstraction is required or provided. Maven enables the reusability of protocol abstractions and component implementations. When we start a project for a new protocol implementation we just need to specify what existing abstractions our implementation depends on. They are automatically fetched and made visible in the new project. This approach also enables deploy-time composition.

4   Case Study: A Scalable, Consistent Key-Value Store

To put into perspective the Kompics concepts, patterns, and different execution modes, we present a case study of a key-value store called CATS that provides a simple API to get and put key-value pairs, while guaranteeing linearizable consistency in partially synchronous, lossy, partitionable and dynamic networks [11]. Kompics was used to develop, deploy, stress-test, and simulate CATS. This is a (non-trivial) large-scale, self-organizing distributed system with dynamic node membership. Each node in the system handles a complex mix of protocols for failure detection, topology maintenance, routing, replication, group membership, agreement, and data consistency. In the next section we highlight the component based software architecture of the system and later we show how the same system implementation designated for deployment is executed in simulation mode for debugging and testing under a wide array of concurrency and failure scenarios.

4.1   CATS Deployment Architecture

Firstly, we provide a general component framework with protocols reusable in many large-scale distributed systems. Such systems typically need a bootstrap procedure to assist newly arrived nodes in finding nodes already in the system in order to execute any join protocols. To this end, we have a BootstrapServer component which maintains a list of online nodes. Every node embeds a BootstrapClient component which provides a Bootstrap service to the node. When a node starts, it issues a BootstrapRequest to the client which retrieves from the server a list of alive nodes and delivers a BootstrapResponse to the node. The node runs a join protocol against one or more of the returned nodes and after joining, it sends a BootstrapDone event to the client, which, from now on, will send periodic keep-alives to the server letting it know this node is still alive. The BootstrapServer evicts nodes who stop sending keep-alives.

Another reusable service, is a monitoring and distributed tracing service. A client component at each node periodically inspects the status of various local components, and may also log network events for tracing. The client periodically sends reports to a monitoring server that can aggregate the status of nodes and present a global view of the system on a web page. The bootstrap and monitoring servers are illustrated in Figure 10 (left), within executable main components.

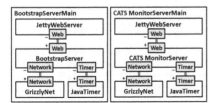
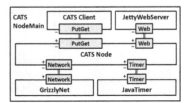

Fig. 10. Bootstrap and monitoring servers (left) exposing a user-friendly web interface for troubleshooting. Component architecture for one CATS node (right). This architecture is designated for system deployment where every CATS node executes on a different machine and communicates with other nodes by sending messages using Grizzly, a Java NIO non-blocking sockets framework.

We embed the Jetty web server library in the JettyWebServer component which wraps every HTTP request into a WebRequest event and triggers it on a required Web port. Both servers provide the Web abstraction, accepting WebRequests and delivering WebResponses containing HTML pages with the node list and global view, respectively.

In Figure 10 (right), we show the component architecture designated for system deployment. Here we have the executable CATS NodeMain component that embeds the CATS node, network, timer, web server, and client application components. The embedded CATS Node exposes its status through a Web port. The HTML page representing the node's status will typically contain hyperlinks to the neighbor nodes and to the bootstrap and monitoring server. This enables users/developers to browse the set of nodes over the web, and inspect the state of each remote node. The CATS Client component may embed a GUI or CLI user interface and issue functional requests to the CATS Node over the PutGet port.

The CATS Node is detailed in Figure 11. By encapsulating many components behind the PutGet port, clients are oblivious to the complexity and event-driven control flow internal to the component. The components used to implement CATS include a PingFailureDetector, a CATS Ring to maintain a distributed hash table, and a One-Hop Router which provides efficient message routing. The One-Hop Router, in turn, uses a service for uniform node sampling, provided by Cyclon Overlay. The Consistent ABD component provides quorum-based read and write operations, again using the One-Hop Router to find the responsible servers.

Every functional component provides a Stat port, accepting StatusRequests and delivering StatusResponses to MonitorClient and JettyWebServer. JettyWeb-Server enables users to monitor a node's components and issue interactive commands to the node through a web browser.

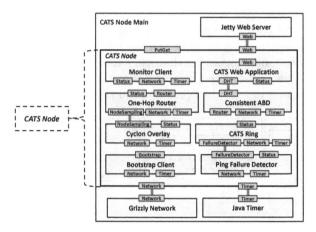

Fig. 11. The architecture of the CATS Node. We omit the channels for clarity. In this scope, all provided ports are connected to all required ports of the same type.

We have deployed and tested CATS on the PlanetLab testbed, on our local cluster, and on Rackspace. Using the web interface to interact with CATS (configured with a replication degree of 5) on the local-area network, resulted in sub-millisecond end-to-end latencies for *get* and *put* operations. This includes the LAN latency (two message round-trips, so 4 one-way latencies), message serialization (4x), encryption (4x), decryption (4x), deserialization (4x), and Kompics runtime overheads for message dispatching and execution. In terms of scalability, for read-intensive workloads, reading 1KB values, CATS scaled on Rackspace to 96 machines providing just over 100,000 reads/sec. We refer the reader to [11] for more details on CATS performance.

4.2   CATS Simulation Architecture

We now show how we can reuse the CATS' components, without modifying their code, to execute the system in simulation mode for testing, stepped debugging, or repeatable simulation studies. Figure 12 (left) shows the component architecture for simulation mode. Here, a generic NetworkEmulator/ExperimentDriver interprets an experiment scenario and issues command events to the CATS Simulator component. A command (triggered through the CATS Experiment port) may tell the CATS Simulator to create and start a new node, to stop and destroy an existing node, or to instruct an existing node to execute a system-specific operation (through its PutGet port). The ability to create and destroy node subcomponents in CATS Simulator is clearly facilitated by Kompics' support for dynamic reconfiguration and hierarchical composition. The NetworkEmulator/ExperimentDriver also provides the Network and Timer abstractions and implements a generic discrete-event simulator.

This whole architecture is executed in simulation mode, i.e., using a simulation component scheduler which executes all components that have received

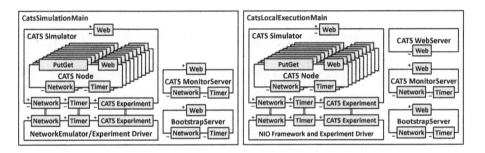

Fig. 12. Component architecture for whole-system simulation (left) / interactive stress-test execution (right). All nodes and servers execute within a single OS process in simulated time (left) / real time (right).

events and when it runs out of work it passes control to the NetworkEmulator/ExperimentDriver to advance the simulation time.

4.3   Local, Interactive, Stress-Test Execution

Using the same experiment scenario used in simulation, the same system code can be executed in an interactive stress-testing execution mode. Figure 12 (right) shows the respective component architecture. This is similar to the simulation architecture, however, our concurrent component scheduler is used and the system executes in real-time.

During development it is recommended to incrementally make small changes and quickly test their effects. The interactive execution mode helps with this routine since it enables us to quickly run a small-scale distributed system (without the need for remote deployment or launching of multiple processes) and we can interact with it using a web browser.

4.4   CATS Experimentation

We designed a Java domain-specific language (DSL) for expressing experiment scenarios for large-scale distributed systems. Such scenarios are interpreted by a NetworkEmulator/ExperimentDriver or NIO Framework and ExperimentDriver component. A scenario is a parallel and/or sequential composition of *stochastic processes*. We start each stochastic process, a finite random sequence of events, with a specified distribution of inter-arrival times.

Here is an example stochastic process:

```
1 StochasticProcess boot = new StochasticProcess() {{
2    eventInterArrivalTime(exponential(2000)); //exponentially distributed, μ = 2s
3    raise(1000, catsJoin, uniform(16)); //1000 joins with uniform IDs from 0..2^16
4 }};
```

This will generate a sequence of 1000 *catsJoin* operations, with an inter-arrival time between two consecutive operations extracted from an exponential distribution with a mean of 2 seconds. The *catsJoin* operation is a system-specific operation with 1 parameter. In this case, the parameter is the ring identifier of the joining node, extracted from an uniform distribution of $[0..2^{16}]$. Here is how the *catsJoin* operation is defined:

```
1 Operation1<Join, BigInteger> catsJoin = new Operation1<Join, BigInteger>() {
2    public Join generate(BigInteger nodeKey) {
3        return new Join(new NumericRingKey(nodeKey));
4 }};
```

It takes one BigInteger argument (extracted from a distribution) and generates a Join event (triggered by the NetworkEmulator/ExperimentDriver on PutGet port). Next, we define a *churn* process which will generate a sequence of 1000 churn events (500 joins randomly interleaved with 500 failures), with an exponential inter-arrival time with a mean of 500 milliseconds.

```
1 StochasticProcess churn = new StochasticProcess() {{
2    eventInterArrivalTime(exponential(500)); //exponentially distributed, μ = 500ms
3    raise(500, catsJoin, uniform(16));        //500 joins
4    raise(500, catsFail, uniform(16));        //500 failures
5 }};
```

Next, we define a process to issues some Lookup events.

```
1 StochasticProcess lookups = new StochasticProcess() {{
2    eventInterArrivalTime(normal(50, 10)); //normally distributed, μ = 50ms, σ = 10ms
3    raise(5000, catsLookup, uniform(16), uniform(14));
4 }};
```

The *catsLookup* operation takes two BigInteger parameters, extracted from a (here, uniform) distribution, and generates a Lookup event that tells CATS Simulator to issue a lookup for key *key* at the node with identifier *node*. As you can see above, a random node in $0..2^{16}$ will issue a lookup for a random key in $0..2^{14}$. 5000 lookups are issued in total, with an exponential inter-arrival time with mean 50 milliseconds.

```
1 Operation2<Lookup, BigInteger, BigInteger> catsLookup
2        = new Operation2<Lookup, BigInteger, BigInteger>() {
3    public Lookup generate(BigInteger node, BigInteger key) {
4        return new Lookup(new NumericRingKey(node), new NumericRingKey(key));
5 }};
```

We defined three stochastic processes: *boot*, *churn*, and *lookups*. The next code snippet shows how we can compose them into a complete experiment scenario. The scenario starts with the *boot* process. Two seconds (simulated time) after *boot* terminates, the *churn* process starts. Three seconds after *churn* starts, the *lookups* process starts, now working in parallel with *churn*. The experiment terminates one second after all lookups are done. Putting it all together, here is how one defines and executes an experiment scenario using our Java DSL:

```
 1  class CatsSimulationExperiment {
 2    static Scenario scenario1 = new Scenario() {
 3      StochasticProcess boot = ...  // see above
 4      StochasticProcess churn = ...
 5      StochasticProcess lookups = ...
 6      boot.start();                                   // start
 7      churn.startAfterTerminationOf(2000, boot);      // sequential composition
 8      lookups.startAfterStartOf(3000, churn);         // parallel composition
 9      terminateAfterTerminationOf(1000, lookups);     // join synchronization
10    }
11    public static void main(String[] args) {
12      scenario1.setSeed(rngSeed);
13      scenario1.simulate(CatsSimulationMain.class); // simulation mode
14      // scenario1.execute(CatsLocalExecutionMain.class);// local, interactive
15  }}
```

Note that the above code is an executable Java main-class. It creates a *scenario1* object, sets an RNG seed, and calls the *simulate* method passing the simulation architecture of your system as an argument (line 14). The *simulate* method instruments the bytecode of the system and executes it in simulation mode, driving the simulation from the given experiment scenario. This is useful for debugging. If you want to run an interactive experiment, comment out line 14 and uncomment line 15. This will run your interactive execution architecture and drive it from the same scenario. You will be able to interact with and monitor the system over the web while the experiment is running.

Discussion and Simulation Performance. We have showed the component based software architecture of a non-trivial distributed system and how the same system implementation designated for deployment can be executed in simulation mode or interactive whole-system execution. We showed how Kompics can be used to build scalable, concurrent middleware using CATS as a case study.

We also ran simulations of CATS and we were able to simulate a system of 16384 nodes in a single 64-bit JVM with a heap size of 4GB. The ratio between the real time taken to run the simulation and the simulated time was roughly 1. For smaller system sizes we observe a much higher simulated time compression effect, as shown in Table 1.

Table 1. Time compression effects observed when simulating the system for 4275 seconds of simulated time.

Peers	Time compression
64	475x
128	237.5x
256	118.75x
512	59.38x
1024	28.31x
2048	11.74x
4096	4.96x
8192	2.01x

5   Related Work

Kompics is related to work in several areas: concurrent programming models [12, 13, 14, 15], reconfigurable component models for distributed systems [5, 6, 16], reconfigurable software architectures [17, 18, 19, 20], and event-based frameworks for distributed systems [7, 21, 22].

Kompics's message-passing concurrency model is similar to the actor model [23], of which Erlang [12], the Unix filter and pipe model, Kilim [14] and Scala [13] are, perhaps, the best known examples. Similar to the actor model, message passing in Kompics involves buffering events before they are handled in a first-in first-out (FIFO) order, thus, decoupling the thread that sends an event from the thread that handles an event. In contrast to the actor model, event buffers are associated with component ports, so each component can have more than one event queue, and ports are connected using typed channels. Channels that carry typed messages between processes are also found in other message-passing systems, such as Singularity [24]. Connections between processes in the actor models are unidirectional and based on process-ids, while channels between ports in Kompics are bi-directional and components are oblivious to the destination of their events.

The main features of the Kompics component model, such as the ability to compose components, support for strongly-typed interfaces, and explicit dependency management using ports, are found in many existing component models, such as ArchJava [20], OpenCOM [5], Fractal [6], LiveObjects [16], and OMNnet++[25]. However, with the exception of LiveObjects, these component models are inherently client-server models, with blocking RPC interfaces.

LiveObjects has the most similar goals to Kompics of supporting encapsulation and composition of distributed protocols. Its endpoints are similar to our ports, providing bi-directional message-passing, however, endpoints in LiveObjects support only one-to-one connections. Other differences with Kompics include: the lack of a concurrency model beyond shared-state concurrency, the lack of reconfigurability, and the lack of support for hierarchical components.

Although there is support for dynamic reconfiguration in some actor-based systems, such as Erlang, Kompics's reconfiguration model is based on reconfiguring strongly typed connections between components. Component-based systems that support similar runtime reconfiguration functionality use either reflective techniques, such as OpenCOM [5], or dynamic software architecture models, such as Fractal [6], Rapide [17], and ArchStudio4/C2 [19]. Kompics's reconfiguration model is most similar to the dynamic software architecture approaches, but a major difference is that the software architecture in Kompics is not specified explicitly in an architecture definition language, rather it is implicitly constructed at runtime.

Other work related to Kompics are non-blocking socket frameworks that support asynchronous event programming, such as Tornado for Python [9] and Lift for Scala actors. Protocol composition frameworks, such as Horus [26], Appia [22] and Mace [27], are also related, but they are specifically designed for building distributed systems by layering modular protocols. Although this approach certainly simplifies the task of programming distributed systems, these frameworks are often designed with a particular protocol domain in mind and this limits their generality. Mace, however, also supports the execution of the same code in both production and simulation. Finally, there are related tools for monitoring distributed systems, such as Dapper [28] by Google, a distributed tracing system that is built-in to a few key modules commonly linked by all applications. In contrast, in Kompics, we have a monitoring client that execute concurrently and can be easily adapted to handle events published by any component.

6   Conclusions and Future Work

In this paper we presented the Kompics component model and programming framework. We showed how complex distributed systems can be built by composing simple protocols. Protocol abstractions are programmed as event-driven, message-passing concurrent components. Kompics contributes a unique combination of features well suited for the development and testing of large-scale, long-lived distributed systems, including: hierarchical component composition, dynamic reconfiguration, message-passing concurrency, publish-subscribe non-blocking component interaction, seamless integration of NIO frameworks, and the ability to run the same code in either production mode or reproducible simulation for testing and stepped debugging. For future work, we are investigating a Kompics front-end in Scala. This would immediately leverage the existing Java components and runtime system. Also, it has the potential for more expressive code and a succint DSL for Kompics operations.

References

1. Chen-Becker, D., Weir, T., Danciu, M.: The Definitive Guide to Lift: A Scala-based Web Framework. Apress, Berkely (2009)
2. Anderson, J.C., Lehnardt, J., Slater, N.: CouchDB: The Definitive Guide Time to Relax, 1st edn. O'Reilly Media, Inc. (2010)
3. Armstrong, J.: Making reliable distributed systems in the presence of software errors. PhD Dissertation, The Royal Institute of Technology, Sweden (2003)
4. Haller, P., Odersky, M.: Scala actors: Unifying thread-based and event-based programming. Theor. Comput. Sci. 410(2-3), 202–220 (2009)
5. Coulson, G., Blair, G., Grace, P., Taiani, F., Joolia, A., Lee, K., Ueyama, J., Sivaharan, T.: A generic component model for building systems software. ACM Trans. Comput. Syst. 26(1), 1–42 (2008)
6. Bruneton, E., Coupaye, T., Leclercq, M., Quéma, V., Stefani, J.B.: The Fractal component model and its support in Java: Experiences with auto-adaptive and reconfigurable systems. Softw. Pract. Exper. 36(11-12), 1257–1284 (2006)
7. Welsh, M., Culler, D., Brewer, E.: Seda: an architecture for well-conditioned, scalable internet services. In: SOSP 2001, pp. 230–243. ACM, New York (2001)
8. Wampler, D.: Scala web frameworks: Looking beyond lift. IEEE Internet Computing 15, 87–94 (2011)
9. Dory, M., Parrish, A., Berg, B.: Introduction to Tornado. O'Reilly Media (2012)
10. Blumofe, R.D., Leiserson, C.E.: Scheduling multithreaded computations by work stealing. J. ACM 46(5), 720–748 (1999)

11. Arad, C., Shafaat, T.M., Haridi, S.: CATS: Linearizability and partition tolerance in scalable and self-organizing key-value stores. Technical Report T2012:04, Swedish Institute of Computer Science (2012)
12. Armstrong, J.: Programming Erlang. In: Pragmatic Bookshelf (July 2007)
13. Odersky, M., Zenger, M.: Scalable component abstractions. In: OOPSLA 2005, pp. 41–57. ACM, New York (2005)
14. Srinivasan, S., Mycroft, A.: Kilim: Isolation-Typed Actors for Java. In: Dell'Acqua, P. (ed.) ECOOP 2008. LNCS, vol. 5142, pp. 104–128. Springer, Heidelberg (2008)
15. Hu, R., Kouzapas, D., Pernet, O., Yoshida, N., Honda, K.: Type-Safe Eventful Sessions in Java. In: D'Hondt, T. (ed.) ECOOP 2010. LNCS, vol. 6183, pp. 329–353. Springer, Heidelberg (2010)
16. Ostrowski, K., Birman, K., Dolev, D., Ahnn, J.H.: Programming with Live Distributed Objects. In: Dell'Acqua, P. (ed.) ECOOP 2008. LNCS, vol. 5142, pp. 463–489. Springer, Heidelberg (2008)
17. Luckham, D.C., Vera, J.: An event-based architecture definition language. IEEE Trans. Softw. Eng. 21(9), 717–734 (1995)
18. Medvidovic, N., Taylor, R.N.: A classification and comparison framework for software architecture description languages. IEEE Trans. Softw. Eng. 26(1), 70–93 (2000)
19. Dashofy, E.M., Asuncion, H.U., Hendrickson, S.A., Suryanarayana, G., Georgas, J.C., Taylor, R.N.: Archstudio 4: An architecture-based meta-modeling environment. In: ICSE Companion, pp. 67–68 (2007)
20. Aldrich, J., Notkin, D.: Architectural Reasoning in ArchJava. In: Deng, T. (ed.) ECOOP 2002. LNCS, vol. 2374, pp. 334–367. Springer, Heidelberg (2002)
21. Krohn, M., Kohler, E., Kaashoek, M.F.: Events can make sense. In: USENIX ATC 2007, pp. 7:1–7:14. USENIX Association, Berkeley (2007)
22. Miranda, H., Pinto, A., Rodrigues, L.: Appia, a flexible protocol kernel supporting multiple coordinated channels. In: Proceedings of the 21st International Conference on Distributed Computing Systems, Phoenix, Arizona, pp. 707–710. IEEE (2001)
23. Agha, G.: Actors: a model of concurrent computation in distributed systems. MIT Press, Cambridge (1986)
24. Fähndrich, M., Aiken, M., Hawblitzel, C., Hodson, O., Hunt, G., Larus, J.R., Levi, S.: Language support for fast and reliable message-based communication in Singularity OS. SIGOPS Oper. Syst. Rev. 40(4), 177–190 (2006)
25. Varga, A., Hornig, R.: An overview of the OMNeT++ simulation environment. In: Simutools 2008 (2008)
26. van Renesse, R., Birman, K.P., Maffeis, S.: Horus: a flexible group communication system. Commun. ACM 39(4), 76–83 (1996)
27. Killian, C.E., Anderson, J.W., Braud, R., Jhala, R., Vahdat, A.M.: Mace: language support for building distributed systems. SIGPLAN Not. 42(6), 179–188 (2007)
28. Sigelman, B.H., Barroso, L.A., Burrows, M., Stephenson, P., Plakal, M., Beaver, D., Jaspan, S., Shanbhag, C.: Dapper, a large-scale distributed systems tracing infrastructure. Technical report, Google, Inc. (2010)

OverStar: An Open Approach to End-to-End Middleware Services in Systems of Systems

Paul Grace[1], Yérom-David Bromberg[2], Laurent Réveillère[2], and Gordon Blair[1]

[1] School of Computing and Communications, Lancaster University, UK
p.grace@lancaster.ac.uk, gordon@comp.lancs.ac.uk
[2] LaBRI, University of Bordeaux, France
{david.bromberg,laurent.reveillere}@labri.fr

Abstract. The increasing complexity of distributed systems, where heterogeneous systems are composed to form systems of systems, pose new development challenges. How can core middleware services, e.g. event communication, resource discovery, etc. be deployed and optimised in an end-to-end manner? Further, how can important properties such as interoperability be managed? In this paper we propose OverStar a framework that generates overlay network based solutions from high-level specifications in order to answer these questions. A middleware service is specified as a self-managing overlay network across heterogeneous systems; timed automata specify how the topology of the network is constructed and the data is exchanged. The key contribution is the open access to individual overlay nodes in order to specify additional flow logic, e.g. the translation of messages to support end-to-end interoperability or the filtering of heterogeneous messages to optimise event dissemination. We evaluate OverStar using service discovery and event communication case studies; these demonstrate the ability to compose heterogeneous systems, achieve end-to-end interoperability and simplify the developer's task. Further, a performance evaluation highlights optimisations that can be achieved.

1 Introduction

Overlay networks are increasingly important in underpinning key middleware functions (e,g. service discovery, multicast, and P2P in various disguises). Indeed they are becoming a pervasive feature of middleware technologies, and their management and co-ordination will be a key requirement in future complex systems. Many different types of overlay networks have been developed to provide virtualised network services for particular environments and requirements, e.g, large-scale resource discovery [22] or multicast [23] in high-churn networks. In addition, software frameworks for overlays: P2 [16], Macedon [21], and OpenOverlays [9] provide tools to rapidly create a tailored overlay network, or incorporate an overlay network as an explicit architectural element of middleware. This work is promising but it falls down in underpinning middleware functions in complex distributed systems-of-systems where there are high levels of *heterogeneity* and *dynamic behaviour*, especially in terms of the middleware

P. Narasimhan and P. Triantafillou (Eds.): Middleware 2012, LNCS 7662, pp. 229–248, 2012.

protocols used by end systems that need to be composed dynamically. These end systems may utilise heterogeneous middleware services, i.e., different event communication middleware (e.g. STOMP[1] or OpenWire[2]) and different resource discovery protocols (e.g. SLP or Bonjour). Hence, there is a need to manage this heterogeneity, especially with respect to interoperability and optimisation.:

- *End-to-End Interoperability.* Heterogeneous local middleware services must interoperate when composed together in order to realise the global functionality of a middleware service.
- *End System Optimisations.* It should be possible to apply service optimisations at the end systems despite the heterogeneous technologies, e.g. applying global message filters locally to reduce both network traffic and protocol message translations.

In this paper, we look at an approach to address these heterogeneity challenges. The OverStar software framework supports the generation of overlay-based middleware services from high-level declarative specifications; in particular it concentrates on supporting the specifications that achieve interoperability and optimisation of heterogeneous systems. For this purpose two separate model specifications are provided:

- *Overlay Specification.* Each heterogeneous middleware service is underpinned by a tailored overlay network. Timed automata are used to specify two aspects of the overlay's behaviour. First, how the overlay topology should best be constructed to integrate the individual end systems (e.g. a tree, ring, etc.). Second, timed automata are also used to model the communication of data in the overlay network, e.g., multicast, anycast, etc.
- *Node Behaviour Specification.* Each overlay node acts as a gateway to the behaviour of the heterogeneous protocols in the local end systems. Protocol transparent middleware behaviour is then specified at each node to achieve interoperability and/or optimise service functionality. Such behaviour is specified using a timed automaton and can contain operations including: message translation, and message filtering.

We evaluate OverStar using a case study based method involving two middleware services in given areas of application: resource discovery and an event service. We show that these services can be specified and optimised in the face of heterogeneous protocols across the end-systems; interoperability can be achieved; and node behaviour specification supports the optimisations of deployments despite the encountered heterogeneity.

The paper is structured as follows. In section 2 we introduce the OverStar approach and associated software framework. In section 3 we then define the formal models that underpin the solution, and in 4 we describe the implementation of the OverStar framework. The evaluation results are given in section 5. In section 6, we analyse the work with respect to the state of the art. Finally, we draw conclusions in Section 7.

---

[1] http://stomp.github.com/
[2] http://activemq.apache.org/openwire.html

2   The OverStar Approach

2.1   Motivation

We use a simple example to motivate the OverStar approach. Fig. 1 illustrates a set of end-systems that employ heterogeneous protocols to provide middleware services in their local domains. Multiple discovery protocols are shown in use: SLP, Bonjour, UPnP and Ariadne [11]. Similarly multiple event communication middleware: Active MQ brokers, XMPP XEP-0060[3] and a publish-subscribe sensor middleware [24]. These can be viewed as isolated islands of interoperability that must be carefully integrated to create resource discovery and event services respectively. Further, in dynamic systems it is unrealistic to predict which end-systems protocols will be employed.

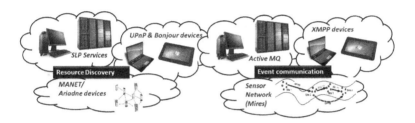

Fig. 1. Heterogeneous middleware services in systems-of-systems

Building global, optimised middleware services across heterogeneous end sys-tems requires a substantial understanding of: distributed algorithms, different communication patterns, interoperability challenges and low-level network pro-gramming. Furthermore, different strategies are required for different contexts (e.g. the solution for resource discovery is different from an event service solu-tion). The potential heterogeneity means that the solution space may rapidly grow, such that a single middleware solution is not sufficient. Hence, we argue that it should be possible to specify the middleware service optimised for the given context and then use this to generate the deployable middleware software.

2.2   The OverStar Middleware Framework

OverStar is a software framework that composes middleware services across het-erogeneous end systems as illustrated in Fig. 2. *OverStar node instances* are deployed in multiple domains to communicate with heterogeneous end systems in order to underpin higher-level middleware services. A node instance is made up of two component types. First, the OverStar nodes must be globally con-nected in order to facilitate the optimised communication between heteroge-neous domains. Overlay networks offer a well established solution for building

---

[3] http://xmpp.org/extensions/xep-0060.html

such virtualised services. However, a single overlay network is not sufficient; for instance, the overlay behaviour required to underpin a resource discovery service may differ from one to underpin publish-subscribe. Hence, the *Overlay Node component* allows different implementations of self-managing overlay behaviour to be created and deployed, e.g., a multicast tree or a DHT ring. Second, service implementation behaviour must be layered atop this overlay; this should connect the legacy systems in such a way that end-to-end interoperability is achieved. Further the service behaviour should be tailored for optimisations, i.e., adding specific service optimisation in spite of the heterogeneity, e.g. applying global publish subscribe filters in the end-system domains. The *Service Node component* allows different behaviours for specific middleware service implementations to be deployed. Finally, each node performs network communication with legacy middleware systems using *data ports*, and with the overlay via the *overlay port*.

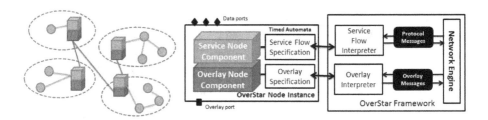

Fig. 2. An overview of the OverStar approach

In order to support the development of services and promote software reuse, the service and overlay node component's behaviour is specified through the use of timed automata (rather than hand-coded), which are finite state automata with a set of clocks, clock constraints, abstract messages, message constraints, queues and actions. We introduce the formal definition of these timed automata in Section 3.1, which are then applied to Overlay Node specifications in 3.2 and Service Node specifications in 3.3. We argue that the use of timed automata fits well with the requirements of global middleware services due to time constrained behaviour, e.g. in the self management of both overlay topologies and the middleware service logic.

The OverStar framework executes on each host and acts as an execution environment for the OverStar node instances. The elements of this framework (illustrated in Fig. 2) behave as follows:

– The *Service Flow Interpreter* interprets the internal model of a Service Node component to achieve the middleware service behaviour, e.g. supporting interoperability. Based upon the timed automata specification the interpreter: i) communicates with end system nodes using their legacy protocols, ii) communicates with other OverStar nodes using an Overlay Node component, and iii) performs middleware logic on the messages received from both.

- The *Overlay Interpreter* interprets the behavior specification of the Overlay Node component and performs the required local node behaviour to construct and maintain the overlay topology, and provide data communication services. That is, react to: join, leave, fail, and data events.
- The *Network Engine* performs two roles to support the two port types. Firstly, it sends the overlay specific messages between nodes in the overlay, i.e., these messages contain the overlay action messages, or forwarded data messages. Secondly, it communicates directly with legacy systems, sending and receiving messages using the required legacy protocol, e.g., it can send and receive SLP messages on the IP multicast channel of SLP.

3   Definition of Models to Specify Component Behaviour

Here we first present the formal definition of the timed automata used in OverStar. We then present the timed automata models for the Overlay node component specifications, followed by the Service node component specifications.

3.1   Timed Automata Specifications

Modeling time dependent behavior. Constraints on clock variables are used to model time dependent behavior. Local clocks are initialized to zero when a node starts and then increase synchronously with the same rate. Clocks associated to transitions act as *clock guards* that restrict the behavior of the automaton. Transitions from one state to another may not be taken according to time constraints, i.e. if a clock guard is not evaluated to true. Clocks may be reset to zero when a transition is taken. Further, to enforce progress properties, i.e. to ensure that nodes do not stay in a state forever, a state may be also associated with a clock constraint, called thereafter, *a local invariant*. For instance, as depicted in Fig. 3,❷, the local invariant $(x < 20)$ associated to state s_1 ensures that the transition from state s_1 to s_5 is only taken if clock x has elapsed (i.e. is evaluated to more than 20 time units). In other terms, a local invariant determines how long an automaton can wait in a particular state for an event to be triggered. If the time expires and there is no transition satisfying the guards, then a violation of the constraints of the system occurs. More precisely, it means that there is a fault in either the specification of guards or invariants in the model; this is what is usually called a timelock. Such locks in OverStar specifications can be avoided thanks to the use of a timelock checker provided by timed automaton analysis tools. Additionally, a state is *urgent* when it has an invariant $x < 0$, with all its incoming transitions resetting x to zero. Hence, in an urgent state, the outgoing transition must be taken immediately (See Fig. 3,❸,❹,❺).

Abstract messages. Triggered events are messages received or sent from either i) the global overlay network referred to as an overlay port, or ii) end systems within a local domain, referred to as one or more data ports; these utilise legacy protocols e.g. SLP, XMPP, etc. for communication. Syntactical description of message data fields, including their data types are formalized through the use

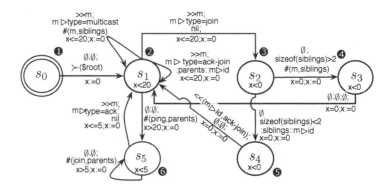

Fig. 3. Timed automaton specifying the self-organizing behavior of an overlay

of abstract messages [4]. An abstract message consists of a set of fields, either primitive or structured. The former is composed of: (i) a label naming the field, (ii) a type describing the type of the data content, (iii) a length defining the length in bits of the field, and (iv) the value, i.e., the content of the field. A structured field is composed of multiple primitive fields. We note $msg \triangleright field$ the operation that selects the $field$ from the abstract message msg. This abstract representation supports the application of additional message logic (e.g. message filtering) irrespective of the concrete packet format of a message.

Message guards. Transitions may also be labeled with a message guard that specifies a set of conjunctions of constraints on triggered events that has the following form: $(msg \triangleright field) \sim rvalue$ with $\sim \in \{<, \leq, =, \geq, >\}$ to evaluate adequately the message field $field$. As a result, a transition from one state to another can be taken only if both its clock and message guards evaluate to true.

Global variables and queues. Message guards may be combined with constraints on either global variables and queues. Both of them are accessible whatever the current state of a timed automaton. Global variables are variables prefixed with the '$' sign whereas queues are variables prefixed with the ':' sign. The term global refers to the states on one node, variables are not global to the distributed system. At any time, a timed automaton is able to store both incoming or outgoing messages to further get them back later.

Actions. When a state is left, actions may be triggered according to the transition to be taken. Available actions are described in Fig. 4 and include forwarding, multicasting, translating, filtering and queuing messages. We are providing a set of key actions to build overlay-based middleware services and provide end-to-end interoperability; however, the set of actions is extensible according to the needs of additional middleware functionality.

Formally, a timed automaton is defined as follows.

Definition 1. *A timed automaton $\mathcal{TA}$ is a tuple $(Q, M, q_0, \mathcal{A}, Evt, \mathcal{C}, Act, \mathcal{V}, \mathcal{F}, \rightarrow, \mathcal{I})$, where Q is a finite set of states, M is a finite set of abstract messages, $q_0 \in Q$ is the starting state and $\mathcal{A} \subset Q$ is a set of accepting states. Evt is a set of event types such that $Evt = \{?, !, \gg, \ll\}$ where ? (resp. !) denotes a received*

Actions	
δm	Translate message m to $f(m)$
$Filter(m,\ fr_1...fr_2)$	Filter message m according to the field content filters $fr_1...fr_2$
$\propto m$	Multicast to the overlay network nodes m
$\succ \$root$	Bootstrap procedure
$: q :: m$	Queue message m in queue q
$\#(m,id_1...id_2)$	Forward message m to overlay nodes $id_1...id_2$
λm	Multicast message m to the local environment

Fig. 4. Available actions in the model

(resp. sent) event from a data port, whereas $\gg$ (resp. $\ll$) denotes a received (resp. sent) event from an overlay port. $\mathcal{C}$ is a finite set of non negative real valued clocks and $\mathcal{B}(\mathcal{C})$ is the set of all clock constraints on $\mathcal{C}$. Act is the set of actions performed when a transition is taken. nil $\in$ Act is an empty action. The set of global variables and queues is respectively $\mathcal{V}$ and $\mathcal{F}$. Additionally, $\mathcal{B}(M,\mathcal{V},\mathcal{F})$ is the set of constraint conjunctions on M, $\mathcal{V}$ and $\mathcal{F}$. Further, $\rightarrow \subseteq Q \times Evt \times M \times \mathcal{B}(M,\mathcal{V},\mathcal{F}) \times Act \times \mathcal{B}(\mathcal{C}) \times Q$ is the set of transitions. Finally, $\mathcal{I}: Q \rightarrow \mathcal{B}(\mathcal{C})$ assigns local invariants to states.

Concretely, transitions have the following form $s_1 \xrightarrow{\mathcal{L}} s_2$ and changes the state of timed automaton from s_1 to s_2 once the label $\mathcal{L}$ is evaluated to true. The transition label $\mathcal{L}$ is defined such as $\mathcal{L} \subseteq Evt \times M \times \mathcal{B}(M,\mathcal{V},\mathcal{F}) \times Act \times \mathcal{B}(\mathcal{C})$, and has the following format:

$$\mathcal{L} = Event|Msg|Data\_guard|Actions|Clock\_guards$$

Correspondingly, four different transitions can be triggered according to events that can occur and are noted as follow (without considering guards and action for the sake of clarity): (i) $s_1 \xrightarrow{?m} s_2$ (resp. $s_1 \xrightarrow{!m} s_2$) if a message m has been received (resp. sent) from a local legacy system, (ii) $s_1 \xrightarrow{\gg m} s_2$ (resp. $s_1 \xrightarrow{\ll(id,m)} s_2$) if a message m has been received (resp. sent to id node) from the underlying overlay network. Further, our model also supports epsilon transitions. However, to avoid non-deterministic timed automata, such transitions must be combined with guards to avoid undeterminism (See for instance Fig. 3, ❸, ❹, ❺). It is important to note that epsilon transitions are only triggered when either timeout occurs or the current state is an urgent state.

3.2   Overlay Specification: Timed Automata to Construct Overlays

The first step in building a middleware service that integrates multiple legacy end systems is to construct the overlay topology and communication services that join them in a manner that the middleware functionality can be layered atop. Using the timed automaton definition, we are able to specify the algorithm to create such an overlay. To ease its understanding, Fig. 3 illustrates the specification of a timed automaton $\mathcal{TA}_{tree}$ deployed at each node to create a self-managing tree overlay.

In particular, $\mathcal{TA}_{tree}$ is an instance of a timed automaton with a global variable $root, two queues named :parents and :siblings, a clock x and three possible actions: bootstrap, forward and queue (respectively noted $\succ$, $\#$ and ::). An overlay node always starts with a bootstrap action that initializes both the $root variable and the clock variable x. The former variable is used to know if an overlay node is or is not the root of the tree based overlay whereas the latter variable is used to control the time dependent behavior (Fig. 3, vertex ❶). Then, overlay nodes must wait at most 20 time units for receiving either: (i) a multicasted data message, (ii) a join request, or (iii) a join acknowledgment (vertex ❷). In the first case, multicasted messages are forwarded to siblings of the overlay node. In the second case, according to size of the siblings queue, the node that has sent the join request may be added or not to the *siblings* queues of the current overlay node (vertex ❸). If it is added then an acknowledgment is sent to the requester (vertex ❺), otherwise the join request is forwarded to the siblings of the current overlay node (vertex ❹). Constraints on the size of the siblings queue enables avoidance of an unbalanced tree. In the third case, the node that receives a join acknowledgment adds the ack sender to its *parents* queue. To ensure that the overlay being built remains connected, each node must probe the liveness of its neighbours. Thus, beyond a delay of 20 time units, if no messages have been received, overlay nodes must poll their parent nodes to check if they are still alive (vertex ❻). If in less than 5 time units, no acknowledgment is received, overlay nodes may have been disconnected from the overlay and thus have to reforward a join request to their parents. Otherwise, if acknowledgments are received, overlay nodes go back to the listening state s_1 to receive messages.

The use of timed automata enables us to specify a fine grained overlay construction algorithm. In particular, it becomes easy to express timed dependent behaviors to perform overlay maintenance, to manage network errors, or to periodically check invariants of the overlay.

3.3 Sevice Specification: End-to-End Middleware Services

Overlay Nodes. At each node in the constructed overlay additional logic is deployed to perform the required middleware functionality that achieves a particular service. Specifically, this logic performs actions on messages received from either the local end systems, or from messages disseminated by the overlay network. As depicted in Fig. 5, all overlay nodes have an *overlay port* through which they can send messages to, and receives messages from other nodes in the overlay (dependent on the network service provided by the overlay, e.g. multicast). Each node also has a set of N *data ports* through which the node communicates with the end systems using the required middleware protocol, e.g. an SLP data port allows the overlay to communicate with end systems using this protocol.

Middleware functionality is then performed as *actions* on the messages received and exchanged between these ports; examples including message translation and filtering are defined in Fig. 4). We use simple examples to then illustrate

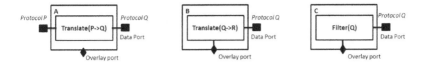

Fig. 5. Middleware logic actions applied at end system nodes

this procedure. Fig. 5A shows that a message received as a *Protocol P* message from a data port is translated to a *Protocol Q* message and sent on the corresponding data port (hence in this example the message is not transmitted to the overlay). Fig. 5B describes similar functionality but this time the message from the data port is translated before it is sent to the overlay. Finally, Fig. 5C illustrates the filtering of messages between the data ports and the overlay port. As previously stated, the approach is extensible to add new message actions to underpin a wider range of middleware services.

Data Flow Specification. Actions themselves are not enough to achieve service functionality; control logic is required to define the flow of data at the individual nodes. Thus, we further employ timed automata to specify the message flow across the overlay; a sequence of middleware, translating, multicast and queuing actions (resp. noted δ, $\propto$ and ::) are constrained by both time and message guards. Hence, it is possible to define different service functionality. For instance, in the case of a global resource discovery overlay integrating heterogeneous end system protocols, one solution is to follow a *translate and multicast strategy*: each node performs local translations between the disparate protocols employed in its domain; if there is no local resource match then the overlay node can pass the request to its neighbours by sending them the received incoming requests and/or their translated forms to increase chances to get successful answers. Fig. 6, illustrates a specification of a timed automaton $\mathcal{TA}_{bonjour1}$ that applies the aforementioned strategy to the *Bonjour* service discovery protocol. As soon as a message m of type DNS_Question is received, it is translated locally according to the underlaying gateway capabilities, to either SLP, UPnP, or other service discovery protocols (and noted $f(m)$) (Fig. 6, ❶). If DNS_Response messages are received locally (i.e. from the local environment) in less than 4 time units, they are sent to the requester (vertex ❺, ❻). Otherwise, the message m and its translated form $f(m)$ are queued and multicasted to overlay neighbors (vertex ❷).

Every 5 time units, if a DNS_Response message is received it is queued to be sent later (vertex ❸). Any other messages received are translated to *Bonjour* (vertex ❼). If the translation is successful, then it means that a DNS_Response has been received and then is queued. If the translation is not successful, the message $f(m)$ is either discarded if it has been already seen by the current node, or multicasted to overlay neighbors otherwise (vertex ❹). Finally, if the delay of 10 time units has passed without receiving any messages then all previously queued DNS_Response responses are sent to the requester, and the queue is flushed (vertex ❺, ❻).

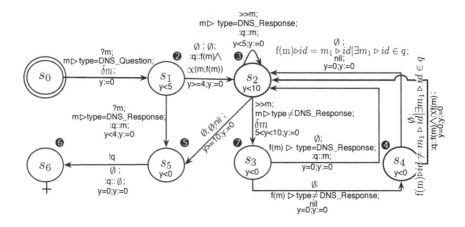

Fig. 6. Translate and forward strategy

From our model it is straightforward to define additional compelling strategies. For instance, in the case where the response time of the global resource discovery service is important, Fig. 6 can be altered to multicast incoming request immediately to find corresponding responses in other networked environment, without waiting for local responses. Further, Fig. 7 shows the node logic for event filtering in a global event service. Here, subscription requests are multicast across the network and translated and applied as local filtering rules. Published events are then translated to an abstract message specification to which the filters are applied. Published Messages that match the filters are translated to the legacy end system protocols and multicasted across either the local network or the overlay according to the messages' origin. This is a relatively simple publish-subscribe service that handles protocol heterogeneity; there are many potential broker strategies, which we believe the overlay and flow specifications are flexible enough to define.

Reusing Overlays for Multiple Middleware Services. The behavior of an overlay, noted $\mathcal{TA_O}$, is modeled through a set of timed automata that are composed together. In a way similar to process algebras such as CCS [18] and FSP [17], we introduce the parallel composition operator $\|$ to compose timed automata. Hence, the behavior of $\mathcal{TA_O}$ consists of individual timed automata that execute their transitions independently. As in our model, each timed automaton is independent from each other, compared to traditional process algebras, our composition operator $\|$ does not provide any synchronization features among composed timed automaton. Further clocks are local to each composed automaton. There are no global or shared clocks variable. So, provisioning n applications using P_1, P_2,..., P_n protocols across an overlay $\mathcal{O}$ is described by the following formula: $\mathcal{TA_O} = \mathcal{TA}_{topology} \| \mathcal{TA}_{P_1} \| \mathcal{TA}_{P_2} \| \mathcal{TA}_{P_3} \| ... \| \mathcal{TA}_{P_n}$. The timed automaton $\mathcal{TA}_{topology}$ describes the self-organization behavior of the overlay and $\mathcal{TA}_{P_1}$, ..., $\mathcal{TA}_{P_n}$ specify the different translation strategy for each

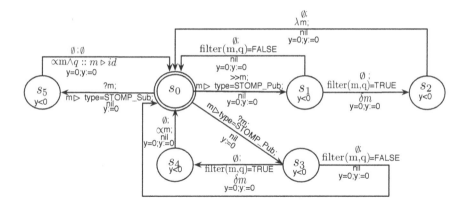

Fig. 7. Event translation and filtering strategy

supported middleware service. The strength of our model comes from its flexibility. Replacing one strategy by another or taking into account a new service and/or a new overlay topology is straightforward as the $\|$ operator enables a modularized specification.

4   The OverStar Framework Implementation

Here we describe the further implementation details of the OverStar software framework. OverStar is implemented in Java and leverages the capabilities of the Starlink framework [4]. There are two key elements to the implementation: i) the implementation of reusable building blocks that underpin the *action* keywords that are performed during the service flow specification logic (e.g. interoperability), and ii) the implementation of the timed automata interpreters.

4.1   Actions: Reusable Software Building Blocks

As previously described, *Actions* are performed to realise the service flow logic behaviour. These are defined as key words in the timed automaton; and these key words relate to reusable software building blocks. Hence, the logic is extensible and adaptable through the creation of new building blocks.

Actions are specified using the Starlink framework. Starlink uses *k-colored automata* to capture the properties of a protocol by a color k and ensures that the messages are sent and received using the appropriate network service. This supports the parsing of a message into the *abstract message* format such that additional logic can be performed on the messages irrespective of the heterogeneous protocols. Hence, an action is a k-colored automata with the message logic relating to the action. When the timed-automata specifies a transition with a particular keyword action then the corresponding coloured automata is executed. To illustrate this method, we present one example in Fig. 8; this is a translation from SLP request messages to UPnP request messages. The original SLP request message is translated to a SSDP request that initiates UPnP behaviour. The bi-coloured state performs the assignment of field data from one message to another. Other examples are: the translation of STOMP to XMPP messages, or the parsing of either of these such that they can be filtered by message topic.

Fig. 8. Starlink merged automaton for SLP to UPnP protocol translation

4.2   Timed Automata Interpreters

Both the Overlay and Service flow interpreters dynamically execute timed automata written in XML (we do not provide a schema here, however, the notation provided in Section 3 offers a concise representation). To illustrate how OverStar operates, we now summarise the behaviour that occurs at the two state types.

At a **receiving state**, the interpreter listens for messages from the overlay or data port. The receiving state parses the message to determine the automaton action e.g. translate, filter, etc. Transitions to other states are taken based upon both action types and guard conditions. For example, where there is a time-guard on the state a timeout exception is used, i.e. the state listens for new events and the timeout value is set to the guard value. If no event is received in the timeframe the exception is caught and the appropriate transition is executed.

At a **sending state**, the interpreter constructs a new instance of an overlay message to be forwarded in the overlay. This consists of the original legacy protocol message with a new OverStar header. The header contains a small amount of data (17 bytes) capturing the message type (e.g. forward, join in 1 byte), a unique message identifier (8 bytes), message source IP (4 bytes), and message source port (4 bytes). The sending state can also send concrete protocol messages to a given legacy end system using the correct protocol behaviour.

5   Evaluation

5.1   Case Study Based Methodology

We employ a case-study approach to evaluate the ability of the OverStar framework to achieve its primary contributions. For this we developed two different but complimentary middleware services to highlight the flexibility of OverStar:

– A resource discovery service that can react to requests from heterogeneous end system protocols (e.g. SLP, Bonjour and UPnP) and ensure that matching service responses are returned.
– An event service that joins end systems using heterogeneous publish-subscribe technologies, e.g., STOMP and XMPP-XE0060 and ensures that events that match subscriptions are received despite the heterogeneous protocols.

The two services employ very different legacy middleware technologies and pose different challenges to applicability of OverStar. The resource discovery and event service solutions were deployed in the emulated complex network environment as described in Section 5.2. Utilising this experimental setup, we performed three measures: i) the end-to-end interoperability achieved by OverStar; ii) specific optimisations within the two services as specified by the service logic; and iii) the overheads occurred during OverStar's operation. These results are used to evaluate the extent to which the primary contributions are achieved.

5.2 Experimental Setup

To evaluate various aspects of OverStar, we have setup a particular network environment enabling reasonably large scale experiments. We have deployed OverStar across heterogeneous domains (e.g. 4, 8, 16) interconnected *via* a network backbone. A heterogeneous domain is instantiated as a Virtual Local Area Network (VLAN). A VLAN contains a set of devices that are logically connected within a single broadcast domain, and located in the same IP subnet. In fact, a one-to-one mapping between VLANs and IP subnets is applied, according to the best practices in network design. Devices may host either the OverStar middleware to act as an OverStar node, or middleware services relying on heterogeneous protocols. The key advantage of using VLANs to interconnect devices is to confine traffic generated by services (e.g. broadcast, multicast and/or unicast) into one domain without interfering with another, while abstracting the underlying physical network topology. Additionally, in our experiments, devices are emulated *via* Linux Kernel-based Virtual Machines (KVM) to use real operating systems and run unmodified both middleware services and OverStar middleware. The whole setup was conducted on a rack server equipped with 4 AMD opteron processors at 2 GHz, including 12-core per processor (for a total of 48 cores), and 32 GB of RAM. The server multiplexes virtual resources such as VLANs, KVMs on top of physical ones, and enables IP routing between domains.

5.3 Interoperability Experiments

In the emulated environment, we deployed a set of heterogeneous end systems across different domain configurations, i.e., four domains, eight domains, and sixteen domains; where in each domain, heterogeneous end systems utilise one of: SLP, Bonjour and UPnP to request or advertise a resource. We then specified and deployed an OverStar service solution using a multicast tree overlay timed-automata to connect the domains (up to sixteen). The service was specified to immediately multicast received requests from the heterogeneous end-systems onto the overlay; when received at the domain nodes these are translated to perform discovery using the local protocols. We measured the number of successful match responses to the requests as the percentage interoperability achieved; this was compared to: i) no interoperability solution deployed, and ii) local bridges (i.e. bridges for SLP to UPnP, Bonjour to SLP, etc. deployed in each domain).

The results in Fig. 9 show that local bridges increase the potential interoperability as they reach more services in the local domain, but OverStar achieves the necessary end-to-end interoperability via the global integrated service (n.b. across the experiment there is a least one matching service, and in many cases multiple matches). A similar experiment was performed for heterogeneous end-system event services (STOMP and XMPP-XE0060). Here the OverStar specification used a multicast tree with the local filtering only timed-automata (see Fig. 7). To measure the interoperability percentage in this case we compared the actual received events as a percentage of the matching events published across the network. Similarly, OverStar is able to achieve end-to-end interoperability in the event service case compared to the local domain approaches. Overall, these results demonstrate that hypothesis one is proven.

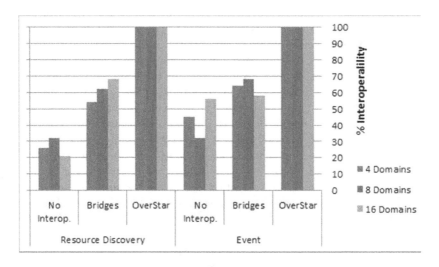

Fig. 9. Percentage interoperability results

5.4   Optimisation Experiments

For the optimisation experiments we use the same experimental setup as with the previous experiment. However, this time we apply different timed-automata strategies for the middleware service specifications. For the resource discovery case: i) multicast and translate (as used in the interoperability experiment), and ii) match service requests locally and multicast to the overlay when there isn't a response (this specification is captured in Fig. 6). For the event service case: i) local filtering only (where all publications are multicast on the overlay and local filters determine which are translated to the end-systems (see Fig. 7), and ii) global filtering where subscriptions are multicast to the OverStar nodes to ensure that only matching publications are sent between domains. The results in Fig. 10 show that for resource discovery, strategy one reduces the maximum response time from a matched service in the global network, but this approach occurs significant message overhead especially as the domain configuration grows larger.

Strategy two reduces this number of messages sent in the network, although the maximum response time is increased. It is interesting to note that the deployment of local bridges in a domain can create a cycle (i.e. the message is translated from one protocol using one bridge and then back to the same protocol by a separate bridge) leading to an infinite number of messages in the domain and across the network. The use of OverStar is shown to prevent such cycles occurring. Finally, in the case of the strategies for the event service, it can be seen that strategy two reduces the overall number of messages in the network compared to strategy one; hence, this minimises the message translations that take place. Overall, these results show that OverStar can be flexibly used to optimise for different domain configurations and requirements and offer initial proof of hypothesis two.

	Resource Discovery						Event Service	
	Strategy One			Strategy Two			Strategy One	Strategy Two
	No.	Min resp.	Max resp.	No.	Min resp.	Max resp.	No.	No.
Domains	msgs	(ms)	(ms)	msgs	(ms)	(ms)	msgs	msgs
4	1593	647	1454	833	672	4673	1372	441
8	3012	638	1625	1343	723	4836	2618	629
16	6206	655	1595	2721	756	4793	453	1074

Fig. 10. Comparison of different service strategies

5.5   Resource Overheads Experiments

Finally, we examine the resource overheads of the OverStar implementation. For this, we measure the time taken to perform three indicative individual actions on each OverStar node: i) the time to translate from an SLP message to a Bonjour message, ii) the time to translate from a STOMP message to an XMPP message, and iii) the time to translate from a STOMP message to an abstract message and then perform filtering. The results in Table. 1 show that OverStar introduces an expected overhead, however, this does not detract significantly from the overall performance of the services (e.g. compared to the overall response time of resource discovery). N.b. the measures are dependent on the protocol types; STOMP to XMPP involves text to XML message translation and hence is slower than SLP to Bonjour which is a binary to binary translation.

Table 1. Direct bridging deployments only

Action	Time (ms)
SLP to Bonjour	0.28
STOMP to XMPP	0.39
STOMP to filter	0.25

6   Related Work

6.1   Interoperability Solutions

Interoperability solutions focus on the search for a universal standard; and where such a standard is agreed and adopted the problem is solved. However, history has shown this approach to be unsuccessful. Two primary examples: the set of CORBA standards from the OMG [10] and the set of Web Services standards [3] from the W3C. However, such one size fits all standards are not suited to the extreme heterogeneity of systems-of-systems, e.g. from small scale sensor applications and embedded devices through to large scale Internet applications.

Rather than seek universal standards, alternative approaches either build direct bridges between systems e.g. the SOAP to CORBA bridge[4], embrace simplicity (i.e. RESTful solutions) or look for transparency (i.e. Service Buses). REST presents a simple uniform API atop a global standard protocol (the HTTP protocol being widely used to connect systems) allowing many interoperability problems at the communication level to be addressed. However, the Restful approach leaves interoperability issues arising at the application behaviour and data level unresolved. For example, a service cannot respond to a GET operation request composed of an operation name and data parameters that has different behaviour and syntax to itself. Opposed to standards, transparent solutions mimic the action of a language interpreter, that is they receive communications from system A and then translate this such that system B can understand and vice versa. Enterprise Service Buses (ESBs) e.g. Artix, INDISS [5], z2z [6], Janus [1] and uMiddle [19], provide such capabilities between multiple "languages". However, transparent solutions are typically restricted to a set of known middleware types, and the development effort required to extend them for new protocols is significant. CONNECT [2] has examined semantics-based solutions to automate this challenging task, however, the focus is single party protocols between two systems; within the CONNECT approach, [13] examines interoperability between heterogeneous multiparty middleware abstractions, but does not consider the underlying deployment complexities of achieving end-to-end interoperability in heterogeneous systems-of-systems.

Analysis. Generally, interoperability has been considered from an enterprise systems perspective, where interactions are point-to-point, planned and long-lived. Hence, they remain limited when considering the dynamic composition of heterogeneous systems, where the knowledge about the services provided by different systems and the protocols they employ are unknown until binding time and a common translation technology cannot be agreed upon in advance.

Further, none of the above solutions considers the cases of interoperation between systems using heterogeneous multi-party communication protocols (e.g. multi-party discovery, group communication, publish subscribe, etc.), they consider only the case where a single system must interact with another. OSDA [15], MUSDAC [20] and SeDiM [7] offer bridging solutions between service discovery

---

[4] http://soap2corba.sourceforge.net/

domains to provide universal solutions i.e. a service lookup request from one domain can be answered in another network domain irrespective of the service discovery protocols employed in that domain. Notably, OSDA uses a peer-to-peer ring to communicate messages between heterogeneous domains. However, the weakness of these platforms are threefold: i) they are specific solutions implemented for service discovery and cannot be flexibly applied to other problem domains e.g. group communication; ii) they employ a transparent intermediary between domains and hence mappers to and from this intermediary must be developed by hand for every protocol, and iii) the intermediary is a 'subset of all protocols' and as such this subset may become too small to underpin interoperability in a general fashion, e.g., if service discovery protocols A and B provide attribute based lookup while protocol C does not then the intermediary cannot include attribute lookup; this lessens any potential interoperation between A and B. In comparison, OverStar supports the specification of end-to-end interoperability solutions between heterogeneous multi-party middleware protocols that span heterogeneous network domains.

6.2 Overlay Networks and Middleware

Overlay networks are virtual communications structures that are logically 'laid over' an underlying physical network. They are established solutions for providing scalable application services across heterogeneous networks, nodes and systems. For example, publish-subscribe and group interaction can be underpinned in the Internet by multicast overlays such as SRM [8]. Similarly, DHT-based peer-to-peer overlays provide reliable resource discovery in large-scale distributed systems e.g. Pastry [22] and Chord [25]. And publish subscribe services are one example of middleware services layered atop DHT, e.g., Scribe [23]. These properties make them suited to connecting heterogeneous systems of systems; yet the different types of middleware protocols suggests that a single network type is insufficient and it must be possible to flexibly specify an overlay to underpin the broad range of potential middleware services.

There exist toolkits that provide principled support for overlay network development. $JXTA^5$ is a framework where p2p applications are developed atop a resource search abstraction; this supports grouping and contacting nodes. This abstraction can be implemented using a number of overlay topologies. This approach involves a full development life-cycle and hence, higher-level declarative languages and models have been produced to simplify the complex task of constructing new overlays. *Macedon* [21] is a state machine compiler for overlay protocol design. Event-driven state machines (EDSMs) have been used over decades for protocol design and specification. Macedon extends this approach to an overlay specific, C++ based language from which it generates source code for overlay maintenance and routing. In the P2/Overlog project [16], applications use a declarative logic language to specify their requirements of the overlay network. This is combined with a data flow approach, as opposed to a finite state

---

5 http://www.jxta.org

machine approach, to maintain the overlay at runtime. Like Macedon, this simplifies the development process of overlays in specific cases. *iOverlay* [14] provides a message switch abstraction for the design of the local routing algorithm. The neighbors of a node are instantiated as local I/O queues between which the user provided implementation switches messages. This simplifies the design of overlay algorithms by hiding the lower networking levels.

Analysis. While suited to the construction and maintenance of overlay networks, the above are limited with respect to the high-level declaration and deployment of the atop application services. That is, it is not possible to specify the data-flow behaviour in terms of handling the problem of end-to-end interoperability. In comparison, OverStar supports the declarative specification of middleware services atop overlay networks in order to optimise the flow of message data and the necessary dynamic translations between protocols .

7   Concluding Remarks and Future Work

In this paper we have highlighted the importance of integration of end systems leveraging heterogeneous middleware; and here, end-to-end interoperability is a key requirement. Indeed, it can no longer be assumed that a single protocol is used across network and organizational boundaries in order to implement network services such as service discovery, multicast, group communication and publish subscribe. Instead, heterogeneous protocols will be employed. In the face of this heterogeneity, new approaches to build global middleware services are required that ensure that all services and devices are connected in an efficient and optimised way in order to effectively coordinate.

For this purpose, we have introduced novel models that specify overlay behaviour to support the development of middleware services that achieve end-to-end interoperability in complex systems-of-systems and an associated software framework (OverStar). The key contributions of which are the use of timed automata for: i) the specification of the topology and maintenance of the overlay network which interconnects heterogeneous protocols across large-scale networks; ii) the specification of the overlay's application service, in this case the logic and flow tailored to the particular middleware service type. We evaluated this framework using both resource discovery and event communication services. Our initial results from the simple case-studies have shown that the OverStar solution increases interoperability within the network and reduces the resource consumption in terms of messages sent compared to bridging solutions.

There are a number of interesting avenues of future work. The first is to extend the models in order to capture improved strategies for performing optimised, scaleable, end-to-end interoperability of resource discovery, group communication, and publish subscribe services. In this regard, overlay networks are well suited to self-organizing behaviour, hence there is the potential for the overlay to monitor the environments and protocols in order to better determine how to optimise the deployed middleware service. The use of interpreted models provides a mechanism to easily adapt the behaviour of the service by dynamically changing the model at runtime. Complimentary to this, the use of machine understandable models, i.e., timed automata, makes machine learning of solutions an interesting way forward; for example, machine learning protocols have been used to learn the automata for individual network protocols [12], and there is the possibility of learning more complex overlay network specifications.

Acknowledgments. This work is part funded by the CONNECT project, funded under the Framework 7 FET Programme: http://www.connect-forever.eu.

References

1. Bissyandé, T.F., Réveillère, L., Bromberg, Y.-D., Lawall, J.L., Muller, G.: Bridging the Gap between Legacy Services and Web Services. In: Gupta, I., Mascolo, C. (eds.) Middleware 2010. LNCS, vol. 6452, pp. 273–292. Springer, Heidelberg (2010)
2. Blair, G.S., Bennaceur, A., Georgantas, N., Grace, P., Issarny, V., Nundloll, V., Paolucci, M.: The Role of Ontologies in Emergent Middleware: Supporting Interoperability in Complex Distributed Systems. In: Kon, F., Kermarrec, A.-M. (eds.) Middleware 2011. LNCS, vol. 7049, pp. 410–430. Springer, Heidelberg (2011)
3. Booth, D., Haas, H., McCabe, F., Newcomer, E., Champion, M., Ferris, C., Orchard, D.: Web services architecture (February 2004)
4. Bromberg, Y.-D., Grace, P., Reveillere, L.: Starlink: Runtime interoperability between heterogeneous middleware protocols. In: 31st International Conference on Distributed Computing Systems, ICDCS 2011, pp. 446–455 (2011)
5. Bromberg, Y.-D., Issarny, V.: INDISS: Interoperable Discovery System for Networked Services. In: Alonso, G. (ed.) Middleware 2005. LNCS, vol. 3790, pp. 164–183. Springer, Heidelberg (2005)
6. Bromberg, Y.-D., Réveillère, L., Lawall, J.L., Muller, G.: Automatic Generation of Network Protocol Gateways. In: Bacon, J.M., Cooper, B.F. (eds.) Middleware 2009. LNCS, vol. 5896, pp. 21–41. Springer, Heidelberg (2009)
7. Flores, C., Blair, G., Grace, P.: An adaptive middleware to overcome service discovery heterogeneity in mobile ad hoc environments. In: IEEE Distributed Systems Online (2007)
8. Floyd, S., Jacobson, V., Liu, C., McCanne, S., Zhang, L.: A reliable multicast framework for light-weight sessions and application level framing. IEEE/ACM Trans. Netw. 5, 784–803 (1997)
9. Grace, P., Hughes, D., Porter, B., Blair, G., Coulson, G., Taiani, F.: Experiences with open overlays: a middleware approach to network heterogeneity. In: Proceedings of the 3rd ACM SIGOPS/EuroSys European Conference on Computer Systems, Eurosys 2008, pp. 123–136. ACM, New York (2008)
10. Object Management Group. The common object request broker: Architecture and specification version 2.0. Technical report (1995)
11. Yih-Chun, H., Perrig, A., Johnson, D.: Ariadne: a secure on-demand routing protocol for ad hoc networks. Wirel. Netw. 11(1-2), 21–38 (2005)
12. Howar, F., Jonsson, B., Merten, M., Steffen, B., Cassel, S.: On Handling Data in Automata Learning - Considerations from the CONNECT Perspective In: Margaria, T., Steffen, B. (eds.) ISoLA 2010, Part II. LNCS, vol. 6416, pp. 221–235. Springer, Heidelberg (2010)

13. Issarny, V., Bennaceur, A., Bromberg, Y.-D.: Middleware-Layer Connector Synthesis: Beyond State of the Art in Middleware Interoperability. In: Bernardo, M., Issarny, V. (eds.) SFM 2011. LNCS, vol. 6659, pp. 217–255. Springer, Heidelberg (2011)
14. Li, B., Guo, J., Wang, M.: iOverlay: A Lightweight Middleware Infrastructure for Overlay Application Implementations, pp. 135–154 (2004)
15. Limam, N., Ziembicki, J., Ahmed, R., Iraqi, Y., Li, D., Boutaba, R., Cuervo, F.: Osda: Open service discovery architecture for efficient cross-domain service provisioning. Computer Communications 30(3), 546–563 (2007)
16. Loo, B., Condie, T., Hellerstein, J., Maniatis, P., Roscoe, T., Stoica, I.: Implementing declarative overlays. In: Proceedings of the Twentieth ACM Symposium on Operating Systems Principles, SOSP 2005, New York, NY, USA, pp. 75–90 (2005)
17. Magee, J., Kramer, J.: Concurrency - state models and Java programs, 2nd edn. Wiley (2006)
18. Milner, R.: Operational and Algebraic Semantics of Concurrent Processes (1990)
19. Nakazawa, J., Tokuda, H., Edwards, W., Ramachandran, U.: A bridging framework for universal interoperability in pervasive systems. In: 26th IEEE International Conference on Distributed Computing Systems, ICDCS 2006 (2006)
20. Raverdy, P., Issarny, V., Chibout, R., de La Chapelle, A.: A multi-protocol approach to service discovery and access in pervasive environments. In: 3rd Annual International Conference on Mobile and Ubiquitous Systems - Workshops, pp. 1–9 (July 2006)
21. Rodriguez, A., Killian, C., Bhat, S., Kostic, D., Vahdat, A.: Macedon: Methodology for automatically creating, evaluating, and designing overlay networks. In: In NSDI, pp. 267–280 (2004)
22. Rowstron, A., Druschel, P.: Pastry: Scalable, Decentralized Object Location, and Routing for Large-Scale Peer-to-Peer Systems. In: Guerraoui, R. (ed.) Middleware 2001. LNCS, vol. 2218, pp. 329–350. Springer, Heidelberg (2001)
23. Rowstron, A., Kermarrec, A.-M., Druschel, P.: SCRIBE: The Design of a Large-Scale Event Notification Infrastructure. In: Crowcroft, J., Hofmann, M. (eds.) NGC 2001. LNCS, vol. 2233, pp. 30–43. Springer, Heidelberg (2001)
24. Souto, E., Guimar, G., Vasconcelos, G., Vieira, M., Rosa, N., Ferraz, C., Kelner, J.: Mires: a publish/subscribe middleware for sensor networks. Personal Ubiquitous Comput. 10(1), 37–44 (2005)
25. Stoica, I., Morris, R., Liben-Nowell, D., Karger, D., Kaashoek, M., Dabek, F., Balakrishnan, H.: Chord: a scalable peer-to-peer lookup protocol for internet applications. IEEE/ACM Trans. Netw. 11, 17–32 (2003)

Opportunistic Multipath Forwarding in Content-Based Publish/Subscribe Overlays

Reza Sherafat Kazemzadeh and Hans-Arno Jacobsen

Middleware Systems Research Group, University of Toronto
{reza,jacobsen}@eecg.utoronto.ca

Abstract. Fine-grained filtering capabilities prevalent in content-based Publish/Subscribe (pub/sub) overlays lead to scenarios in which publications pass through brokers with no matching local subscribers. Processing of publications at these *pure forwarding* brokers amounts to inefficient use of resources and should ideally be avoided. This paper develops an approach that largely mitigates this problem by building and adaptively maintaining a highly connected overlay mesh superimposed atop a low connectivity *primary* overlay network. While the primary network provides basic end-to-end forwarding routes, the mesh structure provides a rich set of alternative forwarding choices which can be used to bypass pure forwarding brokers. This provides unique opportunities for load balancing and congestion avoidance. Through extensive experimental evaluation on the SciNet cluster and PlanetLab, we compare the performance of our approach with that of conventional pub/sub algorithms as baseline. Our results indicate that our approach improves publication delivery delay and lowers network traffic while incurring negligible computational and bandwidth overhead. Furthermore, compared to the baseline, we observed significant gains of up to 115% in terms of system throughput.

1 Introduction

Flexibility, scalability and loose coupling properties of the Publish/Subscribe (pub/sub) model has led to its adoption in a variety of enterprise, datacenter and wide-area network environments [1,2,3,4]. Microsoft, Google and Yahoo, for instance, use pub/sub for end-user notification delivery [5], data dissemination in large-scale server farms [3], and in distributed data storage systems [2]. In enterprise settings, pub/sub has appeared in several contexts and standards including Enterprise Service Bus (ESB) [6,4], algorithmic trading [7], WS-Notifications and WS-Eventing. In wide-area networks, pub/sub messaging has been used in push-based RSS feeds [8], global supply chain data exchange networks [1], and as a potential addressing and routing paradigm for future Internet protocols [9].

Widespread adoption of the pub/sub model further underlines the significance of scalable architectures that can efficiently utilize network resources in order to achieve low message delivery delay and high throughput. A distributed content-based pub/sub system deploys a set of dedicated application layer routers (*a.k.a.* brokers) to form an overlay network [10,11,12,13,14,15,16]. Clients connect to brokers and are offered the flexibility to specify fine-grained filtering constraints on publications they are interested to receive. Publications that satisfy these

P. Narasimhan and P. Triantafillou (Eds.): Middleware 2012, LNCS 7662, pp. 249–270, 2012.
© IFIP International Federation for Information Processing 2012

constraints are forwarded through the overlay towards brokers where interested subscribers reside and are then delivered to those clients.

It is generally infeasible to maintain full connectivity in a large overlay and it becomes imperative to only utilize a selective set of all links. Furthermore, in content-based pub/sub systems the set of matching subscribers to which a given publication must be delivered is highly variable and cannot be determined in advance. This makes it *challenging to build optimal dissemination overlays that only span to brokers with interested local subscribers.* As a result, existing pub/sub systems use a shared dissemination overlay and may forward publications through uninterested (*a.k.a. pure forwarding*) brokers with no local matching subscribers. Processing of publications at pure forwarding brokers increases publication hop count and propagation latency, and therefore amounts to inefficient use of bandwidth and computational resources in the network.

To lower the number of pure forwarders, reconfiguration techniques modify the overlay step-by-step by adding links between brokers with similar subscriber interests and removing links between those with less similarity [17,18]. Altering overlay links in this manner has a large system-wide footprint and while beneficial to some end-to-end publication flows it can at the same time be detrimental to many others. Furthermore, each reconfiguration step requires coordinated updates to routing tables of many brokers, a process that is slow, costly and potentially disruptive. Alternatively, clustering techniques group subscribers with similar interests and move them closer to brokers where publishers reside [19]. In content-based pub/sub systems in which clients may have widely varying interests, the performance of clustering schemes is not always guaranteed. Furthermore, clustering algorithms may prescribe clients with multiple subscriptions to connect to more than one broker, an inconvenience that must ideally be avoided.

A related common problem in virtually all existing pub/sub systems is that overlay forwarding paths are set up in a *fixed end-to-end manner.* In other words, *a publication is forwarded over a fixed path to a destination broker (where matching subscribers are connected) regardless of whether or not the message is of interest to subscribers at intermediate brokers along the path.* This rigidity inevitably results in a large number of pure forwarders, especially in a content-based pub/sub system with highly varied subscriber interests. This deficiency could be mitigated if the overlay connectivity between sources and destinations offered a multitude of redundant forwarding paths giving brokers the flexibility to pick the best forwarding path for each publication on a *one-by-one* basis.

To this end, we propose an adaptive overlay management and dynamic routing approach that constructs a highly connected mesh structure atop a *primary overlay network.* The primary network offers basic connectivity among end-to-end brokers and may use existing routing algorithms. By monitoring ongoing traffic in the primary network, brokers identify popular transit routes and establish additional communication links, referred to as *soft links*. Soft links collectively construct a highly connected overlay mesh and provide a rich set of redundant paths between all source and destination broker pairs. Figure 1 illustrates a snapshot view of the number of end-to-end paths in a running system using this scheme. About 40% of brokers in a network of size 120 have at least one hundred distinct forwarding paths among them. This is increased to more than 1,000 for 13% of brokers in a network of size 250. In our approach, all these routes are readily available for publication forwarding and the decision on which path to take is made at runtime and based on the relative location of matching

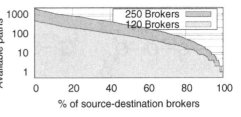

Fig. 1. Number of end-to-end forwarding paths in networks of 120 and 250 brokers (log scale)

subscribers. This is in contrast to most pub/sub systems [13,10,14] which use *fixed end-to-end forwarding paths* and send a message towards a destination broker over the same path regardless of whether or not it matches subscriptions at intermediate brokers. The premise of our approach is that availability of a very large set of alternative routes gives brokers the opportunity to consciously use the path that is best suitable for delivery of the message to all interested subscribers while incurring fewer pure forwarders.

To forward publications in the overlay mesh and determine the relative location of matching subscribers, brokers rely on knowledge of their neighboring brokers within a certain distance, denoted by configuration parameter Δ. This knowledge enables a broker to anticipate how publications flow within its Δ-neighborhood and which alternative routes towards the destinations incur fewer pure forwarders. Furthermore, brokers monitor ongoing traffic to choose the best set of soft links based on three criteria: Avoiding pure forwarding brokers, avoiding slow primary links, and bypassing congested network hotspots. As another advantage of our approach, modifying the overlay mesh of soft links requires only local updates to routing tables. This is a light-weight process and a significant improvement over full overlay reconfiguration techniques [17,18] which require coordinated updates to several brokers' routing tables.

In this paper, we make the following contributions: *(i)* A scheme to adaptively maintain a highly connected overlay mesh for pub/sub systems; *(ii)* techniques to update brokers' routing tables based on network connectivity with no need for coordination among neighbors; *(iii)* four forwarding strategies and efficient cache data structures to realize them; *(iv)* a traffic profiling technique to identify popular transit routes within the overlay; and *(v)* comprehensive experimental evaluations using a Java-based open-source implementation, called *Publiy* [20].

2   Publication Forwarding Strategies

In this section, we give a high level overview of four publication forwarding strategies that we develop in this paper. We defer the details of how each forwarding strategy can be efficiently implemented to subsequent sections.

We use Figure 2 to describe how publication p is forwarded by Broker A in each strategy. In the figure, p matches subscribers local to Brokers N_3, N_5, and

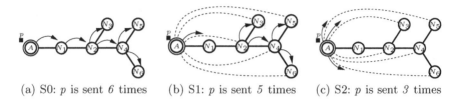

(a) S0: p is sent *6* times   (b) S1: p is sent *5* times   (c) S2: p is sent *3* times

Fig. 2. Forwarding publication p matching subscribers at N_3, N_5, N_6 using different strategies. Primary and soft links are represented by solid and dashed lines, respectively

N_6. Moreover, solid lines represent primary links in the network and dashed lines are extra soft links created and maintained in our approach.

Strategy 0 (S0): This strategy corresponds to conventional pub/sub systems and is presented here mainly as baseline for comparison. Conventional approaches are based on fixed end-to-end forwarding paths [13,14,16] along which matching publications traverse towards interested subscribers. These paths are established over communication links which we refer to as primary links. In Figure 2(a), Broker A sends one copy of p to N_1 which is its immediate neighbor located closer to matching subscribers. Observe that since forwarding paths are maintained in a fixed end-to-end manner, Broker A's decision to send p to this neighbor is not impacted by whether p is of interest to intermediate brokers along p's projected downstream propagation path.

Strategy 1 (S1): Brokers using this strategy take advantage of their neighborhood knowledge to *anticipate the propagation path of publications within their Δ-neighborhoods*. Armed with this knowledge, brokers identify nearby pure forwarders and attempt to bypass them using additional soft links that they possess. S1 allows brokers to utilize both primary links as well as soft links and send publications to their farthest reachable neighbors that are on the intersection of primary paths towards all matching subscribers. In Figure 2(b), the intersection of primary paths from Broker A to Brokers N_3, N_5 and N_6 consists of path $\langle N_1, N_2 \rangle$. As a result, Broker A sends p to N_2 (*i.e.*, the farthest reachable neighbor on this path) thus bypassing N_1. Broker N_2 will then be responsible to forward p to N_3 and N_4. Observe that S1 enables brokers to improve the system's performance by opportunistically bypassing some pure forwarders.

Strategy 2 (S2): This strategy also makes use of both primary and soft links to bypass pure forwarding brokers but compared to S1 this is done in a more aggressive manner. More specifically, brokers that run S2 attempt to directly forward publications towards matching subscribers using their farthest reaching primary and soft links. In Figure 2(c), Broker A uses its soft links and directly forwards separate copies of p to N_3, N_5, and N_6. Note that this strategy improves the chance of bypassing a larger number of pure forwarders. However, this comes at the cost of having Broker A send more copies of publication p.

Strategy Hybrid (SH): The above strategies consume different amount of output bandwidth per processed publication, *e.g.*, Broker A sends three copies of p using S2 while S0 and S1 each require A to send only one copy. Brokers using SH take advantage of this trade-off and dynamically switch between S1 and S2 to tune their output bandwidth consumption. More specifically, a broker with limited output bandwidth uses S1 to minimize utilization of its scarce resources. This, however, can potentially lead to increased network-wide traffic. On the other hand, brokers with no resource constraints use S2 which incurs fewer overall network messages at the expense of more bandwidth utilization at each forwarding broker per publication.

We underscore that the advantages of our forwarding strategies grow in content-based pub/sub systems featuring *selective multicast*. In these systems, publications are likely to match highly varied subsets of subscriptions (the number of these subsets grows exponentially with the system size). Furthermore, interested subscribers are not known in advance and are identified only at runtime. This high degree of unpredictability and matching diversity makes it inherently difficult to optimize the pub/sub overlay when forwarding paths are constructed in a fixed end-to-end manner (*i.e.*, the case of conventional pub/sub systems). In contrast, the flexibility of forwarding publications through a well-connected overlay mesh of soft links in our approach greatly remedies this problem and enables fine-grained tuning of forwarding paths in an *opportunistic manner*.

Realization of our forwarding strategies requires pub/sub brokers to maintain Δ-neighborhood knowledge and perform complex path computations in order to decide how to forward a publication. In the following sections, we elaborate on efficient techniques and data structures to enable brokers to harvest the benefits of high connectivity in the overlay mesh at a negligible overhead.

3   Overlay Maps

We assume that there is an initial pub/sub overlay that provides basic connectivity among brokers. We refer to this overlay and its links as the *primary network* and *primary links*, respectively. In this section, we elaborate on brokers' internal data structures, namely the *Master Overlay Map* and *Working Overlay Map*, used by brokers to make forwarding decisions. Roughly speaking, the former reflects a partial view of the *primary network* which is stable and changes infrequently. The latter, however, acts as an efficient lookup cache and provides a dynamic view of the *overlay mesh* which is built atop the primary network.

Master overlay maps: Brokers store a *partial* view of the primary network in a local data structure called the *Master Overlay Map* (MOM). This partial view is in the form of a subgraph centered at the broker and includes neighboring brokers and their primary links located within distance Δ (i.e., Δ-*neighborhood*). The primary network is stable and changes infrequently, possibly due to occasional broker joins or departures. These changes are propagated hop-by-hop in Δ-neighborhoods so that nearby brokers update their MOMs accordingly.

Working overlay maps: Other than primary links, brokers possess two other types of links, namely *soft links* and *candidate links*. These links construct an

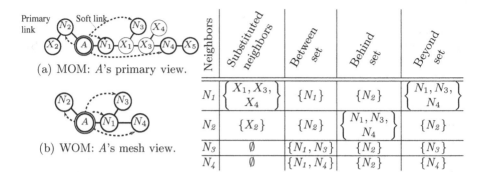

(a) MOM: A's primary view.

(b) WOM: A's mesh view.

Neighbors	Substituted neighbors	Between set	Behind set	Beyond set
N_1	$\left\{ \begin{array}{c} X_1, X_3, \\ X_4 \end{array} \right\}$	$\{N_1\}$	$\{N_2\}$	$\left\{ \begin{array}{c} N_1, N_3, \\ N_4 \end{array} \right\}$
N_2	$\{X_2\}$	$\{N_2\}$	$\left\{ \begin{array}{c} N_1, N_3, \\ N_4 \end{array} \right\}$	$\{N_2\}$
N_3	$\emptyset$	$\{N_1, N_3\}$	$\{N_2\}$	$\{N_3\}$
N_4	$\emptyset$	$\{N_1, N_4\}$	$\{N_2\}$	$\{N_4\}$

Fig. 3. Master and working overlay maps at Broker A ($\Delta = 4$)

Fig. 4. Information in A's WOM ($\Delta = 4$)

overlay mesh that is superimposed atop the primary network. Unlike primary links, soft and candidate links change frequently in order to enable quick adaptation to changes in publication traffic, network and load conditions (details described in Section 6). In order to accommodate this level of dynamism and provide an efficient way to use the connectivity of the overlay mesh for publication forwarding, we devise the *Working Overlay Map* (WOM) data structure. WOM is derived from MOM and transforms the broker's initial knowledge of the primary network into a concise representation in accordance to its current set of primary, soft and candidate links. WOM is *reconstructed locally upon every update to the broker's links* and acts as a pre-computed cache for efficient publication forwarding. In what follows, we describe the steps in construction of WOM from the perspective of Broker A shown in Figure 3.

Step 1: Initially, A's WOM contains all the neighboring brokers and primary links in its MOM, in addition to A's own non-primary links. Since Broker A is often not directly connected to a number of its neighbors, the goal of this step (called edge contraction) is to weed out these neighbors from A's view – thus making it more concise. For this purpose, Broker A considers its neighboring brokers in descending order of distance in the primary network. For each Broker v with no direct link, the edge between v and a closer Broker w is removed and v is substituted with w. Furthermore, all edges incident (attached) to v are removed and attached to w. Once complete, *WOM forms a graph that only contains neighboring brokers to whom A maintains a direct link*. Figures 3(a) and 3(b) illustrate A's MOM and WOM before and after this process, respectively.

Step 2: Broker identifiers in the resulting graph are sorted in an array, denoted by $BrokerArr_A$, in ascending order of their distance in WOM. Henceforth, N_i, refers to the ith broker in this array and we have $dist(N_i) \leq dist(N_{i+1})$.

Step 3: For each Broker N_i, three *auxiliary sets* are computed that contain identifiers of neighbors located in different relative positions with respect to A and N_i (see Figure 4). These auxiliary sets are as follows:

- $BetweenSet(A, N_i)$ contains N_i and brokers located on the path between A and N_i in the primary network. In Figure 3, $BetweenSet(A, N_4) = \{N_1, N_4\}$.
- $BeyondSet(A, N_i)$ contains brokers located downstream of N_i from A's point of view (including N_i). In Figure 3, $BeyondSet(A, N_1) = \{N_1, N_3, N_4\}$.
- $BehindSet(A, N_i)$ contains brokers located downstream of A from N_i's point of view. In Figure 3, $BehindSet(A, N_1) = \{N_2\}$.

We have now covered how brokers' overlay maps are updated. Next, we discuss maintenance of subscription routing tables.

4   Subscription Routing Tables

Brokers maintain their subscription routing tables in a similar manner as to their views of the primary network and overlay mesh. More specifically, there are two routing tables, namely *Master Subscription Table* and *Working Subscription Table*: Subscription entries in the former table construct end-to-end forwarding paths in the primary network. The entries in the latter, however, adapt these paths to the current overlay mesh connectivity as reflected in the broker's WOM.

Master subscription tables: We introduce the notion of *subscription anchor* used to store subscription information in brokers' routing tables. From the perspective of a broker, an *anchor* for a subscription is a broker located up to Δ hops closer to the issuing subscriber (the anchor of a local subscriber points to the broker itself). Anchors are used to forward matching publications hop-by-hop (or multiple hops at a time) towards subscribers. The advantage of using anchors in this manner is that brokers are able to anticipate the propagation path of matching publications within their Δ-neighborhoods and foresee forwarding paths towards all matching subscribers inside and outside of their neighborhoods. Availability of this information allows brokers to choose the actual publication forwarding path from a wealth of alternative routes within their neighborhoods (strategies that are used for this purpose are discussed in Section 5).

The anchor placement algorithm works as follows:[1] Subscriptions are issued by clients and are propagated throughout the network along the primary links *only*. Starting from the broker that a subscriber is connected to, each receiving broker stores a copy of the subscription in a set data structure called the *Master Subscription Table* (MST). Subscription entries in this set are in the form of $s = \langle id, preds, anchor, ppath \rangle$, where id is a unique subscription identifier, $preds$ are predicates specifying client interests, $anchor$ is the subscription anchor, and $ppath$ is the propagation path of the subscription *through the primary network*. As a subscription propagates in the primary network, we require its *anchor* to be adjusted at each intermediate broker as follows: If the issuing subscriber is within distance $\Delta - 1$, the *anchor* remains unchanged; otherwise, the *anchor* is set to the identifier of the broker which is one hop closer to the subscriber than the subscription's previous *anchor*. For example, in Figure 3(a), the *anchor* of a subscription s issued by X_5 will be updated to N_4 before N_1 sends the

---

[1] Applicability of our approach extends to other pub/sub routing schemes that can accommodate the placement of subscription anchors in brokers' Δ-neighborhoods.

subscription to Broker A ($\Delta = 4$). Note that the information to correctly adjust the anchors is readily available locally at brokers as part of their MOM.

Working subscription tables: Similar to how WOM is derived from MOM, brokers derive the *Working Subscription Table* (WST) from their MST and use it for publication forwarding. Construction of WST uses information pre-computed in WOM as follows: For each subscription, $s_{mst} \in MST$, a new subscription, s_{wst}, with identical *preds* and *id* fields but with an updated *anchor* is added into the WST. The *anchor* of s_{wst} is the identifier of the broker that $s_{mst}.anchor$ was substituted with during Step 1 in the construction of WOM (see Section 3). WST is updated upon every change to brokers' links and in order to adapt routing tables to the state and connectivity of the overlay mesh. However, once constructed, all subsequently issued subscriptions (and unsubscriptions) are simultaneously added to (and removed from) both MST and WST.

Subscription Covering: Subscription covering is an important optimization technique that improves matching performance by compacting brokers' routing tables. Subscription s_1 is said to *cover* s_2, *iff*, all publications that match s_2 also match s_1. We compute covering sets for subscriptions with identical anchors. A publication is forwarded over a link if it matches at least one of the subscriptions in the corresponding covering set. Section 7 investigates the impact of broker parameters on performance gains brought about by the covering techniques.

5   Publication Forwarding

This section presents efficient techniques to realize the publication forwarding strategies of Section 2. Regardless of the exact strategy used, the processing of publications involves two steps: *publication matching* and *path computation*. In the first step, brokers use their WST and a matching algorithm to identify the set of subscriptions that match the publication's content. The exact implementation of the matching algorithm is outside the scope of this paper and has been investigated extensively in the literature. We only assume that the output of the algorithm is in the form of a set of broker identifiers corresponding to the *anchor* of matching subscriptions in the WST. We use $Anchors(p)$ to denote this set for publication p. In the next step (i.e., path computation), the broker uses its WOM and computes a final set of neighbors to which it has direct links. This set is denoted as $Fwrd(p)$, and once computed, the broker forwards p accordingly (if the publication matches a local subscription, the issuing subscribers receive a copy of the publication). This section presents how $Fwrd(p)$ is computed.

Path Computations for S0: This strategy concerns conventional pub/sub systems [13,14,16,10] and is presented here purely as a baseline for comparison. Brokers do not establish and maintain soft links and Δ can effectively be set to 1. Furthermore, subscription anchors in WST only consist of immediate neighbors in the primary network. As a result, we have $Fwrd(p) = Anchors(p)$.

Path Computations for S1: In this strategy, brokers possess soft links and exploit them in order to bypass uninterested neighbors. At the same time, a

```
1: function COMPUTE_FORWARDING_S1(Anchors(p)) ▷Input: p's matching anchors.
2:     Anchors(p) ← {X ∈ Anchors(p)∧ primary path to X does not intersect with
       primary propagation path of p}                    ▷ Only keep downstream anchors.
3:     Intersection ←∅; Fwrd(p) ← ∅
4:     for all (Nᵢ ∈ Anchors(p)) do
5:         if (Intersection ∩ BetweenSet(A, Nᵢ) = ∅) then
6:             Intersection ← Intersection ∪ BetweenSet(A, Nᵢ)
7:         else
8:             Intersection ← Intersection ∩ (BetweenSet(A, Nᵢ) ∪ BehindSet(A, Nᵢ))
9:     j ← |BrokerArr_A|
10:    while (j > 0 ∧ Anchors(p) ≠ ∅) do
11:        if (Anchors(p) ∩ BeyondSet(A, Nⱼ) ≠ ∅ ∧ Nⱼ ∈ Intersection) then
12:            Fwrd(p) ← Fwrd(p) ∪ {Nⱼ}
13:            Anchors(p) ← Anchors(p) − BeyondSet(A, Nⱼ)
14:        j ← j − 1
15:    return Fwrd(p)
```

Fig. 5. Path computation for S1 at Broker A

forwarding broker attempts to achieve this goal by sending the publication to the
farthest reachable brokers on the *intersection of the primary paths* to neighbors
in $Anchors(p)$. For efficient path computation, the broker takes advantage of the
pre-computed *auxiliary sets* in its WOM as shown in Figure 5. In Lines 4–8, the
set of brokers on the intersection of primary paths to $Anchors(p)$ is computed:
Intersection. This is carried out via a series of set operations over the pre-
computed auxiliary sets. Next, the **while** loop in Lines 10–14 processes brokers,
N_j, on the intersection of the paths in *descending order of distance*. If there is a
broker in $Anchors(p)$ that is beyond N_j (*i.e.*, $BeyondSet(A, N_j) \cap Anchors(p) \neq
\emptyset$), then N_j is added to $Fwrd(p)$ and all brokers located beyond N_j (including
N_j itself) are removed from $Anchors(p)$ (Line 13). The rationale behind this is
once N_j receives the publication, it sends the publication to all other downstream
brokers, *i.e.*, $BeyondSet(A, N_j)$. Finally, when $Anchors(p)$ becomes empty all
matching subscription anchors have been accounted for and $Fwrd(p)$ is returned.

Path Computations for S2: The goal of brokers in S2 is to directly send
publications to all reachable anchors in $Anchors(p)$ excluding those that have a
closer reachable broker on their primary path. This is different from S1 where
publications are likely to be sent to pure forwarding brokers located on the
intersection of paths to the anchors. Figure 6 presents the path computation
algorithm. Intuitively, the brokers in $Anchors(p)$ are considered in ascending
distance (*i.e.*, from lower subscripts to higher). Each such broker is added to
$Fwrd(p)$ in Line 6, and all its downstream brokers are removed from $Anchors(p)$
in Line 7. Finally, when $Anchors(p)$ becomes empty $Fwrd(p)$ is returned.

Path Computations for SH: Brokers that use the hybrid strategy SH monitor their output publication traffic and use a threshold (*e.g.*, 80% of their uplink
capacity) to decide when to switch between S1 and S2. Once the link utilization

passes this limit, the broker uses S1 to preserve its bandwidth. If the link utilization is lower than the limit brokers use S2 which more aggressively attempts to bypass pure forwarding brokers.

Implementation Notes: The size of all auxiliary sets is bounded by the number of brokers' links. Since this is relatively small, bit-vectors can provide an efficient implementation for the set operations in the algorithms: Broker N_i in WOM is associated with the i-th bit in a bit-vector and set union, and intersection operations are carried out via bit-wise '&' and '|', respectively.

```
1: function COMPUTE_FORWARDING_S2(Anchors(p))  ▷ Input: p's matching anchors.
2:     Anchors(p) ← {X ∈ Anchors(p)∧ primary path to X does not intersect with
       primary propagation path of  p}                    ▷ Only keep downstream anchors.
3:     j ←1 ; Fwrd(p) ← ∅
4:     while (j ≤ |Links| ∧ Anchors(p) ≠ ∅) do
5:         if (Nⱼ ∈ Anchors(p)) then
6:             Fwrd(p) ← Fwrd(p) ∪ {Nⱼ}
7:             Anchors(p) ← Anchors(p) − BeyondSet(A, Nⱼ)
8:         j ← j + 1
9:     return Fwrd(p)
```

Fig. 6. Path computation for S2 at Broker A

6 Managing Broker Links

In large overlays, the overhead of establishing many connections makes it infeasible to maintain full network connectivity. We would therefore like to have brokers selectively establish a small set of "good" soft links. A good soft link contributes most to the system performance and has three characteristics: First, it transmits a large volume of traffic; second, it bypasses a large number of intermediate pure forwarding brokers in the primary network; and, third, the more overloaded the bypassed brokers are the better a soft link is. In what follows, we first introduce *candidate* links and then devise a profiling scheme to identify "good" soft links.

A broker, say A, can have three types of links: *(i)* primary links (denoted by $pLinks_A$) are designated communication links in the primary network over which end-to-end forwarding paths are constructed; *(ii)* soft links (*i.e.*, $sLinks_A$) augment the primary network and build a highly connected mesh overlay; and *(iii)* candidate links (*i.e.*, $cLinks_A$) are not real communication links and only act as temporary stubs in the routing tables to facilitate the process of identifying good soft links. We use the term broker *degree* to refer to the number of primary links a broker has, and the term *fanout* for the maximum number of communication links, i.e., primary and soft links combined. Finally, we use $Links_A$ to denote the set of all links at Broker A, *i.e.*, $Links_A = pLinks_A \cup sLinks_A \cup cLinks_A$.

Publication Traffic Profiling: We define the *gain* of a link over time interval T as the number of brokers that the link bypasses in the primary network times the number of publications that are sent over the link during T times a scaling parameter that factors in the load of bypassed intermediate neighbors. More precisely, Broker A computes the gain of its own link to Broker N as follows:

$$gain(N) = (\# \text{ pubs sent to } N \text{ during } T) * (dist(A, N) - 1) * loadScalingFactor(N)$$

The *loadScalingFactor* is intended to further boost the gain of a link that bypasses overloaded intermediate brokers. It is defined as follows:

$$loadScalingFactor(N) = \Pi_{\forall X}(1 + min(0, normalizedLoad(X) - loadThreshold))$$

where *normalizedLoad*(X) is the normalized load of Broker X located on the primary path between A and N. We considered output publication rate as our preferred broker load metric as opposed to input publication rate. This is due to the fact that a portion of brokers' input publication traffic is destined to local subscribers and cannot be avoided. In contrast, the output publication traffic is more indicative of the volume of publications that a broker relays. Relayed traffic can be opportunistically reduced using soft links that bypass pure forwarders.

Candidate Links: *Prospective soft links* with unknown gains that are first considered for profiling are called candidate links. A candidate link acts as a stub in the broker's WOM and WST and enables publication profiling in a similar way to primary and soft links. In contrast to primary and soft links, however, a candidate link does not have a network connection and publications that are intended to be sent over a candidate link are transparently funnelled over a primary or soft link to another neighbor that is closer in the primary network. Candidate links allow brokers to locally estimate their gain without going through the link establishment process. Once a candidate link is determined to be "good", it is promoted to become a soft link and its corresponding connection is established.

Soft Link Management: Brokers periodically examine the gain of their links and decide which ones to keep and which ones to discard. The total number of links in each round is constrained by the configuration parameter *maxlinks* and consists of at most *fanout* primary/soft links and ($maxlinks - fanout$) candidate links. Broker links are ranked based on their measured gains. Soft links with low gains are discarded and candidate links with high gains are promoted to become soft links. In this process, brokers respect the *fanout* limit on their maximum number of communication links. Finally, brokers may add new candidate links to be profiled in the next round. New candidate links are chosen based on the following heuristics: If an existing link to a neighbor, say X, has a high gain, then there is some chance that direct links to X's neighbors also achieve a good gain. This is especially true if X's high gain is due to the traffic that will eventually be relayed to its neighbors. To determine such cases, the broker considers the neighbors of a high gain link as new candidate links. If such links indeed prove to deliver a good gain, they will be promoted to soft links in the future rounds.

To adapt to network conditions, brokers exchange load information and measure their communication links' round trip times. This information is used in the candidate selection process by prioritizing soft links that bypass slow links and overloaded neighbors. This simple cost model effectively enables brokers to explore their neighborhoods in search of viable soft links at a low cost.

Primary Link Management: The techniques presented so far enable brokers to choose their soft links based on publication traffic and neighbors' load conditions. Addition and removal of soft links is a light-weight process and only requires local (not coordinated) routing table updates. Hence, brokers can afford to employ this technique frequently and adapt swiftly to network and traffic changes. The soft link management scheme may also allow brokers to deal with transient crash or temporary disconnection of their neighbors [21]. In contrast, primary links are meant to be more stable, mainly since changes to the primary network require *costly coordinated updates* to MOMs and MSTs of many *affected* brokers (this cost is unavoidable in the case of permanent crash or departure).

We now present the primary network reconfiguration procedure in the form of a Δ-*move* whereby a broker disconnects one of its primary links and establishes a new primary link to another broker within its original Δ-neighborhood. Any form of overlay modification can then be carried out via a series of Δ-moves, joins and departures of edge brokers. Figure 7 illustrates the state of the primary network before (left) and after (right) Broker A moves from N to B. Solid lines in the figure represent primary links and the *move path*, $\mathcal{P}_{A:N \to B} = \langle N, N_2, \cdots, B \rangle$, is the primary path between Broker N and B. The figure also illustrates subscription anchors in nearby brokers' MSTs (*i.e.*, dashed arrows) that are affected by the move. We use Figure 7 to describe the move procedure via which Broker A's and other nearby brokers' *MOMs* and *MSTs* are updated. Note that the update process only concerns the *master data structures*. Furthermore, in order to ensure that the state of the network remains consistent, the move process uses an external coordinator to prevent concurrent moves from taking place within overlapping neighborhoods. Also, note that while a move is pending, the primary network can still enjoy a high level of adaptation that is brought about using soft links.

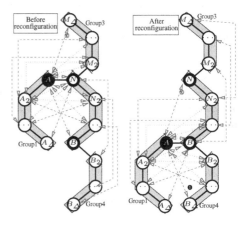

Fig. 7. Overlay before (left) and after (right) Δ-move of Broker A. Solid and dashed lines are primary links and subscription anchors at affected brokers, respectively.

Updating MOMs and MSTs: Following a move by Broker A from N to B, brokers within the old and new Δ-neighborhood of A must update their MOMs as well as the subscription anchors in their MSTs accordingly in order to correctly reflect the state of the primary network following the move. These brokers are said to be *affected* by A's move and can carry out updates as follows: An affected broker needs three pieces of information to compute its new MOM: Its initial MOM, as well as Broker A's initial and final MOMs. The update is done by excluding neighbors of A that are no longer within distance Δ and adding ones in A's new Δ-neighborhood that fall within distance Δ. Likewise, an affected broker needs three pieces of information to compute new anchors for the subscriptions in its MST. The information needed includes: Its old and new MOMs (the new MOM is computed as discussed above) as well as the move path $\mathcal{P}_{A:N\rightarrow B}$. The move procedure, described next, ensures that the information required in the above update process (*i.e.*, the move path and Broker A's old and new MOMs) is provided to affected brokers. As a result, affected brokers can locally compute their new MOMs and MSTs that reflect the state of the network after the join.

The Δ-move Procedure: The move procedure involves the following phases:

Preparation Phase: Before starting a move, Broker A contacts the coordinator for permission. Once granted, it contacts the destination Broker B and receives B's MOM. This will be used by A to construct temporary MOM_{tmp} and MST_{tmp} that reflect the state of its post-move Δ-neighborhood and subscription anchors.

Initialization Phase: Broker A injects a special *move initiation message, m_{init},* at Broker N. The move initiation message is propagated within Broker A's old Δ-neighborhood and receiving brokers discard any soft or candidate links that they may have that bypass Broker A and refrain from creating new ones until the move completes. This step completes once A receives a confirmation message from N indicating completion of propagation of m_{init} in A's Δ-neighborhood.

Update Phase: Broker A issues a move *in-progress message, m_{inprog},* at B that includes information about its old and new MOMs as well as the moving path $\mathcal{P}_{A:N\rightarrow B}$. This message is propagated within A's post-move Δ-neighborhood and receiving brokers construct a temporary MOM_{tmp} and MST_{tmp} which includes the state of their new Δ-neighborhoods and subscription anchors after the move. These brokers use MOM_{tmp} and MST_{tmp} for forwarding of publications from this point on. At the same time, they also refrain from creating any soft or candidate links that bypass Broker A. While the move procedure is in progress, Broker A may receive duplicate publication messages routed via Brokers N and B. As a matter of fact, the rationale behind the restriction of requiring nearby brokers to not bypass Broker A while the move is still in progress is to allow effective duplicate detection and elimination at a single broker (*i.e.*, Broker A). Broker A properly discards the duplicates and forwards the publications it receives for the first time according to its new MOM_{tmp} and MST_{tmp}. Finally, propagation of the m_{inprog} message completes when a corresponding confirmation message arrives at Broker A. At this point, Broker A proceeds to the final phase.

Wrap-Up Phase: Broker A ends its move by issuing a *move end message, m_{end},* at Brokers N and B. This message propagates within the Δ-neighborhood of Broker N prior to the move and the Δ-neighborhood of Broker B after the move (*i.e.*, to all brokers affected by the move). Receiving brokers that are no longer in A's Δ-neighborhood, discard portions of their MOMs that are downstream of A (including Broker A itself) and substitute subscription anchors that point to A with a broker located at distance Δ on the moving path. Furthermore, brokers that remain or have entered A's new Δ-neighborhood discard their old MOM and MSTs and replace them with their temporary counterparts constructed earlier as part of the move procedure (i.e., MOM_{tmp} and MST_{tmp}). From this point on, these brokers can create soft or candidate links that bypass Broker A.

7   Evaluation

We carried out large-scale experimental evaluations on the SciNet cluster [22] as well as PlanetLab [23] using Publiy, our Java-based open-source pub/sub system [20]. SciNet machines each have eight 2.66 GHz 64-bit Intel Xeon CPU cores with 8 GB of memory and PlanetLab machines are a mix of single, dual, and quad core Intel-family $1.8 - 3.2$ GHz CPUs equipped with $1 - 3$ GB of memory. We used several network configurations and pub/sub workload datasets to compare our proposed forwarding strategies against S0, as baseline. Our experimental setups are designed with the anticipated use cases of large-scale pub/sub systems in datacenter or wide-area environments in mind. They are varied in terms of network size, subscription matching distribution, and system parameters such as *fanout*, and bandwidth capacity. Table 1 summarizes different network configurations used in this section. Henceforth, we use the short names, e.g., C1, C2, etc., to refer to the network configuration setups in Table 1.

Table 1. Experimental configurations

Config.	Net. size	Broker degree	Platform
C1	120	3	SciNet
C2	250	3	SciNet
C3	500	3	SciNet
CPL	21	3	Planetlab

In the beginning of each experimental run, brokers propagate subscriptions in the network. In principle, each subscription can be originated from a separate subscriber process. However, due to scarcity of our resources running thousands of clients was infeasible. Instead, we skipped last mile message delivery to clients and only considered publication forwarding within the broker overlay network. We thus had brokers to locally log delivered publications instead of sending them to an actual subscriber (each broker runs on a dedicated CPU core). We believe that this approach is fair for our comparative study, since direct delivery to subscribers incurs the same amount of processing and bandwidth in all strategies.

Figure 8(a) summarizes the matching distribution of the subscription and publication workload datasets used in our experiments. These datasets are either based on real-world traces of user interactions in social networks [24] (i.e., dataset DT-FB) or are synthesized using a Zipf distribution. This choice was motivated by the study of Liu et al. who showed that the popularity of RSS feeds in real-world application scenarios follows Zipf distributions [25]. Figure 8(b) compares the matching distribution of three of our synthesized datasets by illustrating what percentage of publications matches what percentage of subscriptions in

Dataset	Config	Subs count	Matching subs per pub
DT1	C1	6,552	8% (Sparse)
DT2		19,472	53% (Dense)
DT3	C2	28,690	9% (Sparse)
DT4	CPL	900	9% (Sparse)
DT5		6,000	54% (Dense)
DT-C	C3	10,000	4% (Covering)
DT-FB	C1	120,000	6.5% (Sparse)

(a) Datasets summary.

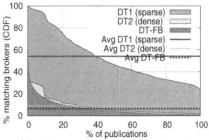

(b) Subscription matching distribution for DT1, DT2, and DT-FB.

Fig. 8. Workload specification

the system. As such, datasets with fewer or larger average number of matching subscriptions per publication are categorized as *sparse* or *dense*, respectively. Finally, dataset DT-C has subscriptions that also have covering relationships.

In all the experimental runs in this section, we set Δ to 4. Although a larger value was in principle possible, it complicates the move procedure (which, as stated in Section 6, is complementary to our approach) by increasing the number of affected brokers within Δ-neighborhood of a moving broker. A smaller Δ, on the other hand, limits the range of *fanout* values that we can experiment with. This is due to the fact that brokers only connect to neighbors that are Δ hops away and the size of Δ-neighborhoods indirectly constrains the maximum *fanout*.

Publication Forwarding Path Length: Publication hop count provides valuable insight into the internal workings of the system in each strategy and has a direct impact on delivery delay, throughput and ultimately system scalability. It is expected that if brokers maintain a larger number of soft links the overlay mesh becomes more connected, offering more optimized forwarding paths in the network. Brokers can selectively pick the best forwarding route based on the strategies used in order to reduce the number of pure forwarders. We compared publication hop counts incurred using different strategies experimentally. The results are illustrated in Figure 9 which plots the cumulative distribution function (CDF) of publication propagation path lengths for executions of configuration C1 with datasets DT1 (sparse) and DT2 (dense). The Δ and broker *fanout* parameters in all executions were set to 4 and 35, respectively. Measurements were carried out within a 10 min interval in which exactly the same number of publications are injected in the system at a low rate of 3,600 msg/sec. At this rate, *no network hotspots* are formed and *all strategies deliver the same number of publications*. This allows us to compare different strategies based on the publication hop count metric independently of other interfering factors.

As shown in Figure 9, compared to S0, strategies S1 and S2 substantially lower publication hop count (data points in the graphs are shifted left). Fewer hops also imply that publications are matched against subscriptions fewer times. Furthermore, as there are no overloaded brokers, SH performs similar to S2. An

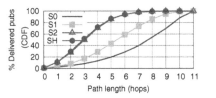 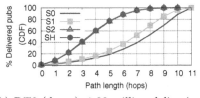

(a) DT1 (sparse): 348 thousand deliveries. (b) DT2 (dense): 1.03 million deliveries.

Fig. 9. Publication propagation path lengths using configuration C1 and *fanout* of 35

interesting effect to observe in the graphs is that the difference between S0 and S1 is smaller in the dense dataset compared to the sparse dataset. This is due to the fact that publications in the dense dataset match more subscriptions and the intersection of primary paths (as computed in S1) is likely to bypass fewer neighbors. This brings the performance of S1 closer to S0.

Number of Pure Forwarding Brokers: As mentioned earlier, due to the selectivity of content-based forwarding, some brokers inevitably relay publications that are not of interest to their local subscribers. Availability of a diverse set of alternative forwarding paths in our overlay mesh enables brokers to reduce such occurrences by tailoring the actual propagation path of publications based on the relative location of matching subscribers at runtime. Our measurements are reported in Table 2 and show that compared to S0, our forwarding strategies cut the number of pure forwarders by up to 70%. Furthermore, if we consider the *yield* of a pub/sub system as the total number of publications delivered (i.e., arrive at brokers with local matching subscribers) over the total number of publications sent between brokers (including those relayed by pure forwarders), we see that S2 achieves a yield of up to 77%. This is an indication that the system operates more efficiently and better utilizes its resources.

Table 2. Pure forwarding and system yield for different strategies (Configuration C1)

(a) C1/DT1: 348,000 pubs delivered.

Strategy	Number of pure forwarders	System yield
S0	559,000	38%
S1	348,000	50%
S2	216,000	61%
SH	195,000	64%

(b) C1/DT2: 1,034,000 pubs delivered.

Strategy	Number of pure forwarders	System yield
S0	1,010,000	50%
S1	687,000	60%
S2	325,000	76%
SH	300,000	77%

Publication Delivery Delay: Figure 10 plots average publication delivery delay (vertical axis) for pairs of brokers that host subscribers and publishers (horizontal axis).[2] The overall average delay for S0 (baseline) is 14.0 ms. This is

---

[2] SciNet uses infiniband interconnect with ultra low latency. We have therefore injected a delay of 1 ms for broker-to-broker communication to account for networking delay.

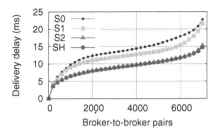
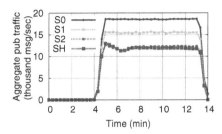

Fig. 10. Publication delivery delay: x-axis shows pairs of source-destination brokers; y-axis is avg. delay for corresponding pair (Conf. C1/DT2, $\Delta = 4$, $fanout = 35$)

Fig. 11. Aggregate network traffic using different strategies (Conf. C1/DT2, $\Delta = 4$, $fanout = 35$). During first 4 mins subscriptions are propagated (traffic not shown).

lowered to 12.5 ms for S1 and 9.3 ms for S2 and SH (up to 50% improvement over the baseline). Also, note that this improvement would have been even greater if the input publication traffic was higher and caused the network to congest.

Network Traffic: Fewer pure forwarders and higher yield implies that the system can deliver the same number of publications by sending fewer messages among brokers. This lowers network traffic and improves efficiency of bandwidth utilization. Using the same configurations as before, Figure 11 illustrates the aggregate network traffic in terms of the number of publications transmitted. The average network traffic in strategies S0, S1, S2 and SH is $3,400$ msg/sec, $2,850$ msg/sec, $2,200$ msg/sec and $2,200$ msg/sec, respectively. Compared to the baseline, this represents up to 35% improvement in bandwidth utilization. Furthermore, the traffic resulting from load exchange messages (in S1, S2 and SH) incurs less than 2% of the total bytes sent and received. This implies that the bandwidth conservation achieved in our strategies still outperforms its overheads.

Computational Overhead: Strategies S1, S2 and SH update WOM and WST after changes to broker links. Our measurements indicate that each update to WOM takes about 0.8 ms. This has a negligible amortized overhead considering the fact that this update takes place roughly every 20 seconds in our implementation. Construction of WST, on the other hand, is dependent on the size of the subscription routing table and takes about 17 ms for a workload that consists of $6,500$ subscriptions (*i.e.*, DT1). Finally, thanks to our efficient MOM data structure and the use of bit-vectors for path computation the time that it takes for S1 and S2 to forward publications remains unchanged. Detailed measurements regarding computational and memory costs are available in [26].

Impact of *fanout* on Broker Performance: Increasing *fanout* improves overlay connectivity but comes at the cost of maintaining a larger number of concurrent network connections. This incurs an overhead related to buffer management and TCP's congestion control mechanism. Additionally, as we investigate experimentally in this section, a larger *fanout* limits the advantages brought about by subscription covering techniques and contributes to a degradation in matching performance. This effect is due to *fragmentation* of the subscription space. To clarify this point consider the following simple example: If subscription s_1 covers s_2 and s_2 covers s_3, a broker that possesses only one link (*fanout* = 1) computes $\{s_1\}$ as the covering set. Therefore, publications are matched against *one subscription only*. On the other hand, if the broker possesses two or more links, the covering sets are likely to grow larger making matching more expensive. For example, if s_1's anchor is downstream one link and s_2 and s_3's anchors are downstream of another link, then the broker computes two covering sets each with one subscription, i.e., $\{s_1\}$ and $\{s_2\}$. As a result, matching becomes more time consuming. The exact size of the covering sets, of course, depends on subscription predicates and relative location of issuing subscribers in the network.

We investigated this phenomenon using configuration C3 with 500 brokers and dataset DT-C with covering relationships. We measured publication matching performance in a system using different *fanout* values. Figure 12 illustrates the results normalized based on smallest *fanout* value of 5. The checkered bars represent average size of covering sets over a 120s interval. It is evident that the fragmentation caused by larger *fanout* values increases the size of covering sets. Furthermore, larger covering sets translate to an even sharper increase in predicate evaluation operations needed to match each publication. For example, between *fanout* of 5 and 10 there is a 12% jump in covering set size and a 34% jump in predicate evaluations. This discrepancy is due to the fact that covering subscriptions are more generic and usually come with fewer predicates than covered subscriptions which in turn are more specific and contain more predicates.

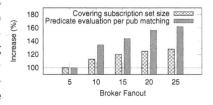

Fig. 12. Larger *fanout* lowers benefits of covering techniques (data normalized based on *fanout* = 5)

System Throughput: In large-scale messaging systems that serve thousands of clients in a datacenter or an enterprise, throughput is perhaps the most important aspect of the system. The reduction in the number of pure forwarders in our strategies frees up brokers' valuable bandwidth and processing resources. These resources can be put to use for disseminating a larger number of publications, therefore improving throughput. To study this effect, we carried out extensive experimental analysis using different configurations and datasets on SciNet [22] and PlanetLab [23]. Figure 13(a) illustrates the results using configuration C1 and datasets DT1 (left) and DT2 (right). We used a high aggregate publishing rate of 72,000 msg/min to push the system to the edge. At this rate, the number of deliveries within our 10 min measurement interval gives a clear comparative understanding of the system throughput in each strategy (i.e., some strategies deliver more publications). Two trends are visible in the figure. First, increasing *fanout* from 5 to 35 significantly improves the number of publication deliveries. Second, our forwarding strategies

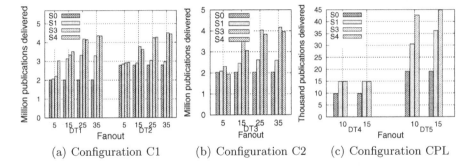

(a) Configuration C1   (b) Configuration C2   (c) Configuration CPL

Fig. 13. Publications delivered within a fixed measurement interval

outperform S0 (the baseline) by up to 115%. Both trends are also present in Figure 13(b) in which configuration C2 and dataset DT3 were used. An interesting observation in both figures is that S2 tends to marginally outperform SH. This is indeed expected since at our very high publishing rate many brokers become overloaded and adaptively switch to S1. Although this strategy reduces the load on such overloaded brokers but produces more publications in the network as a whole (compare number of publications sent in Figure 2(b) and Figure 2(c)). This excess traffic degrades the performance of the system as a whole.

In practice, however, brokers are generally provisioned to operate within a safe buffer from their full capacity. Despite this, broker heterogeneity or traffic imbalances may develop occasional network hotspots. In these scenarios, the adaptive nature of SH is useful to prevent formation of network bottlenecks. To investigate this effect, we re-ran configuration C1/DT1 with a low publishing rate of 7,200 msg/min but throttled brokers' uplinks to be capped at 150 msg/sec. At this rate, some overlay hotspots are formed and the ability of overloaded brokers to dynamically switch to S1 prevents excessive use of their scarce bandwidth. Figure 14 illustrates the throughput and average publication hop count in this scenario using different strategies. It can be seen that SH outperforms S2 in terms of the number of deliveries as it is less likely to develop hotspots.

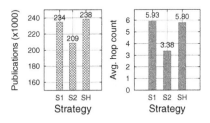

Fig. 14. Performance of different strategies (brokers uplink capped at 150 msg/sec)

PlanetLab Results: We verified our results on the shared PlanetLab environment where nodes' CPU and bandwidth capacity is limited and variable. Figure 13(c) illustrates the results of our throughput analysis with configuration CPL and datasets DT4 (left graph) and DT5 (right graph). The measurement interval is 5 minutes, aggregate publishing rate is 3,300 msg/min and the brokers' uplinks are capped at 10 KB/s. At this rate, the system using DT4 and S0 becomes congested and delivers fewer messages than expected. However, S1 and S2 both reach full delivery goals. Similarly, using DT5, S0 delivers the least number of publications while S1 and S2 achieve much higher (but not full) deliveries.

Facebook Dataset: We verified our results using dataset DT-FB which was extracted from real-world traces of user interaction in online social networks [24] (see [26] for methodology and details). In a deployment using configuration C1 with aggregate publishing rate of $3,600$ msg/min and *fanout* of 20, our measurements indicate that S1 and S2 outperform S0 by 37% and 115%, respectively.

8   Related Work

Our approach is related to Resilient Overlay Networks (RON) [27] which uses mesh-based overlay routing to deal with failures. However, unlike RON which targets generic unicast routing, our techniques are specifically tailored for selective publication multicast in content-based pub/sub systems. Furthermore, in contrast to RON which maintains a full-mesh, the use of Δ-neighborhoods in our approach, improves scalability and keeps the overhead to a negligible limit.

Snoeren *et al.* forward publications over *multiple* disjoint paths in a mesh network [15]. Instead of improving bandwidth efficiency, their scheme is concerned with exploiting path redundancy to guarantee message delivery. Overlay reconfiguration techniques adapt the broker overlay by creating links between brokers with similar subscriptions [17,18]. We see these techniques as complementary to our approach. However, as noted in Section 6, changes to the primary network require costly coordinated updates to routing tables of many brokers. Our use of soft links to adapt the overlay avoids the high cost of such full reconfigurations.

In MEDYM [28], the first broker computes a dissemination tree that spans only to brokers with local matching subscribers. The message piggybacks this tree and is used by other brokers in a source routing-like manner. This has the advantage that the propagation tree has *no pure forwarding brokers*. However, inclusion of routing information in publications incurs high overhead, especially for messages destined to a large number of brokers. Li *et al.* [29] create redundant forwarding paths in a cyclic overlay using overlapping advertisement trees. The quality and diversity of the paths, however, depend heavily on overlapping advertisements and their nondeterministic propagation patterns in the overlay. In contrast, our approach actively creates soft links to maintain redundant forwarding paths after taking broker load and link quality into account.

9   Conclusions

In this paper, we developed a novel approach to adapt a pub/sub overlay based on publication traffic and network conditions by selectively creating special links, called soft links. Soft links boost the network connectivity and provide a large number of end-to-end forwarding paths. The diversity of these redundant paths in the resulting overlay mesh is particularly suited for content-based pub/sub systems in which recipients of a given publication are not known in advance and are only determined at runtime after subscription matching. Furthermore, thanks to the notion of Δ-neighborhoods our approach does not require coordinated route updates and each broker unilaterally decides which soft links to establish. Our extensive experimental results carried out on a cluster and Planetlab confirm that our approach significantly improves the system's throughput and efficiency.

References

1. Global Data Synchronization Network (GDSN): http://www.gs1.org
2. Cooper, B.F., et al.: Pnuts: Yahoo!'s hosted data serving platform. PVLDB (2008)
3. Google Publish/Subscribe (GooPS): CANOE summer school (2009)
4. Li, G., Muthusamy, V., Jacobsen, H.-A.: A distributed service-oriented architecture for business process execution. TWEB 4(1) (2010)
5. Adya, A., Dunagan, J., Wolman, A.: Centrifuge: integrated lease management and partitioning for cloud services. In: NSDI (2010)
6. Oki, B., Pflügl, M., Siegel, A., Skeen, D.: The information bus – an architecture for extensible distributed systems. In: SOSP, pp. 58–68 (1993)
7. Sadoghi, M., et al.: Efficient event processing through reconfigurable hardware for algorithmic trading, vol. 3, pp. 1525–1528. VLDB Endowment (2010)
8. PubSubHubBub, http://code.google.com/p/pubsubhubbub/
9. Publish Subscribe Internet Routing Paradigm (PSIRP), http://www.psirp.org
10. Fidler, E., Jacobsen, H.-A., Li, G., Mankovski, S.: The PADRES distributed publish/subscribe system. In: ICFI (2005)
11. Bhola, S., Strom, R.E., Bagchi, S., Zhao, Y., Auerbach, J.S.: Exactly-once delivery in a content-based publish-subscribe system. In: DSN (2002)
12. Papaemmanouil, O., Cetintemel, U.: SemCast: Semantic multicast for content-based data dissemination. In: ICDE (2005)
13. Carzaniga, A., Rosenblum, D.S., Wolf, A.L.: Design and evaluation of a wide-area event notification service. ACM TOCS (2001)
14. Cugola, G., et al.: The JEDI event-based infrastructure and its application to the development of the OPSS WFMS. IEEE TSE (2001)
15. Snoeren, A.C., Conley, K., Gifford, D.K.: Mesh-based content routing using XML. In: SOSP (2001)
16. Chand, R., Felber, P.: XNET: A reliable content-based publish/subscribe system. In: SRDS (2004)
17. Baldoni, R., et al.: Efficient publish/subscribe through a self-organizing broker overlay and its application to SIENA. Computer Journal 50(4), 444–459 (2007)
18. Migliavacca, M., Cugola, G.: Adapting publish-subscribe routing to traffic demands. In: DEBS (2007)
19. Cheung, A.K.Y., Jacobsen, H.-A.: Dynamic Load Balancing in Distributed Content-Based Publish/Subscribe. In: van Steen, M., Henning, M. (eds.) Middleware 2006. LNCS, vol. 4290, pp. 141–161. Springer, Heidelberg (2006)
20. Publiy project, http://msrg.utoronto.ca/~reza/
21. Kazemzadeh, R.S., Jacobsen, H.-A.: Reliable and highly available distributed publish/subscribe service. In: SRDS, pp. 41–50. IEEE (2009)
22. University of Toronto SciNet Consortium, http://www.scinet.utoronto.ca
23. PlanetLab testbed, http://www.planet-lab.org/

24. Wilson, C., Boe, B., Sala, A., Puttaswamy, K.P.N., Zhao, B.Y.: User interactions in social networks and their implications. In: EuroSys (2009)

25. Liu, H., Ramasubramanian, V., Sirer, E.G.: Client behavior and feed characteristics of RSS, a publish-subscribe system for web micronews. In: IMC (2005)

26. Kazemzadeh, R.S., Jacobsen, H.-A.: Adaptive multi-path forwarding in the Publiy distributed publish/subscribe systems. Tech. rep. (2011), http://msrg.org

27. Andersen, D.G., Balakrishnan, H., Kaashoek, M.F., Morris, R.: Resilient overlay networks. Computer Communication Review 32(1) (2002)

28. Cao, F., Singh, J.: MEDYM: Match-early and dynamic multicast for content-based publish-subscribe service networks. In: ICDCSW (2005)

29. Li, G., Muthusamy, V., Jacobsen, H.-A.: Adaptive Content-Based Routing in General Overlay Topologies. In: Issarny, V., Schantz, R. (eds.) Middleware 2008. LNCS, vol. 5346, pp. 1–21. Springer, Heidelberg (2008)

PolderCast: Fast, Robust, and Scalable Architecture for P2P Topic-Based Pub/Sub

Vinay Setty[1], Maarten van Steen[2], Roman Vitenberg[1], and Spyros Voulgaris[2]

[1] Department of Informatics, University of Oslo, Norway
{vinay,romanvi}@ifi.uio.no
[2] Department of Computer Science, VU University, Amsterdam, The Netherlands
{steen,spyros}@cs.vu.nl

Abstract. We propose POLDERCAST, a P2P topic-based Pub/Sub system that is (a) fault-tolerant and robust, (b) scalable w.r.t the number of nodes interested in a topic and number of topics that nodes are interested in, and (c) fast in terms of dissemination latency while (d) attaining a low communication overhead. This combination of properties is provided by an implementation that blends deterministic propagation over maintained rings with probabilistic dissemination following a limited number of random shortcuts. The rings are constructed and maintained using gossiping techniques. The random shortcuts are provided by two distinct peer-sampling services: CYCLON generates purely random links while VICINITY produces interest-induced random links.

We analyze POLDERCAST and survey it in the context of existing approaches. We evaluate POLDERCAST experimentally using real-world workloads from Twitter and Facebook traces. We use widely renowned Scribe [5] as a baseline in a number of experiments. Robustness with respect to node churn is evaluated through traces from the Skype superpeer network. We show that the experimental results corroborate all of the above properties in settings of up to 10K nodes, 10K topics, and 5K topics per-node.

Keywords: Publish/Subscribe, Peer-to-Peer, Gossiping.

1 Introduction

Publish/subscribe (pub/sub) has become a popular communication paradigm that provides a loosely coupled form of interaction among many publishing data sources and many subscribing data sinks[8]. Many applications report benefits from using this form of interaction, such as application integration [20], financial data dissemination [2], RSS feed distribution and filtering [15], and business process management [14]. As a result, many industry standards have adopted pub/sub as part of their interfaces. Examples of such standards included WS Notifications, WS Eventing, OMG's Real-time Data Dissemination Service, and the Active Message Queuing Protocol.

In pub/sub, subscribers convey their interests in receiving messages and publishers disseminate publication messages. The language and data model to

P. Narasimhan and P. Triantafillou (Eds.): Middleware 2012, LNCS 7662, pp. 271–291, 2012.
© IFIP International Federation for Information Processing 2012

subscribe and publish vary among systems. In this paper, we focus on the topic-based pub/sub model. In a topic-based system, publication messages are associated with topics and subscribers register their interests in receiving all messages published to topics of interest. While traditional pub/sub implementations are either centralized or based on a federated organization of cooperatively managed servers, an increasingly higher number of pub/sub applications are being deployed in P2P environments [22]. Following this trend, a number of decentralized topic-based pub/sub systems have been proposed over the last decade [3, 5, 7, 9, 16, 19, 27, 28]. These systems build a decentralized infrastructure in which the nodes are first dynamically organized into an application-level overlay network, and the resulting network is subsequently used for event routing.

The designers of these systems are facing an uphill struggle because of the distinctively high number of desirable characteristics that a large-scale P2P pub/sub system has to possess all at once in order to be a viable practical solution. In particular, the list includes: (1) Correct delivery of all publications, i.e., absence of false negatives or deterministic 100% hit-ratio guarantee in a failure-free run, (2) *High hit-ratio* under realistic node churn, (3) Fast recovery at the end of a churn period and mending of the overlay so as to achieve 100% hit-ratio, (4) *Low degree* of overlay nodes, (5) *Relay-free routing* (also called topic-connectivity), which means that only subscribers interested in a topic are involved in routing events for that topic, (6) *Scalability* with the number of nodes, topics, number of nodes interested in a topic, and number of topics a node is interested in, (7) Effective dissemination: *fast*, with as *little duplicate delivery* as possible, and *fair distribution of load* due to routing and processing, and (8) *Low overhead* of overlay maintenance. The design challenge is amplified due to a number of trade-offs: low node degree and relay-free routing, robustness under churn and lack of duplicate delivery, scalability and precise delivery with few false negatives and false positives are fundamentally at odds with each other. Furthermore, each of the principal solution approaches provides a bundle of desirable and undesirable properties at the same time: dissemination over multicast trees is fast and without duplication but it is fragile, whereas gossiping is robust but lacking deterministic delivery guarantees.

In this paper, we present POLDERCAST[1], a P2P architecture for topic-based pub/sub. To the best of our knowledge, POLDERCAST is the first solution that takes all of the above factors into account and harmonizes them. In order to substantiate this claim, we present a survey of existing approaches and analyze their performance with respect to most of the above characteristics.

This combination of desirable properties is provided by an implementation that blends deterministic propagation over maintained rings with probabilistic dissemination following a limited number of carefully selected random shortcuts. Per-topic rings allow for relay-free routing and 100% hit-ratio in absence of node churn, yet they are constructed in such a fashion so as to reuse the same links

---

[1] The term is inspired by the Dutch *polder model*, in which diverse societal groups collaboratively negotiate to obtain broadly supported solutions.

for multiple rings thereby minimizing the average node degree. Although at a conceptual level this overlay structure encompasses a separate Hybrid Dissemination [25] overlay *per-topic*, our design leverages interest locality to produce a single composite overlay with substantially fewer links and hence, lower node degrees. Our implementation is based on a new efficient epidemic-based algorithm for creating and maintaining the proposed overlay in a self-organizing way.

We evaluate and validate the properties of our system using extensive simulations in large-scale settings of up to 10K nodes, 10K topics, and 5K topics per-node. We use real-world traces from Twitter and Facebook social networks to model subscriptions. Robustness with respect to node churn is evaluated through traces from the Skype super-peer network. We empirically show that our system (1) converges fast, (2) provides 100% hit-ratio in the absence of node churn and reasonably good hit-ratio in the presence of node churn, (3) has logarithmic dissemination speed in terms of number of hops and (4) has constant factor traffic overhead. We use Scribe [5] as a baseline in a number of our experiments.

2   Preliminaries

The system consists of a set $\mathcal{V}$ of nodes. Each node in the system has a *unique* identifier (e.g., a hash of its IP address), assigned to it when joining the system. Node identifiers are assumed to be sortable and to occupy a circular value space. We assume that the underlying communication network is fully connected, in the sense that *any* node can send a message to *any* other node, provided it knows its IP address.

The topic-based publish/subscribe communication system is organized around a set $\mathcal{T}$ of topics. Each node can play the role of a subscriber or publisher or both. A subscriber v expresses its interest in a set of topics $\mathcal{T}_v \subseteq \mathcal{T}$. We call $|\mathcal{T}_v|$ the *subscription size* of node v. A publisher posts an event on exactly one topic t. The published event should be delivered to *all* $|\mathcal{V}_t|$ ($\mathcal{V}_t \subseteq \mathcal{V}$) subscribers interested in t (no false negatives) and *only* to them (no false positives).

Both publishers and subscribers are allowed to join and leave at any moment, without any prior notice. Node crashes are, therefore, inherently dealt with as ungraceful leaves. In fact, there is no way to distinguish between the two. We assume that a node that leaves and rejoins after a while can remember its prior state.

3   Survey of Related Approaches

In practice, a pub/sub system should satisfy a wide spectrum of desirable properties in the context of high robustness, low dissemination latency, low communication overhead, and high scalability. Many of those properties exhibit an inherent trade-off with each other so that striking the right balance is a central challenge in a pub/sub system design and a guiding objective for our approach.

Table 1 compares the characteristics of POLDERCAST with principally different approaches for P2P topic-based pub/sub systems.

Table 1. Comparison of State of the Art with POLDERCAST

Property\System	Scribe[5]	Vitis[19]	SpiderCast[7]	StAN[16]	daMulticast[3]	POLDER-CAST
Central nodes*	RV	RV&GW	WB	None	None	None
High hit-ratio under churn?	✗, see Sec. 6.6	✓	N/A	N/A	✓	✓
100% hit-ratio in absence of churn?	✓	✓	N/A	N/A	✗	✓
TCO?	✗	✗	Prob.	Prob.	Det.	Det.
Degree of node v	$O(\log |\mathcal{V}|)$	$O(1)$	$O(|\mathcal{T}_v|)$	$O(|\mathcal{T}_v|)$	$\Theta(|\mathcal{T}_v|)$	$O(|\mathcal{T}_v|)$
Incl. dissemination?	✓	✓	✗	✗	✓	✓
Average Duplication Factor	None	Scoped flooding	N/A	N/A	Gossiping	$\leq$ Fanout(f)
Average Delay	$O(\log |\mathcal{V}|)$	$O(\log^2 |\mathcal{V}|)$	N/A	N/A	$O(\log |\mathcal{V}_t|)$	Typically $O(\log |\mathcal{V}_t|)^{\#}$

* RV: Rendezvous. GW: Gateway. WB: Weak bridge.
\# For more details refer to Sec. 6.4 and the discussion below in this section.

With respect to robustness, a pub/sub system should ideally guarantee both 100% hit-ratio without node churn and high hit-ratio in presence of node churn. Consider that existing approaches to P2P pub/sub either utilize epidemic dissemination (daMulticast [3]), or build specialized dissemination overlays. It is well-known that while robust under churn, epidemic dissemination does not provide full reliability, even in a completely static system. On the other hand, most existing dissemination overlays for topic-based pub/sub are fragile (such as dissemination trees in Scribe [5], Magnet [9], or Bayeux [28]) or at least they rely on designated nodes whose existence is critical for correct operation of distributed matching. For example, Scribe and Vitis [19] have a dedicated rendezvous node for each topic. Additionally, Vitis builds subclusters for each topic and the communication between subclusters is handled by gateway nodes. While these systems provide a number of churn-handling mechanisms, fragility of dissemination overlays or reliance on central nodes conceptually limit the potential for high hit-ratio under churn, as we further explore in our evaluation in Sec. 6.6. SpiderCast [7] builds an unstructured overlay that strives to maximize clustering of nodes according to their interest in topics. As observed in [16], this approach may yield an overlay in which highly-connected clusters are interconnected by few links, which we call *weak bridges*. Existence of such weak bridges also impacts the robustness of the system under churn.

POLDERCAST combines deterministic dissemination over a ring with probabilistic dissemination similar to gossiping. The former mechanism guarantees 100% hit-ratio in a static system while the latter provides a high hit-ratio under churn. This is further corroborated by the experimental evaluation in Sec. 6.6.

Consider the characteristics of the overlay built in various existing approaches: A low number of relay nodes is instrumental in reducing the communication and processing cost of dissemination as well as propagation latency expressed by path lengths. Furthermore, guaranteed absence of relays, a.k.a. *topic-connectivity* [6], simplifies message routing mechanisms. On the other hand, fanout is a common minimization parameter in overlay design, which strongly affects system scalability.

Unfortunately, the desirable characteristics of having a low node degree and relay-free routing exhibit a fundamental trade-off [6]. At one extreme is having a fixed node degree independent of the number of topics a node is interested in. Such an approach is proposed in Vitis. This results in a relatively high number of subclusters that need to be connected by additional means, such as gateways, rendezvous nodes, and relays. Scribe builds dissemination structures on top of an underlying DHT whose node degree might be either constant or logarithmic with the total number of nodes in the system. In these systems, a pair of nodes interested in the same topic might be connected by a chain of $\Theta(\log |\mathcal{V}|)$ relays.

At the other extreme of the trade-off are systems that build and maintain a separate overlay for each topic independently, such as Tera [4] and systems that employ gossiping on a per-topic basis, such as daMulticast. These approaches guarantee topic-connectivity during stable periods without churn. However, the degree of node v in these systems is in the order of the number of subscriptions: $\Theta(|\mathcal{T}_v|)$.

SpiderCast and StAN strive to maintain a topic-connected overlay by building random links between the nodes while exploiting the correlation between node interests in order to minimize the degree. Since correlations are typically present in pub/sub workloads, this results in a lower degree compared to Tera or daMulticast. After the system becomes stable, these systems will eventually produce a topic-connected overlay with high probability. Yet, the guarantee of relay-free routing is only probabilistic, which yields low overhead and latencies, but requires additional mechanisms to route messages across potentially disconnected clusters.

The POLDERCAST approach we propose in this paper provides a deterministic guarantee of relay-free routing similar to Tera or daMulticast. At the same time, the degree is similar to that of SpiderCast or StAN due to exploiting correlations. As shown in Table 1, SpiderCast and StAN focus on overlay construction and maintenance and do not propose any specific routing algorithm, thereby rendering the discussion about message dissemination properties as well as hit-ratio nonapplicable to these systems.

For the rest of the approaches, we consider two salient factors that determine the efficiency of message dissemination:

(a) **Average Message Duplication Factor** per node: the number of times (excluding the first) that the same published message is received by a node on average. When the routing is relay-free, average message duplication factor directly translates into the communication cost of message dissemination.

In Scribe, Magnet, and Bayeux, a routing tree is used to disseminate publications, which eliminates any duplication of messages. In the hybrid overlay approach of Vitis, the node floods a published message to those of its neighbours that are interested in the message topic. Even though Vitis has a fixed total degree per node, this fanout may be high enough so as to lead to a high number of duplicate deliveries for the same published message. In daMulticast, the configurable fanout of the epidemic dissemination used for propagating published messages governs the duplication factor. In POLDERCAST there is a fixed maximum dissemination fanout f (typically $f = 2$) for each topic. Each node interested in the topic forwards a message only once (the first time the node receives the message) along at most f links, which gives a bound of f on the duplication factor.

(b) **Average Path-Length:** the average number of hops required for a message to reach a node interested in that message. As shown in Table 1, all of the structured and hybrid overlay approaches have an expected path length that is logarithmic or square logarithmic with the total number of nodes $|\mathcal{V}|$ in the system. Yet, the inclusion of relays nodes (both at the DHT level and pub/sub implementation level) into the dissemination path causes path lengths for some nodes being significantly longer than $O(\log |\mathcal{V}|)$, as we show in Sec. 6.4. DaMulticast performs gossiping on a per-topic basis so that the expected path length is logarithmic with the number of nodes $O(\log |\mathcal{V}_t|)$ interested in the topic.

In our approach, we also strive to achieve expected path lengths that are logarithmic with $O(\log |\mathcal{V}_t|)$ due to the random shortcuts links used for dissemination. From the results in [25], it can be derived that if there is a sufficient number (f-1) of random shortcut links between the nodes interested in a particular topic, POLDERCAST guarantees average dissemination path lengths for that topic to be asymptotically logarithmic. However, our dissemination mechanism uses a fixed number of random links independently of the number of topics a node is interested in. This may potentially render the dissemination mechanism ineffective for a node that is interested in many topics, in which case the average path length may become linear with $|\mathcal{V}_t|$ due to the use of ring links only. Fortunately, this scenario does not manifest itself for typical pub/sub workloads, as confirmed by the empirical results in Sec. 6. Note that the dissemination fanout f determines the base of the logarithm and as such, governs the trade-off between the dissemination speed and duplication factor.

Based on the analysis in this section, we conclude that the solution for topic-based pub/sub we propose is (a) free from rendezvous and relay nodes (b) robust and resistant to churn, and (c) it facilitates efficient message dissemination.

4   POLDERCAST: Disseminating Events

We present POLDERCAST in a top-down approach. In this section we describe the structure of the target overlay and we explain how dissemination is performed once this overlay is in place. Then, in Sec. 5, we dive into the mechanisms in charge of building and maintaining such an overlay.

4.1   The Dissemination Overlay

At a conceptual level we maintain a separate ring per topic augmented by random links shared across the topics. Each ring connects *all* subscribers of the corresponding topic and *only* them. Individual topic rings altogether form a single, connected, and navigable overlay. Ensuring connectivity among all subscribers of a topic, a property known as *topic connectivity*, allows for relay-free routing

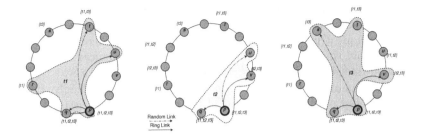

Fig. 1. Topology for three topics $\{t1, t2, t3\}$, showing the ring neighbor links and random neighbor links originating from the node p. Note that q serves as successor of p for all three topics, and v serves as predecessor of p for topics $t1, t2$ illustrating link sharing.

among them. It is the reason why POLDERCAST achieves 100% hit-ratio in the absence of node churn: When an event for a certain topic reaches *any* subscriber of that topic, it is guaranteed to reach *all* remaining subscribers by being propagated along that topic's ring. While this distribution mechanism alone might be adequate for topics with a moderate number of subscribers, its linear dissemination speed does not scale with the popularity of topics. This is the reason why we introduce random links serving as dissemination shortcuts. Propagating events across (some of the) random links to arbitrary other subscribers of the same topic, accelerates dissemination to exponential speed. It additionally provides a controlled degree of redundancy that increases robustness and hit-ratio under node churn.

In this work, we request that a publisher on topic t subscribes to t prior to publishing events, thus becoming a part of the dissemination ring. This overhead for publishers is considered acceptable by most applications and in many existing pub/sub systems.

The rings for each topic are *bidirectional* and nodes are placed into rings in the order of their node ids. That is, a node p maintains, with respect to each topic t in its subscription, two links: one to its t-successor and one to its t-predecessor. The t-successor of node p is defined as the node with the *closest higher* than p's id (in modulo arithmetic), among all subscribers of topic t. The t-predecessor is defined likewise for the *closest lower* id. Fig. 1 gives a sample topology of three topics, and the respective intermingling rings.

It should be observed that while the use of rings in hybrid dissemination structures has appeared in the past [25], their application to topic-based pub/sub is new. The main challenges of using ring in pub/sub lies in combining such structures, one per topic, into a single manageable overlay. In practice, maintaining a separate ring per topic is very expensive, notably for nodes subscribed to many topics. However, it has been observed that subscriptions tend to be strongly correlated [15]. Our approach exploits this correlation in order to substantially lower the number of links maintained: A single link can serve as a ring link for multiple topics.

It is possible to build an overlay with link consolidation across the topics as the central optimization metric in mind. This approach minimizes node degree but may result in a per-topic ring being partitioned into multiple sub-rings. In order to avoid this risk, POLDERCAST takes a more balanced approach and builds a guaranteed ring for each topic separately but in such a way that links have a higher chance of being reused in multiple topics. Specifically, rings are constructed based on node ids instead of their subscriptions. Assume nodes p and q are both subscribed to t_1 and t_2, and they are ring neighbors for t_1. This means that they are both on the ring for t_2 and their ids are numerically close, thereby increasing the chance that they will be ring neighbors for t_2 as well. We further investigate the effect of link consolidation in our experiments in Sec. 6.

With respect to random links, their choice and quantity may have a profound impact on the performance, as discussed in Sec. 3. POLDERCAST combines a configurable number of random links of two types: interest-induced links formed between subscribers with similar subscriptions shorten average dissemination path lengths. At the same time, uniform random links help overcome partitions under node churn and improve load balancing by diverting incoming links from nodes that subscribe to many topics, which become a likely target for interest-induced links. We describe the algorithm for random link formation in Sec. 5 and consider the importance of the links of each type in Sec. 6.

4.2   Event Dissemination

Our event dissemination protocol is inspired by that of RingCast [25] (the protocol is parameterized by a dissemination fanout, f): A node receiving an event for topic t for the *first time*, propagates it f times. Specifically, if the event has been received through the node's t-successor (or t-predecessor), it is propagated to its t-predecessor (or t-successor) and f-1 arbitrary subscribers of t. If the event was received through some third node, or if it originated at the node in question, it is propagated to both the t-successor and the t-predecessor, as well as to f-2 other subscribers of t. Finally, if a copy of this event has already been received in the past, it is simply ignored.

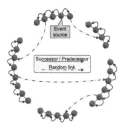
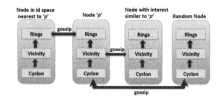
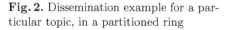

Fig. 2. Dissemination example for a particular topic, in a partitioned ring

Fig. 3. Three-layered architecture. Each layer gossips with the respective layer in other nodes.

From the results in [25], it can be derived that if there is a sufficient number (f-1) of random shortcut links between the nodes interested in a particular topic, POLDERCAST guarantees average dissemination path lengths for that topic to be asymptotically logarithmic. Even under node churn POLDERCAST tries to achieve complete dissemination as shown experimentally in Sec. 6.6. Fig. 2 gives an intuitive illustration of dissemination in a partitioned ring.

Since we apply this dissemination protocol for multi-topic pub/sub, however, analyzing its performance in POLDERCAST is significantly more difficult because the random links are shared across multiple topics and the number of utilizable random links varies for each and every node. Furthermore, some of the random links are skewed towards peers with multiple overlapping topics. This may interfere with the nice property of exponential dissemination speed that is inherent to many gossiping protocols. It may also cause a node whose subscription is similar to those of many other peers to become a hotspot due to a high number of incoming random links. We evaluate these aspects experimentally in Sec. 6.

5   POLDERCAST: Building the Overlay

POLDERCAST's overlay management mechanism is built around three modules: RINGS, VICINITY, and CYCLON, as shown in Fig. 3. Each module maintains its own view, managed by a separate gossiping protocol, which gossips periodically, asynchronously, and independently from the other two modules. In table below we list the parameters controlling the number of neighbors maintained (*view size*), and the maximum number of neighbors included in a gossip message (*gossip size*), per module.

module name	view size	gossip size
RINGS	ℓ_{ring} (per subscribed topic)	g_{ring}
VICINITY	ℓ_{vic} (in total)	g_{vic}
CYCLON	ℓ_{cyc} (in total)	g_{cyc}

Considering a node p with topics $\mathcal{T}_p$, the three modules operate as follows. With respect to each topic $t \in \mathcal{T}_p$, the RINGS module on p is responsible for discovering p's t-successor and t-predecessor. It achieves this by considering a few links to arbitrary subscribers of t as a starting point, and periodically gossiping with them to trade them for other subscribers of t of gradually closer ids.

The VICINITY module is responsible for feeding the RINGS module with a few neighbors for each topic $t \in \mathcal{T}_p$, of arbitrary ids. It is based on VICINITY [23], a topology management protocol that strives at discovering for each node the *closest* other nodes based on some *proximity function*. Per the proximity function introduced in the context of POLDERCAST, the more topics two nodes share the closer they are ranked. Moreover, as detailed in Sec. 5.2, our proximity function dynamically adapts to favor topics currently under-represented in the RINGS module.

Finally, the CYCLON module [24], is a lightweight peer sampling service [12], providing each node with a continuous stream of neighbors chosen uniformly at random from the whole network. As detailed in Sec. 5.3, this is essential for keeping the whole overlay connected, and enabling flexible overlay maintenance in the face of failures and node churn.

For any of the three modules, node q being a *neighbor* of node p means that p has a copy of q's *profile* in the respective module's view. A node's profile contains (i) its IP address and port number, (ii) its (unique) node id, and (iii) the ids of topics the node is subscribed to, each annotated with a *priority* that node assigns to finding neighbors of that topic. The priority of a topic is determined by the number of neighbors it has in the RINGS module: topics with fewer RINGS neighbors are assigned higher priority. Clearly, two or more copies of a node's profile may be different, notably when the node updates its subscriptions, or reports different priorities for its topics. When gossiping to a neighbor, a node sends a fresh copy of its profile, reflecting its current state.

Note that the three gossiping protocols comprising POLDERCAST are executed continuously. In a network characterized by dynamicity, due to nodes departing or joining at any time, crashing, or merely changing their subscriptions, there is no notion of *final* convergence. Instead, nodes engage in a constant convergence process.

5.1   The Rings Module

The RINGS module manages the ring links. That is, it aims at discovering a node's successor and predecessor for each topic in its subscription, and at quickly adapting to new successors/predecessors in dynamic networks.

In that respect, each node maintains ℓ_{ring} neighbors for each topic in its subscription: $\ell_{ring}/2$ with lower and $\ell_{ring}/2$ with higher id. It periodically picks a node from its RINGS view, and the two nodes exchange up to g_{ring} neighbors to help each other improve their RINGS views.

Assume p selects its neighbor q for gossiping. First, p collects *all* subscribers of topics which p and q have *in common*, considering the union of views of *all three modules*. Second, it sorts them by id, and for each topic in common with q it selects the $\ell_{ring}/2$ ones with just lower and the $\ell_{ring}/2$ ones with just higher id than q's id. If more than g_{ring} nodes have been selected, it randomly picks g_{ring} of them. Finally, it sends the selected nodes (i.e., the respective node profiles) to q. Node q does the same in return.

Although the dissemination protocol requires just two ring links per topic, namely the topic successor and predecessor, RINGS maintains up to ℓ_{ring} links per topic. This provides stand-by successors and predecessors to be used in case of failures or node churn. Additionally, it helps nodes navigate to their direct ring neighbors faster, once they have reached the proximity of their ids.

Finally, in order to increase the diversity of neighbors contacted for gossiping, the RINGS module employs a Least Recently Used (LRU) selection policy. This prevents contacting the same neighbor twice in a short interval, when it probably has no new useful information, at the expense of not contacting some other neighbor for a much longer duration. The LRU policy also plays an important role in churn handling by POLDERCAST, thus its implementation details are deferred to Sec. 5.4.

5.2   The Vicinity Module

The VICINITY module is responsible for maintaining interest-induced random links, that is, randomly chosen links between nodes that share one or more topics. Such links serve as input to the RINGS module, as detailed in Sec. 5.1. Additionally, they are used by the dissemination protocol to propagate events to arbitrary subscribers of a topic, as explained in Sec. 4.2.

Interest-induced random links are handled by VICINITY [23], a generic protocol for topology construction and management that lets nodes find their *closest* neighbors out of the whole network, based on some *proximity function*. In short, each node maintains a view of ℓ_{vic} neighbors and periodically gossips with them to discover nodes of even closer proximity, in which case it retains them in place of the least proximal neighbors.

Let p choose q for gossiping. Node p merges its views from all three modules. Then, it selects the g_{vic} nodes closest to q by applying the proximity function on its behalf, and ships them over to q. Upon reception, q merges the received neighbors with the union of all its views, and updates its VICINITY view to the ℓ_{vic} closest neighbors. Finally, q responds by selecting and shipping back its g_{vic} closest to p nodes.

Clearly, the proximity function plays a crucial role in VICINITY. In the context of POLDERCAST, the proximity function is designed to ensure that the RINGS module is supplied with (arbitrary) neighbors for *all* its topics. In that respect, candidates subscribed to topics annotated with higher priority by the target node are ranked closer compared to candidates of lower priority topics. Among candidate nodes that rank equally in terms of topic priorities, proximity is determined by the number of topics shared with the target node: the more shared topics, the closer their ranking.

5.3   The Cyclon Module

Uniform random links are handled by the CYCLON peer sampling service [24]. This module's purpose is twofold. First, it keeps the whole set of subscribers connected in a single partition, even in the presence of churn, large scale failures, or subscription changes. Connectivity is crucial to let new subscribers find their way to their appropriate neighborhood sets, irrespectively of where they initially joined the network. Second, it constitutes a source of links selected uniformly at random from the whole network. Such a source of random links is fundamental to the operation of the other two modules. Further details about the CYCLON protocol can be found in [24].

5.4   Churn Handling

It is a key design goal of POLDERCAST to provide a high hit-ratio and reasonably low delivery latency under node churn, while keeping the number of duplicate messages controllably small. To that end, POLDERCAST should adapt promptly to two types of changes. First, information updates, such as newly joining nodes, new subscriptions, etc. should be propagated fast. Second, the system should quickly detect the disconnection (graceful or due to failures) of nodes, and discard related information from the network.

With respect to propagating new information fast, POLDERCAST relies on its fast convergence properties. When a node joins the network, for example, its VICINITY module will quickly find some neighbors for each topic. Once a neighbor has been found for some topic, the RINGS module can quickly locate the appropriate successor and predecessor in an already largely connected topic ring. When a node's subscription changes, VICINITY will adjust its topic priorities to boost under-represented (new) topics. We further explore the convergence speed of POLDERCAST experimentally in Sec. 6.2.

With respect to ridding the system from outdated links, POLDERCAST employs a proactive mechanism for removing dead neighbors from node views. Whenever a node p gossips with a neighbor q, it temporarily removes q from the respective module's view, anticipating that q will respond and will be inserted anew in p's view. This way, dead neighbors are silently discarded, while alive ones are refreshed. To prevent dead neighbors from remaining indefinitely in a view, a node always selects to gossip with its least recently refreshed neighbor.

Freshness of a neighbor is approximated by an *age* field, associated with every view entry. Once per cycle, a node increments the ages of all its neighbors by one. A neighbor's age is zeroed when a gossip message (or response) is received from that neighbor. A neighbor's age is retained also when that neighbor is handed from one node to another. This way, a dead node's links will have increasingly higher chance to be selected for gossiping (and consequently discarded), even if they are copied among third nodes.

Although the age mechanism provides only an approximation of a link's freshness, it turns out to work sufficiently well for fast removal of dead links. We investigate the impact of node churn on the performance of POLDERCAST in Sec. 6.6.

6   Experimental Evaluation

We evaluate POLDERCAST by simulation based on real-world traces. We focus on the overlay properties (such as the node degree), efficiency of dissemination (delays and duplicate delivery), communication overhead of overlay maintenance, and performance under node churn (hit-ratio for message delivery and speed of convergence for overlay construction). We also compare the performance of POLDERCAST with Scribe[5] as a baseline.

We implement both POLDERCAST and Scribe using the widely adopted *Peer-Sim simulator* [17]. Scribe is implemented as an application atop Pastry DHT[21]. We use the implementation of Pastry for *PeerSim*, publicly available at [1]. We evaluate both POLDERCAST and Scribe at a scale of up to 10K nodes. Experiments of similar scale are common in this area [18, 19].

Unless otherwise mentioned, the view sizes of CYCLON and VICINITY (ℓ_{cyc} and ℓ_{vic}, respectively) were set to 20 entries each, and the gossip lengths in all three protocols (g_{cyc}, g_{vic}, and g_{ring}) were set to 10 entries. The configuration parameters for Scribe are $b = 4$ which defines the base $2^b = 16$ for the log structure of Pastry DHT and $l = 32$ for the leaves of the DHT routing table.

6.1   Experimental Settings

Subscription Workload: Our subscription workloads come from massively deployed social networks, namely Twitter and Facebook.

(1) Twitter Dataset: We used a public Twitter dataset [13], containing 41.7 million distinct user profiles and 1.47 billion social followee/follower relations. In Twitter, when a user posts a message (known as a *tweet*), the tweet is delivered to all followers of that user. As such, each user is modelled as a topic and all its followers are the respective subscribers. Similarly the set of users (followees) a user Alice follows, form Alice's subscription set. Note that in Twitter, relations are unidirectional, i.e., user Alice following user Bob does not require also Bob following Alice.

(2) Facebook Dataset: We used a public Facebook dataset [26], with over 3 million distinct user profiles and 28.3 million social relations as a second workload for our evaluations. Similarly to Twitter, users are modelled as topics as well as subscribers. However, in Facebook relations are bidirectional, therefore two friends in the Facebook social graph subscribe to each other in our model.

Our simulations were performed with workloads of 10K nodes (i.e., up to 10K topics and 10K subscribers), extracted from the original Twitter and Facebook social graphs in a methodology inspired from [18, 19]. More specifically, starting with a random set of a few users as seeds, we traversed the social graph using breadth first search, until the target number of nodes was reached, and all edges between them were extracted to our sample.

Fig. 4 shows the complementary cumulative distribution function (CCDF) of follower/followee counts for both the original Twitter(TW) and Facebook(FB) datasets, as well as for our respective extracted datasets in the inner plot. The plots indicate that the original dataset properties were retained in our extracted sample.

Publication Workload: Due to lack of publicly available real world publication workload we synthetically generate publications. We post one publication event for *each* topic, initiated by a randomly picked subscriber of that topic. Although in practice, event arrival rate may vary across different topics, we use a uniform publication rate since it has no effect on the metrics we consider in this paper.

Latency and Churn Datasets: We use the *King dataset* [11] to model communication latency between nodes. Finally, we evaluate our system under node churn, using real world churn traces: *Skype dataset*. We use Skype super-peer

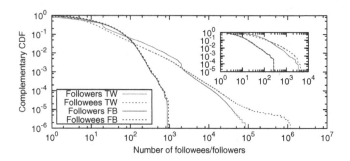

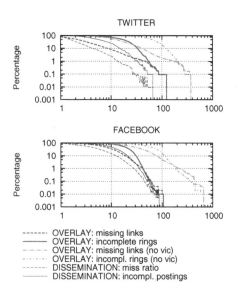

Fig. 4. Distribution of followers and followees, for the Twitter (41.7M users) and Facebook (3M users) traces. Inner plot: trace samples used (10K users).

churn traces from [10], which tracked joining and leaving timestamps of 4000 nodes for one month, starting on September 12, 2005.

6.2 Speed of Convergence

Fig. 5. Convergence speed

We first evaluate the time it takes to jump-start a POLDERCAST overlay from scratch. We start by 10,000 nodes that are already running CYCLON (i.e., each node has ℓ_{cyc} links to random other nodes), but whose VICINITY and RINGS views are completely empty, and we let them gossip to self-organize in a POLDERCAST overlay. Observe that fast convergence to an optimal overlay upon the extreme case of simultaneous bootstrapping typically implies fast reconciliation after a period of milder churn.

Given the input, we start by an offline construction of correct target rings to which the systems should converge over time. Then, we deploy POLDERCAST.

At each cycle, we measure the percentage of target ring links that are *not* yet in place (missing links), as well as the percentage of topics for which the ring has not converged yet (incomplete rings). Fig. 5 shows these metrics for the Twitter and Facebook workloads, respectively.

In order to assess the overlay's efficiency in disseminating events, we conduct another experiment by "freezing" the overlay at the end of each cycle, and posting one event for each topic. We record the percentage of nodes that *missed* an event they should have received (miss ratio), as well as the percentage of events that did *not* make it to all subscribers of their topic (disconnected topics). These measurements are also shown in Fig. 5.

The results show that the overlay converges quite fast: Within 60 cycles, 99% of topic rings are complete. They also indicate that the POLDERCAST overlay is highly efficient even with partially complete rings because it takes fewer cycles to achieve a connected overlay (0% miss ratio) per topic. This is due to propagating events across random links, provided by the combination of VICINITY and CYCLON views.

We also show that our three-layered architecture explained in Sec. Sec. 5 is essential to improve the speed of convergence. In Fig. 5 we compare the convergence speed of POLDERCAST, without the VICINITY layer in the middle, and we can see that it takes almost 3-6 times longer to converge. This is because VICINITY provides interest-induced random links, essential for speeding up the construction process.

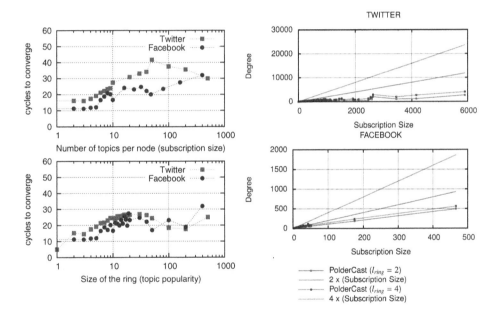

Fig. 6. Correlation between convergence speed and size of the subscription/ring

Fig. 7. Node degree in Rings layer

Apart from the speed it is also important to make sure that the overlay construction is scalable with respect to the number of nodes that participate in a ring (topic popularity) and the number of topics a node is interested in (subscription size). As shown in Fig. 6, even a node interested in over 400 topics converges reasonably fast. This is mainly due to having a higher number neighbours compared to a node interested in a few topics only, which offer it much higher reachability for a large number of topics.

6.3 Overlay Degree

In Fig. 7 we assess the effect of a node's subscription size on its RINGS view size. Due to interest locality, a single neighbor may serve multiple of its topics. This helps the node retain its RINGS outdegree low, and effectively contributes to higher scalability with respect to the subscription size of nodes. We do not consider the degree due to random links here since their number is fixed and small compared to that of ring links.

For the Twitter data, POLDERCAST manages to exploit correlation in the subscriptions to a large extent. However, for Facebook data, the node degree grows almost linearly with subscription size suggesting less subscription correlation. In Scribe, the average degree of a node v in the system is bounded by the number of nodes in the Pastry routing table that point to node v. This number is logarithmic with the total number of nodes and independent of the number of topics that node is subscribed to. This may be an important advantage in the case of an extremely high number of topics a node is interested in.

6.4 Event Dissemination

We now analyze the event dissemination protocol proposed in Sec. 4.2. We measure (1) the dissemination delay, in terms of number of hops required for a publication to reach the subscribers and (2) the duplication factor, namely the ratio between the number of *all* event messages received over the number of *distinct* event messages received. The measurements were taken by injecting the publications as described earlier and averaging the two metrics for 1000 cycles. From this point on, we run POLDERCAST with only Facebook data with 10K nodes, omitting results for Twitter data due to lack of space.

As one can see in Fig. 8(a), with the increase in dissemination fanout the average dissemination delay significantly decreases. However, this decrease takes place at the cost of an increase in the average number of duplicate messages seen by nodes as shown in Fig. 8(b). To compare Scribe with POLDERCAST we plot the average delay in Fig. 8(a). We can see that the average dissemination delay in Scribe is almost 1.7 times higher than the worst-case dissemination delay of POLDERCAST. This is due to the long chain of nodes induced by Scribe dissemination trees, even though DHT gurantees $\log|\mathcal{V}|$ hops delay. These longer chains stem from the inclusion of relay nodes, both at the Scribe and Pastry level.

As shown in plots in Fig. 8(a,b), the choice of random shortcut links has an interesting trade-off between dissemination delay and duplicate messages. At one extreme, if we use the CYCLON view as a source for random shortcut links, neither the dissemination delay decreases, nor the duplication factor increases with the increase in fanout f. This is attributed to the fact that since the CYCLON view is limited in size, and its view is chosen in an interest-agnostic way, the random shortcuts for a topic the node is interested in are not useful for the topics of interest, forcing the dissemination protocol to fall back on ring links. On the other extreme, if we only use the VICINITY view as a source of random links, it leads to a significant decrease in average delay, at the cost of an increase

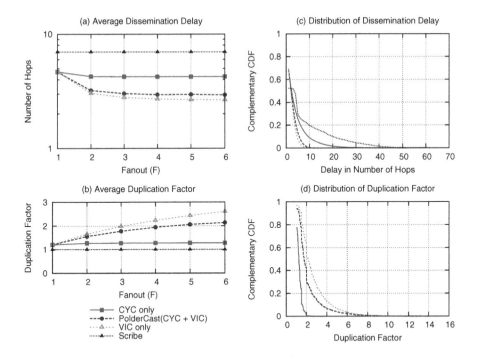

Fig. 8. Event Dissemination Analysis

in the average number of duplicates. In POLDERCAST we balance this trade-off by combining the CYCLON and VICINITY views, which results in the middle ground both for average delay and average duplication factor.

The choice of random shortcuts also has implications on the balancing of load on the nodes. In Fig. 8(d) one can see that if only VICINITY is used for random shortcut links, around 20% of the nodes receive messages at least 4 times. This is due to the fact that nodes that are interested in many topics (> 100) have a high chance to be present in the VICINITY view of many nodes. Since we use both VICINITY and CYCLON views for random shortcuts, it reduces the number of duplicate messages for nodes interested in many topics. It should be noticed that Scribe does not have any duplicate messages since messages in Scribe are disseminated using multicast trees.

In Fig. 8(c) we can see a similar pattern for dissemination delay and we again take the middle ground between the two extremes. Fig. 8(c) also shows that there is a significant number of messages in Scribe with a relatively high dissemination delay, as we explained above.

6.5 Overlay Maintenance

The next experiment aims at evaluating the overhead in overlay maintenance. We measure the number of control messages sent and received by each node to

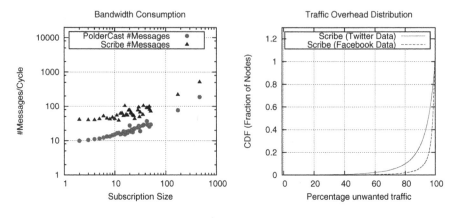

Fig. 9. Bandwith consumption   **Fig. 10.** Traffic Overhead

maintain the overlay. Note that as shown in Fig. 9 nodes interested in many topics (> 100) transmit a higher number of messages. This is due to the fact that they are more frequently selected as a target for gossiping. This factor does not play a significant role: the cycle duration can be chosen to be as high as 1 minute in real scenarios thereby rendering the bandwidth overhead negligible. On the other hand, more intensive control communication by nodes interested in many topics contributes to faster overlay convergence.

It is clear from Fig. 9 that Scribe incurs a higher communication overhead. The number of control messages sent and received by a node v in Scribe is proportional to the number of subscriptions v is interested in. Even though each node has a limited number of children in the multicast tree to maintain, Scribe sends regular heartbeat messages for each topic (both topics of interest and topics for which v is a relay) to keep the trees connected.

The existence of relays and lack of topic-connectivity in Scribe additionally causes unwanted traffic passing through the nodes. We measure the amount of overall traffic (both control and application traffic) passing through each Scribe node and distinguish between the traffic relevant to the subscription topics of the node and unwanted traffic. In Fig. 10 we show the amount of unwanted traffic at each node. We can see that over 90% of the nodes receive more than 80% of unwanted traffic. Such an overhead does not exist in POLDERCAST since topic-connectivity ensures that each node receives only the traffic relevant to the node's subscription topics.

6.6   Message Dissemination under Churn

In this experiment we evaluate POLDERCAST and Scribe publication dissemination under the churn model described earlier. We inject publications as explained earlier with fanout f set to 2. We maintain two successors and two predecessors for each topic ($\ell_{ring} = 4$). To assess the resilience of our protocol to node churn, at the end of each cycle we freeze the overlay and we measure the miss-ratio, i.e., the fraction of nodes that missed at least one publication event. It is worth noting that we set the cycle duration to be 1 minute. As a consequence, we introduce 60 times more node churn during each cycle than originally provided by the churn traces. When measuring the miss-ratio, we exclude the warm-up period of 10 seconds after the node joins the network.

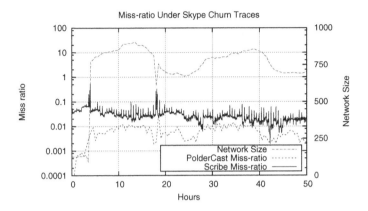

Fig. 11. Message Dissemination Under Churn

As shown in Fig. 11, for the Skype churn model the miss-ratio in POLDERCAST never grows beyond 0.01 except when there is a sharp drop in network size. In that case, the miss ratio momentarily grows to 0.04, but stabilizes quickly. This is due to (1) the use of random shortcuts, keeping the dissemination structure connected even though the ring is partitioned, and (2) since $\ell_{ring} = 4$, with the failure of one successor/predecessor the ring can still stay connected. When hundreds of nodes are joining the system (i.e., when there is a flash crowd), POLDERCAST continues to maintain the miss-ratio below 0.01.

From Fig. 11 it can be seen that Scribe has almost 10 times higher miss-ratio than POLDERCAST. Especially during the flash crowd at the beginning Scribe has a significantly higher miss-ratio due to a slower construction of the multicast trees when around 600 nodes join. Similarly we can see a spike in the miss-ratio when a sharp drop in network size occurs after around hours 18. There is a spike in the miss-ratio of POLDERCAST as well, but the relatively higher miss-ratio of Scribe is caused by the sudden departure of several rendezvous nodes.

7 Conclusions

In this paper we presented POLDERCAST, a P2P architecture for topic-based pub/sub which aims to achieve relay-free, fast and robust dissemination over a scalable overlay with a minimal maintenance cost. POLDERCAST achieves a delicate balance between these conflicting but desirable properties. We evaluated POLDERCAST with Scribe as baseline, using large scale simulations with publicly available real world traces from Facebook [26] and Twitter [13].

References

1. An implementation of the Pastry protocol for PeerSim, http://peersim.sourceforge.net/code/pastry.tar.gz
2. Tibco rendezvous, http://www.tibco.com
3. Baehni, S., Eugster, P.T., Guerraoui, R.: Data-aware multicast. In: DSN (2004)
4. Baldoni, R., Beraldi, R., Quema, V., Querzoni, L., Tucci-Piergiovanni, S.: Tera: topic-based event routing for peer-to-peer architectures. In: DEBS (2007)
5. Castro, M., Druschel, P., Kermarrec, A.M., Rowstron, A.I.T.: Scribe: a large-scale and decentralized application-level multicast infrastructure. IEEE Journal on Selected Areas in Communications 20, 1489–1499 (2002)
6. Chockler, G., Melamed, R., Tock, Y., Vitenberg, R.: Constructing scalable overlays for pub-sub with many topics. In: PODC (2007)
7. Chockler, G., Melamed, R., Tock, Y., Vitenberg, R.: Spidercast: a scalable interest-aware overlay for topic-based pub/sub communication. In: DEBS (2007)
8. Eugster, P.T., Felber, P.A., Guerraoui, R., Kermarrec, A.M.: The many faces of publish/subscribe. ACM Comput. Surv. 35, 114–131 (2003)
9. Girdzijauskas, S., Chockler, G., Vigfusson, Y., Tock, Y., Melamed, R.: Magnet: practical subscription clustering for internet-scale Pub/Sub. In: DEBS (2010)
10. Guha, S., Daswani, N., Jain, R.: An Experimental Study of the Skype Peer-to-Peer VoIP System. In: IPTPS (2006)
11. Gummadi, K.P., Saroiu, S., Gribble, S.D.: King: estimating latency between arbitrary internet end hosts. In: SIGCOMM (2002)
12. Jelasity, M., Montresor, A., Babaoglu, Ö.: T-Man: Gossip-based fast overlay topology construction. Computer Networks 53(13), 2321–2339 (2009)
13. Kwak, H., Lee, C., Park, H., Moon, S.: What is Twitter, a social network or a news media? In: WWW (2010)
14. Li, G., Muthusamy, V., Jacobsen, H.A.: A distributed service-oriented architecture for business process execution. ACM Trans. Web. 4, 2:1–2:33 (2010)
15. Liu, H., Ramasubramanian, V., Sirer, E.G.: Client behavior and feed characteristics of RSS, a publish-subscribe system for web micronews. In: IMC (2005)
16. Matos, M., Nunes, A., Oliveira, R., Pereira, J.: Stan: exploiting shared interests without disclosing them in gossip-based publish/subscribe. In: IPTPS (2010)
17. Montresor, A., Jelasity, M.: PeerSim: A scalable P2P simulator. In: P2P Computing (2009)
18. Patel, J.A., Rivière, É., Gupta, I., Kermarrec, A.M.: Rappel: Exploiting interest and network locality to improve fairness in publish-subscribe systems. Computer Networks 53, 2304–2320 (2009)
19. Rahimian, F., Girdzijauskas, S., Payberah, A.H., Haridi, S.: Vitis: A gossip-based hybrid overlay for internet-scale publish/subscribe enabling rendezvous routing in unstructured overlay networks. In: IPDPS (2011)
20. Reumann, J.: GooPS: Pub/Sub at Google. Lecture & Personal Communications at EuroSys & CANOE Summer School (2009)
21. Rowstron, A., Druschel, P.: Pastry: Scalable, Decentralized Object Location, and Routing for Large-Scale Peer-to-Peer Systems. In: Guerraoui, R. (ed.) Middleware 2001. LNCS, vol. 2218, pp. 329–350. Springer, Heidelberg (2001)

22. Triantafillou, P., Aekaterinidis, I.: Peer-to-peer publish-subscribe systems. In: Encyclopedia of Database Systems 2009, pp. 2069–2075 (2009)
23. Voulgaris, S.: Epidemic-Based Self-Organization in Peer-to-Peer Systems. Phd thesis, VU Universiteit Amsterdam (2006)
24. Voulgaris, S., Gavidia, D., van Steen, M.: Cyclon: Inexpensive membership management for unstructured P2P overlays. Journal of Network and Systems Management 13, 197–217 (2005)
25. Voulgaris, S., van Steen, M.: Hybrid Dissemination: Adding Determinism to Probabilistic Multicasting in Large-Scale P2P Systems. In: Cerqueira, R., Campbell, R.H. (eds.) Middleware 2007. LNCS, vol. 4834, pp. 389–409. Springer, Heidelberg (2007)
26. Wilson, C., Boe, B., Sala, A., Puttaswamy, K.P.N., Zhao, B.Y.: User interactions in social networks and their implications. In: EuroSys (2009)
27. Wong, B., Guha, S.: Quasar: a probabilistic publish-subscribe system for social networks. In: IPTPS (2008)
28. Zhuang, S.Q., Zhao, B.Y., Joseph, A.D., Katz, R.H., Kubiatowicz, J.D.: Bayeux: an architecture for scalable and fault-tolerant wide-area data dissemination. In: NOSSDAV (2001)

Unification of Publish/Subscribe Systems and Stream Databases

The Impact on Complex Event Processing

Joseph Sventek and Alexandros Koliousis

School of Computing Science, University of Glasgow
{joseph.sventek,alexandros.koliousis}@glasgow.ac.uk

Abstract. There is increasing demand for complex event processing of ever-expanding volumes of data in an ever-growing number of application domains. Traditional complex event processing technologies, based upon either stream database management systems or publish/subscribe systems, are adept at handling many of these applications. However, a growing number of hybrid complex event detection scenarios require features of both technologies. This paper describes a unification of publish/subscribe and stream database concepts to tackle all complex event processing scenarios, with particular emphasis upon hybrid scenarios. The paper describes the architecture for this unified system, the automaton programming language that it supports, and the run-time system that animates automata. Several examples of automata that exploit the system's unified nature are discussed. Raw automata performance is characterised, and its relative performance against Cayuga with respect to stock trend analysis is presented.

Keywords: complex event processing, user-defined functions, streams, automata, publish, subscribe, cache.

1 Introduction

There is increasing demand for complex event processing of ever-expanding volumes of data in an ever-growing number of application domains. This explosive growth is fueled by a number of trends in the industry: the availability of inexpensive wireless sensor nodes, the rapid penetration of smart phones in the mobile telephony market, and the growth in availability and sophistication of cloud computing resources. The data deluge resulting from the convergence of these trends dictates that we develop ever more functional and performant complex event processing systems in order to mine the data for information of business or personal importance.

Complex event processing is traditionally achieved using two different technologies: stream database management systems, in which one is able to look backward in time via select statements, and publish/subscribe systems, in which one is able to look forward in time via subscriptions to notifications. Some event processing scenarios naturally fall into one or the other of these

P. Narasimhan and P. Triantafillou (Eds.): Middleware 2012, LNCS 7662, pp. 292–311, 2012.

categories; increasingly, there are a number of hybrid scenarios in which both capabilities are required – i.e. the ability to process received notifications is dependent upon access to global and local state representing historical and/or active policy information that is crucial to the correct processing of the data.

This paper describes a unification of publish/subscribe and stream database concepts to address these hybrid scenarios. At the same time, the resulting system should also handle scenarios for which the unified nature is not required. The keystone of this unified system is a topic-based, publish/subscribe cache (henceforth, the *Cache*). Topics are organised in memory as either append-only stream tables or static relational tables. Ad hoc select queries, enhanced with time windows, can be presented to the cache at any time. An imperative programming language – viz., the Glasgow Automaton Programming Language (GAPL) – is used to program automata to detect complex event patterns over the cached streams and relations. When registered against the cache, each automaton subscribes to chosen topics and receives each event inserted into those topics through the publish/subscribe infrastructure for further processing. Automata can also access (modify) the relational tables, publish new tuples into stream tables, and send events to external processes.

The remainder of the paper is organised as follows. Firstly, we describe related work to place our system in context (§2). This is followed by a discussion of the Cache architecture (§3), the automaton programming language (§4), and the automaton execution model (§5). We then proceed with an evaluation of the system's performance from a number of perspectives, including a performance comparison against Cayuga for several, relevant stock analysis queries (§6). The paper concludes with a discussion of the impact that such a unified system has on future complex event processing (§7), and future work (§8).

2   Related Work

Codd's relational model structures data into a mathematical object, a relational database, where new information can be extracted using algebraic operators such as projection, selection, union, or join [1]. The ordering of columns (attributes) and rows (tuples) in a relational database is immaterial. On the other hand, data streams are modelled as append-only databases supporting continuous queries for which the relative temporal ordering of tuples is significant.

The continuous semantics of queries were first defined in Tapestry, a database system for mail and bulletin board messages [2]. Roughly speaking, a continuous query is a monotonic query – or, equivalently, a non-blocking query [3] – that yields incremental results over a sliding time window whose duration is defined by the current execution time and the last timestamp observed in the previous result set. Fig. 1 shows a variant of the basic continuous query execution model, as proposed in Tapestry. This model inspired the first generation of interactions with the Cache, where continuous queries over network flow streams were used to produce real-time visualisations of home networking traffic [4]. Fig. 1 also shows an equivalent implementation of the continuous query model in GAPL, as an

```
 1 # Let T be a table with attribute x.
   Set τ = -∞
   Set S = ∅
   FOREVER DO
 5   S = {select x from T [since τ]}
     # Each tuple j in S has a timestamp tⱼ.
     τ = arg max_{j∈S} tⱼ
     Return results to user
     Sleep for some period of time, t sec.
10 ENDLOOP
```

```
11 subscribe e to T; # A new tuple e of T.
   subscribe p to Timer;
   window S;
   int period, τ;
   initialization {
16   S = Window(sequence, SECS, t);
     period = t;
     τ = 0;
   }
   behavior {
     if (currentTopic() == 'T')
22     append(S, Sequence(e.x), e.tstamp);
     else { # The current topic is Timer.
       τ += 1;
       if (τ % period == 0) {
26       send(S); # Return results.
         S = Window(sequence, SECS, t);
       }
     }
30 }
```

Fig. 1. The continuous query execution model [2] (left); and its equivalent Glasgow automaton (right). Our [since τ] extension to select (line 5) guarantees to return all tuples that have been inserted into table T in the last t seconds. On the other hand, the automaton reacts upon every insertion of a tuple e to table T, populating a time-based sliding window S of duration t (lines 16, 22). Every t seconds, the automaton sends this window to its registering process (line 26).

introductory example to our automata and the unified nature of the Cache. The nature of this unification, as well as our language features, will become apparent in the subsequent sections.

Since TQL, Tapestry's query language, numerous variants of SQL, the language of Codd's relations, have been introduced in the literature, capturing those continuous semantics. CQL, for instance, the continuous query language of the STREAM data management system [5], provides users with a comprehensive list of time- or count-based sliding window operators to express non-monotonic relations over stream attributes – in other words, stateful relations. Thus, it became apparent to us that the use of sliding windows in stream processing is two-fold. Apart from producing incremental results, sliding windows are also used to maintain the intermediate state necessary for order-agnostic operators – mainly, aggregation and join.

Closely related to this work are user-defined aggregate functions, e.g. like those provisioned in Aurora's SQuAl [6]. A user-defined aggregate function consists of three parts: an initialization function that defines (local) state, opening a window within which the computation takes place; an iteration function that updates state; and a termination function that returns state, when the window closes. User-defined aggregates have been proven to be a sufficient extension to SQL for modeling complex patterns over data streams as finite state machines [3]. At this point, two further analogies can be drawn between user-defined functions and Glasgow automata.

First, an automaton can not only update local state, but also append tuples to other streams, locally (via a publish command) or remotely (via a send command). Second, in contrast to other event query languages, state need not necessarily be local: using associations, an automaton can modify relational tables, whose current state is immediately available to the rest of the system.

Non-deterministic finite state automata, a computational model used in the event query languages of Cayuga [7,8] and SASE [9,10,11], further extend the notion of user-defined aggregates by expressing complex patterns as composites of ordered sequences of events. The FOLD operator of Cayuga, for example, iterates over an *a priori* unknown sequence of events until a terminating predicate is satisfied, maintaining aggregate statistics in the process; or, the skip till next match operator of SASE maintains intermediate state in arrays in order to express Kleene closures, an operator that has recently received considerable attention in complex event detection [12]. For non-deterministic finite automata, the complexity of a pattern lies in determining what comes "next" in event processing [13]. But apart from folding (or skipping) events, it is hard to specify patterns with branching in a Cayuga or SASE automaton. Indeed, a stream has to be replicated and each branch of the pattern must be represented as a different automaton. Finally, it is not always possible to express nested patterns, e.g. a query that uses the local state maintained by another.

The Cache was first used as a stream database of network flows and related policies that govern a home network. Network monitoring and management scenarios have been featured heavily in stream database research. The Tribeca query language [14], for example, supported demultiplexing and multiplexing of packet streams. The demultiplexing of streams, while similar to the group by SQL operator, enables processing of sub-streams beyond mere aggregate statistics using pipes to transform streams at several stages. The importance of multiplexing (merging) network streams has also been stressed in Gigascope, a high-performance network monitoring tool [15]. Gigascope has a two-level query architecture to process packets on high-speed links. High performance is achieved by pushing low-level queries (e.g., protocol filtering or aggregation) closer to the physical network interface. High-level queries then perform more complex tasks.

A number of packet stream processing algorithms focus on the frequency of certain flow attributes, e.g. the throughput to (from) an IP address or a transport port. The problem has been formally characterized as mining the frequent items in data streams [16], and its applications to network monitoring include finding the heaviest bandwidth consumers (heavy-hitters), or finding the heaviest connection initiators (super-spreaders) [17]. These algorithms are expressible, as we will demonstrate, in GAPL. Finally, modern traffic analysis tools also query the implicit structure of flows in a traffic mix, in an attempt to match application labels to the underlying flow patterns, and vice versa. Thus, flow monitoring queries are not just mere counters of some traffic volume metric, e.g. of the number of bytes or packets. Besides identifying frequent items, patterns of temporally correlated flows are used for classification or intrusion detection and are usually expressed as sequences of events [18].

3   The Topic-Based Publish/Subscribe Cache

There are many situations in which detection of interesting events requires the ability to receive raw events as they occur and the ability to query, as well as modify, global state. In many deployment scenarios, these actions need to be done in real-time. This section describes a topic-based publish/subscribe cache that facilitates such real-time processing.

A working system consists of our centralised Cache and a varying number of applications that use it; the applications and the Cache interact through a custom RPC mechanism. There are three distinct roles that applications can assume with respect to this system:

- populate tables with raw events via insert commands;
- retrieve data from tables periodically via select commands; and/or
- register interest to be notified when complex event patterns are detected.

The Cache supports the usual SQL commands for creating tables and inserting tuples into tables. The Cache supports two types of tables, *ephemeral* tables, append-only streams for which the primary key is the time of insertion, and *persistent* tables, time-varying relations for which the primary key is the first defined field of the table schema. Tuples inserted into ephemeral tables are stored in a circular memory buffer,[1] while tuples inserted into persistent tables are stored in the heap. For persistent tables, an on duplicate key update modifier to the insert command is used to update, rather than append, a row in the heap, while maintaining the temporal order of events. Thus, when retrieving tuples from the Cache, the default order for either table type is the time of insertion, unless overridden by an order by modifier.

For monitoring applications, the selection operator has been augmented with appropriate time and count window extensions to reflect the continuous nature of the events. Thus, apart from typical order by and group by operators, *ad hoc* select queries over cached streams can use time interval expressions that narrow the scope of results to a particular time period, e.g. select * from table [since τ], where τ is the timestamp of the last retrieved tuple. Typically, monitoring applications submit such queries periodically.

The third role of applications, viz. reaction applications, is enabled by the unification of this stream database view of events with a publish/subscribe infrastructure, achieved as follows. Every table created in the Cache, whether ephemeral or persistent, corresponds to a publish/subscribe topic with the same name. Whenever a tuple is inserted into a table, that tuple is published as an event to its associated topic. Applications can register automata (i.e., complex event patterns) against the database. As new tuples are inserted into a table, all automata that have subscribed to that topic will receive events for processing. If, while processing an event, an automaton determines that it has detected a pattern of interest, it may send information about the complex event to the application that registered the automaton.

---

[1] This is the reason that the component is called the Cache.

Table 1. Description of data types

Type	*Basics*
int	64-bit integer
real	Double-precision floating point
tstamp	64-bit unsigned integer (*nsec* since the epoch)
bool	True or false
string	Variable-length UTF-8 character array

Type	*Aggregates*
sequence	Ordered set of heterogeneous basic data type instances
map	Map from an identifier to an instance of the bound type
window	Collection of bound type instances, constrained either to a fixed number of items or a fixed time interval
identifier	Key used in maps
iterator	Used to iterate over all instances in a map (keys) or window (data values)

Additionally, during normal processing of events, an automaton may publish (append, insert, or update) a new tuple into another table in the Cache, whether ephemeral or persistent. This unity allows for complex patterns to be presented as materialised views in the stream database and, vice versa, materialised views to be used to derive complex patterns. A typical reaction application (e.g., a policy management engine) registers one or more automata with the Cache.

4 The Automaton Programming Language

4.1 Language Design Principles

Support for complex event pattern matching, requiring both consumption of raw publish/subscribe events and access to static relations, dictated the following features of the Glasgow Automaton Programming Language:

- the ability to subscribe to one or more topic streams over which raw events are conveyed;
- the ability to publish raw or derived events to other publish/subscribe topics;
- the ability to store local state across many event deliveries to an automaton;
- the ability to query one or more persistent tables to access and/or modify static, global relations; and
- the ability to send information about complex event occurrences back to an automaton's registering application.

Furthermore, one requires a small set of basic data types, a small set of aggregate data structures, and a small set of control constructs to store and filter events locally. The basic data types are described in Table 1. The language also defines a minimal set of aggregate types, e.g. a sequence, a map, or a window, and types required to manipulate these aggregate types, e.g. an iterator over a window.

Every aggregate type is instantiated with a constructor. Note that a sequence instance can contain heterogeneous basic type instances, while each map or window instance is bound to a particular type, basic or aggregate. In fact, the ability to instantiate windows of sequences or maps of sequences enables the creation of ephemeral or persistent tables, respectively, that are truly local within the context of an automaton thread. Finally, the language supports if then else and while constructs. It also supports a typical set of operators for arithmetic, conditional expressions, and assignment.

Overall, the C-like syntax for GAPL was chosen to facilitate the coding of commonly-used stream processing algorithms (cf. §6.4), while enabling high-performance filtering of events.

4.2 General Form for an Automaton

In its general form, an automaton program consists of subscriptions, associations, declarations, an initialization clause, and a behavior clause – in that order.

Each automaton source starts with binding a local variable to each publish/-subscribe topic to which it wishes to be subscribed. Every time an event is delivered on any subscribed topic, the bound local variable refers to the last received event over that topic. Attribute values are assigned automatically to variables with names and types being determined by the corresponding table schema. These variables are accessed using the dot notation. For example, variable e.x holds the value of attribute x of event e. The Cache provides a built-in topic, Timer, which delivers a tuple every second consisting simply of a timestamp data type attribute.[2] All other topics must have been created earlier by create table calls made by applications (or during Cache initialization, from a configuration file). An automaton must always subscribe to at least one topic.

Associations are used to bind a local map variable to a persistent table in the Cache. The automaton can then access and modify tuples in the associated persistent table through calls to lookup() and insert() methods on that map variable, respectively. Subsequent declarations in an automaton enable the programmer to declare additional local variables needed for processing.

The initialization clause of an automaton is executed once, after successful compilation. It is usually used to initialise local variables, but therein a programmer can perform any actions supported by the language. The behavior clause, on the other hand, is executed each time an event is delivered to any of the subscribed topics.

4.3 Example Hybrid Automaton

This section describes an automaton that implements a hybrid application scenario, one in which the the processing of events depends upon access to global persistent policy state, taken from the current deployments of the Cache – i.e., as part of a home network router [4].

---

[2] This is an example of punctuation-carrying heartbeat functionality [19].

```
31 create table Flows (
      proto integer,
      saddr varchar(16), sport integer,
      daddr varchar(16), dport integer,
      npackets integer, nbytes integer)

32 create persistenttable Allowances (
      ipaddress varchar(16) primary key,
      nbytes integer)

33 create persistenttable Usage (
      ipaddress varchar(16) primary key,
      nbytes integer)
```

```
34 subscribe f to Flows;
   associate a with Allowances;
   associate b with Usage;
   int n, limit;
   identifier ip;
   sequence s;
   behavior {
      ip = Identifier(f.daddr);
      if (hasEntry(a, ip)) {
         limit = seqElement(lookup(a, ip), 1);
         if (hasEntry(b, ip))
            n = seqElement(lookup(b, ip), 1);
         else
            n = 0;
         n += f.nbytes;
         s = Sequence(f.daddr, n);
         if (n > limit)
            send(s, limit, 'limit exceeded');
         insert(b, ip, s);
      }
54 }
```

Fig. 2. Tables associated with the bandwidth usage consumption automaton

Fig. 3. Bandwidth usage consumption automaton

Households occupied by multiple, sometimes unrelated adults (e.g., students sharing a flat) often opt for broadband plans with rapidly escalating charges if a per month bandwidth allowance is exceeded. These households wish to control bandwidth consumption as it nears the monthly allowance. Additionally, it is often the case that a single member of the household is usually the cause of exceeding the monthly allowance; therefore, there is a desire to track the usage of a subset of the members of the household.

The three tables used to demonstrate this functionality are shown in Fig. 2. Table Flows is an ephemeral table populated with periodic aggregate statistics of home networking traffic (i.e., per flow number of bytes and number of packets accumulated every second). The other two tables are persistent. The Allowances table is populated with a monthly download byte-limit per monitored IP address using a network management utility; and the Usage table records accumulated bandwidth usage, reset to zero by a network management utility at an appropriate frequency.

Fig. 3 shows an automaton that tracks the bandwidth usage per monitored IP address, generating a notification to the registering application (i.e., a policy-based management system) when a limit has been exceeded. The automaton subscribes to Flows events; and associates maps a and b with tables Allowances and Usage, respectively. Upon receipt of each Flows event, it does the following:

- it generates an identifier ip from the flow's destination address;
- if no entry for ip is found in Allowances, it stops processing;
- otherwise, it looks up an allowance for this ip address;
- if there is an entry for ip in table Usage, it fetches the accumulated usage;
- otherwise, it sets usage n to zero;

- it increments n by the number of bytes in the Flows tuple;
- if ip's limit is exceeded, it sends an event to the registering application; and
- it updates the usage for this IP address in the Cache.

5 Automaton Execution Model

When an application registers an automaton against the Cache, it provides the source code for the automaton along with data required for the Cache to create an RPC channel back to the registering application (i.e., a host, a port, and a service name). The source code is then compiled into instructions for a stack machine. If a compilation error is detected, information about the error is communicated back to the registering application, and the RPC channel is closed. Upon successful compilation, a new Pthread is created to animate the automaton, and an identifier is returned instead; this identifier can be used by the registering application to manage the automaton at a later time (e.g., to unregister it).

When the Pthread is created, the byte code sequences resulting from the compilation of the initialization and behavior clauses are bound to an instance of a stack machine interpreter. The initialization sequence is executed once and the thread then enters a continuous loop, awaiting an event on one of its subscribed topics (a tuple insertion); the runtime system guarantees that tuples are delivered to an automaton in strict time-of-insertion order. Upon receipt of an event, the behavior sequence is executed. If an automaton executes a send in the behavior sequence, an RPC call, containing the send() arguments, is made to the registering application. If the automaton executes a publish in the behavior sequence, a tuple is inserted into the table (topic) specified in the publish() arguments, potentially triggering other automata to execute. The default Pthread scheduling algorithm is used by the Cache and appropriate conditional critical regions are used to guarantee safe execution amongst multiple automata threads.

The runtime implements an aggressive garbage collection policy as soon as it knows that heap allocated storage is no longer in use; the delete procedure can be optionally invoked by code to advise when storage is no longer in use.

5.1 Optimizations Enabled by the Execution Model

Many complex event processing systems based upon the stream database model require the creation of multiple temporary event streams for their operators to perform the requisite aggregations and disaggregations demanded by a pattern matching logic. This leads to a very large number of operators that must be scheduled, and a very large number of additional tuples that need to be delivered to a directed acyclic graph of operators that represent the query. The imperative structure of GAPL, together with the ability to declare and manipulate an automaton's local state, enable combinations of multiple operators into a single automaton, thus reducing the scheduling stress on the Cache. The following example, documented fully in [20], demonstrates this effect.

The DEBS 2012 Grand Challenge posed two complex queries with regards to monitoring manufacturing equipment. Here we discuss the first query, illustrated

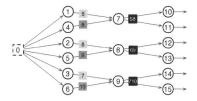

Fig. 4. The DEBS 2012 Grand Challenge query

in Fig. 4. The query consists of fifteen operators (circles), generating nine intermediate streams (squares). Operators 1 and 4 compute a state transition by correlating consecutive events inserted into the initial stream 0; once a pattern is detected by either of them, events are published to operator 7. In turn, operator 7 looks for events in stream 5 followed by events in stream 8. Since this logic is sequential, GAPL allows us to combine these three operators together, in one automaton. Also, operators 10 and 11 have different functionality but they maintain the same state, a 24-hour sliding window over stream 58. If these operators were to be treated separately, then the same window would be maintained twice. Since their logic is independent, this duplication can also be avoided by merging them in one automaton. The other ten operators simply replicate the aforementioned functionality but on different attributes. In fact, our final solution merged all fifteen operators into a single automaton – i.e. one execution thread – avoiding the use of intermediate streams all together. By doing so, the throughput increased by 57% and the execution time decreased significantly, as opposed to having one automaton per operator [20].

5.2   Multi-query Optimizations

Sharing derived events amongst Glasgow automata is currently a programmer's task and it is achieved by explicitly publishing these events to intermediate streams that are, in turn, accessible by other automata running in the context of the Cache; it is not an automated process. Managing these events programmatically, using basic or aggregate data type instances, is one of the key features that enable high-performance event filtering.

A limitation, however, of user-defined optimisations is that multiple automata registrations are not open to multi-query optimisations possible in other query engines. Cayuga, for example, merges equivalent automaton states into a directed acyclic graph using YFilters [21,7], whose edges represent static or dynamic predicates that determine state transitions. This trade-off, where on one hand scaling to thousands of queries requires multi-query optimisations, while on the other hand high performance and expressiveness requires user-defined optimisations, is an open research question; we explore it by investigating the use of GAPL as an intermediate language between the two approaches.

```
55 subscribe t to Timer;
   int i;
   int limit;
   tstamp start;
   int dt;
60 # built-in specific declarations, e.g. sequence s; int x;
   initialization {
     limit = 100000;
63   # built-in specific initialization, e.g. s = Sequence('A', 1);
     print('Start of <built-in> test');
   }
   behavior {
     i = 0;
     start = tstampNow();
     while (i < limit) {
70     # invoke built-in, e.g. x = seqElement(s, 1);
       i += 1;
     }
     dt = tstampDiff(tstampNow(), start);
     print(String('<built-in>: ', float(dt)/100000000.0));
75 }
```

Fig. 5. Built-in cost template automaton

6 Evaluation

Experiments are run on two AMD Athlon 64 dual core 2.7GHz processors with 4GB of RAM running Ubuntu Linux 2.6 and Windows 7, respectively. The Cache is implemented as a multi-threaded process. Its main thread handles RPC requests (e.g., tuple insertions, automaton registrations) from other processes serially; new threads are created upon each successful automaton compilation. The remainder of this section documents the performance of automata in this environment.

6.1 Cost of Built-In Functions

Automata are interpreted programs, thus it is important to characterise the costs of invoking built-in functions in the language. The automaton template in Fig. 5 was used to measure the execution costs to invoke a representative set of the built-in functions supported by the language. The built-in specific declarations (line 60), initialization (line 63), and invocation (line 70) were incorporated into the template as appropriate. The print function was used to display the results on standard output; the number printed is the number of microseconds required for each invocation of the built-in under test. Each automaton was executed for two minutes on an unloaded machine.

Fig. 6 shows the minimum, 25-th, 50-th, 75-th percentiles, and maximum of execution times recorded for each built-in.[3] Several things are apparent from this data:

---

[3] The overhead of the while loop was subtracted from the values produced by the automaton.

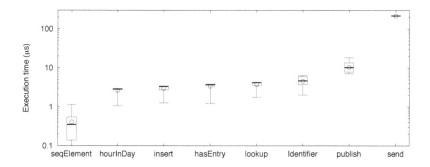

Fig. 6. The execution cost of built-in functions

- the average cost of basic built-in functions (e.g. insert, lookup) is $\sim 3\mu s$;
- identifier generation, which requires access to the heap and copying of strings, is about twice as expensive as a basic built-in;
- publishing an event to another topic is about three times the basic built-in cost; and
- sending an event to an external process takes $\sim 200\mu s$.

6.2 Performance at Scale

As the number of simultaneously subscribed automata increases, one expects the scheduling delay for each automaton to increase. Thus, it is important to understand how the Cache performs as the number of automata and also the frequency of tuple insertion scale up.

To stress the system, we vary the number of automata that subscribe to the Flows topic (cf. §4.3). Independently, we vary the frequency of tuple insertion into the Flows table. An important measure of the ability for the system to handle the increased scale is the delay between when a tuple is inserted into the table/topic, and when each subscribed automaton processes the event. This is measured using the automaton in Fig. 7. For each automaton, a different value is assigned to id (line 85); the subsequent log generated by the automaton is analysed for mean and standard deviation of the average delay observed across all automata, as well as for minimum and maximum delays observed (lines 91-93). The independent parameters for the experimental runs are the number of automata simultaneously subscribed and the cycle period of tuple insertion into Flows, Δt.

Fig. 8 displays the measured delay parameters for $\Delta t = 8ms$. It is clear that the average delay grows linearly as the number of automata scales from one to eight. Note that, in the deployments to date, the typical number of flow tuples inserted are approximately 100 events/second; $\Delta t = 8ms$ corresponds to an insertion rate of 125 tuples/second. It is also important to note that it is quite uncommon in our experience to have several automata subscribed to high frequency topics like Flows.

```
76 subscribe f to Flows;
   real min, max, mean, dt;
   int count, nsecs;
   string id;
   initialization {
       min = 1000.;
       max = 0.;
       mean = 0.;
       count = 0;
85     id = 'A';
   }
   behavior {
       count += 1;
       nsecs = tstampDiff(tstampNow(),
           f.tstamp);
       dt = float(nsecs)/1000000.;
91     mean = mean + (dt - mean) /
           float(count);
       if (dt > max) max = dt;
93     if (dt < min) min = dt;
       if (count >= 1000) {
           print(String(id, ':', mean,
               ',', min, ',', max));
           min = 1000.;
           max = 0.;
           mean = 0.;
           count = 0;
       }
101 }
```

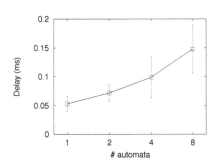

Fig. 8. Delay vs. # automata, $\Delta t = 8ms$

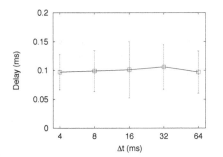

Fig. 7. Performance at scale template automaton

Fig. 9. Delay vs. event inter-arrival rate with 4 automata running

Fig. 9 shows the measured delay parameters for four automata as Δt scales from $4ms$ to $64ms$ (insertion rates of 250 events/second to 16 events/second). The average and variance of the delay remain essentially constant across this range of packet insertion rates.

Thus, the system scales well with number of automata and frequency of tuple insertion. The linear growth in average and standard deviation of delay with number of automata is consistent with scheduling increasing numbers of Pthreads. The constancy of average and variance against insertion frequency indicates that there is plenty of execution capacity in the Cache for the loads presented.

6.3   Performance at Stress

Another important measure of the capacity of the system is the maximal rate at which it can absorb and generate RPC requests and responses. To measure this, we executed the automaton of Fig. 10 to measure one-way and two-way stress performance, with a single application performing insert calls into a Test table as rapidly as possible. Note that to measure two-way stress performance, simply uncomment line 117 in the automaton.

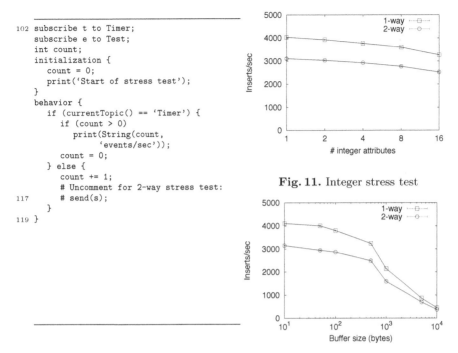

```
102 subscribe t to Timer;
    subscribe e to Test;
    int count;
    initialization {
        count = 0;
        print('Start of stress test');
    }
    behavior {
        if (currentTopic() == 'Timer') {
            if (count > 0)
                print(String(count,
                    'events/sec'));
            count = 0;
        } else {
            count += 1;
            # Uncomment for 2-way stress test:
117         # send(s);
        }
119 }
```

Fig. 11. Integer stress test

Fig. 10. Performance at stress template automaton

Fig. 12. Character string stress test

The performance as the number of integer fields in the Test table schema varies from 1 to 16 is shown in Fig. 11. Fig. 12 shows the performance as the number of characters in a schema consisting of a single varchar field varies from 1 to 10,000. The RPC system performs fragmentation/reassembly at 1024-byte boundaries, so the drop with buffer size is to be expected.

6.4 Finding Frequent Items

This section evaluates the implementation of the "frequent" algorithm, a one-pass algorithm for finding the top-k items in a data stream [16], as a Glasgow automaton (Fig. 13). The algorithm stores $k-1$ out of n items, according to their popularity; after processing n events, the approximate result set will contain at least those items that have occurred n/k times. The input data to the automaton are 264,745 out-going HTTP requests (appended to an ephemeral table Urls) to 5,572 unique hosts, as logged by a router running in a small office environment at the University of Glasgow. Fig. 14 shows the Zipfian frequency distribution of the data set, where hosts are ranked by their popularity, a well-known characteristic of Web traffic.

An alternative approach is to introduce the algorithm as a built-in procedure in the language, a *de facto* approach in traditional query languages. Indeed,

```
120 subscribe e to Urls;
    map T;
    iterator i;
    identifier id;
    int count;
    int k;
    initialization {
        k = k;
        T = Map(int);
    }
    behavior {
        id = Identifier(e.host);
        if (hasEntry(T, id)) {
            count = lookup(T, id);
            count += 1;
            insert(T, id, count);
        } else if (mapSize(T) < (k-1))
            insert(T, id, 1);
        else {
            i = Iterator(T);
            while(hasNext(i)) {
                id = next(i);
                count = lookup(T, id);
                count -= 1;
                if (count == 0)
                    remove(T, id);
                else
                    insert(T, id, count);
            }
        }
    }
150 }
```

Fig. 13. The frequent algorithm [16]

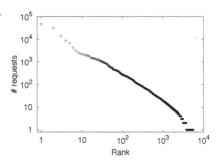

Fig. 14. Number of requests per Web page ordered by popularity

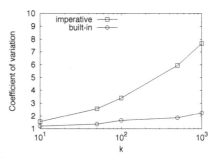

Fig. 15. Imperative *vs.* built-in execution time of the frequent algorithm

```
151 subscribe e to Urls;
    map T;
    initialization { T = Map(int); }
154 behavior { frequent(T, Identifier(u.host), k); }
```

Fig. 16. The frequent algorithm as a built-in function

there might be situations where, despite the efficient code generated from the GAPL compiler, an interpreted solution may be insufficiently performant.

To demonstrate this, we also implemented the frequent algorithm as a built-in function in the language and evaluated the two approaches – namely, the automaton of Fig. 13 and the automaton of Fig. 16. From an algorithmic perspective, the execution time of these automata is dominated by $O(1)$ operations (e.g. inserting into T) and $O(k)$ operations (e.g., iterating over T). As k increases, the number of $O(1)$ operations increases, and the $O(k)$ operations become more expensive. Thus, it is expected that as k increases, the mean execution time (μ) will decrease and the standard deviation (σ) will increase. Fig. 15 shows the coefficient of variation (σ/μ) for both the imperative and the built-in implementation of the frequent algorithm.

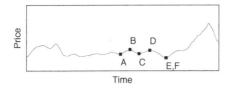

Fig. 17. An M-shaped pattern in the dataset illustrated

6.5   Comparison with Cayuga

This section evaluates the performance of the Cache against the Cayuga query engine [7]. Most of the examples in the Cayuga distribution, as well as the data sets provided, are related to complex event processing for stock market investors. We evaluate three exemplar Cayuga queries against equivalent implementations in GAPL. The dataset used contains 112,635 anonymised stock events whose schema consists of a timestamp, an identifier as a company's name, and a price.

The first query is an example of a basic built-in operator that simply publishes incoming events to another stream. In the Cayuga Event Language (CEL), the query is:

```
155 SELECT * FROM Stock PUBLISH T
```

The equivalent Glasgow automaton is one that subscribes to stream Stock and publishes an event to another stream T with the same schema. I.e.,

```
156 subscribe s to Stock;
157 behavior { publish('T', s); }
```

The second query is an example of a Cayuga automaton with multiple states that detects a double-top formation in the price chart of any stock – this is a well-known pattern amongst trade analysts, also known as an M-shaped pattern. Fig. 17, for example, shows one of the M-shaped patterns found in the data set. The CEL query that detects such patterns is illustrated in Fig. 18. Certain details of the query have been omitted, while others have been simplified; we summarise its functionality in the following.[4]

Starting from the innermost expression (lines 174-176), Cayuga correlates two consecutive Stock events for the same company until the price rebounds. The engine then attaches a new automaton instance to the next query state, continuously iterating over an *a priori* unknown number of Stock events for the same company, as long as its price monotonically increases. This is achieved by the inner FOLD operator (line 177). Cayuga proceeds outwards in the query, transiting to the next Cayuga automaton state, looking for a monotonic decrease in that stock's price, and so on, spawning new automaton instances along the way and storing valleys and peaks of a given stock's price in attributes A to F of the resulting schema.

---

[4] The complete queries summarised in Figures 18 and 19 are available at
www.dcs.gla.ac.uk/~koliousa/middleware.html.

```
158 SELECT Name, A, B, C, D, E, Price as F
    FROM
    FILTER {...} ( # Price increases.
    FILTER {...} ( # Price decreases.
    SELECT Name, A, B, C, D, Price as E
    FROM
    FILTER {...} ( # Price increases.
    SELECT Name, A, B, C, Price as D
    FROM
    FILTER {...} ( # Price decreases.
    SELECT Name, A, B, Price as C
    FROM
    FILTER {...} ( # Price increases.
    SELECT Name, A, Price as B
    FROM
    FILTER {...} ( # Price decreases.
174 SELECT Name, Price as A
    FROM Stocks
176 NEXT {$1.Name=$2.Name} Stock
177 ) FOLD{...} Stock # Price increasing.
    ) FOLD{...} Stock # Price decreasing.
    ) FOLD{...} Stock # Price increasing.
    ) FOLD{...} Stock # Price decreasing.
    ) NEXT {$1.Name = $2.Name} Stock
182 ) PUBLISH T
```

Fig. 18. M-shaped pattern in Cayuga

```
183 subscribe s to Stock;
    map m;
    identifier id;
    sequence stock;
    real a, ..., f, previous;  # Prices
    bool A, ..., F;            # States
    initialization { m = Map(sequence); }
    behavior {
        id = Identifier(s.id);
        if (! hasEntry(m, id)) {
            # Init states & prices for stock id
            stock = Sequence(s.price, false, ...);
            insert(m, id, stock);
        } else {
            stock = lookup(m, id);
            previous = seqElement(stock, 0);
            # A is the 1st element, B the 2nd, etc.
            # ...
            if (previous < s.price) {
                # Monitor increasing...
            } else if (previous > s.price) {
                # Monitor decreasing...
            }
        }
    }
207 }
```

Fig. 19. M-shaped pattern in GAPL

```
208 subscribe s to Stock;
    map stocks;
    identifier id;
    sequence tuple, updated;
    initialization { stocks = Map(sequence); }
    behavior {
        id = Identifier(s.id);
        if (! hasEntry(stocks, id)) {
            # New run; set count to 1.
            tuple = Sequence(s.price, s.time, 1,
                s.price, s.time);
            insert(stocks, id, tuple);
            publish('Folded', 'create', s.id,
                tuple);
        } else { # Existing run; update.
            tuple = lookup(stocks, id);
            if (s.price > seqElement(tuple, 3)) {
                # Price is increasing;
                # Incr. count (l. 228)
                updated = Sequence(
                    seqElement(tuple, 0),
                    seqElement(tuple, 1),
228                 seqElement(tuple, 2) + 1,
                    s.price, s.time);
                insert(stocks, id, updated);
                publish('Folded', 'change',
                    s.id, updated);
            } else {
                remove(stocks, id);
                publish('Folded', 'remove',
                    s.id, tuple);
            }
        }
    }
237 }
```

```
238 subscribe f to Folded;
    map m;
    window w;
    identifier id;
    sequence s;
    iterator i;
    initialization { m = Map(window); }
    behavior {
        id = Identifier(f.id);
        if (f.command == 'create') {
            w = Window(sequence, ROWS, 1000);
            s = Sequence(f.price1, f.time1,
                f.count, f.price2, f.time2);
            append(w, s);
            insert(m, id, w);
        } else if (f.command == 'change') {
            w = lookup(m, id);
            s = Sequence(f.price1, f.time1,
                f.count, f.price2, f.time2);
            append(w, s);
        } else { # Removed from map stocks.
            w = lookup(m, id);
            i = Iterator(w);
            while (hasNext(i)) {
                s = next(i);
                publish('T', s);
            }
            remove(m, id);
        }
    }
265 }
```

Fig. 20. Detecting sequences of increasing stock prices

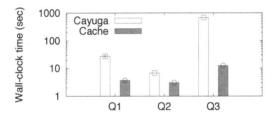

Fig. 21. Benchmarking against Cayuga

Our implementation (simplified) is shown in Fig. 19. The automaton maintains booleans A to F, together with their associated price values (a to f), in a map of sequences; each entry represents a small state machine for a given stock. Once all states A to F for a stock are true, then the M-shaped pattern has been detected. Depending on the current stock price, the algorithm backtracks to previous states or proceeds to the next (ascending or descending price runs) accordingly. Note here that our solution is algorithmic, using the if then else constructs of GAPL.

The final query is an example use of the FOLD operator to perform aggregate computations across multiple iterations. The CEL query has the form:

```
266 SELECT *
    FROM (
    SELECT *, 1 AS counter FROM Stock
    ) FOLD {$1.Name = $2.Name, $.Price < $2.Price, $.counter + 1 AS counter} Stock
270 PUBLISH T
```

The desired behaviour is to detect continuous runs of increasing prices for each stock, and to display the sequence of events that constituted each run. This has been implemented using the two Glasgow automata illustrated in Fig. 20. The automaton on the left maintains a map entry (a sequence) for a given company (s.id) as long as its price is monotonically increasing. At the end of each run, i.e., when the stock's price decreases, the sequence contains the current lowest price, the start time, the length of the run, and current highest price, and the end time. In order to also display the sequence of events that constitute each run, we publish to another topic, Folded, and implement a custom state management system – with states create, change, and remove – in the automaton on the right.

Fig. 21 shows the results from comparing the execution time of the three CEL queries with their equivalent implementations in the automaton programming language. The Cayuga engine best compiles in Microsoft's Visual Studio, thus the experiments were run on a Windows platform. The Cayuga execution times are the elapsed time after all events have been loaded into memory and until all events have been processed. The Cache was never provisioned for post-hoc analysis of in-memory data: all events are processed in real-time. For a fair comparison, we derive our timings by first appending all events in a window, and then iterate over the window and execute the queries.

For the first query, the performance improvement against Cayuga is an order of magnitude. This strengthens the argument of the efficacy of the automaton execution model and the efficient unification of the publish/subscribe infrastructure with the data stream management code. For the second query, the automaton detects the pattern twice as fast as Cayuga. This is another example of the ability to implement multiple state machines under a single execution thread, which contributes to this performance enhancement. Finally, for the third query, our implementation is dramatically faster ($\times 50$) than Cayuga's equivalent.

7   The Impact on Complex Event Processing

We have proposed an algorithmic, imperative approach to complex event processing. The first impact of this work is Turing completeness, something that was proposed from a theoretical basis in [3]. Some event languages have a solid background in event calculi and result in one-line expressions that are compact implementations, but are not open to user optimizations – apart from physical query execution plans. For example, there is a large body of complex event language research on Kleene closures [9]. Although not explicitly documented here, we have implemented SASE's Kleene closure operator (e.g., based on partition contiguity) with a map of windows in GAPL.

Our experiences thus far are that the imperative programming style of GAPL enables it to be used in many domains: home network management [4], industrial applications [20], and, given the present comparisons to Cayuga, stocks. In addition to its expressiveness, this imperative model has been shown more performant than a declarative event language (CEL). Thus, it may be viewed as an intermediate language between SQL-like queries (logical query plans) and their execution interpretation (physical query plans).

8   Conclusions

It is clear that the automaton language, as integrated into the Cache, provides a very high-performance complex event processing capability. It can be criticized for its imperative, C-like structure, in terms of usability by individuals wanting to deploy their own automata. We have started to investigate compilation of stream expressions for complex event patterns, such as Cayuga's, into equivalent automata. An alternative approach is to compile stream expressions directly into instructions for the stack machine that underlies the Cache.

In comparing with Cayuga, we have determined that we need to be able to create streams on the fly. This will enable exploration of the dynamic demultiplexing of streams, as lately discussed in [22]. We continue our comparative endeavours with the Linear Road Benchmark [23].

References

1. Codd, E.F.: A relational model of data for large shared data banks. Commun. ACM 13, 377–387 (1970)
2. Terry, D., Goldberg, D., Nichols, D., Oki, B.: Continuous queries over append-only databases. In: Proceedings of the ACM SIGMOD (1992)

3. Law, Y.N., Wang, H., Zaniolo, C.: Query languages and data models for database sequences and data streams. In: Proceedings of the VLDB (2004)
4. Sventek, J., Koliousis, A., Dulay, N., Pediaditakis, D., Rodden, T., Lodge, T., Sharma, O., Sloman, M., Bedwell, B., Glover, K., Mortier, R.: An Information Plane Architecture Supporting Home Network Management. In: Proceedings of the IFIP/IEEE IM (2011)
5. Arasu, A., Babu, S., Widom, J.: The CQL continuous query language: semantic foundations and query execution. The VLDB Journal 15, 121–142 (2006)
6. Abadi, D.J., Carney, D., Çetintemel, U., Cherniack, M., Convey, C., Lee, S., Stonebraker, M., Tatbul, N., Zdonik, S.: Aurora: a new model and architecture for data stream management. The VLDB Journal 12, 120–139 (2003)
7. Demers, A., Gehrke, J., Hong, M., Riedewald, M., White, W.: Towards Expressive Publish/Subscribe Systems. In: Ioannidis, Y., Scholl, M.H., Schmidt, J.W., Matthes, F., Hatzopoulos, M., Böhm, K., Kemper, A., Grust, T., Böhm, C. (eds.) EDBT 2006. LNCS, vol. 3896, pp. 627–644. Springer, Heidelberg (2006)
8. Brenna, L., Demers, A., Gehrke, J., Hong, M., Ossher, J., Panda, B., Riedewald, M., Thatte, M., White, W.: Cayuga: a high-performance event processing engine. In: Proceedings of the ACM SIGMOD (2007)
9. Agrawal, J., Diao, Y., Gyllstrom, D., Immerman, N.: Efficient pattern matching over event streams. In: Proceedings of the ACM SIGMOD (2008)
10. Wu, E., Diao, Y., Rizvi, S.: High-performance complex event processing over streams. In: Proceedings of the ACM SIGMOD (2006)
11. Gyllstrom, D., Agrawal, J., Diao, Y., Immerman, N.: On supporting kleene closure over event streams. In: Proceedings of the IEEE ICDE (2008)
12. Mozafari, B., Zeng, K., Zaniolo, C.: From regular expressions to nested words: unifying languages and query execution for relational and XML sequences. Proc. VLDB Endow. 3(1-2), 150–161 (2010)
13. White, W., Riedewald, M., Gehrke, J., Demers, A.: What is "next" in event processing? In: Proceedings of the ACM PODS (2007)
14. Sullivan, M., Heybey, A.: Tribeca: a system for managing large databases of network traffic. In: Proceedings of the USENIX ATEC (1998)
15. Cranor, C., Johnson, T., Spataschek, O., Shkapenyuk, V.: Gigascope: a stream database for network applications. In: Proceedings of the ACM SIGMOD (2003)
16. Cormode, G., Hadjieleftheriou, M.: Finding the frequent items in streams of data. Commun. ACM 52, 97–105 (2009)
17. Sekar, V., Reiter, M.K., Zhang, H.: Revisiting the case for a minimalist approach for network flow monitoring. In: Proceedings of ACM IMC (2010)
18. Kandula, S., Chandra, R., Katabi, D.: What's going on?: learning communication rules in edge networks. In: Proceedings of the ACM SIGCOMM (2008)
19. Johnson, T., Muthukrishnan, S., Shkapenyuk, V., Spatscheck, O.: A heartbeat mechanism and its application in Gigascope. In: Proceedings of the VLDB (2005)
20. Koliousis, A., Sventek, J.: DEBS Grand Challenge: Glasgow automata illustrated. In: Proceedings of the ACM DEBS (2012)
21. Diao, Y., Altinel, M., Franklin, M.J., Zhang, H., Fischer, P.: Path sharing and predicate evaluation for high-performance XML filtering. ACM Trans. Database Syst. 28(4), 467–516 (2003)
22. Zeitler, E., Risch, T.: Massive scale-out of expensive continuous queries. PVLDB 4(11), 1181–1188 (2011)
23. Arasu, A., Cherniack, M., Galvez, E., Maier, D., Maskey, A.S., Ryvkina, E., Stonebraker, M., Tibbetts, R.: Linear road: a stream data management benchmark. In: Proceedings of the VLDB (2004)

High-Performance Location-Aware Publish-Subscribe on GPUs

Gianpaolo Cugola and Alessandro Margara

Politecnico di Milano, Dipartimento di Elettronica e Informazione
Piazza Leonardo da Vinci 32, Milan, Italy
{cugola,margara}@elet.polimi.it

Abstract. Adding location-awareness to publish-subscribe middleware infrastructures would open-up new opportunities to use this technology in the hot area of mobile applications. On the other hand, this requires to radically change the way published events are matched against received subscriptions. In this paper we examine this issue in detail and we present CLCB, a new algorithm using CUDA GPUs for massively parallel, high-performance, location-aware publish-subscribe matching and its implementation into a matching component that allows to easily build a full-fledged middleware system. A comparison with the state-of-the-art in this area shows the impressive increment in performance that GPUs may enable, even in this domain. At the same time, our performance analysis allows to identify those peculiar aspects of GPU programming that mostly impact the performance of this kind of algorithm.

Keywords: Publish-Subscribe   Middleware,   Location-Awareness, Content-Based Matching, Parallel Hardware, CUDA GPUs.

1   Introduction

The diffusion of mobile devices, like notebooks, tablets, and smartphones, which characterized the last few years, has enabled *mobile computing* scenarios based on *location-aware services*. In several cases these services involve some form of *event-based interaction* [22] among the different parties, being them the final users or the components of the mobile applications they use. Examples of services that combine these two models of interaction are location-aware advertising (that reach potential clients based on their location and interests), location-aware social networking (that want to let co-located people to "socialize", i.e., communicate and coordinate), traffic information services (where information reaches interested users based on their location), emergency services (that spread some emergency-related information only to the people present in a specific area where the emergency situation occurs), and so on.

From a software engineering standpoint we notice that this model of interaction can be efficiently supported by a *location-aware publish-subscribe* middleware layer, which lets distributed components *subscribe* to the *notification of events* (often simply "events") happening in a given *location* (usually in the neighborhood of the subscriber) and *publish* the events they want to notify to

P. Narasimhan and P. Triantafillou (Eds.): Middleware 2012, LNCS 7662, pp. 312–331, 2012.
© IFIP International Federation for Information Processing 2012

others. In particular, a *content-based* infrastructure [14] is the most suited for the kind of services we mentioned, as it provides the level of expressiveness to allow subscribers to express their interests based on the whole content of the event notifications published.

The key element of every content-based publish-subscribe middleware infrastructure is the *matching component* in charge of filtering incoming events against received subscriptions to decide the interested recipients. If we focus on this component and on the algorithm it implements, we notice that none of those proposed so far [1,14] fits the mobile scenarios we address. Indeed, in order to maximize performance all the matching algorithms assume: (i) that subscriptions are fairly stable and (ii) that they differ from each other (i.e., they include constraints on different attributes[1]), and they leverage these assumptions to index existing subscriptions in complex data structures that minimize the number of comparisons required to match incoming events. Unfortunately, both these assumptions are violated by location-aware publish-subscribe: the location constraint is present in every subscription and subscriptions change frequently since the area of users' interests moves with them.

To overcome these limitations we developed *CLCB - Cuda Location-aware Content-Based matcher*, a new matching algorithm that leverages the processing power of *CUDA Graphical Processing Units (GPUs)* to provide high-performance location-aware content-based matching. In designing CLCB we started from the consideration that modern GPUs in general, and those that implement the CUDA architecture in particular, offer a huge computing power suited for different types of processing, once the right algorithm has been designed. Indeed, GPU programming is a complex task that requires programmers to take into account the peculiarities of the hardware platform, from the memory layout and the way memory is accessed, to the fact that GPU cores can be used simultaneously only to perform data-parallel computations.

In the remainder of the paper we show how CLCB addresses these issues, exploiting all the processing power of CUDA GPUs to minimize both the time to perform location-aware content-based matching of incoming events, and the time to update subscriptions when users move and the area of their interests changes. A comparison against various state-of-the-art systems shows the advantages GPUs may bring to this domain. In particular, next section introduces the location-aware publish-subscribe model we consider, while Section 3 offers an overview of the CUDA programming model. The CLCB algorithm is described in Section 4, while Section 5 evaluates its performance. Finally, Section 6 presents related work and Section 7 provides concluding remarks.

2   The Interaction Model in Details

As the name suggests, location-aware publish-subscribe middleware infrastructures enable a model of interaction among components that extends the

---

[1] See Section 2 for the specific nomenclature we use to refer to the format of events and subscriptions.

traditional publish-subscribe model by introducing a concept of "location". In particular, we assume a data model that is very common among content-based publish-subscribe middleware infrastructures [9], where event notifications are represented as a set of *attributes*, i.e., $\langle name, value \rangle$ pairs, while subscriptions are a disjunction of *filters*, which, in turn, are conjunctions of elementary *constraints* on the values of single attributes, i.e., $\langle name, operator, value \rangle$ triples.

As far as location is concerned, we assume that each event happens in a specific *location*, while filters have an *area of relevance*. Notice that we associate the area of relevance to filters and not subscriptions on purpose. Indeed, this choice allows to easily model the (common) situation of a user that wants to subscribe to events X happening in an area A_X *or* to events Y happening in a different area A_Y.

For simplicity we assume that locations are expressed using Cartesian coordinates and that the area of relevance of each filter is a circle, which we represent using three floats: two for the center of the area and one for its radius[2].

Given these definitions, the problem of location-aware content-based matching we want to solve can be stated as follows: given an event e happening at a location $loc(e)$ and a set of subscriptions $S = \{s_1, ..., s_n\}$, each composed of a set of filters $s_i = \{f_{i_1}, ..., f_{i_m}\}$ with their area of relevance $area(f_{i_1}), ..., area(f_{i_m})$, find those subscriptions s_j such that:

$$\exists k : loc(e) \in area(f_{j_k}) \wedge matches(e, f_{j_k})$$

where $matches(e, f_{j_k})$ iff every constraint in f_{j_k} is satisfied by an attribute in e.

Moreover, the peculiarity of the scenarios we consider is that the area of relevance of filters changes frequently as it reflects the actual location of the subscribers, which are supposed to move at run-time.

3   Parallel Programming with CUDA

Attaining good performance with parallel programming is a complex task. A naïve paralleling of a sequential algorithm is usually not sufficient to efficiently exploit the presence of multiple processing elements, and a complete re-design of the algorithm may be necessary, taking into account the peculiarity of the underlying architecture and its programming model.

Introduced by Nvidia in Nov. 2006, the CUDA architecture offers a new programming model and instruction set for general purpose programming on GPUs. Different languages can be used to interact with a CUDA compliant device: we adopted CUDA C, a dialect of C explicitly devoted to program GPUs. The CUDA programming model is founded on five key abstractions:

Hierarchical Organization of Thread Groups. The programmer is guided in partitioning a problem into coarse sub-problems to be solved *independently* in parallel by *blocks* of threads, while each sub-problem must be decomposed

---

[2] This choice does not impact our algorithm and can be easily changed to represent both the location of events and the area of relevance of filters differently, including 3-dimensional areas.

into finer pieces to be solved *cooperatively* in parallel by all threads within a block. This decomposition allows the algorithm to easily scale with the number of available processor cores, since each block of threads can be scheduled on any of them, in any order, concurrently or sequentially.

Shared Memories. CUDA threads may access data from multiple memory spaces during their execution: each thread has a *private local memory* for automatic variables; each block has a *shared memory* visible to all threads in the same block; finally, all threads have access to the same *global memory*.

Barrier Synchronization. Since thread blocks are required to execute independently from each other, no primitive is offered to synchronize threads of different blocks. On the other hand, threads within a single block work in cooperation, and thus need to synchronize their execution to coordinate memory access. In CUDA this is achieved exclusively through *barriers*.

Separation of Host and Device. The CUDA programming model assumes that CUDA threads execute on a physically separate *device* (the GPU), which operates as a coprocessor of a *host* (the CPU) running a C/C++ program. The host and the device maintain their own separate memory spaces. Therefore, before starting a computation, it is necessary to explicitly allocate memory on the device and to copy there the information needed during execution. Similarly, at the end results have to be copied back to the host memory and the device memory have to be deallocated.

Kernels. They are special functions that define a single flow of execution for multiple threads. When calling a kernel k, the programmer specifies the number of threads per block and the number of blocks that must execute it. Inside the kernel it is possible to access two variables provided by the CUDA runtime: the *threadId* and the *blockId*, which together allow to uniquely identify each thread among those executing the kernel. Conditional statements involving these variables can be used to differentiate the execution flows of different threads.

Architectural Issues

There are details about the hardware architecture that a programmer cannot ignore while designing an algorithm for CUDA. First of all, the CUDA architecture is built around a scalable array of multi-threaded *Streaming Multiprocessors* (*SMs*). When a CUDA program on the host CPU invokes a kernel k, the blocks executing k are enumerated and distributed to the available SMs. All threads belonging to the same block execute on the same SM, thus exploiting fast SRAM to implement the shared memory. Multiple blocks may execute concurrently on the same SM as well. As blocks terminate new blocks are launched on freed SMs.

Each SM creates, manages, schedules, and executes threads in groups of parallel threads called *warps*. Individual threads composing a warp start together but they have their own instruction pointer and local state and are therefore free to branch and execute independently. On the other hand, full efficiency is realized only when all threads in a warp agree on their execution path, since CUDA parallels them executing one common instruction at a time. If threads in the same warp diverge via a data-dependent conditional branch, the warp executes each path serially, disabling threads that are not on that path. Only when all paths complete the threads converge back to the same execution flow.

An additional issue is represented by memory accesses. If the layout of data structures allows threads with contiguous ids to access contiguous memory locations, the hardware can organize memory accesses into several memory-wide operations, thus maximizing throughput. This aspect significantly influenced the design of CLCB's data structures, as we discuss in the next section.

Finally, to give an idea of the capabilities of a modern GPU supporting CUDA, we provide some details of the Nvidia GTX 460 card we used for our tests. It includes 7 SMs, which can handle up to 48 warps of 32 threads each (for a maximum of 1536 threads). Each block may access a maximum amount of 48KB of shared, on-chip memory within each SM. Furthermore, it includes 1GB of GDDR5 memory as global memory. This information must be carefully taken into account when programming: shared memory must be exploited as much as possible to hide the latency of global memory accesses but its limited size significantly impacts the design of algorithms.

4   The CLCB Algorithm

In this section we first explain why existing solutions for content-based matching and spatial searching cannot fully satisfy the requirements of a location-aware publish-subscribe middleware, then we present our CLCB algorithm in details.

4.1   Why a New Algorithm?

To support the model of interaction described in Section 2 a middleware has to perform a location and content-based filtering of incoming events against existing subscriptions, which are two complex and time consuming tasks. In principle, this can be done in three ways::

1. by encoding the location of events as part of their content (i.e., as an ad-hoc attribute) and the area of relevance of filters inside the filters themselves (i.e., as an ad-hoc constraint), using a traditional content-based matching algorithm to filter incoming events against existing subscriptions;
2. by separating the location from the content matching problem, to solve the former through an algorithm explicitly designed for spatial searching and the latter through a traditional content-based matching algorithm;
3. by combining the location and content matching steps in a single, ad-hoc algorithm.

The first approach has two limitations: (*i*) in the mobile scenario we target the area of relevance of filters changes frequently and this would require a frequent update of the location constraints, while traditional content-based matching algorithms organize subscriptions into complex data structures that make updates relatively expensive; (*ii*) the presence of a similar constraint (the one about location) on every filter reduces the efficiency of existing algorithms, which leverage

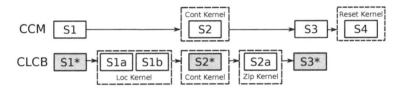

Fig. 1. The CCM and CLCB algorithms compared

the differences among filters to reduce the number of comparisons to perform. In Section 5 we will measure the actual impact of these limitations.

The second approach is the one we take as a benchmark in Section 5, showing that it is outperformed by our CLCB algorithm, which, in turn, follows the third approach. The next two sections describe how it works.

4.2   CLCB: An Overview

To perform the content-based matching part of its job, CLCB exploits a modified version of CCM, our CUDA-based matching algorithm [24]. CCM stores received subscriptions into the GPU memory, organizing the constraints that compose them into groups, based on the name of the attribute to which they apply. To process an incoming event e, CCM moves e into the GPU memory and evaluates all the constraints that apply to e. For each satisfied constraint it increments a counter[3] associated to the corresponding filter. When the counter for filter f equals the total number of constraints in f then f is satisfied and so is the subscription to which f belongs. When this happens, CCM marks the element that corresponds to the satisfied subscription into an ad-hoc bit vector that represents the result of processing. Such vector is kept in the GPU memory and copied back to the CPU memory when the processing of e finishes. To maximize the utilization of the GPU's computing elements, CCM processes all the constraints in parallel, using a different CUDA thread for each of them, and it increases the counters of filters through atomic operations.

In summary, for each incoming event e CCM performs the following steps (see top of Figure 4.2):

S1 copies e and all the data structures required for processing from the CPU to the GPU memory;

S2 uses the GPU to evaluate all the constraints that apply to the attributes of e in parallel, counting the satisfied constraints and setting the bit vector of matched subscriptions;

S3 copies the bit vector of matched subscriptions to the CPU memory.

S4 resets the bit vector of matched subscriptions and the counters of satisfied constraints associated to each filter to 0, ready for processing a new event.

A naïve approach to add location-awareness to CCM would be to add an additional step, before or after the content-based matching, where checking the

---

[3] CCM belongs to the vast category of "counting" algorithms. See Section 6.

location of event e against the area of relevance of stored filters. Unfortunately, this would not attain the best performance. Instead, we followed a different approach (see bottom of Figure 4.2), which combines location and content-based matching in a single, integrated process. In particular, we added two intermediate steps between S1 and S2. For each filter f:

S1a performs an initial content-based pre-filtering, by encoding the names of attributes in e as a Bloom filter [5] that is compared with the pre-calculated Bloom filter that encodes the names of constraints in f. This allows to efficiently[4] compare the two sets of names, discarding f if it includes constraints on attributes not present in e;

S1b checks the area of relevance of f against the location of e.

Both these steps are executed into a single CUDA kernel (named `Loc` in Figure 4.2), using a different CUDA thread to process each filter in parallel.

The presence of the two steps above allowed us to optimize the content-based matching algorithm of CCM (i.e., step S2) to immediately skip those filters whose area of relevance does not match the location of e. We also modified CCM by observing that it was designed for scenarios where a large number of filters is included into a relatively small number of subscriptions. For this reasons it encodes its results (i.e., the set of matched subscriptions) as a bit vector. On the contrary, we expect most location-aware services to have a large number of subscriptions and to select only a small portion of them while processing an event. In this scenario, encoding results as a large and sparse bit vector becomes inefficient. Accordingly, we added the following step just before S3:

S2a converts (using a CUDA kernel named `Zip` in Figure 4.2) the bit vector generated by CCM into an array of matched subscription identifiers.

This is the result that is copied back to the CPU memory at the new step S3*.

Finally, we were able to move most of the processing formerly in S4 into the Loc kernel (which implements steps S1a and S1b), reducing the total number of kernels to launch.

4.3 CLCB in Detail

Data Structures. Figure 4.3 shows the data structures used in CLCB. In particular, Figure 2(a) shows the data structures stored on the GPU memory persistently (across event processing)[5].

Vector `FPos` stores the center (x and y coordinates) of the area of relevance of each filter as two 32 bit floats (more precisely we use a `float2` CUDA type). Nearby is vector `SqDist`, which stores the square of the radius of the corresponding area of relevance. These two data structures are separated from the others to simplify location updates.

---

[4] Comparing two Bloom filters for set inclusion requires a single bit-wise *and* plus a comparison.

[5] We focus on the CLCB specific data structures, leaving aside those used by CCM. The interested reader may find a precise description of these structures in [24].

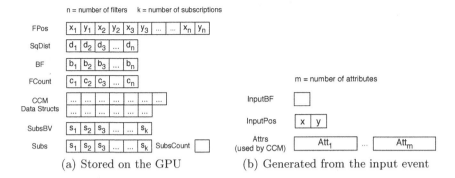

Fig. 2. Data structures of CLCB

BF is a vector of Bloom filters (as 32 bit integers), which encodes, for each filter f, the set of names of the constraints in f (see step S1a above). Notice that 32 bit may seem small for a Bloom filter, but: (i) they are enough to guarantee 10% of false positives with up to 6 constraints per filter (independently from the number of names in the workload); (ii) we use them to quickly identify those filters that have no chance to be matched, i.e., we may tolerate some false positives if this increases performance, and moving to 64 bit or more would greatly reduce performance as the bandwidth toward GPU memory is limited.

Vector **FCount** stores, for each filter f, the number of constraints currently satisfied in f (including the implicit constraint on the area of relevance). As such, it is used both during the location-based filtering step S1b and during the content-based filtering step S2.

SubsBV is the bit vector of matched subscriptions generated after the location-based and content based filtering steps S1a, S1b, and S2 take place.

Finally, vector **Subs** represents the final result of the CLCB computation (generated by step S2a). It stores the (32 bit) identifiers of the subscriptions satisfied by the event. **SubsCount** contains the number of matched subscriptions, i.e., the number of elements actually stored in **Subs**.

Notice that the internal organization of data into **FPos**, **SqDist**, **BF**, and **FCount** allows to store the relevant information regarding filters into contiguous memory regions. This allows to implement steps S1.a and S1.b (i.e., the entire **Loc** kernel) in such a way that threads with contiguous ids access contiguous memory regions: a key choice to allow the CUDA runtime to optimize memory accesses by grouping them into a reduced number of memory-wide operations.

The data structures that encode the relevant information about the event e under processing are shown in Figure 2(b). They are built by the CPU and transferred to the GPU memory for processing. In particular, **InputBF** is the Bloom filter that encodes (as a 32 bit integer) the names of e's attributes; **InputPos** is a **float2** element that represents the coordinates of the location of e. Finally, vector **Attrs** stores the attributes of e, which are used during the content-based filtering step S2.

Algorithm 1. The Loc and Zip kernels in details

```
1: function Loc
2:     id = blockId.x · blockDim.x + threadId
3:     if id ≥ n then
4:         return
5:     end if
6:     if id==0 then
7:         SubsCount = 0
8:     end if
9:     if ! includes(InputBF, BF[id]) then
10:        FCount[id] = 0
11:        return
12:    end if
13:    Pos = FPos[id]
14:    sqDistX = (InputPos.x − Pos.x) · (InputPos.x − Pos.x)
15:    sqDistY = (InputPos.y − Pos.y) · (InputPos.y − Pos.y)
16:    if sqDistX + sqDistY > SqDist[id] then
17:        FCount[id] = 0
18:    else
19:        FCount[id] = 1
20:    end if
21: end function
22:
23: function Zip
24:     id = blockId.x · blockDim.x + threadId
25:     if id ≥ k then
26:         return
27:     end if
28:     if SubsBV[id] == 1 then
29:         SubsBV[id] = 0
30:         position = atomicAdd(SubsCount, 1)
31:         Subs[position] = id
32:     end if
33: end function
```

Processing Kernels. Algorithm 1 shows the Loc and Zip kernels, while the details of the Cont kernel can be found in [24].

The Loc kernel performs steps S1a and S1b. In implementing it, we tried to stop the execution of threads as soon as possible. This increases the chances that all the threads in a warp (the minimum allocation unit for CUDA) terminate, thus freeing resources for other threads. Moreover, this also reduces the number of memory accesses performed by each thread, which often represents the main bottleneck in CUDA. In particular, each thread of the Loc kernel first computes its id and uses it to decide which filter to consider, from 0 to $n - 1$. Since each block consists of a fixed number of threads (usually 256) and threads are allocated in blocks, it is often impossible to allocate the exact number of threads required (n in our case). Accordingly we check, at Line 3, if the current thread is required, discarding useless threads immediately. Line 7 is performed by a single thread (the one with id = 0), which resets the counter of matched subscriptions SubsCount. This is a necessary step to be ready to process the new event and embedding it into this kernel reduces the number of operations that the host program issues to the GPU.

Lines 9–12 encode step S1a above. Each thread performs a preliminary content-based evaluation of the filter f for which it is responsible, by comparing the Bloom filter that encodes the set of constraint names in f (i.e., BF[id]) with the Bloom filter that encodes the set of attribute names in e (i.e., InputBF). This operation only requires to read a 32 bit element (InputBF) shared among threads (automatically cached by modern NVIDIA GPUs), while another 32 bit element for each thread must be read from the main memory (BF[id]). As already mentioned, the layout of the BF data structure and the way it is accessed by threads allows the CUDA runtime to combine the latter reads into a reduced number of memory-wide operations.

If the content-based comparison above succeeds, each thread compares the location of the input event and the area of relevance of the filter it is responsible for. This is done at Lines 13–16. If the comparison succeed the thread sets the counter of satisfied constraints of the current filter (FCount[id]) to 1. In any other case this value is reset to 0 (Lines 10 and 17). Again, this is a necessary step to be ready to process the new event and embedding it into the Loc kernel allows to eliminate kernel Reset, which was originally part of CCM (see Figure 4.2). We also notice that the introduction of kernel Loc allows to modify the CCM algorithm (kernel Cont) so that each thread there immediately checks the value of the counter for the filter it is responsible for. If it is 0 than the thread can immediately terminate as it is sure that either the Bloom filter based content check or the location-based matching did not succeed.

After the Loc and Cont kernel runs, we execute the Zip kernel, whose pseudo-code is shown in Algorithm 1. It executes one thread for each subscription. At the beginning (Line 24) every thread computes its id and immediately terminates if it exceeds the total number of subscriptions. Then, every thread checks one element of the SubsBV bit vector in parallel. If the element is set to 0, the thread can safely terminate. Otherwise, it resets the element to 0 to be ready for the next event and appends the identifier of the corresponding subscription to vector Subs. To do so, it atomically increases SubsCount using the atomicAdd function provided by the CUDA runtime. This function returns the old value of SubsCount, which the thread uses to access the Subs vector.

Reducing Memory Accesses. In the Loc kernel, each thread accesses a different element of vector FCount, setting it to 1 if the filter matches the event and to 0 in the other cases (i.e., to be ready for the next steps). In most application scenarios, we expect that only a (small) fraction of FCount needs to be set to 1, since only a small fraction of the filters is geographically close to the location of the event under processing. Accordingly, we could reduce memory accesses by reducing the number of times we have to reset the FCount elements to 0. To obtain this result we notice that each element of FCount must be a 32 bit integer for architectural reason: the Cont kernel needs to increase it using an atomicAdd operation, which is defined only for 32 bit integers. However, we expect filters to include only a small number of constraints, much less than 256, so a single byte would be enough for our purposes. Moving from these premises, we optimized the Loc and Cont kernels grouping runs by four. At run $r = 1, ..., 4$ we set to 1 the rth byte of FCount[id] if necessary, while we reset the whole 4 bytes only at the first run. This way we reset the FCount vector only once every four runs, which results in an average improvement in processing time of about 20%.

Reducing Latency. Both the operations of launching a kernel and issuing a memcopy between the CPU and the GPU memory in CUDA are asynchronous and initiated by the host CPU. A straightforward implementation could force the CPU to wait for an operation involving the GPU to finish before issuing the following one. This approach, however, pays the communication latency introduced by the PCI-Ex bus for every command sent to the GPU. To solve this issue, CLCB makes use of a *CUDA Stream*, which is a FIFO queue where the CPU can put operations to be executed sequentially on the GPU. This way we may explicitly synchronize the CPU and the GPU only once for each event processed, to make sure that the GPU has finished its processing and all the results have been copied into the main memory before the CPU accesses them. This approach enables the hardware to issue all the instructions it finds on the Stream immediately, paying the communication latency only once.

5 Evaluation

This section evaluates CLCB, comparing it with existing approaches for content-based matching and spatial indexing. We evaluate the time required to match an incoming event and the time required to update the area of relevance of a filter. Moreover, we show how the relatively small amount of memory provided by existing GPUs does not constitute a limitation for our algorithm.

Experiment Setup. To study the performance of CLCB we started from a default scenario (see Table 1) that represents a typical metropolitan situation, with 250k subscribers, each installing 10 filters. The area of relevance of filters is fixed at 0.01% of the entire area under analysis: this is equivalent to consider a circle with 76m radius in a city like Milan. Each filter contains 3 to 5 constraints and is satisfied by 0.5% of incoming events, on the average. We consider subscribers (hence the area of relevance of the filters they sent) to be uniformly distributed. Since in some scenarios this could be a non-realistic assumption, we also considered the case where subscribers are concentrated in certain areas (actually, we will show that this further increases the advantages of CLCB w.r.t. existing approaches). To compute the time required to match each event, we submitted 1000 events having 3 to 5 attributes each, and calculated the average processing time. Similarly, to compute the update time we changed the area of relevance of 1000 filters, calculating the average update time.

All tests have been run on a 64bit Linux PC with an AMD Phenom II x6 CPU running at 2.8GHz and 8GB of RAM. We used GCC 4.6 and the CUDA Toolkit 4.1. The GPU is a Nvidia GTX 460 with 1GB of RAM. We repeated each test several times with different seeds to generate subscriptions and events. For each measure, we report the average value we measured, omitting, for readability, the 95% percentile, which is always below 1% of the measured value.

Limitation of Content-Based Matching Algorithms. As already mentioned in Section 4.1, it is theoretically possible to provide a location-based service using a traditional content-based matching algorithm and encoding the area of relevance of each subscription as a special constraint. Here, we show the limitations of this approach by analyzing the performance of two state of the

Table 1. Parameters for the default scenario

Number of events	1000
Attributes per event, min-max	3-5
Number of subscriptions	250000
Content constr. per filt., min-max	3-5
Filters per subscription	10
Number of distinct names	100
Area covered by each filter	0.01%
Spatial distribution	Uniform
Selectivity of content	0.5%

Table 2. Processing and update times of content-based matching systems

	SFF	BETree
Proc. Time w/o Location	13.78 ms	1.48 ms
Proc. Time w/ Location	118.69 ms	84.09 ms
Update Time	10151 ms	n.a.

art algorithms: SFF [9] v. 1.9.5 and BETree [27]. They are among the fastest implementations of the two main classes of matching algorithms, i.e., counting algorithms and tree-based algorithms, respectively (see Section 6).

The results we collected using the parameters of our default scenario are shown in Table 2. We first consider the average time required to process a single event: in the first line we consider only content-based matching (there is no area of relevance associated to filters). In this scenario SFF requires 13.78ms to process a single events, while BETree requires 1.48ms. In the second line of Table 2, we also consider the area of interest. We observe a significant increase in processing time: SFF becoming 8.6 times slower and BETree becomes 56.8 times slower. This happens because the complexity of both the (classes of) algorithms is influenced by the number of constraints on each event attribute. For this reason, adding the location constraint (that applies to the same attribute of every event) to each filter represents a challenging scenario for these algorithms. By comparison, in the default scenario, CLCB requires 0.306ms to perform both content-based and location-based matching, providing a speedup of 389× over SFF and 275× over BETree.

The third line of Table 2 shows the average time required to update the area of relevance of a single filter. SFF builds some complex indexing structures to speedup the processing: since it was designed to work under the assumption of rare changes in the interests of subscribers, it does not provide primitives to update filters, but completely re-creates all indexes after each update. For this reason, updating the area of relevance requires more than 10s with SFF. As for BETree, we could not made this test directly, as we only had access to an executable binary that implements the BETree algorithm starting from a file that holds all the subscriptions. On the other hand, given the way BETree operates, we expect results similar to those of SFF.

Limitation of Location-Based Filtering Algorithms. Several data structures have been proposed in the literature to store and retrieve localized information. They are generally known as spatial indexing structures and the most widely adopted is R-Tree [20]. In the following we compare CLCB against R-Tree. In particular, we used the R*-Tree variant[6], known for its efficiency [3].

---

[6] We adopted the open source C++ `libspatialindex` library 1.7.0 available at `http://libspatialindex.github.com`

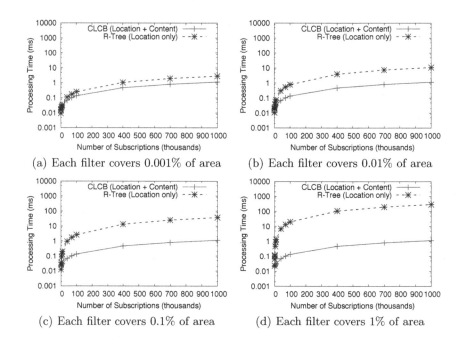

(a) Each filter covers 0.001% of area

(b) Each filter covers 0.01% of area

(c) Each filter covers 0.1% of area

(d) Each filter covers 1% of area

Fig. 3. Matching times of CLCB and R-Tree compared (uniform spatial distribution)

Since the performance of R-Tree is influenced by several parameters, we conducted some preliminary tests to determine the most convenient ones for our scenarios.

Here we compare the event matching and location update times of R-Tree and CLCB while varying (i) the percentage of area covered by each filter and (ii) the geographical distribution of filters and events. All the other parameters are defined as in our default scenario. As for the area of relevance, we consider 4 different coverage percentages: 0.001%, 0.01%, 0.1%, and 1%. In our metropolitan scenario, considering the city of Milan, this means using areas of relevance with a radius of 24m, 76m, 240m, and 759m, respectively. Considering an entire country like Italy these numbers become: 1km, 3km, 10km, and 31km, while in a small city like Pisa they become: 7m, 22m, 71m, and 225m, respectively.

Figure 3 shows the average time required by R-Tree and CLCB to process a single event when using a uniform geographical distribution for events and filters. Notice that CLCB executes both location-based and content-based matching, while R-Tree only provides location-based filtering. First, we observe that the advantage of CLCB increases with the number of subscriptions. With very small problems, R-Tree is more efficient, since CLCB pays the (almost fixed) overhead for launching the kernels and moving input data and results between the CPU and the GPU memory. However, also in these cases, the performance of CLCB and R-Tree are comparable; moreover, CLCB starts to provide better results with about 400 subscriptions (i.e., 4000 filters). Second, the area of relevance of each filter does not impact on the performance of CLCB; on the contrary, it

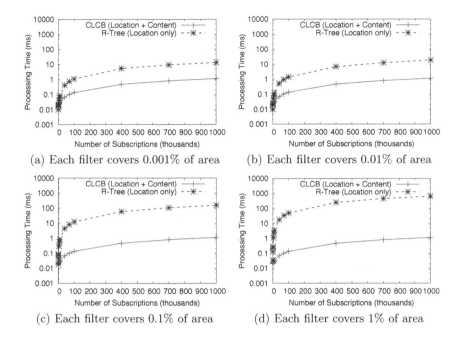

Fig. 4. Matching times of CLCB and R-Tree compared (zipf spatial distribution)

has a great influence on R-Tree, whose performance degrades when the areas of filters overlap. With 1 million subscriptions (10 millions filters), CLCB provides a speedup of 2.47× when each filter covers 0.001% of the area, and 251.7× speedup when each filter covers 1% of the area.

In most application scenarios, we expect events and filters to exhibit an uneven geographical distribution, with higher density of population concentrated around a few areas of interest. We analyze how this aspect impacts on performance in Figure 4, where we use a Zipf power law to generate the location of events and the center of the area of interest of filters. This change does not significantly impact the performance of CLCB. On the contrary, it has a great impact on the matching time of R-Tree, which increases significantly w.r.t. Figure 3. Even in the less expensive scenario in which each filter covers 0.001% of the area (Figure 4 a), it exhibits a matching time of more than 10ms with 700k subscriptions or more. With 1 million subscriptions, CLCB provides a speedup of 11.7×, 16.3×, 132.8×, and 544× with filters covering 0.001%, 0.01%, 0.1%, and 1% of the area, respectively.

Figure 5, shows the average time required to move the area of relevance of a single filter. Since our tests showed that this time is only marginally influenced by the average size of the area of relevance, both for R-Tree and CLCB, Figure 5 shows the results obtained in our default scenario (i.e., when each filter covers 0.01% of the area). Notice also that, according to some preliminary tests we made, the update time is independent from the specific changes we consider, being changes that move the area of relevance a few meters away, or changes that move it far away; and, again, this is true both for CLCB and R-Tree.

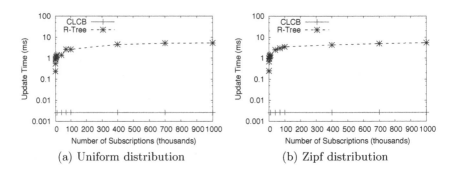

(a) Uniform distribution   (b) Zipf distribution

Fig. 5. Update times of CLCB and R-Tree compared

This means that the results we collect do not depend from the specific pattern of mobility [6] followed by clients. Accordingly we considered 1000 random changes and measured the average time to update the area of interest of filters.

Given these premises, we observe that R-Tree organizes filters into a balanced tree. Moving the area of relevance of a filter requires removing the old area of relevance and adding a new one: in some cases this operation may also require a recursive re-balancing of the tree. The case of CLCB is much simpler since each update only requires the copy of 2 float values (32 bit each) from the CPU to the GPU memory: this takes a constant time of 2.65 microseconds. On the contrary, the update time for R-Tree increases with the number of filters installed. With 1 million subscriptions, the update time is about 5.26ms: in this scenario CLCB provides a speedup of 1985× when considering a uniform distribution for the areas of relevance. By comparing Figure 5 a and b, we observe that, differently from the matching time, the update time is only marginally influenced by the geographical distribution of filters (being uniformly distributed or aggregated around certain areas).

Analysis of CLCB. To better understand the performance of CLCB, we measured the time spent in the five steps described in Section 4 (see Figure 4.2): (*i*) Copy Input, where the CPU generates the input data structures and copies them to the GPU (step S1 in figure); (*ii*) execution of the `Loc` kernel performing location-based filtering; (*iii*) execution of the `Cont` kernel performing content-based filtering; (*iv*) execution of the `Zip` kernel that stores matching subscriptions into a compact array; (*v*) Copy results, where the results are copied back from the GPU to the CPU memory (step S3 in figure).

Figure 6(a) shows the results we measured when changing the number of subscriptions, while the remaining parameters are defined as in our default scenario. First of all, we observe that the first and last steps (copy of input from the CPU to the GPU and copy of results from the GPU to the CPU) require a small amount of time (less than 0.1ms), which does not depend from the number of filters deployed in the system. Moreover, they are dominated by the cost of kernels execution, which increases with the complexity of the problem. This is a significant result: often, when porting algorithms to the GPU, the overhead required for moving information back and forth from the CPU to the GPU

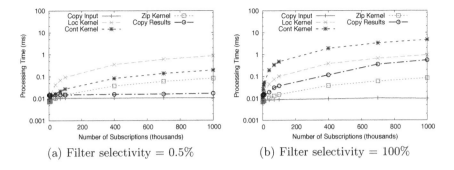

Fig. 6. Distribution of times in CLCB

memory overcomes the benefits of parallel execution. This is not the case for CLCB, which minimizes the amount of information transferred from the CPU to the GPU (only the content of the event under analysis) and from the GPU to the CPU (only the list of matched subscriptions).

To stress the system even more, we considered a second scenario, where the constraints of filters were chosen to select every event. The only form of filtering remaining depends on the location of events and the area of relevance of filters. Albeit unrealistic, this is an interesting scenario for the extreme challenges it brings to CLCB: (*i*) the content-based pre-filtering of events does not provide any advantage; (*ii*) a larger amount of subscriptions is selected and need to be transferred back to the CPU, at the end of computation; (*iii*) the Cont kernel becomes more expensive, since all constraints are satisfied and no thread can be stopped. Figure 6(b) shows the results we measured in this scenario. Interestingly, the execution time of the Loc kernel is only marginally influenced and the same happens to the Zip kernel; moreover, despite the time to copy results back to the CPU memory grows, it remains below 0.6ms even in the larger scenario with 1 million of subscriptions. In practice, the overall running time is dominated by the Cont kernel, which is the one registering the largest growth. This is an inevitable consequence of the extreme scenario. As we already verified, every content-based matching algorithm suffers when filters contain the same names of the event under processing.

Memory Consumption. Memory often represents a serious bottleneck to the scalability of GPU-based algorithms. Indeed, GPUs often host a limited amount of memory w.r.t. CPUs (up to 4GB, at most). Moreover, to increase performance, information needs to be flattened out and stored into contiguous regions, often increasing memory consumption.

Figure 7 shows the GPU memory demand of CLCB when increasing the number of filters deployed. Our reference hardware (which is a cheap card only providing 1GB of RAM) could support more than 1.3 millions subscriptions (13 millions of filters). Considering one subscription (10 filters) per user this means supporting 1.3 millions users (the entire population of a city like Milan) with a single entry-level graphic card. We can reasonably assert that memory consumption does not represent an issue for CLCB.

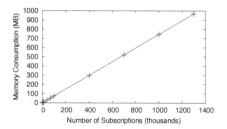

Fig. 7. Memory consumption of CLCB

As a final note, we foresee the possibility to combine CLCB with higher level partitioning algorithms to exploit multiple machines, each one covering a different geographical region.

6   Related Work

This section describes related work in the fields of publish-subscribe middleware and matching algorithms, models and algorithms for location-aware publish-subscribe, and spatial indexing structures.

Publish-Subscribe Middleware. The last decade saw the development of a large number of publish-subscribe middleware [26,2,14,25,12] first exploiting a centralized dispatcher, then moving to distributed solutions for improved scalability. A key aspect of every publish-subscribe middleware is the matching algorithm it uses to evaluate incoming events against installed subscriptions.

Two main categories of matching algorithms can be found in the literature: *counting* algorithms [16,9,24] and *tree-based* algorithms [1,7,27]. In our evaluation, we considered one algorithm for each class: SFF and BETree. SFF maintains a counter for each filter to record the number of constraints satisfied by the current event. On the contrary, tree-based algorithms, like BETree, organize subscriptions into a rooted search tree. Inner nodes represent an evaluation test; leaves represent the received subscriptions. Given an event, the search tree is traversed from the root to the leaves. At every node, the value of a single attribute is tested, and the satisfied branches are followed until the fully satisfied subscriptions are reached at the leaves. To the best of our knowledge, no existing work has demonstrated the superiority of one of the two approaches in every scenario. However, in [27] BE-Tree has been compared against many state-of-the-art matching algorithms, showing best performance in a wide range of scenarios.

Despite the efforts described above, content-based matching is still considered a time consuming task. To overcome this limitation, researchers have proposed to distribute matching among multiple brokers, exploiting covering relationships between subscriptions to reduce the amount of work performed at each node [8]. The use of a distributed dispatching infrastructure is orthogonal w.r.t. CLCB, which can be used in distributed scenarios, contributing to further improve performance. In this field, it becomes critical to efficiently propagate updates to subscriptions through the network of processing brokers. To accomplish this goal, the idea of parametric subscriptions [21] has been proposed. Again, CLCB could play a role here, as it allows to efficiently install updates at each broker.

The idea of parallel matching has been recently addressed in a few works. In [17], the authors exploit multi-core CPUs both to speedup the processing of a single event and to parallelize the processing of different events. Unfortunately, the code is not available for a comparison. Other works investigated how to parallel matching using ad-hoc (FPGA) hardware [28]. To the best of our knowledge, CCM [24] is the first matching algorithm to be implemented on GPUs, and CLCB is the first to explore GPUs for location-based publish-subscribe. Along the same line, in [13] we explored the possibility to use GPUs to support Complex Event Processing.

Location-Aware Publish-Subscribe. Location-aware publish-subscribe has been introduced as a key programming paradigm for building mobile applications [10,15]. Existing proposals mainly focused on techniques for supporting physical and logical mobility of clients in distributed publish-subscribe infrastructures [18], with little or no emphasis on the matching algorithm.

A more general model is represented by context-aware publish-subscribe, in which a generic context (not only location) is associated with each subscription [11,19]. We plan to study how to extend CLCB to efficiently support the expressiveness provided by the context-aware publish-subscribe model.

Spatial Indexing Data Structures. Spatial indexing data structures organize and store information items that have an associated location on a bi-dimensional or multidimensional space. They provide spatial access methods for extracting stored elements through spatial queries (e.g., to extract all elements contained, in a given area, that overlap a given area, etc.). The most known and widely adopted spatial indexing structure is the R-Tree [20], a variant of a B^+ tree in which each inner node stores the minimum bounding rectangle including all the areas defined in its children. The performance of an R-Tree strongly depends on the heuristics used to decide how to keep the tree balanced: the heuristics used by R*-Tree [3] (our reference) are often cited among the most effective.

A few works have been proposed that aim at parallelizing spatial indexing methods. None of them can be directly applied to the problem we target in this paper. In [29] the authors focus on parallelizing spatial join for location-aware databases. Similar results are presented in [4], where the authors discuss how several data mining techniques can be efficiently implemented on GPUs. In [23], a GPU-based implementation of R-Tree is presented: differently from our approach, parallelism is not exploited to increase the performance of a single query, but to run different queries in parallel. Finally, the work in [30] proposes a technique to speedup processing of large R-Tree structures by storing recently visited nodes on the GPU memory and re-use them for future queries. Different from our approach, the authors focus on structures that do not fit in main memory; only a portion of the computation is performed on the GPU and several interactions between the CPU and the GPU may take place while navigating the tree. A maximum speedup of 5× is achieved with this technique, which is significantly below the results provided by CLCB. More generally, none of these works is publicly available for comparison, while, to the best of our knowledge, CLCB is the first solution that combines both location-based and content-based filtering into one solution.

7 Conclusions

In this paper, we presented CLCB, a location-aware content-based matching algorithm for CUDA GPUs. CLCB is designed to enable both high-performance processing of events and low-latency update of the area of relevance associated with subscriptions. As such, it may easily be adopted as the core component of a location-aware event-based middleware infrastructure capable of supporting large scale scenarios. A comparison of CLCB with existing content-based matching algorithms and with algorithms for spatial access, shows relevant speedups both in terms of processing and update time.

Acknowledgment. We would like to thank Prof. Hans-Arno Jacobsen and Dr. Mohammad Sadoghi for giving us access to their BETree prototype and for helping us in using it during our tests. This work was partially supported by the European Commission, Programme IDEAS-ERC, Project 227977-SMScom.

References

1. Aguilera, M.K., Strom, R.E., Sturman, D.C., Astley, M., Chandra, T.D.: Matching events in a content-based subscription system. In: PODC 1999, pp. 53–61. ACM, New York (1999)
2. Baldoni, R., Virgillito, A.: Distributed event routing in publish/subscribe communication systems: a survey. Tech. rep. DIS, Università di Roma "La Sapienza" (2005)
3. Beckmann, N., Kriegel, H.P., Schneider, R., Seeger, B.: The r*-tree: an efficient and robust access method for points and rectangles. In: SIGMOD 1990, pp. 322–331. ACM, New York (1990)
4. Böhm, C., Noll, R., Plant, C., Wackersreuther, B., Zherdin, A.: Data Mining Using Graphics Processing Units. In: Hameurlain, A., Küng, J., Wagner, R. (eds.) Trans. on Large-Scale Data- & Knowl.-Cent. Syst. I. LNCS, vol. 5740, pp. 63–90. Springer, Heidelberg (2009)
5. Broder, A., Mitzenmacher, M.: Network applications of bloom filters: A survey. Internet Mathematics 1(4), 485–509 (2004)
6. Camp, T., Boleng, J., Davies, V.: A survey of mobility models for ad hoc network research. Wireless Communications and Mobile Computing 2(5), 483–502 (2002)
7. Campailla, A., Chaki, S., Clarke, E., Jha, S., Veith, H.: Efficient filtering in publish-subscribe systems using binary decision diagrams. In: ICSE 2001, pp. 443–452. IEEE Computer Society, Washington, DC (2001)
8. Carzaniga, A., Rutherford, M.J., Wolf, A.L.: A routing scheme for content-based networking. In: INFOCOM 2004, Hong Kong, China (March 2004)
9. Carzaniga, A., Wolf, A.L.: Forwarding in a content-based network. In: SIGCOMM 2003, Karlsruhe, Germany, pp. 163–174 (August 2003)
10. Cugola, G., de Cote, J.: On introducing location awareness in publish-subscribe middleware. In: 25th IEEE ICDCS Workshops, pp. 377–382 (June 2005)

11. Cugola, G., Margara, A., Migliavacca, M.: Context-aware publish-subscribe: Model, implementation, and evaluation. In: ISCC 2009, pp. 875–881 (July 2009)
12. Cugola, G., Picco, G.: REDS: A Reconfigurable Dispatching System. In: SEM 2006, pp. 9–16. ACM Press, Portland (2006)
13. Cugola, G., Margara, A.: Low latency complex event processing on parallel hardware. Journal of Parallel and Distributed Computing 72(2), 205–218 (2012)
14. Eugster, P.T., Felber, P.A., Guerraoui, R., Kermarrec, A.M.: The many faces of publish/subscribe. ACM Comput. Surv. 35, 114–131 (2003)
15. Eugster, P., Garbinato, B., Holzer, A.: Location-based publish/subscribe. In: NCA 2005, pp. 279–282 (July 2005)
16. Fabret, F., Jacobsen, H.A., Llirbat, F., Pereira, J., Ross, K.A., Shasha, D.: Filtering algorithms and implementation for very fast publish/subscribe systems. In: SIGMOD 2001, pp. 115–126. ACM, New York (2001)
17. Farroukh, A., Ferzli, E., Tajuddin, N., Jacobsen, H.A.: Parallel event processing for content-based publish/subscribe systems. In: DEBS 2009, pp. 8:1–8:4. ACM, New York (2009)
18. Fiege, L., Gartner, F., Kasten, O., Zeidler, A.: Supporting Mobility In Content-Based Publish/Subscribe Middleware. In: Endler, M., Schmidt, D.C. (eds.) Middleware 2003. LNCS, vol. 2672, pp. 998–998. Springer, Heidelberg (2003)
19. Frey, D., Roman, G.-C.: Context-Aware Publish Subscribe in Mobile Ad Hoc Networks. In: Murphy, A.L., Vitek, J. (eds.) COORDINATION 2007. LNCS, vol. 4467, pp. 37–55. Springer, Heidelberg (2007)
20. Guttman, A.: R-trees: a dynamic index structure for spatial searching. In: SIGMOD 1984, pp. 47–57. ACM, New York (1984)
21. Jayaram, K., Jayalath, C., Eugster, P.: Parametric subscriptions for content-based publish/subscribe networks. In: Gupta, I., Mascolo, C. (eds.) Middleware 2010. LNCS, vol. 6452, pp. 128–147. Springer, Heidelberg (2010)
22. Luckham, D.C.: The Power of Events: An Introduction to Complex Event Processing in Distributed Enterprise Systems. Addison-Wesley, Boston (2001)
23. Luo, L., Wong, M., Leong, L.: Parallel implementation of r-trees on the gpu. In: ASP-DAC 2012, January 30 - Febraury 2, pp. 353–358 (2012)
24. Margara, A., Cugola, G.: High performance content-based matching using gpus. In: DEBS 2011 (2011)
25. Mühl, G., Fiege, L., Gartner, F., Buchmann, A.: Evaluating advanced routing algorithms for content-based publish/subscribe systems. In: MASCOTS 2002 (2002)
26. Mühl, G., Fiege, L., Pietzuch, P.: Distributed Event-Based Systems. Springer (2006)
27. Sadoghi, M., Jacobsen, H.A.: Be-tree: an index structure to efficiently match boolean expressions over high-dimensional discrete space. In: SIGMOD 2011, pp. 637–648. ACM, New York (2011)
28. Tsoi, K.H., Papagiannis, I., Migliavacca, M., Luk, W., Pietzuch, P.: Accelerating publish/subscribe matching on reconfigurable supercomputing platforms. In: MRSC 2010, Rome, Italy (March 2010)
29. Yampaka, T., Chongstitvatana, P.: Spatial join with r-tree on graphics processing units. In: IC2IT (2012)
30. Yu, B., Kim, H., Choi, W., Kwon, D.: Parallel range query processing on r-tree with graphics processing unit. In: DASC 2011, pp. 1235–1242 (December 2011)

Enabling Efficient Placement of Virtual Infrastructures in the Cloud

Ioana Giurgiu[1], Claris Castillo[2], Asser Tantawi[2], and Malgorzata Steinder[2]

[1] Systems Group, Dept. of Computer Science, ETH Zurich
igiurgiu@inf.ethz.ch
[2] IBM T.J. Watson Research Center
{claris,tantawi,steinder}@us.ibm.com

Abstract. In the IaaS model, users have the opportunity to run their applications by creating virtualized infrastructures, from virtual machines, networks and storage volumes. However, they are still not able to optimize these infrastructures to their workloads, in order to receive guarantees of resource requirements or availability constraints. In this paper we address the problem of efficiently placing such infrastructures in large scale data centers, while considering compute and network demands, as well as availability requirements. Unlike previous techniques that focus on the networking or the compute resources allocation in a piecemeal fashion, we consider all these factors in one single solution. Our approach makes the problem tractable, while enabling the load balancing of resources. We show the effectiveness and efficiency of our approach with a rich set of workloads over extensive simulations.

Keywords: Network-aware virtual machine placement, Cloud, Performance.

1 Introduction

In enterprise data centers, infrastructure architects tailor hardware and software configuration to optimize for their workloads. To run a production application, the administrator provisions physical machines, storage, networks, middleware, and application code such that the application is resilient to hardware failures and performance bottlenecks. The Cloud changes the infrastructure provisioning model. A typical IaaS offers virtualized building blocks, such as virtual machines, storage volumes, and networks, which users of the Cloud connect together to create virtualized infrastructures for their workloads. Very little control is given to a user with respect to the layout of these virtualized building blocks on the physical infrastructure. As a result, it is impossible for the user to build a virtualized infrastructure that guarantees, for example, high communication bandwidth between virtual machines, proximity to storage, or spreading of multiple virtual machines across different racks for availability reasons. As a matter of fact, the only support for workload optimization available in today's Cloud is via prebuilt virtual infrastructures which are tuned to specific workloads. For instance, Amazon EC2 offers high performance computing (HPC) instances [1].

P. Narasimhan and P. Triantafillou (Eds.): Middleware 2012, LNCS 7662, pp. 332–353, 2012.

We believe that this cookie-cutter approach hinders further adoption and development of the technology. Instead, Cloud users should be able to design and deploy virtual infrastructures that optimize for their workload. We refer to these virtual infrastructures as Virtual Network Infrastructures (*VNI*). More specifically, a VNI is represented as a set of heterogeneous virtual machines with constraints governing the performance of these virtual machines as a whole in order to satisfy application requirements. In this work we address one crucial problem in enabling this vision. We are concerned with developing placement techniques that allow the Cloud to efficiently and effectively allocate resources that satisfy VNI constraints and Cloud level goals. We consider VNIs consisting of virtual machines with compute and network demand, as well as availability requirements.

A VNI can be represented as an attributed graph. As such, the VNI placement problem is equivalent to the problem of graph monomorphism and therefore is NP-hard [2]. The complexity of the problem arises from its combinatorial nature, thus efficiency is a major challenge. Others in the community have tackled less constrained versions of this problem [3,4,5]. The proposed approaches however, address the placement problem in a piecemeal fashion: they either focus on the aspects pertaining to network performance leaving aspects of the allocation of compute resources as a secondary objective or vice versa, or suffer from high complexity. Our approach is unique in that it tackles the problem in a comprehensive manner by factoring in network, compute and availability performance aspects into one single solution.

We have developed a novel placement framework that makes the problem tractable and is generic enough to support increasing complexity. The core of the framework is the introduction of a novel resource abstraction, called a *cold spot* from here on. A cold spot consists of a collection of compute nodes that exhibit high availability of compute resources and network connectivity. Cold spots identify subsets of resources where VNIs should be best deployed. They help reduce and guide the search space for the optimization problem. Our placement framework consists of four steps: (a) identifying cold spots, (b) clustering virtual machines to reduce overall communication traffic and reduce placement complexity, (c) identifying candidate cold spots whose features are similar to those of the VNI in order to increase the chances of deployment, and (d) performing the actual placement by using efficient graph-based search algorithms that optimize for load balancing.

The main contributions of this work can be summarized as follows:

- We develop a placement framework that breaks down the placement problem into four tractable subproblems.
- We introduce a novel resource abstraction called *cold spot* that effectively reduces the search space and improves performance.
- We present experimental results that show the efficiency and effectiveness of our approach in large data centers.

The remainder of this paper is organized as follows. We formulate the problem in Section 2. Section 3 overviews all four stages of our technique in detail, while Section 4 presents our experimental results. Finally, in Section 5 we discuss open questions and future work. Section 6 provides an overview of the current state of the art and positions our work. And, we conclude in Section 7.

2 Problem Formulation

We consider a data center which consists of a collection of physical machines (PM) that are inter-connected by a network consisting of a set of links (LK). Every PM can host one or more virtual machines (VM). A VNI comprises a set of networked and constrained VMs and is the deployable unit within the data center. The placement problem consists of mapping VMs in a given VNI to PMs in the data center. Next, we describe the physical infrastructure and VNI characterization in more detail. Table 1 summarizes the most common terms used throughout the paper.

Let $\mathcal{PM} = \{PM_i | i = 1, 2, ..., n_{PM}\}$ denote the set of physical machines in the data center. Each PM has a set of resources $\mathcal{R} = \{r_m | m = 1, 2, ..., n_R\}$, such as *CPU*, *memory*, and *disk storage*. The total capacity of resource r_m on PM_i is denoted by $rc_{i,m}$, whereas $ru_{i,m}$ represents its usage on the same PM, $ru_{i,m} \leq rc_{i,m}$. We define the amount of resource available for r_m on PM_i as $ra_{i,m} = rc_{i,m} - ru_{i,m}$. We assume that a PM is connected to a switch through an edge link, and that switches are interconnected through core links.

The network is modeled as a graph, where PMs and switches are vertices, while links are edges. We denote the set of links as $\mathcal{LK} = \{LK_k | k = 1, 2, ..., n_{LK}\}$. Each link is characterized by a communication bandwidth. The total bandwidth capacity of LK_k is denoted by bc_k, whereas bu_k represents its usage, $bu_k \leq bc_k$. The amount of available bandwidth is defined as $ba_k = bc_k - bu_k$. We characterize data center $\mathbf{D}$ by the tuple $(\mathcal{PM}, \mathcal{LK})$.

A VNI $\mathbf{P}$ is characterized by the tuple $(\mathcal{VM}, \Lambda, S)$. The set $\mathcal{VM} = \{VM_j | j = 1, 2, ..., n_{VM}\}$ represents the collection of virtual machines which constitute the

Table 1. Common terminology

Term	Description	Term	Description
r_m	Resource (e.g., CPU)	ba_k	Bandwidth available in LK_k, i.e., $bc_k - bu_k$
$rc_{i,m}$	Total capacity of resource r_m on PM_i	bu_k	Bandwidth usage of LK_k
$ru_{i,m}$	Usage of resource r_m on PM_i	bc_k	Total bandwidth capacity of LK_k
$ra_{i,m}$	Availability of resource r_m on PM_i, i.e., $rc_{i,m} - ru_{i,m}$	$rd_{j,m}$	Resource demand of VM_j on resource r_m
$\lambda_{i,j}$	Network demand between VM_i and VM_j	$n_{PM_{CS}}$	Cardinality of the set of PMs belonging to cold spot CS
$l_{i,j}$	Locality constraint between VM_i and VM_j $(\infty, -\infty)$	$path(i,j)$	Set of links on path between PM_i and PM_j
n_{VM}	Cardinality of the set of VMs belonging to a VNI	n_{PM}	Cardinality of the set of PMs in data center

VNI. VM_j is characterized by a set of resource demands $rd_{j,m}$, one per resource type in $\mathcal{R}$. These resource demands are considered when placing a specific VM onto a PM, in order to make sure that there are enough available resources on the PM to satisfy the VM demands. The communication bandwidth demand between VM_i and VM_j is denoted by $\lambda_{i,j} \geq 0$, where $1 \leq i, j \leq n_{VM}$ and $\lambda_{i,i} = 0$. We assume that the matrix $\Lambda = [\lambda_{i,j}]$ is symmetrical with zero diagonal. In other words, bandwidth requirements among VMs in a given VNI may be modeled as an undirected graph, where the vertices are VMs and the edges are pairwise communication demands.

Availability constraints are characterized as follows. We consider a data center which is partitioned into a hierarchy of availability zones, where PMs in the same zone have similar availability characteristics. As an example, a hierarchy of availability zones may be induced by the containment hierarchy of PMs, blade centers, racks, cluster and data centers. In such case, one may model this hierarchy as a tree, where the leaves are the PMs and the intermediate node represents a zone of availability. Thus, we associate an availability level, $V_l, l = 0, \cdots, L$, for a node at level l in the tree, where $l = 0$ represents the leaves, i.e., PMs, and $l = L$ represents the root of the tree with height L, i..e, highest level switch. We assume that $V_0 \leq V_1 \cdots \leq V_L$, since two PMs in distant availability zones have higher chances of having one of them available. Using this tree model, two PMs PM_i and PM_j with the lowest common ancestor at level l have $v_{i,j} = V_l$ (Clearly, $v_{i,i} = V_0$). For convenience we define $g_i(l), i = 1, \cdots, n_{PM}$ and $l = 0, \cdots, L$ as the set of PMs such that for $PM_j \in g_i(l)$ we have $v_{i,j} = V_l$. Following these observations, availability constraints can be directly mapped into locality constraints. More specifically, to represent location constraints between VMs, we define the matrix $S = [s_{i,j}^l]$, where $s_{i,j}^l$ represents the type of location constraint between VM_i and VM_j, where $1 \leq i, j \leq n_{VM}$ and $i \neq j$ and l refers to the availability zone level required by the constraint. In this paper we assume two distinct types, namely $s_{i,j}^l \in \{+\infty, -\infty\}$, corresponding to *colocation* and *anti-colocation*, respectively. To illustrate, an *anti-colocation* constraint at the PM-level ($l = 0$) between VM_i and VM_j indicates that VMs must be placed on different PMs and is associated with an infinitely large communication cost between them. Alternatively, a *colocation* constraint means that the VMs must be placed on the same PMs and is associated with a small communication cost.

We denote by $\pi(\mathbf{P}, \mathbf{D})$ a particular placement of VNI $\mathbf{P}$ in data center $\mathbf{D}$. For brevity we will write it as $\pi(\mathbf{P})$. $\pi(\mathbf{P})$ is a vector of length n_{VM}, where $\pi_j(\mathbf{P})$ is the PM onto which VM_j is placed. The placement process maps every VM in $\mathcal{VM}(\mathbf{P})$ to a particular PM in $\mathcal{PM}$, such that (a) the VM's resource demands are satisfied by the PM, (b) the bandwidth constraints between any two communicating VMs are met by the links of the data center connectivity network, (c) the pairwise location constraints are satisfied.

Placement Goals. We consider two classes of objectives in our placement technique: *system behavior objectives* (1-2) and *performance objectives* (3-5):

1. *Efficient and scalable placement* – We need to place VNIs in such a way that (a) the performance of the application is maximized (e.g., fewer hops

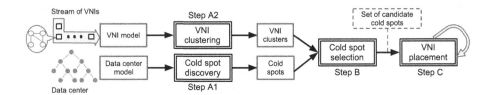

Fig. 1. VNI placement process

between communicating VMs reduces network delay), and (b) the placement
time scales with the increasing size of the data center.

2. *High VNI acceptance rate* – The placement algorithm must maximize the
   number of VNIs for which constraints are satisfied.
3. *Load balancing* – For all placed VNIs, we seek to balance allocation of all
   resources across the data center.
4. *Resource constraints* – We assume that resources are not over-committed.
   Hence, VNI resource demands must be met by the corresponding resources
   available on the data center. Formally, $\forall PM_i \in \mathcal{PM}$, $\forall r_m \in \mathcal{R}$,

$$ru_{i,m} \equiv \left[\sum_{\mathbf{p}} \sum_{VM_j \in \mathcal{VM}(\mathbf{p})} rd_{j,m} \; \mathbf{I}_{\pi_j(\mathbf{p}),PM_i} \right] \leq rc_{i,m},$$

where $\mathbf{p}$ runs over all placed VNI and $\mathbf{I}$ is the indicator function. Furthermore, $\forall LK_k \in \mathcal{LK}$,

$$bu_k \equiv \left[\sum_{\mathbf{p}} \sum_{VM_i, VM_j \in \mathcal{VM}(\mathbf{p})} \lambda_{i,j} \; \mathbf{I}_{LK_k \in path(\pi_i(\mathbf{p}), \pi_\mathbf{j}(\mathbf{p}))} \right] \leq bc_k,$$

where $path(PM_i, PM_j)$ represents the set of links along the path between
PM_i and PM_j. For simplicity, we assume that the traffic demand between
two PMs is routed through a single path in the network.

5. *Hard location constraints* – The colocation and anti-colocation constraints
   must be satisfied for all placed VNIs. As we explain later, softening con-
   straints can be easily achieved. That is, $\forall \mathbf{p}$, $\forall VM_i, VM_j \in \mathcal{VM}(\mathbf{p})$,

$$s_{i,j}^l = +\infty \;\; \Rightarrow \;\; VMj \in g_i(l), s_{i,j}^l = -\infty \;\; \Rightarrow \;\; VMj \notin g_i(l).$$

3   Placement Algorithms

Our approach to meet the constraints and performance objectives presented
earlier is to divide the placement problem into four steps as shown in Figure 1.
In this section, we discuss these steps in detail.

3.1   Cold Spot Discovery

One key component of our placement technique is the concept of *cold spot*. A cold spot is a resource construct consisting of a collection of physical computing nodes that exhibit high availability of compute resources and ample network connectivity to other PMs. In principle, any property of interest can be considered when constructing cold spots. This step is concerned with discovering such cold spots in the system and is invoked periodically and asynchronously relative to the placement request. This observation is important since performing any analysis on the data center graph is expected to be computationally intensive.

The intuition behind this stage is twofold. First, it reduces the search space when placing a VNI within the data center, which results in an overall lower placement time and hence better scalability. Second, cold spots improve resource utilization by reducing resource fragmentation. We demonstrate these benefits in Section 4. This step takes as input the data center model, its state (which includes resource allocation), as well as a dynamic parameter, called *threshold* and produces a set of cold spots. This stage is further divided into two main steps: ranking the PMs and generating a set of cold spots.

Ranking of Physical Compute Nodes. The first step ranks all the PMs in the data center based on their resources availability. We define the availability of a particular PM_i by a measure, RA_{PM_i}, which is based on the compute resources and the network bandwidth of all outgoing links, namely,

$$RA_{PM_i} = \sum_{r_m \in \mathcal{R}} w_m \, ra_{i,m} \cdot \sum_{LK_k \in links(PM_i)} ba_k,$$

where w_m is a weight which can be adjusted in order to tailor the PMs ranking relative to a specific type of resource and $links(PM_i)$ represents the set of links connected to PM_i (via NICs).

We want PMs with ample network connectivity to other PMs in the system to be ranked higher, as they have a higher potential to satisfy the needs of VNIs. To this end, we propose a heuristic that has a long-sighted view of the PMs network connectivity. That is, to compute the rank of a given PM the heuristic first identifies the PM's neighborhood as the set of PMs that are K hops away, and then computes its network connectivity to these PMs as a function of network bandwidth. K is a parameter which could be set in relation to the data center diameter or VNI size. This step generates a list of all PMs in decreasing order of their availability, computed with the heuristic NRA_{PM_i} defined as,

$$NRA_{PM_i} = \frac{\sum_{PM_j \in neighbors(PM_i, K)} \frac{RA_{PM_i} + RA_{PM_j}}{2} \, min_{LK_k \in path(PM_i, PM_j)}(ba_k)}{\mid neighbors(PM_i, K) \mid}$$

where $neighbors(PM_i, K)$ is the set of PMs that are at most K hops away from PM_i. Notice that the heuristic accounts for the minimum available bandwidth on the path between PM_i and a neighbor PM_j to characterize the network component, as well as for both PM_i's and PM_j's compute resources availability.

Cold Spots Generation. Cold spots are constructed by continuously adding PMs to already existing collections based on several heuristics. To keep track of the non-added PMs we maintain an updated list. The first entry in the list, which corresponds to the PM with the highest rank, becomes the root of the new cold spot. In order to decide whether a particular not-yet-added PM_i should be added to the new cold spot, we define the measure $Potential_{PM_i}$ as follows. Let CS denote the currently identified cold spot. We define the potential of PM_i as the weighted sum,

$$Potential_{PM_i} = (1 - w)R_i + w\sqrt{\frac{H_i^2 + B_i^2}{2}}$$

which includes three terms: R_i, H_i, and B_i. They are defined as,

$$R_i = \sum_{r_m \in \mathcal{R}} w_m \, ru_{i,m},$$

$$H_i = \frac{\sum_{PM_j \in CS} \frac{hops(PM_i,PM_j)-1}{hops(PM_i,PM_j)+1}}{n_{PM_{CS}}}, B_i = \frac{\sum_{PM_j \in CS} 1 - \frac{hops(PM_i,PM_j)}{\sum_{LK_k \in path(PM_i,PM_j)} \frac{1}{1-bu_k}}}{n_{PM_{CS}}}$$

where R_i is a measure of resource utilization of PM_i, H_i captures the distance, expressed in number of hops ($hops(PM_i, PM_j)$), between PM_i and all PMs that have been already added to the cold spot CS, and B_i the bandwidth utilization between all the links connecting PM_i to all PMs in the cold spot. Both H_i, and B_i terms are expressions of the network connectivity aspect. As such, the weight w provides better controllability of the algorithm over the characteristics of the cold spot. The complexity of the algorithm is $O((n_{PM} + n_{PM_{CS}}n_{VM}) log_{n_{VM}})$. It is important to note that our network metrics can be easily modified to accommodate for network technologies wherein the number of hops is not a metric of relevance, e.g., flat networks, by only incorporating link utilization.

PMs that have lower potential values are more desirable, thus a PM_i is included as part of CS if $Potential_{PM_i} \leq threshold$. The *threshold* is a parameter that greatly influences the features of the resulting cold spots. Fig. 2(a) provides an example of how cold spots are discovered for a data center consisting of 16 PMs, depending on the variance of the resources load on PMs and the threshold value. If the load variance on the PMs is low, then the prevailing factor for adding new PMs to a cold spot is their distance to PMs already found in the cold spot. In the opposite scenario, the cold spot discovery step groups PMs with similar characteristics of their compute loads and neighborhood qualities, even beyond the first-level switch. The algorithm is driven by the threshold value. The lower it is, the more selective the filtering (i.e., adding PMs to a cold spot) is, and vice-versa. Thus, with a threshold of 0.2 and a low load variance, the algorithm groups together PMs under the same first-level switch.

3.2   VNI Clustering

The clustering step groups the highly communicating VMs of a VNI in order to reduce traffic, while at the same time satisfying the location constraints.

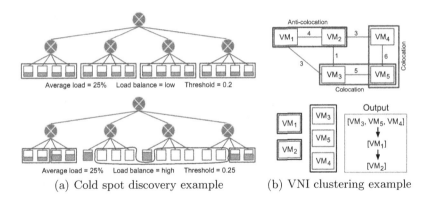

(a) Cold spot discovery example   (b) VNI clustering example

Fig. 2. Cold spot discovery and VNI clustering examples

The purpose of performing the clustering is to guide and simplify the placement, by establishing the order in which the VMs should be considered by the placement algorithm to improve network utilization–while respecting locality constraints.

Our proposed algorithm is based on stochastic flow injection [6]. Due to space constraints we omit the description of the algorithm and refer the reader to [6]. We extended this technique to also consider locality constraints between pairs of VMs as follows. Since anti-colocation and colocation constraints translate to either placing VMs separately on different PMs or placing them together, we add logical links between location-constrained VMs with ∞ or $-\infty$ weights, as expressions of communication demands. The algorithm complexity is $O(n_{LK_{CS}}n_{VM}^2)$ where LK_{CS} corresponds to the number of links in the cold spot. Notice that other clustering techniques such as K-mean clustering could have been used and extended to incorporate locality constraints.

To illustrate consider a VNI composed of 5 VMs as shown in Fig. 2(b). Assume that VM_3 has the highest average compute demand followed by VM_5, VM_1, VM_4 and VM_2. The communication links between VMs have demands expressed in Mbps (e.g., 3Mbps between VM_1 and VM_3). Additionally, we include two colocation and one anti-colocation constraints. By applying the algorithm, we generate 3 clusters of VMs, satisfying all location constraints. As expected, VM_1 and VM_2 need to be placed on different PMs, while all remaining VMs must be colocated – with these being hard requirements. The last step orders the VMs within each cluster based on their average compute demands, followed by a sorting between clusters. We can easily see that the first cluster considered in the placement step contains VM_3, VM_4 and VM_5, since VM_3 is the most demanding VM. Similarly, VM_1 precedes VM_2 at placement.

3.3 Cold Spot Selection

This step compares specific VNI features against the properties of the available cold spots and selects those cold spots that have an increased chance of allocating resources to match the VNI demands. To do this we introduce a metric $Score_{CS}$ which is used to rank all cold spots. Let us consider a VNI $\mathbf{P}$, then $Score_{CS}$ is defined as,

$$Score_{CS} = (n_{PM_{CS}} - sparsity_{\mathbf{P}}) * Avg_{CS,P} * Dev_{CS,P}.$$

We describe in detail each of the three components that make up $Score_{CS}$.

$Sparsity_{\mathbf{P}}$ provides a lower-bound in the number of PMs needed for placing $\mathbf{P}$ if all the resources in the cold spot were fully available. We omit the algorithm to compute this metric due to space constraints. Instead, we explain by example. Suppose we have a VNI $\mathbf{P}$ is composed of VM_1, VM_2, and VM_3. Also, suppose that there is an anti-colocation constraint between VM_2 and VM_3. This means that we need at least 2 PMs to place the VNI, since VM_2 and VM_3 need to be placed on different machines. A similar approach is followed for colocation constraints.

$Avg_{CS,P}$ is the average remaining availability over all n_R resources and the links. To define it, consider cold spot CS and the set of physical machines in CS as $\mathcal{PM}_{CS} = \{PM_i | i = 1, 2, ..., n_{PM_{CS}}\}$. Further, let $\mathcal{LK}_{CS} = \{LK_k | k = 1, 2, ..., n_{LK_{CS}}\}$ be the set of links in CS. Let the VNI under consideration include the set of VMs, $\mathcal{VM}_P = \{VM_j | j = 1, 2, ..., n_{VM}\}$. We define

$$rr_m = \frac{1}{n_{PM_{CS}}} \left[\sum_{i=1,2,...,n_{PM_{CS}}} ra_{i,m} - \sum_{j=1,2,...,n_{VM}} rd_{j,m} \right]$$

as the average remaining availability of resource r_m, $m = 1, 2, ..., n_R$, in CS after satisfying the resource demand of VNI, $\mathbf{P}$.

Further, we define

$$br = \frac{1}{n_{LK_{CS}}} \left[\sum_{k=1,2,...,n_{LK_{CS}}} ba_k - \sum_{i,j=1,2,...,n_{VM}; i>j} \lambda_{i,j} \right]$$

as the average remaining bandwidth over all links in the CS after satisfying the bandwidth demand of VNI, $\mathbf{P}$.

Thus, we can now define

$$Avg_{CS,P} = \frac{\sum_{m=1,2,...,n_R} rr_m + br}{n_R + 1}.$$

$Dev_{CS,P}$ is the absolute deviation in remaining resource availability, given by

$$Dev_{CS,P} = \sum_{m=1,2,...,n_R} |rr_m - Avg_{CS,P}| + |br - Avg_{CS,P}|.$$

In a nutshell, the first term of the equation evaluates whether the size of the cold spot is bigger than the sparsity of the VNI. The second term computes for each resource the difference between the average aggregate cold spot availability

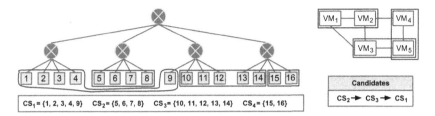

Fig. 3. Cold spot selection example for clustered VNI and a data center with 16 PMs

and the average aggregate VNI demand. Finally, the last term computes the overall variance we would obtain if the VNI was placed in the given cold spot – the smaller the variance, the better. The score needs to be positive for the cold spot to be considered a candidate and we always choose the cold spot with the minimum score value. The intuition behind the $Score_{CS}$ metric is that the cold spots whose features are most similar to those of the VNI should be ranked higher, and therefore tried first for placement. The algorithm complexity is $O(n_{PM_{CS}} \log n_{PM_{CS}})$ for each cold spot found.

Consider the scenario from Fig. 3, with the same VNI as in Fig. 2(b) and four cold spots, each having 2, 4, 5 and 5 PMs, respectively. Assume that the VNI to be placed has the sparsity value 3, given by the location constraints and the fact that the PMs capacity allows neither VM_1 or VM_2 to be placed together with the cluster VM_3, VM_4, and VM_5. Thus, the first step of the algorithm already eliminates CS_4, by comparing its size with the sparsity metric, and builds the candidates set with the remaining cold spots. Consider, in the second step, that by computing $Avg_{CS,P}$ and $Dev_{CS,P}$, all candidates obtain similar values and the metric differentiating them is the size against sparsity. Given the way we score the candidates, the cold spot with the smallest size (CS_2) is ranked first in the placement step, while the largest ones are last.

3.4 VNI Placement

The final step performs the actual VNI placement within the current cold spot, selected from the candidate list. We employ a breadth-first search algorithm, which attempts to retrieve the optimal path from the search tree based on heuristics. We describe the optimization goal later in this section. The search tree is an expression of the optimization problem of finding the optimal placement for a VNI. Its root is the starting search point (i.e., no VM placed yet), the inner nodes correspond to partial placements and leaf nodes to complete placements. The search tree is dynamically constructed at runtime by iteratively creating successor nodes linked to the current node. This is achieved by considering the possible placements for VMs sequentially, depending on how VMs are ordered as a result of the clustering step. A heuristic function, estimating the cost of the paths from the root to the current node, is used. At each step during traversal, the node with the lowest heuristic value is chosen. In what follows, we discuss our heuristic used in the search algorithm given in Algorithm 1.

Algorithm 1. VNI placement algorithm

Params: VNI $\mathbf{P} = (\mathcal{VM}, \lambda, S)$, $\mathcal{VM} = \{\text{VM}_1, ..., \text{VM}_{n_{VM}}\}$,
    $\text{CS} = \{\mathcal{PM}_{CS}, \mathcal{LK}_{CS}\}$, $\{\mathcal{PM}_{CS} = \{\text{PM}_1, ..., \text{PM}_{n_{PM_{CS}}}\}$, path

1: *Initialize* pending, placed, path, V, *and* S *to* $\emptyset$
2: *For each* VM $\in$ P, *add* VM *to* pending
3: **while** pending <> $\emptyset$ **do**
4:     $\text{VM}_{current}$ ← pending[0]
5:     **if** placed == $\emptyset$ **then**
6:         *For each* PM $\in$ CS, *add* ($\text{VM}_{current}$, PM, h) *to* S
7:         *Add* ($\text{VM}_{current}$, PM) $= min_{k \in S}\{\text{h}\}$ *to* path
8:     **else**
9:         V ← getPMsForConstraints($\text{VM}_{current}$, path)
10:         *For each* PM $\in$ V, *add* ($\text{VM}_{current}$, PM, h) *to* S
11:         *Add* ($\text{VM}_{current}$, PM) $= min_{k \in S}\{\text{h}\}$ *to* path
12:     **end if**
13:     *Remove* $\text{VM}_{current}$ *from* pending
14:     *Add* $\text{VM}_{current}$ *to* placed
15: **end while**

Our cost heuristic is an expression of the *resource fragmentation* in the cold spot caused by the partial placement decisions, from the root to the current node in the search tree. Since the algorithm always advances on the path with minimum cost, i.e., minimizing resource fragmentation, our heuristic is effectively seeking at balancing the cold spot resources utilization. Thus, for cold spot CS, we introduce the cold spot fragmentation measure denoted by h_{CS}, which includes contributions due to (1) *network fragmentation*, expressed as the number of *isolated regions*, and (2) *resource imbalance*, expressed as the deviation of utilized CPU, disk storage, and memory resources within the cold spot. We define an *isolated region* as a set of PMs that share a link whose utilization is higher than 90% when communicating to the rest of the network starting from the first level switch. To illustrate, all the PMs contained in a bladecenter whose link connecting to the rack-level switch is 92% utilized would comprise an isolated region. Let $N_{isolatedregions}$ be the number of isolated regions in CS. In order to compute its value, we implemented a recursive algorithm that we omit due to space limitation. As described earlier, the cold spot CS consists of the set of physical machines $\mathcal{PM}_{CS} = \{PM_i | i = 1, 2, ..., n_{PM_{CS}}\}$. We define, $ra_m = \frac{1}{n_{PM_{CS}}} \sum_{i=1,2,...,n_{PM_{CS}}} ra_{i,m}$, as the average availability of resource $r_m, m = 1, 2, ..., n_R$, in CS. Further, we define

$$Avg_{CS} = \frac{1}{n_R} \sum_{m=1,2,...,n_R} ra_m \text{ and } Dev_{CS} = \sum_{m=1,2,...,n_R} | ra_m - Avg_{CS} |,$$

as the average availability over all n_R resources in CS and the absolute deviation in resource availability, respectively.

We denote the cold spot fragmentation measure as

$$h_{CS} = \frac{N_{isolatedregions} * Dev_{CS}/n_R}{Avail_{CS}},$$

where $Avail_{CS}$ denotes the overall availability of CS and is given by

$$Avail_{CS} = \frac{\sum_{i,j=1,2,\ldots,n_{PM_{CS}};\, i>j} \frac{(ra_{PM_i}+ra_{PM_j})}{2} * min_{k\in path(PM_i,PM_j)}\, ba_k}{n_{PM_{CS}}\,(n_{PM_{CS}} - 1)},$$

where

$$ra_{PM_i} = \frac{1}{n_R} \sum_{m=1,2,\ldots,n_R} ra_{i,m}.$$

The algorithm complexity is $O(n_{PM_{CS}} + n_{VM}{}^2)$. In order to speedup the VNI placement, we consider a simple, but effective variant based on beam search. Instead of accounting for all valid PMs for the current VM (i.e., by satisfying the location constraints relative to VMs already placed), only a reduced number of PMs are processed. Given the previously placed VMs, for the current VM we consider those PMs that are closest, in number of hops, to all the PMs already allocated. Only if, by computing the heuristic, none of the closest PMs have the necessary resources for the current VM, we expand the search by including the PMs that have not been considered in the first step. In most cases, the solution found by applying beam search will be suboptimal, but significantly faster.

4 Evaluation

In this section we present simulation results to demonstrate the performance of our VNI placement technique. We use the method of batch means to estimate the performance parameters we consider (and which we discuss shortly), with each batch consisting of 15 runs. For every run, the following methodology is used. We start with an empty data center and sequentially place VNIs until its average compute load – as mean over CPU, memory, and disk storage utilization– reaches 25%, 50% and 75%. Next, we remove random placed VNIs and add new ones with an exponential distribution, such that the average compute load remains stable around the respective targeted values. Each experiment is run such that 50% of the initially placed VNIs are replaced by new VNIs and we collect the performance metrics periodically. Our simulator is written in Java and the experiments were performed on a ThinkPad T520, with 4GB RAM and Intel Core i3-2350m processor, running Ubuntu 11.04.

We consider three types of performance metrics which capture the perspective of the *VNI*, *user* and the *system*. The average path length per placed VNI represents the VNI metric and captures the distance in number of hops between VMs belonging to the same VNI instance. We consider three user metrics: (1) placement time, which represents the time it takes to solve the placement problem, (2) number of attempts, which captures the average number of attempts or cold spots considered until successfully placing a VNI, and (3) drop rate, which is a ratio of the number of rejected VNIs over the total number of offered VNIs. Finally, the system metrics include the (1) average network utilization, (2) average network congestion, defined as the mean over most congested links per placed VNI, (3) network variance, and (4) compute resources variance.

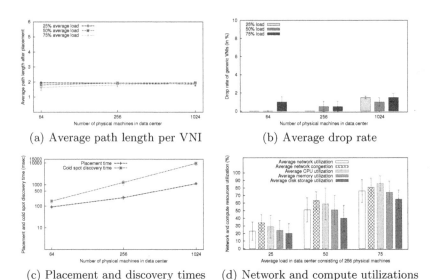

(a) Average path length per VNI   (b) Average drop rate

(c) Placement and discovery times   (d) Network and compute utilizations

Fig. 4. Results for the generic VNI workload with various data center sizes

Tree networks are widely adopted in data centers due to their cost-effectiveness and simplicity. Therefore, we consider a data center consisting of a three level tree structure. Following a bottom-top order it can be described as follows: the first level consists of PMs, the second level consists of bladecenters – with each bladecenter containing 16 PMs, the third level consists of racks – with each rack containing 4 bladecenters. We vary the number of racks to produce data centers of different capacities, where by capacity we refer to the size of the data center in number of PMs. We consider three data center sizes: 64, 256, and 1024 PMs. Each PM has 32 cores, 64GB RAM, and 4TB storage capacities, while each network link has 1Gbps capacity. Additionally, between any two PMs there exists a unique path in the data center. Following, the data center diameter (i.e., maximum number of hops between any two PMs) is 4 for 64 PMs, 6 for 256 PMs, and 8 for 1024 PMs. Note that our technique is applicable to any network topology.

We consider a rich set of workloads. We first evaluate our technique against a generic VNI mix in Section 4.1 and show the impact that each placement stage has on the performance of our approach. Second, we consider a more realistic workload mix consisting of cache, hadoop, and three-tiered like VNIs as described in Section 4.3. Finally, we report on the impact that the threshold value has on the cold spot discovery step (Section 4.4) and compare our approach to a technique proposed for virtual network embedding [7] in Section 4.5.

4.1   Generic VNI Mix

We consider three types of VNIs: small, large, and extra-large consisting of small, large, and extra-large VM instances, respectively. The resource demands of the VMs follow the specifications of Amazon EC2 instances [8]. That is, their respective resource demands are: (1 core, 1.7GB memory, 160GB storage), (4 cores,

7.5GB memory, 850 GB storage), and (8 cores, 15GB memory, 1690 GB storage). A generic mix is composed of 60% small VNIs, 25% large VNIs, and 15% extra-large VNIs. The number of VMs per VNI is between 2 and 10 following a uniform distribution. For every pair of VMs, we create network demand and locality constraints with probability 0.5 and 0.1, respectively, with the ratio of colocation to anti-colocation constraints being 0.5. The network demands between small, large, and extra-large pairs of VMs are 5, 20, and 50Mbps, respectively.

Results are shown in Fig. 4. As it can be observed, the average path length for placed VNIs remains stable at a value of 2 hops and is independent of the data center diameter, thus demonstrating the scalable nature of our approach. This is due to the fact that cold spots enable keeping network traffic under the first-level switch, hence reducing network traffic across higher-level switches. We also note that the average number of attempts to place a VNI varies between 1 and 2, which demonstrates that our selection techniques is effective at ranking cold spots as a function of how their features compare to the offered VNI.

Fig. 4(b) depicts a low drop rate of less than 2%. More specifically, for the 64-PM, 256-PM, and 1025-PM data center, (62, 118, and 184), (239, 468, and 723), and (977, 1858, and 2820) VNIs are offered in total, respectively for the 25%, 50%, and 75% loads. As expected, we observe in Fig. 4(c) that the placement time increases linearly with the size of the data center, going from 90 ms for 64 PMs to 1100 ms for 1024 PMs. Similarly, the cold spot discovery time increases as the data center becomes larger, from $\approx$170 ms for 64 PMs, to $\approx$1255 ms for 256 PMs, and to $\approx$9590 ms for 1024 PMs. However, recall that this time is amortized since the cold spot discovery step is executed asynchronously to VNI placement calls.

Fig. 4(d) considers the 256-PM data center and shows the average compute and network utilizations, as well as their corresponding variances, as measures of resource load balancing. Note that Amazon EC2 instances are CPU intensive, therefore the CPU load for all three loads (i.e., 25%, 50%, 75%) is slightly higher than memory and disk storage. To characterize the data center network, we measure the average utilization and the average congestion. The network utilization has similar values as the compute one and its deviation is less than 16%. As expected, the network congestion is higher than the utilization, since for every placed VNI it accounts only for the most congested link on the path between the corresponding PMs. We observe that the maximum network congestion VNIs experience is 81% corresponding to a load of 75%.

4.2   Breaking Down the Placement Technique

In this section we investigate the impact that each individual placement step has on the overall performance. To do this we repeat the experiments with each individual step disabled or modified as described below.

VNI Clustering. First, we repeat the experiment for the 256 PMs data center with the VNI clustering step disabled. As it can be observed in Fig. 5(a), without clustering the network utilization and congestion increases by 10–25% and 10–30%, respectively. Furthermore, the variance in the links utilization is higher by up to 60% for lower data center loads, while the congestion variance is higher

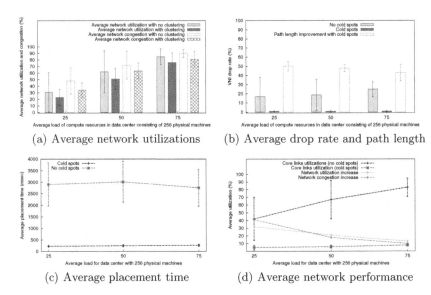

(a) Average network utilizations   (b) Average drop rate and path length

(c) Average placement time   (d) Average network performance

Fig. 5. Network performance with vs. without VNI clustering (a) and cold spot vs. data center level (b-d) in a 256-PM data center

by up to 45%. We conclude that the clustering step is effective at ensuring that highly-communicating VMs are placed in close proximity, which, as a result, improves network utilization and load balancing.

Cold Spot Discovery. Next, we compare our previous results for the generic VNI workload mix with those obtained when disabling the cold spot discovery step. That is, for every incoming VNI, the placement considers all the PMs in the data center for placement. We plot the results in Fig. 5(b)– 5(d). We observe that without cold spots the average path length for placed VNIs increases by a factor of 2. That is, VMs belonging to the same VNI are placed further apart from each other, thus impacting the traffic in the core links. In fact, we observe the core links utilization increases up to 10x factor. As a consequence, the drop rate increases from less than 2% to up to 25%. This is due to the fact that as core links become congested, the network becomes fragmented and it is more difficult to find a feasible placement for incoming VNIs. A secondary effect is observed in the increased average network utilization and congestion by up to 40% for lower loads of the data center. Finally, given that to place a VNI the algorithm considers all the PMs in the data center, the placement time increases by 10–12x factor as shown in Fig. 5(c).

Random Cold Spot Selection. Further, we are interested in assessing our cold spot selection technique. To do this we consider a selection algorithm wherein cold spots are selected in a random fashion. Fig. 6 shows the average placement attempts and variance of compute resources. As observed, randomly selecting cold spots increases the number of attempts required for successful placements by a factor of 1.5–2x. In addition, the compute resources variance is higher by 15%

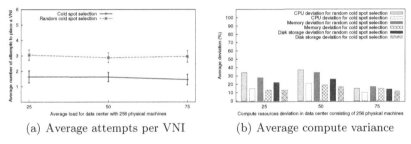

(a) Average attempts per VNI   (b) Average compute variance

Fig. 6. Random cold spot selection vs. our default algorithm in a 256-PM data center

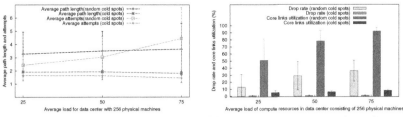

(a) Path length and attempts per VNI (b) Drop rate and core links utilization

Fig. 7. Comparison between random cold spots and our default algorithm on 256 PMs

to 55%, with the more significant impact for lower data center loads. Similarly, the network utilization and congestion are also increased by up to 40% and 15%, respectively. We conclude that the cold spot selection step intelligently chooses the best candidate cold spots for each VNI, to achieve better load balancing and VNI performance in the data center.

Random Cold Spot Discovery. Finally, we evaluate how our cold spot discovery technique influences the performance of our placement technique (Fig. 7). We consider a cold spot discovery algorithm wherein PMs are randomly added to cold spots, as opposed to being added based on their rankings. In this algorithm, the size of the randomly generated cold spots corresponds to the average observed in our previous experiments which is 16. This step is invoked every 20 new incoming VNIs. As expected, the average path length of the placed VNIs increases to 3–4 hops and in some cases even reaches the data center diameter. We also observe an increase in the average number of attempts to place VNIs. Given the random locality in the data center of the VMs within one cold spot, many VNI placements impose demands on the core links. As such, we notice an increase to up to 90% utilization, as opposed to utilizations under 10% with our technique. An important effect of the core links congestion is the increased drop rate, to up to 36% of the total number of offered VNIs.

4.3   Placing Cache, Hadoop, and Three-Tiered VNIs

The second part of the evaluation considers realistic workloads, composed of cache, hadoop, and three-tiered VNIs, and measures the effectiveness of our

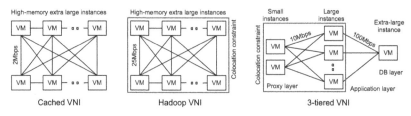

Fig. 8. Topologies for the cache, hadoop, and three-tiered VNIs

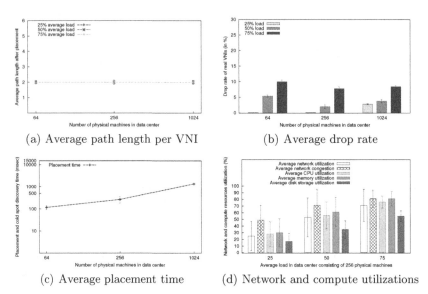

(a) Average path length per VNI

(b) Average drop rate

(c) Average placement time

(d) Network and compute utilizations

Fig. 9. Results for mix VNI workload with various data center sizes

placement technique for the performance metrics considered in the previous section. Fig. 8 shows the topologies corresponding to these specific VNIs.

Note that cache and hadoop VNIs have identical topologies, where all VMs communicate in a full mesh model and their number varies between 6 and 12. The compute demands match the specifications of Amazon EC2's high-memory extra large instances (6.5 cores, 17.1GB memory, 420GB storage). The network demands are 2Mbps and 25Mbps for the cache and hadoop VNIs, respectively. Whereas, the cache VNI has no location constraints, the VMs of hadoop VNIs need to be placed on PMs located under the same first-level switch (bladecenter). The three-tiered VNIs contain a proxy layer with 2 small EC2-like instances, an application layer, consisting of 5 to 10 large EC2-like instances, and the database layer with 1 extra-large EC2-like instance. The network connectivity between layers is full mesh, with 10Mbps demand for proxies and 100 Mbps for the database instance. The location constraints apply to the VMs belonging to the application and proxy layers, such that they need to be placed on PMs located under the same first-level switch.

Fig. 9 reports the results obtained when placing a mix of realistic VNIs, where 50% are three-tiered, 25% are cache and the remaining 25% are hadoop.

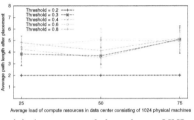
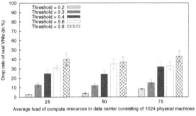

(a) Average path length per VNI   (b) Average drop rate

Fig. 10. Results with different threshold values in a 1024-PM data center

We observe that the average path length per placed VNI is 2 and remains independent of the data center diameter. It is also noticeable that the network constrained nature of the cache and hadoop VNIs results in higher drop rate of up to 8% when the average load in the data center is 75% and longer placement time by at most 20% as compared to placing generic VNIs. This results in an increase in the number of attempts to place a VNI to an average between 2 and 3.2. In Fig. 9(d) we note that the average memory load is higher than both CPU and disk storage. This effect is due to the higher memory footprint of both cache and hadoop VNIs. We also observe that network congestion increases by up to 30% for lower loads as compared to when generic VNIs are used due to the higher network demand of the VNIs.

4.4 Cold Spot Discovery Threshold

Next, we investigate how the threshold used in the cold spot discovery step influences the properties of the cold spots and the effectiveness of our technique. To do this we run our simulation with the mix of realistic workloads on a 1024 PMs size data center for various threshold values. Selective results are shown in Fig. 10. We notice an increase in average path length per VNI placed as the threshold increases. Over extensive experiments, we found that a value of 0.2 results in cold spots that are balanced and PMs are closely located. With other values, one can easily generate cold spots that are either too small in size, and thus not suitable for the offered VNIs, or too large, and thus making the placement process less effective. As a result, the drop rate increases with higher thresholds, reaching 43% in some cases. This follows intuition since VMs are located further from each other, which means core links quickly become congested. We conclude that choosing different thresholds can impact the performance of our technique. In Section 5 we discuss this aspect further.

4.5 Comparison to VNM

Finally, we want to compare our approach with previous techniques. The closest work to ours is a virtual network mapping (VNM) technique previously proposed in [7]. In [7], the authors recognize the need to consider both physical node and links optimizations together throughout the placement process. Additionally, the algorithm controls the network allocation (routing) and therefore

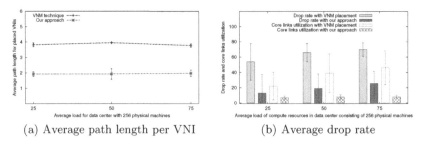

(a) Average path length per VNI   (b) Average drop rate

Fig. 11. Comparison between our approach and the VNM technique proposed in [7]

has more flexibility at finding a feasible placement. The algorithm in [7] finds a cluster of physical nodes that are lightly loaded without considering the network connectivity of the physical nodes and solves the routing problem of connecting physical nodes based on the topology of the virtual network. To match the authors' assumption that one physical node can only allocate resources for one virtual node, we apply our placement technique on generic VNIs whose VMs and links require at least 50% of a PM's compute resources and bandwidth capacity. We note that this is an unrealistic assumption since in practice, VM to PM densities as high as 100 VMs per PMs are the norm in cloud environments. However, it allows us to perform a more fair comparison between both techniques.

Our results for a 256-PM data center are presented in Fig. 11. As expected, satisfying the compute constraint of 50% demand imposes additional difficulty on our algorithm, which results in an increased drop rate to up to 25%. However, since the VNM technique does not consider the ample network connectivity of physical nodes, the resources chosen do not properly match the nature of VNIs. Consequently, the drop rate increases to up to 70% and the core links utilization increases as the average load of the data center increases. Similarly, the average path length per placed VNI is higher by a 2x factor. We conclude that considering locality and neighborhood quality in the cold spot discovery are primary factors for resource allocation in data centers.

5   Discussion

In this section, we briefly address some additional considerations towards a more complete VNI placement framework to be considered as future work.

VNI-Aware Dynamic Cold Spot Discovery: We have shown that constructing cold spots based on network and compute resource availability suffices to achieve good placement performance for workloads with compute, network, and availability constraints. As workloads become more complex, the process of cold spot discovery needs to be extended to address workloads characteristics, e.g., proximity to specific storage devices. We favor an online approach wherein via learning mechanisms the cold spot discovery process is tuned to identify cold spots whose properties are aligned with the incoming workload.

Integration into a Real System: Our technique is model driven, therefore to adopt it in a real environment one requires to build a model of the data center and the workloads. This is a simple software engineering task. In fact, significant part of the placement technique presented in this paper has been deployed in a data center environment.

Optimizations: First, we foresee being able to merge and split cold spots in order to produce cold spots with specific characteristics for different workloads. Second, when VNIs are destroyed, we do not keep track of their placement scheme. This could be used to improve the placement efficiency of future VNIs. Third, the placement algorithm could be improved by using A* algorithms so that partial placement decisions are based on estimations of the final resource fragmentation. This enhancement has the potential of pruning paths in the search space even further and achieve better placement outcomes.

6   Related Work

Following we present a comparative analysis of similar research problems, as well as simpler versions of the VNI placement problem.

Virtual Network Placement. The VNI placement problem shares similarities with the Virtual Network Mapping (VNM) problem which plays a central role in building a virtual network (VN). During the mapping process each virtual node (link, respectively) is assigned to a node (path, respectively) of the physical network such that a set of resource constraints is satisfied. In the VNI problem however, we are concerned with a broader and finer-grained set of constraints in addition to network and compute resources. Several efficient heuristics have been developed to solve the VNM problem in the past [9,10,11,12]. Some of these restrict the search space by assuming the node place is given in advance and only solve the link embedding problem [12]. Others [11] rely on probabilistic meta-heuristics such as simulated annealing and reduce complexity by type-casting the virtual routers and physical nodes. In [10] the authors reduce complexity by decomposing the network substrate and the virtual networks into known topologies and assume that a substrate node can only host one virtual node. Others such as [9] only focuses on the network aspects of the problem.

Topology-Aware Task Mapping. The problem of placing task graphs in parallel computers is also similar to our problem. Tasks nodes must be placed on processors nodes while respecting the network communication constraints and the resource constraints of the processors. In the task graph placement problem however, compute resources are specified coarsely. Therefore, existing solutions focus on maximizing communication throughput. Typically, task-mapping algorithms consist of two stages: partitioning and mapping. In the partitioning stage, a *clustering* process groups together task nodes with high communication requirements. In our technique we have adopted and extended an existing clustering technique used in [6] for task graphs to cluster virtual machines. In [13] the authors present a topology-aware placement technique that considers the topology of the processor network when making placement decisions. Note that both works focus on the network aspects of the problem.

Network-Aware Virtual Machine Placement. In [5] the authors formulate the network aware virtual machine placement problem as an optimization problem and prove its hardness. The heuristic proposed assumes a homogeneous *slot* resource model, thus each physical machine can allocate a fix number of virtual machines and is only concerned with network and compute resources. Furthermore, its complexity is $O(n^2)$ where n is the number of physical machines. Our technique, in contrast, addresses the exploding combinatorial nature of the problem by identifying *cold spots* in advance and thus achieving better performance. In [4] a novel cloud network platform is proposed which extends the provisioning model of the Cloud to include a rich set of network services. In CloudNaas the placement of virtual machines and network demand is fully decoupled, i.e., a bin-packing technique is used to decide on the allocation of compute resources, while a separate technique is used to handle the allocation of network demand. This approach leads to resource fragmentation since compute and network resources can be unevenly utilized. We advocate for a more coupled approach that considers the management of both network and compute resource into one single integrated solution. Finally, in [3] the authors propose using a placement engine based on an optimization solver to orchestrate multiple resources. This solver can take up to 6.1 seconds to load balance 1000VMs on a 15 PMs Cloud when only compute resources are considered. This is another evidence of the scalability challenge faced in provisioning resources in the Cloud. Note that we target solving the initial placement problem in sub-seconds on much larger systems.

7   Conclusions

We have considered the problem of placing virtual infrastructures with compute, network, and availability constraints in the Cloud. Unlike previous approaches, that address the placement problem from either the network or computer resources perspective, our approach factors in both in one integrated solution. We have developed a novel placement framework which makes the problem tractable and is generic enough to support increasing complexity. The center of our technique lies in the introduction of *cold spots*, defined as resource constructs that reduce the combinatorial complexity of the problem, while enabling the load balancing of resources. We have shown the effectiveness and efficiency of our approach with a rich set of workloads over extensive simulations.

References

1. Amazon: HPC Applications (2012), http://aws.amazon.com/hpc-applications/
2. Bengoetxea, E.: Inexact graph matching using estimation distribution algorithms. Ecole Nationale Supérieure des Télécommunications, Paris (2002)
3. Liu, C., Loo, B.T., Mao, Y.: Declarative automated cloud resource orchestration. In: Proceedings of SOCC 2011, pp. 1–8. ACM (2011)
4. Benson, T., Akella, A., Shaikh, A., Sahu, S.: CloudNaaS: a cloud networking platform for enterprise applications. In: Proceedings of SOCC 2011, pp. 1–13 (2011)

5. Meng, X., Pappas, V., Zhang, L.: Improving the scalability of data center networks with traffic-aware virtual machine placement. In: Proceedings of the 29th IEEE Conference on Computer Communications (INFOCOM 2010), pp. 1–9. IEEE (2010)
6. Taura, K., Chien, A.: A heuristic algorithm for mapping communicating tasks on heterogeneous resources. In: Proceedings of HCW 2000, pp. 102–115 (2000)
7. Zhu, Y., Ammar, M.: Algorithms for assigning substrate network resources to virtual network components. In: Proceedings of INFOCOM 2006, pp. 1–12 (2006)
8. Amazon: EC2 instances (2012), http://aws.amazon.com/ec2/instance-types/
9. Yu, M., Yi, Y., Rexford, J., Chiang, M.: Rethinking virtual network embedding: substrate support for path splitting and migration. SIGCOMM Computing Communications Review, 17–29 (2008)
10. Zhu, X., Santos, C., Beyer, D., Ward, J., Singhal, S.: Automated application component placement in data centers using mathematical programming. International Journal of Network Management 18, 467–483 (2008)
11. Ricci, R., Alfeld, C., Lepreau, J.: A solver for the network testbed mapping problem. SIGCOMM Computing Communications Review 33, 65–81 (2003)
12. Szeto, W., Iraqi, Y., Boutaba, R.: A multi-commodity flow based approach to virtual network resource allocation. In: Proceedings of GLOBECOM 2003 (2003)
13. Agarwal, T., Sharma, A., Laxmikant, A., Kale, L.: Topology-aware task mapping for reducing communication contention on large parallel machines. In: Proceedings of IPDPS 2006 (2006)

A Scalable Inline Cluster Deduplication Framework for Big Data Protection

Yinjin Fu[1,2], Hong Jiang[2], and Nong Xiao[1,*]

[1] State Key Laboratory of High Performance Computing,
National University of Defense Technology, China
[2] Department of Computer Science and Engineering, University of Nebraska-Lincoln, USA
yinjinfu@gmail.com, jiang@cse.unl.edu, nongxiao@nudt.edu.cn

Abstract. Cluster deduplication has become a widely deployed technology in data protection services for Big Data to satisfy the requirements of service level agreement (SLA). However, it remains a great challenge for cluster deduplication to strike a sensible tradeoff between the conflicting goals of scalable deduplication throughput and high duplicate elimination ratio in cluster systems with low-end individual secondary storage nodes. We propose Σ-Dedupe, a scalable inline cluster deduplication framework, as a middleware deployable in cloud data centers, to meet this challenge by exploiting data similarity and locality to optimize cluster deduplication in inter-node and intra-node scenarios, respectively. Governed by a similarity-based stateful data routing scheme, Σ-Dedupe assigns similar data to the same backup server at the super-chunk granularity using a handprinting technique to maintain high cluster-deduplication efficiency without cross-node deduplication, and balances the workload of servers from backup clients. Meanwhile, Σ-Dedupe builds a similarity index over the traditional locality-preserved caching design to alleviate the chunk index-lookup bottleneck in each node. Extensive evaluation of our Σ-Dedupe prototype against state-of-the-art schemes, driven by real-world datasets, demonstrates that Σ-Dedupe achieves a cluster-wide duplicate elimination ratio almost as high as the high-overhead and poorly scalable traditional stateful routing scheme but at an overhead only slightly higher than that of the scalable but low duplicate-elimination-ratio stateless routing approaches.

Keywords: Big Data protection, cluster deduplication, data routing, super-chunk, handprinting, similarity index, load balance.

1 Introduction

The explosive growth of data in volume and complexity in our digital universe is occurring at a record rate [1]. Enterprises are awash in digital data, easily amassing petabytes and even exabytes of information, and the risk of data loss escalates due to the growing complexity of data management in Big Data. No matter how the data is lost, it is costly for an enterprise [2]. One of the best protection strategies against threats is to backup data locally or remotely. The frequency, type and retention of

---

* Corresponding author.

P. Narasimhan and P. Triantafillou (Eds.): Middleware 2012, LNCS 7662, pp. 354–373, 2012.

backups vary for different kinds of data, but it is common for the secondary storage in enterprises to hold tens of times more data than the primary storage, and more data stored and moved for disaster recovery. The sprawling of backup storage systems not only consumes more data storage space, power and cooling in data centers, it also adds significant administration time and increases operational complexity and risk of human error. Meanwhile, to satisfy the high velocity requirements in modern storage systems, memory becomes the new disk, and disk becomes the new tape. Managing the data deluge under the changes in storage media to meet the SLA requirements becomes an increasingly critical challenge for Big Data protection.

Data deduplication, a specialized data reduction technique widely deployed in disk-based backup systems, partitions large data objects into smaller parts, called chunks, and represents and replaces these chunks by their hash fingerprints for the purpose of improving communication and storage efficiency by eliminating data redundancy in various application datasets. IDC data shows that nearly 75% of our digital world is a copy [4], while ESG points out that over 90% data is duplicated in backup datasets [5]. To satisfy scalable capacity and performance requirements in Big Data protection, cluster deduplication [6,7,8,9,11,12] has been proposed to provide high deduplication throughput in massive backup data. It includes inter-node data assignment from backup clients to multiple deduplication nodes by a data routing scheme, and independent intra-node redundancy suppression in individual nodes. Unfortunately, cluster deduplication at large scales faces challenges in both inter-node and intra-node scenarios. For the inter-node scenario, there is a challenge called *deduplication node information island*, which means that deduplication is only performed within individual servers due to overhead considerations, and leaves cross-node redundancy untouched. Thus, data routing becomes a key issue in cluster deduplication to concentrate data redundancy within individual nodes, reduce cross-node redundancy and balance load. For the intra-node scenario, it suffers from *the disk chunk index lookup bottleneck*. That is, the chunk index of a large dataset, which maps chunk fingerprint to where that chunk is stored on disk in order to identify the replicated data, is generally too big to fit into the limited memory of a deduplication server and causes the parallel deduplication performance of multiple data streams from backup clients to degrade significantly due to the frequent and random disk I/Os to look up the chunk index.

There are several existing solutions that aim to tackle these two challenges of cluster deduplication by exploiting data similarity or locality. Locality based approaches, such as the stateless routing and stateful routing schemes [6], exploit locality in backup data streams to optimize cluster deduplication. These schemes distribute data across deduplication servers at coarse granularity to achieve scalable deduplication throughput across the nodes, while suppress redundant data at fine granularity in individual servers for high duplicate elimination ratio in each node. However, to achieve high cluster deduplication effectiveness, it requires very high communication overhead to route similar data to the same node. Similarity based methods leverage data similarity to distribute data among deduplication nodes and reduce RAM usage in individual nodes [8]. These methods can easily find the node with highest similarity by extracting similarity features in the backup data streams, while they often fail to obtain high deduplication effectiveness in individual deduplication servers. A more recent study, called SiLo [18], exploits both locality and similarity in backup streams to achieve a near-exact deduplication but at a RAM cost that is much lower than locality-only or similarity-only based methods. However, it only addresses the intra-node challenge of single deduplication server. Inspired by SiLo, we aim to exploit data similarity and locality to strike a sensible tradeoff between the goals of high deduplication effectiveness and high performance scalability for cluster deduplication.

In this paper, we propose Σ-Dedupe, a scalable source inline cluster deduplication framework, as a middleware deployable in data centers and cloud storage environments, to support Big Data protection. The main idea behind Σ-Dedupe is to optimize cluster deduplication by exploiting data similarity and locality in backup data streams. To capture and maintain data locality in individual deduplication server, we adopt the notion of super-chunk [6], which represents consecutive smaller chunks of data, as a unit for assigning data to nodes. We extract the super-chunk feature by using handprinting technique, a new application of deterministic sampling, to detect resemblance among super-chunks. According to the super-chunk handprint, we design a similarity based stateful data routing algorithm to route each super-chunk to a target node with highest discounted resemblance by storage usage. After the target node selection, all the fingerprints of those chunks belonging to the super-chunk are sent to the target node to determine whether these chunks are duplicate or unique. Finally, the backup client only needs to send the unique chunks of the super-chunk to the target node. To reduce the overhead of resemblance detection in each node, we build a similarity index to store the handprints of the stored super-chunks in each node, which also helps to alleviate the chunk disk index bottleneck for the deduplication processes in individual nodes by combining it with the conventional container-management based locality-preserved caching scheme [3].

The proposed Σ-Dedupe cluster deduplication system has the following salient features that distinguish it from the existing state-of-the-art cluster deduplication schemes:

- Σ-Dedupe exploits data similarity and locality by applying a handprinting technique at the super-chunk level to direct data routing from backup clients to deduplication server nodes to achieve a good tradeoff between the conflicting goals of high cluster deduplication effectiveness and highly scalable deduplication throughput.
- Σ-Dedupe builds a similarity index over the traditional container-based locality-preserved caching scheme to alleviate the chunk disk index lookup bottleneck for the deduplication process in each deduplication server node. The similarity index balances between memory overhead and deduplication accuracy for intra-node redundancy suppression by dynamically adjusting the handprint size.
- Evaluation results from our prototype implementation of Σ-Dedupe show that it consistently and significantly outperforms the existing state-of-the-art schemes in cluster deduplication efficiency by achieving high global deduplication effectiveness with balanced storage usage across the nodes and high parallel deduplication throughput at a low inter-node communication overhead. In addition, it maintains a high single-node deduplication performance with low RAM usage.

2   Background and Motivation

In this section, we first provide the necessary background and related work for our research by introducing the cluster deduplication techniques, and then present data similarity analysis based on a handprinting technique to motivate our research in the scalable inline cluster deduplication for Big Data protection.

2.1   Cluster Deduplication Techniques

Deduplication can be divided into four steps: data chunking, chunk fingerprint calculation, chunk index lookup, and unique data store. Source deduplication is a popular scheme that performs the first two steps of the deduplication process at the client side and decides whether a chunk is a duplicate before data transfer to save network bandwidth by avoiding the transfer of redundant data, which differs from target deduplication that performs all deduplication steps at the target side. To immediately identify and eliminate data redundancy, inline deduplication is a process that performs deduplication on the traditional data I/O path with some impact on I/O performance. The throughput and capacity limitations of single-node deduplication have led to the development of cluster deduplication to provide high deduplication throughput in massive backup data. In our scheme, in order to shorten the backup window and improve the system scalability by reducing data transfer over the network, we choose source inline cluster deduplication to optimize the backup data storage in large-scale storage systems. However, in cluster deduplication design, in addition to the design challenge of the traditional chunk index structure in single-node deduplication, the design of data routing for the assignment of data to deduplication nodes has become a difficult challenge in achieving high global duplicate elimination ratio and scalable performance with balanced workload across the deduplication nodes.

Many existing cluster deduplication schemes, such as EMC Data Domain's global deduplication array [24], IBM's ProtecTier [22], and SEPATON's S2100-ES2 [25], are designed to work well in small clusters. But using these technologies to scale to thousands of nodes in cloud datacenters would most likely fail due to some of their shortcomings in terms of cluster-wide deduplication ratio, single-node throughput, data skew, and communication overhead. Hence, the design of inter-node data routing scheme and intra-node redundancy suppression in large-scale cluster deduplication has become increasingly critical in recent years.

HYDRAstor [9] performs deduplication at a large-chunk (64KB) granularity without data sharing among the nodes, and distributes data at the chunk level using distributed hash table (DHT). Nevertheless, 64KB is still too limited to capture and preserve sufficient amount of locality for cluster deduplication purposes. While its chunk-level DHT based data routing is effective in lowering communication overhead and avoiding data sharing across the deduplication nodes, the intra-node local duplicate elimination ratio is reduced due to the large chunk size that tends to evade redundancy detection.

EMC's super-chunk based data routing [6] exploits data locality to direct data routing at the super-chunk level. It can route data evenly at the coarse-grained super-chunk level to preserve data locality and keep load balanced for scalable deduplication performance, and perform a fine-grained chunk-level redundancy suppression to achieve high deduplication effectiveness for intra-node local deduplication. Depending on whether the information on previously stored data is used, super-chunk based data routing can be divided into stateless routing and stateful routing. Stateless routing is also based on DHT with low overhead and can effectively balance workload in small clusters, but suffers from severe load imbalance in large clusters. Stateful routing is designed for large clusters to achieve high global deduplication effectiveness by effectively detecting cross-node data redundancy with the state information, but at the cost of very high system overhead required to route similar data to the same node.

Extreme Binning [8] is a file-similarity based cluster deduplication scheme. It can easily route similar data to the same deduplication node by extracting similarity characteristics in backup streams, but often suffers from low duplicate elimination ratio when data streams lack detectable similarity. It also has high data skew for the stateless routing due to the skew of file size distribution as studied in [13] and [17]. Similar to Extreme Binning, a new file-similarity based data routing scheme is proposed by Symantec [23] recently, but only a rough design is presented.

Table 1 compares some of the typical and representative cluster deduplication schemes, as discussed above. In relation to these existing approaches, our Σ-Dedupe is most relevant to Extreme Binning, and EMC's super-chunk based data routing (Stateless and Stateful). It aims to overcome many of the weaknesses described about these schemes. Comparing with Extreme Binning, Σ-Dedupe performs stateful data routing with a strong ability to discover similarity at the super-chunk level instead of the file level to enhance cluster-wide deduplication ratio and reduce data skew. Similar to EMC's super-chunk based data routing, Σ-Dedupe can preserve data locality at the super-chunk granularity, but is different from the former in that it exploits strong similarity at the super-chunk level to route data by a handprinting technique and only performs local stateful routing to keep load balanced and lower system overhead.

Table 1. Comparison of key features among representative cluster deduplication schemes

Cluster Deduplication Scheme	Routing Granularity	Deduplication Ratio	Throughput	Data Skew	Overhead
NEC HydraStor	Chunk	Medium	Low	Low	Low
Extreme Binning	File	Medium	High	Medium	Low
EMC Stateless	Super-chunk	Medium	High	Medium	Low
EMC Stateful	Super-chunk	High	Low	Low	High
Σ-Dedupe	Super-chunk	High	High	Low	Low

2.2   Super-Chunk Resemblance Analysis

In the hash based deduplication schemes, cryptographic hash functions, such as the MD5 and SHA families of functions, are used for calculating chunk fingerprints due to their very low probability of hash collisions that renders data loss extremely unlikely. Assume that two different data chunks have different fingerprint values; we use the *Jaccard index* [14] as a measure of super-chunk resemblance. Let h be a cryptographic hash function, $h(S)$ denote the set of chunk fingerprints generated by h on super-chunk S. Hence, for any two super-chunks S_1 and S_2 with almost the same average chunk size, we can define their resemblance measure $r(S_1, S_2)$ according to the Jaccard index as expressed in Eq (1).

$$r(S_1,S_2) \triangleq \frac{|S_1 \cap S_2|}{|S_1 \cup S_2|} \approx \frac{|h(S_1) \cap h(S_2)|}{|h(S_1) \cup h(S_2)|} \tag{1}$$

Our similarity based data routing scheme depends on the creative feature selection on super-chunks by a handprinting technique. The selection method is based on a generalization of Broder's theorem [15]. Before we discuss the theorem, let's first introduce the min-wise independent hash functions.

Definition 1. A family of hash functions $H = \{h_i: [n] \rightarrow [n]\}$ (where $[n] = \{0, 1, \ldots, n-1\}$) is called *min-wise independent* if for any $X \subset [n]$ and $x \in X$, it can be formally stated as in Eq. (2), where $\Pr_{h \in H}$ denotes the probability space obtained by choosing h uniformly at random from H.

$$\Pr_{h \in H}(\min\{h(X)\} = h(x)) = \frac{1}{|X|} \tag{2}$$

As the truly min-wise independent hash functions are hard to implement, practical systems only use hash functions that approximate min-wise independence, such as functions of the MD/SHA family cryptographic hash functions.

Theorem 1. (Broder's Theorem): For any two super-chunks S_1 and S_2, with $h(S_1)$ and $h(S_2)$ being the corresponding sets of the chunk fingerprints of the two super-chunks, respectively, where h is a hash function that is selected uniformly and at random from a min-wise independent family of cryptographic hash functions. Then Eq. (3) is established.

$$\Pr(\min\{h(S_1)\} = \min\{h(S_2)\}) = r(S_1,S_2) \tag{3}$$

Considering that h is a min-wise independent cryptographic hash function, for any $x \in S_1$, $y \in S_2$, the probability of x equaling y is the Jaccard index based resemblance $r(S_1, S_2)$, then we have a result as expressed in Eq. (4). Since there are $|S_1|$ choices for x and $|S_2|$ choices for y, Eq. (3) in the above theorem is established.

$$\Pr(\min\{h(S_1)\} = h(x) \wedge \min\{h(S_2)\} = h(y) \wedge h(x) = h(y)) = \frac{r(S_1,S_2)}{|S_1| \bullet |S_2|} \tag{4}$$

We consider a generalization of Broder's Theorem, given in [10], for any two super-chunks S_1 and S_2, and then we have a conclusion expressed in Eq. (5), where $\min_k$ denotes the k smallest elements in a set. It means that we can use the k smallest chunk fingerprints as representative fingerprints of a super-chunk to construct a *handprint* for it to find more similarity in datasets. With k being the handprint size, two super-chunks will more likely be found similar.

$$\begin{aligned} &\Pr(\min_k\{h(S_1)\} \cap \min_k\{h(S_2)\} \neq \varnothing) \\ &= 1 - \Pr(\min_k\{h(S_1)\} \cap \min_k\{h(S_2)\} = \varnothing) \\ &\geq 1 - (1 - r(S_1,S_2))^k \geq r(S_1,S_2) \end{aligned} \tag{5}$$

We evaluate the effectiveness of handprinting on super-chunk resemblance detection in the first 8MB super-chunks of four pair-wise files with different application types, including Linux 2.6.7 versus 2.6.8 kernel packages, and pair-wise versions of PPT, DOC and HTML files. We actually use the Two-Threshold Two-Divisor (TTTD) chunking algorithm [16] to subdivide the super-chunk into small chunks with 1KB, 2KB, 4KB and 32KB as minimum threshold, minor mean, major mean and maximum threshold of chunk size, respectively. TTTD is a variant of the basic content defined chunking (CDC) algorithm that leads to superior deduplication. We can calculate the real resemblance value based on the Jaccard index by the whole chunk fingerprint comparison on each pair of super-chunks, and estimate the resemblance by comparing representative fingerprints in handprint comparison with different handprint sizes. The estimated resemblance, as shown in Figure 1 as a function of the handprint size, approaches the real resemblance value as the handprint size increases. An evaluation of Figure 1 suggests that a reasonable handprint size can be chosen in the range from 4 to 64 representative fingerprints. Comparing with the conventional schemes that only use a single representative fingerprint (when handprint size equals to 1), our handprinting method can find more similarity for file pairs with poor similarity (with a resemblance value of less than 0.5), such as the two PPT versions and the pair of HTML versions.

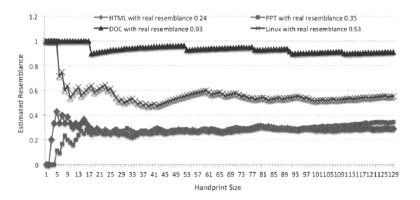

Fig. 1. The effect of handprinting resemblance detection

3   Σ-Dedupe Design

In this section, we present the design of the Σ-Dedupe cluster deduplication system. Besides the high throughput requirement in individual deduplication nodes, any cluster deduplication system must support scalable performance without significantly sacrificing capacity saving. We use the following design principles to govern our design for system architecture and data routing scheme:

— **Throughput.** The cluster deduplication throughput should scale with the number of nodes by parallel deduplication across the cluster nodes. Deduplication nodes should perform near-raw-disk data backup throughput by eliminating index lookup bottleneck, implying that our scheme must optimize for cache locality even with some but acceptable penalty on capacity saving.

— **Capacity.** In backup data streams, similar data should be forwarded to the same deduplication node to achieve high duplicate elimination ratio. And capacity usage should be balanced across nodes to support high scalability and simplified system management. If system resources are scarce, deduplication effectiveness can be sacrificed to improve the system performance.

— **Scalability.** The cluster deduplication system should easily scale out to handle massive data volumes with balanced workload among deduplication nodes, implying that our design must not only optimize the intra-node throughput by capturing and preserving high locality, but also reduce inter-node communication overhead for data routing by exploiting data similarity.

To achieve high deduplication throughput and good scalability with negligible capacity loss, we design a scalable inline cluster deduplication framework in this section. In what follows, we first show the architecture of our inline cluster deduplication system. Then we present our similarity based data routing algorithm to achieve scalable performance with high deduplication efficiency. This is followed by the description of the similarity index based lookup optimization for high deduplication throughput in deduplication nodes.

3.1   System Overview

The architecture of our cluster deduplication system is shown in Figure 2. It consists of three main components: backup clients, deduplication server cluster and director.

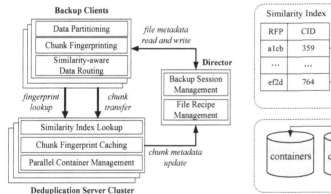
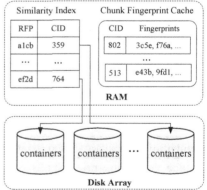

Fig. 2. Σ-Dedupe architectural overview   **Fig. 3.** Data structures in deduplication server

Backup Clients. There are three main functional modules in a backup client: data partitioning, chunk fingerprinting and data routing. The backup client component backs up and restores data streams, performs data chunking with fixed or variable chunk size and super-chunk grouping in the data partitioning module for each data stream, and calculates chunk fingerprints by a collision-resistant hash function, like MD5, SHA-1 or SHA-2, then selects a deduplication node for the routing of each super-chunk by the data routing scheme. To improve cluster system scalability by

saving the network transfer bandwidth during data backup, the backup clients determine whether a chunk is duplicate or not by batching chunk fingerprint query in the
deduplication node at the super-chunk level before data chunk transfer, and only the
unique data chunks are transferred over the network.

Deduplication Server Cluster. The deduplication server component consists of three
important functional modules: similarity index lookup, chunk index cache management and parallel container management. It implements the key deduplication and
backup management logic, including returning the results of similarity index lookup
for data routing, buffering the recent hot chunk fingerprints in chunk index cache to
speedup the process of identifying duplicate chunks and storing the unique chunks in
larger units, called containers, in parallel.

Director. It is responsible for keeping track of files on the deduplication server, and
managing file information to support data backup and restore. It consists of backup
session management and file recipe management. The backup session management
module groups files belonging to the same backup session of the same client, and file
recipe management module keeps the mapping from files to chunk fingerprints and all
other information required to reconstruct the file. All backup-session-level and file-
level metadata are maintained in the director.

3.2   Similarity Based Data Routing Algorithm

As a new contribution of this paper, we present the similarity based data routing algorithm. It is a stateful data routing scheme motivated by our super-chunk resemblance
analysis in Section 2. It routes similar data to the same deduplication node by looking
up storage status information in only one or a small number of nodes, and achieves
near-global capacity load balance without high system overhead. In the data partitioning module, a segment of the data stream is first divided it into n small chunks, that
are grouped into a super-chunk S. Then, all the chunk fingerprints $\{fp_1, fp_2, ..., fp_n\}$
are calculated by a cryptographic hash function in the chunk fingerprinting module.
The data routing algorithm, shown below, performs in the data routing module of
backup clients.

Algorithm 1. Similarity based stateful data routing

Input: a chunk fingerprint list of super-chunk S, $\{fp_1, fp_2, ..., fp_n\}$
Output: a target node ID, i

1. Select the k smallest chunk fingerprints $\{rfp_1, rfp_2, ..., rfp_k\}$ as a handprint for the
    super-chunk S by sorting the chunk fingerprint list $\{fp_1, fp_2, ..., fp_n\}$, and sent the
    handprint to candidate nodes with IDs $\{rfp_1 \bmod N, rfp_2 \bmod N, ..., rfp_k \bmod N\}$ in
    the deduplicaton server cluster with N nodes;
2. In deduplication server cluster, obtain the count of the existing representative fin-
    gerprints of the super-chunk in the candidate nodes by comparing the representa-
    tive fingerprints of the previously stored super-chunks in the similarity index. The
    returned k count values, one for each of the k candidate nodes, are denoted as $\{r_1,
    r_2, ..., r_k\}$, which are corresponding to the resemblances of S in these nodes;

3. Calculate the relative storage usage, which is a node storage usage value divided by the average storage usage value, to balance the capacity load in the candidate nodes by discounting the resemblance value with it, and the relative storage usage values in the k candidate nodes, are denoted as $\{w_1, w_2, \ldots, w_k\}$;
4. Choose the deduplication server node with ID i that satisfies $r_i/w_i = \max\{r_1/w_1, r_2/w_2, \ldots, r_k/w_k\}$ as the target node.

Our similarity based data routing scheme can achieve load balance for the k candidate nodes by adaptively choosing deduplication server node. We now prove that the global load balance can be approached by virtue of the universal distribution of randomly generated handprints by cryptographic hash functions, in Theorem 2 below.

Theorem 2. If each super-chunk handprint includes k fingerprints, and a local load balancing scheme is considered for the k candidate nodes with a mapping based on a modulo operation, then loads on all deduplication nodes can approach a global load balance.

Proof. We prove the proposition by contradiction. Assume that the deduplication cluster consists of N nodes, where $N \gg k$. Now, we assume that our proposition is false. It means that there are at least two capacity load levels in the deduplication cluster without a global load balance. We can divide all nodes into two groups by load level, denoted $\{H_1, \ldots, H_i\}$ for the high load level and $\{L_1, \ldots, L_j\}$ for the low load level, where $i + j = N$. For any super-chunk, the fingerprints in its handprint all map to either the high-load group or the low-load group, which means that all the super-chunks can be divided into two groups with the same cryptographic hash function. If all fingerprints in the handprint of super-chunk A map to the high-load group while all fingerprints in the handprint of super-chunk B map to the low-load group, then we can easily construct a super-chunk C, for which half of the fingerprints in its handprint are from super-chunk A and the other half are from super-chunk B. Now we find that super-chunk C belongs to neither high-load group nor low-load group. This contradicts to our deduction for cryptographic hash functions when the proposition is false. Hence, our proposition must be true. We will further evaluate the theorem by experiments on real datasets in Section 4.

3.3   Similarity Index Based Deduplication Optimization

We outline the salient features of the key data structures designed for the deduplication server architecture. As shown in Figure 3, to support high deduplication throughput with low system overhead, a chunk fingerprint cache and two key data structures, similarity index and container, are introduced in our design.

Similarity index is a hash-table based memory data structure, with each of its entry containing a mapping between a representative fingerprint (RFP) in a super-chunk handprint and the container ID (CID) where it is stored. To support concurrent lookup operations in similarity index by multiple data streams on multicore deduplication nodes, we adopt a parallel similarity index lookup design and control the synchronization scheme by allocating a lock per hash bucket or for a constant number of consecutive hash buckets.

Container is a self-describing data structure stored in disk to preserve locality, similar to the one described in [3], that includes a data section to store data chunks and a metadata section to store their metadata information, such as chunk fingerprint, offset and length. Our deduplication server design supports parallel container management to allocate, deallocate, read, write and reliably store containers in parallel. For parallel data store, a dedicated open container is maintained for each coming data stream, and a new one is opened up when the container fills up. All disk accesses are performed at the granularity of a container.

Besides the two important data structures, the chunk fingerprint cache also plays a key role in deduplication performance improvement. It keeps the chunk fingerprints of recently accessed containers in RAM. Once a representative fingerprint is matched by a lookup request in the similarity index, all the chunk fingerprints belonging to the mapped container are prefetched into the chunk fingerprint cache to speedup chunk fingerprint lookup. The chunk fingerprint cache is a key-value structure, and it is constructed by a doubly linked list indexed by a hash table. When the cache is full, fingerprints of those containers that are ineffective in accelerating chunk fingerprint lookup are replaced to make room for future prefetching and caching. A reasonable cache replacement policy is Least-Recently-Used (LRU) on cached chunk fingerprints. To support high deduplication effectiveness, we also maintain a traditional hash-table based chunk fingerprint index on disk to support further comparison after in-cache fingerprint lookup fails, but we consider it as a relatively rare occurrence.

To backup a super-chunk, after selecting the target node by our data routing algorithm, we resort to looking up the representative fingerprints in the similarity index. When a representative fingerprint is matched, we find the mapped container in the chunk fingerprint cache. If the container is already cached, we compare the fingerprints in the super-chunk with all the chunk fingerprints in the corresponding container; otherwise, we prefetch the fingerprints of that container from its metadata section before further comparison. After the search in all containers of the matched representative fingerprints, the unmatched fingerprints will be compared with the on-disk chunk fingerprint index. Finally, the chunks corresponding to the unmatched fingerprints are stored in an open unfilled container or a new container. Our similarity-index based optimization can achieve high throughput with less system RAM overhead by preserving strong chunk-fingerprint cache locality over container management.

4   Evaluation

We have implemented a prototype of Σ-Dedupe as a middleware in user space using C++ and pthreads, on the Linux platform. We evaluate the parallel deduplication efficiency in the single-node multi-core deduplication server with real system implementation, while use trace-driven simulation to demonstrate how Σ-Dedupe outperforms the state-of-the-art cluster deduplication techniques by achieving a high cluster-wide capacity saving that is very close to the extremely high-overhead stateful approach at a slightly higher overhead than the highly scalable stateless approach, while maintaining a scalable performance in large cluster deduplication. In addition, we conduct sensitivity studies to answer the following important design questions:

- What is the best chunk size for the single-node deduplication to achieve high deduplication efficiency?
- How does similarity index lock granularity affect the representative fingerprint index lookup performance?
- How sensitive is the cluster deduplication ratio to handprint size?

4.1   Evaluation Platform and Workload

We use two commodity servers to perform our experiments to evaluate parallel deduplication efficiency in single-node deduplication servers. All of them run Ubuntu 11.10 and use a configuration with 4-core 8-thread Intel X3440 CPU running at 2.53 GHz and 16GB RAM and a SAMSUNG 250GB hard disk drive. One server serves as both the backup client and director, and the other as the deduplication server. Our prototype deduplication system uses GBit Ethernet for internal communication. To achieve high throughput, our backup client component is based on an event-driven, pipelined design, which utilizes an asynchronous RPC implementation via message passing over TCP streams. All RPC requests are batched in order to minimize the round-trip overheads. We also perform simulation on one of the two servers to evaluate the cluster deduplication techniques.

Table 2. The workload characteristics of the real-world datasets and traces

Datasets	Size (GB)	Deduplication Ratio
Linux	160	8.23(CDC) / 7.96(SC)
VM	313	4.34(CDC) / 4.11(SC)
Mail	526	10.52(SC)
Web	43	1.9(SC)

We collect two kinds of real-world datasets and two types of application traces for our experiments. The Linux dataset is a collection of Linux kernel source code from versions 1.0 through 3.3.6, which is downloaded from the website [19]. The VM dataset consists of 2 consecutive monthly full backups of 8 virtual machine servers (3 for Windows and 5 for Linux). The mail and web datasets are two traces collected from the web-server and mail server of the CS department in FIU [20]. The key workload characteristics of these datasets are summarized in Table 2. Here, the "size" column represents the original dataset capacity, and "deduplication ratio" column indicates the ratio of logical to physical size after deduplication with 4KB fixed chunk size in static chunking (SC) or average 4KB variable chunk size in content defined chunking (CDC).

4.2   Evaluation Metrics

The following evaluation metrics are used in our evaluation to comprehensively assess the performance of our prototype implementation of Σ-Dedupe against the state-of-the-art cluster deduplication schemes.

Deduplication Efficiency: A simple metric that encompasses both capacity saving and system overhead in deduplication process. It is well understood that the deduplication efficiency is proportional to deduplication effectiveness that can be defined by deduplication ratio (*DR*), which is the ratio of logical size to physical size of the dataset, and inversely proportional to deduplication overhead that can be measured by deduplication throughput (*DT*), which is the ratio of logical dataset size to deduplication process time. Based on this understanding and to better quantify and compare deduplication efficiency of a wide variety of deduplication techniques, we adopt a metric, called "bytes saved per second", which is first defined in [13], to measure the efficiency of different deduplication schemes in the same platform by feeding a given dataset. It is calculated by the difference between the logical size *L* and the physical size *P* of the dataset divided by the deduplication process time *T*. So, deduplication efficiency (*DE*) can be expressed in Eq. (6).

$$DE = \frac{L-P}{T} = (1 - \frac{1}{DR}) \times DT \qquad (6)$$

Normalized Deduplication Ratio: The metric is designed for cluster deduplication effectiveness. It is equal to the cluster deduplication ratio divided by deduplication ratio achieved by a single-node, exact deduplication system. This is an indication of how close the deduplication ratio achieved by a cluster deduplication method is to the ideal cluster deduplication ratio.

Normalized Effective Deduplication Ratio: A single utility measure that considers both cluster-wide deduplication effectiveness and storage imbalance. It is equivalent to normalized deduplication ratio divided by the value of 1 plus the ratio of standard deviation σ of physical storage usage to average usage α in all deduplication servers, similar to the metric used in [6]. According to the definition of normalized deduplication ratio by cluster deduplication ratio (*CDR*) and single-node deduplication ratio (*SDR*), normalized effective deduplication ratio (*NEDR*) can be expressed in Eq. (7). It indicates how effective the data routing schemes are in eliminating the deduplication node information island.

$$NEDR = \frac{CDR}{SDR} \times \frac{\alpha}{\alpha + \sigma} \qquad (7)$$

Number of Fingerprint Index Lookup Messages: An important metric for system overhead in cluster deduplication, which significantly affects the cluster system scalability. It includes inter-node messages and intra-node messages for chunk fingerprint lookup, both of which can be easily obtained in our simulation to estimate cluster deduplication overhead.

4.3   Parallel Deduplication Efficiency on Single-Node Server

As deduplication is a resource intensive task, we develop parallel deduplication on multiple data streams for each node with multi-thread programming in pthreads to leverage the compute capabilities of multi-core or many-core processor of modern commodity servers. In our design, we adopt the RAM file system to store the workload and avoid unique data write to disks to eliminate the disk I/O performance bottleneck, due to our low disk I/O configuration. Meanwhile, we assign a deduplication thread for each data stream to read in parallel different files that are stored in RAM to create multiple data streams. We measure the throughput of parallel chunking and hash fingerprinting at backup clients as a function of the number of data streams. Considering the fact that static chunking has negligible overhead, we only test Rabin hash based content defined chunking (CDC) for chunking throughput by implementing it based on the open source code in Cumulus [21] with 4KB average chunk size. The implementation of the hash fingerprinting is based the OpenSSL library. Figure 4(a) shows the experiment results of CDC and MD5/SHA-1 based fingerprinting in the backup client. The throughput of chunking and fingerprinting can scale almost linearly and reach their peak values (148MB/s for CDC, 980MB/s for SHA-1 finger printing and 1890MB/s for MD5 fingerprinting) with 4 or 8 data streams, since the processor at the client is a 4-core 8-thread CPU. To find more data redundancy in backup datasets, CDC may affect the performance of deduplication for its low throughput and high deduplication time. We select SHA-1 to reduce the probability of hash collision even though its throughput is only about a half that of MD5.

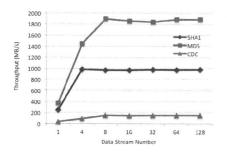

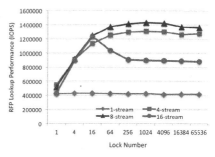

(a) Chunking and fingerprinting throughput in backup client

(b) The performance of similarity index parallel lookup

Fig. 4. Intra-node parallel deduplication performance

To exploit the multi-core or many-core resource of the deduplication server node, we also develop parallel similarity index lookup in individual deduplication servers. For our multiple-data-stream based parallel deduplication, each data stream has a deduplication thread, but all data streams share a common hash-table based similarity index in each deduplicaiton server. We lock the hash-table based similarity index by evenly partitioning the index at the single-hash-bucket or multiple-contiguous-hash-bucket granularity to support concurrent lookup. We test the performance of the parallel similarity index when all index data is loaded in memory. To avoid the possible performance bottleneck of a single backup client, we feed the deduplication server with chunk fingerprints generated in advance. Figure 4(b) shows the performance of the parallel index lookup for multiple data streams as a function of the number of locks. When the number of locks is greater than 1024, the performance drops as the lock overhead becomes non-negligible. 8 data steams still perform the best because the CPU supports 8 concurrent threads, while the performance of 16 streams drops when the number of locks is larger than 16 because of the overhead of thread context switching that causes data swapping between cache and memory.

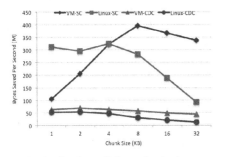

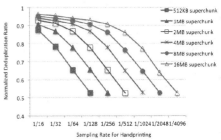

(a) Deduplication efficiency in single server

(b) Deduplication effectiveness as a function of the sampling rate and super-chunk size

Fig. 5. Sensitivity study on chunk size and handprint size

We measure the deduplication efficiency in a configuration with a single backup client and a single deduplication server to show the tradeoff between deduplication effectiveness and overhead. To eliminate the impact of the disk bottleneck, we store the entire workload in memory and perform the deduplication process to skip the unique-data-chunk store step. The deduplication effectiveness is affected by the data chunking method and the selected chunk size. High deduplication effectiveness can be achieved by using small chunk size and the CDC scheme instead of the Static Chunking (SC) scheme. This high effectiveness, however, comes at the expense of the increased amount of metadata necessary to manage the increased number of chunks and variable chunk size, negatively impacting system's performance. To assess the impact of the metadata overhead on deduplication efficiency, we measure "Bytes Saved Per Second", the deduplication efficiency as defined in Section 4.2, as a function of the chunk size. The results in Figure 5(a) show that SC outperforms CDC in deduplication efficiency due to the former's low overhead in data chunking. The deduplication efficiency is dynamically changing with the selected chunk size, and also depends on the workload. The single deduplication server can achieve the highest deduplication efficiency when the chunk size is 4KB for statically chunked Linux workload, 8KB for statically chunked VM workload and 2KB for both workloads with CDC. As a result, we choose to perform chunking with the SC scheme and select 4KB as the chunk size in the following experiments for high deduplication efficiency.

In our Σ-Dedupe design, handprinting plays a key role in similarity-index based deduplication optimization since the container ID is indexed by the representative fingerprints of a handprint. Handprinting is a novel use of deterministic sampling, where we define the *handprint-sampling rate* as the ratio of handprint size to the total number of chunk fingerprints in a super-chunk. This sampling rate affects both the deduplication effectiveness and RAM usage in each node. We turn off the traditional chunk index lookup module in our prototype, and conduct a series of experiments to demonstrate the effectiveness of the handprint-based local deduplication in Σ-Dedupe. Figure 5(b) shows the deduplication ratio produced by applying our similarity-index-only optimization (without traditional chunk index) to the Linux workload, normalized to that of the traditional single-node exact deduplication with a chunk size of 4KB, as a function of the handprint-sampling rate and super-chunk size. As can be seen, the deduplication ratio falls off as the sampling rate decreases and as the super-chunk size decreases, and the "knee" point for the 16MB super-chunk at the sample rate of 1/512 is a potentially best tradeoff to balance deduplication effectiveness and RAM usage, and it translates to a handprint size of 8. Meanwhile, the results further suggest that, interestingly, the deduplication ratio remains roughly constant if the sampling rate is halved and super-chunk size is doubled at the same time. As a result, we can find that 8 representative fingerprints in a handprint are sufficient to achieve a deduplication ratio that is close to that of the exact deduplication approach with high RAM utility. Furthermore, and importantly, Σ-Dedupe only uses 1/32 of the RAM capacity required by the traditional chunk index to store our similarity index to achieve about 90% of the deduplication effectiveness when the super-chunk and handprint sizes are 1MB and 8 respectively.

A first-order estimate of RAM usage, based on our earlier analysis, indicates that, comparing with the intra-node deduplicaition scheme of the EMC super-chunk based data routing—DDFS [3], and the intra-node deduplication of Extreme Binning, for a 100TB unique dataset with 64KB average file size, and assuming 4KB chunk size and 40B index entry size, DDFS requires 50GB RAM for Bloom filter, Extreme Binning uses 62.5GB RAM for file index, while our scheme only needs 32GB RAM to maintain similarity index. We can further reduce the RAM usage by adjusting super-chunk size or handprint size with the corresponding deduplication effectiveness loss.

4.4   Cluster-Deduplication Efficiency

We route data at the super-chunk granularity to preserve data locality for high performance of cluster-wide deduplication, while performing deduplication at the chunk granularity to achieve high deduplication ratio in each server locally. Since the size of the super-chunk is very sensitive to the tradeoff between the index lookup performance and the cluster deduplication effectiveness, as demonstrated by the sensitivity analysis on super-chunk size in [6], we choose the super-chunk size of 1MB to reasonably balance the conflicting objectives of cluster-wide system performance and capacity saving. In this section, we first conduct a sensitivity study to select an appropriate handprint size for our Σ-Dedupe scheme, and then compare our scheme with the state-of-the-art approaches that are most relevant to Σ-Dedupe, including EMC's super-chunk based data Stateful and Stateless routing and Extreme Binning, in terms of the effective deduplication ratio, normalized to that of the traditional single-node exact deduplication, and overhead measured in number of fingerprint index lookup messages. We emulate each node by a series of independent fingerprint lookup data structures, and all results are generated by trace-driven simulations on the four datasets under study.

Handprint-based Stateful routing can accurately direct similar data to the same deduplication server by exploiting data similarity. We conduct a series of experiments to demonstrate the effectiveness of cluster deduplication by our handprint-based deduplication technique with the super-chunk size of 1MB on the Linux workload. Figure 6 shows the deduplication ratio, normalized to that of the single-node exact deduplication, as a function of the handprint size. As a result, Σ-Dedupe becomes an approximate deduplication scheme whose deduplication effectiveness nevertheless improves with the handprint size because of the increased ability to detect resemblance in super-chunks with a larger handprint size (recall Section 2.2). We can see that there is a

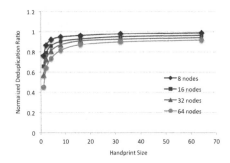

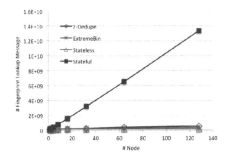

Fig. 6. Cluster deduplication ratio (DR), normalized to that of single-node exact deduplication, as a function of handprint size

Fig. 7. System overhead in terms of the number of fingerprint-lookup messages

significant improvement in normalized deduplication ratio for all cluster sizes when handprint size is larger than 8. This means that, for a large percentage of super-chunk queries, we are able to find the super-chunk that has the largest content overlap with the given super-chunk to be routed by our handprint-based routing scheme. To strike a sensible balance between the cluster-wide deduplication ratio and system overhead, and match the handprint size choice in single-node, we choose a handprint consisting of 8 representative fingerprints in the following experiments to direct data routing on super-chunks of 1MB in size.

To compare Σ-Dedupe with the existing data routing schemes in cluster deduplication, we use the effective deduplication ratio (EDR), normalized to the deduplication ratio of the single-node exact deduplication, to evaluate the cluster-wide deduplication effectiveness with the load-balance consideration. We compare our Σ-Dedupe scheme with the state-of-the-art cluster-deduplication data routing schemes of Extreme Binning (ExtremeBin), EMC's stateless (Stateless) and EMC's stateful (Stateful) routing schemes, across a range of datasets. Figure 8 plots EDR as a function of the cluster size for the four datasets and four algorithms. Because the last two traces, Mail and Web, do not contain file-level information, we are not able to perform the file-level based Extreme Binning scheme on them. In general, Σ-Dedupe can achieve a high effective deduplication ratio very close that achieved by the very costly Stateful data routing. More specifically, the Σ-Dedupe scheme achieves 90.5%~94.5% of the EDR obtained by the Stateful scheme for a cluster of 128 server nodes on the four datasets, while this performance margin narrows to 96.1%~97.9% when averaging over all cluster sizes, from 1 through 128. Stateless routing consistently performs worse than Σ-Dedupe and Stateful routing due to its low cluster-wide data reduction ratio and unbalanced capacity distribution. Extreme Binning underperforms Stateless routing on the VM dataset because of the large file size and skewed file size distribution in the VM dataset, workload properties that tend to render Extreme Binning's similarity detection ineffective. Σ-Dedupe outperforms ExtremeBinning in EDR by up to 32.8%

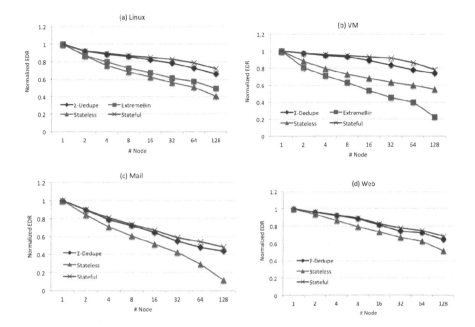

Fig. 8. Effective deduplication ratio (EDR), normalized to that of single-node exact deduplication, as a function of cluster size on four workloads

and 228.2% on the Linux and VM datasets respectively for a cluster of 128 nodes. For the four datasets, Σ-Dedupe is better than Stateless routing in EDR by up to 25.6%~271.8% for a cluster of 128 nodes. As can be seen from the trend of curves, these improvements will likely be more pronounced with cluster sizes larger than 128.

In cluster deduplication systems, fingerprint lookup tends to be a persistent bottleneck in each deduplication server because of the costly on-disk lookup I/Os, which often adversely impacts the system scalability due to the consequent high communication overhead from fingerprint lookup. To quantify this system overhead, we adopt a metric used in [6], the number of fingerprint-lookup messages. We measure this metric by totaling the number of chunk fingerprint-lookup messages on the two real datasets of Linux and VM, for the four cluster deduplication schemes. As shown in Figure 7 that plots the total number of fingerprint-lookup messages as a function of the cluster size, Σ-Dedupe, Extreme Binning and Stateless routing have very low system overhead due to their constant fingerprint-lookup message count in the cluster deduplication process, while the number of fingerprint-lookup messages of Stateful routing grows linearly with the cluster size. This is because Extreme Binning and Stateless routing only have 1-to-1 client-and-server fingerprint-lookup communications for source deduplication due to their stateless designs. Stateful routing, on the other hand, must send the fingerprint lookup requests to all nodes, resulting in 1-to-all communication that causes the system overhead to grow linearly with the cluster size even though it can reduce the overhead in each node by using a sampling scheme. As described in Algorithm 1, the main reason for the low system overhead in Σ-Dedupe is that the pre-routing fingerprint-lookup requests for each super-chunk only need to be sent to at most 8 candidate nodes, and only for the lookup of representative fingerprints, which is 1/32 of the number of chunk fingerprints, in these candidate nodes. The total number of fingerprint-lookup messages for Σ-Dedupe is the sum of after-routing message number, which is almost the same as Extreme Binning and Stateless routing, and pre-routing message number, which is a quarter (8×1/32) that of after-routing. So the fingerprint lookup message overhead will not exceed 1.25 times that of Stateless routing and Extreme Binning in all cluster sizes.

5   Conclusion

In this paper, we describe Σ-Dedupe, a scalable inline cluster deduplication framework for Big Data protection, which achieves a tradeoff between scalable performance and cluster-wide deduplication effectiveness by exploiting data similarity and locality in backup data streams. It adopts a handprint-based local stateful routing algorithm to route data at the super-chunk granularity to reduce cross-node data redundancy with low overhead, employs similarity index based optimization to improve deduplication efficiency in each node with very low RAM usage. Our real-world dataset-driven evaluation clearly demonstrates Σ-Dedupe's significant advantages over the state-of-the-art cluster deduplication schemes for large clusters in the following important two ways. First, it nearly (over 90%) achieves the cluster-wide deduplication ratio of the extremely costly and poorly scalable Stateful cluster deduplication scheme but only at a slightly higher overhead than the highly scalable Stateless and Extreme Binning schemes. Second, it significantly improves the Stateless and Extreme Binning schemes in the cluster-wide effective deduplication ratio while retaining the latter's high system scalability for low overhead. Meanwhile, high parallel deduplication efficiency can be achieved in each node by exploiting similarity and locality in backup data streams. In the near future, we will implement our scalable data routing scheme in large-scale cluster deduplication systems.

Acknowledgements. We thank other members of ADSL in UNL and the anonymous reviewers for their helpful comments and valuable suggestions to improve our paper. This research is partially funded by the 863 Program of China under Grant No. 2011AA010502, the National Natural Science Foundation of China under Grants No. 61025009, 61120106005, 61232003, 60903040 and 61170288, China Scholarship Council, and the US NSF under Grants IIS-0916859, CCF-0937993, CNS-1016609 and CNS-1116606.

References

1. Villars, R.L., Olofson, C.W., Eastwood, M.: Big Data: What It Is and Why You Should Care. White Paper, IDC (2011)
2. Kolodg, C.J.: Effective Data Leak Prevention Programs: Start by Protecting Data at the Source-Your Databases. White Paper, IDC (2011)

3. Zhu, B., Li, K., Patterson, H.: Avoiding the Disk Bottleneck in the Data Domain Deduplication File System. In: Proc. of USENIX FAST (2008)
4. Gantz, J., Reinsel, D.: The Digital Universe Decade-Are You Ready? White Paper, IDC (2010)
5. Biggar, H.: Experiencing Data De-Duplication: Improving Efficiency and Reducing Capacity Requirements. White Paper. The Enterprise Strategy Group (2007)
6. Dong, W., Douglis, F., Li, K., Patterson, H., Reddy, S., Shilane, P.: Tradeoffs in Scalable Data Routing for Deduplication Clusters. In: Proc. of USENIX FAST (2011)
7. Douglis, F., Bhardwaj, D., Qian, H., Shilane, P.: Content-aware Load Balancing for Distributed Backup. In: Proc. of USENIX LISA (2011)
8. Bhagwat, D., Eshghi, K., Long, D.D., Lillibridge, M.: Extreme Binning: Scalable, Parallel Deduplication for Chunk-based File Backup. In: Proc. of IEEE MASCOTS (2009)
9. Dubnicki, C., Gryz, L., Heldt, L., Kaczmarczyk, M., Kilian, W., Strzelczak, P., Szczepkowski, J., Ungureanu, C., Welnicki, M.: HYDRAstor: a Scalable Secondary Storage. In: Proc. of USENIX FAST (2009)
10. Bhagwat, D., Eshghi, K., Mehra, P.: Content-based Document Routing and Index Partitioning for Scalable Similarity-based Searches in a Large Corpus. In: Proc. of ACM SIGKDD (2007)
11. Yang, T., Jiang, H., Feng, D., Niu, Z., Zhou, K., Wan, Y.: DEBAR: a Scalable High-Performance Deduplication Storage System for Backup and Archiving. In: Proc. of IEEE IPDPS (2010)
12. Kaiser, H., Meister, D., Brinkmann, A., Effert, S.: Design of an Exact Data Deduplication Cluster. In: Proc. of IEEE MSST (2012)
13. Fu, Y., Jiang, H., Xiao, N., Tian, L., Liu, F.: AA-Dedupe: An Application-Aware Source Deduplication Approach for Cloud Backup Services in the Personal Computing Environment. In: Proc. of IEEE Cluster (2011)
14. Jaccard Index, http://en.wikipedia.org/wiki/Jaccard_index
15. Broder, A.Z., Charikar, M., Frieze, A.M., Mitzenmacher, M.: Min-wise Independent Permutations. Journal of Computer and System Sciences 60(3), 630–659 (2000)
16. Eshghi, K., Tang, H.K.: A framework for Analyzing and Improving Content-based Chunking Algorithms. Technical Report, Hewlett Packard (2005)
17. Wallace, G., Douglis, F., Qian, H., Shilane, P., Smaldone, S., Chamness, M., Hsu, W.: Characteristics of Backup Workloads in Production Systems. In: Proc. of FAST (2012)
18. Xia, W., Jiang, H., Feng, D., Hua, Y.: Silo: a Similarity-locality based Near-exact Deduplication Scheme with Low RAM Overhead and High Throughput. In: Proc. of USENIX ATC (2011)
19. The Linux Kernel Archives, http://www.kernel.org/
20. FIU IODedup Traces, http://iotta.snia.org/traces/391
21. Vrable, M., Savage, S., Voelker, G.M.: Cumulus: Filesystem Backup to the Cloud. In: Proc. of USENIX FAST (2009)
22. IBM ProtecTIER Deduplication Gateway, http://www-03.ibm.com/systems/storage/tape/ts7650g/index.html
23. Efstathopoulos, P.: File Routing Middleware for Cloud Deduplication. In: Proc. of ACM CloudCP (2012)
24. EMC Data Domain Global Deduplication Array, http://www.datadomain.com/products/global-deduplication-array.html
25. SEPATON S2100-ES2,
    http://www.sepaton.com/products/SEPATON_ES2.html

CloudPack*
Exploiting Workload Flexibility through Rational Pricing

Vatche Ishakian, Raymond Sweha, Azer Bestavros, and Jonathan Appavoo

Computer Science Department, Boston University
Boston, MA 02215, USA
{visahak,remos,best,jappavoo}@cs.bu.edu

Abstract. Infrastructure as a Service pricing models for resources are meant to reflect the operational costs and profit margins for providers to deliver virtualized resources to customers subject to an underlying Service Level Agreements (SLAs). While the operational costs incurred by providers are dynamic – they vary over time depending on factors such as energy cost, cooling strategies, and aggregate demand – the pricing models extended to customers are typically fixed – they are static over time and independent of aggregate demand. This disconnect between the dynamic cost incurred by a provider and the fixed price paid by a customer results in an economically inefficient marketplace. In particular, it does not provide incentives for customers to express workload scheduling flexibilities that may benefit them as well as providers. In this paper, we utilize a dynamic pricing model to address this inefficiency and give customers the opportunity and incentive to take advantage of any flexibilities they may have regarding the provisioning of their workloads. We present CLOUDPACK: a framework for workload colocation, which provides customers with the ability to formally express workload flexibilities using Directed Acyclic Graphs, optimizes the use of cloud resources to minimize total costs while allocating clients' workloads, and utilizes Shapley valuation to rationally – and thus fairly in a game-theoretic sense – attribute costs to the customers. Using extensive simulation, we show the practical utility of our CLOUDPACK colocation framework and the efficacy of the resulting marketplace in terms of cost savings.

Keywords: Cloud computing, resource provisioning, scheduling.

1 Introduction

Motivation: Cloud computing has emerged as compelling paradigms for the deployment of distributed applications and services on the Internet. Critical to this, are Infrastructure as a Service (IaaS) providers which own and maintain large physical datacenter installations and use virtualization technologies to provide customers with resources in the form of Virtual Machines. By relying on

---

* This research was supported in part by NSF awards #0720604, #0735974, #0820138, #0952145, and #1012798.

P. Narasimhan and P. Triantafillou (Eds.): Middleware 2012, LNCS 7662, pp. 374–393, 2012.
© IFIP International Federation for Information Processing 2012

virtualized resources, customers are able to easily deploy, scale up or down their applications [3].

IaaS providers incur a significant capital investment as part of creating and providing such services. A data center's return on investment (profit) relies heavily on decreasing its overall cost through efficient cooling and energy conservation [16, 33], while increasing its overall utilization (Revenue) as customers' adoption of cloud services increases.

Minimizing the overall cost involves a non-trivial optimization that depends on many factors, including time and location dependent factors. For example, in some cities, the cost of energy is variable depending on time of day [1, 32], while the cost of cooling might be higher during peak utilization times. The location of allocated virtual resources in the data center can also be a crucial factor in cost reduction. An efficient allocation can lead to powering down of resources [16], or in decreased cost of cooling [2]. These approaches are but examples of what providers must consider in order to decrease their overall costs.

Problem Description: Despite the complexities associated with minimizing the overall cost of cloud providers, the pricing models extended to cloud customers are typically fixed – they are static over time and independent of aggregate demand. For example, the pricing model of IaaS providers such as Amazon and Rackspace for leasing resources is in the form of *fixed-price SLAs*, which do not vary with resource availability, seasonal peak demand, and fluctuating energy costs.[1] From the customers' perspective, fixed pricing has its advantages due to its simplicity and the fact that it provides a sense of predictability. That said, fixed pricing has many disadvantages for customers and providers alike due to the fact that it does not allow *both* of them to capitalize on customer-side flexibility.

Under a fixed pricing model, customers do not have any incentive to expose (or the means to capitalize on) the flexibility of their workloads. By workload flexibility, we refer to scheduling flexibilities that customers may be able to tolerate, such as requesting a virtual machine for backup operations which can run anytime during a day. This customer-side *demand flexibility* could be seen as an asset that may benefit *both* customers and providers. From the provider's perspective, demand flexibility could be seen as an additional lever in the aforementioned optimization of operational costs, whereas from the customer's perspective, demand flexibility could be seen as a feature of their workloads that should translate to cost savings. Fixed pricing models do not enable demand flexibility to play a role in the marketplace, effectively resulting in an inefficient marketplace [24].

Leveraging customer-side demand flexibility requires the development of dynamic (as opposed to fixed) pricing mechanisms and associated flexible SLA models that provide customers with proper incentives and assurances. In particular,

---

[1] Amazon spot instance is a prime example of flexible pricing, but unlike our CLOUD-PACK framework, it does not provide customers any guarantees in terms of when and for how long a customer's demand is going to be honored.

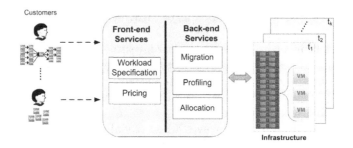

Fig. 1. CLOUDPACK Colocation Framework

the pricing mechanism must provably reward (and certainly never mistreat) customers for expressing the scheduling flexibilities in their workloads.

Scope and Contribution: In this paper, we present CLOUDPACK: (see Section 3) a colocation framework that achieves the above-stated goals by giving customers both the means and the incentive to express any flexibilities they may have regarding the provisioning of their workloads. Architecturally, our framework can be described as illustrated in Figure 1: it consists of two major services, *Back-end services* and *Front-end services*. The CLOUDPACK framework can be incorporated into an offering by cloud providers; it can be implemented as a value-added proposition or as a secondary market by IaaS resellers; or it can be directly leveraged in a peer-to-peer fashion by IaaS customers.

Front-end services are exposed to the IaaS customers and consists of two components: Workload Specification Component (Section 3.1), and Pricing Component (Section 3.4). The workload specification component provides customers not only the ability to state their requests in terms of virtualized resources subject to SLAs, but also to express their allocation flexibilities represented as Directed Acyclic Graphs (DAGs). The pricing component not only attributes accrued costs rationally – and thus fairly in a game-theoretic sense – across customers, but also provides incentives for customers to declare their flexibilities by guaranteeing that they will not be mistreated as a consequence.

Back-end services are oblivious to the IaaS customers and are utilized by the provider to control its resources. The Back-end services consist of the following components: An Allocation Component (Section 3.2) that colocates workloads (virtual resource requests) from multiple customers on the same set of physical resources. The main objective of the Allocation component is with the aim of minimize the total cost of used IaaS resources, while adhering to customers' SLAs provided using the Workload Specification Component. Profiling or monitoring Component whose main purpose is to provide customers with the raw data that enables them to adjust their reservations as well as gaining insight and visibility into resource utilization, overall performance. Finally the migration component is used to eliminate hotspots, enable load balancing, and allow for physical resource maintenance.

Profiling [8, 13, 37, 39] and Migration [20, 21, 25, 27] Components have been extensively studied in the literature and are implemented as standard features in widely popular virtualization technologies such as Xen and VMware, thus we consider them to be beyond the scope of this work.

To demonstrate the promise of using CLOUDPACK framework to manage the colocation of different workloads, using simulation (Section 4), we perform an extensive experimental evaluation of our framework using synthetically generated workloads, selected from a set of representative real workload models. The results highlight the practical utility of our dynamic pricing mechanism, the efficacy of our algorithm in colocating workloads, and the rationally fair distribution of costs among customers.

2   CLOUDPACK: Background and Setting

In this section, we present an IaaS resource cost model utilized by CLOUDPACK along with assumptions about the underlying IaaS setting needed to instantiate our colocation framework.

2.1   IaaS Resource Cost Model

As we alluded before, fixed resource pricing does not reflect the time-variant expenses incurred by providers and fails to capitalize on the scheduling flexibilities of customers. Expenses incurred by providers are affected by different criteria such as datacenter utilization, efficient cooling strategies, ambient temperature, total energy consumption, and energy costs. Indeed, studies indicate that the amortized cost of energy and physical resources account for 30% and 45% of the cost of datacenters, respectively [3, 15]. In addition, it is becoming a norm for datacenters to be charged a variable hourly rate for electricity [32], or for peak usage [15]. Accordingly, in this paper, we consider two factors to be the primary determinants of the costs incurred by providers: (1) the variable cost of electricity as a function of the time of the day, and (2) the level of utilization of resources, and hence the power consumption, at each point in time.

In order to pursue this notion further, we need an accurate model of resource energy consumption. Recent work on energy [12, 14, 33] suggest that a physical machine's power consumption increases linearly with the system load, with a base idle power draw – power consumed by an idle physical machine – of 60%. Under this simple model one can already observe a generic notion of fixed and variable costs. In addition, Ranganathan et al. [35] suggest a linear relationship between watts consumed for powering and watts consumed for cooling. Using this knowledge, it is reasonable to assume that the total expense of operating a physical resource j during time t is:

$$P_j + f(t, U_j(t))$$

where P_j reflects an amortized fixed cost of the resource j. The function $f(t, U_j(t))$ is the energy cost consumed by resource j at time t under utilization $U_j(t)$. we define $f(t, U_j(t))$ as follows:

$$f(t, U_j(t)) = \alpha(t)(v_0 + (1 - v_0)U_j(t) * R_j)$$

where $\alpha(t)$ is a coefficient reflecting the energy cost at time t, and v_0 is the energy fraction consumed by the resource when idle,[2] and R_j is the fixed capacity of resource j which is generic enough to reflect a single host, a single rack, or an entire datacenter.[3] Note that $f(t, U_j(t))$ has also a fixed part reflecting the cost of operating the resource if the resource is turned on and is in an idle state.

2.2 IaaS Setting

As an underlying infrastructure for CLOUDPACK, we assume an IaaS setting consisting of any number of possibly heterogeneous resources, (e.g. physical machines). Each resource is characterized by a number of dimensions (e.g., CPU, network, memory, and disk space) which constitute dimensions of the resource capacity vector. The cost of resources follows the IaaS resource cost model presented in the previous section.

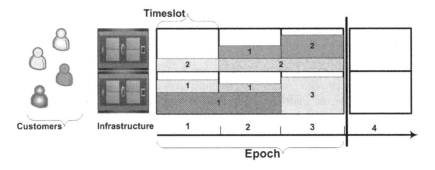

Fig. 2. CLOUDPACK Epoch Example

A fundamental principle in the instantiation of our colocation framework is the concept of epochs. We consider an epoch to be a sequence of periodic timeslots during which the workloads of customers can be colocated. The determination of colocation configurations is calculated at the beginning of an epoch, and is fixed for the entire duration of that epoch. Figure 2 illustrates an example epoch consisting of three timeslots, through which customers' requests (virtual machines) are allocated on the physical machines.

Customers who are not able to join at the beginning of an epoch will only be considered for colocation during the next epoch. Similar to grid markets, we envision different marketplaces operating at different timescales, with epochs ranging from days to weeks to months. One way to minimize customer wait time is to instantiate marketplaces with overlapping epochs of the same duration. Another method would be to have multiple marketplaces of epochs with exponentially increasing time scales, where a customer can colocate in a logarithmic number of shorter time-scale epochs before reaching the epoch he desires to join [18].

---

[2] Throughout this paper, we take v_0 to be 60% [12,14,33].

[3] Although we take energy as an example of time variant cost, our model could apply any other time variant cost.

3   CLOUDPACK: The Framework

In this section, we present the three major components of the CLOUDPACK colocation framework: Workload Specification, Allocation, and Pricing.

3.1   CLOUDPACK: Workload Specification Component

We propose an expressive resource specification language for customer workloads, which allows them to declare their quantitative resource requirements as well as any associated temporal flexibilities.[4] Our resource specification language is XML based, we omit the syntax due to space constraints. A workload is represented as a DAG. A node in the graph represents a single task (virtual machine), to be mapped to a resource, and consumes some of the resource dimensions. A task has two attributes: The total number d of timeslots (periods) during which the task must remain on the same resource, and a quantitative resource request matrix $V \in \mathbb{R}^{m \times d}$ where d represents the required duration and m represents the different dimensions requested during each period. The directed edges in the graph represent the temporal dependencies between tasks. An edge between node k and k' dictates that task k needs to finish execution before task k' starts execution. The weight on an edge $w \geq 0$ designates the maximum delay a customer can tolerate between releasing a resource by task k and acquiring a resource for the execution of task k'. In addition, a customer i specifies an execution window (T_i^s, T_i^e), where T_i^s is the workload earliest start time, and T_i^e is a deadline for the completion of the workload. This formally declared temporal flexibility by a customer will be exploited by our framework to achieve better colocation.

This model is expressive enough for various types of applications. Figure 3 (a) shows a sample specification for a batch workload. Such a workload is representative of bulk data transfer or backup applications. The workload consists of five tasks with different utilization levels and durations. The tasks are not temporally dependent, thus there are no edges between them, implying that they may be satisfied in any order within the execution window. Specifying a web server, which requires the workload to execute on the same resource would result in representing the workload as one node with a duration equal to 24 and volume V of size $m \times 24$ that varies accordingly. Figure 3 (b) illustrates a pipelined workload with 24 nodes, where tasks need to execute in sequence throughout an entire day with different utilizations, and the delay between the execution of two consecutive tasks is zero.

The above example illustrates a scenario in which the customer has no scheduling flexibilities. Figure 3 (c) illustrates a typical MapReduce workload, where a scheduling task needs to execute, followed by a set of independent *map* tasks, and finishing with a *reduce* task. Figure 3 (d) is a constrained version of the

---

[4] We note that our workload specification language allows customers to specify additional dimensions associated with each node (e.g., location, operating system, etc.). Without loss of generality, in this paper, we only consider dimensions related to consumable physical resources.

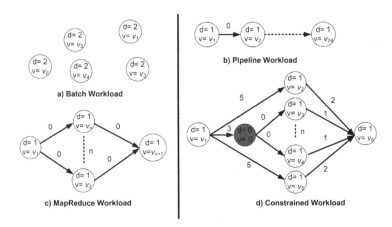

Fig. 3. An example illustrating different workload models

MapReduce workload, where some communicating tasks need to run concurrently. We introduce a *marker* node, (in red), that has a duration of zero and a utilization of zero; it forces a number of tasks to run concurrently once the marker node is scheduled. This feature is essential for High Performance Computing workloads.

Note that current customers of cloud offerings such as Amazon need to specify and map their actual applications to resource requests as part of their adequate resource reservation (e.g. small, medium, large). Profiling and benchmarking techniques such as the ones described in [8, 39] can be used to predict an applications resource consumption.

3.2   CLOUDPACK: Allocation Component

In the previous section, we presented our workload specification language, which allows IaaS customers to describe their workloads. In this section, we formulate the allocation problem and present a linear programming optimization solution. The objective of the system is to fulfill the requests of all customers, taking into consideration their flexibility (constraints) while incurring the minimal total cost. The aggregate load on the system can be represented by the graph $G = < V, E >$, representing the union of the DAGs $G_i = < V_i, E_i >$ representing the workloads of all customers $i \in U$ – namely, $V = \bigcup_{\forall i} V_i$ and $E = \bigcup_{\forall i} E_i$.

We define $Y(t, j)$ to be a binary decision variable that equals to one when resource j is in use at time t. We also define $X(j, t, k, l)$ to be a binary decision variable such that

$$X(j, t, k, l) = \begin{cases} 1 \text{ If resource } j \text{ at time } t \text{ is assigned to node } k\text{'s duration } l. \\ \\ 0 \text{ Otherwise} \end{cases}$$

We formulate our colocation optimization problem as follows, (verbal description to follow):

$$\min \sum_{\forall t,j} (Y(t,j) \times P_j + Y(t,j) \times (\alpha(t) \times v_0)$$

$$+ \alpha(t) \times (1 - v_0)U_j(t) \times R_j) \tag{1}$$

Subject to:
$$\sum_{\forall l} X(j,t,k,l) \leq Y(t,j) \qquad \forall t,j,k \tag{2}$$

$$\sum_{\forall k, 1 \leq l \leq d_k} X(j,t,k,l) \times u(k,l) \leq R_j \qquad \forall j,t \tag{3}$$

$$\sum_{\forall j,t} X(j,t,k,l) = 1 \qquad \forall k \in V, 1 \leq l \leq d_k \tag{4}$$

$$X(j,t,k,l) = X(j,t+1,k,l+1) \tag{5}$$
$$\forall j,t,k \in V, 1 \leq l < d_k$$

$$X(j,t,k,l) = 0 \qquad \forall j,k \in V_i, t < T_i^s, 1 \leq l \leq d_k \tag{6}$$

$$X(j,t,k,l) = 0 \qquad \forall j,k \in V_i, t > T_i^e, 1 \leq l \leq d_k \tag{7}$$

$$\sum_{j,t<t'} X(j,t,k,d_k) \geq \sum_{j'} X(j',t',k',1) \quad \forall t', (k,k') \in E \tag{8}$$

$$\sum_{j} X(j,t',k,d_k) \leq \sum_{j',t'<t\leq t'+W_e+1} X(j',t,k',1) \tag{9}$$
$$\forall t', (k,k') \in E$$

where P_j and R_j are the cost and capacity of a specific physical resource j, $u(k,l)$ is the utilization request of a nodes k's duration l, $U_j(t)$ is the total utilization of resource j at time t is formally defined as $(\sum_{\forall k, 1 \leq l \leq d_k} X(j,t,k,l) \times u(k,l))/R_j$, v_0 is the energy consumed by resource j while idle, and $\alpha(t)$ is the cost of energy at time t. This formulation is a general enough to model different types of resources. Intuitively, the optimization problem aims to minimize the cost of resources across time while keeping in line with each customer's specified flexibility. The objective function is the sum of three parts, reflecting the cost of leasing the resource: $Y(t,j) \times P_j$ reflects the fixed cost of leasing the resource, $Y(t,j) \times \alpha(t) \times v_0$ is the initial cost of energy to run the resource at an idle state if that resource is in use at time selected at time t, and $\alpha(t) \times (1 - v_0)U_j(t) \times R_j$ stands for the additional (variable) cost as a consequence for utilizing the resource.[5]

Equation (2) ensures that a resource j is utilized at time t, by setting $Y(j,t)$ to one if that resource is used to serve the requests of any customer during

---

[5] We do not multiply the third component of Equation (1) by $Y(t,j)$, since if the resource j is not assigned during time t, then its $U_j(t) = 0$.

that time. Equation (3) ensures that the utilization of a single resource does not exceed a fixed capacity R_j. This constraint is needed not to overprovision the resources. Equation (4) guarantees that all periods of each task are fulfilled exactly once. Equation (5) ensures that a task's periods are allocated consecutively on the same resource. This constraint is essential for fulfilling requirements of workloads such as a WebServer. Equation (6) and (7) ensure that the time of execution of customer i's tasks are between the start time T_i^s and end time T_i^e specified by the customer. Finally, Equation (8) and (9), guarantee that the allocation of resources respects the client's edge constraints (flexibility). In particular, Equation (8) constrains the allocation of the first timeslot of a request k' to follow the resources allocated to the last timeslot of request k, while Equation (9) guarantees that such an allocation happens within the specified client's delay W_e on edge (k, k').

3.3 CLOUDPACK: Greedy Heuristic

The optimization problem defined in the previous section is a variant of mixed-integer programming, which is known to be NP-hard in general[6]. Therefore, in this section, we propose a greedy algorithm that results in solutions to our allocation problem, which we show to be effective in our experiments. The algorithm starts from an initial valid solution and iterates over several greedy *moves* until it converges. The final solution is the configuration based on which physical resources are going to be allocated to the customers.

The initial solution is generated by randomly assigning workloads to resources, such that each workload's specific constrains are satisfied. Naturally, the initial solution's total cost is far more expensive than an optimal solution.

At each greedy move (iteration), the algorithm chooses a workload which has the highest current-to-optimal cost ratio r among all customer workloads. Calculating the optimal cost of a workload is not trivial, however, we can calculate the *utopian* cost, a lower bound on the optimal workload cost efficiently, where the utopiancost of a workload reflects only the cost of energy and resources that the workload actually uses. The utopian cost is calculated under the assumption that there is a perfect packing of the workload, with the energy cost being the minimum throughout the customer's specified workload start and end times.

Once the workload with the highest r is identified, we proceeds to relocate it such that r is minimized. If the relocation results in reducing the total cost of the solution, then the relocation (move) is accepted, the solution is updated, and the process is repeated. Otherwise, the algorithm chooses the workload with the second highest ratio r and iterates. The algorithm stops when the iteration step fails to find a move for any of the workloads.

3.4 CLOUDPACK: Pricing Component

The allocation component is designed to minimize the total aggregate cost of using resources. However, we need a pricing component to apportion (distribute)

---

[6] The proof of NP-hardness is omitted due to space limitations.

this total cost across all customers. This component requires an appropriate pricing mechanism, which ensures that the interests of customers, particularly fairness in terms of costs that customers accrue for the resources they acquire, and provides guarantees of no mistreatment of a customer's flexibility.

There are many ways to apportion the total cost across customers. For instance, one option would be to divide the cost equally among customers. Clearly, this mechanism will not be fair as it does not discriminate between customers with large jobs and customers with small jobs. Another option would be to charge each customer based on the proportional cost of each resource they utilize. As we will show next, such an option is also not fair.

Consider an example of two customers A and B each with a single task workload with 50% resource utilization. Customer A is constrained to run during the highest energy cost period. Customer B has no such constraint. Let c_l be the cost of running during low energy period, and c_h be the cost of running during high energy period. An optimized solution would colocate customer A and B to run during the highest energy cost period with a total cost of c_h. For all costs of $c_h > 2 \times c_l$, a proportional share pricing mechanism would divide the total cost across both customers, thus forcing unfairly customer B to pay more than what he/she would have paid (c_l) had he/she run by herself at the lowest cost period.

A "rationally fair" pricing mechanism allocates the total cost over the customers in accordance with each customer's marginal contribution to the aggregate cost of using the resources. Such mechanism should take into consideration not only the actual customer workload demands, but also the effects of the workload constraints.

To quantify per-customer contribution, we resort to notions from economic game theory. In particular, we adopt the concept of Shapley value [29], which is a well defined concept from coalitional game theory that allows for fair cost sharing characterization among involved players (customers).

Given a set of n customers U, we divide the total cost of the system $C(U)$ by ordering the customers, say $u_1, u_2, \cdots, u_n$, and charging each customer his/her marginal contribution to the total system cost. Thus, u_1 will be charged $C(u_1)$, u_2 will be charged $C(u_1, u_2) - C(u_1)$, etc. Since the ordering of customers affects the amount they will be charged, a fair distribution should take the average marginal cost of each customer over all possible ordering permutations. Then the marginal cost of $\phi(C)$ of each customer u is defined as follows:

$$\phi_u(C) = \frac{1}{N!} \sum_{\pi \in S_N} (C(S(\pi, u)) - C(S(\pi, u) \setminus u)) \tag{10}$$

where $S(\pi, u)$ is the set of players arrived in the system not later than u, and π is a permutation of arrival order of those customers. Thus player u is responsible for its marginal contribution $v(S(\pi, u)) - v(S(\pi, u) \setminus u)$ averaged across all $N!$ arrival orders of π.

Looking back at the previous example of two customers A and B, there are two possible ordering: B, A and A, B. For the first, the cost of $B = c_l$ and the cost of $A = c_h - c_l$. For the second, the cost of $A = c_h$, and the cost of

$B = 0$. After averaging both costs, we end up with a rationally fair individual cost distribution: $B = \frac{c_l}{2}$ and $A = c_h - \frac{c_l}{2}$.

By adopting Shapley value as a rationally fair mechanism for allocating costs, customers have the incentive to declare the flexibility (if any), because the pricing mechanism guarantees that a customer's cost will not increase because of flexibility. We formalize this notion in the following theorem.

Theorem 1. *The fair pricing mechanism under Shapley value guarantees no mistreatment as a result of customer flexibility, i.e., $\phi_i(C) - \phi_i(C)_F \geq 0$, where $\phi_i(C)$ is the cost of customer i and $\phi_i(C)_F$ is the cost of flexible customer i under Shapley value.*

Proof. The proof is by contradiction. Assuming that the opposite is true, i.e., $\phi_i(C) - \phi_i(C)_F < 0$, implies that there exists at least one permutation where $C(S(\pi,i)) - C(S(\pi,i) \setminus i) - C(S(\pi,i))_F + C(S(\pi,i) \setminus i)_F < 0$. Since the configuration of other players did not change, then $C(S(\pi,i) \setminus i)_F = C(S(\pi,i) \setminus i)$. Thus, $C(S(\pi,i)) - C(S(\pi,i))_F < 0$. This implies that the optimization solution $OPT(i)$ resulting in $C(S(\pi,i))$ is better than the optimization solution $OPT(i)_F$ resulting in $C(S(\pi,i))_F$. But if $OPT(i)$ is better than $OPT(i)_F$ then the optimization should have found it, since the flexibility of the customer contains the constrained version as well – a contradiction.

While computing the exact cost for each customer using Equation (10) is straightforward for small number of customers, finding the exact cost becomes infeasible as the number of customers increases. Thus, we resort to computing an estimate of the Shapley value using sampling.[7] We utilize Castro's [7] polynomial time estimation of Shapley value, which not only achieves a good estimation of the original Shapley value, but also provides bounds on the estimation error.

Let the vector of estimated Shapley values based on all possible $N!$ permutations be $Sh = (\phi_1(C), \phi_2(C), \cdots \phi_n(C))$; Let the vector of estimated Shapley values based on m sample permutations be $\hat{Sh} = (\hat{\phi}_1(C), \hat{\phi}_2(C), \cdots, \hat{\phi}_n(C))$. Using the central limit theorem, Castro's technique calculates the number of permutations m needed such that $P(|\phi_i(C) - \hat{\phi}_i(C)| \leq \epsilon) \geq 1 - \alpha$, where ϵ is the error bound, and α is the confidence factor. Calculating the number of samples m required to achieve the bound $P(|\phi_i(C) - \hat{\phi}_i(C)| \leq \epsilon) \geq 1 - \alpha$ requires knowing the standard deviation σ, which is an unknown value. In our setting, to calculate σ, we first (conservatively) take the standard deviation σ_i of each customer to be $\omega_h - \omega_l$: ω_l reflects the cost incurred by the customer under the assumption that there is an optimal packing of the workload with minimum cost of energy, and ω_h reflects the cost incurred by the customer under the assumption that the workload is the only workload in the system with a maximal cost of energy. A worst case value on σ could be calculated by taking $\sigma = \max(\sigma_1, \sigma_2, \cdots, \sigma_i)$ for all customers i.

Let $\hat{\phi}_i(C)_F$ be the flexibility of a customer using a Shapley value sampling technique. The mistreatment guarantee by the system no longer holds. However,

---

[7] Estimating Shapley value has proven to be effective in calculating the contribution of customers to the effective network peak demand [36].

as we show in Theorem 2, we can bound the mistreatment of the customer based on the original Shapley value.

Theorem 2. *The fair pricing mechanism under an estimated Shapley value bounds the mistreatment of a customer as a result of his/her flexibility from the original Shapley value to be $\leq \epsilon$ i.e., $P(\hat{\phi}_i(C)_F - \phi_i(C) \leq \epsilon) \geq 1 - \frac{\alpha}{2}$, where $\hat{\phi}_i(C)_F$ is the sampled cost of flexible customer i, $\phi_i(C)$ is the cost of customer i under Shapley value, ϵ is the error bound, and α is the confidence factor.*

Proof. Using a Shapley value sampling technique, we have $P(|\hat{\phi}_i(C)_F - \phi_i(C)_F| \leq \epsilon) \geq 1 - \alpha$, thus, $P(\hat{\phi}_i(C)_F - \phi_i(C)_F \leq \epsilon) \geq 1 - \frac{\alpha}{2}$. But we know from Theorem 1 that $\phi_i(C)_F \leq \phi_i(C)$, thus, $P(\hat{\phi}_i(C)_F - \phi_i(C) \leq \epsilon) \geq 1 - \frac{\alpha}{2}$.

Since comparison against Shapley valuation is impractical because of it computational inefficiency, which might not provide confidence for customer to be flexible, A further motivation is provided by bounding the flexible Shapley value with the estimated Shapley value.

Theorem 3. *The fair pricing mechanism under estimated Shapley value bounds the mistreatment of a customer as a result of his/her flexibility to be $\leq \epsilon_1 + \epsilon_2$, i.e. $\hat{\phi}_i(C)_F \leq \hat{\phi}_i(C) + \epsilon_1 + \epsilon_2$ with probability $(1 - \frac{\alpha}{2})^2$, where $\hat{\phi}_i(C)_F$ is the sampled cost of flexible customer i, $\hat{\phi}_i(C)$ is the sampled cost of customer i, ϵ_1 and ϵ_2 are the sample error bounds, and α is the confidence factor.*

Proof. Using the Shapley value sampling technique, we have the following results: $|\phi_i(C) - \hat{\phi}_i(C)| \leq \epsilon_1$ and $|\hat{\phi}_i(C)_F - \phi_i(C)_F| \leq \epsilon_2$ with probability $(1 - \alpha)$. Thus, $P((\phi_i(C) - \hat{\phi}_i(C)) \leq \epsilon_1) \geq 1 - \frac{\alpha}{2}$ and $P(\hat{\phi}_i(C)_F - \phi_i(C)_F \leq \epsilon_2) \geq 1 - \frac{\alpha}{2}$. Since the sampling process is independent, The probability of $(\phi_i(C) - \hat{\phi}_i(C)) \leq \epsilon_1$ and $\hat{\phi}_i(C)_F - \phi_i(C)_F \leq \epsilon_2$ is equal to $(1 - \frac{\alpha}{2})^2$.

In addition, from Theorem 1, we have $\phi_i(C)_F \leq \phi_i(C)$. Therefore we have $\hat{\phi}_i(C)_F \leq \epsilon_2 + \phi_i(C)_F \leq \epsilon_2 + \hat{\phi}_i(C) + \epsilon_1$ with probability $(1 - \frac{\alpha}{2})^2$.

Finally, an added property of Shapley and sampled Shapley value is budget balance *i.e.* the total cost of customers is always equal to the total cost of the resources used. This property works as incentive for providers or resellers, since it guarantees that they are going to get a revenue which covers the resources they lease.

4   CLOUDPACK: Experimental Evaluation

In this section, we present results from extensive experimental evaluations of CLOUDPACK colocation framework. Our main purpose is to establish the feasibility of our proposed framework as an underlying mechanism to make effective use of a provider's IaaS and still achieve a fair distribution of costs among customers, by (1) establishing the efficacy of our greedy heuristic by comparing it to optimally allocated workloads, (2) evaluating the cost incurred by the customer

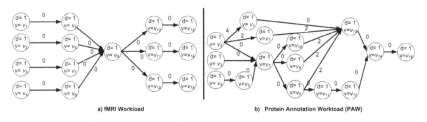

a) fMRI Workload   b) Protein Annotation Workload (PAW)

Fig. 4. High Performance Computing Workloads

to use such a system to allocate a workload compared to the utopian cost, and (3) measure the benefit of a customer from flexibility.

Workload Models: To evaluate our experiments, we synthetically generate workloads based on the workload models (shown in Figure 3), such as batch, and MapReduce workloads. We generate two pipeline workload versions: Webserver which has a single node with an execution length equal to the length of the epoch, and a *chain* workload which has a variable number of sequential tasks.[8] In addition, we enrich our set of workloads with two additional High Performance Computing workloads (c.f. Figure 4) for Protein annotation workflow (*PAW*), and Cognitive Neuroscience (*fMRI*) [40]. We believe that this set of workload models is representative for many cloud based applications. We assume homogeneous resources with the fixed cost part equal to 10 cents per hour, a resource capacity equal to one, and an epoch consisting of twenty four hours where customers configurations are calculated at the beginning of the epoch. To calculate the number of samples m required to estimate a Shapley costs, we take $\epsilon = 0.1$, and $\alpha = 0.05$. Based on available server power consumption measurements provided by Koomey [23], specifically for mid-range server, we assume that a physical resource's power consumption is 500 watts per hour.

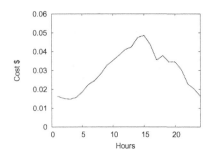

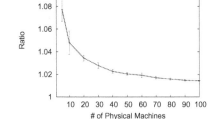

Fig. 5. Energy Cost (KW/H)   **Fig. 6.** Packing Ratio (Heuristic/Optimal)

Energy Cost: To model the energy cost for our framework, we use real energy costs from the Ameren website [1]. Ameren publishes energy costs daily on an

---

[8] We vary the length of the chain workload in our experiments.

hourly basis. We get energy cost for a one month period (from 08/01/11 to 08/31/11) and average them per hour. Figure 5 shows the average price of energy for this period over a 24-hour period. The cost of energy reflects a diurnal pattern – higher during the day and cheaper at night.

Efficacy of Our Greedy Heuristic: In this experiment, we evaluate the performance of our greedy heuristics compared to an optimal allocation of tasks. Since knowing an optimal allocation is difficult (bin packing is NP-hard), we resort to generating workloads for which we know (by construction) that an optimal allocation exists.

We do so by simulating a set of physical machines for the duration of an epoch, and repeatedly creating fragments that sum up to a physical machine's full capacity. We generate fragments based on a uniform distribution between zero and one, thus the average number of fragments per resources is two.[9] Similar results for physical machine's fragmentation were observed given other distributions but were omitted due to lack of space. We proceed in a round-robin fashion over the set of workload models in our disposal (except the batch), and greedily embed each workload over the physical machines. Once no more workloads can be embedded, we assign the remaining unembedded fragments as part of a batch workload. By construction, we know that a "perfect" allocation exists (with every resource being fully utilized for the entire epoch).

We set the start time and end time of all workloads to be the beginning and end of the epoch, respectively. Next, we place the resulting workloads to be the input to our greedy heuristic. Our purpose from this experiment is to evaluate how far our heuristic is from an optimal allocation. Therefore, we assume that the cost of electricity is fixed (i.e., independent of time).

Figure 6 shows the ratio of allocation achieved using our algorithm relative to an optimal allocation. The x-axis shows the number of physical machines used, and the y axis shows the ratio of workload allocation achieved using our heuristic over that of an optimal allocation. The results are reported with 95% confidence. The figure shows that our algorithm's performance is highly comparable to the optimal. Furthermore, as we increase the number of physical machines, the ratio decreases.

Fair Pricing Scheme vs. Utopian Customer Cost: Unlike the previous experiment, which aimed to show the efficacy of our heuristic by comparing its performance to an optimally-allocated set of workloads, the purpose of this experiment is to highlight the fairness of our game-theoretic inspired pricing scheme in comparison to the utopian cost of the customer. As we alluded before, the utopian cost is the (possibly unrealistic) minimal possible cost – reflecting only the cost of the energy and resources the customer actually uses.

To generate workloads, we start by selecting a workload model based on a uniform distribution where each workload model: HPC (fMRI, PAW), WebServer, MapReduce (MR), Chain, and batch get equal percentages (20%) of the total

---

[9] If the generated fragment is greater than the leftover resource capacity, then we assign the fragment the remaining resource capacity.

workload population. Once a workload is selected, we generate a start time randomly for the workload to execute, and set the end time of the workload to be the start time plus the length of execution of the workload. This is an easy step since all of the workloads except chain have fixed structures. For chain workloads, we generate the number of consecutive resource requests based on an exponential distribution with a mean of six. If the end time is greater than the duration of the epoch, then we exclude that workload, and proceed to generate a new one, otherwise we accept the generated workload as part of the overall workload population.

To model the utilization of the webserver workload, we use a standard method of generating the workloads based on an exponential distribution whose mean is modulated by a Sine function. This is done to model the diurnal pattern of higher web server load during the day, and lower web server load at night. For the remaining workload models, we generate the utilization of requests based on a uniform distribution between 0.2 and 1.

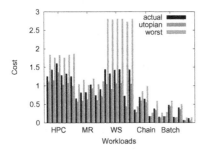
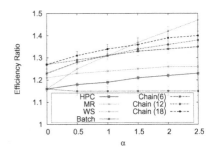

Fig. 7. Per workload cost comparison

Fig. 8. Effect of energy fluctuation on workload cost

Figure 7 shows the distribution of costs based on sampled Shapley value for 30 workloads, where all workload models have equal percentage of workload population (20%). We also show the utopian cost, as well as the cost incurred by the customer had she opted to execute her workload by herself (i.e. no colocation), which we denote as *Worst* cost. As shown, approximate Shapley value is close to the utopian cost. An interesting observation is the ratio between the utopian and approximate cost is highest for webserver workloads, while batch workloads are very close to the utopian. In fact, we also observe that batch workloads can even pay *less* than their utopian. This is due to the fact that batch workloads are the least restrictive workloads in terms of modeling (no edges between tasks), and have complete time flexibility, while webservers have the least flexibility.

To further investigate this phenomena, we proceed to measure the sensitivity of workload costs to fluctuation in energy costs. To model variability in energy cost, we use the distribution of energy highlighted in Figure 5, and modulate it by multiplying it with α, where α varies between 0 and 2.5. For each workload model, we generate 50 workloads and calculate the cost of colocation using the modulated energy cost. We generate two additional variations of chain workloads with length based on exponential distribution with mean 12 and 18 respectively. We define the efficiency ratio as the ratio between the actual customer cost over the utopian cost. Figure 8 highlights our results. The x-axis plots the changing values of α. For $\alpha = 1$, the cost of energy reflects the actual cost shown in Figure 5. As highlighted, inflexible workloads, such as the webserver suffer most as a result of increase in energy cost with overall increase of more than 20 percent, while batch workloads do not show any increase.

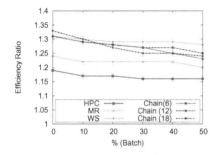

Fig. 9. Workloads with batch mix

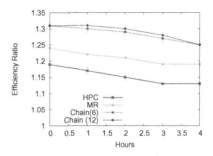

Fig. 10. Effect of Flexibility

Given the fluidity (maximal flexibility) of batch workloads, we investigate their effect when colocated with other workload models. We performed experiments using the same settings as the previous experiment: set the value of $\alpha = 1$, and for each workload, we mix it with different percentages of batch workloads. Figure 9 shows the measured efficiency ratio for different percentages of batch workload mix. We observe that pipeline based workloads like chain and webserver are a better fit for batch workloads than HPC or MR workloads. One reason which is based on observing the actual allocation outcome is due to the existence of parallel branches in MR and HPC models, which provides these workloads – unlike chain and webserver workloads – an additional opportunity for allocation.

Benefit from Flexibility: To measure the effect of flexibility on the overall reduction in cost, we performed experiments using the same setting as before, while allowing the extension of start time and end time of workloads by σ, for different values of σ (hours). Figure 10 shows the effect of customer flexibility on workloads.[10] As expected, the more flexible a workload is, the better the efficiency ratio.

5   Related Work

Economic Models for Resource Management: Several resource management techniques have been proposed for large-scale computing infrastructures using various micro-economic models such as auctions, commodity markets, and

---

[10] We do not include models of webserver and chains with average length 18 since they do not allow for much flexibility in a 24-hour epoch.

iterative combinatorial exchange [4, 6, 30, 38]. Amazon EC2 spot instance is a prime example of one of these markets. Customers bid for resources, and will be allocated such resources as long as their bid is higher than the market price at the time of allocation. Unlike EC2 spot instance which does not provide an SLA regarding the allocation period, in CLOUDPACK, customers are guaranteed to execute throughout the entire time of their allocation.

Ishakian et al, [20] develop a colocation service which allows for migration, profiling and allocation of workloads. In that setting, a customer's workload consists of a *single* task and interactions are driven by the rational behavior of customers, who are free to relocate as long as the relocation minimize their cost. In this Setting, a customer's workload consists of multiple tasks and we optimize the allocation of resources and apportion costs using the game-theoretic-inspired Shapley concept – what we devise is a pricing mechanism and not a game. As a result, each customer ends up paying a marginal cost.

Unlike all of the models referenced above, CLOUDPACK allows for an explicit consideration of the flexibility of customers (as opposed to having such a flexibility be expressed through the strategic choices of customers).

Data Center Energy Management: Minimizing the operating cost of data centers is a very active research topic. Along these lines, there has been significant breakthroughs in terms of optimizing the use of resources through efficient server power management [14, 33], optimized workload distribution and consolidation [16, 32] or better cooling [31]. The authors in [33] motivate the need for coordination among different energy management approaches because they may interfere with one another in unpredictable (and potentially dangerous) ways. They present a power management solution that utilizes control theory for coordination of different approaches.

A common characteristic in the above-referenced, large body of prior work is that the IaaS provider is doing the optimization, which does not provide any incentive for customers. In our model, we aim to minimize the overall operational cost of the datacenter, and provide the transparency that allows flexible customers to take advantage of their flexibility.

Workflow Scheduling: Different workflow management and scheduling tools have been proposed that focus on scheduling DAGs with the purpose of optimizing the makespan and consider QoS properties like deadlines and/or budget constraints [17, 26, 34, 40]. Henzinger et al [17] provide a static scheduling framework that is based on small state abstractions of large workloads, Similar to previous work, Our model aims to minimize the overall operational cost of the datacenter. However, we provide a provably fair pricing mechanism which distributes the cost of leasing resource over customers and provides them with the incentive to declare their flexibility.

Service Level Agreements: There has been significant amount of research on various topics related to SLAs. The usage , specification, and economic aspects of resource management in grids have been considered in [5, 9, 22, 28]. An inherent assumption in such systems is that the customer's SLAs are immutable.

We break that assumption by allowing the customer to provide multiple yet functionally equivalent forms of SLAs. Our framework utilizes this degree of freedom to achieve a better colocation.

Languages and Execution Environments: Workflow/dataflow languages have been proposed since the sixties, with IBM job control language [19] a prime example. Since then, different languages and execution engines have been developed [10, 11, 30]. These languages modeled coordination or dependencies among tasks (programs) as DAGs. Task dependencies reflect data dependencies between tasks. In our language, workloads define resource requests and dependencies are model customer temporal tolerance or flexibility.

Parkes et al [30] outline a tree based bidding language (TBBL), where resources are mapped to the leaves of the tree, and inner nodes model logical operations. TBBL can be used to describe customer requests, however, a such description would be inefficient due to the exponential increasing number of nodes resulting from a customer's flexibility.

6   Conclusion

In this work, we proposed a new pricing model for cloud resources that better reflects the costs incurred by IaaS providers, and gives cloud customers the opportunity and incentive to take advantage of any scheduling flexibilities they might have. We presented CLOUDPACK: a framework for colocation of customer workloads. Our framework provides (1) a resource specification language that allows customers to formally express their flexibility, (2) an algorithm that optimizes the use of cloud resources, and (3) a game-theoretic inspired pricing mechanism that achieves a rationally fair distribution of incurred costs over customers. We presented performance evaluation results that confirm the utility and potential of our framework.

Our on-going research work is pursued along three dimensions. Along the first, we are investigating extensions to our specification language to allow for yet more expressive forms of SLAs – *e.g.*, non-parametric constraints, such as geographic location, anti-colocation, and network proximity, as well as providing customers with a *choice* construct that allows them to specify alternative workload configurations and physical resource flexibilities. Our second line of work is focusing on extending CLOUDPACK to allow for resource allocation with uncertainty, i.e., account and provide cost for resource failures. Our third line of work is focused on developing a prototype of a our colocation framework that will allow us to conduct experiments in a dynamic setting that is subject to the overheads resulting from actual allocation and relocation of workloads. Elements of this prototype have been developed as part of our earlier work on XCS a VM cloud colocation service [20].

References

1. Ameren real-time prices (March 2011),
   https://www2.ameren.com/RetailEnergy/realtimeprices.aspx

2. Ahmad, F., Vijaykumar, T.N.: Joint optimization of idle and cooling power in data centers while maintaining response time. In: ASPLOS 2010, pp. 243–256. ACM, New York (2010)

3. Armbrust, M., Fox, A., Griffith, R., Joseph, A., Katz, R., Konwinski, A., Lee, G., Patterson, D., Rabkin, A., Stoica, I., et al.: A view of cloud computing. Communications of the ACM 53(4) (2010)

4. AuYoung, A., Buonadonna, P., Chun, B.N., Ng, C., Parkes, D.C., Shneidman, J., Snoeren, A.C., Vahdat, A.: Two auction-based resource allocation environments: Design and experience. In: Buyya, R., Bubendorfer, K. (eds.) Market Oriented Grid and Utility Computing, ch. 23. Wiley (2009)

5. Barmouta, A., Buyya, R.: GridBank: A Grid Accounting Services Architecture (GASA) for Distributed Systems Sharing and Integration. In: IPDPS 2003. IEEE Computer Society Press, Washington, DC (2003)

6. Buyya, R., Yeo, C.S., Venugopal, S., Broberg, J., Brandic, I.: Cloud computing and emerging it platforms: Vision, hype, and reality for delivering computing as the 5th utility. Future Generation Computer Systems 25(6) (2009)

7. Castro, J., Gómez, D., Tejada, J.: Polynomial calculation of the shapley value based on sampling. Computers & Operations Research 36(5) (2009)

8. Chen, J., Wang, C., Zhou, B.B., Sun, L., Lee, Y.C., Zomaya, A.Y.: Tradeoffs between profit and customer satisfaction for service provisioning in the cloud. In: HPDC, New York, USA (2011)

9. Czajkowski, K., Foster, I., Kesselman, C., Sander, V., Tuecke, S.: SNAP: A Protocol for Negotiating Service Level Agreements and Coordinating Resource Management in Distributed Systems. In: Feitelson, D.G., Rudolph, L., Schwiegelshohn, U. (eds.) JSSPP 2002. LNCS, vol. 2537, pp. 153–183. Springer, Heidelberg (2002)

10. Dean, J., Ghemawat, S.: MapReduce: Simplified data processing on large clusters. Communications of the ACM 51(1) (2008)

11. Deelman, E., Blythe, J., Gil, Y., Kesselman, C., Mehta, G., Patil, S., Su, M., Vahi, K., Livny, M.: Pegasus: Mapping scientific workflows onto the grid. In: Grid Computing, pp. 131–140. Springer (2004)

12. Fan, X., Weber, W.D., Barroso, L.A.: Power provisioning for a warehouse-sized computer. In: ISCA, New York, USA (2007)

13. Ferguson, A.D., Bodík, P., Kandula, S., Boutin, E., Fonseca, R.: Jockey: guaranteed job latency in data parallel clusters. In: EuroSys, pp. 99–112 (2012)

14. Gandhi, A., Harchol-Balter, M., Das, R., Lefurgy, C.: Optimal power allocation in server farms. In: SIGMETRICS 2009. ACM, New York (2009)

15. Greenberg, A., Hamilton, J., Maltz, D.A., Patel, P.: The cost of a cloud: Research problems in data center networks. CCR Online (Janaury 2009)

16. Heller, B., Seetharaman, S., Mahadevan, P., Yiakoumis, Y., Sharma, P., Banerjee, S., McKeown, N.: ElasticTree: Saving energy in data center networks. In: NSDI (2010)

17. Henzinger, T., Singh, V., Wies, T., Zufferey, D.: Scheduling large jobs by abstraction refinement. In: Proceedings of the Sixth Conference on Computer Systems, pp. 329–342. ACM (2011)

18. Hua, K., Sheu, S.: Skyscraper broadcasting: A new broadcasting scheme for metropolitan video-on-demand systems. ACM SIGCOMM Computer Communication Review 27 (1997)

19. IBM: Job Control Language. (May 2011), http://publib.boulder.ibm.com/infocenter/zos/basics/index.jsp?topic=/com.ibm.zos.zcourses/zcourses_jclintro.html

20. Ishakian, V., Sweha, R., Londoño, J., Bestavros, A.: Colocation as a Service. Strategic and Operational Services for Cloud Colocation. In: IEEE NCA (2010)

21. Clark, C., Fraser, K., Hand, S., Hansen, J.G., Jul, E., Limpach, C., Pratt, I., Warfield, A.: Live Migration of Virtual Machines. In: NSDI, pp. 273–286. USENIX Association, Berkeley (2005)

22. Keller, A., Ludwig, H.: The WSLA Framework: Specifying and Monitoring Service Level Agreements for Web Services. J. Netw. Syst. Manage. 11, 57–81 (2003)

23. Koomey, J.: Estimating total power consumption by servers in the us and the world (2007)

24. Lai, K.: Markets are dead, long live markets. SIGecom Exch. 5(4), 1–10 (2005)

25. Liu, H., Jin, H., Liao, X., Hu, L., Yu, C.: Live Migration of Virtual Machine Based on Full System Trace and Replay. In: Proc. of the 18th ACM HPDC (2009)

26. Mandal, A., Kennedy, K., Koelbel, C., Marin, G., Mellor-Crummey, J., Liu, B., Johnsson, L.: Scheduling strategies for mapping application workflows onto the grid. In: HPDC, Washington, DC, USA (2005)

27. Nelson, M., Lim, B.H., Hutchins, G.: Fast Transparent Migration for Virtual Machines. In: ATEC 2005: Proceedings of the Annual Conference on USENIX Annual Technical Conference, pp. 25–25. USENIX Association, Berkeley (2005)

28. Netto, M.A., Bubendorfer, K., Buyya, R.: SLA-Based Advance Reservations with Flexible and Adaptive Time QoS Parameters. In: Proceedings of the 5th International Conference on Service-Oriented Computing (2007)

29. Nisan, N.: Algorithmic game theory. Cambridge Univ. Press (2007)

30. Parkes, D., Cavallo, R., Elprin, N., Juda, A., Lahaie, S., Lubin, B., Michael, L., Shneidman, J., Sultan, H.: ICE: An iterative combinatorial exchange. In: Proceedings of the 6th ACM Conference on Electronic Commerce, pp. 249–258. ACM (2005)

31. Parolini, L., Sinopoli, B., Krogh, B.: Reducing data center energy consumption via coordinated cooling and load management. In: USENIX Conference on Power Aware Computing and Systems (2008)

32. Qureshi, A., Weber, R., Balakrishnan, H., Guttag, J., Maggs, B.: Cutting the electric bill for internet-scale systems. In: SIGCOMM, pp. 123–134 (2009)

33. Raghavendra, R., Ranganathan, P., Talwar, V., Wang, Z., Zhu, X.: No "power" struggles: coordinated multi-level power management for the data center. In: ASPLOS 2008, pp. 48–59 (2008)

34. Ramakrishnan, L., Chase, J.S., Gannon, D., Nurmi, D., Wolski, R.: Deadlinesensitive workflow orchestration without explicit resource control. J. Parallel Distrib. Comput. 71, 343–353 (2011)

35. Ranganathan, P., Leech, P., Irwin, D., Chase, J.: Ensemble-level power management for dense blade servers. In: ISCA, pp. 66–77 (2006)

36. Stanojevic, R., Laoutaris, N., Rodriguez, P.: On economic heavy hitters: Shapley value analysis of 95th-percentile pricing. In: Proceedings of the 10th Annual Conference on Internet Measurement. ACM (2010)

37. Verma, A., Cherkasova, L., Campbell, R.H.: Resource provisioning framework for mapReduce jobs with performance goals. In: Kon, F., Kermarrec, A.-M. (eds.) Middleware 2011. LNCS, vol. 7049, pp. 165–186. Springer, Heidelberg (2011)

38. Wolski, R., Plank, J.S., Bryan, T., Brevik, J.: G-commerce: Market Formulations Controlling Resource Allocation on the Computational Grid. In: IPDPS (2001)

39. Wood, T., Cherkasova, L., Ozonat, K., Shenoy, P.D.: Profiling and Modeling Resource Usage of Virtualized Applications. In: Issarny, V., Schantz, R. (eds.) Middleware 2008. LNCS, vol. 5346, pp. 366–387. Springer, Heidelberg (2008)

40. Yu, J., Buyya, R., Tham, C.: Cost-based scheduling of scientific workflow application on utility grids. In: Proceedings of the First International Conference on e-Science and Grid Computing, pp. 140–147. IEEE Computer Society (2005)

Dynamic Software Deployment from Clouds to Mobile Devices

Ioana Giurgiu[1], Oriana Riva[2,*], and Gustavo Alonso[1]

[1] Systems Group, Dept. of Computer Science, ETH Zurich
[2] Microsoft Research, Redmond

Abstract. With the functionality of mobile applications ever increasing, designers are often confronted with either the resource limitations of the devices or of the network. As pointed out by recent work, application partitioning between mobile devices and clouds, can be used to solve some of these issues, improving performance and/or battery life. In this paper, we argue that the static decisions made in existing work cannot leverage the full potential of application partitioning. Thus, to allow for variations in the execution environment, we have developed a system that dynamically adapts the application partition decisions. The system works by continuously profiling an applications performance and dynamically updating its distributed deployment to accommodate changes in the network bandwidth, devices CPU utilization, and data loads. Using several real applications, we show that our approach provides performance gains as high as 75% over traditional approaches and achieves lower power consumption by a factor close to 45%.

Keywords: Mobile cloud computing, dynamic distribution, modularity.

1 Introduction

Today's mobile users demand increasingly ubiquitous applications and ever richer functionality on their devices. They want to create panoramas from photo collections, manage their finances, and even run augmented reality or data analytics applications while interacting spontaneously and expecting fast response times. These demands and expectations create a complex design problem. On the one hand, running the applications entirely on the mobile is limited by the computational resources of the devices. On the other hand, running the applications remotely is limited by the network bandwidth and often raises usability issues due to varying latency. Thus, recent research efforts have proposed to offload parts of an application from the mobile device to the cloud [6,8,9,11,26], thereby demonstrating important gains in battery life and performance. Code offloading raises two important questions: *what* and *when* to migrate for remote execution. While most techniques exclusively focus on what to offload, by making offline partitioning decisions, we advocate that understanding when it becomes beneficial to offload code is just as important. Changes in the network bandwidth or latency,

---

* Work done while being at ETH Zurich.

P. Narasimhan and P. Triantafillou (Eds.): Middleware 2012, LNCS 7662, pp. 394–414, 2012.
© IFIP International Federation for Information Processing 2012

sudden increases of the CPU load on the mobile device, and variations in the user's inputs during interactions can dramatically impact the performance and responsiveness of most applications, an aspect often ignored in existing work.

Consider an example from furniture houses where computer-based applications can help customers visualize the possible arrangement of furniture items in their homes. Static approaches would store the furniture catalog and perform the image rendering remotely, independent of any changes in environmental factors. However, one can easily imagine situations in which varying network conditions result in significantly slower application responsiveness (e.g.,, due to a drop in available bandwidth). In such scenarios, an adaptive system would recognize that the network is the bottleneck and not the device's CPU, and would promptly limit data transfers and move more computation to the mobile device. A similar decision can be made based on the amount of data involved, something that depends on what the user wants to upload in every interaction. There will always be situations where static partitioning has chosen the wrong configuration.

In this paper, we address the challenges of (1) what parts of an application to offload and (2) when, by considering the changing conditions one is likely to encounter when operating with mobile devices. Our system explores an adaptive deployment model where the cloud moves part of the application to the mobile device to improve user experience and minimize data transfers. To ensure high flexibility in what application parts to offload, we assume applications are modularized. Writing modular applications is already a well-established practice with increasing software support [10,19,23] and various projects recognize the benefits of decoupling an application's functionalities into pluggable modules [4,12,27]. Thus, given a modular application, we deliver an automatic pipeline of operations that optimally partitions it on-the-fly between the cloud and the mobile device according to the device's CPU load, network conditions, or user inputs. Full automation is key to improve user experience and to ensure the user does not have to be involved in what are complex architectural decisions. Thus, the dynamic aspects of our system guarantee that on-the-fly acquisition of an application does not result in unacceptable delays. Additionally, we introduce a novel mechanism to allow devices to autonomously and dynamically adjust an application configuration based on the user's inputs.

Our system runs on Android [3] and Amazon EC2 instances [1]. It was evaluated with three applications: a service for ticket purchase, an indoor localization application and a text-to-speech synthesizer. In all cases, for small, medium and large EC2 instances, we observe significant gains (i.e., reduced interaction time by up to 75% and lower power consumption by up to 45%), while considering all data and code migration costs. The system dynamically adapts to changes in the data load or the execution environment, by promptly finding and switching to the optimal configuration. An additional benefit of our approach is that applications that could not otherwise be run on the mobile device (except maybe for very small data loads), execute successfully for all data inputs, while minimizing the overall interaction time. An example is FreeTTS [13], a text-to-speech synthesizer application which we used in the evaluation. If running entirely on the mobile device, FreeTTS works up to a maximum input of only 5 KB of text, showing after that an exponential increase in the execution time. We show that with our technique this restriction does no longer hold and the application performance is significantly improved.

The rest of the paper is organized as follows. In the next section, we discuss related work. Section 3 describes the system's goals and design principles, while Section 4 gives insights on its implementation. In Section 5, we describe our applications and present results in Section 6. Finally, we conclude in Section 7.

2   Related Work

An increasing amount of work is being done in the context of application partitioning and offloading to remote servers or the cloud. However, most systems tackle the static problem, that of making partitioning decisions before an application interaction is initiated and without readjusting the offloading scheme at runtime. More recently, the dynamic aspect has gained more attention and several approaches have emerged [7–9, 22] although they are all based on very different premises and present different limitations.

MAUI [9] and CloneCloud [7,8] aim at improving the performance and battery life on the mobile device by offloading application state to either remote servers or cloud clones. Both require the application to be pre-installed at the device, which creates problems with the number of platforms to be supported and as software evolves. Our system provides on-demand installation, which removes the need of having the software pre-installed and makes it significantly easier to evolve the application. Furthermore, MAUI's offloading unit (i.e., method) is finer-grained compared to ours (i.e., OSGI modules [19]). Thus it becomes unfeasible for applications with more than tens of methods, since their algorithm requires exponential time to traverse the entire search space. Finally, although MAUI can react to CPU or network changes, it cannot adapt to varying user inputs. Our approach uses a caching algorithm to solve this problem.

CloneCloud shows the effectiveness of static analysis of Java code to manage dynamic offloading. However, their evaluation shows significant gains only for large inputs, i.e., 100 photos, as only then the achieved speedup on the clones becomes significant. A serious drawback is that the gains observed do not consider the bandwidth cost. CloneCloud assumes that the device and remote server have fully synchronized file systems and removes the cost of such synchronization from the measurements. As soon as dynamic data is involved the observed cost in battery and performance is likely to be dominated by the data transfer. In our scenarios, we consider the cost of data transfers an integral part of the problem. Thus, we account for the data migration overhead and observe significant performance improvements by doing so even with modest amounts of data involved. Odessa [22] has also recognized the need to dynamically adjust offloading decisions, and proposes a technique to structure the parallelism across mobile devices and remote servers for streaming applications. More recently, [17] has proposed a fault-tolerant approach to save energy on mobile devices by server offloading without partitioning. The application is present at both ends and only state is migrated to switch from local to remote executions. State migration, however, has the same problems as data migration as the overhead typically comes from the user data and cannot be ignored. Therefore, most of these dynamic approaches offload the application state only, while ignoring the hurdles of both code and data migration. We argue these problems are essential and need to be addressed, thus our system provides support to offload code and data on-the-fly.

Static approaches have been proposed in the context of "cyber foraging"' [5, 25]. Spectra [5, 11] and Chroma [6] partition applications into local and re-moteable tasks, pre-installed on surrogates. Task partition is based on manu-ally specified execution plans. Other systems use virtual machine techniques to increase flexibility. Slingshot [28] and Goyal and Carter's prototype [15] allow users to install their own functionality on surrogates. These systems are different from ours in that they rely on the developer to manage the partitioning process and require application pre-installation. In the context of program partitioning, Coign [16] provides static partitioning of COM components, while Wishbone [18] and Abacus [2] focus on partitioning either stream or data-intensive applications. However, none of these systems readjust their partitioning decision at runtime. Other work tackled the migration of Java applications [20] remotely. In addition to their static approach, their offloading unit (i.e., Java classes) is unsuitable for large applications. Other systems have treated applications as three-tier struc-tures [29–31] to simplify partitioning. Although they put little burden on the programmer, there is no support for dynamic migration of components.

3   System Overview

Our system's goal is to make cloud applications not originally designed for mobile platforms capable of running on mobile devices in a resource-efficient manner, while maintaining high performance under dynamic conditions. In order to pro-vide an improved user experience for a wide range of applications (with long- and short-term interactions), our approach addresses several requirements.

On-the-fly application installation and updates. In practice, it is not possible to assume that a device has all necessary applications pre-installed. Moreover, for cloud providers it is important to reduce the data transfer to its clients at in-stallation time and provide support for versioned updates. Our system eliminates full code pre-installation and enables application updates at runtime.

Dynamic and optimal application partitioning. The decision on how to dis-tribute an application between the cloud and the mobile device is not obvious, but highly application- and platform-specific. Moreover, mobile devices can ex-perience changes in connectivity due to mobility and network instability, as well as variations in the application load (both in CPU and data transfer) due to multiple concurrently-running applications. Our system considers an appli-cation's structure, resource requirements and device constraints to identify its best mobile-cloud partition and adjust it online. In addition, it reconfigures the current application deployment without interrupting ongoing interactions. In Al-fredO, an *optimal* partitioning is the application distribution that results in the lowest interaction time. It is equivalent to the graph cutting problem and can be solved with linear programming, as described later in Section 3.3.

Adaptation to varying data inputs. The number and size of data inputs (e.g., size of images to process, length of text to synthesize, etc.) can impact an application's execution time, and thus its optimal partitioning between client and cloud. As user inputs cannot be easily predicted, it is hard to know a priori which partitioning configuration suits best a particular user interaction. Rather than deferring the partitioning decision to the cloud side, our system allows clients to autonomously decide which configuration to adopt once the user inputs have been submitted to the application.

The system builds on top of our previous work [14, 24], where we tackled the problem of static code offloading, based on offline profiling of applications.

3.1   Architecture

To benefit from our model, applications must be built in a modular fashion, where ideally *modules* contain highly-cohesive functionalities and communicate through low-coupled *dependencies*. The steps taken to distribute a modular application between the cloud and the mobile device are shown in Fig. 1. First, on the cloud, the *application profiler* instruments the application to extract a compact description of its modular structure, as well as CPU and communication statistics (step 1a). On the client, the *mobile device's profiler* collects measurements of the CPU load, network status and available storage space (step 1b). Both profilers submit this information to the *graph generator* component, which uses these measurements to generate a compact specification of the application and environment, in the form of a resource consumption graph (step 2). Based on this description, the optimizer identifies the best distribution of modules and configures the deployment accordingly (step 3a). For different simulations of the user inputs, the optimizer computes asynchronously the most suitable partitions and caches them on the mobile device (step 3b).

At bootstrap, our system offloads the minimum functionality required to start the application on the mobile device. Once the first code migration phase has completed and the acquired components are active, the user can start using the application. At runtime, due to different user inputs, fluctuations in the network connectivity, or changes in load on the mobile device (e.g., users switch from WiFi to 3G, move to low bandwidth areas or increase the device's CPU load by starting more applications) the profilers and optimizer are constantly running such that the partitioning configuration can be changed on the fly.

Fig. 1 also shows that our system runs on top of the R-OSGi [23] and OSGi [19] platforms, that provide module management and remote communication capabilities across application modules.

3.2   Code Pre-installation and Updates

Our approach removes the need to pre-install an application on the mobile device before interaction and provides users with on-the-fly installations and updates.

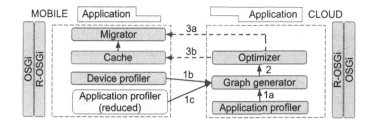

Fig. 1. Architecture and pipeline of operators

This flexibility comes from the modular nature of our design principles (i.e., supported by the OSGI management system our system relies on), and proves to be not only efficient, but also convenient for both cloud providers and clients.

On-demand migration, especially for large applications, is significantly more efficient than full pre-installation. For example, FreeTTS [13], used in our evaluation, has a small code base of 4 MB. If application updates are constantly made available, with a code pre-installation approach the application has to be fully downloaded each time, as versioning is not supported. With AlfredO, only the code necessary to enable the interaction is fetched on the mobile device, merely 260 KB for this application. Once one starts using the application, our system acquires on-the-fly the code necessary to provide users with an optimal interaction. Moreover, by supporting versioning, when code updates are available, AlfredO fetches only the newly modified modules. Additionally, modularity allows us to naturally foster the deployment of applications that contain critical or security restricted pieces of code (i.e., banking). With our system, only those components that have no privacy issues can be installed on the client. This means that software or service providers can still benefit from increased security, while improving user experience on the device.

3.3   Optimal and Dynamic Application Partitioning

Our system partitions applications between the cloud and mobile device while optimizing interaction time and bandwidth utilization. We describe how the optimal partition of an application is identified and how is adapted at runtime.

Application Instrumentation and Profiling. The profiler is responsible for characterizing the structure and behaviour of a given cloud application, as well as collecting measurements at every user interaction. First, it extracts the inter-module dependencies which have a direct impact on bootstrapping and executing the application, as well as the partitioning decision. Dependencies impose the order in which modules need to be started and restrict their location. The more dependencies a module has, the more expensive its remote invocations become if moved to the mobile device. Second, for each module, the profiler measures its code size, the amount of sent and received data, and its execution time.

From the network perspective, mobile devices connect to the outside world through 3G or WiFi, if available. The differences in their data rates are well known, with a theoretical maximum below 14 Mbps for 3G (HSDPA) and 54 Mbps for WiFi (802.11g). In practice, the gap is much higher and mobility makes network conditions even more unstable. Thus, the profiler monitors on the device which network interface is currently in use and what are the bandwidth and latency on the link. Section 4 provides more details on the profiling step.

Application and Network Specification. The profiled data is used to provide a compact description of each application module. A *module* is a logical unit encompassing one or more application functions. An example of module specification provided by the profiler is the following:

```
module 'mPayment' {
    deps: [mRSA, mBank]; type: [nIO, movable]; CPU: 168ms;   size: 17kB}
wire 'wPR': ('mPayment', 'mRSA', 50kB)
wire 'wPB': ('mPayment', 'mBank', 7kB)
network: ('WiFi', 6Mbps, 87ms)
```

A module, such as the *mPayment* used in the ticket machine application, has a number of dependencies (*deps*) on other modules (i.e., it uses functions provided by such modules). In this case, *mPayment* depends on *mRSA* and *mBank*. Its *type* property specifies whether it communicates with components outside the application (type=IO) or only with internal modules (type=nIO). In addition, as not all modules can be migrated to a mobile device (e.g., due to privacy issues, database management), they are also classified into *movable* and *non-movable*. Some of these properties can be automatically extracted by processing a module's dependencies (e.g., database connections), but, if not obvious, it is also possible for the developer to manually annotate them. *CPU* and *size* report the average execution time for such module and its code size. A *wire* specifies how much data is transferred between two inter-connected modules, while *network* specifies the type of network connection the device is currently using (WiFi or 3G), as well as its measured bandwidth and latency.

Application Optimization. Based on the application and network specifications, the optimizer decides how to partition the application while minimizing the overall interaction time and respecting device-specific constraints, such as maximum storage space available for installing modules and maximum amount of data which can be transferred to the cloud.

The application specification is represented through a *consumption graph*, which captures both the application structure and the gathered statistics. It consists of a directed acyclic graph $G = \{M, D\}$, where a vertex M_i is a module and an edge d_{ij} models a dependency between M_i and M_j. Each vertex M_i has a cost expressed through two parameters: the code size c_i and the execution time t_i of the corresponding module. Each edge d_{ij} has a cost expressed by the size of data transferred between the connecting modules, $in_{ij} + out_{ji}$.

Given the consumption graph, the optimization problem consists of finding a cut in the graph such that some application modules execute on the device and the rest on the cloud. Let us consider an application with n modules, M_1, M_2, ..., M_n and a partition $P = P_{device} \bigcup P_{cloud}$, where $P_{device} = \{M_p | p \in [1, ..., k]\}$ is the set of modules to migrate on the mobile device and $P_{cloud} = \{M_s | s \in [1, ..., l]\}$ is the set of modules residing in the cloud. The objective function minimizes the overall interaction time of the application, while taking into account the overhead of acquiring and installing the necessary modules on the device, as well as generating proxies for all remote dependencies.

$$min\ O_P = min\ (\sum_{i=1}^{k} \frac{c_i}{B} + t_{is} * k + t_p * r + \sum_{i=1}^{k} t_i + \sum_{j=1}^{l} t_j + \sum_{i=1}^{t \leq k} \sum_{j=1}^{w \leq l} \frac{(in_{ij} + out_{ji})}{B})$$

$$such\ that:\ \sum_{i=1}^{k} c_i \leq C_{MAX}\ and\ \sum_{i=1}^{t \leq k} \sum_{j=1}^{w \leq l} in_{ij} \leq D_{MAX}$$

The first part in the function models the cost of migrating k modules to the mobile device over a link of bandwidth B, installing and starting them $(t_{is} * k)$, as well as generating the proxies for all remote dependencies $(t_p * r)$. As we explain in Section 4, in order to become active, modules need to be installed and started, and proxies must also be established to manage the client-cloud communication. Our measurements show that the overall installation and starting time of an application's partition linearly increases with the number (k) of modules fetched on the device. t_{is} is a parameter characteristic of the phone platform, which can be measured at bootstrap. For the phone platform we used, for instance, we found $t_{is} = 1700\ ms$. The proxy generation time depends on the number of remote dependencies (r) the fetched modules require. We found the startup time per proxy (t_p) to be in average 360 ms (300 ms for WiFi, 420 ms for 3G).

The second part of the function models the computation time of the modules executing on the client and on the cloud. We explain in Section 4 how the client's CPU time is estimated. Finally, the last term in the function captures the time necessary for transferring data between the distributed modules. The solution to the problem must also satisfy a group of user-defined constraints. The example above shows constraints on the maximum size of bytecode to be migrated to the mobile device and on the data transferred from the device to the cloud at each application invocation. To find the optimal partition we modify the *ALL* algorithm proposed in [14] to account also for the CPU and network analysis. The *ALL* algorithm takes as input the consumption graph and generates all possible partitioning configurations obtained by traversing the graph in an adapted topological order that combines both breadth-first and depth-first search. The algorithm first eliminates the configurations that do not satisfy the user's constraints, and then evaluates the objective function for each valid configuration such that the optimum can be found. Its complexity is $O(|M||D|log|D|)$.

Dynamically Adjusting Partitions. Since the execution environment changes dynamically (variations in CPU load on the mobile phone, network bandwidth, etc.) our system needs to be able to promptly switch from an application distribution to another, if necessary. In order to do this, the optimizer periodically runs and detects when the current partitioning is no longer optimal. In replacing a current distribution with a newer (optimal) one, it is important to minimize the application's interruption time, and possibly carry out most of the reconfiguration work in parallel to the ongoing execution. To reduce the overall bootstrap cost, our technique takes into account which modules have been fetched and installed on the mobile device by the previous distribution. The optimizer searches for the optimal configuration, and, if different from the current one, it transfers the missing modules to the mobile device. While the previous configuration continues to operate, the system installs the newly fetched modules. Once the initialization of the new configuration has finished, if there is an ongoing interaction, at its termination our system seamlessly switches to the new configuration which will be used from the next interaction onwards.

Adaptation to Varying Data Inputs. Besides variations in CPU load and network, a user's data inputs can significantly affect the partitioning decision. This is relevant for a large class of interactive applications that our system targets. While in some applications, user inputs are relatively standardized or it is possible to build an accurate approximation model (e.g., a ticket machine), for other applications it is hard to predict properties such as number, type, and size of the inputs. For instance, in an image processing application, the size and number of images during a user session are relevant factors in determining the CPU and network requirements of the application. Likewise, for a text-to-speech synthesizer, the text size to be translated can impact the application's behavior.

We exclude the possibility of running the optimizer on the client side because this would involve extra communication for collecting the profiling information from the cloud side, as well as extra CPU overhead for running the algorithm. Instead, we allow clients to *cache* some of the optimizer's solutions and autonomously decide on which partitioning configuration to use.

The optimizer first computes the optimal partitioning with the current network conditions and some default user inputs. It then generates additional solutions by simulating possible operating scenarios. Scenarios are defined by varying various *features*, describing both the operating environment and user inputs. For instance, the *network bandwidth* feature has the format *network(lower, upper)* and examples are *wifi(0.0,3.0)*, *wifi(3.1-6.0)*, *3G(0.0,1.5)*, *3G(1.6-3.0)*. The *input* feature has the format *input([lower_num,upper_num],[lower_size,upper_size])* and qualifies number and size ranges of a specific input (e.g., images submitted to an image-processing application, text sent to a speech synthesizer). Examples are *intext([1-5],[1-500])*, *intext([1-5],[501-1000])*, *intext([6-10],[1-500])*.

By generating all the possible combinations of such features, a pool of scenario configurations is derived. The optimizer computes the optimal partitioning for each configuration and returns to the client a report consisting of tuples <*configuration_type,solution*>. At each interaction with the application, the client consults the cached report and based on the inputs received and the operating conditions, it autonomously decides on which configuration to adopt.

A potential risk with this approach is that by considering all possible values that the features might take, the number of scenarios to process grows exponentially.

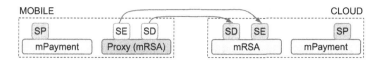

Fig. 2. Example of bundle deployment using R-OSGi

To limit this number, the server maintains a history of the minimum and maximum values previously observed for each feature and computes a maximum number of ranges for each one (typically in the order of 4 ranges). In addition, the features are manually specified by developers such that only relevant aspects are monitored. If a new input does not fit in any of the ranges, then the chosen configuration will be done corresponding to the range closest to the input.

4   Implementation

Our system is implemented for the Android platform and is based on ApacheFelix [10] (i.e., a Java implementation of the OSGi module management system), with the addition of R-OSGi [23] for remote execution across platforms. The architecture is shown in Fig. 1. The runtime on the cloud includes the application profiler, the consumption graph generator and the optimizer. The optimizer returns to the mobile device the list of modules, *bundles* in OSGi terminology, to fetch using the migrator, and a pool of selected configurations to cache. The client runs the device profiler and a reduced version of the application profiler collecting only CPU statistics.

Flexible Bundle Deployment. Bundles are reusable pieces of software packaged in binary components, containing bytecode and metadata (i.e., versioning and dependencies). Modular designs encourage the coupling of related functions in the same bundle, exposed through a *service interface*. Any bundle that wants to use another bundle needs references to the registered services, thus being oblivious to any implementation details. OSGi allows an application to install, start, stop and uninstall bundles, as well as register services.

Since OSGi is restricted to single machines, our system requires an additional layer for remote communication, namely R-OSGi. R-OSGi's main goal is to provide dynamism and full location transparency for bundles, without changing their implementation or structure. To provide remote communication across bundles, R-OSGi generates a *proxy* on the calling bundle's side, which delegates service calls to the remote side. The proxy is registered with the local service registry as an implementation of the remote bundle service. An alternative to proxy generation is the actual fetching and installation of the remote bundle.

In Fig. 2, we consider a cloud application consisting of two bundles *mPayment* and *mRSA*, with their services *SP*, *SE* and *SD*, such that SP depends on both SE and SD. Initially only *mPayment* is fetched on the mobile device and remote proxies are generated for *mRSA*'s services. As the optimal distribution can dynamically change, our goal is to switch between partitions without interrupting an ongoing interaction, by exploiting R-OSGi's dynamic bundle management. Changing a configuration means acquiring the new bundles, installing and starting them, stopping and uninstalling the currently running ones, as well as generating the necessary remote proxies. Let us assume that the optimizer decides to fetch also *mRSA* on the mobile device. To initialize *mRSA* on the client, our system performs the following operations: (a) it migrates the code of *mRSA* to the device; (b) it installs and starts *mRSA*; (c) it generates remote proxies for all dependencies on *mRSA*; (d) it removes its proxy used by *mPayment*. When the process is completed, the new configuration is ready to be used. With the exception of operation (d), all other steps can occur in parallel with an ongoing interaction, without the need for the current configuration to stop.

Profiling with Structural Reflection. Application profiling uses load-time reflection at bytecode level. Every bundle has a MANIFEST file with metadata on versioning, services and dependencies on other bundles. For each service, the profiler identifies the Java classes implementing it and injects in all methods code to measure the execution time and the size of I/O parameters. The overall execution time per bundle is the sum of the running times of all executed methods. Measuring the data transfer between bundles allows us to identify which bundles are closely coupled and can benefit from colocation. The execution time helps to identify computational-intensive bundles which might cause performance degradation if ran on the mobile device. Finally, by inspecting the JAR package of a bundle, the profiler extracts its bytecode size, which is relevant to estimate the bundle's migration time and the storage required on the mobile device.

The first time an application is profiled, all static (i.e., bytecode size, services and dependencies) and dynamic (i.e., running time and I/O data size) parameters are measured on the cloud. At runtime, the profiler monitors only the dynamic variables. To avoid flapping in the measurements, it maintains a history of measurements and computes exponentially smoothed moving averages.

CPU, Network and Power Profiling. Our system does not assume offline profiling for all applications and mobile platforms. Relative to CPU, this would require running all configurations for every application on the mobile device, and measuring the execution time for each invocation. In practice, we found a simple approximation to be accurate enough for our optimization problem, with the benefit of a small overhead on the client. The execution time of each bundle on the device is approximated as $t_c = t_s * K$, where t_s is its execution time on the cloud and K is a factor indicating how much slower the client's CPU is compared to the remote machine. Offline, we experiment with various mobile platforms and estimate the corresponding K parameters. In our setup, we found *K=3* to work well for all our applications. At the beginning of a user interaction, the optimizer uses the estimated K parameter, and then dynamically corrects the initial estimation based on the CPU execution time of all bundles running on the device. In addition, on the mobile side we periodically obtain the current CPU load of the device, over all active processes, from Android API functions.

Relative to network, the profiler detects whether the user is using WiFi or 3G by parsing the content of *proc/net/dev*. To estimate the bandwidth and latency of the current network, the system prunes the network by periodically sending 50 kB of data to the cloud. We found 50 kB to be a good representative size for our applications. Measurements are carried out every 30 seconds, but once an application interaction starts, *opportunistic profiling* is used instead: the bandwidth estimation is based on transfers carrying actual application data.

In order to profile the power consumed by running application bundles on the mobile device, our system uses PowerTutor [21], an online power estimation system that has been implemented for the Android platform. Since CPU and network are prime factors for application bundle distribution, we profile the CPU and WiFi/3G statistics provided by PowerTutor and define the power consumption as $Power_{total} = Power_{WiFi|3G} + Power_{CPU}$. Measuring the power consumed by an application can validate whether our latency-based model is effective in both minimizing the interaction time and reducing the device's energy consumption. Thus, we require that the power consumed with the optimal configuration found by the system is smaller than those experienced when the entire application is running either on the device or in the cloud. Our results in Section 6 validate these conditions.

5   Applications

We briefly describe the three prototype applications we used to evaluate our system: indoor localization (IL), text-to-speech synthesizer (TTS) and ticketing machine (TM). IL and TTS belong to the *maps* and *media* application categories, while TM is an example of infrastructure service. The class of applications we target are computationally and network intensive, and are characterized by request-reply interactions. However, the model can be extended to other categories, such as streaming, by incorporating queuing networks to naturally emulate the behavior of application modules and capture clients arrival rate.

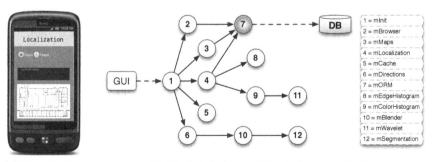

(a) Localization   (b) Modularization of the indoor localization

Fig. 3. IL application on Android and its modularization scheme

We developed IL and TM from scratch, and modularized an already existing TTS synthesizer [13]. A screenshot of the IL application is shown in Fig. 3(a). The IL application provides users with visualization facilities of a building map, including map tracking, browsing and directions to people and places within the building. Localization is carried out using the phone camera. As shown in Fig. 3(b), these functions were implemented using 12 bundles. *mInit* sets parameters and user preferences. *mMaps* and *mBrowser* allow the user to choose buildings, places and people for which *mORM* retrieves maps from a database. *mCache* can save the searched maps for future use. To locate themselves inside a building, users take photos of their surroundings, which are then compared for similarity against existing snapshots in the database. To determine the similarity degree, photos are decomposed in wavelets and features, such as color and edge histograms (*mWavelet*, *mColorHistogram*, *mEdgeHistogram*). The average values are then compared to the precomputed ones in the database. Finally, *mDirections* displays a map highlighting the path from the user's current position to the browsed place or person. *mBlender* and *mSegmentation* use image processing algorithms to draw the required directions. Only *mORM* is marked as *non-movable* to the mobile device, since it is strongly coupled with the database.

For the TTS and TM applications we only provide a brief description. TTS supports two operations: (a) the translation of a text extracted from a photo taken with the device's camera, and (b) the generation of speech from the translated text. The application has been implemented by adapting modules from the FreeTTS [13] synthesizer. The application was modularized in 10 bundles. Finally, the TM application was the result of a joint project with the Swiss national railway (SBB). TM allows users to purchase train tickets, browse train routes, check prices and receive electronic tickets from their mobile devices. The application's functions were split into 10 bundles, out of which some contained private data of SBB and therefore were bound to remain in the cloud. For both applications the graph obtained by modularization is similar to the one in Fig. 3(b).

6   Evaluation

We evaluate how our system meets the following goals: (a) improving an application's performance in the cloud-mobile device setup, (b) dynamically switching between partitioning configurations, (c) reacting to variations in CPU load, network and user inputs, and (d) maintaining a reasonable overhead on the device. In the tests we use the three applications described and all experiments consider 15 repetitions. The client runs on a HTC Desire smartphone and the server on small, medium or large standard Amazon EC2 instances. The HTC Desire phone runs Android 2.1, has a Qualcomm QSD 8250 1 GHz processor and 576 MB of RAM. The smartphone communicates with the server using WiFi or 3G.

To show that AlfredO chooses the optimal configuration, in all experiments we consider all possible distributions of the applications and execute them in the setup described above. Then, by comparing the measurements obtained against the optimizer output, we can argue whether AlfredO's decision matches reality.

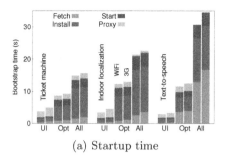

(a) Startup time

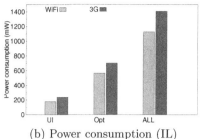

(b) Power consumption (IL)

Fig. 4. Startup time and power consumption on HTC Desire for the three applications on EC2 US-East instances (WiFi and 3G in use)

6.1   Initialization Cost

First, we characterize the performance overhead of our system on the Android platform. On the HTC Desire, the start up consists of launching the client components shown in Fig. 1 and registering their inter-dependencies. This takes on average 12–14s. Once the system is running, the startup time of an application varies depending on the module distribution between client and cloud.

Fig. 4(a) shows the installation times for all three applications. For each application, we report 3 pairs of bars. For each pair, the first represents the WiFi case and the second one the 3G case. The first set of bars reports the installation time for the UI configuration, in which only the user interface is fetched on the mobile device. The second set (Opt) represents the installation time for the optimal distribution, while the last (All) evaluates the case in which the entire application is installed on the client. Fig. 4(b) reports how much power is consumed for the IL application for all three configurations (UI, Opt and All). The purpose of this experiment is to show how the time and power consumption for an application deployment can be greatly reduced by acquiring only parts of it on the device. For the TTS application, the gap between the Opt and All installation times is of almost 18s, which is a considerable overhead for a mobile device. We also notice a significantly less power consumption by 600–700mW when installing the optimal distribution, compared to acquiring the whole application locally. On the other hand, when comparing the Opt and UI configurations, one may think that acquiring only the user interface represents always the quickest option. In the next set of experiments, we show that the problem is more complex, and analyze how the resulting application interaction time and power consumption varies with the chosen partitioning configuration.

A more detailed analysis of Fig. 4 also shows the overall installation time breakdown. This includes the overhead for fetching, installing and starting the selected bundles, as well as generating proxies for remote dependencies. The fetching time depends on the bundles' code size, while the installation-start time is typically around 1.7s per bundle. Generating one remote proxy takes around 300ms for WiFi and 420ms for 3G. For the IL application (see Fig. 3(b)), the UI setup acquires 1 bundle and generates 5 proxies, while the Opt configuration

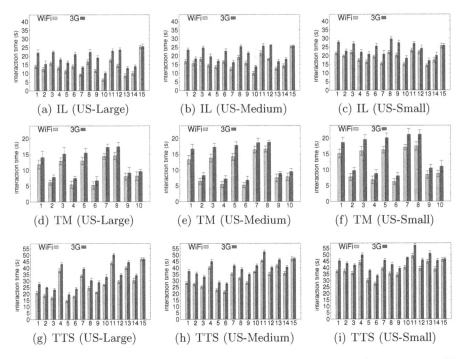

Fig. 5. Interaction time for the three applications with varying configurations, on different EC2 instances (WiFi and 3G in use)

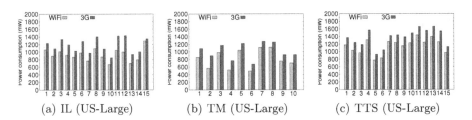

Fig. 6. Power consumption for the three applications with varying configurations, on EC2 US-Large instances (WiFi and 3G in use)

fetches 6 bundles and generates 3 proxies. The time required to stop-uninstall a bundle is in the range of 1.6s and a proxy removal requires around 350–400ms.

6.2   Steady-State Behaviour

Next, we consider the system's steady state, when all required bundles for a configuration have been fetched, installed and started. Fig. 5 reports the observed interaction time for a subset of the possible partitionings for the three applications on three EC2 instance types (small, medium and large). Configurations are ordered by increasing number of bundles acquired on the client.

Acquiring more bundles on the mobile side does not necessarily improve performance, and installing only the user interface (configuration 1 in all figures) is not always the optimal choice. In general, how an application's performance varies is not so easily correlated to how many modules are moved to the client or what their size is. These results motivate the need for a partitioning algorithm capable of picking the most suitable partition. The optimal partitioning for IL depends on the EC2 instance type, with configuration 10 for large and medium instances and 13 for small machines. Similarly, for TTS configuration 5 is best for large instances and 6 for medium and small ones. In the case of TM, the optimal configuration is 6 for all instances. Fig. 6 reports the power consumed by the same configurations for all applications, but only on large EC2 instances. Our measurements confirm that the optimal configuration in terms of interaction time is also the most power-efficient for all applications. In addition, we observe similar trends between the power consumption and interaction times for small and medium EC2 instances, where the best configurations for both IL and TTS applications change. The results show that an interaction latency-based model is enough to find those distributions that are also the most power-efficient. The reasoning behind is that network operations are more expensive in terms of mWs consumed, and therefore solving the partitioning problem with the goal of minimizing overall data transfers also achieves optimal power consumptions.

Next, we apply our solving algorithm and measure the achieved improvement on the interaction time and power consumption. For all our applications, the algorithm is able to select the best configuration. Table 1 reports the interaction time and power consumption of the optimal configuration, as well as the algorithm solving time. The performance gain on the mobile device is very promising. For TM the gain in performance is up to 61%, when we compare with the two extreme cases, All and UI. For IL and TTS, the improvements are even higher, up to 75% and 69% respectively. Finally, the comparison on power consumption presents similar trends and gains for all three applications by 20–46%, with smaller values for 3G as expected due to its increased latency. The percentages

Table 1. Gains on performance and power consumption (on EC2-Large)

Solver		TM (0.16s)		IL (0.2s)		TTS (0.17s)	
		Time(s)	Power(mW)	Time(s)	Power(mW)	Time(s)	Power(mW)
Opt	WiFi	5.17	493	6.13	668	14.14	774
	3G	6.72	673	10.01	848	19.05	928
All	WiFi	33%	30%	75%	46%	69%	21%
	3G	29%	27%	60%	38%	58%	18%
UI	WiFi	57%	43%	56%	37%	31%	34%
	3G	52%	39%	54%	32%	29%	32%

are computed as the ratio between $Diff_t$ and Opt_t, where $Diff_t$ represents the difference between the execution time obtained with ALL or UI depending on the case and the execution time obtained with Opt, while Opt_t is the optimal interaction time.

To understand how performance is improved we need to consider the applications' bundle structure. In the case of IL, shown in Fig. 3(b), the best configuration contains *mInit, mCache, mMaps, mBrowser, mDirections* and *mBlender*. For this application, it is not convenient to fetch more bundles because they are too computational intensive for the mobile platform and their execution time on the client exceeds the time required for data transfers to the cloud.

Once the optimizer has identified the optimal configuration, the mobile client fetches, installs and starts the corresponding bundles, and sets up the remote proxies. However, the more the user interacts with the application, the faster the initialization cost is amortized. We measured the number of invocations necessary to fully amortize the initialization cost. For WiFi at most two interactions are sufficient to pay off the initial overhead, while for 3G already one invocation is enough to amortize the overhead. This confirms that our approach can bring such a high performance improvement to fully hide the installation overhead, and thus makes it suitable for both long-term short-term interactions.

6.3   Dynamic Optimization and Redeployment

We investigate which configuration is optimal at bootstrap, when no bundle has been acquired yet on the mobile device. Ideally, in choosing the best partitioning one should consider the number of user interactions. In the case of one interaction, the configuration with minimal installation time is probably better, while for more interactions, having a lower invocation time is more important. As the number of interactions cannot be easily known a priori, our system makes the decision entirely online and periodically re-evaluates it, as shown in Fig. 7(a).

Consider a user performing three consecutive interactions with the IL application. The optimizer processes the objective function every 10s and returns the best configuration. At time 0 (no code is acquired yet on the device), the optimizer picks configuration 2 (*c2*), which does not provide the lowest interaction time, but minimizes the overall time for initialization and interaction. As some bundles have already been fetched on the client, at time 10, the optimizer picks the configuration with the lowest interaction time, *c10*. Installing the new distribution is done in parallel to the application running. Its cost is roughly 8s, since c2 is already active, and it can be used already for the second interaction.

Fig. 7(a) shows the benefits of initializing *c10* in parallel to the application execution (*Parallel*). In this way, before *c10* becomes active, there is an interruption of only 1.2 s (*Sp*) due to the removal of the 3 remote proxies used by *c2*. This is the only operation that cannot be executed concurrently, but its overhead is negligible compared to the performance gain. In fact, when comparing against the case when the initialization happens sequentially (*Sequential*), the parallel approach allows the user to carry out 3 full interactions in the time the sequential one completes 2.

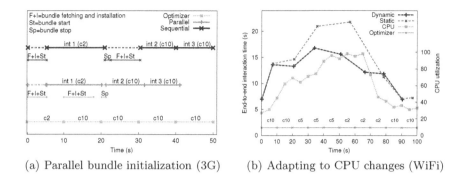

(a) Parallel bundle initialization (3G)   (b) Adapting to CPU changes (WiFi)

Fig. 7. Parallel bundle initialization and adapting to CPU changes (IL)

Moreover, in the sequential approach, the application is not available for roughly 10s (represented with a dotted line).

6.4   Reactivity to CPU Load

The ability of reconfiguring an application online allows the system to quickly react to changing network conditions or CPU load. We give an example of the latter in the next experiment. We cause an increase in the device's CPU utilization to 67% and 95%, by running for a few minutes a CPU-intensive process. The optimizer reacts to the CPU variations by choosing a "cheaper" configuration in terms of consumed CPU. Fig. 7(b) shows the performance improvements our approach (*Dynamic*) has over the *Static* one, which always runs with the configuration chosen at the first interaction.

As shown in Fig. 7(b), the first interaction with IL uses *c10*. When the CPU increase to 67% occurs, based on new profiled data the optimizer decides to switch to *c5*, which contains 4 of the 6 bundles from *c10*. This decision improves performance by roughly 5s over the static approach (visible in the 4th interaction). Between the 4th and 5th interactions, an additional increase to 95% occurs. Again, the optimizer reacts by choosing *c2*, which reduces the number of bundles running on the mobile device to 2. The performance improvement of the dynamic approach compared to the static case is even larger. Finally, we decrease the CPU utilization to 37% and the optimizer decides to switch back to *c10*. Its bootstrap is done in parallel to the 7th interaction and the performance becomes similar to the static case. Given that application interactions running with specific configurations are not interrupted once the optimizer switches to different partitionings, allows our approach to become stable. This stability comes from the fact that the optimizer is given the opportunity to periodically verify and strengthen its decision while the application is executing.

This test shows the efficiency of our dynamic approach over a static one. The same mechanism has shown to be effective in reacting to changes in network bandwidth caused by unstable wireless connectivity or switching between WiFi

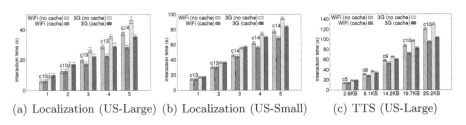

(a) Localization (US-Large) (b) Localization (US-Small)   (c) TTS (US-Large)

Fig. 8. Reactivity to changing user inputs for the IL and TTS applications

and 3G. Due to space restrictions we only briefly present our observations. By reducing the available bandwidth on the device, for WiFi the optimizer switches from $c10$ to $c13$, which brings more bundles locally and reduces the remote data transfer. By doing so, a user is able to perform 11 interactions in the same time 8 interactions are executed with the static approach. For 3G, $c14$ is chosen and more bundles than in the WiFi scenario are brought on the device. This is due to the lower available bandwidth with 3G connections. The dynamic AlfredO manages to perform 8 interactions compared to 6 with the static approach.

6.5   Adapting to Changing User Inputs

Next, we consider the system's ability to adapt to changing user inputs, based on a set of usage scenarios and associated configurations cached on the device. We evaluate this feature with the IL and TTS applications.

In Fig. 8, we compare the interaction time when the cache is disabled or enabled. If disabled, the device adopts the configuration used for the previous interaction. If enabled, the client chooses the best configuration depending on the inputs. For IL, we test by increasing the set of inputs from 1 to 5 images, each 300 kB in size. For TTS, we vary the size of the text from 2.6 kB to 25.2 kB.

On large EC2 instances, both applications show gains of 20-25% with cache enabled. For IL, Fig. 8(a) shows that already with 3 photos it is best to switch from $c10$ to $c13$. With 5 or more photos moving to $c14$ is optimal. In the TTS application (Fig. 8(c)), the system changes from $c5$ to $c9$ at the first increase in text size. With a text increase to 19.7kB, the best configuration becomes $c10$ and improves performance by over 25s for both WiFi and 3G. For small EC2 instances, the cache decides to switch from $c13$ to $c14$ with 3 input photos (Fig. 8(b)), when in fact $c13$ has a lower interaction time for 3G. This is due to the generic nature of the cached solutions, which cannot cover all possible scenarios. Even so, the penalty in performance is very small (1.5s).

6.6   Resource Overhead

Finally, we discuss the system's overhead on the mobile platform. The code size of all components residing on the mobile device is 178 kB, while on the cloud side is 903 kB. The memory footprint is typically less than 7 MB and is comparable to other applications or processes running simultaneously on the Android platform.

Profiling requires code injection for all bundles. The code increase depends on the number of classes and methods to be profiled, but it typically does not exceed 2–3 kB for a bundle of 20–25 kB. We observed that the performance degradation due to profiling is under 8% for all bundles. The data generated by the profiler represents the statistics collected at each user interaction. In average, the logged measurements require less than 2 kB of data.

7   Conclusions

With the ever richer functionality of mobile applications, users are confronted with either the computational limitations of their devices or the network limitations. Recent work has proposed application partitioning between mobile devices and remote servers or clouds, to improve performance and battery life. In this paper, we argue that static decisions or ignoring the effects of user data cannot leverage the full potential of code offloading when variations in network, device CPU load, or user inputs occur. Our system shows that dynamically adapting partitioning decisions is key to improve user experience. Our experiments over different networks and cloud infrastructures show that our approach significantly reduces interaction time and power consumption by (1) fetching application parts to the mobile device when appropriate, (2) dynamically adjusting the distributed configuration to changes in the network conditions, client load and user inputs, and (3) caching deployment settings for efficient execution with varying application inputs. Additionally, our system offers a greater degree of flexibility for applications on mobile devices as it supports a wider range of scenarios than just services running completely in the cloud.

References

1. Amazon EC2, http://aws.amazon.com/ec2/
2. Amiri, K., Petrou, D., Ganger, G., Gibson, G.: Dynamic Function Placement for Data-intensive Cluster Computing. In: Proc. of USENIX, pp. 307–322 (2000)
3. Android, http://code.google.com/android
4. Google AppInventor, http://appinventor.googlelabs.com/about
5. Balan, R., Flinn, J., Satyanarayanan, M., Sinnamohideen, S., Yang, H.: The case for cyber foraging. In: Proc. of the 10th Workshop on ACM SIGOPS European Workshop: Beyond the PC, pp. 87–92. ACM (2002)
6. Balan, R.K., Satyanarayanan, M., Park, S.Y., Okoshi, T.: Tactics-based remote execution for mobile computing. In: Proc. of MobiSys, pp. 273–286. ACM (2003)
7. Chun, B., Ihm, S., Maniatis, P., Naik, M., Patti, A.: CloneCloud: Elastic execution between mobile device and cloud. In: Proc. of EUROSYS. ACM (2011)
8. Chun, B., Maniatis, P.: Augmented smarphone applications through clone cloud execution. In: Proc. of the 12th USENIX HotOS Workshop (2009)
9. Cuervo, E., Balasubramanian, A., Cho, D., Wolman, A., Saroiu, S., Chandra, R., Bahl, P.: MAUI: making smartphones last longer with code offload. In: Proc. of MobiSys, pp. 49–62. ACM (2010)
10. Apache Felix, http://felix.apache.org/site/index.html

11. Flinn, J., Park, S., Satyanarayanan, M.: Balancing performance, energy and quality in pervasive computing. In: Proc. of ICDCS, pp. 217. IEEE (2002)
12. Fragments, http://android.com/guide/topics/fundamentals/fragments.html
13. FreeTTS, http://freetts.sourceforge.net/docs/index.php
14. Giurgiu, I., Riva, O., Juric, D., Krivulev, I., Alonso, G.: Calling the Cloud: Enabling Mobile Phones as Interfaces to Cloud Applications. In: Bacon, J.M., Cooper, B.F. (eds.) Middleware 2009. LNCS, vol. 5896, pp. 83–102. Springer, Heidelberg (2009)
15. Goyal, S., Carter, J.: A lightweight secure cyber foraging infrastructure for resource-constrained devices. In: Proc. of WMCSA, pp. 186–195 (2004)
16. Hunt, G., Scott, M.: The coign automatic distributed partitioning system. In: Proc. of OSDI, pp. 187–200. USENIX (1999)
17. Kwon, Y.-W., Tilevich, E.: Power-efficient and fault-tolerant distributed mobile execution. In: Proc. of ICDCS (2012)
18. Newton, R., Toledo, S., Girod, L., Balakrishnan, H., Madden, S.: Wishbone: Prole-based Partitioning for Sensornet Applications. In: Proc. of NSDI, pp. 395–408 (April 2009)
19. OSGi Alliance. OSGi Service Platform, Core Specification, v4.1, Draft (2007)
20. Ou, S., Yang, K., Zhang, J.: An effective offloading middleware for pervasive services on mobile devices, vol. 3, pp. 362–385. Elsevier Science (2007)
21. Powertutor (2009), http://ziyang.eecs.umich.edu/projects/powertutor/
22. Ra, M.-R., Sheth, A., Mummert, L., Pillai, P., Wetherall, D., Govindan, R.: Odessa: enabling interactive perception applications on mobile devices. In: Proc. of MobiSys (2011)
23. Rellermeyer, J.S., Alonso, G., Roscoe, T.: R-OSGi: Distributed Applications Through Software Modularization. In: Cerqueira, R., Campbell, R.H. (eds.) Middleware 2007. LNCS, vol. 4834, pp. 1–20. Springer, Heidelberg (2007)
24. Rellermeyer, J.S., Riva, O., Alonso, G.: AlfredO: An Architecture for Flexible Interaction with Electronic Devices. In: Issarny, V., Schantz, R. (eds.) Middleware 2008. LNCS, vol. 5346, pp. 22–41. Springer, Heidelberg (2008)
25. Satyanarayanan, M.: Pervasive computing: vision and challenges. IEEE Personal Communications 8(4), 10–17 (2001)
26. Satyanarayanan, M., Bahl, P., Caceres, R., Davies, N.: The case for VM-based cloudlets in mobile computing. IEEE Pervasive Computing 8(4), 14–23 (2009)
27. Microsoft Silverlight, http://www.silverlight.net
28. Su, Y., Flinn, J.: Slingshot: deploying stateful services in wireless hotspots. In: Proc. of MobiSys, pp. 79–92. ACM (2005)
29. Yang, F., Gupta, N., Gerner, N., Qi, X., Demers, A., Gehrke, J., Shanmugasundaram, J.: Computation offloading to save energy on handheld devices: A partition scheme. In: Proc. of CASES, pp. 238–246. ACM (2001)
30. Yang, F., Gupta, N., Gerner, N., Qi, X., Demers, A., Gehrke, J., Shanmugasundaram, J.: A unified platform for data driven web applications with automatic client-server partitioning. In: Proc. of WWW, pp. 341–350. ACM (2007)
31. Yang, F., Shanmugasundaram, J., Riedewald, M., Gehrke, J.: Hilda: A high-level language for data-driven web applications. In: Proc. of ICDE, pp. 32–43. IEEE Computer Society (2006)

Enhancing the OS against Security Threats in System Administration

Nuno Santos[1], Rodrigo Rodrigues[2], and Bryan Ford[3]

[1] MPI-SWS
[2] CITI / Universidade Nova de Lisboa
[3] Yale University

Abstract. The consequences of security breaches due to system administrator errors can be catastrophic. Software systems in general, and OSes in particular, ultimately depend on a fully trusted administrator whom is granted superuser privileges that allow him to fully control the system. Consequently, an administrator acting negligently or unethically can easily compromise user data in irreversible ways by leaking, modifying, or deleting data. In this paper we propose a new set of guiding principles for OS design that we call the *broker security model*. Our model aims to increase OS security without hindering manageability. This is achieved by a two-step process that (1) restricts administrator privileges to preclude inspection and modification of user data, and (2) allows for management tasks that are mediated by a layer of trusted programs—*brokers*—interposed between the management interface and system objects. We demonstrate the viability of this approach by building BROKULOS, a Linux-based OS that suppresses superuser privileges and exposes a narrow management interface consisting of a set of tailor-made brokers. Our evaluation shows that our modifications to Linux add negligible overhead to applications while preserving system manageability.

1 Introduction

Security threats related to system administrator ("admin") activity are receiving increasing attention, fueled by a series of events that highlighted the damage that such activities can inflict [6,19,22]. Traditionally, system maintenance requires superuser privileges for a range of operations. As a result, admins holding such privileges can put user data at risk through leakage, corruption, or loss. These hazards have raised concerns in many organizations [12,13], and become even more relevant as companies [5] and government agencies [1] outsource IT management to third parties such as cloud providers. In the space of operating system design, in particular, these concerns have in part motivated research in "least-privilege" system designs that reduce the TCB size [16,25,37], offer more fine-grained protection [11], harden the TCB using formal verification [21], or use labeling to reason about and control information flow [33,36].

A unifying goal underlying the existing body of work is to build *untrusted-admin* systems, i.e., systems that can be used by users who wish to store and process sensitive data (either locally or "in the cloud") without requiring trust

P. Narasimhan and P. Triantafillou (Eds.): Middleware 2012, LNCS 7662, pp. 415–435, 2012.

in the administrators of either their own systems or the cloud platform. The focus of this body of work has been on low-level kernel or hypervisor mechanisms, and little attention has been devoted to the higher-level challenges of building untrusted-admin systems that actually remain *administerable*. For example, in the influential Decentralized Information Flow Control (DIFC) model exemplified by the HiStar OS [36], building an untrusted-admin system requires not just the DIFC-enforcing kernel but also a set of user-level processes with *declassification* privileges, which users (data owners) must trust to handle their data appropriately during management activities that by nature must touch or affect this data. If a cloud system is to offer data backup services, for example, then the system must include some form of trusted daemon or declassifier that can read the user's data and forward it to the backup destination (perhaps after encryption). However, HiStar did not look into the problem of how to securely design these trusted daemons or declassifiers so as to cope with the range of management tasks performed by the admins.

The main challenge in finding a solution to this problem lies in a tension between security and manageability. In practice, operating systems require a wide variety of tasks to keep the system operational, some of which may touch or otherwise impact sensitive user data and processes, e.g., adding and removing software packages and drivers, loading kernel modules, applying security patches, managing user accounts, backing up and restoring user data, etc. Any of these "standard" administrative actions, if not handled carefully, could give an untrusted admin access to sensitive data either directly (e.g., a compromised backup daemon or declassifier) or indirectly (e.g., if an admin can "upgrade" a correct kernel module to an insecure version). Actually designing realistic and usable mechanisms and tools enabling administrators to *do their job* of managing OSes, in an untrusted-admin model, remains a largely unexplored challenge.

To address this challenge, we introduce and explore an untrusted-admin system design model that we call the *broker security model*, which we apply to the design of operating systems, but is a software system design model that can be applicable to a range of software systems. Our model is inspired by the central observation that users must in practice trust admins for *resource availability*, even if they do not wish to trust admins for *information security*. For example, a malicious or merely negligent admin can always "pull the plug," drop network connectivity, or fail to migrate data or virtual machines off of old hardware to be decommissioned. Such availability failures are typically obvious to users, however, and leave a clear "accountability trail"; a cloud provider will not survive as a business if it fails to maintain promised resource availability.

Thus, we aim to create a clean OS design separation between *resource availability* mechanisms, over which admins must have control in order to do their job, and *information security* mechanisms, over which admins *must not* have control. To meet this goal, our model only allows the admin to access and manipulate system objects in well-formed ways through a set of trusted programs called *brokers*. Brokers *never* concede the admin superuser privileges. Instead, they only provide him with the specific functionality that is necessary to manage the system (e.g., create a user account) and control the resources (hence data availability) while ensuring that users gain control over the confidentiality and integrity of their data. To enforce this policy, the model defines three security invariants that the brokers must preserve; insofar as the these invariants are met, the system designer is free to specify the number and functionality of brokers that can better assist the admin in managing the system and to devise the most adequate mechanisms to enforce the model's security invariants.

To validate the broker security model, we present the design and implementation of a proof-of-concept OS called *Broker Umbrella for Linux-based OSes* (BROKULOS), which is based on a Debian Linux distribution enhanced with tailor-made broker extensions. One key design challenge is related to the fact that the management tasks in Linux are numerous, heterogeneous, and ill-defined. Since superuser privileges can no longer be granted to the admin, it is not clear which functions must be implemented to provide full OS manageability and whether these tasks can be performed without violating the model's security constraints. We address these questions by (1) characterizing the broker functionality based on a comprehensive survey of the fundamental tasks for maintaining a vanilla Debian distribution, and (2) specifying how exactly this functionality must be adapted in order to preserve the invariants of the broker model. We find that this functionality can be implemented by extending well-known Linux mechanisms and therefore show that the degree of protection proposed by the broker model is practical on commodity OSes, and does not require the use of niche research systems like HiStar (though these systems could also benefit from adopting our model).

In summary, our contributions are as follows. First, we characterize the important problem of enhancing the security of software systems in general (and OSes in particular) against administration threats while retaining system manageability. Second, we propose a principled way to approach this problem by introducing the broker security model. Third, we comprehensively study OS platforms and design BROKULOS, a system that demonstrates that enforcing this model on commodity OS platforms is possible with relatively few changes to existing Linux mechanisms. Finally, we evaluate our prototype, showing that BROKULOS preserves manageability, adds modest overhead to the management operations performed by the admin, and negligible overhead to the system.

2   Goals, Assumptions, and Threat Model

Our main goal is to devise a security model for enhancing the security of software systems against mismanagement threats. We focus, in particular, on administration roles that target the OS and require superuser privileges, e.g., installing applications, configuring devices, setting up security policies, creating user accounts, etc. We aim to find a sweet spot in the design space that strikes a balance between limiting the power of the admin and providing the functionality that is required for maintaining the system. We envision that the principles of our security model will be applicable to a range of software systems that currently depend on granting superuser privileges in their specific domains (e.g., database servers or web applications). To demonstrate the feasibility of our model, our

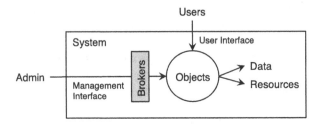

Fig. 1. Software system under the broker security model

solution should not require deep changes to existing OSes and should mostly preserve compatibility with legacy applications.

Our model rests upon several assumptions. We consider that the implementation of the OS trusted computing base (TCB) is correct. Our focus is not minimizing the TCB size; such goal is complementary to our work and has been the focus of various other research projects [24, 25, 34, 37]. For this reason, our design is centered on a monolithic kernel with a large TCB. Nevertheless, we discuss in Section 8 a possible approach to reducing the TCB size by using an information flow kernel such as HiStar [36]. Additionally, we assume that the machine that hosts the system is physically secure, and that the system exposes a management interface that allows the admin to manage the system remotely. This situation is common in many organizations that host and process sensitive data, such as cloud providers [15].

We characterize our threat model. We assume that the admin has access to the machine through its management interface and uses the operations exposed by this interface to maintain the system and access user data (either on disk or memory). In a commodity OS, for example, this interface consists of all operations that require superuser privileges and therefore need to be performed from the root account or through a *sudo* gateway. In particular, if the management interface allows the admin to reboot the system, which is a necessary capability in the case of an OS, the admin can bypass the system security protections and have access to the persistent system state stored on disk. However, the admin cannot exploit vulnerabilities in the TCB code, for instance, to perform privilege escalation attacks, nor perform physical attacks on the machine. In addition, we do not consider side channel attacks.

3   Broker Security Model

The broker security model enhances the security of a software system by weakening the trust requirements relative to the system admin. In particular, it precludes the admin from compromising the confidentiality and integrity of user data and computations, while preserving manageability.

Figure 1 shows how the broker security model extends a software system. The base system (which follows a conventional system design) is modeled as a collection of objects, each of them containing data and holding a set of hardware resources. In an OS, for example, these objects include files, processes, user accounts, etc. The system allows users and admin to access and manage objects through two interfaces—a user interface and a management interface. In the base system the management interface gives the admin superuser privileges, which allow him to fully control all system objects and therefore access user data without restrictions. Under the broker security model, however, the management interface no longer grants superuser privileges but only allows the admin to execute a set of trusted programs called *brokers*.

Brokers mediate the access to objects in a well-formed manner as to (1) provide the functionality that is necessary and sufficient to manage objects properly (e.g., create user accounts) and (2) let the admin retain control over resource availability while shifting control over user data confidentiality and integrity to users. To make sure that users retain control over their data security, brokers must maintain the following three security invariants:

1. Information security. A broker does not allow user data to be output or modified in ways that violate the confidentiality and integrity of that data. For example, allowing a debugger to be attached to a user process without the user being aware of or having authorized this operation violates this property.

2. Identity protection. A broker does not allow user identities and associated credentials to be hijacked or overridden. Otherwise, the admin could abuse this privilege to impersonate a user and access his data. For example, allowing the admin to change user passwords arbitrarily breaks this requirement.

3. System integrity. A broker ensures that the system can only transition between system states that preserve security invariants 1 and 2. For example, a broker cannot allow arbitrary kernel modules to be loaded because this feature could be exploited for privilege escalation: loading a malicious module could subvert brokers' security mechanisms.

This simple model can then be applied to enhance the security of software systems (and OSes in particular) by adopting a two-step methodology. First, one must specify the broker layer by identifying the *functionality* that the set of brokers need to offer while simultaneously obeying the three security invariants prescribed by the model. Second, one needs to devise the *mechanisms* that implement brokers' functionality and enforce the security invariants. We next apply these steps to an OS.

4   OS Broker Functionality

A natural way to enforce the broker security model in an OS is to start from a point that is secure by design yet overly restrictive, and then add carefully crafted brokers to regain manageability. In particular, a natural starting point is a design that forces the admin to operate from a regular user account, i.e., suppress the root account and prevent unrestricted execution of privileged commands through `sudo`. The challenge then becomes specifying and designing a set of brokers that (1) do not overlook functionality that is necessary for keeping the system administrable and yet (2) enforce the security invariants of the broker model.

To achieve this, we start with a thorough characterization of the set of commands that brokers should support by surveying the most fundamental management tasks performed by admins. The tools that support these tasks can then provide the baseline mechanisms needed to implement the brokers. Since these tools are likely to violate the broker model invariants, it is necessary to validate whether and how such violations take place so that we can enhance these tools to build brokers that satisfy the invariants.

Table 1 shows the list of tasks that we surveyed along with an indication of how the various tasks violate the three security invariants we listed previously. This list combines the results of two approaches. In a bottom-up approach, we studied a collection of packages and respective tools available in a basic Debian distribution, identified the functionality of each tool, and used our judgment to assess whether its functionality is fundamental for the admin. In a top-down approach, we studied the system administration literature and identified the high level tasks that an admin needs to perform. Overall, we manually inspected 902 executables included in 100 packages[1] and studied three different textbooks [14, 17, 35]. We then converged on a single (coarse-grained) task list, which we have examined with professional system administrators from the host institution of one of the authors to make sure it reasonably characterizes the management activity of a typical OS admin.

The tasks that violate the information security (IS) invariant mostly involve processes, files, and volumes and their primary goal is to manage resources and user data. For example, to learn about the memory utilization and open files by user processes, tools like `ps` and `lsof` reveal sensitive information that may be contained, e.g., in command line arguments of the process or in the names of user files. Similarly, tools for backing up and restoring user data (e.g., `tar` and `gzip`) would allow the admin to inspect and modify user data.

The tasks that breach the identity protection (IP) invariant are mostly related to user accounts and group management. User account operations include the ability to arbitrarily set and modify the identity and credentials of a user account (e.g., changing the password of an account using `passwd`). Group management enables adding and removing users from groups with tools like `useradd` and `usermod`. These capabilities would allow the admin to access files and processes owned by the user, in the first case, or shared within a group, in the second case.

The tasks that compromise the system integrity (SI) invariant are mostly related to software and system management. Typical OSes allow the admin to install arbitrary software, which can affect both the TCB (e.g., by upgrading the kernel, installing OS services, loading kernel modules) as well as shared applications. With this capability the admin could escalate his privileges to access user data by tampering with the TCB or by installing backdoors in shared applications. Admins can also set up devices to compromise the system integrity. For example, the ability to set the system time can be used to launch replay attacks.

---

[1] These packages were selected from a minimal Debian distribution according to two criteria: they contain the basic tools (package "Priority" is "Required" or "Important") and provide system administration support (package "Section" is "Admin").

Table 1. Management tasks grouped into categories: Tasks are grouped by category. For each task we indicate the security invariants they violate: information security (IS), identity protection (IP), and system integrity (SI).

Category	Management task	IS	IP	SI
Software	List, install, upgrade, and remove shared applications and libraries			×
	List, install, upgrade, and remove system services and kernel images			×
	Configure software and diagnose errors			×
	Apply security patches			×
	Manage local system documentation			×
Accounts	Create, modify, and delete user accounts		×	
	Disable user accounts temporarily			
	Modify account credentials		×	
	Force users to modify their credentials			
Groups	Create, modify and delete user groups		×	
Processes	Monitor and limit memory utilization by user processes	×		
	Check for runaway processes	×		
	Modify process execution priorities	×		
	Check for unattended login sessions	×		
Files	Perform backup and restore of user data	×		
	Set and view disk quotas			
	Check file space utilization	×		
	Remove temporary files (in /tmp and in /lost+found)	×		
	Re-distribute disk space in the filesystem	×		
	Mount and unmount filesystems			
	Check filesystem integrity and fight fragmentation	×		
	Check disk space	×		
	Create, modify, and format partitions			
System	Restart the system after panics, crashes, and power failures			
	Load, list, and unload kernel modules			×
	Start and stop services			×
	Automate and schedule system administration tasks with cron			
	Check and clear system log files	×		
	Configure and modify swap space			
	Configure init and runlevels			×
	Configure the network and check open connections	×		
	Setup system clock			×
	Setup and check the status of the printer			

Note that the purpose of Table 1 is not to enclose *all* management tasks. Instead, it comprises only the set of fundamental broker operations, which admins can then rely upon for more complex tasks. For example, for diagnosing resource misuse, admins can use various brokers, e.g., for checking runaway processes, unattended login sessions, and process memory utilization. In fact, it is typical to use helper tools to identity the source of such problems. Another example, for recovering from system bugs, admins can use brokers for securely installing software and backing up / restoring user data. Indeed, rather than fixing compromised systems, the common practice for system recovery is to make clean-slate software reinstalls and restore user data from backups; this method guarantees that the system state is again known and trustworthy.

Ideally, the table should list all the tasks that are necessary and sufficient to meet all needs of OS admins. In spite of our best efforts and positive feedback

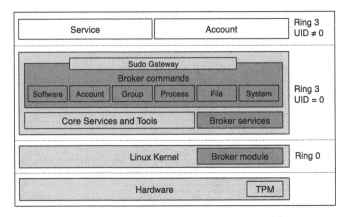

Fig. 2. Broker-enhanced OS architecture

from expert system administrators, however, this table is not necessarily complete and may need to be adapted by adding, modifying, or removing entries depending on the concrete OS, deployment environment, and admin needs.

Now that we have characterized the functionality that should be offered by the broker layer, we present an OS design that implements it.

5 Broker-Enhanced OS Design

We start with an overview of the OS architecture that we propose and then describe how each security invariant is enforced by the brokers.

5.1 Architecture

Figure 2 illustrates the internals of a broker-enhanced OS. Since it is not our primary goal to minimize the size of the TCB, we simply extend a vanilla Debian Linux distribution with a set of components that implement the broker extensions for the system. These components consist of broker commands, dedicated services, and an LSM kernel module.

In contrast to the vanilla Debian distribution, there is no superuser account (root) nor any other way that the admin can obtain superuser privileges. Instead, both users and the admin run their processes in protection domains with UID > 0. UID 0 is then reserved for the components that need to run in privileged mode such as OS services (e.g., init, sshd), and broker commands. The space of unprivileged domains (UID > 0) is split into two parts: UIDs $\leq u_t$, which are reserved for services that do not need to run in privileged mode, and UIDs $> u_t$, which are reserved for user accounts (where u_t is a configurable threshold).

Brokers consist of a well-defined set of trusted programs that run in privileged mode (UID = 0). Table 2 shows examples of the most representative brokers, grouped into categories according to their semantics. To allow for invoking brokers from a non-privileged account, we rely on the well known sudo gateway, which also authorizes broker execution based on the role—admin or user—associated with each account. To bootstrap the creation of admin accounts, the admin role is assigned to the first account to be created; the admin can then define the role of the subsequent user accounts.

Next, we describe in more detail the mechanisms introduced by the broker extensions that provide support for the management tasks in Table 1 while preserving the security invariants required by the model. We structure this presentation according to the invariants that are to be preserved.

5.2 Enforcing the Information Security Invariant

The information security invariant stipulates that the admin cannot access user data through the system management interface. This is the model's most fundamental requirement because otherwise user data confidentiality and integrity could be directly violated. To meet this requirement, the protection domains of the admin and users should be perfectly isolated from each other. However, this can be challenging when user domains must be crossed over, particularly for resource management and data management tasks. We discuss these in turn.

Managing Account Resources. The admin must be able to control the resources associated with a user account (e.g., set user quotas for CPU and memory). This control, however, requires permission to access the resources allocated to user data. Without the proper protections, however, such access could allow the admin to access user data, thereby compromising its confidentiality and integrity. To enforce a clean separation between resources and data, we propose taking the following steps.

The first step is to conservatively isolate the protection domains of admin and users. To start, we can use the UID-based protection domains to prevent direct access to user files and processes that are not explicitly shared by the users. However, it is also necessary to prevent information leakage through the /proc filesystem. The Linux kernel exposes extensive information relative to user processes in a collection of files located under /proc/PID, where PID is the process number. The kernel generates the content of these files on the fly whenever they are opened and sets the permissions of many of them to publicly readable. However, making some of these files public violates the information security invariant (e.g., files stat or cmdline expose many details about the memory usage or the command line of processes, respectively). To prevent access to this information with minimal kernel changes, we simply override the file permissions to make them private to the process owner and accessible to the system brokers. We preserve kernel compatibility by adding these changes in an LSM module.

To enable the admin to manage account resources, the second step is to provide a set of specific brokers for process and file management. These brokers, however, only let the admin "see" an account as a bundle of CPU, memory, and storage resources whose utilization he can observe, restrict (by setting quotas), and deallocate *as a whole*. For example, brokers for process management only output aggregate information of resource utilization and always operate on all

Table 2. List of representative brokers grouped into categories: Describes each broker's functionality and command name (in parenthesis)

Category	Examples of representative brokers
Packages	list packages (pkg-list), get package (pkg-get), install package (pkg-install), upgrade package (pkg-upgrade), remove package (pkg-remove), flush package cache (pkg-flush)
Accounts	create account (acc-create), disable account (acc-disable), enable account (acc-enable), force password reset (acc-force), reset password (acc-passwd), delete account (acc-delete), load user policy (acc-polload)
Groups	create group (grp-create), list groups (grp-list), delete group (grp-delete), add member (grp-addmem), list members (grp-lstmem), remove member (grp-remmem)
Processes	list resource utilization (ps-list), kill account processes (ps-kill), set account process priority (ps-renice)
Files	backup account files (fls-backup), restore account files (fls-restore), list storage usage (fls-du), move account (fls-move), clean temp (fls-cltmp)
System	insert module (mod-insert), remove module (mod-remove), list services (svc-list), start service (svc-start), stop service (svc-stop), reboot (sys-reboot), setup system clock (dev-clock), setup network card (dev-net)

processes of an account (e.g., by applying kill and renice to all processes). Brokers for file management follow the same approach. As another example, monitoring the storage consumed by a user and moving user files to another volume only reveals aggregate disk utilization and displaces all files located in users' home directories or in user-approved subdirectories, respectively.

Exporting Account Data. The aforementioned techniques allow for resource management without user data access. However, in certain operations like backing up and restoring user data the admin needs to export user data from the user account's protection domain, where the data is secured, to another machine. To support these operations while preserving information security, the system encrypts the data and appends integrity checks before the data leaves the protection domain. However, we need to ensure that, when restoring the data, the backed up data can only be decrypted (1) on machines booting an untampered version of BROKULOS and (2) by the original owner of the data. To guarantee this property, the user data is encrypted and decrypted with a *seal key*. The seal key is a unique cryptographic key that the system associates with each newly created account. To enforce requirement (1), we take advantage of TPM primitives, which allow us to encrypt (seal) the seal key such that it can only be decrypted (unsealed) if the machine boots a correct BROKULOS binary. If the booted system is correct, the system then ensures that the seal key is only accessible to the owner's account, thereby ensuring requirement (2). To support recovering data on a different machine, e.g., because the original one was decommissioned, sealing could be extended to allow for unsealing to take place on any machine with a similar configuration. This extension could be done by coupling BROKULOS with Excalibur [32], a trusted computing system that enforces access control policies for multi-node environments.

5.3   Enforcing the Identity Protection Invariant

With the protection mechanisms for the enforcement of information security in place, the admin no longer has direct access to user data. Nevertheless, these

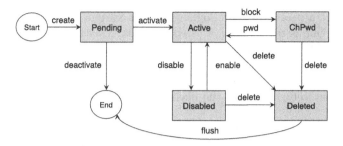

Fig. 3. State transitions between account states: The user must explicitly accept that the account is valid before it can be used. In the active state, the admin can temporarily disable the account or force the user to change authentication credentials. The resources of a deleted account can be released at a later point in time.

protections could be circumvented if the identity protection invariant is not assured. This invariant requires that the admin cannot control user credentials and identities, otherwise he could impersonate users and access their data directly. Thus, ideally, users should be able to control their own identities without hindering the admin's ability to control resources. In practice, however, shifting control to users entails some loss of management flexibility for the admin. Therefore, we need to design brokers for managing accounts and groups that provide reasonable manageability without sacrificing the identity protection invariant, as we describe next.

Managing User Accounts. In managing user accounts, we enforce the identity protection invariant by offering a set of brokers for regulating an account's life cycle such that user login credentials are strictly controlled by the user.

The basic life cycle of a user account is shown in Figure 3. An account is created by the admin; he specifies the initial configuration of the account (e.g., user name, home directory) and an initial login credential, which is only going to be used once. The first time the user logs in with the initial login credential, he must ensure that he has exclusive access to the account by claiming it. This process involves running a secure protocol which serves two purposes. First, it provides a report describing the initial account's configuration and state. If the account has been set up with initialization scripts or if somebody has logged into it before, the user will be able to detect these irregularities and abort the operation. If, however, the report shows no problems, the user can set up his authentication credentials (e.g., by uploading the user's public key) without admin interference. This process will disable the initial login credential and lock the user name associated with the account. From this point onwards, only the user can login to his account and he has full control over its content, but not its resources. The admin can still adjust the resources associated with the account, disable user login temporarily (e.g., in the case of a misbehaving user), force a user to change credentials, and, whenever necessary, delete the account.

Changing credentials is done by users themselves using the credentials they have uploaded to the system. To address the concern that losing user credentials would prevent a user from ever logging in, our system supports two override mechanisms. One is to rely on a trusted third party, either a single entity or a quorum, to reset the user credentials. Another is to increase redundancy by registering multiple credentials and using various authentication mechanisms (e.g., public key, password, passphrase). Although this approach does not eliminate the problem entirely, it reduces the likelihood of permanent loss of access.

Managing Group Membership. Aside from allowing users to control their own identities and credentials, user groups' members need to be properly authenticated. Otherwise, the admin could gain access to group-shared data by creating fake identities and registering them as legitimate group members. To enforce the identity protection invariant when managing groups, the BROKULOS admin is still allowed to create and delete user groups, but adding and removing members is delegated to users themselves. The approach we use for delegation is to designate a (per-group) *group leader* that makes group membership authorization decisions. The group leader must validate users' identities before adding them to a group. Since relying on user names chosen by the admin is insecure for authentication, the group leader must check users' credentials (e.g., a certificate of the user's public key).

5.4   Enforcing the System Integrity Invariant

The mechanisms we have introduced thus far can effectively enforce both the information security and identity protection invariants. However, if the admin can compromise these mechanisms, these assurances can no longer be guaranteed. Thus we next propose a mechanism for enforcing the system integrity invariant, taking into account two aspects of the problem: managing TCB components and shared applications.

Managing TCB Components. Managing TCB components involves installing, upgrading, configuring and removing software components that run in privileged domains—either in the kernel space (i.e., the kernel itself or kernel modules) or in the user space with UID 0 (e.g., services, system libraries, system tools, and brokers)—and configuring devices (e.g., setting up the network and the system timer). To enforce the integrity of the TCB, all these operations must be validated, and this is done using special-purpose brokers.

In particular, for installing TCB components, brokers only authorize this operation if the new TCB component is "trusted". Several definitions of trust could be used, for example, in an ideal world, the system would automatically verify if the implementation is correct. BROKULOS uses a simple model where a TCB component is trusted if its compliance with the broker security model is endorsed by one or multiple third parties that are mutually trusted by both the admin and users, referred to as Mutually Trusted Signers or MTSes. (Users' consent is necessary otherwise a misbehaved admin could use this mechanism to modify the TCB.) To enforce this consent, admins set up the initial MTS certificates in the system and users must approve or reject them whenever they claim their accounts. MTS certificates can be changed over time—e.g., when renovating or revoking them, or when adding new MTSes—by either establishing a chain of trust that only accepts new MTS certificates signed by a preexisting MTS, or by polling all users before accepting a new MTS certificate. The MTS role can be performed by any entity mutually approved by admin and users (e.g., certification organizations, software development companies, specific administration roles within the organization, or open source communities).

Regarding device configuration, we again only accept configurations that are vouched for by an MTS. The notion of what is expected from a trusted configuration is device-specific. Therefore device-specific brokers are expected to perform the appropriate validations. A particularly interesting case is the system clock, where the system time should not be set arbitrarily. Therefore, we restrict time updates to trusted NTP servers sent over secure channels. This is done by requiring the NTP configuration file (which identifies addresses and credentials of the NTP servers) to be signed by an MTS. Given the large number of devices, we did not design brokers for all of them, but new devices could easily be accommodated by incorporating appropriate brokers.

In addition to enforcing TCB integrity, it is necessary to assure users of its enforcement. This is because the admin can circumvent the TCB protection mechanisms by rebooting the machine and tampering with the TCB binaries on disk. We offer these guarantees by means of a remote attestation protocol, which users run when they claim their accounts. Our protocol is based on a standard attestation protocol [30], which transmits the boot time measurements (hash) of the TCB components signed by the TPM. We then extend it to include the MTS identities as well as the user account report (see Section 5.3). Thus, when users claim their accounts they can validate the hashes of the TCB binaries and the MTS identities, thus assessing the integrity of the TCB.

Managing Shared Applications. Finally, another type of software that must be trusted to correctly manipulate user data are shared applications (e.g., MySQL). To give users the flexibility of choosing which applications they trust, we let them define *user policies* that express their restrictions. The policy language expresses a list of rules, each of them consisting of comparisons among four attributes we currently support: package maintainer, package name, package version, and filename.

To enforce these policies, we developed a special purpose LSM kernel module. The LSM module overrides the standard DAC permissions and enforces the user policy at runtime: whenever the user runs an external program, the LSM module intercepts this operation, evaluates the policy, and aborts the execution if the policy evaluation fails. To evaluate each policy rule, the LSM module checks the attribute conditions specified in the policy against a set of extended filesystem attributes featuring the executable. The filesystem attributes are attached by the broker layer whenever the executable's package is installed. The broker responsible for installing the packages obtains the attributes for each program from a manifest contained in the program's package. Users load their policies into the LSM module once they claim their accounts.

6   Implementation

Our BROKULOS prototype is based on the Debian GNU/Linux 6.0 ("Squeeze") distribution running Linux 2.6.39.3. Our implementation effort includes the broker layer, which we implemented in about 4,400 lines of Python code, and the LSM kernel model, coded in less than 1,000 lines of C code. For convenience, brokers take advantage of basic tools such as dpkg, gpg, and useradd to perform the low level changes to the system. These tools are included in the core packages of BROKULOS, which comprises 77 packages, out of a total of 266 packages. This package configuration is based on Debian's minimal setup, which is then extended with BROKULOS's functionality.

The LSM module implements the protection mechanisms for overriding the DAC permissions of the /proc files and evaluating user policies. To implement this functionality, it places handlers in two LSM hooks (bprm_check_security and inode_permission). The LSM module provides an interface via VFS under the mount point /brokulos for loading the user policies into the module.

Our current prototype uses TPMs to support remote attestation and secure storage. We use TrustedGRUB [3] to measure the integrity of the files of core packages and extend the PCR registers with these measurements accordingly. Then, we use the TPM's quote primitive to generate and sign an attestation report when requested by the users. This procedure requires setting up an AIK key so that the TPM can sign the report. The implementation of secure storage has some limitations: we keep the entire system on an encrypted partition using LVM, but, as of now, we have not modified LVM so that the encryption keys are protected using the sealing primitives of the TPM. This technique, however, poses no particular challenges and is already used in Windows by BitLocker [26].

7   Evaluation

We now evaluate the security, manageability, and compatibility of BROKULOS, and experimentally gauge its performance overheads.

7.1   Security

BROKULOS improves security in three main aspects. First, it significantly reduces the management interface exposed to the admin. Unlike a commodity Linux distribution where the admin is endowed with superuser privileges, in BROKULOS the admin can only perform the privileged operations exposed through the broker layer. The broker layer makes the management interface explicit, and narrows it to a relatively small numbers of trusted programs. Thus, provided these programs are correctly implemented, the admin cannot acquire privileges not contemplated in the broker model.

Second, BROKULOS explicitly restricts the software that can run in a privileged domain, i.e., that belongs to the TCB. In a commodity Linux distribution, because the admin can install arbitrary software in the privileged protection domain, it is not possible to foresee which security properties are guaranteed by the system. In BROKULOS, however, only the software that is signed by an MTS can run in the privileged domain. Thus, provided that MTSes are trustworthy, the system enforces the well-defined security invariants of the broker model.

Finally, BROKULOS allows users to specify the software they trust to process their data. BROKULOS conservatively prohibits the execution of all shared programs (i.e., not owned by the user) and allows the user to open exceptions based on a user policy. This mechanism prevents the user from accidentally running applications that could compromise the security of his data.

An orthogonal aspect of the system security is shrinking the TCB size to reduce the likelihood of code vulnerabilities. As we mentioned, this aspect was not the emphasis of our work and we therefore see it as being complementary and a follow up to BROKULOS. Nevertheless, we note that while brokers add code to the TCB, it is only a small additional fraction of much simpler code when compared to the OS kernel. Furthermore, we expect to make broker programs trustable by releasing their source code.

7.2   Manageability

The ideal way to evaluate the system manageability would be through the practical experience of deploying and managing the system in a real setting. Not having access to such a deployment, our methodology is to validate the whether BROKULOS provides adequate broker coverage to accommodate all the management tasks we have surveyed (see Table 1).

Our current prototype provides a set of 41 brokers spanning multiple task categories. In some cases there is a one-to-one correspondence between the task and a particular broker (e.g., backing up data is supported by `file-backup`), whereas in others a single broker serves multiple tasks (e.g., `ps-list` lists both the CPU and memory allocated to an account). Overall, BROKULOS currently covers the most crucial set of management tasks. We provide only limited support for tasks related to devices (e.g., managing the printer) and filesystems (e.g., format partitions and fight fragmentation). Overall, out of the 33 coarse-grained tasks of the table, our system fully supports 29. Although devising brokers to support the remaining tasks constitutes a challenge when compared to the brokers we have built so far, the high fraction of management tasks covered by the existing brokers shows that our system provides extensive management support.

7.3   Compatibility

Overall, BROKULOS preserves compatibility with existing Linux mechanisms and applications. Our solution requires no modifications to the Linux kernel besides plugging in a kernel module to the standard LSM interface. The system leaves ABI / APIs unchanged, thereby preserving application compatibility. However, some popular administration tools are disabled, since they violate the broker model. This is the case, for example, `lsof`, which prints out a list of every file that is in use in the system. As a result, the admin may have to adapt and possibly change his scripts to use BROKULOS's brokers.

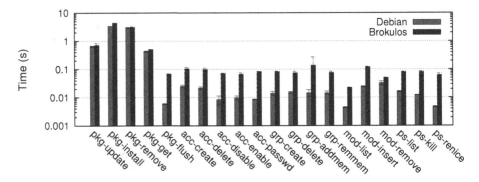

Fig. 4. Performance of brokers when executed by the admin: Covers representative brokers relative to package, account, group, module, and process management. The brokers for installing, getting, and removing packages use the `hello` package, which suffices for measuring the broker overhead for any package.

7.4 Performance

To evaluate the performance of our prototype, we focused on the places where BROKULOS introduces overheads to the vanilla Debian distribution: the broker layer, which affects management operations, and the LSM module, which impacts the execution latency of all programs in the system. (Recall that the LSM handler code runs every time the `exec` system call is executed.)

Our evaluation methodology is as follows. To study the broker layer overhead we use microbenchmarks. For each broker, we measure its execution time, measure the execution time of a vanilla Debian operation whose functionality is comparable to the broker's (e.g., user account creation), and then compare both values to analyze the performance penalty incurred by BROKULOS's management tasks. For each experiment, we run 10 trials and report the mean time and standard deviation. To study the overhead of the LSM module we measure the impact of policy evaluation on the execution time of a large task, namely compiling the Linux kernel 2.6.39.3. We measure the overall execution time with and without policy evaluation, using a policy with 266 rules, where each of them tests a package installed in the system. We use an Intel Xeon machine with a 2.83GHz 8-core CPU, and 1.6GB of RAM.

Figure 4 plots the results of the broker layer evaluation. It shows only the subset of system brokers that (1) require sanitization of standard admin tools to enforce compliance with the broker model (e.g., resetting the network card is not shown), and (2) have a direct correspondence with a vanilla Debian operation (e.g., the backup broker is not shown). There is a significant disparity in the performance overhead among brokers. Brokers whose Debian counterpart execute in the order of 10ms undergo a performance penalty of around one order of magnitude. For execution times above the 0.1s threshold, however, the performance between the two cases is comparable. The high overhead of short-lived brokers is partly due to the extra functionality, but mostly due to being implemented in Python, whereas their Debian counterparts are implemented more efficiently in C. If we consider, e.g., the `ps-renice` broker, which sets the same priority to all the processes of a user, and its counterpart, which corresponds to the command `renice -u`, the 10-fold increase is simply due to Python overhead. Since the broker functionality is not significantly more complex than that of pre-existing tools', we believe that implementing brokers from scratch and in C should produce comparable performance to the Debian distribution.

Our LSM module study shows that policy evaluation is efficient. The overall execution times of the kernel compilation in Debian and in BROKULOS show no differences, which means that the LSM module adds negligible overhead to long running tasks. These results are expected since the LSM module handlers perform very little work and only when a program is executed.

8   Discussion

In this section we discuss several issues regarding possible design extensions and the deployment of the system.

Shrinking the TCB Size. Several directions could be taken to reduce BROKULOS's TCB size. One direction is to leverage existing sandboxing mechanisms for Linux such as UserFS [20] in order to run some of the trusted programs (e.g., privileged services) in an unprivileged environment. Thus, exploiting one of these services would not compromise the entire system. To avoid depending on the correctness of the large Linux kernel, a second direction is to explore designs based on microkernels [21] or on DIFC kernels [23, 36]. The important thing to note is that the broker security model is also applicable in these settings, with the added advantage that brokers can set fine-grained policies; e.g., the `ps-list` broker can be constrained to only be able to read the `/proc` files. Thus, in the event of an exploit, the attacker could only leak information from those files and nothing else, thereby improving security.

Extension to Medium- and Large-Scale Deployments. In real deployments, a machine rarely operates autonomously; it may rely on networked services for storing data (e.g., NFS), authentication (e.g., LDAP), or upgrading software (e.g., package repositories), for example. In cloud computing or grid platforms, each machine is itself a constituent of a larger distributed system. Although in this paper we have focused on securing a single machine, we believe that the same principles can be applied to a distributed setting by propagating trust across components using secure channels and remote attestation mechanisms. However, we have not yet explored these extensions.

9   Related Work

We organize related work into security models, systems that restrict admin privileges, and security mechanisms for Linux.

Security Models. Bell-LaPadula [8] and Biba [9] are well known information flow security models for multilevel security that can express confidentiality and integrity policies, respectively. These and other IFC models [28], however, focus on how information flows in a system and have not looked at expressing the range of management operations required by admins (e.g., for managing software), which is the focus of our work. Clark-Wilson (CW) [10] is an informal security model concerning data integrity, which aims to prevent users from manipulating data objects arbitrarily. Our broker model shares similarities with CW in that CW also relies on trusted programs to streamline the way data objects can change. In contrast, we focus not on users' access control but on admins', and we go beyond CW in prescribing concrete invariants that trusted programs must adhere to in order to secure the system's management interface.

Systems That Restrict Admin Privileges. Despite apparent similarities with some of our design choices, current commodity OSes rely on a fully trusted admin. In particular, although Ubuntu [4] does not have a root account, the admin can still acquire superuser privileges and perform arbitrary operations through a trusted program. The Plan9 [31] distributed system was the first OS without superuser. Plan9 comprises multiple nodes, each of which is managed independently by a node's owner. Although there is no system-wide superuser, the owner of each node can control not only the node resources, but also compromise the security of the user data located on the node. More recently, HiStar [36] showed that the separation between resource management and data management is possible using DIFC. However, HiStar only provides the DIFC foundations for data protection and does not consider the high-level manageability issues addressed in BROKULOS. Similarly, trusted computing systems [25, 33] have focused on securing user data and computations from the admin by using confinement [25] and labeling [33] techniques, but without specific concerns for preserving manageability. In the hypervisor world, the work by Murray et al. [27] and more recently CloudVisor [37] allow for management of VMs without admin interference, but address different challenges than BROKULOS's, which targets OSes rather than virtualized platforms.

Security Mechanisms for Linux. Many mechanisms have been specifically designed to improve Linux security. A large body of these mechanisms aim to confine untrusted code to some kind of sandboxing environment, e.g., chroot, Jails [18], Linux containers [2], and UserFS [20]. Other mechanisms such as SELinux [29] and AppArmor [7] provide some specific support for MAC in Linux. Each of these mechanisms cannot per se address the manageability issues that constitute the focus of our work. Nevertheless, some of these proposals share similarities with BROKULOS's user policies. SELinux also allows defining policies based on specific programs, but it differs from BROKULOS in that SELinux policies are defined by the admin, whereas BROKULOS's policies are defined by the users. AppArmor allows attaching policies to programs based on file paths, which BROKULOS also supports. However, in AppArmor, if a program has no policy associated with it, then it is by default not confined. Thus, contrary to BROKULOS, it cannot protect users from accidentally executing malicious programs not covered by the policies. Note, however, that BROKULOS's key contribution is not so much in proposing fundamentally new mechanisms, but in showing that, by putting together and adapting well known Linux mechanisms, enhancing Linux according to the broker model is possible, adds little impact to performance, and provides good manageability.

10   Conclusion

This paper introduced the broker security model, a general security model aimed at protecting the confidentiality and integrity of user data from system administration errors. By only trusting admins for resource availability and not for information security, this model improves data protection with little impact on system manageability. It achieves this property by relying on a layer of *brokers*—trusted programs that mediate access to system objects. We showed that this model is practical for OSes by implementing and evaluating BROKULOS, our proof-of-concept broker-compliant OS. The broker model lays out important principles in the design of untrusted-admin systems. We envision applying it to other software systems (e.g., databases and web applications) and improving the mechanisms necessary to enforce this model (e.g., by reducing the TCB size).

Acknowledgements. We would like to thank Carina Schmitt and Jörg Herrmann for sharing with us their experience as professional system admins. We are also grateful to the anonymous reviewers for their feedback. This work was partly supported by the National Science Foundation under grant CNS-1149936. The research of Rodrigo Rodrigues is supported by an ERC starting grant.

References

1. Federal Government's Cloud Plans: A $20 Billion Shift,
   http://www.cio.com/article/671013/Federal_Government_s_Cloud_Plans_A_20_Billion_Shift
2. Lxc Linux Containers, http://lxc.sourceforge.net
3. Trusted GRUB, http://trousers.sourceforge.net/grub.html
4. Ubuntu, http://www.ubuntu.com/
5. Verizon to Put Medical Records in the Cloud,
   http://www.networkcomputing.com/cloud-computing/229501444
6. Insecurity of Privileged Users: Global Survey of IT Practitioners. Tech. rep. Ponem Institute and HP (2011),
   http://h30507.www3.hp.com/hpblogs/attachments/hpblogs/666/62/1/HP%20Privileged%20User%20Study%20FINAL%20December%202011.pdf
7. AppArmor, http://www.novell.com/linux/security/apparmor
8. Bell, E.D., La Padula, J.L.: Secure computer system: Unified exposition and Multics interpretation. Tech. rep. MITRE Corp. (1976)
9. Biba, K.J.: Integrity considerations for secure computer systems. Tech. rep. MITRE Corp. (1977)

10. Clark, D.D., Wilson, D.R.: A Comparison of Commercial and Military Computer Security Policies. In: IEEE Symposium on Security and Privacy (1987)
11. Colp, P., Nanavati, M., Zhu, J., Aiello, W., Coker, G., Deegan, T., Loscocco, P., Warfield, A.: Breaking up is hard to do: security and functionality in a commodity hypervisor. In: SOSP (2011)
12. ENISA: Cloud Computing - SME Survey (2009), http://www.enisa.europa.eu/act/rm/files/deliverables/cloud-computing-sme-survey/
13. ENISA: Cloud Computing Risk Assessment (2009), http://www.enisa.europa.eu/act/rm/files/deliverables/cloud-computing-risk-assessment
14. GBdirect: Linux System Administration (2004), http://training.gbdirect.co.uk
15. Hamilton, J.: An Architecture for Modular Data Centers. In: CIDR (2007)
16. Härtig, H., Hohmuth, M., Feske, N., Helmuth, C., Lackorzynski, A., Mehnert, F., Peter, M.: The Nizza Secure-system Architecture. In: CollaborateCom (2005)
17. Esteve, J., Boldrito, R.: GNU/Linux Advanced Administration (2007)
18. Kamp, P., Watson, R.N.M.: Jails: Confining the omnipotent root. In: SANE 2000 (2000)
19. Keeney, M.: Insider Threat Study: Computer System Sabotage in Critical Infrastructure Sectors. Tech. rep. U.S. Secret Service and CMU (2005), http://www.secretservice.gov/ntac/its_report_050516.pdf
20. Kim, T., Zeldovich, N.: Making Linux Protection Mechanisms Egalitarian with UserFS. In: USENIX Security Symposium 2010 (2010)
21. Klein, G., Elphinstone, K., Heiser, G., Andronick, J., Cock, D., Derrin, P., Elkaduwe, D., Engelhardt, K., Kolanski, R., Norrish, M., Sewell, T., Tuch, H., Winwood, S.: seL4: Formal verification of an OS kernel. In: SOSP (2009)
22. Kowalski, E.: Insider Threat Study: Illicit Cyber Activity in the Information Technology and Telecommunications Sector. Tech. rep. U.S. Secret Service and CMU (2008), http://www.secretservice.gov/ntac/final_it_sector_2008_0109.pdf
23. Krohn, M., Yip, A., Brodsky, M., Cliffer, N., Kaashoek, M.F., Kohler, E., Morris, R.: Information Flow Control for Standard OS Abstractions. In: SOSP (2007)
24. McCune, J.M., Li, Y., Qu, N., Zhou, Z., Datta, A., Gligor, V.D., Perrig, A.: TrustVisor: Efficient TCB Reduction and Attestation. In: IEEE Symposium on Security and Privacy (2010)
25. McCune, J.M., Parno, B., Perrig, A., Reiter, M.K., Isozaki, H.: Flicker: An Execution Infrastructure for TCB Minimization. In: EuroSys (2008)
26. Microsoft: BitLocker Drive Encryption, http://www.microsoft.com/whdc/system/platform/hwsecurity/default.mspx
27. Murray, D.G., Milos, G., Hand, S.: Improving Xen Security Through Disaggregation. In: VEE (2008)
28. Myers, A.C., Liskov, B.: A Decentralized Model for Information Flow Control. In: SOSP (1997)
29. NSA: Security-Enhanced Linux (SELinux) (2001), http://www.nsa.gov/selinux
30. Parno, B., McCune, J.M., Perrig, A.: Bootstrapping Trust in Commodity Computers. In: IEEE Symposium on Security and Privacy (2010)
31. Cox, R., Grosse, E., Pike, R., Presotto, D., Quinlan, S.: Security in Plan 9. In: USENIX Security Symposium 2002 (2002)
32. Santos, N., Rodrigues, R., Gummadi, K.P., Saroiu, S.: Policy-Sealed Data: A New Abstraction for Building Trusted Cloud Services. In: USENIX Security (2012)

33. Sirer, E.G., de Bruijn, W., Reynold, P., Shieh, A., Walsh, K., Williams, D., Schneider, F.B.: Logical Attestation: An Authorization Architecture for Trustworthy Computing. In: SOSP (2011)
34. Steinberg, U., Kauer, B.: NOVA: A Microhypervisor-Based Secure Virtualization Architecture. In: Eurosys (2010)
35. Wirzenius, L., Oja, J., Stafford, S., Weeks, A.: The Linux System Administrator's Guide (1993-2004), http://tldp.org/LDP/sag
36. Zeldovich, N., Boyd-Wickizer, S., Kohler, E., Mazières, D.: Making Information Flow Explicit in HiStar. In: OSDI (2006)
37. Zhang, F., Chen, J., Chen, H., Zang, B.: CloudVisor: Retrofitting Protection of Virtual Machines in Multi-tenant Cloud with Nested Virtualization. In: SOSP (2011)

On the Practicality of Practical Byzantine Fault Tolerance

Nikos Chondros, Konstantinos Kokordelis, and Mema Roussopoulos

University of Athens

Abstract. Byzantine Fault Tolerant (BFT) systems are considered to be state of the art with regards to providing reliability in distributed systems. Despite over a decade of research, however, BFT systems are rarely used in practice. In this paper, we describe our experience, from an application developer's perspective, trying to leverage the publicly available, highly- studied and extended "PBFT" middleware (by Castro and Liskov), to provide provable reliability guarantees for an electronic voting application with high security and robustness needs.

We describe several obstacles we encountered and drawbacks we identified in the PBFT approach. These include some that we tackled, such as lack of support for dynamic client management and leaving state management completely up to the application. Others still remaining include the lack of robust handling of non-determinism, lack of support for web-based applications, lack of support for stronger cryptographic primitives, and more. We find that, while many of the obstacles could be overcome, they require significant engineering effort and time and their performance implications for the end-application are unclear. An application developer is thus unlikely to be willing to invest the time and effort to do so to leverage the BFT approach.

Keywords: Byzantine Fault Tolerance, Reliability, Distributed Systems.

1 Introduction

Byzantine Fault Tolerant (BFT) systems are considered by the systems research community to be state of the art with regards to providing reliability in distributed systems. A BFT system implements a replicated state machine [1] typically consisting of $n = 3f + 1$ replica servers that each provide a finite state machine and execute operations from clients in the same order. BFT systems assume a pessimistic failure model, based on the classic Byzantine generals' problem [2] which provides agreement amongst a set of nodes where at most f nodes display arbitrarily incorrect behaviors, known as Byzantine faults.

BFT systems are attractive because they provide guaranteed safety and liveness properties when the assumption of up to f faulty nodes hold. Early work on BFT systems was widely considered to be impractical for use by real systems because they were either too slow to be used in practice or assumed synchronous environments that rely on known message delay bounds. However, the seminal

P. Narasimhan and P. Triantafillou (Eds.): Middleware 2012, LNCS 7662, pp. 436–455, 2012.

work of Castro and Liskov [3], published in 1999, changed this view. This work proposed and implemented *Practical Byzantine Fault Tolerance* achieving an impressive peak throughput of several tens of thousands (null) operations per second, previously thought unattainable. As has been noted by others [4], over the last thirteen years, the research community has seen a flurry of excitement with several efforts to improve the performance and/or cost of BFT replication systems. These efforts include studies aimed at increasing throughput or reducing latency of client requests [5–12, 4, 13], efforts to reduce the number of replica servers needed to withstand f faults to achieve lower replication cost [5, 14, 13], and efforts to boost the robustness of the protocol under both faulty servers and faulty clients [15, 4]. A large majority of these systems [5, 6, 11, 15, 4, 10, 13] are direct descendents of the Castro and Liskov system, hereonin referred to as the PBFT approach (for Practical Byzantine Fault Tolerance). Both the implementations and evaluations of these systems depend on the initial PBFT code base.

Despite BFT's attractive correctness guarantees, BFTs are still rarely used in practice. This is unfortunate, given the ever-increasing need for reliability in real-world distributed systems. More and more applications require high security and reliability to be both trustworthy to users and successful in use (e.g, electronic voting and digital preservation). The lack of wide deployment of state-of-the-art BFT technologies is puzzling. The open-source PBFT code initially provided by Castro and later modified by others has been publicly available for several years, and while readily sized up by the academic community for research purposes, it has not been used in practice in real-world systems.

In this paper, we examine, from the perspective of an application developer, the *practicality*, i.e., feasibility, of using the PBFT protocol and accompanying implementation to provide provable reliability guarantees for a real-world application. Our motivating application is a state-of-the art electronic voting system, offered as a public Internet service. The current version is centralized [16]. Given the critical nature of the application, our aim is to build a system that has *no centralized component*. Every aspect of the system's design should be distributed to avoid single points of attack and failure. Our aim is to leverage the correctness guarantees provided by PBFT systems to improve the security and reliability properties of the system. In such a system, clients (on behalf of users/voters) connect to the voting service, view the election procedures in which they have a right to participate, send the user's vote, and potentially reconnect at a later point to view the progress and/or results of the election. Our aim has been to gauge, from the perspective of a developer in need of providing reliability beyond simple crash-fault recovery, how easily the PBFT approach and accompanying system could be molded to fit the application developer's needs.

We have focused on the original PBFT implementation for several reasons. First, over the past thirteen years, the large majority of research efforts on improving BFT systems have relied on the PBFT approach and implementation. The PBFT codebase is the most stable and complete (in terms of implemented features), and it has been widely studied and extended over several years by several research groups. Second, this is the only publicly-available implementation for which a proof of correctness under a formal model has been completed [17]. Third, even as the debate over improving BFT systems continues, the interface to application developers provided by the PBFT middleware remains the same. This means that any later developments in the PBFT system suite can be easily leveraged by applications. Fourth, our particular electronic voting application is written in C; the PBFT code base is written in C++. A recent effort, called UpRight [18] aimed at easing the application developer's effort to make use of BFT technology is written in Java, still has several key features missing (e.g., view changes are unimplemented), and seems to be a work-in-progress that has not seen much development in the last two years. Thus, for a developer wanting to leverage the attractive reliability guarantees of BFT *now*, the original PBFT system offers more promise. Finally, we studied quorum-based BFT systems, using Q/U (e.g., [7]) as well as the study in [19], but found that these approaches are not suitable for our application, as we anticipate a high level of concurrency in our replicated service.

We describe our experience trying to leverage the PBFT approach and code base to enhance the reliability of our e-voting application. We describe several obstacles we encountered and drawbacks we identified in the PBFT approach. One key drawback we identified is that PBFT-based systems assume static membership – ie., clients and replica servers know each other apriori before system initialization. Most Internet services require support for dynamic client management, particularly when the number of envisioned clients is large. The PBFT literature (original as well as all subsequent descendants of PBFT) does not address this issue. Another key drawback is that PBFT leaves state management completely to the application developer, who is required to manually manage a raw memory region, while also issuing notifications to the library before changing memory contents. This may be fine when developing system services, but is not a convenient base for an application. Additionally, PBFT treats a replica server's memory as stable storage, by assuming the use of uninterruptable power supplies [3]. Many Internet application services, particularly an electronic voting system, cannot afford to rely on this assumption and instead require traditional ACID semantics to ensure data stored is consistent and persists despite crashes and faults. The PBFT system suite leaves state management to the application developer. This means that an application developer wishing to make use of an available legacy database to provide ACID semantics is faced with the decision of implementing these semantics into the application from scratch or retrofitting the BFT middleware to interface with and support the legacy database.

In addition to the above, we describe a number of other drawbacks including: the mechanism used by PBFT to handle nondeterminism in applications, the lack of support for stronger cryptography, the lack of support for web-based applications, and others. The description of our experience may seem pedantic, with many minute low-level details, but we provide these here to give the reader a clear understanding, from a holistic systems perspective, of the obstacles faced by a developer trying to put the PBFT system to real, practical use. These are details that are often considered "not important enough" to warrant attention in many research papers (and prototype implementations, for that matter), usually due to time and space constraints. Nonetheless they can trip up a third-party developer hoping to make use of the novel research prototype. In practice, it is the details that make or break the widespread deployment and use of a system.

We find that while many of the obstacles we describe could be overcome with a "better" or "revised" BFT middleware implementation that is tuned specifically for the needs of the particular application, they require significant engineering effort and time. More importantly, the performance implications of the changes required to meet the application's needs are unclear. For example, we describe how we overcome the first two drawbacks above. While adding support for dynamic client management does not significantly affect system performance, measured in *null* operations per second, retrofitting the PBFT middleware to support a legacy database reveals a throughput performance of *real* operations that is two orders of magnitude smaller than the *null* ones, advertised by prior BFT studies.

To date, only two publications on BFT that we are aware of have noted that reporting null operations per second as throughput is not representative of real applications and thus not helpful to the end-developer [20, 13]. This is understandable, as the focus of most BFT research efforts has not been on end-application use but on improving the BFT middleware itself and null operations provide a basis for comparison. Nonetheless, a developer faced with having to make a slew of modifications to the BFT middleware to get an end-system that has unknown performance properties is hesitant to invest the effort to do so.

This paper makes the following contributions:

- We identify a number of drawbacks in the PBFT protocol suite, from the perspective of an end-application developer trying to leverage PBFT reliability guarantees and we describe solutions to address these. The sheer number of drawbacks severely affects the ease with which a developer can leverage the PBFT approach.
- We present changes we made to the PBFT protocol and implementation to enable dynamic client management, a must for many Internet service applications in use today. We show that these changes can be made with minimal additions to the PBFT protocol, thus not affecting its provable reliability guarantees. We demonstrate, via empirical experiments, that support for dynamic client management can be achieved with minimal performance impact.
- We evaluate the performance impact of retrofiting the PBFT middleware to support ACID semantics via a widely-used legacy database to ease the state management burden of many applications requiring these semantics. We evaluate the impact on performance of this change, and show that for *non-null* operations, the throughput can be many times smaller than the tens of thousands of *null* operations per second presented in prior studies.

The source code for our modifications to the PBFT protocol and implementation is available online at *http://sourceforge.net/p/p2bft*.

2   Background

2.1   Original Algorithm

The Castro-Liskov algorithm for Practical Byzantine Fault Tolerance [3] (abbreviated as *PBFT*) is a replication algorithm that can tolerate arbitrary faults. It is based on State Machine Replication [21, 1] where transitions are applied to an instance of the application's state and result in a new, deterministic instance of the state. The general idea is that a group of replicas form a static group that provides a service. At each instance in time, one of them is the primary and is responsible for sequencing the requests, providing total order. This in turn guarantees linearizability [22], which is a correctness condition for concurrent objects where a concurrent computation is equivalent to a legal sequential computation. A view is the epoch where the primary is stable. The remaining replicas monitor client requests and the primary's behavior and, if the latter is found misbehaving, begin a view change procedure to elect a new primary.

The algorithm is asynchronous and provides liveness and safety guarantees when less than a third of the replicas are faulty. More specifically, to tolerate f Byzantine faults, the group needs at least $3f + 1$ members. Safety, formally proved by using the I/O Automaton model [23], guarantees that replies will be correct according to linearizability. Liveness assures that clients will eventually receive replies to their requests. The algorithm does not rely on synchrony to provide safety but does rely on a weak synchrony assumption to provide liveness: that *delay(t)* does not grow faster than t indefinitely. Here, *delay(t)* represents the time interval between initial message transmission *(t)* and message delivery to the replica process. For the protocol to be live, the client is expected to keep retransmitting its request until it finally obtains the reply. Further assumptions include independence of node failures and inability of an attacker to subvert cryptographic protocols.

In normal operation, the client sends a request to the primary. The primary assigns a monotonically increasing sequence number to the request and begins a 3-phase agreement protocol with the other replicas, at the end of which each node executes the request and directly transmits the reply to the client. The latter will accept the reply as correct only when $f + 1$ replies match. The 3-phase protocol consists of the exchange of the following messages, where the target of a multicast is the set of replicas:

1. *Pre-prepare*, multicast from the primary, which assigns a sequence number to a request and forwards its contents
2. *Prepare*, multicast by each replica, agreeing to the sequence number assignment
3. *Commit*, multicast by each replica, which helps guarantee total ordering across views

After the commit, each replica will execute the request and transmit the reply directly to the client. In all of the above message exchanges, the sender is expected to sign the contents with his private key.

Certain optimizations were applied by Castro and Liskov to this basic mode of operation to improve the latency and throughput of the system. First of all, the use of asymmetric cryptography was reduced, by introducing Message Authentication Codes. The client assigns a different key to each replica and sends the key to it, signed with the node's public key. From then on, all requests are accompanied by an 'authenticator', which is a structure that contains one MAC for each replica. This considerably boosts performance, as we confirm in Section 4. Another optimization is the tentative execution of requests before the commit phase. The client cooperates in this mode of operation as it expects $2f + 1$ tentative replies (marked as such by each replica) instead of the normal $f + 1$. If such a quorum is not assembled, the client simply retransmits the request message. As the replicas will in turn retransmit the last reply for this client (which by now should be marked as stable, since the Commit phase should be over), a smaller quorum of f+1 stable (non-tentative) replies may be enough.

Yet another optimization is the special treatment of *read-only* and *big* requests. A request is considered *big* if its size exceeds a configurable threshold, while the *read-only* status is explicitly set by the client. These differentiated requests are multicast from the client to all replicas, to relieve the primary of this burden. The default configuration of the original PBFT implementation sets the threshold to 0, resulting in all requests being treated as *big*. The *read-only* requests are specially treated and are executed as soon as they are received, sequencing permitting, of course. Finally, *request batching* is employed to minimize network usage and agreement latency. A *congestion window* is defined as the number of requests that have been received but not yet executed by the primary; its size is an adjustable parameter of the system. When the primary receives a request message, it calculates the difference between the last locally executed sequence number and the sequence number assigned to the new request. If this difference exceeds the defined *congestion window*, it postpones issuing the *pre-prepare* message, giving itself time to catch up on request execution. Once it does, it includes in a single *pre-prepare* message, as many outstanding request messages as possible, thus minimizing latency due to individual agreement. Note that batched requests capture parallelism from different clients, as each client is allowed a single outstanding request only.

The original PBFT implementation was developed by Castro, and published as open-source along with his dissertation. The environment chosen was: Linux, C++, UDP as the network protocol, the Rabin assymetric cryptosystem, UMAC32 for MACs and MD5 for digests. This implementation defines application "state" as a single continuous virtual memory region. In fact, it splits this region in two, the first part for the internal library needs and the second part for the application. The library has a subsystem that manages the synchronization and checkpointing of this state using copy-on-write techniques and Merkle (hash) trees [24]. The general idea is that the state is divided in pages of equal length. A hash tree is formed where the leaves are the actual data pages while the inner nodes are the hashes of their children (either of the data pages at level *height-1*, or of the hash text at smaller depths). At the root, a single digest uniquely identifies the complete memory region.

A checkpoint message communicates this root hash to the rest of the replicas to agree that the state is properly synchronized. If a peer finds itself out of sync, an efficient tree walking algorithm is started from the root, to identify the (hopefully few) data pages that are different and have them retransmitted by the rest of the group.

The server part of an application wishing to use PBFT services is expected to initialize the library and then wait for up-calls from it, to service requests and produce replies. While executing, it has free read access to arbitrary memory regions inside the "state" managed by PBFT, but is expected to notify the library **before** making any changes.

2.2   Reasoning about the Default Implementation

It is very hard to reason about the behavior of a distributed system when it is run on multiple hosts, without a common clock. To address this hardle, we modified the library to be able to run multiple times on the same host, using different port numbers. We also created a log of all messages exchanged between replicas that, given the common clock, allowed us to reason about the behavior of the system, by creating UML sequence diagrams depicting the operation of the system as a whole. All further observations are based on this groundwork.

2.3   Authenticators and Erratic Recovery Behavior

To better understand the recovery process, we stopped and restarted a replica, using the default optimal configuration. We immediately witnessed erratic behavior in the recovery process, which started and re-synchronized the state to the latest checkpoint, but was unable to execute the few requests remaining in the log after that point because they failed the authentication test. Upon investigation, we found that the use of authenticators, introduced for efficiency, impeded the recovery process, because the transient state of the restarted replica had no recording of the authenticators to use for validating client requests. The solution the existing system implements, is the periodic retransmission of the authenticators from each client to all replicas, based on a timer. This way, once the recovering replica receives the authenticators of the clients, it will be able to resume the recovery process from the next checkpoint. The only way to lower the timeframe for this service interruption, is to reduce the authenticator retransmission timeout, which results in increased load for the network. We investigated other solutions including on-demand retransmission of the authenticators; we did not pursue this however, because retransmissions can introduce denial-of-service vulnerabilities, as a faulty replica could simply bombard the clients with authenticator retransmission requests.

2.4   PBFT Behavior on UDP Packet Loss

The definition of a Byzantine fault is any possible fault, including an error as trivial as a UDP packet loss. This creates interesting behaviors. We observed that UDP packets were indeed lost in our experiments, even in the loop-back interface, due to congestion caused by stress-testing the system. The impact of this is profound, as such an error will leave a replica lagging behind in transaction execution and will cause the recovery process to commence on the next checkpoint. Although elegant in theory, this approach will not work in a production environment where it is unacceptable to lose replicas from such trivial errors. One obvious solution would be the use of TCP for its reliability; that however is not trivial to implement as it requires switching from a message-oriented network layer to a connection-oriented one. The use of SCTP, which allows reliable message-oriented communication looks more suitable, as long as all replica hosting platforms implement it of course.

The *big* request optimization described above combined with a trivial UDP packet loss can adversely affect the robustness of the system. In this case, *big* requests are multicast to all replicas only once, from the client. The primary will then use only the digest of the request body for further communication with the rest of the replicas. Consider what happens if one of the packets traveling from the client to one of the replicas is dropped on the way. All replicas will begin the three-phase protocol to commit and execute the request, but when execution time comes, the replica that missed the request body will be unable to execute, and will be stuck at this point until the next checkpoint arrives and the recovery process kicks in. For a request not marked as *big* though, the process is different and more stable. Here, if the request from the client to the primary is dropped, the client will timeout and retransmit the request, resulting in a request execution workflow where either all or no replica at all participates.

2.5   PBFT Handling of Non-determinism

In the original PBFT implementation, a feature was introduced to resolve the non-deterministic characteristics of most applications. The primary makes an application-specific up-call, which returns a set of values that are attached by the primary to the Pre-Prepare message. This data becomes common to all replicas executing the request, thus providing deterministic behavior on request execution. Subsequent work on the PBFT protocol [25] added an extra mechanism to validate this data on each replica. A new application-specific up-call was established that, when passed the non-deterministic data, is expected to validate it and return success or failure. For example, the primary attaches the system clock to the Pre-Prepare message and each replica validates the passed value against its own clock to make sure it is appropriate.

However, the handling of non-determinism described above introduces a subtle issue. It is not always clear how the application can validate the non-deterministic data passed to it via the new upcall. The hurdle for such a validation is the instance in time it is supposed to happen. In the normal, fault-free lifetime of a request, the validation happens as soon as the Pre-Prepare message is received, which is almost immediately after it is transmitted. Thus validating against a time delta is viable. However, when a request is replayed from the log during recovery, the time drift can be quite large and validating using a time delta will fail and impede the recovery process. A solution to this issue would be to differentiate message processing for the recovery process and completely skip non-deterministic data validation during recovery. This however is again a non-trivial exercise, as message execution in the original PBFT implementation is completely agnostic to message origin.

3   PBFT Deployment Drawbacks, Obstacles, and Solutions

3.1   Dynamic Client Membership

The existing PBFT protocol and implementation assumes completely static membership where each node in the system, client or replica, needs a priori knowledge of the address, port, and public key for every other node. Although this approach was sufficient for the proof-of-concept prototype, it is too limiting for real world use, particularly Internet service applications with a large number of clients. Our goal is to remedy this to enable clients to join and leave the replicated service dynamically, while letting the replicas remain statically bound to one another. The end result is that clients only need information regarding replicas, but no information regarding other clients, allowing for a more scalable deployment.

To achieve support for dynamic client membership, replicas need to identify each client in an identical (deterministic) manner. This leads us to store the client identifiers in the shared state of the service (i.e., in the continuous memory region). When a client requests to join or leave the group, each replica needs to process the request using the same version of the shared state. Thus, all such client requests need to be totally ordered, at least with respect to one another.

We define two special system requests, namely a *Join* and a *Leave*, which follow the same life-cycle as all other application-level (client) requests. This results in a single total order across all requests, application or system, fulfilling our requirement. The *Join* and *Leave* system requests are processed by the middleware library and are invisible to the application.

We introduce a level of indirection between what the PBFT library already uses as a node identifier and what the client reception module assigns to new clients, for efficiency of message evaluation. Instead of using a single address range of $[0..max\_clients]$, an arbitrary identifier is assigned to each new client and a table maps this number to the index in the array of client and server node entries. This way, when a client request arrives, the system first checks to see if the identifier exists in the redirection table before going into the more lengthy process of verifying its signature or authenticator.

Originally, our idea was for the client to multicast a simple Join system request to all replicas, carrying its address, its public key and a random nonce, signed with its private key. Each replica would assign the same new identifier and transmit it back in the reply. However, a malicious client could initiate an infinite number of connections, using phony addresses, thus exhausting the bounded maximum number of node entries in each replica. To address this vulnerability, we improve the connection process by splitting the Join operation into two phases. In the first phase, the client submits its data as previously described and awaits a challenge. Upon receiving the challenge, the client calculates a response and transmits it back to the replicated service in the second phase of the Join. Only then will the replicas add the client to the system as a full member. This approach ensures the client indeed owns the address he claims, since receiving the challenge is necessary to compute the response.

We also add an application-level identification buffer to the Join message. This buffer is passed to the application for authorization. It might include, for example, an encrypted user id and password. The application then returns an identifier to be associated with this client (e.g., the user id). The middleware guarantees that only a single session can be active at a time for this specific identifier, by terminating all previous sessions when a new one is established. This way, even in a distributed denial of service attack, the attacker can only establish as many sessions as the number of credentials he has managed to obtain.

The Leave system request is much simpler. It simply instructs each replica to remove the client from its internal tables. All further communication with the service is prohibited for this client.

We add timeouts to enforce cleanup of stale sessions once the node structures are full. To achieve some common ground regarding time across all replicas, all requests are timestamped with the time of the primary. When each request is executed, its timestamp is recorded for each client. When a join request arrives that cannot be serviced because the client/server node table is full, a cleanup process is started that will locate all clients with a last executed request older than the current join request minus a configurable threshold. All such sessions are cleared to make room for the new connection. If no such stale sessions are found, the new Join request is denied.

Note we have enhanced the PBFT protocol with support for dynamic client membership without changing the inherent properties and message exchanges of the protocol. Thus, our changes do not affect the safety and liveness guarantees offered by PBFT.

3.2   A Higher Level State Abstraction

In a replicated state machine, the term 'state' is an abstract definition of the persistent workspace of the application. PBFT defines state to be a continuous virtual memory region where both the application and the middleware library store their non-transient state in contiguous non-overlapping partitions. The middleware library has full access to this memory region while the application code is not executing, since it is responsible for managing replication and synchronization of this state across replicas. The application, on the other hand, has free read access to it, but is required to notify the library before making changes to any region, thus permitting copy-on-write optimizations of state synchronization.

While this approach relieves the application considerably from having to deal with state synchronization, it creates a number of questions which the application developer must face: What can a modern application do with just a pointer to a memory region? How is this state persistently stored on disk when the service stops? And how does the developer avoid the havoc caused by a misbehaving application which fails to notify the library before modifying memory? To address these questions in a satisfactory manner, we decided to adapt an embedded relational database engine, to intervene between the PBFT middleware library and the application. This way, the application will have SQL-level access to its state and the embedded engine will take care of interfacing with the PBFT library to satisfy its requirements.

In our search for an embedded relational database engine, the major feature we were after was storage of data in a single file, which we could map to virtual memory. We selected SQLite [26] because it exhibits this feature and because it is mature and widely deployed. SQLite is an embedded, in-process library that implements a self-contained relational database engine using SQL as its command language and a C call level interface for the application. It stores all data objects in a single database file that is binary compatible across machine architectures (endianness) and word sizes.

In SQLite's quest to be a multi-platform product, the authors have defined an abstraction layer called VFS (Virtual File System), that sits between the relational engine and the operating system. By hooking into this subsystem, we can manage memory mapping and perform PBFT-required memory modification notifications, as well as re-implement non-deterministic functions, such as system time and random values, by using the upcalls described in Section 2. Interaction with VFS is illustrated in Figure 1.

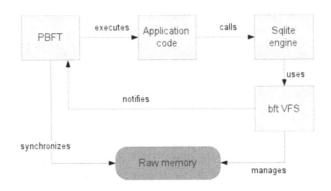

Fig. 1. SQLite with its VFS inside a PBFT application

SQLite uses two disk files to manage the database, for reliability reasons. The first file is the actual database, which we map to virtual memory. The second file is the rollback journal (or write-ahead-log, in a different mode of operation), which is used to rollback failed transactions. We leave this second file to be stored on disk, since it allows the engine to recover in the case of system failure and it is not actually part of the application state. The database file is synchronized with its disk image on transaction commit.

We gain many advantages with this approach. First, a committed transaction will be durable, even in the case of a system crash. That is, when the replica node restarts operation, its state will include the last committed transaction, and PBFT recovery will commence from this point. Second, even if the node is to be removed from the replicated service, its data will be usable on its own, being just another database file. Moreover, an uncommitted transaction will be rolled back on the next attempt to access the database file, from the replicated service or on its own. These advantages are simply the by-product of the ACID semantics that SQLite provides and excellent reasons why developers will likely want to take advantage of it.

One obstacle we faced was that while SQLite can freely manage the growth and shrinkage of its database file, PBFT is not so permitting, because it requires knowledge of the size of the memory region that represents the state, during its initialization. To alleviate this, we use a sparse file that is defined to be a large enough size on initialization, without actually occupying that space on disk, a solution that is reasonable in modern 64-bit operating systems with large virtual memory address ranges.

The application code now simply passes the name of the database file to the PBFT initialization function responsible for starting up the replica server and setting up any data structures needed by the middleware. The function returns to the application code a standard SQLite database handle. Using this handle, the application can call standard SQLite library functions (e.g. sqlite3_exec, sqlite3_prepare_v2, sqlite3_step) to access the database while executing during the appropriate PBFT upcall. This way, an application already using SQLite is immediately portable to the PBFT middleware with only minor changes to the initialization code. Our approach thus guarantees that, whenever the application is called to execute a request, it will have a database consistent with all other replicas. This is achieved by the PBFT middleware library, which manages the raw memory content where the database file is mapped, as it was designed to.

3.3   Remaining Issues

Cryptography. Applications requiring strong cryptography, such as private key generation and storage on the server side of the application, are not well supported by the current PBFT implementation. For key generation, strong random values are required. Unfortunately, even if the primary obtains such strong randomness from its local OS services, for example via /dev/random, there is no way such values can be verified from the remaining replicas, by their very definition of being random. Because of this, an adversary can obtain access to one of the execution replicas, wait until it becomes the primary and use predetermined values instead of random values. In this manner, the adversary can trigger the generation of well-known private and public keys and thus violate confidentiality. To alleviate such attacks, one solution would be to enforce a threshold signature scheme [27] for such authentication requirements, provided for by the middleware library. In such a scheme, private key information for each replica would never be transmitted over the network, as it would not be stored in shared state. In a $(f + 1, n)$ (where $n = 3f + 1$) threshold signature scheme, the set of n replicas would collectively generate a digital signature despite up to f byzantine faults. The PBFT protocol would have to be modified to provide for such cryptographic operations.

Another confidentiality issue is the matter of protecting storage of sensitive information. This has been studied by Yin et al [5], who propose separating the agreement part of the PBFT protocol from the execution part, while also adding an intermediate cluster of 'privacy firewall' nodes. In this layout, $3f+1$ *agreement* nodes receive the client requests and forward them to $2f + 1$ *execution* nodes for execution. To ensure that a faulty execution node cannot disclose sensitive information, an $h + 1$ rows by $h + 1$ columns *privacy firewall* set of nodes is positioned between the agreement and execution cluster, which allows tolerating up to h faulty firewall nodes. This approach however, increases both deployment complexity and request execution latency.

Stateless Applications Only. The original PBFT implementation purposely ignores the notion of client-specific state. This, however, severely limits the target applications to those that are either stateless in nature, or manage session state on their own using their global state abstraction; the latter will need to pass session identifiers inside the request and reply bodies, without any assistance from the middleware library. This is not an inherent limitation of the State Machine Replication approach. It is simply a consequence of the lack of appropriate mechanisms in the PBFT library. With our addition of application level sign-on messages to the protocol, resulting in identification of specific sessions, a library-level subsystem can now be developed that will map parts of the state to a specific session. This enables easier porting of stateful applications to the BFT world.

Web Applications. Our end goal is to provide a web application to end users, which provides them hassle-free access to the server counterpart of the e-voting service. We aim to achieve this while providing end-to-end BFT semantics. To this end, the browser-hosted part of the application, typically written in JavaScript, will have to directly access each and every replica. This communication however cannot be carried over UDP because this protocol is not allowed in the JavaScript runtime environment. Moreover, binary messages are highly inconvenient in this context. Higher level protocols, such as WebSocket, and structures like JSON or XML need to be used. Support for these technologies needs to be incorporated in the middleware library, a task not so trivial because of the need to switch from a point-to-point message-based communication to a connected channel-oriented communication. Additionally, cryptographic functions will need to be available in the browser-hosted client part, which requires transitioning from Rabin to more widely available cryptosystems, such as RSA.

Additionally, we aim to have the replicas placed in different physical locations, to obtain real independance of faults caused by network partitions. This requirement dictates operation in a Wide Area Network environment, where the quadratic message complexity of PBFT will most probably prove costly regarding request latency. Although we tried to simulate a WAN deployment scenario using BFTsim [19], the simulator could not scale to a large enough number of nodes (> 100) to obtain meaningful results. This issue has been studied in [28], but no open-source implementation is readily available.

Summary: The above issues can be overcome, but require a significant amount of engineering effort. An application developer wanting to leverage and deploy PBFT *now* is likely to be unwilling to invest the time and effort required to retrofit the PBFT approach to match the needs of his/her application.

4   Evaluation

In this section we present empirical measurements of the PBFT library, both with and without our modifications supporting dynamic client and seamless state management for applications requiring ACID semantics provided by a legacy database. We test the PBFT library and our modifications to it on a cluster of 8 machines connected with a 1Gbit Ethernet switch. The first four machines are Intel Xeon E5620 at 2.40 GHz under CentOS 5.5 with Linux kernel 2.6.18-194. The remaining four are Intel Core 2 Duo E6600 at 2.40 GHz under Debian 5.0 with Linux kernel 2.6.26. All eight machines run 64 bit versions of their corresponding operating systems. Ping roundtrip time is measured at 134-183 microseconds between all hosts. Bandwidth is measured, using iperf, at 938 Mbits/sec. For all tests, we generate a server and client executable using a particular library configuration set so as to measure the effect of turning on or off a particular optimization and/or modification. We design the client to connect to the library and wait for a signal. On signal reception, it records the current time, starts its operation and then measures and reports elapsed time. To coordinate all processes running on different hosts while at the same time collecting and aggregating measurements, we implement a test framework using Python and netcat, where the latter runs on each host and allows a single controller to submit scripts (i.e., experiments) and collect the results.

4.1   Non-SQL Experiments

We first conduct an experiment without the SQL state abstraction modifications we made to benchmark the original PBFT implementation. Our goal is to measure the impact on system throughput of turning on/off the optimizations described in Section 2. Recall that the use of certain optimizations (such as the use of MACs and special handling of *big* requests) increases performance at the cost of decreased robustness (e.g., slow recovery) of the system.

Table 1. PBFT library configurations we test. sta=static clients, transactions are null requests/responses of 1024 bytes.

Name	TPS	StDev
sta_mac_allbig_batch	17.014	66
sta_mac_allbig_nobatch	1.051	56
sta_mac_noallbig_batch	3.030	57
sta_mac_noallbig_nobatch	1.109	103
sta_nomac_allbig_batch	1.291	4
sta_nomac_allbig_nobatch	1.199	12
sta_nomac_noallbig_batch	992	2
sta_nomac_noallbig_nobatch	1.186	7
nosta_nomac_noallbig_batch	988	1
nosta_nomac_noallbig_nobatch	1.205	1

We generate and test a series of PBFT library configurations, shown in Table 1. The first configuration is the default configuration preferred and recommended by Castro, with all optimizations enabled, including the use of MACs, special treatment of all requests as *big* requests, and request batching. Since batching is the only optimization for which we did not observe faulty behavior, we isolate it and test all other combinations of configurations with batching enabled and disabled, to show its impact. The last four rows of Table 1 depict the most robust configurations (use of MACs and big request handling turned off). Since our particular application has stringent security and reliability requirements, we choose to measure the impact of adding support for dynamic client management using these configurations. We believe other Internet service applications with similar high security and robustness needs would need to run the PBFT library using these configurations. The client and server programs built to measure throughput transmit null requests and responses of varying sizes, of 256, 1024, 2048, and 4096 bytes. We test the system using 12 clients spread evenly across 4 machines while being serviced by 4 replicas, each running alone on a single host. In all cases, IP-level multicasting was turned off, as the networks we are targeting (WANs) do not support it. The results for each of the request and response sizes are similar, so for brevity we show a representative plot, for size of 1024 bytes in Figure 2.

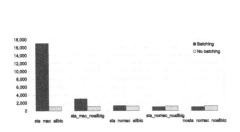

Fig. 2. PBFT tests

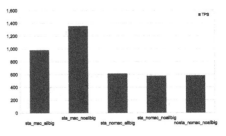

Fig. 3. PBFT + SQL benchmark

From Table 1 and Figure 2, it is clear that the first configuration, which is the default configuration of the PBFT library with all optimizations turned on achieves the best throughput performance. In our experiments, this configuration achieves approximately 17000 null operations per second, while for the most robust configurations the throughput drops to about 1000 null operations per second.

We observe that disabling the batching optimization seriously affects performance when using MACs. When switching to signing with private keys, the delay introduced is so large that batching can no longer assist in any way. Moreover, when disabling big request handling, performance drops to 18% of the optimal, while disabling the use of MACs causes performance to drop to 7.5% of the optimal respectively. Disabling both big request handling and MAC use causes performance to drop to 6% of the optimal. While we observe a difference in performance amongst these configurations where some subset of optimizations is turned off, the bottom line is that performance takes a big hit when turning off any of the optimizations. However, for an application with high security requirements, we conjecture robustness is favored over performance.

We evaluate the impact on performance of adding support for dynamic client management using the most robust configurations. The performance decrease is 0,5% (988 vs 992), which is negligible. This negligible decrease in performance is attributable to the cost of accessing the redirection table that converts assigned customer ids to indexes in the tables tracking participating nodes (clients and servers). We emphasize that the above tests are *artificial* because they are testing "null" operations. The software on the replica spends no time executing application code; it simply manages the network protocol. The large majority of prior BFT studies present throughput in terms of null operations per second. This is understandable as the focus is on providing a baseline benchmark against which varying BFT protocols can be compared, but is not helpful to the application developer who needs to understand how the system would behave using real application requests.

4.2   SQL State Abstraction Experiments

In this subsection, we evaluate the performance of adding seamless state management for applications requiring ACID semantics provided by a legacy database. Null operations are thus not realistic to use in this setting. For our client application request we choose the insertion of a single row into a database table. This is the operation our e-voting service must perform to record a user's vote in an ongoing election. The tuple inserted into the database includes a simple key and value text (representing voter identity and accompanying vote), in addition to a timestamp and a random value. We purposefully added the timestamp and random value to test that replies are indeed identical across all replicas. For this experiment, we enable request batching and vary turning on and off the remaining options (use of MACs, big request handling, and support for dynamic clients). ACID semantics are provided using the rollback journal mode of

SQLite. Throughput performance, measured as database insertion transactions per second, is illustrated in Figure 3.

In this experiment, the big request handling optimization pays no dividends because the system now spends time executing a real, non-null request which requires accessing the hard disk. This dominates the overall request execution lifetime. At any rate, the most robust configuration with dynamic clients enabled is now at 43% of the best (sta_mac_noallbig). Since disk access is a big factor in this experiment, we perform two more experiments to isolate its impact. In these experiments, we measure the most robust configuration (where the use of MACs and big request handling are disabled) with dynamic clients and ACID semantics (as above) and we measure another configuration without ACID semantics (no rollback journal and no flushing to disk on each operation). The ACID version achieves 534 TPS while the No-ACID version achieves 1155 TPS, an approximately $2x$ performance boost.

Summary: The optimizations turned on by default in the PBFT library, lead to the high throughput numbers reported in prior studies, but as we have shown in Section 2, using some simple fault scenarios (such as UDP packet loss), the high performance numbers come at the cost of decreased robustness of the system. Moreover, the performance numbers reported by a large majority of prior BFT studies are based on a metric of null operations per second. This is not a helpful metric for the end-application developer, particular for a developer whose application makes use of a legacy database for ACID semantics.

5   Related Work

Since the 1999 publication on PBFT by Castro and Liskov [3], there has been a flurry of research activity focused on improving the BFT middleware performance [5–8, 10–12, 4, 9, 13], replication cost [5, 14, 13], and robustness under both faulty servers and faulty clients [15, 4]. A large majority of these systems [5, 6, 11, 15, 4, 10, 13] are direct descendents of the Castro and Liskov PBFT system and reuse and build upon the Castro codebase. Thus, the obstacles we encountered as application developers in using the PBFT system apply to its descendents as well.

Wood et al. [13] write "no commercial data center uses BFT techniques despite the wealth of research in this area" and posit that this is due to the high cost of replication required by BFT protocols. They aptly point out that, for applications such as web servers and database servers, it is the execution of client requests and not the agreement of request ordering that dominates the performance of a BFT protocol. They propose lowering the number of active execution replicas to $f + 1$ by using virtual machines as execution nodes and ZFS snapshots for quick state checkpointing. When the $f + 1$ replicas produce inconsistent replies, a paused execution node is revived and starts executing requests immediately. The middleware library fetches the state needed by these requests on demand, to amortize the cost of state transfer. The paper claims that for applications running over a WAN environment, the time to perform state transfer is minimal compared to WAN latencies. The focus of the paper is on reducing replication cost while maintaining good performance. While this is welcome for an application to be deployed in a data center, the paper does not address how the application developer can easily make use of the system, stating simply that applications must be rewritten to take advantage of the system.

Clement et al. [18] introduce *UpRight*, with the goal of making it easy for application developers to convert a crash-fault tolerant application into a BFT application. It includes a number of state-of-the-art BFT techniques, including separation of agreement from execution, insights from the Aardvark protocol [4] on dealing with faulty clients and alleviating denial-of-service attacks, as well as more flexible state management (but not at such a high level as a relational engine). It also allows individual tailoring of crash-fault (Up) and arbitrary-fault (Right) tolerance. Unfortunately, it is still a work in progress. with several key features missing (e.g., view changes are unimplemented) and does not seem to have seen much development since March 2010 [29], so it is not helpful to a developer wishing to make use of BFT techniques now.

Several attempts have been made to address the inability of replicated BFT services to mesh with the rest of the infrastructure in today's multi-tier world. Merideth et al. [30] introduced *Thema*, which aims to mask BFT complexity from the application developer of web services based applications. An agent, visible to the unaffected outside world, plays the role of the client of a BFT system. Additionally, a proxy collects the multiple out-call requests from the replicas of a BFT system, and issues the actual out-call on their behalf, returning the reply when available. Unfortunately, both the agent and the proxy are centralized components which are inappropriate for applications such as ours which require completely distributed design.

Pallemulle et al. [31] focus on interoperability between BFT systems, while enforcing fault isolation and introduce a new protocol, named *Perpetual* to achieve this. Sen et al. [20] in a system called Prophecy, designed to increase BFT performance, introduce a *Sketcher* component, that tries to trade space for performance, by storing a historical log of request/reply pairs and allowing the application to differentiate its requests, asking for possible log-based replies. In its distributed incarnation, *D-Prophecy* is simply an attempt to avoid re-execution of repetitive requests. In the centralized version, *Prophecy*, the *Sketcher* completely avoids BFT access but now becomes a single point of failure.

Amir et al. [28] introduce *Steward*, a hierarchical BFT architecture, that tries to scale BFT to a wide-area network, by introducing an abstraction layer above PBFT using a Paxos-based protocol. It uses a threshold signature scheme to ensure the recipient of a cross-domain message that enough replicas at the originating site agreed with the request. Both these features are welcome to security-conscious Internet application services. Unfortunately, no source code is available.

Vandiver et al. [12] and Garcia et al. [10] introduce middleware for BFT database replication. Incoroporating legacy databases into a BFT system is important for a wide range of Internet applications. Unfortunately, both systems assume closed systems with a finite number of clients. The developer of an Internet-facing application service must still deal with the issue of having end-user clients issue requests to the replicated database system. Either these systems need to provide support for dynamic client management or they must offload the Internet-facing application component accepting customer/user requests to a centralized component, something not appropriate for our particular application.

Finally, Guerraoui et al. [17] introduce a new abstraction allowing for the construction of new BFT protocols with a fraction of the code currently necessary, thus vastly simplifying the BFT researcher's task. Having waded through the 20,000 lines of PBFT code, we applaud this effort and emphasize here the need to simplify the end application developer's task as well.

6   Conclusion

This paper is a call to the research community to look more closely at BFT middleware from the perspective of a real-world application developer. Our experience in trying to apply the PBFT approach to a real-world application with stringent security and reliability needs reveals a slew of difficulties that the application developer must face if he wants to use even the highly- studied and several-times extended PBFT protocol and codebase upon which a large majority of subsequent BFT middleware is based. While the difficulties encountered by the developer can be overcome, they require significant engineering effort and have unclear performance ramifications. These two characteristics are likely to make the developer hesitant to invest the effort to leverage BFT techniques.

The systems community prides itself on building and measuring real systems. We believe that improving BFT middleware performance and robustness remain important. However, if BFT middleware are to see widespread deployment in real-world systems, then the research community needs to focus on the *usability* of BFT algorithms from the perspective of the application developer.

References

1. Schneider, F.: Implementing fault-tolerant services using the state machine approach: a tutorial. ACM Computing Surveys 22(4), 299–319 (1990)
2. Lamport, L., Shostak, R., Pease, M.: The byzantine generals problem. ACM TPLS 4(3), 382–401 (1982)
3. Castro, M., Liskov, B.: Practical byzantine fault tolerance. In: OSDI (February 1999)
4. Clement, A., Wong, E., Alvisi, L., Dahlin, M.: Making byzantine fault tolerant systems tolerate byzantine faults. In: NSDI (April 2009)
5. Yin, J., Martin, J.P., Venkataramani, A., Alvisi, L., Dahlin, M.: Separating agreement from execution for byzantine fault tolerant services. In: SOSP (October 2003)
6. Kotla, R., Dahlin, M.: High throughput byzantine fault tolerance. In: DSN (June 2004)
7. Abd-El-Malek, M., Ganger, G., Goodson, G., Reiter, M., Wylie, J.: Fault-scalable byzantine fault-tolerant services. In: SOSP (October 2005)

8. Cowling, J., Myers, D., Liskov, B., Rodrigues, R., Shrira, L.: Hq relication: A hybrid quorum protocol for byzantine fault tolerance. In: OSDI (November 2006)
9. Distler, T., Kapitza, R.: Increasing performance in byzantine fault-tolerant systems with on-demand replica consistency. In: EuroSys (April 2011)
10. Garcia, R., Rodrigues, R., Preguica, N.: Efficient middleware for byzantine fault tolerant database replication. In: EuroSys (April 2011)
11. Kotla, R., Alvisi, L., Dahlin, M., Clement, A., Wong, E.: Zyzzyva: Speculative byzantine fault tolerance. In: SOSP (October 2007)
12. Vandiver, B., Balakrishnan, H., Liskov, B., Madden, S.: Tolerating byzantine faults in transaction processing systems using commit barrier scheduling. In: SOSP (October 2007)
13. Wood, T., Singh, R., Venkataramani, A., Shenoy, P., Cecchet, E.: Zz and the art of practical bft. In: EuroSys (April 2011)
14. Distler, T., Kapitza, R., Popov, I., Reiser, H., Schroder-Preikschat, W.: Spare: Replicas on hold. In: NDSS (February 2011)
15. Amir, Y., Coan, B., Kirsch, J., Lane, J.: Byzantine replication under attack. In: DSN (June 2008)
16. Kiayias, A., Korman, M., Walluck, D.: An internet voting system supporting user privacy. In: ACSAC (December 2006)
17. Guerraoui, R., Knezevic, N., Quema, V., Vukolic, M.: The next 700 bft protocols. In: EuroSys (April 2010)
18. Clement, A., Kapritsos, M., Lee, S., Wang, Y., Alvisi, L., Dahlin, M., Riche, T.: Upright cluster services. In: SOSP (October 2009)
19. Singh, A., Das, T., Maniatis, P., Druschel, P., Roscoe, T.: BFT protocols under fire. In: NSDI (2008)
20. Sen, S., Lloyed, W., Freedman, M.: Prophecy: Using history for high-throughput fault tolerance. In: NSDI (April 2010)
21. Lamport, L.: The implementation of reliable distributed multiprocess systems. Computer Networks 2 (1978)
22. Herlihy, M., Wing, J.M.: Linearizability: A correctness condition for concurrent objects. ACM TPLS 12(3), 463–492 (1990)
23. Lynch, N.: Distributed Algorithms. Morgan Kaufmann (1996)
24. Merkle, R.C.: A Digital Signature Based on a Conventional Encryption Function. In: Pomerance, C. (ed.) CRYPTO 1987. LNCS, vol. 293, pp. 369–378. Springer, Heidelberg (1988)
25. Castro, M., Rodrigues, R., Liskov, B.: BASE: Using abstraction to improve fault tolerance. ACM TOCS 21(3) (August 2003)
26. Sqlite embedded database engine, http://www.sqlite.org
27. Desmedt, Y.G., Frankel, Y.: Threshold Cryptosystems. In: Brassard, G. (ed.) CRYPTO 1989. LNCS, vol. 435, pp. 307–315. Springer, Heidelberg (1990)
28. Amir, Y., Danilov, C., Dolev, D., Kirsch, J., Lane, J., Nita-rotaru, C., Olsen, J., Zage, D.: Steward: Scaling byzantine fault-tolerant systems to wide area networks. In: DSN (2006)
29. Upright: Making distributed systems up (available) and right (correct), http://code.google.com/p/upright/w/list
30. Merideth, M., Iyengar, A., Mikalsen, T., Tai, S., Rouvellou, I., Narasimhan, P.: Thema: Byzantine-fault-tolerant middleware for web-service applications. In: SRDS (October 2005)
31. Pallemulle, S.L., Thorvaldsson, H.D., Goldman, K.J.: Byzantine fault-tolerant web services for n-tier and service oriented architectures. In: ICDCS (June 2008)

SCORe: A Scalable One-Copy Serializable Partial Replication Protocol*

Sebastiano Peluso[1,2], Paolo Romano[2], and Francesco Quaglia[1]

[1] Sapienza University, Rome, Italy
{peluso,quaglia}@dis.uniroma1.it
[2] IST/INESC-ID, Lisbon, Portugal
{peluso,romanop}@gsd.inesc-id.pt

Abstract. In this article we present SCORe, a scalable one-copy serial-izable partial replication protocol. Differently from any other literature proposal, SCORe jointly guarantees the following properties: (i) it is gen-uine, thus ensuring that only the replicas that maintain data accessed by a transaction are involved in its processing, and (ii) it guarantees that read operations always access consistent snapshots, thanks to a one-copy serializable multiversion scheme, which never aborts read-only transactions and spares them from any (distributed) validation phase. This makes SCORe particularly efficient in presence of read-intensive workloads, as typical of a wide range of real-world applications. We have integrated SCORe into a popular open source distributed data grid and performed a large scale experimental study with well-known benchmarks using both private and public cloud infrastructures. The experimental results demonstrate that SCORe provides stronger consistency guaran-tees (namely One-Copy Serializability) than existing multiversion partial replication protocols at no additional overhead.

Keywords: Distributed Transactional Systems, Partial Replication, Scalability, Multiversioning.

1 Introduction

In-memory, transactional data platforms, often referred to as NoSQL data grids, such as Cassandra, BigTable, or Infinispan, have become the reference data man-agement technology for grid and cloud computing systems. For these platforms, data replication represents the key mechanism to ensure both adequate perfor-mance and fault-tolerance, since it allows (a) distributing the load across the different nodes within the platform, and (b) ensuring data survival in the event of node failures.

* This work has been partially supported by national funds through FCT - Fundação para a Ciência e a Tecnologia, under projects PTDC/EIA-EIA/102496/2008 and PEst-OE/EEI/LA0021/2011, by the EU project Cloud-TM (contract no. 57784) and by COST Action IC1001 EuroTM.

P. Narasimhan and P. Triantafillou (Eds.): Middleware 2012, LNCS 7662, pp. 456–475, 2012.

A common design approach for these data platforms consists in the adoption of relaxed data-consistency models, such as eventual consistency [1] and non-serializable isolation levels [2], or restricted transactional semantics, such as single object transactions [3] and static transactions [4]. These schemes have been shown to yield significant performance advantages with respect to classic strongly consistent transactional paradigms. Unfortunately, these advantages come at the cost of additional complexity for the programmers, who have to reason on the correctness of complex applications in presence of weak consistency guarantees and/or may need to identify non-trivial work-around solutions to circumvent the limitations of constrained programming paradigms.

Some recent proposals have been targeted at more strict consistency models, such as One-Copy Serializability, and have been based on the usage of (optimistic) atomic broadcast protocols [5]. Unfortunately, these solutions have been tailored for the case of full replication (in which each node maintains a copy of the entire data-set), which is a clearly not viable option for large scale systems. Indeed, the adoption of partial data replication schemes appears to be an essential requirement for large scale systems. In this context, a key requirement to maximize scalability is to ensure *genuineness* [6,7], namely to guarantee that only the sites that replicate the data items accessed within a transaction exchange messages to decide its final outcome (hence excluding solutions that rely on centralized components or that involve every site in the system). Unfortunately, several partial replication protocols, such as [8,9], do not exhibit this property, thus again hampering scalability. On the other hand, some genuine protocols proposed in literature, such as [7], require read-only transactions to undergo a remote validation phase. This is also quite undesirable from a performance perspective, especially for geographically dispersed infrastructures, given the predominance of read-intensive workloads in typical applications [10].

Genuine protocols guaranteeing relatively strong consistency levels, while also avoiding the validation of read-only transactions have been recently presented in [11,12]. However, these protocols do not ensure One-Copy Serializability (1CS). In particular, the protocol in [11] only ensures Extended Update-Serializability (EUS), which allows different client applications, during the execution of read-only transactions, to observe the commits of non-conflicting update transactions as serialized in different orders. Similar considerations can be made for the protocol in [12], with the additional note that the above anomalies can also involve the commits observed by update transactions.

In this paper we present SCORe, namely a scalable one-copy serializable replication protocol. SCORe overcomes the above drawbacks by employing a genuine partial replication scheme which guarantees that read-only transactions always observe a consistent snapshot of the data, hence avoiding to incur in expensive remote validation phases. This result is achieved by combining a local multiversion concurrency control algorithm with a highly scalable distributed logical-clock synchronization scheme that only requires the exchange of a scalar clock value among the nodes involved in the handling of a transaction. All the above features jointly allow SCORe to be performance effective, highly scalable, and able to provide supports for a wider set of applications, including those that impose strict data consistency requirements.

We have implemented SCORe within Infinispan, a mainstream open source data grid framework developed by Red Hat [13]. We have assessed the effectiveness of SCORe via an extensive experimental study based on both the TPC-C [14] and YCSB [15] benchmarks, using as experimental testbeds a private cluster with up to 20 nodes, and a public cloud (FutureGrid) with up to 100 nodes. Major outcomes from the study entail demonstrations of linear scalability by SCORe across a wide range of workloads, and no overheads compared to state of the art genuine partial replication solutions [11] guaranteeing weaker consistency semantics (namely EUS).

The remainder of this paper is organized as follows. In Sect. 2 we discuss related work. The model of the system we are targeting is provided in Sect. 3. The SCORe protocol is presented in Sect. 4. The proof of correctness is provided in Sect. 5. The results of the experimental analysis are reported in Sect. 6.

2   Related Work

The issue of transactional systems replication has been thoroughly addressed in literature. Most of the existing proposals have been targeted at the case of full replication, where a copy of each data item is retained at each involved site. In this context, solutions have been provided coping with aspects such as protocol specification [16], and design of replication architectures based on middleware level approaches [17,18] and/or on extensions of the inner logic of individual transactional systems [16]. Comparative studies [19] have demonstrated how the solutions that coordinate the replicas via total order group communication primitives, such as [20,21], exhibit the potential for improved performance levels. Also, total order based protocols relying on speculative transaction processing schemes, such as [22,23], have been shown to further reduce the impact of distributed synchronization on both latency and throughput. On the other hand, compared to all these proposals, in this paper we address performance and scalability of the replicated system from an orthogonal perspective since our focus is on architectures making use of partial data replication, as opposed to full replication.

When considering partial replication schemes, literature proposals can be grouped depending on (i) whether they can be considered genuine, and on (ii) the specific consistency guarantees they provide. The works in [8,9] provide non-genuine protocols where the commitment of a transaction requires interactions with all the sites within the replicated system. Compared to these approaches, genuine partial replication schemes have been shown to achieve significantly higher scalability levels [11]. The protocol in [7] provides a genuine solution also supporting strict consistency, namely 1CS. However, differently from the present proposal, this protocol imposes that read-only transactions undergo a distributed validation phase. Also, these transactions are potentially subject to rollback/retry. Instead, the SCORe protocol we propose never aborts read-only transactions, since it guarantees that they always observe a consistent snapshot of data, and consequently spares them from expensive remote validations.

Analogously to SCORe, the solutions proposed in [11,12] are genuine and do not require read-only transactions to be remotely validated. However, differently from SCORe, they do not guarantee that read operations behave as if they were performed within transactions executed on a given serial schedule. For the protocol in [11], this anomalous behavior can occur only for read-only transactions, while for the protocol in [12] it may arise also for update transactions. Overall, both these protocols target weaker consistency semantics than SCORe. Similar arguments can be used when comparing SCORe with the recent proposal in [24], which does not guarantee strong consistency in the case of read operations performed on nodes maintaining distinct partitions of the replicated data.

As for the reliance on multiversions, our proposal is also related to the one in [25], where a multiversion concurrency control mechanism is provided in order to cope with distributed transaction processing in the context of distributed software transactional memories. However this protocol does not cope with (partially) replicated data and it guarantees Snapshot Isolation (SI).

3   Model of the Target System

We consider a classic asynchronous distributed system model composed of $\Pi = \{N_1, \ldots, N_n\}$ nodes, each one representing a transactional process within the replicated system. We consider the classic crash-stop failure model. Hence, nodes may fail by crashing, but never behave maliciously. A node that never crashes is said to be correct, otherwise it is said to be faulty. We assume that nodes only communicate through message passing, thus not having access to a shared memory nor to a global clock. Messages are delivered via reliable asynchronous channels, i.e., messages are guaranteed to be eventually delivered unless either the sender or the receiver crashes. However, messages may experience arbitrarily long (but finite) delays, and we assume no bound on relative process speeds or clock skews.

We assume a simple key-value model for the data maintained by the nodes in Π. Also, data are assumed to be multiversioned, hence each data item d, maintained by whichever node, is represented as a sequence of versions $\langle k, val, ver \rangle$, where k is a key representing d's identifier, val is its value and ver is a scalar, monotonically increasing logical timestamp that identifies (and totally orders) the versions of data item d. Each node N_i is assumed to store a partial copy of the whole data set. We abstract over the data placement policy by assuming that data are subdivided across m partitions, and that each partition is replicated across r nodes. We denote with $\Gamma = \{g_1, \ldots, g_m\}$ the set of groups of nodes belonging to Π, where g_j represents the group of those nodes that replicate the j-th data partition. Each group is composed of exactly r nodes (the value of r being selected in order to ensure the target replication degree), of which at least one is assumed to be correct. Given a data item d, we denote as $replicas(d)$ the set of nodes that maintain a replica of d, namely the nodes of group g_j that replicate the data partition containing d. The same notation is used to indicate sets of nodes maintaining replicas of sets of data items. As an example, $replicas(S)$, with $S = \{d, d'\}$, is used to indicate the set of nodes maintaining a copy of d or a copy of d'.

In order to maximize flexibility of the data placement strategy, we do not require groups to be disjoint (they can have nodes in common), and assume that a node may belong to multiple groups, as long as $\bigcup_{j=1...m} g_j = \Pi$. We highlight that the assumed partitioning model allows capturing a wide range of data distribution algorithms, and, in particular, algorithms based on consistent hashing, which are very popular in NoSQL transactional data stores thank to their ability to: (i) minimize data transfers upon joining/leaving of nodes (which, for ease of presentation, we do not model explicitly in this work, although we will briefly discuss how to cope with dynamic groups in Sect. 4.4); (ii) ensure the achievement of target replication degrees; and (iii) avoid distributed lookups to retrieve the identities of the group of processes storing the replicas of the requested data items.

We model transactions as a sequence of read and write operations on data items, which are preceded by a begin operation, and are followed by a commit or an abort operation. A transaction can be originated on whichever node $N_i \in \Pi$, and can read/write data belonging to any partition. Also, we do not assume any a-priori knowledge on the set of data items that will be read or written by transactions. In addition a history over a set of transactions consists of a partial order of events that reflects the operations (begin, read, write, abort, commit) of those transactions.

4   The SCORe Protocol

4.1   Overview

SCORe is a genuine (hence highly scalable) partial replication protocol that implements a one-copy serializable distributed multiversion scheme. As in typical non-distributed multiversion algorithms [26], SCORe replicas store multiple versions of the data items that they maintain, each tagged with a scalar timestamp. However, SCORe introduces a novel distributed timestamp management scheme that addresses two main issues: (i) establishing the snapshot visible by transactions, i.e. selecting which one, among the multiple versions of a datum (replicated across multiple nodes) should be observed by a transaction upon a read operation; (ii) determining the final global serialization order for update transactions via a distributed agreement protocol that takes place during the transactions' commit phase.

To this end SCORe maintains two scalar variables per node, namely $commitId$ and $nextId$. The former one maintains the timestamp that was attributed to the last update transaction when committed on that node. $nextId$, on the other hand, keeps track of the next timestamp that the node will propose when it will receive a commit request for a transaction that accessed some of the data that it maintains.

Snapshot visibility for transactions is determined by associating with each transaction T a scalar timestamp, which we call *snapshot identifier* or, more succinctly, *sid*. The *sid* of a transaction is established upon its first read operation. In this case the most recent version of the requested datum is returned, and the transaction's *sid* is set to the value of *commitId* at the transaction's originating node, if the read can be served locally. Otherwise, if the requested datum is not maintained locally, $T.sid$ is set equal to the maximum between *commitId* at the originating node and *commitId* at the remote node from which T reads. From that moment on, any subsequent read operation is allowed to observe the most recent committed version of the requested datum having timestamp less than or equal to $T.sid$, as in classical multiversion concurrency control algorithms.

SCORe relies on a genuine atomic commit protocol that can be seen as the fusion of the Two-Phase Commit algorithm (2PC) and the Skeen's total order multicast [6]. 2PC is used to validate update transactions and to guarantee the atomicity of the application of their post-images. Overlapped with 2PC, SCORe runs a distributed agreement protocol, similar in spirit to Skeen's total order multicast algorithm, which allows to achieve a twofold goal: (i) totally ordering the commit events of transactions that update any data item in a partition j among all the nodes that replicate j (namely, g_j); (ii) tracking the serialization order between *update* transactions that exhibit (potentially transitive) data dependencies by totally ordering them via a scalar *commit timestamp* that is also used as version identifier of the post-images of committed transactions.

A key mechanism used in SCORe to correctly serialize transactions, and in particular to track write-after-read dependencies [26], is to update the *nextId* of a node upon the processing of a read operation. Specifically, if a node receives a read operation from a transaction T having a *sid* larger than its local *nextId*, this is advanced to $T.sid$. This mechanism allows to guarantee that any update transaction T^{up} that requests to commit on node N_i at time t is attributed a commit timestamp larger than the timestamp of any transaction T that read a value from N_i before time t, hence ensuring that T^{up} is serialized after T.

Finally, since a transaction is attributed a snapshot identifier upon its first read, which is used throughout its execution, SCORe guarantees that the snapshot read by a transaction is always consistent with respect to a prefix of the (equivalent serial) history of committed transactions. As a consequence, in SCORe read-only transactions never abort and do not need to undergo any distributed validation.

The pseudocode of the SCORe protocol is reported in Algorithms 1, 2, 3, 4, and discussed and analyzed in the following. For the sake of presentation, we will first assume that the transaction's coordinator does not crash, and then discuss how to relax this assumption in Sect. 4.4.

4.2   Handling of Read and Write Operations

SCORe buffers write operations of transactions in a private writeset (denoted as ws in Algorithm 1), which is only made visible upon transaction's commit.

Read operations on a datum d first check whether d has already been updated by the transaction, returning in this case the value present in the transaction's writeset. Otherwise, it is necessary to establish which of the versions of d is visible to the transaction. As already mentioned, transactions establish the sid that they use to determine version's visibility upon their first read. If this read operation is local, the transaction's sid is simply set equal to the originating node's $commitId$. Otherwise, it is set equal to the maximum between the $commitId$ of the remote node from which the data is read and the $commitId$ of the transaction's originating node. Further, if the transaction's sid is higher than the node's $nextId$, the latter is set equal to $T.sid$. This ensures that update transactions that subsequently issue a commit request on that node are serialized after T.

Next, the version visible by transaction T is determined, as in conventional MVCC algorithms [26], by selecting the most recent version having commit timestamp less than T's snapshot identifier. Before doing so, however, T first waits for the completion of the commit phase of any transaction T' that i) is updating d, and ii) is currently in its commit phase. In fact, in case T' is committed successfully, as it will be clearer in the following, it might be attributed a timestamp smaller than $T.sid$. Hence, T' would be totally ordered before T and the version of d created by T' would be visible to T. If T' aborted, on the other hand, T should not see its updates. In order to enforce the correct tracking of this read-after-write dependence, SCORe forces any transaction T reading a data item d to wait until there are no longer transaction commit events pending on d and with a (either final or temporary) commit timestamp smaller than $T.sid$

The logic for handling remote read operations is defined by Algorithm 2. It is worthy to highlight that, even though transactions update their own sid only upon their first read operation, a node attempts to advance its local timestamps $commitId$ and $nextId$ whenever it receives a message (associated with the request or the response of a read operation) from another node in the system informing it that snapshots with higher timestamps have been already committed. This mechanism, which aims to maximize the freshness of visible snapshots, is encapsulated by the $updateNodeTimestamps$ function. This function advances immediately the $nextId$ timestamp, which is used to determine the timestamp proposed for future commit requests. However, additional care needs to be taken before advancing the node's $commitId$ timestamp. As this timestamp determines the (minimum) snapshot visible by locally generated transactions, in fact, it can be increased to a new value, say $commitId'$, only if it is found that there are no committing transactions that may be given a timestamp less than or equal to $commitId'$.

Finally, SCORe includes a simple, yet effective, optimization that consists in immediately aborting update transactions which, based on their snapshot identifier, are forced to observe, upon a read operation, data item versions that have been already overwritten by more recently committed transactions.

Algorithm 1. Begin, read and write events (node N_i).

upon $Write(Transaction\ T,\ Key\ k,\ Value\ val)$ **do**
$\quad T.ws \leftarrow T.ws \setminus \{< k, - >\} \cup \{< k, val >\};$

upon $Value\ Read(Transaction\ T,\ Key\ k)$ **do**
$\quad$**if** $(\exists < k, val > \in T.ws)$ **then**
$\quad\quad$**return** $val;$
$\quad$**if** (is first read of T) **then**
$\quad\quad T.sid \leftarrow N_i.commitId;$
$\quad$**if** $N_i \in replicas(k)$ **then**
$\quad\quad < val, maxCommitted, mostRecent > \leftarrow doRead(T.sid, k);$
$\quad$**else**
$\quad\quad$**if** (is first read of T) **then**
$\quad\quad\quad$**send** READREQUEST$[T,\ k,\ T.sid,\ \top]$ **to all** $N_j \in replicas(k);$
$\quad\quad$**else**
$\quad\quad\quad$**send** READREQUEST$[T,\ k,\ T.sid,\ \bot]$ **to all** $N_j \in replicas(k);$
$\quad\quad$**wait receive** READRETURN$[T,\ val,\ maxCommitted, mostRecent]$ **from** $N_j \in replicas(k);$
$\quad$**if** (is first read of T) **then**
$\quad\quad T.sid \leftarrow maxCommitted;$
$\quad$**if** $T.isUpdate \wedge \neg mostRecent$ **then**
$\quad\quad T.abort();$
$\quad T.rs \leftarrow T.rs \cup \{< k, val >\};$
$\quad$**return** $val;$

function $< Value, SnapshotId, boolean > doRead(SnapshotId\ sid,\ Key\ k)$
$\quad$// Track write-after-read dependence
$\quad N_i.nextId \leftarrow max(N_i.nextId, readSid);$
$\quad$// Enforce read-after-write dependence
$\quad$**wait until** $(N_i.commitId \geq readSid \vee k.exclusiveUnlocked());$
$\quad Version\ ver \leftarrow k.getLastVersion();$
$\quad$**while** $ver.vn > sid$ **do**
$\quad\quad ver \leftarrow ver.prev;$
$\quad$**return** $< ver.value, N_i.commitId, k.isLastVersion(ver) >;$

Algorithm 2. Handling of remote reads (node N_i).

upon receive READREQUEST$[T,\ k,\ readSid,\ firstRead])$ **from** N_j **do**
$\quad SnapshotId\ newReadSid \leftarrow readSid;$
$\quad$**if** $firstRead \wedge N_i.commitId > newReadSid$ **then**
$\quad\quad newReadSid \leftarrow N_i.commitId;$
$\quad < Value, mostRecent > val \leftarrow doRead(newReadSid, k);$
$\quad$**send** READRETURN$[T,\ val, mostRecent, N_i.commitId];$
$\quad updateNodeTimestamps(readSid);$

upon receive READRETURN$[T,\ val, lastCommitted, mostRecent]$ **from** N_j **do**
$\quad updateNodeTimestamps(lastCommitted);$

function $updateNodeTimestamps(SnapshotId\ lastCommitted);$
$\quad$// Update global snapshot knowledge
$\quad N_i.nextId \leftarrow max(N_i.nextId, lastCommitted);$
$\quad N_i.maxSeenId \leftarrow max(N_i.maxSeenId, lastCommitted);$

upon $N_i.maxSeenId > N_i.commitId \wedge pendQ.isEmpty() \wedge stableQ.isEmpty()$ **atomically do**
$\quad N_i.commitId \leftarrow max(N_i.maxSeenId, N_i.commitId);$

4.3 Commit Phase

As already mentioned, with SCORe read-only transactions can be committed without undergoing distributed validation phases (unlike, for instance, in [7]).

Update transactions, on the other hand, execute a Two-Phase Commit protocol, which is detailed in the following. To guarantee genuineness, SCORe involves in the commit phase of a transaction T only the nodes that maintain replicas of the data items that T accessed. More in detail, when a node N_i requests to commit transaction T, it broadcasts a PREPARE message to all nodes N_j belonging to $Replicas(T.rs \cup T.ws)$. Upon the receipt of this message, node N_j verifies whether the transaction can be serialized after every transaction that has locally committed so far. To this end, it attempts to acquire exclusive, resp. shared, locks for the data in T's writeset, resp. readset, that it locally maintains. This lock acquisition is non-blocking since the node waits for a busy lock only for a certain amount of time, which is determined by means of a configurable timeout parameter. Next, if the acquisition of the locks succeeds, the node validates T's readset, verifying that none of the items read by T has been overwritten by a more recently committed transaction. If any of these operations fails, T is simply rolled back, which will yield to the abort of the whole distributed transaction, as in classic 2PC.

If the transaction passes the validation phase, however, the VOTE message of 2PC is exploited to overlap a distributed agreement scheme similar in spirit to Skeen's total order multicast algorithm that aims to establish the final serialization order for the transaction. More in detail, N_j increments the $nextId$ timestamp, inserts the pair $< T, N_j.nextId >$, defined on the domain $TransactionId \times SnapshotId$ in a queue of pending committing transactions (denoted as $pendQ$) ordered by $SnapshotId$, and sends back to the transaction coordinator the value of $N_j.nextId$ in piggyback to the VOTE message. The coordinator gathers the VOTE messages (aborting the transaction in case one of the contacted node does not respond within a predefined timeout), determines the final commit timestamp for T as the maximum among the timestamps proposed by the transaction's participants, and broadcasts back a DECIDE message with the transaction's final commit timestamp.

Upon the receipt of the DECIDE message with a positive outcome, unlike classical 2PC, the transaction is not necessarily immediately committed. In fact, as each data item is replicated over more than one node, and since we want to ensure 1CS without requiring the validation of read-only transactions, SCORe guarantees that the commit events of all update transactions (even non-conflicting ones) are totally ordered across all the replicas of a same partition. To ensure this result, when a DECIDE message is received on N_j for transaction T with final commit timestamp fsn, T is removed from the pending queue and is immediately committed (atomically increasing $N_j.nextId$) only if there are no other transactions in both the pending queue and a second queue, denoted as $stableQ$, with snapshot id less than fsn. If this is not the case, T is buffered in $stableQ$, which is ordered by $SnapshotId$ as well, till it can be ensured that no other pending transaction will ever receive a final commit snapshot id less than fsn (see Algorithm 4).

We conclude by remarking that the idea of intertwining an atomic commit algorithm and the Skeen's total order multicast algorithm was, to the best of our knowledge, first employed in our recent proposal GMU [11]. Differently from SCORe, however, GMU relies on a vector-clock-based timestamping mechanism that guarantees a weaker consistency criterion (Extended Update-Serializability [10]).

Algorithm 3. Commit phase (node N_i).

---

upon *boolean Commit(Transaction T)* **do**
    if $T.ws = \emptyset$ **then**
        return $\top$;
    boolean outcome $\leftarrow \top$;
    Set proposedSn $\leftarrow \emptyset$;
    send PREPARE$[T, T.sid, T.rs, T.ws]$ **to all** $N_j \in replicas(T.rs \cup T.ws)$
    for all $N_j \in T.involvedNodes$ **do**
        wait receive VOTE$[T, sn, res]$ **from** N_j **or timeout**;
        if $(res = \bot \vee$ **timeout**$)$ **then**
            $outcome \leftarrow \bot$;
            break;
        else
            $proposedSn \leftarrow proposedSn \cup sn$;
    $T.sid \leftarrow max(proposedSn)$;
    send DECIDE$[T, T.sid, outcome]$ **to all** $N_j \in T.involvedNodes$
    wait until $T.completed = \top$;
    return $T.outcome$;

upon receive PREPARE$[T, sid, rs, ws])$ **from** N_j
    boolean outcome $\leftarrow (getExclLocksWithTimeout(ws) \wedge getSharedLocksWithTimeout(rs)$
    $\wedge\ validate(rs, sid));$ SnapshotIdsn $\leftarrow NULL\_SID$
    if *outcome* **then**
        $sn \leftarrow N_i.nextId \leftarrow N_i.nextId + 1$;
        $pendQ \leftarrow pendQ \cup \{< T, sn >\}$;
    send VOTE $[T, sn, outcome]$ **to** N_j;

upon receive DECIDE$[T, fsn, outcome])$ **from** N_j **atomically do**
    if *outcome* **then**
        $N_i.nextId \leftarrow max(N_i.nextId, fsn)$;
        $stableQ \leftarrow stableQ \cup \{< T, fsn >\}$;
    $pendQ \leftarrow pendQ \setminus \{< T, - >\}$;
    if $\neg outcome$ **then**
        $releaseSharedLocks(T.rs)$;
        $releaseExclusiveLocks(T.ws)$;
        if $T.origin = N_i$ **then**
            $T.outcome \leftarrow \bot$;
            $T.completed \leftarrow \top$;

boolean validate(Set readSet, SnapshotId sid) **do**
    for all $k \in readSet$ **do**
        if $k.getLastVersion().vn > sid;$ **then**
            return $\bot$;
    return $\top$;

4.4 Garbage Collection and Fault-Tolerance

For space constraints we can only briefly overview which standard mechanisms could be integrated in SCORe to deal with garbage collection of obsolete data versions and fault-tolerance.

Algorithm 4. Finalizing the commit phase of transaction T (node N_i).

```
 1: upon ∃ < T, fsn > : {< T, fsn > = stableQ.head ∧
 2:       (∄ < T', sn > : < T', sn > = pendQ.head ∧ sn < fsn} atomically do
 3:    apply(T.ws, fsn);
 4:    releaseSharedLocks(T.rs);
 5:    releaseExclusiveLocks(T.ws);
 6:    stableQ ← stableQ \ {< T, fsn >};
 7:    if T.origin = N_i then
 8:        T.outcome ← ⊤;
 9:        T.completed ← ⊤;
10:
```

As in non-distributed MVCC algorithms, versions of a data item d having timestamps less than the *sid* of any active transaction can be safely removed, provided that most recent versions of d have already been committed. In a distributed platform, it is required to disseminate the information on the *sid* of the oldest active transaction at each node. This information can be spread by relying, e.g., on lazy approaches based on piggybacking or gossip [27].

For simplicity, we have opted to present SCORe as layered on top of a 2PC protocol, which is well known to be blocking upon failure of the coordinator. However, the issue of how to ensure high availability of the transaction coordinator state is well understood, and a range of orthogonal solutions have been proposed in literature to deal with such failure scenarios. One may use, for instance, protocols such as Paxos Commit [28] or other consensus based abstractions [29], to replicate the state of the coordinator of a transaction T across the replicas of any of the data partitions accessed by T. Note that, as we are assuming that at least one process is correct for each replica group, failures of transactions' participants will not lead to blocking scenarios during the execution of a remote read operation. Failures of transactions' participants can, instead, lead to aborts during the commit phase, as the coordinator unilaterally aborts the transaction if it times out while waiting for some reply during the prepare phase. To ensure the liveness of the commit protocol, SCORe relies on an underlying Group Communication System [5] in order to handle the removal of faulty replicas from the system and manage its reconfiguration, which may imply the re-distribution of data across replicas to guarantee a desirable replication degree.

Aiming at ensuring 1CS, SCORe opts for sacrificing availability (by aborting transactions that span remote nodes) in order to ensure consistency in presence of network partitions. This is not surprising, given the existence of well known results, such as the CAP theorem [30], concerning the impossibility of achieving both availability and consistency in presence of partitions.

Finally, SCORe does not introduce additional issues concerning the management of dynamic process groups with respect to classic 2PC-based transactional replication systems. Conversely, its supports for multiversion simplify significantly the design of state-transfer mechanisms [31] aimed to synchronize the state of newly joining nodes.

5   Correctness Proof

Preliminary Definitions. Let us start by briefly recalling some basic notions and nomenclature on multiversioned histories [26]. Let us denote as x_i the version of data item x committed by transaction T_i. A multiversioned history H defines a partial order on the operations executed by transactions on the multiversioned dataset, and each operation can be a *read*, a *write*, a *begin*, a *commit* or an *abort* operation. We use the following notation for the five types of operations: b_i denotes the begin of a transaction T_i, while c_i and a_i represent respectively its commit and its abort; the notation $r_i(x_j)$ is used to indicate the transaction T_i performs a read on the version x_j, while $w_i(x_i)$ denotes a write of a new version x_i issued by transaction T_i. In addition, a multiversioned history H implicitly defines a total order $\ll_x$ for each data item x. A version order $\ll$ on H is the union of the $\ll_x$ for each x in H.

Given a multiversioned history H and a version order $\ll$ on the written data item versions, a *Direct Serialization Graph $DSG(H, \ll)$* (as in [10,26]) is a direct graph having a vertex V_{T_i} for each committed transaction T_i in H (i.e. c_i is in H) and a direct edge $V_{T_i} \xrightarrow{E} V_{T_j}$ from a vertex V_{T_i} to a vertex V_{T_j} if one of the following statements holds:

- T_j *directly read-depends on* T_i $(V_{T_i} \xrightarrow{wr} V_{T_j})$. There exists a data item x such that both $w_i(x_i)$ and $r_j(x_i)$ are in H.
- T_j *directly write-depends on* T_i $(V_{T_i} \xrightarrow{ww} V_{T_j})$. There exists a data item x such that both $w_i(x_i)$ and $w_j(x_j)$ are in H and version x_i immediately precedes version x_j according to the total order defined by $\ll$.
- T_j *directly anti-depends on* T_i $(V_{T_i} \xdashrightarrow{rw} V_{T_j})$. There exists a data item x and a committed transaction T_k in H such that $k \neq i$, $k \neq j$, both $r_i(x_k)$ and $w_j(x_j)$ are in H and version x_k immediately precedes version x_j according to the total order defined by $\ll$.

A multiversioned history H is *One-Copy Serializable* iff there exists a version order $\ll$ such that the $DSG(H, \ll)$ graph does not contain any oriented cycle.

One-Copy Serializability. Our proof is based on establishing a mapping between each vertex V_{T_i} in $DSG(H, \ll)$ and the value of the commit timestamp of T_i, denoted as $commitSId(T_i)$. We prove the acyclicity of the $DSG(H, \ll)$ by showing that for each edge $V_{T_i} \xrightarrow{E} V_{T_j} \in DSG(H, \ll)$ SCORe guarantees that $commitSId(T_i) \leq commitSId(T_j)$.

Note that, if T_i is a read-only transaction, $commitSId(T_i)$ is equal to the *sid* assigned to T_i upon its first read operation. On the other hand, in case T_i is an update transaction, $commitSId(T_i)$ is computed during T_i's commit phase and is equal to the maximum identifier among the ones proposed by the nodes involved in the commit of T_i .

Let us start by assuming that E is a direct write-dependence edge, and show that SCORe ensures that $commitSId(T_i) < commitSId(T_j)$. This is because T_i and T_j are both update transactions and they commit on a common subset S of the nodes in the system (at least the nodes storing the data item on which the write-dependence is materialized). In fact, in accordance with the design of the commit phase, it is ensured that: (i) T_j cannot enter the commit phase of the protocol before T_i has committed, since T_j has to wait for the release of some exclusive lock owned by T_i at least on the nodes in S; (ii) T_i updates the $nextId$ on the nodes in S to a value at least equal to $commitSId(T_i)$ before finalizing its commit; (iii) the $commitSId(T_j)$ is chosen as the maximum among the $nextId$ values, incremented by one, of the nodes involved in the commit of T_j.

Now assume that E is a direct read-dependence edge. This means that T_j has read a version committed by T_i. Therefore the snapshot identifier used by T_j to perform read operations, i.e. $T_j.sid$, is greater than or equal to the T_i's commit snapshot identifier due to the reading rule defined by the protocol. So, if T_j is a read-only transaction, this entails that $commitSId(T_i) \leq T_j.sid = commitSId(T_j)$; otherwise, if T_j is an update transaction its commit snapshot identifier will be always greater than its reading snapshot identifier, since the value proposed by each node involved in the commit of T_j (i.e. the incremented $nextId$) is greater than every snapshot seen by T_j. As a consequence, $commitSId(T_i) < commitSId(T_j)$ holds.

Finally, if E is a direct anti-dependence edge, we have to distinguish two scenarios. In the former, if T_i is a read-only transaction, then the $commitSId(T_j)$ is greater than $commitSId(T_i)$ since (i) the T_j's commit snapshot identifier is at least equals to all the values proposed for its commit and (ii) there exists a value among the one proposed that is guaranteed to be greater than T_i's reading snapshot identifier (i.e. $commitSId(T_i)$ in this scenario) due to the visibility rule adopted on each read operation of T_i. In particular, T_i performs a read operation on a data item x of a node N only after it has ensured that (i) the $nextId$ value on N will be greater than its reading snapshot identifier and (ii) no transaction will commit an update on x using a snapshot id not greater than $commitSId(T_i)$. Otherwise, if T_i is an update transaction, it is guaranteed that at the time T_j commits, T_i has been already successfully committed otherwise T_i's read-set would have been invalidated by T_j. This case is analogous to the one in which E is a write-dependence edge since we have two update transactions, T_i and T_j, that commit on a common subset of nodes S, and T_i commits before T_j; therefore $commitSId(T_i) < commitSId(T_j)$ holds.

Executing 1CS. Indeed, the SCORe protocol provides a consistency criterion stronger than 1CS. In fact, the protocol ensures that the read operations issued by every transaction $T \in H$, even those that eventually abort, observe the state generated by a sequential history equivalent to H. This is verifiable by considering that: (i) since a write operation is externalized only upon a successful commit, a live or an aborted transaction at time t can be considered as a read-only committed transaction that contains its read prefix performed until t, except the operation which has triggered an abort (if any); (ii) the $DSG(H, \ll)$ graph has a node for each committed transaction or an aborted/live transaction reduced to its read prefix.

This property, which was also called Executing 1CS by Adya [10], is also implied by the more recent Opacity [34] property. However, it is easy to show that, since SCORe fixes the timestamp of a transaction upon its first read operation, it does not guarantee real-time ordering, as required by Opacity.

6   Experimental Data

In this section we report the results of an experimental study aimed at evaluating the performance and scalability of SCORe. This study is based on a prototype implementation of SCORe[1] that has been integrated within the Infinispan data grid system, a JAVA based open source NoSQL data platform developed by Red Hat [13]. Similarly to what done by other distributed, in-memory data platforms, Infinispan externalizes a simple key-value store interface. Also, it targets scalability by natively relying on weak data consistency models, and on a lightweight consistent hashing scheme [32], which allows partitioning data efficiently across the nodes, while ensuring good load balancing and minimum reshuffling of keys in presence of joins/departures of nodes from the platform. Further, Infinispan natively supports partial replication, allowing to store each key across a fixed, user-tunable number of replicas.

The strongest consistency level ensured by Infinispan is Repeatable Read [2] (RR), which guarantees that no intermediate or aborted values are ever observed, and that no two reads on the same key within the same transaction can return different values. RR is definitely weaker than Serializability, as it allows the commit of (both read-only and update) transactions that observe non-serializable schedules [10]. To provide some more architectural details, Infinispan relies on an encounter based two-phase-locking scheme, which is applied only to write operations and that does not synchronize reads. Repeatability of read operations is instead guaranteed by storing (locally caching) the read data items, and returning the stored copies upon subsequent reads. For what concerns the native replication protocol supported by Infinispan, it relies on a classical 2PC-based distributed locking algorithm [33].

Being Infinispan designed to achieve high scalability in the context of weak data consistency models, we argue that it represents an ideal baseline to evaluate the costs incurred in by the SCORe protocol in order to provide 1CS (i.e. strong consistency) guarantees.

Benchmarks. We have evaluated SCORe using two different benchmarks. The first one is a porting of TPC-C [14] adapted to execute on a NoSQL platform such as Infinispan. TPC-C is a benchmark representative of OLTP environments, and is characterized by complex and heterogeneous transactions, with very skewed access patterns, and hence non-minimal conflict probability. In our study we configured the benchmark to generate two workloads: one including 50% of update transactions, and a second one including 90% of read-only transactions.

---

[1] The SCORe prototype is publicly available at the URL http://www.cloudtm.eu

The second benchmark is YCSB (Yahoo! Cloud Serving Benchmark) [15], which is specifically targeted at the assessment of key-value data grids and cloud stores. This benchmark is somehow complementary to TPC-C since its transactional profile is characterized by simpler transactions that rarely conflict.

Test-bed Platforms. We performed our study on two different experimental testbeds. The first one, denoted as Cloud-TM platform, is a dedicated cluster of 20 homogeneous nodes, where each machine is equipped with two 2.13 GHz Quad-Core Intel(R) Xeon(R) E5506 processors and 16 GB of RAM, running *Linux 2.6.32-33-server* and interconnected via a private Gigabit Ethernet. This platform is representative of small/medium private clouds or data-center environments, with dedicated servers and a fairly large amount of available (computational and memory) resources per node. In all the experiments performed on the Cloud-TM platform we used four threads per node to inject transactions (in closed loop), which guaranteed a high utilization of the machine's resources without overloading them, which would otherwise lead to unreliable results in terms of assessment of the distributed protocol used to handle partial replication.

The second used platform is FutureGrid, which is a public distributed test-bed for parallel and cloud computing. This platform allowed us to evaluate SCORe in environments representative of public cloud infrastructures, which are typically characterized by more competitive resource sharing, ample usage of virtualization technology, and relatively less powerful virtualized nodes. On top of the FutureGrid platform we performed experiments using up to 100 virtual machines, equipped with 4GB RAM, two 2.93GHz cores Intel Xeon CPU X5570, running CentOS 5.7 x86_64. All the VMs were deployed in the same physical data-center and interconnected via Gigabit Ethernet. Also, again in order not to saturate machine's resources, in all the experiments performed on FutureGrid we used two threads per node to inject transactions (in closed loop).

Finally, for both deploys on the above described platforms, we have set the replication degree of each data item to the value 2.

Results. In Fig. 1 we show the achieved throughput values for TPC-C on top of the Cloud-TM platform while varying the number of involved nodes between 2 and 20. The plots in the top row refer to the workload composed at the 90% by read-only transactions, denoted as Workload A. The left plot reports the throughput for write transactions, whereas the right plot reports the throughput for read-only transactions. We contrast the performance of SCORe, with that of the native RR scheme supported by Infinispan, and with that of the GMU protocol presented in [11], which has also been integrated within Infinispan. As already discussed, GMU ensures a consistency criterion (namely EUS - Extended Update-Serializability [10]) weaker than 1CS, but stronger than RR. In other words, GMU exhibits intermediate consistency semantics with respect to the other two analyzed protocols.

The plots highlight that SCORe attains throughput values that are even slightly better than those achieved by GMU. This phenomenon is explainable

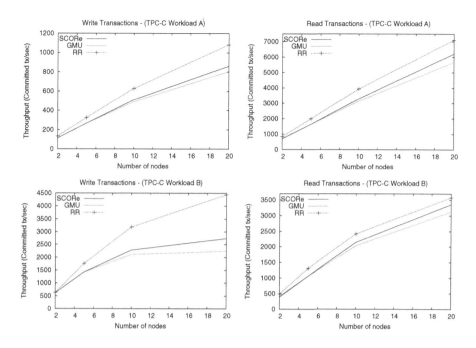

Fig. 1. TPC-C Benchmark (Cloud-TM)

by considering that, while SCORe relies on a timestamping mechanism based on scalar clock values, GMU uses vector clocks, which introduce higher overheads with respect to scalar clocks as the number of nodes in system grows.

The plot in the bottom row of Fig. 1 reports the results for TPC-C, obtained on top of the Cloud-TM platform, for the scenario encompassing 50% of read-only transactions, denoted as Workload B. While the comparative behavior of SCORe vs GMU follows trends similar to those observed for 90% read-only transactions, this time the performance loss of SCORe vs RR for update transactions grows significantly. This is essentially due to the fact that the increased volume of update transactions leads to an increased abort rate caused predominantly by failures during the validation phase of the transaction's read set (interestingly, the aborts due to failures in the lock acquisition phase turned out to be statistically marginal). In other words, as the update rate grows, the probability for an update transaction to access a stale snapshot accordingly grows. In particular, for the case of 20 nodes, the abort probability for update transactions with SCORe is on the order of 43%, while RR only exhibits around 8% abort rate for update transactions, with aborts exclusively caused by deadlocks. However, when considering the total throughput for Workload B (including both read-only plus update transactions), SCORe exhibits similar scalability trend when compared to RR. Overall, the data show that, for increased contention scenarios, strong consistency semantics do pay a performance toll, which, in this specific configuration, corresponds to a throughput reduction up to 22% (at 20

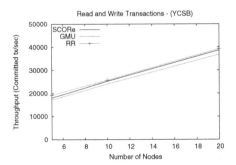

Fig. 2. YCSB Benchmark (Cloud-TM)

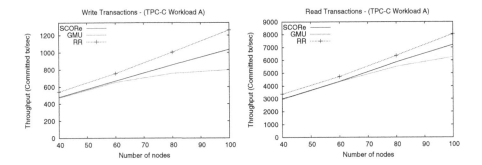

Fig. 3. TPC-C Benchmark (FutureGrid)

nodes). On the other hand, we argue that this is an unavoidable cost to pay in applications whose correctness can be endangered by adopting non-serializable isolation levels.

In Fig. 2 we show the results obtained by running YCSB on the Cloud-TM platform. We used Workload A [15] of the benchmark, which is an update intensive workload (comprising 50% of update transactions) simulating a session store that records recent client actions. We report the maximum throughput (committed transactions per second) achievable by the three considered protocols. The plot shows that the average reduction in throughput for both SCORe and GMU, compared to RR, oscillates around 8%, and that, again, the throughput scales linearly at the same rate as RR, providing an evidence of the efficiency and scalability of the proposed solution when considering transaction profiles featuring applications natively tailored for key-value data stores.

In Fig. 3 we present the results obtained by running Workload A of TPC-C on FutureGrid. The data confirm the general trends already observed on the Cloud-TM platform, highlighting both the high scalability of the proposed solution and its high efficiency when compared to vector-clock-based solutions, such as GMU, whose overheads grow linearly with the scale of the platform.

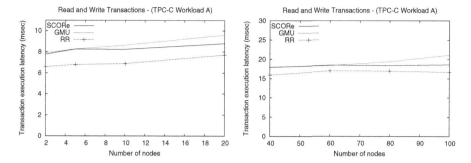

Fig. 4. Average transaction execution latency (TPC-C Workload A) for both Cloud-TM (left) and FutureGrid (right)

Finally, for completeness of the analysis, we report in Fig. 4 the average transaction execution latency for the case of TPC-C (Workload A) run on both Cloud-TM and FutureGrid. By the data we observe that, for all the protocols, latency values stay almost flat while increasing the size on the underlying platform (and consequently of the total workload sustained), which again supports the claim of good scalability of SCORe. Further, the relevance of this result is supported by the fact that all the reported values were related to scenarios where the utilization of infrastructural resources was high (as an example, for the tests with TPC-C on top of FutureGrid the CPU utilization was constantly observed to be over the 80%). Hence, the data refer to scenarios where the throughput was relatively close to the maximum sustainable one.

7   Conclusions

In this article we introduced SCORe, which is, to the best of our knowledge, the first partial replication protocol that jointly guarantees the following properties: (i) genuineness, which maximizes system scalability by demanding that only the replicas that maintain data accessed by a transaction are involved in its processing; (ii) strong consistency of the snapshots observed by read operations, thanks to a one-copy serializable multiversion scheme, which never aborts read-only transactions and that spares them from any (distributed) validation phase.

We integrated SCORe in Infinispan, a popular open source distributed data grid, and evaluated its performance by means of an experimental study relying on well-known benchmarks and on the usage of both private and public cloud infrastructures. The experimental results demonstrate that SCORe can scale up to a hundred nodes, delivering throughput and latency comparable to schemes that ensure much weaker consistency criteria.

We argue that the ability of SCORe to ensure strong consistency guarantees without hampering scalability can enlarge significantly the spectrum of applications commonly deployed on large scale NoSQL data grids.

References

1. DeCandia, G., Hastorun, D., Jampani, M., Kakulapati, G., Lakshman, A., Pilchin, A., Sivasubramanian, S., Vosshall, P., Vogels, W.: Dynamo: amazon's highly available key-value store. In: Proc. of the 21st ACM SIGOPS Symposium on Operating Systems Principles, pp. 205–220 (2007)
2. Berenson, H., Bernstein, P., Gray, J., Melton, J., O'Neil, E., O'Neil, P.: A critique of ANSI SQL isolation levels. In: Proc. of the ACM SIGMOD International Conference on Management of Data, pp. 1–10 (1995)
3. Lakshman, A., Malik, P.: Cassandra: a decentralized structured storage system. ACM SIGOPS Operating Systems Review 44, 35–40 (2010)
4. Aguilera, M.K., Merchant, A., Shah, M., Veitch, A., Karamanolis, C.: Sinfonia: a new paradigm for building scalable distributed systems. ACM SIGOPS Operating Systems Review 41, 159–174 (2007)
5. Defago, X., Schiper, A., Urban, P.: Total order broadcast and multicast algorithms: Taxonomy and survey. J. ACM Computing Surveys 36, 372–421 (2004)
6. Guerraoui, R., Schiper, A.: Genuine atomic multicast in asynchronous distributed systems. J. Theoretical Computer Science 254, 297–316 (2001)
7. Schiper, N., Sutra, P., Pedone, F.: P-Store: Genuine Partial Replication in Wide Area Networks. In: Proc. of the 29th IEEE Symposium on Reliable Distributed Systems, pp. 214–224 (2010)
8. Armendáriz-Iñigo, J.E., Mauch-Goya, A., González de Mendívil, J.R., Muñoz-Escoí, F.D.: SIPRe: a partial database replication protocol with SI replicas. In: Proc. of the 2008 ACM Symposium on Applied Computing, pp. 2181–2185 (2008)
9. Serrano, D., Patiño-Martínez, M., Jiménez-Peris, R., Kemme, B.: Boosting Database Replication Scalability through Partial Replication and 1-Copy-Snapshot-Isolation. In: Proc. of the 13th Pacific Rim International Symposium on Dependable Computing, pp. 290–297 (2007)
10. Adya, A.: Weak Consistency: A Generalized Theory and Optimistic Implementations for Distributed Transactions. PhD Thesis, Massachusetts Institute of Technology (1999)
11. Peluso, S., Ruivo, P., Romano, P., Quaglia, F., Rodrigues, L.: When Scalability Meets Consistency: Genuine Multiversion Update-Serializable Partial Data Replication. In: Proc. of the IEEE 32nd International Conference on Distributed Computing Systems, pp. 455–465 (2012)
12. Sovran, Y., Power, R., Aguilera, M.K., Li, J.: Transactional storage for geo-replicated systems. In: Proc. of the 23th ACM Symposium on Operating Systems Principles, pp. 385–400 (2011)
13. Marchioni, F., Surtani, M.: Infinispan Data Grid Platform. PACKT Publishing (2012)
14. TPC Council: TPC-C Benchmark, Revision 5.11 (2010)
15. Cooper, B.F., Silberstein, A., Tam, E., Ramakrishnan, R., Sears, R.: Benchmarking cloud serving systems with YCSB. In: Proc. of the 1st ACM Symposium on Cloud Computing, pp. 143–154 (2010)
16. Kemme, B., Alonso, G.: Don't Be Lazy, Be Consistent: Postgres-R, A New Way to Implement Database Replication. In: Proc. of the 26th International Conference on Very Large Data Bases, pp. 134–143 (2000)
17. Lin, Y., Kemme, B., Patiño-Martínez, M., Jiménez-Peris, R.: Middleware based Data Replication providing Snapshot Isolation. In: Proc. of the 2005 ACM SIGMOD International Conference on Management of Data, pp. 419–430 (2005)

18. Thomson, A., Abadi, D.J.: The case for determinism in database systems. J. VLDB Endowment 13, 70–80 (2010)
19. Wiesmann, M., Schiper, A.: Comparison of Database Replication Techniques Based on Total Order Broadcast. J. IEEE Transactions on Knowledge and Data Engineering 17, 551–566 (2005)
20. Pedone, F., Guerraoui, R., Schiper, A.: The Database State Machine Approach. J. Distributed and Parallel Databases 14, 71–98 (2003)
21. Thomson, A., Diamond, T., Weng, S., Ren, K., Shao, P., Abadi, D.J.: Calvin: fast distributed transactions for partitioned database systems. In: Proc. of the 2012 ACM SIGMOD International Conference on Management of Data, pp. 1–12 (2012)
22. Carvalho, N., Romano, P., Rodrigues, L.: SCert: Speculative certification in replicated software transactional memories. In: Proc. of the 4th Annual International Conference on Systems and Storage, pp. 10:1–10:13 (2011)
23. Palmieri, R., Quaglia, F., Romano, P.: OSARE: Opportunistic Speculation in Actively REplicated Transactional Systems. In: Proc. of the IEEE 30th International Symposium on Reliable Distributed Systems, pp. 59–64 (2011)
24. Baker, J., Bond, C., Corbett, J., Furman, J.J., Khorlin, A., Larson, J., Leon, J., Li, Y., Lloyd, A., Yushprakh, V.: Megastore: Providing Scalable, Highly Available Storage for Interactive Services. In: Proc. of the 5th Biennial Conference on Innovative Data Systems Research, pp. 223–234 (2011)
25. Bieniusa, A., Fuhrmann, T.: Consistency in hindsight: A fully decentralized STM algorithm. In: Proc. of the 2010 IEEE International Symposium on Parallel and Distributed Processing, pp. 1–12 (2010)
26. Bernstein, P.A., Hadzilacos, V., Goodman, N.: Concurrency Control and Recovery in Database Systems. Addison-Wesley (1987)
27. van Renesse, R., Birman, K.P., Vogels, W.: A Robust and Scalable Technology For Distributed Systems Monitoring, Management, and Data Mining. J. ACM Transactions on Computer Systems 21, 164–206 (2003)
28. Gray, J., Lamport, L.: Consensus on transaction commit. J. ACM Transactions on Database Systems 31, 133–160 (2006)
29. Frølund, S., Guerraoui, R.: Implementing E-Transactions with Asynchronous Replication. J. IEEE Transactions on Parallel and Distributed Systems 12, 133–146 (2001)
30. Brewer, E.A.: Towards robust distributed systems (abstract). In: Proc. of the 19th Annual ACM Symposium on Principles Of Distributed Computing, pp. 7 (2010)
31. Jiménez-Peris, R., Patiño-Martínez, M., Alonso, G.: Non-Intrusive, Parallel Recovery of Replicated Data. In: Proc. of the 21st IEEE Symposium on Reliable Distributed Systems, pp. 150–159 (2002)
32. Karger, D., Lehman, E., Leighton, T., Panigrahy, R., Levine, M., Lewin, D.: Consistent hashing and random trees: distributed caching protocols for relieving hot spots on the World Wide Web. In: Proc. of the 29th Annual ACM Symposium on Theory of Computing, pp. 654–663 (1997)
33. Gray, J., Helland, P., O'Neil, P., Shasha, D.: The dangers of replication and a solution. In: Proc. of the ACM SIGMOD International Conference on Management of Data, pp. 173–182 (1996)
34. Guerraoui, R., Kapalka, M.: On the Correctness of Transactional Memory. In: Proc. of the 13th ACM SIGPLAN Symposium on Principles and Practice of Parallel Programming, pp. 175–184 (2008)

P3S: A Privacy Preserving Publish-Subscribe Middleware

Partha Pal, Greg Lauer, Joud Khoury, Nick Hoff, and Joe Loyall

BBN Technologies
Cambridge, MA 02138
{ppal,glauer,jkhoury,nhoff,jloyall}@bbn.com

Abstract. This paper presents P3S, a publish-subscribe middleware designed to protect the privacy of subscriber interest and confidentiality of published content. P3S combines recent advances in cryptography, specifically Ciphertext Policy Attribute Based Encryption (CP-ABE) and Predicate Based Encryption (PBE) with an innovative architecture to achieve the desired level of privacy. An initial P3S prototype has been implemented on top of a COTS JMS platform (ActiveMQ). Results of preliminary security analysis and initial evaluation of latency and throughput indicate that the P3S design is both practical and flexible to provide different levels of privacy for publish-subscribe messaging over various message sizes and network bandwidth settings.

Keywords: publish-subscribe, architecture, security, privacy, performance.

1 Introduction

Message-oriented middleware supporting publish-subscribe (pub-sub) interaction has become fairly common in military and commercial applications. In pub-sub messaging, information consumers and producers do not need to establish a connection between them a-priori (often described as loose coupling). Pub-sub style messaging also provides selective filtering of information so that the consumers only receive messages they are interested in (often described as brokering). The combination of brokering and loose coupling facilitates scalability: instead of n entities each connecting to each other (n^2 connections), in a typical pub-sub system they just need to connect to the broker (n connections). However, loose coupling and brokering make it hard to maintain information privacy. Subscriber interest is usually visible at the broker because it needs to do the matching and filtering, and standard encryption cannot be used to protect the published content because there is no end to end security association between the information producer and the ultimate receiver of the content.

This drawback limits the use of pub-sub messaging in a wide range of system and application contexts. For example, in the commercial context, parties pursuing a merger and acquisition (M&A) deal may be interested in receiving updates on various topics, but the knowledge that party X is interested in topic Y may tip the hand of X. In a military context, intelligence analysts in a coalition environment may be

P. Narasimhan and P. Triantafillou (Eds.): Middleware 2012, LNCS 7662, pp. 476–495, 2012.

interested in receiving updates on information that they have agreed to share, but the knowledge that country A is interested in topic B may compromise country A's strategy. Also, in both the commercial and military contexts, information updates may have associated "need to know" type requirements stipulating that published content should not be visible to anyone other than the subscribers with matching interest—for example, the broker or other parties who are not interested in "Lehman Brothers" should not receive updated information about Lehman Brothers.

Techniques like sharing encryption keys among publishers and consumers, re-encryption, onion-routing etc. have been used to provide a level of privacy in pub-sub systems. We discuss a number of such approaches in Section 7; however, none of these provide a satisfactory solution to keeping subscriber interests private.

The main contributions of this paper are as follows:

- Design and implementation of a pub-sub middleware with a strong cryptographic guarantee of the privacy of subscriber interest and confidentiality of published content. To the best of our knowledge, no such system exists today.
- Performance analysis indicating that such privacy guarantee can be provided at a reasonable cost over a variety of combinations of message size, match rate and network bandwidth.
- Innovative combination of advanced cryptography with sophisticated architecture design as a blueprint for developing advanced security capabilities in the middleware.

The rest of the paper is organized as follows. Section 2 describes the privacy properties and performance characteristics that P3S set out to achieve. Section 3 presents the basics of the advanced cryptographic techniques used in P3S. Section 4 and 5 presents the P3S architecture design and current implementation respectively. Section 6 reports our preliminary analysis of privacy and performance. Section 7 summarizes related work, and Section 8 concludes the paper.

2   Terminology, and Privacy and Performance Targets

We use standard pub-sub terminology throughout the paper with a few exceptions. **Publisher** is an entity that wishes to make information content available to subscribers, and **subscriber** is an entity that registers subscription interest and receives the content that matches the interest. **Payload** refers to the content that a publisher wants to publish. The term **metadata** is used to refer to the description of a payload. **Interest** is a predicate about metadata and the term **matching** refers to the action of determining if the metadata describing a published payload satisfies the subscriber's interest. Among the less common terms, we use **third party** to denote an entity that is neither a publisher nor a subscriber. In P3S, there are four third parties namely, the Repository Server, the Distribution Service, the PBE Token Server and the Attribute-Based Access Control and Registration Authority (ARA). They will be introduced in more detail in Section 4. Finally, we also use the term **participant** to mean a publisher, a subscriber or a third party.

The P3S middleware aims to satisfy a set of privacy and performance requirements above and beyond the traditional pub-sub functional requirements.

Basic P3S **functional requirements** are as follows. Publishers should not be aware of subscribers; P3S is expected to deliver published items to subscribers with matching interest. Matching is done based on metadata associated with published items, described as attribute-value pairs chosen from a fixed, predefined space of attributes and their values (metadata space). Subscriber interest is expressed as a conjunctive predicate over the attribute value pairs from the metadata space. The predicates may have wildcard (*) for values indicating interest in any value of the corresponding attribute. P3S should deliver a published item to a subscriber if and only if the latter is interested in the item. P3S should be open in the sense that legitimate clients may, within a metadata space, register any subscription. Controlling what subscription predicates a subscriber can issue is beyond the scope of the current paper; however we assume that a legitimate client behaving honestly will not subscribe with wildcards for all attributes.

The P3S **privacy requirements** are focused on protecting subscriber interest and minimizing the exposure of published content. Subscriber interests are private; other participants should not learn the interest(s) of a subscriber. Similarly, the publisher should not reveal payloads to subscribers unless their interests match. Furthermore subscribers should not learn anything about published metadata beyond knowing that their predicate does/doesn't match metadata. A publisher may not know if a particular item was matched or not. Other participants may learn that an item was published as long as the participant is unable to identify the item (for example the item is encrypted). An item that has been deleted based on its publisher's intent should not be available to subscribers even if the deleted item's metadata matched the subscriber's interest. Additionally, a participant with access to the original item may not re-publish the item after it has been deleted; he can however, publish the same content as a new item (new identifier, new metadata) as his own.

Finally, in terms of **performance requirements**, P3S aims to keep the average time to process and deliver a publication to an individual matching subscriber within ten times (10x) that of a similar (baseline) system without the privacy protection. Similarly, P3S throughput is also aimed to be no worse than ten times (10x) that of the throughput of a similar system without privacy protection.

3   Cryptographic Background

3.1   Predicate Based Encryption (PBE)

PBE is a 1: n (one-to-many) encryption scheme where encryption depends on the attribute values specified by the encryptor and where decryption keys depend on predicates. Decryption is possible only if the attribute values set by the encryptor (publisher in our case) satisfy the decryptor's (subscriber in our case) predicate. Formally, following the model and notation from [7, 6], let $x = <x_1, x_2, ..., x_l>$ denote the attribute vector with l elements chosen from the alphabet Σ, i.e., $x \in \Sigma^l$, and let y denote the l-element interest vector chosen from the alphabet $\Sigma_* = \Sigma \cup \{*\}$, i.e., $y \in \Sigma_*^l$ where $*$ denotes the wildcard character. Let us also define the conjunctive predicate $\qquad Match: \Sigma^l \times \Sigma_*^l \to \{0,1\} \qquad$ as $\qquad Match(x, y) = 1$ when $x_i = y_i \, \forall i \, for \, which \, y_i \neq *$. As in [7, 6], we focus only on the match predicate since it enables the construction of several other predicates.

Definition: A Public Key Predicate Based Encryption scheme (PK-PBE) consists of the following algorithms:

$Setup(\lambda) \to (PK, SK)$: The setup algorithm takes a security parameter and outputs a master public key PK and master secret key SK.

$Encrypt(PK, x, M) \to CT_x$: Encrypts the message M using the master public key PK and the attribute vector x.

$GenToken(SK, y) \to T_y$: Takes secret key SK and interest vector y and outputs a token T_y.

$Query(T_y, CT_x) \to M$: Takes as input token T_y for some interest vector y and ciphertext CT_x encrypted using some attribute vector x and outputs message M if $Match(x, y) = 1$ and null otherwise.

Semantic security, token security, and collusion-resistance are the security properties generally considered in the context of a predicate encryption scheme. Semantic security requires that no information about the attribute vector x be revealed by the ciphertext. Token security requires that no information about the interest vector y be revealed by the cryptographic token. Collusion-resistance means that multiple tokens do not allow unauthorized decryption of a ciphertext, i.e., at least one of the tokens must match in order to decrypt, hence combining tokens does not release information. The public key encryption schemes in [6] and [7] provide semantic security and collusion-resistance and will be the focus of this work. The schemes do not provide token security. Any party with access to a token T_y and the ability to generate encrypted metadata is able to infer the interest vector y (see [9]).

Hidden Vector Encryption (HVE) [6] is an efficient PBE construction based on composite-order groups that assumes a single predicate – equality $Match$ - and supports large alphabets. Iovino et al. [7] provide a more efficient HVE construction that uses prime-order groups but restricts Σ to the binary alphabet $\Sigma = \{0,1\}$. The current implementation of P3S utilizes the construction and implementation in [7, 10]. While the P3S architecture is open to other PBE implementations, our choice of HVE implies that the supported predicates are conjunctions of equality on a binary alphabet augmented with wildcards. We extend the expressiveness of this binary PBE scheme to support a richer attribute space. Attribute and predicates are represented as bit vectors in HVE. To support a metadata space of N attributes, each of which may take one of 8 values, we construct the 3N-bit vector x where the first 3 bits are used to encode the 1st attribute, the next 3 for the 2nd and so on. We do the same for y and assume a wildcard spans all bits that represent the attribute. Note that the security of our mapping follows directly from the attribute-hiding property of HVE [7].

3.2   Ciphertext Policy Attribute Based Encryption

As in PBE, CP-ABE uses a set of attributes and a predicate over those attributes. However CP-ABE encrypts the ciphertext with a policy (predicate) over the set of attributes, and associates the decryption key with a set of attributes. Decryption of the ciphertext is possible if and only if the decryptor's attributes match under the predicate specified by the encryptor. CP-ABE is thus a 1: n (one-to-many) encryption scheme in which the encryptor of the data (publisher in our case) does not need to explicitly know who the participants (subscribers) are, yet can still constrain which participants may decrypt the data.

> *Definition:* A Ciphertext-Policy Attribute Based Encryption scheme (CP-ABE) [8] consists of the following algorithms:
>
> $Setup(\lambda) \rightarrow (PP, MSK)$: The setup algorithm takes a security parameter and outputs the public parameters PP and master key MSK.
>
> $Encrypt(PP, M, A) \rightarrow CT_A$: Encrypts the message M using the public parameters PP and policy (also called the access structure) A defined over the attribute space. The algorithm outputs the ciphertext CT_A such that only a user that possesses a set of attributes that satisfy A is able to decrypt.
>
> $KeyGeneration(MSK, S) \rightarrow S_k$: Takes master key MSK and set of attributes S and outputs a private key S_k.
>
> $Decrypt(PP, S_k, CT_A) \rightarrow M$: Takes as input the public parameters and secret key S_k and ciphertext CT_A for some policy A. It outputs message M if the attributes satisfy the ciphertext policy.

In terms of its security properties, CP-ABE does not hide the policy A, or the attributes an entity holds. In fact, the policy A is transmitted in the clear with the ciphertext. As with PBE, CP-ABE is collusion-resistant in the sense that combining keys can decrypt a message only if at least one of the keys can decrypt the message on its own.

We used the construction and implementation of Bethencourt et al [8, 15] in P3S. This construction does not support the logical operator NOT in A, a shortcoming that can be addressed by defining NOT of an attribute by a separate attribute, but this essentially doubles the number of attributes.

4   P3S Architecture

4.1   Components

The components of the P3S architecture are:

- Attribute-Based Access Control and Registration Authority (ARA): The ARA acts as the certification authority, and only interacts with other components during registration. During registration it provides the publishers and subscribers with information they need to publish, including the metadata and predicate schema, CP-ABE and PBE keying material (see Section 4.3 for more details).

- Dissemination Server (DS): The DS sets up TLS tunnels to subscribers and publishers and keeps track of how to send information and acknowledgements to them. It receives PBE-encrypted metadata and CP-ABE-encrypted payload from the publishers, and forwards PBE-encrypted metadata to registered subscribers, and the CP-ABE-encrypted payload to the RS.
- Repository Server (RS): The RS stores CP-ABE encrypted payloads along with their associated Globally-Unique-IDs (GUIDs), and sends the encrypted payload associated with a GUID to a subscriber upon request.
- Predicate-Based Encryption Token Server (PBE-TS): The PBE-TS receives cleartext subscription interest (predicate) from the subscriber, and returns the corresponding PBE token to the subscriber.

The P3S architecture is designed to accommodate *anonymization*. If available, subscribers contact PBE-TS and RS via the anonymization service. P3S's basic privacy properties are independent of anonymization, but if incorporated, anonymization enhances privacy protection further by hiding the subscriber identity to PBE-TS and RS.

4.2   High Level Overview

Fig. 1 illustrates the basic high-level P3S information flow. Publishers use CP-ABE to encrypt payload with a policy that specifies what attributes are required to decrypt it. Subscribers have attributes that allow decryption of the CP-ABE encrypted payload if they satisfy the publisher's CP-ABE policy. In this sense, CP-ABE provides a level of access control to protect the confidentiality of the payloads. Subscribers obtain PBE tokens representing their subscription predicates. Publishers PBE encrypt a reference to the payload using the associated metadata and send the encrypted metadata to subscribers, via the DS. Subscribers match their tokens against the encrypted metadata. A successful match yields the only information required to retrieve the payload from the RS. Performing the matching in the subscriber combined with the use of PBE protects the privacy of both subscriber interest and content metadata. The retrieval request is then sent through an anonymization service (if available).

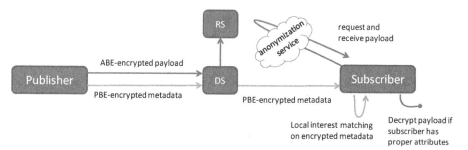

Fig. 1. P3S high level architecture

The CP-ABE encryption allows the publisher to control who can see the payload without requiring the publisher to know which subscriber is receiving it. The PBE encryption allows the subscriber to determine which publications match its interests without the system disclosing the metadata associated with the publication. Recall that the access policy in CP-ABE encryption is "in the clear", and thus the access policies should only refer to attributes that are safe to disclose to subscribers that may fail to decrypt the payload, such as organization names or subscriber roles. PBE encryption does not disclose the values of the attributes used to encrypt the data (except to the extent that a match with subscriber predicates discloses it). However, our current architecture does not provide a mechanism to restrict the types of queries that a subscriber can make. The next section discusses the P3S protocol operation in detail.

4.3   Operation

Initialization: Fig. 2 illustrates the initialization process for Subscribers and Publishers. The ARA provides the subscriber with the PBE metadata format, i.e., field/value information for specifying subscription interests, contact information for the P3S services (RS, DS and PBE-TS) and their public key certificates, a CP-ABE secret key (SKC) based on the client attributes, which is used to decrypt payloads, and a certificate that indicates the participant is a subscriber.

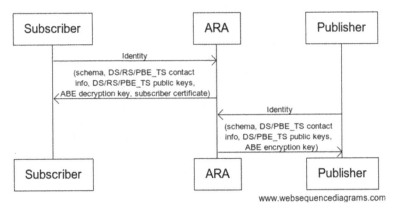

Fig. 2. P3S initialization process

The ARA provides the publisher with the PBE public parameters, metadata format, contact information and public key certificates for the P3S services (DS and PBE-TS), and the CP-ABE policy attributes and the CP-ABE public parameter PKC to be used by the publisher to encrypt the contents it wishes to publish.

Subscription: Fig. 3 illustrates the process of subscription. The subscriber generates a symmetric key K_S and then uses the public key of the PBE-TS to encrypt the 3-tuple $(K_S,\ subscriber\ certificate,\ plaintext\ predicate)$ and sends it to the PBE-TS via the anonymization service. The PBE-TS decrypts the triple and, if the subscriber certificate is valid, computes the PBE token corresponding to the plaintext predicate. It then encrypts the token using the key K_S and sends it back to the (unknown) subscriber via the anonymization service. This process allows the subscriber to obtain the token associated with its plaintext predicate while remaining anonymous to the PBE-TS providing the token. Note that the PBE-TS sees the plaintext predicate.

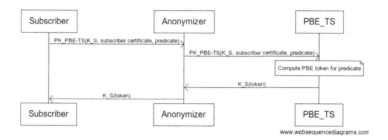

Fig. 3. P3S subscription process

Publication: Fig. 4 illustrates the process of publication. The Publisher has a payload and associated metadata to be published. It generates a unique $GUID$ from a large space (making it hard to guess) and then uses PBE encryption to encrypt that $GUID$. It sends this PBE-encrypted $GUID$ to the DS which then forwards it to all the subscribers. The Publisher then CP-ABE encrypts the 2-tuple $(GUID, Payload)$. The CP-ABE encryption specifies a policy that defines the attributes required by a subscriber if the payload is to be decrypted. The choice of this policy is outside of the scope of this paper, but could be determined by the payload metadata. The Publisher then sends the 3-tuple $(GUID, CP\ ABE\ encrypted(GUID, Payload), T_{GUID})$, where T_{GUID} represents a time to live (TTL) for this item, to the DS which forwards it to the RS. The RS stores the $CP\ ABE\ encrypted(GUID, Payload)$ indexed by the GUID for later retrieval by subscribers. The RS stores the item for at least T_{GUID}, after which it is garbage collected.

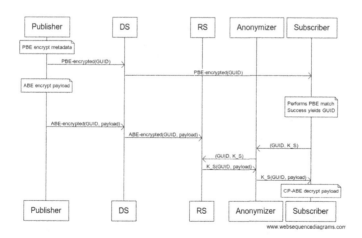

Fig. 4. P3S publication process

The subscribers receive the PBE-encrypted GUID from the DS and attempt to decrypt it using their PBE tokens. If a subscriber's predicate matches the metadata used during the PBE encryption of the GUID, the GUID will be revealed. The subscriber is then ready to request the associated payload. It first generates a symmetric key K_S and then encrypts the 2-tuple $(K_S, GUID)$ with the RS's public key. It then sends this message to the RS via an anonymization service. The RS decrypts the message, retrieves the $CP\ ABE\ encrypted(GUID, Payload)$associated with the GUID, encrypts that $CP\ ABE\ encrypted(GUID, Payload)$ using the key K_S and sends it back to the subscriber via the anonymization service. This process allows the subscriber to request a particular payload without revealing its identity to the RS.

The subscriber decodes the message using the key K_S and then attempts to CP-ABE decode the $CP\ ABE\ encrypted(GUID, Payload)$. If it has the right attributes to successfully decode it then it obtains the payload and associated GUID (which it then uses to correlate the request and response).

Deletion: Deletion is handled by the RS's garbage collection mechanism. The RS has a configurable parameter T_G and each publication provides the item specific TTL T_{GUID} which represents the publisher's intent to delete the content after the specific period of time. The RS deletes the item corresponding to the identifier $GUID$ after $T_{GUID} + T_G$. The reason for the configurable T_G parameter is to provide some accommodation for the uncontrollable delays in a distributed setting and slower consumers. For a strict interpretation of deleting based on publisher's intent T_G can be set to 0, which may result in considerably more failures to fetch the item for some (slower) clients with matched subscription.

5   Current Prototype

We have implemented a P3S prototype using the Apache Active MQ [14] open source Java implementation of the Java Message Service (JMS) standard. The current version of the prototype includes all components and features described above except for the anonymization service and CP-ABE encryption (i.e, the ARA and encryption of published content). We have developed the CP-ABE support functionality using the construction and library described in [8, 15], but it is not yet integrated with the P3S prototype. The PBE encryption support is implemented by enhancing the HVE implementation [7] of the JPBC [10] library, and is integrated in the prototype.

In the current implementation, the DS is implemented by extending the AMQ broker. The P3S subscriber and publisher protocols are implemented by extending the AMQ client libraries. We retained the top level JMS interface, so that existing JMS compliant publishers and subscribers can take advantage of the P3S's privacy preserving properties without code change, once they include the P3S enhanced AMQ client libraries. The RS is implemented as a composition of two services, a Web Service to respond to subscriber's request for content retrieval, and a Persistence Service that subscribes to the DS for encrypted content and uses an embedded Apache Derby database for storing them. The PBE-TS is also implemented as a Web Service that runs within an embedded Jetty container and embeds the extended HVE library. We plan to implement the ARA in a similar manner. Publishers and subscribers interact with the DS over TLS.

6   Analysis of Privacy and Performance Overhead

6.1   Privacy

In this paper we present a semi-formal analysis of privacy. We begin with the threat model considered in the analysis:

> *Definition:* An *Honest but Curious* (HBC) participant only makes well-intentioned requests (honest) but remembers everything that was sent to them (curious). They do not eavesdrop, masquerade as other participants, or hijack communications.

> *Definition:* A *malicious* participant attempts to eavesdrop, performs replay and man-in-the-middle attacks, and masquerades as other participants.

Note that colluding HBC participants may share information without being malicious. Our analysis focuses mainly on privacy under an HBC threat model, but includes colluding HBC subscribers. The ARA, which we assume to be a trusted certification authority, is not part of the analysis. Additionally, integrity and availability are also kept out of scope for the most part except for the following. Because of TLS and the request-response nature of P3S messages, participants can detect if network failures cause message loss at the application level. The basic P3S operation is robust to node failures as well. The RS stores encrypted content on disk. A crashed component can resume publish-subscribe activities after restart without requiring re-encryption of any published content. A restarted subscriber simply needs to (re)register with the DS and (re)obtain its PBE tokens from the PBE-TS. Similarly, upon restart a publisher needs only to (re)register with the DS. A restarted DS needs to wait for subscribers and publishers to (re)register. A restarted RS simply needs to (re)register with the DS.

Structured Analysis Using *Gadgets:* A *gadget* is a simple mechanism we developed to capture information dependency underneath an encryption scheme. In this section we use the PBE gadget that captures PBE information elements and their interdependencies as an illustration. Gadgets for other encryption schemes used (e.g., CP-ABE, Public Key, Symmetric Key) in P3S are similarly constructed.

  More specifically, a gadget is a directed graph $G = (V, E)$ where each node in V is either an information element or an AND gate (&). Nodes in the red boundary are the main information elements, the ciphertext and the token to unlock it. Edges in E represent information dependencies: a directed edge from node u to node v means that information element v depends on u. When u is the & gate, then v depends on all information elements that are incident to u.

  Fig. 5 shows the PBE gadget. Upper case labels like X, Y, T_Y represent the set of all possible information elements represented by their lower case counterparts x, y, T_y. In Fig. 5, PBE ciphertext ct_{PBE} depends on the (plaintext) message m (which in P3S is a GUID) and the attribute vector x (which in P3S is the metadata description) and the PBE master public key pk_{PBE}. The & gate leading to ct_{PBE}

embodies the PBE Encrypt operation described in section 3.1. Similarly, information elements and dependencies underneath the two other major PBE operations, namely GenToken (which takes the interest vector y and the PBE master secret key sk_{PBE} to produce the PBE token T_y corresponding to y) and Query (which takes the ciphertext ct_{PBE} and PBE token T_y to recover m) are also shown in the PBE gadget. A gadget can be extended to represent additional dependencies relevant to the system using the encryption scheme represented by the gadget. For instance, in Fig. 5 nodes connected only by broken edges are additional information and dependency that matters to P3S such as the association x_{pid} between the publisher identity pid and the attribute vector x (representing metadata), and the association y_{sid} between subscriber identity sid and the interest vector y (representing subscriber interest). Nodes in the extended gadget with dark borders represent the information subject to privacy requirements.

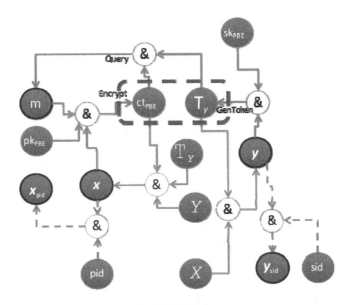

Fig. 5. PBE Gadget

Analysis using the PBE gadget described above involves tracing the execution steps of the P3S system over time focusing on the behavior of individual participants and information they become privy to during execution. We then test whether private information (information elements with dark borders) becomes visible to undesired participants, and if so, under what circumstances (i.e., HBC, malicious or colluding). Undesired exposure of sensitive information M is a threat to the privacy of M.

In any execution of P3S, the PBE-TS can see all subscription interests in plain text. However, because of the anonymizer, the PBE TS cannot associate the subscription interests to subscriber identities. Privacy of y_{sid} is still maintained even though the interest vector y is visible to the PBE-TS. Similarly, anyone who has access to the ciphertext ct_{PBE} and the right PBE token can decrypt it. However, under HBC operation, a subscriber's token is not shared with anyone else, and the PB-TS does not see ciphertext ct_{PBE}. Therefore privacy of m is not threatened.

Analysis using the PBE gadget illustrates the lack of token security in PBE [9]. If a participant is able to obtain a token T_y and create encrypted metadata, it will be able to reveal y by creating encrypted metadata for all attribute vectors (i.e., X) and test them against the token T_y. This threat is indicated by the orange edges connecting the & node with y, X and T_y. In HBC execution of P3S, all non-3rd party participants can encrypt any attribute vector in X, but they only have access to their own tokens. A colluding HBC subscriber S_1 can share its Token T_y with others, but if they can do that, they might share their plaintext interest as well. Even then, such sharing does not reveal any more information than the union of the information revealed by them individually. A malicious non-3rd party participant however can obtain any token T_y, i.e., privacy of y (subscriber interest) is threatened under malicious participants.

Another issue revealed by the gadget is that if a subscriber can subscribe to all or a significant part of the space of all possible subscription interests (i.e., Y) to accumulate T_Y, he can test any given ciphertext ct_{PBE} against all tokens in T_Y to reveal the attribute vector x used to encrypt ct_{PBE}. This is shown by the orange edges connecting the & node with x, Y, ct_{PBE}, and T_Y. HBC and non-colluding execution of P3S will not allow a subscriber to share tokens, however, over time a subscriber might accumulate a large number of tokens, which could be used to launch this attack. We have identified ways to mitigate this threat. One possibility is to time-stamp publications and tokens, making tokens active only within a configurable period of time. This approach has the advantage of providing a token revocation mechanism but requires the clients to be time-synchronized and using time as an additional metadata attribute.

Summary of Non-3rd Party Participant's Visibility: An HBC subscriber does not know about anyone else's subscription interest. It does not know metadata description of published payloads even though it receives all PBE encrypted metadata. PBE matching, even when the match succeeds, does not reveal the metadata description. Matched metadata reveals the GUID, but the subscriber cannot see the corresponding content unless it possesses the appropriate CP-ABE attributes to decrypt the CP-ABE encrypted $(GUID, Payload)$ pair. Being able to decrypt the payload does not reveal the publisher identity unless the identity is included in the content. A subscriber that also publishes of course has full visibility of its publications (content and metadata).

An HBC publisher will have no visibility of content and metadata being published and subscribed by other participants. The publisher does not know whether the content it published matched with anybody's subscription, or the identity of the matching subscriber, or whether anyone actually received its content.

Summary of 3rd Party Participant's Visibility: The HBC RS does not know which publisher has published, since it receives all messages from the DS. It does not know the content of the message since they are CP-ABE encrypted, and as a result does not know anything about the content of the payload it sends to a subscriber. It does not know the metadata associated with the content since that information is PBE encrypted and not delivered to RS. The RS does not know which subscriber has requested a payload, since all such requests are received from an anonymization service. The symmetric key K_S sent with such requests allows the RS to return the payload to the subscriber privately without having to know the subscriber's identity. The RS can keep track of whether a CP-ABE encrypted payload has ever been requested and how many requests have been received for each such encrypted payload. It knows neither the plaintext payload nor the metadata associated with an encrypted payload.

The HBC DS knows nothing about the subscriber interests since those are kept local to the subscribers. The DS does not know the content of the payload, since it is CP-ABE encrypted. It does not know anything about the metadata associated with a payload since that information is PBE encrypted. The DS does not know which payloads have been requested since it does not see any requests for payload from subscribers and, in any event, such requests are encrypted with the RS's public key. The DS does know the size of payloads and the size of encrypted PBE metadata.

The HBC PBE-TS does not know anything about publications as it receives no encrypted metadata and no encrypted payloads. The PBE-TS knows the plaintext predicates generated by subscribers but does not know the binding of subscriber to predicate as all PBE token requests are sent via the anonymization service. The symmetric key K_S sent with such requests allows the PBE-TS to return the token to the Subscriber privately without having to know the Subscriber's identity.

Eavesdroppers and Other Leakage: Eavesdroppers without any CP-ABE or PBE credentials learn nothing about subscriptions, metadata or payload content. Eavesdroppers may learn the GUID sent by the publisher in the clear but may not decrypt the associated CP-ABE payloads[1]. To prevent eavesdroppers from learning if more than one subscriber has received the same payload, transmissions of a payload from the RS to subscribers are super-encrypted with a subscriber-specified symmetric key. Requests for payloads are encrypted with the RS's public key. Legitimate interactions in P3S however reveal a number of auxiliary information about P3S to parties that are not the intended receiver of such information. For example, the size of encrypted content (subscribers and RS are legitimate end users of this interaction) is visible to eavesdroppers as well as the DS. CP-ABE access control policy is visible to the RS (matching subscribers are legitimate end users of this interaction). The RS knows if an encrypted content has sent to some subscriber(s) (i.e., matched). The aggregate rate at which items are being published can be estimated by subscribers from the number of encrypted metadata they're getting. The RS can estimate it by how frequently payloads are stored. Eavesdroppers and the DS know the per-publisher publication rate and number of items published by each publisher. Eavesdroppers and the RS know the aggregate number of items received by subscribing clients.

6.2   Performance

We collected metrics by running the P3S prototype in various configurations such as all parties on one physical server, the DS and RS on a server and a small number of other participants on individual hosts in the network. However, these measurements do not present the true performance characteristics of P3S. Even though only a fraction of the subscriptions may actually match a given publication, it is important to

---

[1] To protect against this the publisher may super-encrypt the GUID with the RS's public key before publishing the payload message.

consider all subscribers in the model because the baseline needs to test each subscription against a publication (impacts the broker's processing load), and encrypted metadata for each publication needs to be disseminated to all clients (consumes network bandwidth). Therefore, we used analytic models with parameter values obtained from the current prototype to get an understanding of the performance at scale (e.g., 100s of subscribers) of the P3S system vis-à-vis a baseline. We used a standard centralized pub-sub system as baseline, where publishers submit their payload and metadata (such as a topic) to a central broker, subscribers register subscriptions with the broker, and the broker sends the payload whose metadata matches with a subscription to the subscriber. In the P3S model, we ignored the anonymizer since as explained in the previous section, anonymization is not necessary for the basic privacy guarantees of P3S. Since CP-ABE is not yet integrated in the P3S prototype, we obtained the CP-ABE timing and ciphertext sizes from the CP-ABE library running standalone. **Table 1** shows the parameters of the model and their values used in the analysis. The two metrics we evaluated are end-to-end latency and throughput:

- **End-to-end Latency:** This is the time taken by a single publication to reach all matching subscribers including the time taken for encryption and decryption.
- **Throughput:** This is the maximum rate at which publications can be injected into the system, such that all are properly matched and delivered.

Table 1. Parameters and values used in performance models

Symbol	Meaning	Input Values
ℓ	Network latency	45 ms
$\mathcal{B}$	Network bandwidth	10 Mbps
M	Size of plaintext payload to be transferred	Varying
P	Size of PBE metadata specification	40 bits
P_P	Size of PBE-encrypted metadata	10KB
M_A	Size of CP-ABE-encrypted payload	$0.6 \times M$
$ser(m)$	Serialization time for message size m	$m/\mathcal{B}$
N_s	Number of subscribers	100
f	Fraction of subscribers that match a given publication	5%
V	Number of attributes in CP-ABE policy	10
K	Security parameter in CP-ABE algorithm	384 bits

Sketch of the End-to-End Latency Model

The major contributors to end-to-end latency are shown in Fig. 6. End-to-end latency for the **baseline** $t^b = t_1^b + t_2^b + t_3^b$, where t_1^b is the time for the publisher to send its message (with metadata) to the broker, t_2^b is the time for the broker to perform the matching operation against all registered subscriptions, and t_3^b is the time for the broker to transmit the message to **all** matching subscribers.

Messages from one node to another incurs a fixed latency ℓ and a serialization time $ser(m)$, where m is the message size. Given a network bandwidth $\mathcal{B}$, $ser(m) = m/\mathcal{B}$. The baseline system may use standard cryptography (e.g., SSL) to encrypt messages, but difference in the size of cleartext and the corresponding cipher-text is insignificant to impact the processing and transmission times, which means $t_1^b = \ell + \frac{M}{B}$. Because the broker needs to send published item to $f \times N_s$ matching subscribers, and sending an item to a single subscriber takes the same time as t_1^bs, $t_3^b = f \times N_s \times t_1^b$. Simple XPath matching operation in a modern desktop takes roughly .05ms, and therefore with N_s subscribers $t_2^b = 0.05 \times N_s \, ms$.

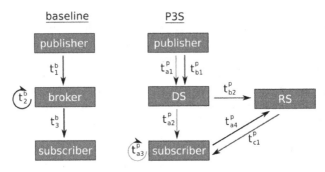

Fig. 6. Contributors to latency for baseline and P3S

End-to-end latency for **P3S** $t^p = \max\left(t_a^p, t_b^p\right) + t_c^p$, where t_a^p is the elapsed time between the publisher sending the encrypted metadata to the time when the RS receives the content retrieval request from the last matching subscriber, t_b^p is the time to send the encrypted item to RS (i.e., content submission), and t_c^p is the time taken for RS to send the encrypted item to requesting subscribers. As shown in Fig. 6 t_a^p has four subcomponents $(t_{a1}^p, t_{a2}^p, t_{a3}^p, t_{a4}^p)$, and and t_b^p has two (t_{b1}^p, t_{b2}^p). Activities contributing to t_a^p and t_b^p can happen in parallel in P3S, but until both complete, the RS cannot serve the requested item, hence we take $\max\left(t_a^p, t_b^p\right)$. This formulation of t^p is actually a worst case estimate, which happens when matching subscribers receive the encrypted metadata last, and the last matching subscriber requests the content first. In practice, activities contributing to t_c^p happen in parallel to t_a^p or t_b^p because a subscriber requests the content as soon as its subscription matches, and the RS may receive the item while some subscribers are still receiving the encrypted metadata.

The time taken to PBE encrypt and send the metadata to the DS (t_{a1}^p) is $\ell + ser(P_P) + enc_P$, where enc_P is the PBE encryption time($\approx 30ms$ in our test environment). The time from when the DS starts dissemination to when the last subscriber receives the transmission $\left(t_{a2}^p\right)$ is $\ell + N_s ser(P_P)$. The time to perform PBE match operation (t_{a3}^p) is $\sim 30ms$ for the $\sim$40KB ciphertext. The last component of t_a^p, $t_{a4}^p = \ell + ser(G)$ where G denotes the size of a GUID, which is $\sim$10 bytes. The component t_{b1}^p includes the time to CP-ABE-encrypt the content and send it to the DS, and is approximated as $\ell + ser(M_A) + enc_A$. CP-ABE encryption is fairly fast ($enc_A \approx 3ms$). The component t_{b2}^p is also estimated to be $\ell + ser(M_A)$ but the serialization times will be different because the bandwidth between the DS and RS is assumed to be 100 Mbps, as might be typical on a LAN, whereas the bandwidth between the publisher and the DS is 10Mbps as shown in Table 1. CP-ABE encryption adds to the size of the message being sent, the size of the CP-ABE ciphertext is estimated from theory to be $M_A = 2VK + M$, where V is the number of attributes in the CP-ABE policy, K is a security parameter, and M is the size of the plaintext payload. Finally, the component t_c^p, corresponding to the time taken to send the payload from the RS to all matching subscribers and subsequent decryption, can be modeled similarly to the dissemination of PBE-encrypted metadata i.e., $t_c^p = \ell + ser(M_A) \times N_s \times f + dec_A$. The last subscriber to get the payload has to wait for the serialization time for all other subscribers, the serialization time for itself, the network latency for itself, and the time to do the CP-ABE decryption ($dec_A \approx 12ms$).

Sketch of the Throughput Model

Fig. 7 shows the major contributors to our throughput model. We determine the maximum rate at which each part of the system can process publications, and find the minimum of those rates. For the baseline, the throughput is $\min(r_1^b, r_2^b)$ where r_1^b is the rate at which the broker can match publications to subscriptions, and r_2^b is the rate at which the broker can send payloads to matching subscribers. Given β hardware threads for matching, $r_1^b = \dfrac{\beta}{N_s \times t_{xpath}}$, and $r_2^b = \dfrac{\beta}{M \times N_s \times f}$.

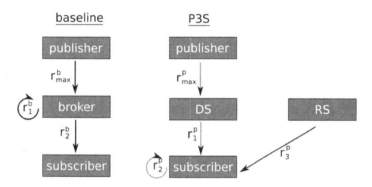

Fig. 7. Major contributors to throughput for baseline and P3S

For P3S, the throughput for P3S is $\min(r_1^p, r_2^p, r_3^p)$, where r_1^p is the rate at which the DS can broadcast metadata items to subscribers and modeled as $r_p^1 = \dfrac{\mathcal{B}}{P_p \times N_s}$; r_2^p is the rate at which a subscriber can perform PBE matches, and modeled as $r_p^2 = \dfrac{\alpha}{t_{PBE}}$, where t_{PBE} be the time required for the subscriber to match their PBE token and α is the number of hardware threads dedicated to matching (currently set to 2); and r_3^p is the rate at which the RS can satisfy payload requests, and modeled as $r_3^p = \dfrac{\mathcal{B}}{M_A \times N_s \times f}$. The subscriber sends a request to the RS when a match occurs, these requests are small and infrequent, and are not a limiting factor.

Results

In this section, the message size in the horizontal axis of all figures refers to clear text payload size. Fig. 8 shows the latency results for $\mathcal{B} = 10Mbps$. For small payloads, the baseline has low latency (Fig. 8(a)) because it only has to serialize a small number of small messages, and matching time is small. As the payloads get larger, latency is dominated by the serialization time in the available bandwidth. The P3S system follows the baseline for large payloads. For large payloads, network serialization time dominates over other factors such as the PBE matching time. For small payloads P3S exhibits a threshold. The PBE matching operation at the subscriber takes approximately 38ms, regardless of clear text payload size. For 1K payloads, all network operations take 1ms or less. Accordingly, for small payloads, the P3S system performance is within ten times the baseline (Fig. 8(b)).

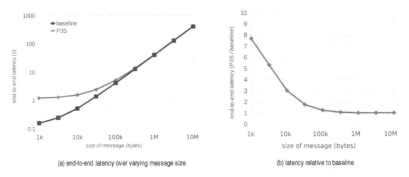

(a) end-to-end latency over varying message size

(b) latency relative to baseline

Fig. 8. End to end latency analysis

Results for the throughput analysis are shown in Fig. 9. As with latency, bandwidth is the dominant factor in the baseline. As payload size increases, throughput decreases because fewer messages per second can be sent out the network interface of the central broker. The P3S system exhibits almost exactly the same behavior as the baseline for large payloads, but it is the bandwidth out of the RS that limits the throughput.

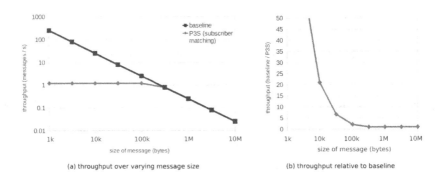

(a) throughput over varying message size

(b) throughput relative to baseline

Fig. 9. Throughput analysis for f = 5%

For small payloads, P3S performance flattens because regardless of the payload size, the DS must send the PBE encrypted metadata (~40KB) to each of the 100 subscribers, which creates a bottleneck in the network interface of the DS. Consequently, P3S performs worse than the baseline for small payloads (Fig. 9(b)). This issue can be addressed by reconfiguring the P3S architecture to use hierarchical dissemination.

P3S throughput relative to the baseline shows no dependence on the number of subscribers for a fixed matching rate f. We also observed that increasing the network bandwidth from 10 to 100 Mbps helps both systems equally. But increasing the match rate benefits P3S. The baseline only disseminates to subscribers who match, whereas P3S must disseminate to all of them, and if more subscribers match, the baseline loses its advantage. Fig. 10 shows the throughput of both P3s and the baseline for $f = 50$. By contrast, the plots in Fig. 9 was for $f = 5\%$. Combining all these results, we can conclude that P3S performs very well (within 10x) compared to the baseline except for small payloads and low matching rates.

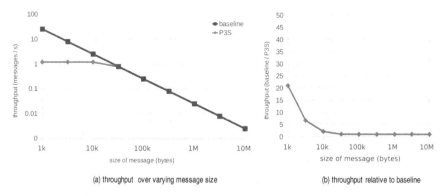

(a) throughput over varying message size

(b) throughput relative to baseline

Fig. 10. Throughput analysis, f = 50%

7 Related Work

Standard security measures such as role-based access control and content encryption in traditional pub-sub middleware offer only a partial solution: the decryption key needs to be shared among potential subscribers and enough metadata and subscription information needs to be visible to the broker. A content-based pub-sub scheme where content decryption keys are shared using Pedersen commitment and matching is performed on blinded attribute-value pairs is presented in [5]. Although their scheme has similar objectives, subscribers need to register a-priori with the publishers, and brokering is limited to equality of strings and numeric comparison. Another approach outlined in [4] makes use of reencryption and onion-routing indirection to dissociate the location of predicate matching the publishers and subscribers. This scheme appears to be specialized for a P2P content sharing network. In [3] a policy-based approach is presented where data owners can specify who can access their publications and under what condition. But the broker and the policy enforcement mechanism can see both the published content and subscriber interest. Contrail [16] presents a novel form of pub-sub for smart phones that uses sender-side content filters for privacy. In this scheme, the association between the publisher and subscriber is pretty strong- the subscriber and publisher perform a handshake to install the sender-side filter. Private stream searching [17] is another relevant research area where the goal is to run encrypted query on unencrypted streams to produce encrypted matching results. Homomorphic encryption [12] offers a potential solution for privacy preserving pub-sub however, homomorphic encryption supporting complex computation performed at the broker is still not practical. We are not aware of any work attempting to preserve the privacy of subscriber interest and confidentiality of published content in the way described here other than the two other projects under the R&D program supporting this work. One uses circuit-based minimal model of secure computation [2] and Barrington's theorem [1] to simulate the complexity class NC^1 using width-5 branching programs. The other uses Oblivious Transfer [13] to achieve the privacy objectives.

8   Conclusion

Current pub-sub systems do not provide privacy of published metadata or subscriber's interest, and can only provide a limited cover for published content. The P3S system is designed to protect the privacy of subscriber interest and confidentiality of published content. A P3S prototype is implemented on a COTS JMS platform (Apache AMQ). The privacy guarantees of P3S come from innovative use of PBE and CP-ABE, and an innovative system architecture that severely limits the exposure of private information by isolating and careful positioning of key underlying information and computation. All components required to support P3S protocol interactions have been developed, the initial integrated P3S prototype integrates all capabilities except for CP-ABE encryption and anonymization of subscriber interactions with the PBE-TS and RS. Initial evaluation shows that P3S overhead is within 10x of the baseline for a variety of payload size, match rate and network bandwidth combinations. Preliminary privacy analysis shows that P3S preserves the privacy of published content and subscriber interest for HBC participants, and even when some of them collude.

Analysis also revealed a number of shortcomings of the current P3S prototype. For example, the PBE-TS is privy to plaintext subscriber interest. Also, there is no subscription control policy enforced on the subscribers. We are currently investigating how to address these shortcomings. One potential approach is to find alternative configurations where subscriber interest never gets out of the subscriber. For instance, the PBE-TS functionality can be embedded in each subscriber instead of being centralized. Another alternative is to frame PBE Token generation as a secure 2-party computation [11] in which the PBE TS has the PBE Master Key, and the subscriber has the interest, and a PBE token is produced by a secure 2-party computation between them without divulging any party's information to the other. Apart from these, we are also exploring innovative uses of the basic privacy-preserving pub-sub middleware such as private multiparty chat or private control channels in a control system. Finally, we are performing formal security analysis of P3S using indistinguishability games to complement the semi-formal analysis presented in this paper.

Acknowledgement. The authors acknowledge the collaboration and guidance of Brent Waters and Vitaly Shmatikov of Univeristy of Texas, Austin in integrating CP-ABE and PBE in P3S.

This work is supported by the Intelligence Advanced Research Project Activity (IARPA) via Department of Interior National Business Center (DoI/NBC) Contract No. DIIPC20195. The U.S. Government is authorized to reproduce and distribute reprints for Governmental purposes notwithstanding any copyright annotation thereon. The views and conclusions contained herein are those of the authors and should not be interpreted as necessarily representing the official policies or endorsements, either expressed or implied, of IARPA, DOI/NBC, or the U.S. Government.

References

1. Barrington, D.: Bounded-width polynomial-size branching programs recognize exactly those languages in NC^1. Journal of Computer and System Sciences 38(1), 150–164 (1989)
2. Feige, U., Kilian, J., Naor, M.: A minimal model for secure computation (extended abstract). In: STOC 1994, pp. 554–563 (1994)
3. Opyrchal, L., Prakash, A., Agrawal, A.: Supporting Privacy Policies in a Publish-Subscribe Substrate for Pervasive Environments. Journal of Networks 2 (February 2007)
4. Klonowski, M., Kutylowski, M., Rozanski, B.: Privacy Protection for P2P Publish-Subscribe Networks, Security and Protection of Information, Brno Univ. of Defense, pp. 63–74 (2005)
5. Nabeel, M., Shang, N., Bertino, E.: Privacy-Preserving Filtering and Covering in Content-Based Publish Subscribe Systems. Purdue University Tech Report 2009-15, June 18 (2009)
6. Boneh, D., Waters, B.: Conjunctive, subset, and range queries on encrypted data. In: Vadhan, S.P. (ed.) TCC 2007. LNCS, vol. 4392, pp. 535–554. Springer, Heidelberg (2007)
7. Iovino, V., Persiano, G.: Hidden-Vector Encryption with Groups of Prime Order. In: Galbraith, S.D., Paterson, K.G. (eds.) Pairing 2008. LNCS, vol. 5209, pp. 75–88. Springer, Heidelberg (2008)
8. Bethencourt, J., Sahai, A., Waters, B.: Ciphertext-Policy Attribute-Based Encryption. In: Proceedings of the 2007 IEEE Symposium on Security and Privacy, pp. 321–334 (2007)
9. Shen, E., Shi, E., Waters, B.: Predicate Privacy in Encryption Systems. In: Reingold, O. (ed.) TCC 2009. LNCS, vol. 5444, pp. 457–473. Springer, Heidelberg (2009)
10. GAS Lab Universita deli Studi di Salerno. jPBC Library,
    http://gas.dia.unisa.it/projects/jpbc/index.html,
    (last accessed May 18, 2012)
11. Jarecki, S., Shmatikov, V.: Efficient Two-Party Secure Computation on Committed Inputs. In: Naor, M. (ed.) EUROCRYPT 2007. LNCS, vol. 4515, pp. 97–114. Springer, Heidelberg (2007)
12. Gentry, C.: Fully homomorphic encryption using ideal lattices. In: Proceedings of the 41st Annual ACM Symposium on Theory of Computing (STOC 2009), New York, pp. 169–178 (2009)
13. Kilian, J.: Founding Cryptography on Oblivious Transfer. In: Proceedings of the 20th Annual ACM Symposium on the Theory of Computation, STOC (1988)
14. Apache Software Foundation. ActiveMQ,
    http://activemq.apache.org/features.html, (last accessed May 18, 2012)
15. Bethencourt, J., Sahai, A., Waters, B.: CP-ABE Library,
    http://acsc.cs.utexas.edu/cpabe, (last accessed May18, 2012)
16. Stuedi, P., Mohammed, I., Balakrishnan, M., Morley Mao, Z., Ramasubramanian, V., Terry, D., Wobber, T.: Contrail: Enabling Decentralized Social Networks on Smartphones. In: Kon, F., Kermarrec, A.-M. (eds.) Middleware 2011. LNCS, vol. 7049, pp. 41–60. Springer, Heidelberg (2011)
17. Ostrovsky, R., Skeith, W.E.: Private Searching on Streaming Data. Journal of Cryptology 20(4), 397–430 (2007)

Author Index